Landscape Restoration
H A N D B O O K

by

Donald Harker • Sherri Evans
Marc Evans • Kay Harker

NEW YORK
AUDUBON
SOCIETY

LEWIS PUBLISHERS
Boca Raton   Ann Arbor   London   Tokyo

Library of Congress Cataloging-in-Publication Data

Catalog information is available from the Library of Congress.

ISBN 0-87371-952-2

Contents

Foreword

Cooperation and communication are the keys to improving the quality of our environment. Cooperation opens the door to a strong, unified effort to advance a progressive environmental agenda. Communication is integral to cooperation. We need to talk about our concerns for the environment and our common responsibility for taking care of our planet. We need to discuss our concerns and responsibilities, as well as our goals and objectives, in order to enhance our ability to actively work together.

In 1887, Frank Chapman, the first president of The Audubon Society of New York State, spoke with women and encouraged them to sign pledge cards that stated their intention to never again wear bird feathers on their hats. The fashion of adorning hats and clothes with feathers nearly caused the extinction of several bird species. By communicating the importance of bird protection to women and by offering them the opportunity to work positively and cooperatively toward protecting birds, Chapman was able to generate a forceful, unified effort toward changing prevalent environmental attitudes. It was from this effort that the Audubon movement and the early stages of today's international bird conservation efforts evolved.

Today, in that same tradition, The Audubon Society of New York State continues its communication efforts by maintaining that every one of us is responsible for taking care of the earth; every one of us should do what we can where we live, work, and recreate to protect the environment. The Audubon Society of New York State offers a cooperative approach to actively care for and protect our environment—The Audubon Cooperative Sanctuary System. The Cooperative Sanctuary System is divided into four programs (Individual, Golf, School, and Corporate and Business) and is designed to encourage landowners and managers to become actively involved in conservation and wildlife enhancement, and to publicly recognize those who are involved in conservation and wildlife enhancement activities.

Over the twenty-odd years that I have been involved in the environmental movement, people have said over and over, "Quit telling me everything you're opposed to and tell me what you're in favor of." Well... here you go. The concepts in the *Landscape Restoration Handbook* are what New York Audubon is for. The United States Golf Association is cooperating with us, along with hundreds of existing golf courses across the country, and many individuals, corporations, and schools. I'd be pretty surprised if any one of the people managing these facilities ever got up in the morning and said, "Let me see. Today I think I'll pollute the environment." My experience has been that what they do say with increasing regularity is "Give me some information, some direction. Tell me how I can help wildlife and the environment."

The *Landscape Restoration Handbook* is our response. It is a cooperative effort between New York Audubon and the United States Golf Association and its purpose is to make information about enhancing the environment available to landowners and land managers. The *Landscape Restoration Handbook* is an important component of The Audubon Cooperative Sanctuary System. But, in reality, **you** are the most important part of The Cooperative System. You, the homeowner, the golf course superintendent, the school official, the corporate land manager, the architect, or the concerned citizen who has this book in your hands; you hold the key to conserving our environment. The key is not this book, though the book will open many doors by making available essential information. It is, in fact, your land, your home, your golf course, your business property, or school that is the key to a healthy environment. The *Landscape Restoration Handbook* is the best information that we could gather to help you achieve both your goal and ours—managing your land with the best interests of the environment in mind.

Thank you for the opportunity to share our thoughts and ideas with you.

Ronald G. Dodson
President
The Audubon Society of New York State

Acknowledgments

The authors are deeply indebted to many people who helped with this book and wish to thank the following:

The United States Golf Association who generously supported this work, and especially the USGA Environmental Research Committee for their support, ideas, and review of the manuscript.

Ron Dodson, President of the New York Audubon Society, for his support of this effort from its conception to its completion. He edited the manuscript, shared ideas, and generously wrote the Foreword. His good cheer and enthusiasm help keep us all going.

Mike Kenna, Research Director of the Greens Section of USGA, for his support, encouragement, and enthusiasm. His editing improved the manuscript and he generously shared ideas that improved this book.

David Snyder, Austin Peay State University, who could not pass up the opportunity to critique two former students and teach them just a little more. David critically read portions of the manuscript.

Stan Beikmann, Director of Fernwood, Inc., who has taught many about gardens and enthusiastically supported the Fernwood Prairie restoration project. Stan critically read portions of the manuscript.

Susan Kiely, who researched, edited, typed, and managed much of the production of this book for the year we all worked on it. Susan is now working on her Masters degree in landscape design.

Cathy Guthrie, for her research on the ecological community descriptions and species lists.

Van Fritts for editing, research, typing, and helping us tend to all of the details.

Deborah White for editing and research on plant species and ecological communities.

Liz Natter for critically reading the manuscript and offering many helpful suggestions.

Hal Bryan, Eco-Tech, Inc., for sharing his vast experience in wetland restoration with us and for critically reading the manuscript and offering many helpful suggestions.

Mary Kay Solecki, Bill Carr, and William Dick–Peddie provided valuable information and suggestions on the ecological communities and species lists.

Leslie Sauer, Andropogon Associates, for reviewing the manuscript and offering helpful suggestions that improved the completeness of this book.

Thomas Heilbron, founder/developer of The Champions golf course, for enthusiasm about the concept and allowing us to use The Champions for the conceptual design work.

Max Medley for reviewing species lists and providing library material.

Bill Martin, Eastern Kentucky University, for sharing ideas, experience, and his library.

Karen Bess for help on The Champions conceptual plan.

Lou Martin for proofing and editing the final manuscript.

Brian Lewis for support, encouragement, and understanding.

April Deluca who did the final layout and design of this book.

Others who helped with research, editing, and/or typing include Laura Dalton, Jim Fries, John Kartesz, Carolyn Wilczynski, Jean Mackay, Francis Harty, Marilyn Wrenn Harrell, Glenn Humphress, Hayden Harker, and Ambika Chawla.

PlanGraphics, Inc., especially John Antenucci, Kaye Brothers, Leann Rodgers, and Jani Sivills for computer assistance.

And last, but not least, to our many friends who always had an encouraging word when we needed it. The authors take responsibility for any errors in this book.

About the Authors

Donald F. Harker, an environmental consultant and co-director of the Kentucky Local Governance Project, received his B.S. degree in biology from Austin Peay State University, Clarksville, Tennessee and his M.S. degree in biology from the University of Notre Dame, South Bend, Indiana, where he studied "killer" bees in Brazil. He is the recent founder of the Center for Sustainable Systems.

Don has been a naturalist, farmer, and environmental consultant. He spent over ten years in Kentucky state government as Director of the Kentucky State Nature Preserves Commission, Director of the Kentucky Division of Water, and Director of the Kentucky Division of Waste Management. Don's consulting and research have taken him to Alaska, Mexico, Venezuela, Ecuador, Brazil, Costa Rica, Bahamas, and throughout the United States.

Sherri Evans, owner and operator of Shooting Star Nursery, Frankfort, Kentucky, received her B.A. in biology and M.A. in zoology from Southern Illinois University, Carbondale, Illinois. She has worked as a wildlife researcher and environmental consultant, and has spent over seven years in state government natural resource management programs.

Shooting Star Nursery was established in 1988, the first nursery in Kentucky to specialize in the propagation and use of native plants for landscaping and restoration. The nursery offers consulting services in landscape and restoration planning and has worked with parks, golf courses, national forests, utility companies, city planners, museums, nature preserves, businesses, and others to create attractive, self-sustaining native plant landscapes.

Marc Evans, Botanist/Ecologist for the Kentucky State Nature Preserves Commission, received his B.A. and M.S. in botany from Southern Illinois University in Carbondale, Illinois.

Marc has been a botanist/ecologist with the Kentucky State Nature Preserves Commission for ten years. He has worked as a biological consultant, researcher, and park naturalist. Marc is co-owner with Sherri of Shooting Star Nursery.

Kay Harker, manager of the groundwater branch of the Kentucky Division of Water, received her B.S. and M.S. degrees in biology from Austin Peay State University, Clarksville, Tennessee, and has completed all the course work toward a PhD in biology at the University of Kentucky, Lexington, Kentucky.

Since 1985 Kay has worked for the Kentucky Department for Environmental Protection on solid waste, hazardous waste, and water issues. Kay has also been a naturalist, college teacher, and high school teacher.

Dedication

This book is dedicated to our children, Heather Harker, Hayden Harker, and Daniel Evans, and the children of their generation, who soon must care for the earth for the next generation. This is how humanity survives.

Landscape Restoration
HANDBOOK

CHAPTER 1

Naturalizing the Managed Landscape

Introduction

Since the beginning of recorded time, human beings have felt both a part of nature, and at the same time, apart from nature. Sometimes we are able to simply enjoy the beauty that nature has to offer. Sometimes we use natural forces to our advantage. At other times, we are at the mercy of nature. The spring rains that moisten the soil and foster lush, green growth can become a deluge, washing the hopes of farmers and homeowners into the nearest stream or river. When challenged by nature's forces, one can work with them, or attempt to control them.

Today, we understand that working with nature, and not against it, makes both environmental and economic sense. Working with nature does not necessarily mean just letting nature take its own course. It means making sound decisions about how to manage the land. It means finding out what will work with the land, given its physical and chemical characteristics. When we view the land, whether it's our own backyard, a forest, a meadow, a park, or a golf course, we each have some vision of how we think that land "ought" to look. Weaving nature into our vision for a landscape means seeing the beauty in a field of wildflowers, instead of thinking it looks like unkempt weeds.

This book is based upon the concept that the managed landscape *can* be naturalized and that the process of naturalizing the landscape makes long–term environmental and economic sense. Naturalizing the landscape means using native plants to restore and beautify the landscape. It is both restoring or creating an ecological community, using as

full a complement of native species as possible, and landscaping with native plants. It takes hundreds or even thousands of years for an ecological community to develop. It may not be possible to completely recreate such a community and certainly, not in a short time. We can, however, begin the process by educating ourselves about what may have been present before the land was altered, and then developing a long–term plan to restore the land, as much as possible, to its former natural condition.

The naturalization process can either be in the form of natural landscaping or ecological restoration. This book provides guidance on both of these, for example, if one chooses a site to create a forest and plants five species of trees from the long list of the oak–hickory forest type, that can be either ecological restoration or natural landscaping. It depends to a large degree upon the goal and outcome of the project. If the intention is to maintain a five–species complex or planting, then it is natural landscaping. If, however, the intention is to add trees, shrubs, and herbaceous species of the oak–hickory forest, and to allow changes that result in the succession of these plants into a more natural ecological community, then it is ecological restoration. Both natural landscaping and ecological restoration have value. Given the size or shape of the site, the surrounding land uses, or unchangeable cultural or developed features, complete restoration of an ecological community may not be possible. This should not keep the land manager from utilizing natural landscaping on the property.

The greenspaces of the earth's landscape mosaic are diminishing. Parks, farms, yards, greenways, wooded river corridors, woodlots, and golf courses are all part of the greenspace patchwork where people seek escape from the stress and noise of cities and highways. All of these areas are, or have the potential to be, important parts of the naturalized landscape. As the natural components of these areas increase, the connection between the natural world and the human–influenced world increases. When naturalized, greenspaces provide birdsong, the flicker of orange or blue from a winging butterfly, prairie grasses blowing in the wind, or a chipmunk scurrying through the leaves—sounds and sights that remind us of our role, our place, in nature.

Golf courses are a kind of managed landscape where "nature by design" is an integral part of the game and the landscape. Over the years, however, particularly in the United States, the human vision of how a golf course "should" look has overshadowed nature's design. The popularity of golf has increased steadily in the United States since 1946. According to the National Golf Foundation, from 1985 to 1990, the number of golfers increased from 17.5 to 25 million. In this same period, the number of rounds of golf played annually increased by 17.6 percent. Between 1968 and 1990, the number of golf facilities increased from 9,600 to 12,800. Today, it is estimated that over 12 percent of the United States population over the age of twelve plays golf. Currently, the National Golf Foundation estimates that there are over 13,951 golf courses in the United States. Assuming an average size of 124 to 180 acres per facility, there are from 1.6 to 2.3 million acres of land dedicated to golf facilities. Opportunities to use natural landscaping or practice ecological restoration abound on each of these facilities. Out–of–play areas, stream corridors, wetland areas, and woodlots can all play important roles for wildlife and environmental conservation. By practicing the principles of natural landscaping and ecological restoration and passing on information concerning those efforts to golfers, we will spread the seeds to encourage individual participation in naturalizing the landscape beyond the golf course.

Naturalizing and restoring the land are parts of an ecological renaissance and plan–of–action for the future. Human progress is now being measured in terms such as "sustainable", "environmentally friendly", and "quality of life." Living within sensible ecological boundaries and restoring parts of the earth to a more natural state are integral parts of that ecological renaissance.

Why Naturalness?

There is broad scientific agreement that the world's biological resources (biodiversity) are being significantly diminished. Protecting these resources and restoring naturalness to human–altered landscapes are important to protecting the world's biodiversity. "Naturalness," simply defined, is "the degree to which the present community of plants and animals resembles the community that existed before human intervention." Restoring naturalness can mean planting a native tree or planting a forest. The act of becoming knowledgeable about and appreciating our natural heritage can lead to a recognition of our common destiny with the natural world, and a desire to both protect and restore the earth's resources.

Some have asked whether we should spend our resources on restoring the earth when so much protection effort is needed to save the natural areas that remain. John Berger (1990), executive director of Restoring the Earth, speaks to the issue. "I have been told that we should not publicize or even propose restoration because society will use it to excuse new assaults on the environment. Yet the technology of resource restoration is developing rapidly and cannot be wished away. Just as our understanding of atomic energy cannot be unlearned, so, too, the genie of restoration is `out of the bottle.' Our task is to see that restoration is used properly — to repair past damage, not to legitimize new disruption. An epochal development has clearly begun: For the first time in human history, masses of people now realize not only that we must stop abusing the earth, but that we also must restore it to ecological health. We must all work cooperatively toward that goal, with the help of restoration science and technology."

Much of the landscape has already been altered from its natural state. Clearly naturalization will, of necessity, play an increasingly significant role in efforts worldwide to preserve the planet's biodiversity.

By increasing the naturalness of our landscape, we become a positive force in contributing to a sustainable world. Landscape restoration affects the world in a variety of ways.

- creates a healthier, sustainable mosaic of land uses on the landscape
- maintains a diversity of plants and animals
- maintains the gene pool of particular plant and animal species, promoting hardiness, disease resistance, and adaptability
- protects ecosystems and ecological communities
- improves water quality
- minimizes erosion
- creates positive, progressive, and constructive attitudes about the natural world
- promotes the concept that natural is beautiful
- creates lower maintenance landscapes, reducing our dependency on water and the production and use of chemicals

The *Landscape Restoration Handbook* is an "ecological call–to–action." It is a call to those who manage yards, farms, corporate land, parks, school yards, roadsides, and golf courses to consider a more natural vision for the human–managed landscape. We are facing ever–increasing demands and impacts on the landscape. The cumulative impacts of our burgeoning population over time are nearly incalculable. Naturalizing and restoring the earth must become the business of everyone. Every attempt at restoration, from planting a tree to restoring a forest, matters, for each one shows that our reconciliation with the earth is desired and is progressing.

There is a story (original teller unknown) about a big storm that came and washed thousands of starfish onto the beach. A little girl came down to the beach and was terribly upset by all of the stranded starfish that would soon die. She began picking up starfish, running down to the ocean, and throwing them back into the sea. A man came along and reasoned with the child that she was wasting her time. There were so many starfish on the beach that her efforts just would not matter. The little girl grabbed up a starfish, ran to the sea, and threw it into the sea. She returned to the man and, with a smile, said "It mattered to that one."

Photo. 1.1. Golf course with a naturalized landscape

Using This Book

This book is divided into several chapters that outline principles for developing a comprehensive naturalization program. A three–part "Greenlinks" program is discussed in Chapter 2, outlining a broad–based program for education, regional planning, and naturalization planning. Also discussed in the book are principles and guidelines for increasing biological diversity (Chapter 3), natural landscaping (Chapter 4), and ecological restoration (Chapter 5). These three chapters provide a basic background for understanding conceptual and detailed naturalization plans. The diversity of landscape conditions, such as soil, slope, and available moisture, demands site specific analyses in order to develop detailed naturalization plans. While such analyses are beyond the scope of this book, the principles in this book can be generally applied by the land manager in developing a naturalization plan.

In addition to the Greenlinks program and principles and guidelines for naturalization, the dominant ecological communities are described for thirty natural regions of the continental United States (Chapter 6 and Appendix A). These descriptions provide a framework for determining which common ecological communities occur or occurred in each region of the country. A list of plant species associated with each ecological community (Appendix A) is included to help the landscaper or restorationist select appropriate species. Characteristics of each species are presented in a woody species matrix and herbaceous species matrix (Appendix B) to help in the selection of species appropriate for the planting conditions and design specifications of a naturalized planting. The matrices include, for each plant, information on its type, environmental tolerances, aesthetic values, wildlife values, flower color, bloom time, and landscape uses. The matrices are organized alphabetically by scientific name.

Appendix C is a list of nurseries which carry native plants that can be used for either natural landscaping or ecological restoration. The nurseries are organized by state for the lower forty–eight states.

The plant lists used in this book have come from a variety of sources. Because of the diverse sources and the age of some sources, all scientific and common names have been synonymized with *Synonymized Checklist of the Vascular Flora of the United States* (Kartesz 1991) and *Common Names for the North America Flora* (Kartesz, 1990).

This book can be read from front to back or used as a reference. Those interested in landscaping or ecological restoration can go directly to the appropriate chapter. For a broader view of landscape restoration, however, a full reading can stimulate imagination and creativity in approaching the naturalization of our human–managed landscapes. In addition, it is hoped that this book will help stimulate a renewed sense of interest in taking active steps to become environmentally sensitive caretakers of the planet earth.

CHAPTER 2

Greenlinks

Introduction

Greenlinks is the name given to a comprehensive program for naturalizing the landscape. It involves both planning and education. A Greenlinks program is divided into three basic parts: (1) introducing a target audience to the idea of naturalizing the landscape through a strong education program; (2) working with adjacent and regional landowners to link more and more greenspaces and natural areas together in a regional context; and (3) developing a detailed naturalization plan for the managed site.

An overall plan for naturalizing managed landscapes generally includes a combination of ecological restoration and natural landscaping. A variety of goals and objectives can be developed for a site. They include improving wildlife habitat, creating more aesthetically pleasing surroundings, restoring natural communities, protecting local rare plants or animals, or preserving the local gene pool of a particular species or natural community.

It is not possible to offer detailed prescriptions of how to restore or landscape every type of site. To develop a detailed site plan requires applying the principles for maintaining natural diversity, ecological restoration, and natural landscaping to specific parcels of landscape. This chapter offers guidelines for developing an educational program, regional overview, and naturalization plan.

Greenlinks Education Program

Any naturalization or ecological restoration project benefits from, and is more successful with, a strong education program. Naturalizing the landscape provides opportunities for education about a region's natural heritage, the value of natural landscaping, and restoring natural communities. We recommend that the opportunity created by a naturalization project be used to educate owners, managers, members, visitors to managed areas, and public officials. Also, a cooperative effort with surrounding landowners can lead to regional naturalization programs that increase biological diversity. This will be especially important if landowners of large natural areas or important corridors become involved.

As development increasingly encroaches on the few remaining natural lands, opportunities to learn about nature are diminished. Restoring ecological communities and establishing natural landscapes play important roles in preserving the unique vegetational character that distinguishes each region of the continent. Naturalization projects on managed landscapes provide an opportunity for the public, members, visitors, and students to learn about the natural heritage of the region. This educational experience will increase awareness and appreciation of efforts to preserve that heritage. What people learn can also be transferred to other areas, such as their yards and the property where they work.

Ecological restoration and natural landscaping serve as excellent examples of how to create less intensively managed landscapes which help reduce maintenance costs, conserve natural resources, increase biological diversity, and benefit wildlife. Keeping the public well informed about the establishment process is very important for maintaining continuous support for these projects. This is especially important since it may take several years for a restoration project or natural landscape to mature

Photo 2.1. Children at Fernwood Prairie getting a lesson about a disappearing ecological community.

and achieve its full aesthetic potential. During the interim, the landscape may appear "weedy" or unkempt to the uninformed viewer. Natural landscapes and ecological communities go through a dynamic process of change as they become established and mature. These changes demonstrate how the forces of nature shape the natural environment and are exciting and educational to observe.

Education occurs when one has a new awareness or experience, learns the name of a plant or bird, or has his consciousness raised about an issue. A comprehensive Greenlinks education program will seek to bring people into the overall planning and development of the program. Various kinds of educational approaches can be used. The following are a few recommended elements in a comprehensive Greenlinks education program.

- Solicit the help of local nature centers, native plant societies, botanical gardens, and local people with expertise in native plants and restoration.
- Involve the public, members and supporters of the managed area, local officials, and

students in planning and implementing the naturalization program.

- Invite adjacent and surrounding land owners to meet and discuss the regional concept of a Greenlinks program. Involve them in developing a regional plan.
- Sponsor educational forums in the community to demonstrate examples and highlight the positive components of Greenlinks.
- Join the Audubon Cooperative Sanctuary Program. This is a program sponsored by the New York Audubon Society which provides an advisory information service promoting the protection and enhancement of wildlife habitats and water resources.
- When a plan is completed, develop informational brochures to provide background on the goals and processes of establishing natural landscapes.
- Be sure your plan includes self–interpreting walking paths with interpretive signs at strategic locations, such as trailheads and in front of natural gardens, to help the public

learn to recognize native species of plants, the wildlife they attract, and other benefits of using native plants.

Regional Overview Plan

One of the first recommendations of the New York Audubon Cooperative Sanctuary Program is to create a resource committee. A principal task for that committee can be to obtain aerial photographs, soil maps, and topographic maps and use them to examine the regional ecological context of the particular site. Attention should be given to the habitats surrounding the site, the location of streams and rivers, and the current and potential land uses of the area. If a regional Greenlinks program is attempted, this exercise will provide a good idea of the opportunities available for linking patches of natural communities and greenspaces together. Regional landscape approaches are necessary to maintain plant and animal diversity. It cannot be done by creating many small patches of habitat on one small site.

"The regional landscape approach to preservation should therefore recognize the importance of broad corridors connecting habitat islands. Fence rows and shelterbelts should be widened whenever possible. Regional planners should draw corridors of natural habitat onto their blueprints. Park planners might connect significant patches of habitat within a given park, which would minimize island effects while still permitting development of considerable land area. Stream corridors, which can be effective avenues of dispersal for terrestrial as well as aquatic organisms, particularly if they are wide and contain some upland habitat, should be protected wherever possible (Noss 1983)."

There is also a temporal dimension to any site. In other words, one must consider what will happen to the area over time. The concern is not just what will happen to the site, but what will happen to the surrounding landscape. If development is occurring in a particular adjoining area, then visual screening may be appropriate. Effective screening may take years to develop. Activities upstream affect the quality and quantity of water downstream. Wildlife corridors can be broken by many types of activity. Working with adjacent landowners on a regional plan can pay great dividends in the future.

Figure 2.1 shows the region around The Champions golf course in the central Bluegrass Region of Kentucky. This area is heavily impacted by agriculture, horse farms, and development, with very few natural areas or high quality greenspaces left. The regional context suggests that corridors to natural areas in the region can be established through a naturalized stream corridor network, wooded fencerows, and wooded patches. The Kentucky River is a primary corridor that remains wooded. It runs from the Eastern Kentucky mountains to the Ohio River. Providing links to this area will increase the wildlife for a site. There are also some large natural areas (wooded but impacted) in the Sinking Creek area. These are important to the regional biota and should be part of a Greenlinks program. A comprehensive Greenlinks program will require developing these ideas and bringing together the landowners, citizens, and local officials who can help make such an idea a reality.

The Naturalization Plan

Basic to the concept of naturalizing a managed site is the development of the naturalization plan. The four main components of the plan are 1) a statement of objectives, 2) a synthesis and analysis of baseline information on existing site conditions, 3) a conceptual design plan identifying potentials for natural landscaping and restoration, and 4) a program for establishment and maintenance that includes a reasonable timetable and an estimate of costs. Component four is part of a detailed site plan and beyond the scope of this book.

Site Objectives

An important first step in the planning process is to define the objectives for naturalizing the managed site. In many cases there will be multiple objectives. They may be functional, such as controlling erosion; aesthetic, such as visually screening an unpleasant view or creating a colorful wildflower garden; economic, such as reducing dependency on chemicals used for landscape maintenance; or biological, such as increasing diversity or protecting a rare species. Many of these objectives are interrelated, and multiple objectives are often attainable on a given site when each is considered fully and early in the planning process. For example, many of the most showy or fragrant flowers

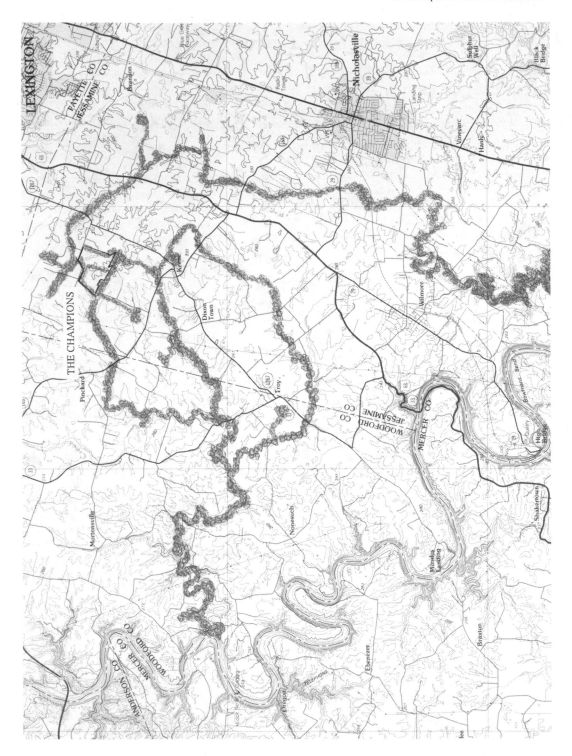

Fig. 2.1. This figure shows one proposal for using wooded rivers, streams, fencerows, railroad rights–of–way, and roads to connect woodland patches throughout the landscape.

suitable for landscaping are also excellent nectar–producing plants that will attract wildlife. Many native trees and shrubs with showy flowers or brilliant autumn color also provide valuable cover or food for wildlife as well as welcome shade on a hot summer day.

Baseline Information

Synthesis and analysis of baseline information help guide decisions concerning the possibilities and limitations for naturalizing the site. The end result is the delineation of naturalized landscapes to be created, restored, or enhanced. A site survey should be conducted that includes the biota and an analysis of the light, moisture, soils, slope, altitude, wind, and micro–climate. This information is then used to select appropriate ecological communities as landscape models. The plant and animal data are especially useful to help identify the potential of existing communities for preservation, restoration, or enhancement.

Baseline information forms the framework of the naturalization plan. Baseline data is usually presented on a base map which provides a visual record of the plan. The size of the planning site dictates the scale of the base map, but a scale of one–quarter inch to the foot is generally the minimum used for effective planning (Weddle 1983). Some types of baseline information to be included on the base map are features such as property boundaries; easement boundaries; above and below ground utility and communication rights–of–way; existing trees, shrub borders, meadows, water bodies, and other natural features; and buildings, paved roads, and other permanent structures, with access and service corridors noted. Symbols may be used to identify orientation, predominant seasonal wind patterns, and seasonal changes in the angle of sunlight. Information on existing local ordinances governing vegetation, minimum setbacks, and other restrictions should be included. A series of transparent overlays can be used to record physical, biotic, and visual survey data.

A series of landscape surveys may be needed to obtain accurate baseline data, especially when knowledge of measurable quantities and qualities of the site is desired. Surveys are often a compilation of existing data from architectural drawings, maps, and aerial photographs, combined with on–site inventories of physical, biotic, and visual characteristics. Survey results are presented as drawings, photographs, and written documentation.

Physical survey data on soils, geology, topography, and hydrology can often be compiled from U.S. Geological Survey topographic and geologic maps, and county–based soil surveys. Soil survey data can be misleading in areas disturbed by past construction activities, in which case samples from test holes can be used to plot topsoil and subsoil layers across a site. Soil tests, available through local Cooperative Extension Service offices, analyze soil fertility and acidity.

A biotic or ecological survey is often needed to assess the quality of existing natural communities. The survey should produce a complete record of plant and animal life, including the identification of rare or sensitive species requiring special consideration during site planning and development. The relative abundance of non–native species and a recommended eradication program should be included as part of the report. At the very least, an assessment of the relative quality of existing natural communities within a regional context should be included. The species composition of the plant communities can be used as an indicator of local environmental conditions.

A viewshed survey may be desirable to qualitatively evaluate the visual character of the landscape. The visual survey may encompass visual horizons, water, vegetation patterns, and visual attributes and intrusions of adjacent land. The beyond–site viewsheds are judged subjectively as attractive or intrusive, often as viewed from one or more pre–selected locations on the site. Recommendations are made as to the potential to open or reduce viewsheds from various areas. Photographic documentation, particularly with a panoramic series, provides a permanent record for later reference.

The Conceptual Design Plan

The landscape can be considered as patches within patches. One can look at a large piece of landscape and see fields, streams, and forest. At that scale the forest or field may seem homogeneous. A closer look reveals that each is, in reality, many smaller patches. Each separate patch is considered a site or planning unit for developing a naturalization plan.

The conceptual plan identifies the patches or planning units potentially available for restoration or natural landscaping. These planning units are discrete parcels of similar physical makeup that will receive similar treatment. A planning unit can be a portion of hillside with the same soil type, exposure, and moisture regime on which the same ecological community will be restored.

A conceptual design has been developed to illustrate some of the restoration and landscaping principles that can be applied to an existing golf course. The design was created for The Champions golf course (Fig. 2.2) located in the Bluegrass Region of Kentucky near Lexington. Photos 2.2 through 2.13 show how the course currently looks.

The concepts illustrated in the design created for The Champions golf course include the following:

Ecological Restoration

- Upland Ecological Community Restoration— The central Kentucky Bluegrass region had a variety of upland plant communities. They included the oak–ash savanna, oak–hickory forest, and canebrakes. All of these communities are used in the concept plan.
- Wetland Ecological Community Restoration—Two natural wetland communities are recommended. Below the spillway of the large impoundment is a good location for a marsh. This marsh will increase the plant and animal diversity and act as a water quality improvement system for runoff coming into the lake and out through the spillway.
  The other wetland is a wooded area at the head of the impoundment. It is recommended that this area be expanded. Part of this planning unit is currently forested and part is old field with an existing pond located on adjacent property under the same management. This pond should be left and surrounded by woods. This forested wetland area can serve as a buffer to the impoundment by trapping sediment and agricultural runoff from the surrounding area.
- Corridors—The concept plan maximizes the idea of connecting patches of forest, wildflower meadows, canebrakes, wetlands, and savannas. These corridors will allow animals to move throughout the area more readily. The corridors also connect patches on the golf course with areas off the course. This will bring more species onto the course from outside. It actually creates a two–way path, with animals moving both ways.
- Vegetative Structure—The types and availability of habitat are significantly increased with increased vegetative structure. This means tree, shrub, and herbaceous layers should be planned and allowed to develop corridors. Dead and fallen logs and leaf litter should not be removed.

Natural Landscaping

- Enhancement Zones—Certain edge areas with high visibility have been selected as enhancement zones. These zones are considered landscaping because they will have a high concentration of showy prairie wildflowers rather than the normal dominance of grasses. It will cost more to develop these areas than native savanna, so they are restricted in size.
- Screening—The entire perimeter of the site will be screened from the road and surrounding area. This screening increases privacy, reduces noise from traffic, and provides more habitat.
- Special Features—Three special features were identified on the site. They are generally described as follows:
  The first special feature is a natural outcropping of limestone. Fortunately, a number of mature trees were left standing in this area (see Photo. 2.11). It is recommended that a bench be placed here. Recommended plantings include native flowering shrubs and herbs.
  The second special feature is a spring head that has a stone spring house built around it. Unfortunately, it occurs in an open area; however, it will be much more attractive with a backdrop of trees (see Photo. 2.12).
  The third special feature is a natural seep in an area with some topographic relief. The area was left with mature trees. It will be very attractive with a planting of large native ferns such as cinnamon fern and royal fern and a diversity of wildflowers adapted to moist soils (see Photo. 2.13).

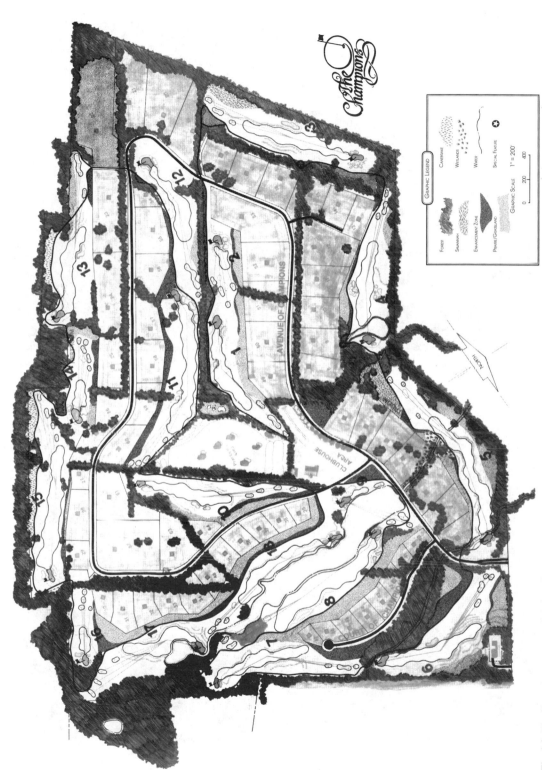

Fig. 2.2. The Champions conceptual design plan

Photo. 2.2. Overview of portion of course

Photo. 2.3. Fairway with patches of natural woodland left on either side

Photo. 2.4. Golf cart path goes through edge of natural woods

Photo. 2.5. View from golf cart path into natural woods

Photo. 2.6. Row of trees currently raked and mowed

Photo. 2.7. Row of trees with shrub layers, herbaceous layers, and leaf litter left on the ground

Photo. 2.8. Woodland that can be naturalized to screen a road

Photo. 2.9. Open area available for naturalization including shrub and herbaceous layers

Photo. 2.10. Open area available for native grassland restoration and enhancement zone

Photo. 2.11. Special feature No. 1 is a natural limestone outcropping

Photo. 2.12. Special feature No. 2 is a natural spring with a stone springhouse

Photo. 2.13. Special feature No. 3 is a natural spring

CHAPTER 3

Principles for Maintaining and Restoring Natural Diversity

Introduction

An effective naturalization plan is based on the application of principles for maintaining natural diversity in a managed landscape. Diversity, as used here, is not the diversity of a zoo, but is diversity as seen in natural communities and ecosystems. The aim is not to plant as many different kinds of trees as possible on a particular site, but to restore a natural community on a site with as full a complement of native species as possible. Restoration of a natural plant community provides a variety of habitats valuable to a variety of animals. These principles are not prescriptive; they are designed to help people think about the use of a particular parcel of land. Application of the principles will enable managers of golf courses, parks, recreation areas, farms, schools, and other parcels of land to increase the diversity of plants and animals on their land. If applied widely within a region, these principles can result in a new landscape mosaic that increases overall naturalness and regional diversity of native plant and animal species. Restoring many small areas to natural communities contributes to increased individual, population, and community diversity.

Maintaining and restoring natural diversity to our increasingly fragmented landscape is our challenge. A number of studies address this issue. For example, as forests in the northeastern United States were converted to farmland in the late 1800s and early 1900s, the number of species of migratory songbirds using these areas declined. But, as small forest patches were reestablished in the latter half of this century, the number of bird species increased. A study of small urban and suburban forest preserves of less than 247 acres suggests that populations of many species may not be self-sustaining in a small preserve, but are instead an important part

of a larger, regional population (Askins and Philbrick 1987). The study illustrates that diversity can increase in an area even when the creation of a large preserve is not possible. When created, small preserves can play an important role in restoring our natural heritage without diminishing the intended human use of the land.

Small areas will not satisfy all the needs of all species that occur within a region. However, by analyzing specific characteristics of an individual area and consulting the lists of native plants for that ecological community, the landscaper can determine the types of plants that will best survive and prosper at a specific site. In restoring native plant communities, the landscaper provides an opportunity for the animal species associated with those communities to find suitable shelter, food, and areas for raising young. Although only a few species may be present on any given restored site, the total of all restored sites will preserve a large number of species and create diversity within a region. To preserve the regional diversity of native plants and animals, it is important to restore many small sites.

This chapter provides principles, guidelines, and design suggestions for increasing and maintaining a diversity of plants and animals on parcels of managed land. Each parcel, whether a golf course, school, yard, farm, park, or unused corporate land, can play an important role in maintaining regional diversity. The principles and designs suggested in this chapter can be used to increase species diversity, increase the populations of particular species, and assist in restoration of specific ecosystems. These principles can be applied during the establishment of a new managed area or on an area currently in use.

What Is Diversity?

Biological diversity, or biodiversity, refers to the variety of life in all its forms and levels of organization (Hunter 1990). Deliberations on biological diversity include discussions of genetic diversity of individuals within a species, diversity of populations, diversity of communities, and diversity of ecosystems and regional vegetation types called biomes. This chapter discusses four levels of biological organization: individuals, populations, communities, and ecosystems.

Scientists identify all individual plants or animals by a two-part scientific name. The first word is the genus to which the species belongs and the second word is the specific epithet, or species name. Each species is adapted to survive in a certain range of conditions. All individuals of a species differ slightly from one another in their abilities to adjust and respond to a particular range of environmental conditions. These slight differences represent diversity within the species. Since all environments are continually changing, this diversity is important in the long-term survival of species.

A population is defined as a group of individuals of a single species that interact, interbreed, and live in a given area. The individuals in a population are genetically diverse, and a viable population has sufficient genetic diversity to withstand changes in the environment. All environments change. In genetically diverse populations, some individuals may die as a result of changes, but many survive and the population survives. Usually a large population contains more genetic diversity than a small population and thus has a better chance of surviving environmental change. Density, or the number of organisms per unit area, is one measure used by scientists to characterize a population.

An ecological community is an interrelated assemblage of plants and animals associated with the abiotic or physical environment. A community type repeats itself, with variations, under similar conditions across the local landscape (or within an ecoregion). Through time, species within a community have developed complex relationships and interactions. Competition among similar species for scarce food supplies is a common occurrence in communities. Predation of one species upon another affects the number of different kinds of species in a community. Studies of competition, preda-

tion, decomposition, and many other relationships among species within communities suggest that preservation of a single species isolated from its community is difficult, and often impossible. Because of the many varied relationships, interactions, and requirements of species, studies of the needs of a given species are often incomplete and are always time consuming to conduct. Although autecological studies (studies of individual species' needs) may be very successful in preserving a species, time and financial constraints make such studies of all species within a community impractical. An effective and less expensive means of preserving a species is usually through preserving or restoring its natural community. Restoration of natural communities does not require knowledge of all requirements of all species.

An ecosystem is a complex system of biotic and abiotic components and relationships. It includes not only the plant and animal communities, but also the microorganisms, climate, sunlight, water, and soil that interact with communities and with each other. Nutrients, water, and energy cycle through the system. Animals use other animals or plants as food. Slightly different soils, slopes, and many other factors make for subtle differences in each locale or habitat within a given ecosystem. An ecosystem usually contains, or can include, many different ecological communities and may cover a large area.

The place that a plant or animal lives is its habitat. Plants and animals of a given species have specific requirements which must be met in order to survive. Each site or parcel of landscape has characteristic soil, exposure, moisture, and temperature ranges which meet the requirements of a given assemblage of plants. Each community of plants provides habitat for a particular group of animals. Wetland and upland trees may be found in the same geographic area, but the two types of trees are not found in the same habitat. Each has different requirements for soil type and moisture. It is better to restore or preserve an upland site and a wetland site, than attempt to artificially recreate such a site where it did not exist.

The intricate interdependencies of living things dictate that restoration and conservation efforts be focused on the habitat and community levels. The north-facing and south-facing slopes of a hill in the eastern deciduous forest provide different habitats and thus different communities of plants and animals. These differences result from different amounts of direct sunlight that fall on the hillsides which, in turn, affect the moisture and temperature regimes in the soil. These two communities in the same ecosystem are different.

Since the 1800s, ecologists have attempted to define criteria that determine the numbers and kinds of organisms that live in any given ecosystem. In one woodland ecosystem in England, scientists have attempted to list all species of plants and animals. This effort has taken several years, does not include microorganisms, and is not complete (Hunter 1990). Because ecosystems are so complex and are continually changing, ecologists frequently study a particular group of organisms such as rodents, birds, trees, or grasses, or an individual species. From these studies they attempt to develop general rules of ecosystem function or preservation.

Scientists measure and evaluate biological diversity in several ways. One concept of diversity is the number of different types or species of organisms within an ecosystem or over a defined parcel of landscape. In order to compare different sites and different studies, ecologists have developed ways to measure diversity. One of the simplest measurements of diversity is the number of species that dwell in a habitat. The number of species is referred to as species richness. Habitats with more species are considered more diverse. But simple numbers of species often do not tell the entire story of diversity. A forest with 90 percent of one tree species and 5 percent each of two other species is different from a community containing the same three tree species but at densities of 25, 35, and 40 percent. Each forest has the same richness with three species of trees, but the forest with the more even distribution is considered more diverse. The distribution of abundance among different species or the relative abundance of species is referred to as evenness. Forests with high evenness are considered more diverse than forests with low evenness. Ecologists have developed several different equations combining richness and evenness to measure diversity. In these equations richness, or number of species, is a more important factor than evenness. Frequently, ecologists use only the number of species, or richness, when studying an area.

Diversity can be increased to very high levels.

But diversity is not our only goal. We would like also to maintain or restore the natural communities that occurred in a region. Restoration of natural communities is suggested for two main reasons. First, by using plants that originally occurred in an area, the manager will also be more likely to attract and reestablish native animals within the area. Trees, for example, attract fewer bird species when planted in areas in which they are not native. Exotic pine trees in France (Constant et al. 1973) and Australia (Disney and Stokes 1976) contain fewer species of birds than are found in pine plantations in their native countries. Eucalyptus trees are not native to California, Sardinia, or Chile (Smith 1974) and plantations in these areas contain few bird species. Eucalyptus trees, however, support a diverse community of birds in their native Australia. The implications of these studies are clear. Native populations of plants will maximize the diversity of native animal species. A second reason to restore natural communities is that current scientific methods do not provide the means to understand all relationships and individual species' requirements necessary to create a community. Diversity may be increased without understanding all the reasons for that increase. Restoration of a natural community should include as many of the components of the community as possible, to ensure that the requirements of individual species are met.

Principles of Diversity

Landscape restoration is based on an understanding of how ecosystems work. Studies of species' requirements, maintenance of natural areas and biological diversity, island biogeography, landscape ecology, and ecosystems have led to the recognition of specific principles that can be applied to managed parcels of land to maintain and restore natural diversity.

Ecology is the study of how organisms interact with each other and with their environment. Ecologists are often satisfied with general explanations of why certain things happen. However, managers of golf courses, recreation areas, or parks want to predict the outcome of particular action under specified conditions. Because of the complex relationships within an ecosystem, the predictive powers of ecology are limited. But some ecological principles are understood well enough to be applied, resulting in increased diversity. Application of these principles will increase the diversity on small tracts of land and at the same time increase the aesthetic value and preserve the functionality of the tract.

"The key to planning the management for all species of wildlife is to know the species' habitat requirements and provide a variety of habitat components in a desirable combination that will meet the needs of as many species as possible" (Schneegas 1975). To increase the diversity of native plants requires the evaluation of existing site conditions and the application of ecological and horticultural principles in using native plants. Most plants, being rooted in the soil, are totally dependent on the site conditions. For animals, we may analyze why certain species or combinations of species are found in certain places, and recreate the conditions specifically related to those species. Alternatively, we may recreate the native plant community and rely upon immigration of animal species (Fig. 3.1).

Animals require food, shelter from predators and the weather, and breeding habitats to ensure the best chances of securing mates, nesting, and raising young. The challenge with managed areas is to restore or retain sufficient characteristics of the natural community to maintain a high diversity of plants and animals and at the same time allow human use of the area.

The principles outlined in this book are to some degree hierarchical and overlapping. For example, the theoretical best restoration of a disturbed site is a large, circular (maximize interior, minimize edge) preserve that represents the original community found on that site. The minimum size will depend upon whether it is a forest or grassland community. If the site is to have a variety of uses, however, then perhaps the original community cannot be restored. An alternative is to restore a few smaller patches of different habitat communities none of which may contain a full complement of species.

Some of the principles have a threshold of applicability. If a 500-acre forest exists, most species that normally inhabit a forest, including most of those that inhabit deep forest, will be found in this area. If half of that 500 acres were changed to native grasslands, both the forest species and grassland species would be found on that same 500 acres. If the forest acreage is reduced to below the size and shape that will support the entire complement of forest species, then a reduction in the number of species occurs as the parcel is further subdivided (Fig. 3.2). Knowing the limitations of when and how the principles are applied requires some understanding of natural communities. Discussion with ecologists, botanists, and zoologists familiar with the local communities may aid in determining which principles to use in any given area.

Beginning in the late 1800s, scientists noted that islands contain fewer species than continental land areas of equal size. In 1967, MacArthur and Wilson formally developed the theory of island biogeography. Much of today's landscape is divided into island-like habitat patches that are decreasing in size, becoming more isolated, and disappearing. Habitat patches

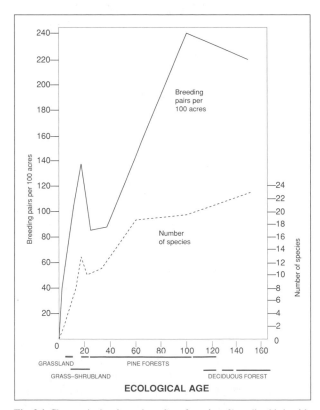

Fig. 3.1. Changes in density and number of species of breeding birds with advance of community development from abandoned agricultural fields to climax forest. Ecological age is in approximate years. (After Johnston and Odum 1956)

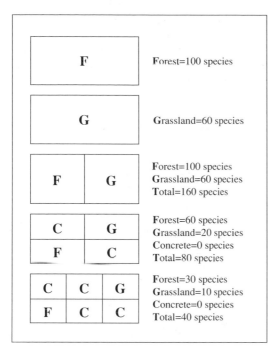

Fig. 3.2. Theoretical effects of fragmentation on species on a parcel of land. Numbers of species are for illustrative purposes only. The total number of individuals within each species will also diminish as the degree of fragmentation increases.

display some similarities with islands. Which species can reach a patch? How diverse is each patch? What is the relationship between patch size and its diversity? These are concepts that have analogous island concepts.

Scientists continue to debate specifics of the theory of island biogeography and other ecological concepts, but a few principles for explaining diversity have emerged: smaller islands contain fewer species; islands further from the mainland contain fewer species; boundaries (edges) between different vegetation types contain more species of both plants and animals; more extinctions of species occur in smaller areas; and reductions in the pool of species for immigration will reduce the number of species and the relative abundance of species in a community. Although many authors apply the theory of island biogeography to the design of natural reserves in order to maintain plant or animal communities, there is not agreement on all management strategies.

Golf courses, recreation areas, farms, schools, and parks may be managed to increase diversity by applying ecological principles. The following is a synopsis of ecological principles that represent current scientific thinking on how diversity is maintained, and suggestions for applying these principles to preserve, recreate, or restore natural areas. We have divided the principles into those relating to the spatial aspects of ecosystems on the landscape (Table 3.1) and those relating to the community or biological aspects of ecosystems (Table 3.2). These principles summarize concepts and ideas derived from scientific studies. A more detailed discussion of each spatial and community principle comprises the remainder of this chapter. The reader may elect to skip the detailed discussions of the principles that follow or read about the principles that are of particular interest.

Table 3.1. Spatial Principles and Guidelines

- **Large areas of natural communities sustain more species than small areas**—Preserve as many large natural communities as possible in single tracts for each ecosystem, or increase the size of existing patches to the minimum size needed to sustain viable wildlife populations.
- **Many small patches of natural communities in an area will help sustain regional diversity**—Where there is no opportunity to preserve, increase, or create large natural community patches, increase the number of small community patches.
- **The shape of a natural community patch is as important as the size**—Modify or design the shape of natural community patches to create more interior habitat. If space is limited, a circular area will maximize interior habitat.
- **Fragmentation of habitats, communities, and ecosystems reduces diversity**—Avoid fragmentation of large patches of natural vegetation. Even a narrow access road through a forest can be a barrier to movement of small organisms, eliminate interior habitat, and introduce unwanted species.

■ **Isolated patches of natural communities sustain fewer species than closely associated patches**—
Minimize the isolation of patches. Corridors and an increased number of patches can prevent
isolation.

■ **Species diversity in patches of natural communities connected by corridors is greater than
that of disconnected patches**—Maintain or develop many corridors of similar vegetation to
connect isolated patches of the same or similar community types. Opportunities exist along
roadways, rivers and streams, urban ravines, fencerows, hedgerows, railroad rights-of-way, to name
a few. Wider corridors provide more wildlife benefits and protect water quality better than narrower
ones. Breaks in the corridor should be avoided.

■ **A heterogeneous mosaic of natural community types sustains more species and is more likely
to support rare species than a single homogeneous community**—On large parcels, mosaics of
natural communities should be restored as the diversity of the landscape allows. Smaller parcels should
be evaluated within a regional context with the goal of developing such mosaics on the landscape.

■ **Ecotones between natural communities are natural and support a variety of species from both
communities and species specific to the ecotone**—Ecotones (transition zones between communities) should be allowed to naturally develop between adjacent communities. The amount of area
in ecotones can be increased by increasing the interspersion of community types on a given parcel,
but this should not be done at the expense of reducing interior habitat.

Table 3.2. Community Principles and Guidelines

■ **Full restoration of native plant communities sustains diverse wildlife populations**—The more
fully restored natural community has a higher diversity. This means introducing as many components of the natural community as possible.

■ **An increase in the structural diversity of vegetation increases species diversity**—The vegetational structure of a community can be enhanced by restoring tree, shrub, and herbaceous layers that
are reduced or lacking. Dead logs and litter should also be left.

■ **A high diversity of plant species assures a year-round food supply for the greatest diversity
of wildlife**—Introduce as many species known to be part of the natural community as possible. Also
retain dead, standing, and fallen trees as they provide important nesting sites for many cavity nesting
species and a source of food for other species.

■ **Species survival depends on maintaining minimum population levels**—Different species will
have different minimum population requirements. The minimum population in a particular parcel
will depend upon factors listed above, such as how connected patches are.

■ **Low intensity land management sustains more species and costs less than high intensity
management**—The maintenance costs and environmental impacts associated with landscape
management can often be reduced by reducing management intensity. Management intensity can
be reduced by converting areas to native vegetation adapted to site conditions. Natural forest,
grassland, and wetland communities are low intensity landscapes.

Spatial Principles

The landscape is a mosaic of land uses, such as
fields, wetlands, woods, and asphalt. Patches are
areas of habitat different from the surrounding area
(called a matrix). The study of natural patches
provides insight into the ecological mechanisms
controlling which species inhabit them. Remnants
are isolated patches of persistent, regenerated, or

restored native ecosystems. In many areas of the
United States, previously disturbed patches may
regenerate to the original ecosystem. This regeneration is the regrowth of a natural community
through natural succession. The ability of a patch to
regenerate will depend on its size, degree of isolation, and how severely it has been disturbed. Restoration can recreate natural ecosystems in areas
where regeneration is not possible. Additionally,

restoration can reestablish ecosystems more rapidly than regeneration. Principles of restoration and succession are discussed in chapter 4.

Principle One—Large areas of natural communities sustain more species than small areas

Species richness within communities follows a consistent pattern of an increasing number of species with increasing size of the area. One method of showing the relationship between number of species and area size is the species-area curve. Scientists plot the number of species on one axis of a graph and the area on the other axis. The number of species in any given ecosystem will increase rapidly as the tract size increases up to a certain point, and then increases less rapidly (Dunn and Loehle, 1988). The species-area curve is different for different vegetation types and for their associated animals. A first estimation of the number of species expected in an area of a certain size can come from studies of species-area curves. To achieve maximum diversity for different types of organisms in different regions, areas of different minimum sizes are required, as illustrated by the species-area curves in Figure 3.3.

The optimum method to maintain maximum diversity is to preserve many large areas. The larger the area the more species preserved. Very large areas ensure the preservation of rare species and large predators. Predators such as hawks and owls require larger patches for survival than do songbirds.

Different geographic regions exhibit different numbers of total species on the same size area. Climate is one of the most important factors affecting geographic variability in species richness. Benign climates have greater species richness than harsh climates (Fig. 3.4). Stable climates have a larger number of species than variable climates (Currie 1991). To protect all or most of the species representative of a particular community or habitat, an area of minimum size must be established. The minimum size area may be different in different ecosystems and the total number of species that can be expected will differ in different areas of the country.

To preserve all species in a forest, large tracts must be preserved. Forest interior species will not occur in small forests. Freemark and Marriam (1986) concluded that large tracts of forest are needed to provide habitat for forest interior birds. Bird species richness increases significantly through a forest island size of approximately sixty acres and is likely to continue increasing significantly at forest sizes greater than sixty acres. Forest interior bird species began appearing in two acre forests (Galli et al. 1976). The interior structure of grassland can be achieved in a smaller area than is required for the establishment of a forest interior. A smaller area can thus provide sufficient habitat for grassland interior birds.

Principle Two—Many small patches of natural communities in an area will help sustain regional diversity

The scientific literature contains many articles debating whether a single large or several small preserves of equivalent total area will contain more species. No clear, general answer on either theoretical or empirical grounds has emerged. Even though it is desirable to preserve large areas, fragmentation of natural communities and the mounting pressures from expanding human populations preclude the establishment of large tracts of natural communities in many areas. When preservation of large areas is not possible, the next best option is to preserve many small areas.

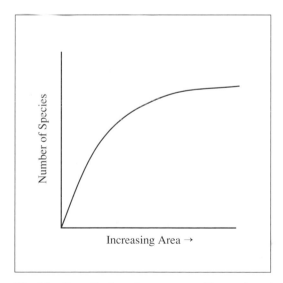

Fig. 3.3. Generalized species–area curve. The number of species increases as the area of a patch or island increases. The actual shape of the curve varies with the type of animal.

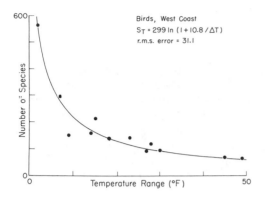
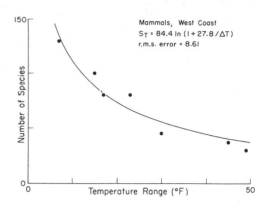

Fig. 3.4. Relationship between temperature fluctuations and species richness in west coast birds from Panama to Nome, Alaska, (a) and mammals from southern Mexico to Nome, Alaska (b). Areas with larger temperature ranges have fewer species. Point for Panama is taken from *Geographical Ecology* (MacArthur 1972, page 135). Mammal data are from Simpson 1964. (reprinted with permission from MacArthur 1975)

The number of species in any area is determined chiefly by the number of different habitats (Forman and Godron 1986). Increasing the size of an area increases subtle habitat differences. Differences in soil, slope, moisture, and associated species affect the composition of the community. Even if sites are chosen randomly, rather than selected to maximize diversity, it is likely that groups of separate sites will encompass various habitats. Each small area will, because of the subtle habitat differences, contain different species. Any single small area may not contain as many species as a large tract, but the total number of species from all smaller tracts may equal or exceed the number of species in a single large tract.

By maintaining several similar patches, the likelihood of all individuals of a species being destroyed is reduced. Random events such as epidemics, parasitic infections, or fires may exterminate a species in a patch. If one large patch containing all the individuals of the species is lost, the species will become extinct. But if several small patches contain the species, it is unlikely that an epidemic or fire will spread to all patches, so some individuals will survive. The last population of Heath Hens was found on an island. A large fire and an epidemic among the hens occurred. These combined natural disasters exterminated this last population (Hunter 1990). Had there been populations on other islands or tracts of mainland, some probably would have survived and could have func-

tioned as a source of immigrants for reestablishing the population on the devastated island.

At any moment several small patches may contain different species due to local extinctions. If the region as a whole is made up of many different patches, then each of the small reserves may support a different group of species and the total number of species conserved might exceed that in a large reserve containing a single or few habitat types. Additionally, the different patches serve as a source of species to emigrate to new patches. Studies summarized by Simberloff and Abele (1982) indicate that for plants in England, birds and mammals on mountaintops in the American Great Basin, and lizard species in Australia, several small reserves contain more species than one large reserve. They theorize that the increase is due to subtle habitat variations. Simberloff and Abele (1984) conclude that the ideal strategy is to have many large reserves, but that smaller reserves are useful. For low density species such as predators, however, large reserves are clearly essential.

Blake and Karr (1984) presented data showing that two smaller forest tracts are more likely to have a greater number of bird species but a single large tract will retain more long distance migrants and forest interior species that are dependent on large forest tracts. A single small patch will not preserve as many species as a larger patch. To maximize species diversity several small patches are needed.

Principle Three—The shape of a natural community patch is as important as the size

Patches of natural habitat occur in many shapes. Depending on the patch, the shape may affect its utility in preserving and creating diversity. Long, thin reserves are optimal for catching immigrants, and functioning as corridors to help direct emigrants to suitable larger reserves; but they do not allow development of distinct interior habitats. A circle is the shape with the least edge per unit area. Use a circular area if space is limited and interior habitat is desired.

Most natural areas are surrounded by human activity that can affect the natural area. Human activities produce disturbances that reduce the number of species. The further the natural area is from human activities, the less likely it is that the system will experience a reduction in the number of species. The edge of a natural area is impacted by surrounding human activities. Oblong or irregularly shaped patches contain a larger portion of edge than round patches or squares with the same total area (Fig. 3.5). Thus round areas have a larger area that experiences less disturbance and will be more likely to have a higher species richness.

When habitat with a distinct interior is to be preserved or created, the optimal shape to use is a circle. If paths are to be created in a natural area, they should be placed as near the edge of the patch as possible and still allow people using the path to experience the natural communities. Placing paths close to the edge of the natural area leaves a larger central area with less disturbance.

Principle Four—Fragmentation of habitats, communities, and ecosystems reduces diversity

Fragmentation can be viewed in several ways. Morrison, et al. (1992) define it as the increase in isolation and decrease in size of resource patches. For the purposes of this book we define fragmentation as the process of altering the landscape, eventually leading to the creation of isolated remnants of natural communities that had once covered the entire landscape. Fragmentation ranges from putting a road through a forest to the elimination of a forest. For the purposes of emphasis and explanation we have specifically chosen to separate the closely related concepts of isolation, corridor de-velopment, and size, shape, and number of patches from the overall concept of fragmentation.

Much research has focused on fragments and their relationship to islands, and the application of island biogeographic theory to fragments. Porosity—the measure of density of patches—decreases as fragmentation increases. This means the distance from one patch to another increases. Reduction of species richness within fragments is a generally accepted phenomenon. Agricultural or urban landscapes that surround native habitat patches are

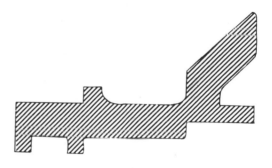

Total area: 96.4 acres
Core area: 0 acres
Species sensitive to fragmentation: 0/16

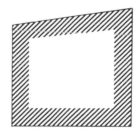

Total area: 116.1 acres
Core area: 49.4 acres
Species sensitive to fragmentation: 6/16

Fig. 3.5. The shape of the patch dictates the amount of edge and interior. (Temple 1986)

radically but not totally different from the native habitat. Some of the native plants and animals still exist in the agricultural or urban landscape, yet the diversity is greatly decreased and they exist isolated from a natural community.

Long-term fragmentation of natural landscapes has been documented in Wisconsin from 1831 to 1950, and in England between 1759 and 1978 (Shafer 1990). A commonly accepted theory is that habitat loss through fragmentation is the leading cause of species extinctions (Norton 1986). As the remaining patches of natural habitat become smaller and smaller, the diversity of animals and plants decreases (Fig. 3.6). Fragmentation of natural communities is occurring on every continent. In some parts of the world, few fragments of natural areas remain. The pattern of decreasing size and increasing modification of fragments is similar on every continent except Antarctica.

Ecological communities and habitats are lost as a result of fragmentation. Fragmentation may result in the complete loss of some habitats and their associated species. The small patches that result from fragmentation may not contain a minimum viable population of a species (i.e., the number of individuals of a given species sufficient to sustain the population). If individuals can move from patch to patch and breed with individuals from other patches, genetic diversity, which is necessary for

the long-term survival of a species, is maintained. If individuals cannot move among patches, the population may be reduced below the minimum size needed to preserve the population, or the genetic diversity may be lowered to a harmful level. As fragmentation progresses, the patches of original habitat become further apart. The increasing distance between similar patches decreases the likelihood that species can migrate among patches. As species are exterminated within a given patch, new individuals cannot immigrate and diversity is decreased.

Rare species and species with patchy distributions are more susceptible to extinction as a result of habitat loss through fragmentation than are common species with an even distribution. As populations in habitat patches are exterminated, the likelihood of extermination of other populations dependent on that species increases.

Effects of fragmentation can be reduced by maintaining or establishing corridors to connect patches. From earlier discussions of eastern woodlots, we have seen that the effects of fragmentation can be reversed as patches of woods are reestablished in farmlands. If large tracts of natural communities exist, every effort should be made to prevent fragmentation. Paths, service corridors, rights-of-way, and roads should be placed on the margins of natural areas. Buildings and areas used by humans should be clustered near the edges of natural communities.

Principle Five—Isolated patches of natural communities sustain fewer species than closely associated patches

Insularization is the process by which fragments of the original ecosystem become more and more isolated from one another thus becoming more like islands. Insularization can decrease or even stop colonization of patches from outside areas. The patches become too far apart to allow individuals to move from one patch to another. Ran-

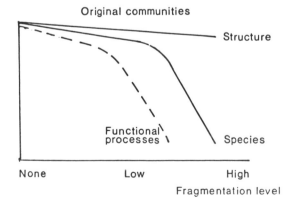

Fig. 3.6. Predicted changes in functional process (e.g. predation, pollination, herbivore), vegetative structure (e.g. stem density) and species numbers (Hansson and Angelstam 1991).

dom events such as epidemics may cause the death of all individuals in a patch. Without the possibility of immigration, the diversity is thus permanently reduced. Insularization can remove resources that species in the reserve depend on for survival (Wilcox 1980). As the patches become so small that species requirements are not met, extinction occurs. Extinction of a species in turn affects other species and may result in a further decrease in species richness (Balser et al. 1981).

In the book *Wildlife—Habitat Relationships* (Morrison et al. 1992), the authors state that "over time, individuals in local patches or groups of patches might become extinct from chance variations in survivorship and recruitment or from catastrophic or systematic declines in the resource base." Figure 3.7 (a-f) is taken from Morrison as an example of this point.

Patch size and degree of isolation affect both the species composition of bird communities (Whitcomb et al. 1981, Butcher et al. 1981) and the local abundance of birds (Lynch and Whigham 1984). Patch size, acreage of nearby forests, and the distance to extensive forest tracts affect the number of bird species (Opdam et al. 1985). In Maryland, forest fragments of at least three acres will permit most forest interior bird species to breed if the tract is near enough to a larger forest fragment to allow recruitment of individuals (Whitcomb 1977, Whitcomb et al. 1977). Although patches this small might not ensure survival of forest interior bird species over long periods of time (Whitcomb et al 1981), they do contribute to genetic diversity, reduce the effects of random events, and allow more individuals to produce young each year.

Morrison et al. (1992) states that "connectivity of patches and permeability of edges vary according to a species' body size, habitat specificity, and area of home range. What acts as habitat entirely suitable in type and amount for sustaining a small-bodied, habitat-specific species such as the red tree vole *(Arborimus longicaudus)*, a specialist on Douglas-fir, also might act, at a much wider scale, merely as a dispersal stepping-stone for a larger-bodied, less habitat-specific species such as the mountain lion *(Felis concolor)*."

Columbian ground squirrels may move between habitat patches, but they do not colonize some new patches because emigrants only settle near other squirrels of the same species rather than in all vacant patches. Movement into a new patch is related to distance from a source of squirrels, but not to the size of the patch (Weddell 1991). Thus for some mammal species location of patches near colonizing sources is important for establishing new populations. Isolation will reduce colonization in these species.

If large tracts of land must be subdivided or fragmented, the resulting smaller areas should be kept close together or connected by corridors to prevent isolation.

Principle Six—Species diversity in patches of natural communities connected by corridors is greater than that of disconnected patches

Corridors are narrow strips of habitat that allow movement between patches of similar habitat (Fig. 3.8). The concept of corridors resulted from studies of species on islands, peninsulas, and mainland fragments. Mainland fragments typically contain more species than islands of the same size. Yet peninsulas or islands that are part of an island group, with some islands near the mainland, have more species than isolated islands. As species become extinct in fragments, corridors allow new species to move into the fragments. Since random events commonly cause local extinctions, corridors are important in maintenance of diversity.

Even small corridors may be effective in providing a path for movement of small mammals, amphibians, and reptiles that travel on the ground and have limited mobility. Some exterminations are inevitable in small reserves or islands. Colonization, the movement of a species into an area not previously inhabited, may enable a small patch to maintain its diversity in spite of exterminations. The maintenance of species diversity is highly dependent on the ability of individuals to recolonize habitat patches after local exterminations. Corridors increase the chances for colonization.

Stepping stones, or closely spaced suitable habitats, may function similarly to corridors. Thus very small patches of natural vegetation may not provide a habitat suitable for a species entire life, but they may serve as important stepping stones allowing emigration into suitable patches. Shelterbelts of the Great Plains are composed of trees and shrubs and may serve as stepping stones between habitats containing trees adjacent to riv-

Fig. 3.7 (a–f). Schematic representation of landscape dynamics of patch colonization and occupancy (Morrison et al. 1992).

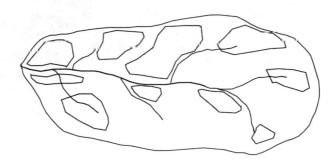

3.7a. Occurrence of ten patches of old-growth forest within a watershed

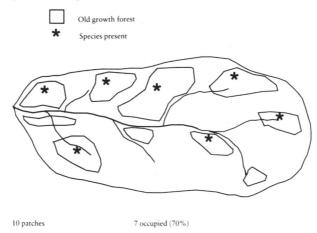

☐   Old growth forest

＊   Species present

10 patches   7 occupied (70%)

3.7b. Occurrence of old-growth obligate vetebrate in seven of the ten patches

☐   Old growth forest   ▨   Clearcut

＊   Species present

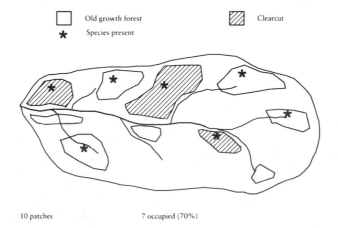

10 patches   7 occupied (70%)

3.7c. Selection of three patches for clear-cut timber harvesting

Fig. 3.7.

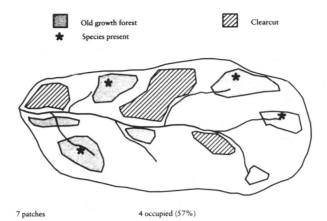

7 patches   4 occupied (57%)

3.7d. Immediate result of harvest disturbance: loss of the species in three patches

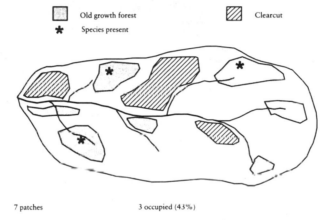

7 patches   3 occupied (43%)

3.7e. Later loss of the species in a distant, isolated, smaller forest patch (faunal relaxation)

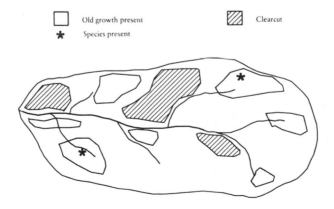

3.7f. Still later loss of the species in a larger forest patch recently isolated

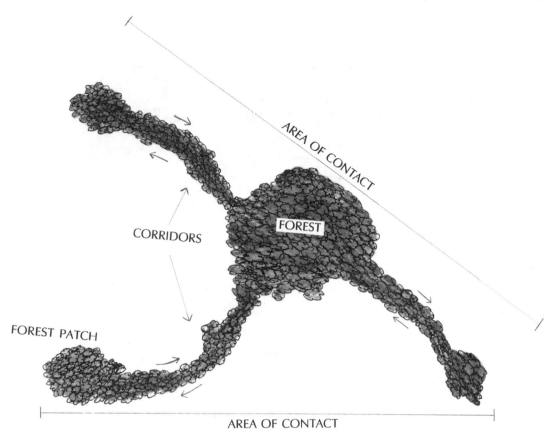

CORRIDORS

FOREST

AREA OF CONTACT

FOREST PATCH

AREA OF CONTACT

Fig. 3.8. Corridors facilitate movement between patches and broaden the area of contact for species moving across a landscape.

ers. They are especially effective for such highly mobile species as birds.

In addition to providing a means to reestablish populations that have been exterminated in a patch, corridors facilitate genetic exchange among small populations. Such exchange is important in maintaining the viability of small populations. The literature includes many articles discussing minimum population size necessary to ensure that a species does not become extinct. Many events can cause drastic reductions in population size. Reduced populations typically exhibit a loss in the genetic variability of the species. Reduced genetic variability may endanger populations because the reduced genetic diversity lowers the chances that at least some individuals in a population will be genetically equipped to endure changes in the environment. The population may thus be reduced further, and loose more genetic variability. As the population becomes smaller, inbreeding occurs, further im-

pairing the ability of the species to survive. Inbreeding of closely related individuals increases the probability that harmful genetic traits will be expressed in their offspring. Movement of individuals among patches reduces inbreeding. Many animals disperse long distances from their parents before they themselves begin breeding. Corridors increase movement of adults among patches and dispersal of young. Both increase genetic diversity.

Abandoned ravines in urban settings, riparian (river edge) areas, utility rights-of-way, roadsides, railroad rights-of-way, hedgerows, and fence lines may function as corridors. For some species it is not important that corridors be of the same vegetation type as the natural areas they connect, but only that they be different from the surrounding croplands or urban areas (Marriam 1984). In designing corridors, connections to existing corridors as well as patches should be incorporated into the design of a site. In urban areas habitat islands are often small, isolated from natural habitats, experience much disturbance, and thus experience high extinction rates (Davis and Click 1978). It is important to create corridors that connect with existing corridors and patches to insure their maximum effectiveness.

In arid regions, areas along rivers (riparian habitats) frequently contain trees not found in adjacent grasslands or deserts. Riparian woodlands maintained along streams in arid regions function as corridors for movement between natural patches.

Forested riparian corridors are also important in agricultural and urban settings. For example, in the cultivated landscape of Kentucky's Bluegrass region several species of salamanders and mammals occur only along the "mainland" wooded corridor of the Kentucky River. Bryan (1991) found smoky shrews, *Sorex fumeus,* only in the deep forest litter of the wooded ravines of the river.

Forested corridors are often important resting and feeding areas for migrating birds (Sprunt 1975). They help maintain suitable water temperatures for aquatic life, improve water quality, and preserve stream integrity. Forested areas along streams should be preserved during development of golf courses and other managed areas. To protect water quality, forest filter strips bordering streams in flat terrains should be at least twenty-five feet wide and increase two feet in width for each one percent of slope (Trimble 1959). In municipal settings the filter strip should be doubled in width (Trimble and Sartz 1957). Filter strips for wildlife may need to be even wider. Stauffer and Best (1980) studied riparian communities of breeding birds in the Central Plains and found that for wooded study plots to contain the maximum diversity of twenty species, a minimum width of 660 feet was needed. A strip 297 feet wide had only thirteen of the twenty species and strips less than twenty-three feet wide contained seven of the twenty.

Two characteristics of corridors—breaks and nodes—have significant implications in increasing and maintaining diversity (Fig. 3.9). Breaks in corridors are long or short areas in which the corridor community is interrupted by the surrounding habitat. Corridors of trees and shrubs around agricultural fields are often interrupted in areas where gates or connections between fields occur. Animal movement along corridors may be reduced or eliminated by such breaks (Forman and Godron 1986). If breaks are necessary, they should be as small as possible. Corridor breaks as small as 50-100 meters may be significant to birds, bats, and other small mammals. Exposure to predation may be a primary reason for avoidance of such openings.

Nodes are areas in which the corridors are wider. Nodes often occur at the junction of two corridors or, in the case of riparian corridors, in the inside of river bends. Increases in species diversity are documented for nodes along fence rows although the nodes show relatively small increases in width compared to the corridor (Forman and Godron 1986).

Opportunities for corridors along roads are often excellent. A slightly wider right-of-way to accommodate native grasses, shrubs, and trees creates an effective corridor. Areas around buildings can serve as screening as well as corridors.

Principle Seven—A heterogenous mosaic of natural community types sustains more species and is more likely to support rare species than a single homogenous community

Sampson and Knopf (1982), in discussing forest management, stressed that managers should strive for a diversity of ecological communities not maximum diversity within one community. Maximum diversity means conserving the greatest number of species possible on one tract of land. Preserving a diversity of ecological communities means preserving many different habitat types on many different tracts of land. Each tract will contain slightly different environmental factors and thus slightly different communities of plants and animals. Each individual tract may not represent its highest potential diversity. Yet a diverse array of species associated with each tract will be preserved. Preserving many tracts of land in many different locations takes advantage of slightly different habitats at each location. Specialized habitats that occur only on a few locations are thus more likely to be preserved and rare species that are found in only these habitats will survive.

In nature, many communities form a natural mosaic of small patches over the landscape. Using the earlier example of north- and south-facing slope communities, we saw this natural mosaic effect. Several distinct communities and habitats may occur in an area of hills with north-facing slopes, south-facing slopes, and wet areas such as springs,

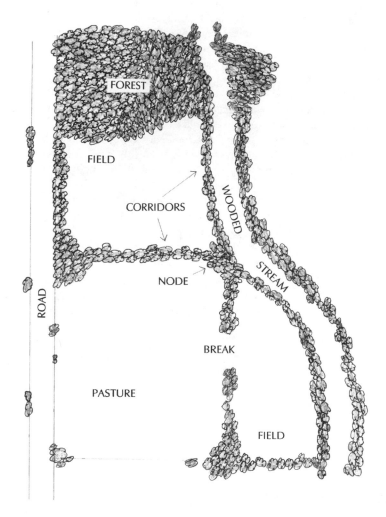

Fig. 3.9. The trees and shrubs along the fence rows, streams, and road connect two forest patches. Nodes and breaks are labeled.

storing the natural communities as much as possible, we will restore the natural mosaic of communities.

Principle Eight—Ecotones between natural communities are natural and support a variety of species from both communities and species specific to the ecotone

Ecotones are the transition zones or boundaries between two habitats, community types, or ecological systems. The boundary may be between a hay field and a forest or between a natural grassland and a forest (see fig. 3.10). Typically the edges of the two ecosystems are not distinct lines, but the transition from one ecosystem to another occurs over some area. This area of transition is called an ecotone. An ecotone may be as abrupt as the edge between a lake and the forest on its shore. Larger ecotones exist in the transition from forest type to forest type as latitude or altitude increases. More species exist in ecotones than in the individual adjacent communities (Forman and Godron 1986). Certain species from each of the two bordering ecosystems, as well as species that exist only in edges, are found in the ecotone, and thus a greater number of species occur in the ecotone than in either ecosystem alone. However, interior species from the two ecosystems are not found in ecotones. Ecotones are transition zones and not all species can live in transition zones.

Ecotones consist of a mosaic of plants from the two adjacent ecosystems, as well as obligate ecotone species. Freemark and Marriam (1986) found that for birds the mosaic of different habitats in ecotones is important in the maintenance of populations of migratory birds. Migratory birds that spend their winters in the tropics form the majority of species in the ecotone between the boreal and

seeps, and streams at the bases of the slopes. Disturbed areas and old growth fields form other patches. Each species has very specific requirements that are satisfied in a particular habitat. The goal should be to preserve different habitats rather than attempt to create a habitat that does not naturally occur in an area. Restoration of an existing south-facing slope community would be easier than attempting to create a north-facing slope community in an area that does not possess the appropriate exposure to sunlight, soils, or hydrology. Restoration of the community that originally occurred in an area will more likely be successful, will require less management, and will exhibit more long-term viability. By analyzing an area and re-

eastern deciduous forests (Clark et al. 1983). Creating a mosaic of habitats generates ecotones, thus increases species diversity.

The edge effect, or the increase in species richness in ecotones (Fig. 3.11), is important in design consideration but cannot be separated from the area effect. If only a small piece of land is available, a forest interior cannot be created, and species limited to forest interior cannot be established. But trees, shrubs, and herbs can be established that will increase the number of species that are not dependent on interior forests. For eastern deciduous forests, sixty-two acres contain 75 percent of bird species and represent the point on the species-area curve at which rapid increases in species ceases (Tilghman 1987).

A circle provides the highest probability of maintaining or establishing an interior forest and reduces the edge effect to a minimum. Shafer (1990) suggests that shape is not important as long as reserves are not very thin (e.g. 600 feet), in which case edge effect becomes overwhelming. In natural settings ecotones increase diversity. Fragmentation, over most of the world, has reduced natural communities to small isolated patches. Edges are abundant between forest and fields because of agriculture. The challenge is to protect, restore, or recreate tracts that contain enough area to provide interior habitats and to allow the natural ecotones between communities to develop over larger areas of landscape. Natural ecotones such as where a wetland meets a lowland forest or where an upland forest joins wooded, streamside bottomlands are more desirable than human-created edge.

Community Principles

Principle One—Full restoration of native plant communities sustains diverse wildlife populations

The physical conditions of a particular site determine what community of plants will survive for the long term without special care. When con-

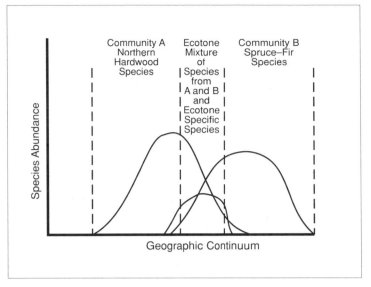

Fig. 3.10. The ecotone between two natural forest communities will include species from both and species that only occur in the ecotone.

fronted with a previously farmed or otherwise disturbed area, it may be difficult to determine the vegetation history of the site. The soil series on a site is one of the best clues to the original vegetation. The techniques described in Chapter 5 can be used to analyze the site. Restoring the fullest possible complement of those plant species that would most likely have occupied an area originally, while retaining the characteristics of the site needed to maintain its human uses, results in an increase in native animals (Fig. 3.12).

Principle Two—An increase in the structural diversity of vegetation increases species diversity

Physiognomy, or vegetation structure, is important since it affects the variety of habitats available for animals and plants. A forest with a shrub understory has more structure and more habitat types than one without a shrub layer. Most species are habitat specific. Some ecosystems naturally have a lower diversity of habitats and species than others. Birds that inhabit grasslands are usually quite characteristic of, and restricted to, the grassland vegetation type. Both diversity and density of bird species are low in grasslands, compared to other habitats (Cody 1985).

When migratory birds return to the forests of the eastern United States to breed, they frequently

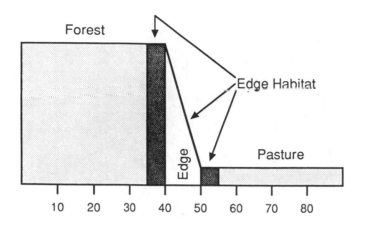

Fig. 3.11. Edge habitat created at the junction of a forest patch and pasture. Edge effects develop in both the forest and the pasture (Luken 1990).

lishing shrubs along roads, as screening around maintenance buildings, and between fairways can increase the populations of sparrows in mixed grass prairie regions.

In shelterbelts in the Great Plains, multiple rows of trees and shrubs provide more structure than single rows. They provide more winter cover and therefore more bird species than single row shelterbelts (Schroeder 1986). Multirow shelterbelts also provide cover for deer and other mammals. The most effective configuration of plants in shelterbelts is tall trees in the middle rows and lower shrubs in the outer rows of the belt. Maximum species richness occurred in shelterbelts of eight or more rows and ninety or more feet in width. In the Central Plains of Iowa, Stauffer and Best (1980) showed that vertical stratification of vegetation, sapling and tree species richness, and sapling and tree size all correlated positively with bird species richness. In this same study it was shown that removal of the shrub and sapling layer adversely affected eleven species and benefited four species. Maximum numbers of bird species occur when three distance layers exist: herbaceous, shrub, and trees over twenty-five feet tall (MacArthur and MacArthur 1961).

Although small mammal populations increase in response to seed production in arid areas and after forest clearing, vegetation cover is the single most important factor affecting small mammal species richness in fence rows of the eastern United States (Asher and Thomas 1985). Structure is also critical to the small mammal community. The biomass and diversity of mice, voles, and shrews are related to the lower strata of vegetation and the depth and friability of the litter and soil humus layers. (Bryan pers. com.)

Vegetation structure is increased by establishing several layers of vegetation including herbs, shrubs, understory trees, and canopy trees. Litter and dead logs also increase structure and should not be removed. Horizontal logs retain leaves and build litter layers which enhances habitat for small mammals, amphibians, and retiles.

return to the same area year after year. They need food sources, perches from which they sing to attract mates, and nest sites, all of which are affected by vegetation structure. Components of the vegetation that correlate with song posts and nest sites include canopy tree volume, tree cover, tree height and size, number of trees, ground cover, and number and type of shrubs (Clark et al. 1983). This and similar studies in other forested communities suggest that the natural association of trees, shrubs, and ground cover is needed to attract and maintain a diverse bird population in eastern forests. Manicured forests with a diminished shrub layer and reduced ground cover and litter will attract fewer birds and provide less protective cover for small mammals, reptiles, insects, and amphibians. One study found that the development of a good ground cover resulted in the addition of one or two bird species; a shrub layer added one to four species. A tree layer added approximately twelve species, with the addition of three more species as the trees developed (Willson 1974).

In the Northern Great Plains, the reduced number of sparrows on unreclaimed mine spoils was shown to be related to the loss of sagebrush habitat. Sparrows used the sagebrush as singing posts, for nesting, and for perches from which to feed on grass seeds. A second factor associated with the abundance of sparrows was the presence of litter (Schaid et al. 1983). Litter should be left in place in both forest and shrub communities. Preserving or estab-

Principle Three—A high diversity of plant species assures a year-round food supply for the greatest diversity of wildlife

Seeds are energy rich and are frequently used by animals as food. Management of areas should include a system to allow seed production. This is especially true for arid areas and grasslands.

Grassland environments exhibit large, unpredictable changes from year to year (Collins and Glenn 1991). A high degree of annual fluctuation in temperature and precipitation occurs with no apparent trend. The amount and timing of precipitation determine the production of seed crops upon which grassland birds depend. Thus it is not surprising that grassland birds are opportunistic. Unlike birds of the eastern forests, they do not return to the same site each year for nesting, but instead seek the most suitable site for reproduction each year. Establishment of natural vegetation will provide song posts, food supplies, cover, and nesting materials and sites. Since the essentials for survival and reproduction exist at these sites, they will be selected by birds. Grassland birds often feed on seeds and insects. Management of grassland should include allowing grasses to produce seeds. The grass stems should be left standing to provide perches from which the birds hunt for insects.

Increases in small mammal populations are often related to increased supplies of food such as seeds. In arid regions, small mammal population increases are correlated with increased seed production. Forest clearings or disturbed areas exhibit an increase in deer mice resulting from increased supplies of seeds and insects (Ahlgren 1966). Butterflies, especially their caterpillars, can have very specific food requirements. This requires the planting of particular plant species if those butterflies are desired or considered part of the particular community being restored. Berries, nuts, nectar, leaves, and twigs may all be used as food sources. Some

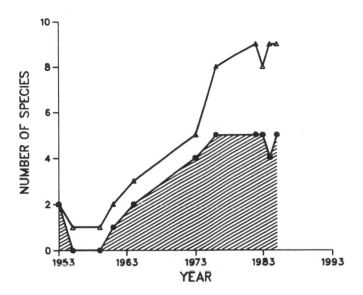

Fig. 3.12. This figure shows the return of interior edge birds (unshaded) and forest interior birds (shaded) in an old field that was allowed to return to natural forest (Askins and Philbrick 1987).

species feed on different food sources during different times of the year. A diversity of plants assures a year-round supply of food for different species.

Principle Four—Species survival depends on maintaining minimum population levels

The size of a reserve affects the number of individuals of any species that can live in that reserve. Every individual of a population requires a certain amount of space. The amount of space is dependent upon food sources and preferences, species interactions, and reproductive needs. Additionally, a minimum number of individuals of a given species is necessary to maintain genetic diversity and long-term survival of the species.

Much research has focused on the minimum population size needed to prevent a species from becoming extinct. One definition of a minimum viable population is the smallest isolated population having a 99 percent chance of persisting for 100 years in spite of random effects. Random effects include demographic, environmental, and genetic events and natural catastrophes (Shafer 1990). The minimum viable population size thus obviously varies among species.

Early suggestions stressed the need for a large

population of between 50 and 500 animals to maintain sufficient within-population variation to prevent negative genetic effects. However, since not all individuals in a population are part of the mating system, more than 50 to 500 individuals may be needed (Boecklen and Simberloff 1986). Recent papers have focused on the subdivision of populations as a means of maintaining genetic diversity rather than trying to determine the minimum population size. This recalls the idea of many small reserves linked by corridors to allow for migration among populations.

In nature, plants frequently exist in small populations. Higher plants, being rooted to one spot, are often highly site-specific. The most favorable sites are a few environmentally heterogeneous reserves of sufficient size to minimize edge effects. Some plants have the ability to propagate asexually. The majority of higher plants are bisexual. Asexual reproduction and bisexuality implies that minimum population sizes for maintenance of genetic diversity can be half those of populations requiring two individuals to reproduce (Ashton 1988). For these reasons plants often need less space than animals to support a viable population.

Principle Five—Low intensity land management sustains more species and costs less than high intensity management

Managed areas in the United States receive a range of treatments, but are often kept neat and tidy. Leaves, dead limbs, fallen trees and limbs, and debris are immediately removed. Grass is mowed on all accessible spots. The resulting communities lack diversity of habitats, do not exhibit complex vegetation structure, and contain reduced food supplies. Diversity of plants and animals is reduced. Reduced management and maintenance provide the opportunity for increased diversity. Dead leaves, twigs, and other debris are a food source for insects which are an important food source for small mammals and birds. Dead limbs provide nest cavities and harbor insects as food supplies for birds. Mature grass provides seed supplies and a more complex vegetation structure. Decreased management intensity increases complex structure of the environment and food supplies, and costs less than intensive management.

Stauffer and Best (1980), in a study of breeding birds of the Central Plains, found that snags (dead, standing trees) were more important than live trees or dead limbs as nesting sites for the ten bird species requiring cavities for nests. Snags or fallen logs also provide food and shelter for many bird species. Mammals, amphibians, and reptiles may also use cavities in snags and logs for shelter. In addition to providing food and shelter, dead logs and snags function in nutrient and energy recycling. Larger species such as the pileated woodpecker can only use trees of a certain minimum size, but small species can use large or small snags. Hunter (1990) suggests that a minimum size of snag to provide for larger species is a thirty foot tall snag with a diameter of twenty inches. Additionally, snags should be distributed throughout the forest since birds establish territories and cannot be crowded into small, localized areas. Explicit equations have been developed to estimate numbers of snags needed to support the maximum number of some woodpeckers. But the autecology of all cavity nesting woodpeckers, much less all species, is too poorly understood to allow the determination of precise numbers of snags needed. Foresters and wildlife managers have generally recommended two to four snags per acre. For North American species this is supported by some empirical data (Hunter 1990).

Conclusion

Forests in Massachusetts represent a transition zone between the hardwood forests of northern New England and the oak-hickory forest of southern New England. Studies of thirty-two woodlands ranging in size from 2 to 170 acres showed that the size of the woodland was the primary influence on diversity. Forests with manicured understories were not included in the study. The number of species of birds increased rapidly as the size of the woodlots increased from two to sixty-two acres, but increased more slowly thereafter. At sixty-two acres, 75 percent of the bird species were present. Management conclusions from this study include the following (Tilghman 1987):

- establish or maintain woodlands greater than sixty-two acres;
- maintain natural vegetation in the shrub layer;
- include a variety of microhabitats such as small scattered openings;
- create some form of water in, or adjacent to, the woods;
- include patches of conifers or wetland;
- eliminate buildings adjacent to the woods; and,
- limit the number of trails.

Similar recommendations exist for prairie communities (Verner 1975):

- preserve as large an area as possible;
- provide a heterogeneous mosaic of grasses and forbs rather than a uniform stand of either;
- provide cattails of intermediate stem density, rather than bulrushes, for nesting;
- increase the structural complexity of the vegetation by increasing the vertical profile and increasing the percent vegetation cover and total volume of vegetation;
- make every effort to avoid single species plant communities or at least to reduce monocultures to small, intermingled patches;
- provide song posts;
- provide nest cavities; and,
- allow enough vegetation to provide cover for nests.

The studies cited above support the principles outlined in this chapter and the idea that restored or existing natural areas should be allowed to remain in their natural state. Grasses should not be mowed. Limbs, dead trees, litter, and debris should be left in place to produce a varied array of habitats.

The principles in this chapter will not all be used on any one site. However, for each site the use of even one or two of the principles will increase diversity. During development of a site the creative incorporation of these principles, when appropriate, will increase diversity.

CHAPTER 4

Principles and Practices of Natural Landscaping

Introduction

Natural landscaping as used in this book is defined as the art of capturing the character and spirit of nature in a designed landscape. The objective of natural landscaping is to restore the natural beauty of the landscape by utilizing native plants in a community context. Unlike ecological restoration, which attempts the replication of an ecological community with a full complement of species, natural landscaping uses nature as a model for landscape designs. Once the local site conditions are analyzed and appropriate ecological communities are chosen as models, the landscaper is free to choose any number of species which characterize those models. Species selection often depends as much on the landscaper's personal vision of natural beauty as on other factors.

The term "natural" landscape is commonly used, when a more accurate term might be "naturalized" (or "naturalistic") landscape. The designed landscape may resemble a natural one, but it requires planning, site preparation, installation, and maintenance. Natural landscaping should be viewed as a long–term process that ultimately results in a self–sustaining landscape. But you are not trying to recreate the complexities and balance of ecological systems.

The planning unit size often dictates whether ecological restoration or natural landscaping is more appropriate to achieve planning objectives. Both forms of naturalizing use the ecological community as the basis for design. Well–developed ecological communities are highly expressive of the land and its history, and have achieved a balance with the natural forces that shape the landscape (Diekelmann and Schuster 1982). They are not only aesthetically appealing, but are relatively stable and self–perpetuating. The species composition of each community is indicative of the local light, moisture, soil, and other environmental factors. The plants that characterize a particular community are compatible, both in terms of their growing requirements, and their ability to compete with each other for available resources. Such communities serve ideally as models for plantings, as well as indicators of local site conditions. As is true in ecological restoration, care should be taken to model the planting after a community having minimal past disturbance from logging, grazing, fire, construction, or other kinds of development. State natural heritage agencies, native plant societies, university and local botanists, and regional and local offices of The Nature Conservancy can often identify high quality ecological communities to serve as local models.

One approach to designing a naturalized landscape is to first select a desirable ecological community model and then attempt to create site conditions favorable to developing that community. While this method may sometimes work, it can require considerable effort and expense with no guarantee of success. A more effective approach is to determine the existing site conditions and select one or more natural communities adapted to these conditions as landscaping models. This requires a thorough analysis of site conditions and a working knowledge of locally adapted ecological communities. The ecological community descriptions in Appendix A and the species matrices in Appendix B are designed to guide the landscaper in selecting the community models and native species appropriate to the planting site.

The species matrices present information on the aesthetic attributes, wildlife values, environmental tolerances, and suggested landscape uses for plant species listed for each ecological community. This information is particularly helpful to the landscaper for selecting species compatible with design criteria. The list of nursery sources in Appendix C can be used to locate the nearest possible sources of nursery–propagated plants and seeds of selected species.

Landscaping With Native Species

Intrinsic to natural landscaping is the use of native or indigenous species of plants adapted to local site conditions. The term "native" refers to a species' place, or region, of origin. A native species is one that occurs in a particular region as a result of natural forces and without known or suspected human cause or influence. The natural range of a species, in which it is considered native, is the area it grows in naturally, without human intervention. Natural range can vary considerably from species to species. For example, white oak is native to a large area of the eastern United States, while willow oak is native to only the southeastern United States. Both of these oaks, if planted outside their natural range, are considered non–native or exotic. According to Dr. David Northington, director of the National Wildflower Research Center, a native plant is one that was here, growing in the wild, before European settlement began 300 years ago. Native plants are part of the natural history of a region. They form naturally diverse communities and are well adapted to the climate, soils, and other biotic and abiotic components of their region of origin. An indigenous plant is one native to a particular range. A plant is exotic if it is growing out of its natural range. A naturalized plant is an exotic that has been introduced to an area and is able to perpetuate on its own. Queen Anne's lace is an example, as is, unfortunately, kudzu. Botanists strongly discourage the use of exotics for fear that successful introductions will displace natives.

When incorporating native plants into a designed landscape, it is preferable to use material from a source as close to the planting site as possible to assure it is hardy and adaptable to local growing conditions. While some ecologists believe that source materials obtained from outside a 50– or 100–mile radius of the planting site could contaminate the local gene pool, most would agree that use of such material is preferable to the use of cultivars or non–native species for restoration projects. Compelling reasons for using native plants in designed landscapes are the desire to have nature's beauty close at hand, conserve natural resources, reduce maintenance costs, preserve biological diversity, and prevent species extinctions.

Most state roadside wildflower programs are beginning to rely more on using wildflowers native to the planting region than they have in the past. The sentiments of Mike Creel, a public information director with the South Carolina Department of Wildlife and Marine Resources, concerning the use of native species for roadside beautification, is applicable to managed landscapes in general: "In beautifying [South Carolina's] roadsides, our basic rule should be to follow nature's lead. We must recognize and inventory existing stands of wildflowers, shrubs, and trees that are already growing along our highways. We must consider ways of conserving these existing stands, ways of improving their growing conditions, and ways of expanding their acreage. The native flora and natural habitats of South Carolina are part of our heritage. Our region's special diversity paints a natural tapestry unlike anywhere else in the world. Those interested in conservation and nature should strive to attain a ["South Carolina]–scape" in their wild acreage..." (Shealy 1989).

Approximately 20,000 species of flowering plants are native to North America (Xerces Society 1990). Just a few years ago the scarcity of native plant materials available from reputable nurseries was a barrier to creating an attractive naturalized landscape. As interest in natural landscaping has "blossomed," so have the number and diversity of mail–order nurseries catering to this demand. Today, it is possible to select from a wider offering of native trees, shrubs, vines, herbs, and grasses than ever before, and to select species that are indigenous to each region of the country. This presents exciting, new opportunities to design with nature and to bring some of nature's inspiration and beauty closer to home.

Cumulative environmental impacts (i.e., from the use of chemicals or mowing) and the costs associated with grounds maintenance can be reduced by using native plants in designed landscapes. Americans are increasingly concerned about environmental quality and are searching for effective alternatives to turf grass and other intensively managed landscapes that consume resources and contribute to environmental pollution. Native plants are adapted to the climatic and environmental conditions of their indigenous regions. When used in appropriate growing conditions, they thrive with minimal need for water, mowing, and chemicals such as fertilizers and pesticides.

The importance of biological diversity to maintaining ecological balance is a motivating reason to use native plants in the naturalized landscape. The loss of native plant communities is a principle cause of species extinction. In the United States alone, some 220 acres of habitat are lost each hour to highway and urban development. About 15 percent of the native plants of North America are presently threatened with extinction. Some biologists estimate there is one plant species for every ten or more animal species, therefore the loss of even one plant species can potentially affect the ecology of a number of animals (Xerces Society 1990). Many plants, in turn, depend on animals for such biological services as pollination and seed dispersal. The value of natural landscaping to preserving biological diversity depends on the type and size of the landscape and its relation to other kinds of land uses. Even on a small scale, however, such landscapes not only protect plant species but also provide food and cover for many kinds of beneficial insects, songbirds, and other animals that are increasingly impacted by habitat loss.

The philosophy behind preserving biodiversity through landscaping works only if we are careful not to contribute to the loss of wild plants. By using only nursery–propagated plants and seeds we can add to the existing flora. Removing plants from the wild disturbs their natural habitats and results in a net loss of plants since only a percentage survive transplanting. Care must also be exercised to avoid introducing native plants into new regions. Many introductions do not adapt, while others become aggressive and invasive into natural habitats to the detriment of native plants and animals. The list in Appendix C can be used to locate the nearest sources of nursery–propagated native plants and seeds. Before ordering plants be sure to ask if the nursery propagates their plants or collects them

from the wild. Do not order from nurseries that wild collect.

Opportunities for Natural Landscaping

Opportunities for natural landscaping abound in all types of managed parcels, from small urban lots to extensive national parks. An urban lot is typically a high intensity management system that relies on a steady regime of mowing, pruning, irrigating, fertilizing, and controlling pests for maintenance. Undeveloped parklands occur at the opposite end of the spectrum, representing low intensity management systems in which maintenance may be limited to provision of access and other low level amenities. On any single managed parcel, there may be one to many levels of management intensity depending on the objectives and uses of different planning units. One goal of using natural landscaping is to reduce management intensity on as many units as possible. Every time we can lower the intensity from high to moderate or low, we reduce the costs and environmental impacts associated with landscape maintenance while increasing aesthetic, wildlife, and interpretive values.

Some examples of places where natural landscaping can be effectively implemented include:

- Entranceways to a parcel, around signs and kiosks, trailheads.
- Lodge, club house, visitor center, meeting, restaurant, and maintenance facilities.
- Roadsides, foot paths, and hiking trails.
- Picnic and camping sites.
- Parking areas.
- Borders around other kinds of gardens (e.g., vegetable).
- Transition areas between mowed and undeveloped areas.
- Lake, pond, stream, and wetland margins.
- Drainage ditches and septic cells.
- Areas too steep, isolated, or otherwise difficult to mow.

A golf course is an excellent example of varying degrees of landscape management intensity on a single site. The intensity is greatest on the greens, progressively less on the tees and fairways, and minimal in areas of rough (Green and Marshall 1987). The latter areas can comprise more than 50 percent of the total area of a course and afford numerous opportunities for natural landscaping. The degree of difficulty of a course is often related to the extent and severity of hazards such as the rough (Green and Marshall 1987). More difficult courses may provide greater opportunities for natural landscaping to achieve multiple objectives of aesthetics, conservation, and economics. Natural wetlands are being incorporated into the fairways and roughs of golf courses.

Many opportunities exist to use natural landscaping around fairways. Port Ludlow of Washington, ranked in the top 1 percent of the nation's best designed golf courses by the American Society of Golf Course Architects, uses wildflowers to accent out–of–play areas, knolls between greens, and doglegs on fairways. Larger areas near entrances, the back of the driving range, and around tee boxes are other suitable locations (Stroud 1989). In intervening areas between fairways, natural landscaping can be used to create a sense of mystery and anticipation as the player moves between fairways, or to visually distinguish one or a series of fairways. Where long–distance views must remain unbroken or where tall vegetation may interfere with play, establishing meadow landscapes may be desirable; elsewhere, wooded landscapes may be more appropriate.

Often, when assessing a managed site for landscaping potential, the planner can identify areas that have a low level of use but are in a high intensity management program. Such areas can often be converted to natural landscapes and be maintained at a fraction of the cost (Photo. 4.1). Golf course superintendents have reported savings of 25 to 30 percent compared to turf, largely resulting from reduced mowing, irrigating, and fertilizing (Stroud 1989). States that have implemented aggressive roadside wildflower programs have reported similar savings. The Georgia Department of Transportation (DOT) reported a 25 to 30 percent savings in maintenance costs for areas previously mowed (Corley 1989). In Florida, Gary Henry, a DOT landscape architect, explains: "In the past it would have been seven mowings a year, and now that is reduced to two or three" (Weathers and Hunter 1990). One annual mowing is all that may be needed in some locations.

In addition to reduced maintenance costs, such programs elicit extremely positive public response, increasing tourism and visitor enjoyment. Golf course superintendents view wildflower plantings as one of their biggest marketing tools, noting that the positive response from guests has been "overwhelming" (Stroud 1989). One South Carolina DOT landscaper reported receiving "about twenty calls and letters a day" from motorists enthused

Photo 4.1. Naturalized landscapes add beauty and lower maintenance costs..

about roadside wildflower plantings. The North Carolina DOT program was described by landscaper Bill Johnson as "the most popular program instituted in DOT." Again, the response was described as overwhelming (Weathers and Hunter 1990). The Texas roadside wildflower program has been around a long time, but has really exploded in the past five years. With renewed efforts beginning in 1980, the statewide mowing budget declined from $33 million annually to $21 million, saving $12 million (Weathers and Hunter 1990). Comparable savings can be realized on any size site, from a corner suburban lot to extensive rural acreage.

An increasing number of government programs are available to help land managers convert managed lands to natural vegetation. For highway projects, monetary support is mandated by the 1987 Surface Transportation and Uniform Relocation Act, which requires that twenty-five cents out of every $100 allocated for landscaping federally funded highways be spent on wildflower plantings. The U.S. Department of Agriculture's Agricultural Stabilization and Conservation Service has a relatively new program to provide cost sharing to landowners establishing native vegetation. Many state agencies now have habitat improvement and forest stewardship programs that offer technical assistance with restoration planning and cost sharing to implement revegetation programs. Additional assistance is sometimes available through local Cooperative Extension Service and Soil and Water Conservation District offices. Local restoration experts are often the most knowledgeable about the assistance programs available in their area.

Landscape Planning

Site Analysis

The process used to develop a plan for naturalizing is presented in Chapter 2. An important part of that process is assembling baseline information about the site and analyzing that information to develop specific design criteria. Physical survey data are used to identify micro–climatic effects and characterize topography (and exposures to light and wind), hydrology, and soils. This information is used to select appropriate ecological communities as landscaping models. Biotic survey data are used to characterize vegetation and identify the potential of existing ecological communities for preservation, restoration, or enhancement. This section describes some of the factors to consider when analyzing a site for natural landscaping.

Climate

The effects of climate and existing physical features on establishing or enhancing the naturalized landscape should be evaluated. Large–scale patterns of temperature and precipitation influence the predominant vegetation of a region, but climate can also reflect local influences. Heat reflected off pavement in urban areas, for example, can greatly increase air temperatures. Local climate data should be compared to regional data to determine whether local differences may affect vegetation patterns. The creation of a favorable micro–climate may be an essential part of the design, enabling the establishment of certain plant species which do not presently exist on the site. In all regions, the south side of a building is warmer than the north side, but seasonal changes in the length and angle of sunlight and their effects in each region should also be considered (Diekelmann and Schuster 1982).

In the northeast, winds come predominantly from the southwest in summer and the west and northwest in winter, but local influences can alter this pattern drastically. Tall buildings and certain topographic features can influence wind velocity; winds passing over water may be cooler or warmer, depending on the water body, but are generally more humid. Shelterbelt plantings are often used to modify the patterns and drying effects of wind on a site, as well as to reduce exposure to sunlight and to screen views. The protected micro–climate of a woodland environment can be created or enhanced by planting overstory trees to reduce exposures to sunlight and wind and modify the effects of these elements on soil moisture, and air and soil temperatures. Use of understory trees, shrubs, and vines can further these effects and create additional micro–climatic effects at various vertical above–ground heights. Conversely, pruning or removing woody vegetation can have the opposite effect on a site (Diekelmann and Schuster 1982).

Topography

The existing contours of a site often dictate the placement of roads and other structural components (Weddle 1983). Proper conservation practices dictate that roads be routed along the contours of a slope to prevent soil erosion as well as to minimize long–term maintenance costs. Topography also has a direct effect on the micro–climate of a site and can affect the selection of an appropriate plant community type. North– and east–facing slopes generally have less exposure to wind and sunlight, and being more mesic than south– and west–facing slopes support a greater diversity of plant and animal species. Slopes are better drained than level bottoms and terraces, which may be subject to periodic or prolonged flooding or saturated soil conditions.

Topography can be used to screen an undesirable view or as a focal point to display ornamental plantings. Where the topography is relatively flat, construction of berms can add vertical diversity and mystery to the landscape by hiding or revealing different landscape features.

Hydrology

Aquatic features such as streams, springs, and ponds contribute to the aesthetic and biological diversity of a landscape, and should be retained and enhanced wherever possible. Water adds a refreshing element to the landscape, both visually and audibly, and can be the focus of a landscape design. Even small, shallow pools and muddy depressions can present opportunities to establish different kinds of vegetation and are valuable to wildlife. The potential for creating new water bodies on a site should be carefully evaluated. It is often possible to increase the water–retention capabilities of a site simply by modifying existing drainage practices or structures. The benefits of creating new water bodies by damming or otherwise altering natural hydrology, however, should be carefully evaluated in terms of the objectives delineated in the landscape plan. Water bodies impacted by pollution should be examined to determine the potential for improving water quality and establishing natural vegetation in the water and along the shorelines.

Soils

The condition of the soil at various locations within a planning site may affect the potential for establishing different types of natural communities. Areas with naturally hydric soils suggest high water retention and good potential for the establishment of a wet prairie or even an aquatic community. Fertile soils with good drainage can support many kinds of forest and prairie communities in the eastern region. Excessively well–drained soils with low fertility will support a prairie or barrens community in the east, or a desert community in the southwest. Modern soil improvement techniques make it possible to grow plants on naturally poor or highly degraded sites, however, the costs of replenishing soil structure, moisture retention capability, fertility, and other qualities should be considered (Green and Marshall 1987).

Vegetation

To promote aesthetic and biological diversity, good quality representatives of existing ecological communities should be retained and protected to the extent possible during all phases of planning and implementing a naturalization plan. Such communities should be considered as site amenities that influence the overall landscape design. Retaining existing desirable vegetation can reduce the overall costs of implementing the plan. Trees are a long–term investment in the landscape, and healthy trees should always be retained where possible. Even undesirable trees can often be retained to provide needed shelter for new plantings until they are well established.

Landscape Design Considerations

The presence and quality of existing natural communities, as well as the prevailing natural character of the surrounding landscape will, in large part, influence the design. Knowledge of how the pre–developed landscape appeared is helpful in developed areas. Existing ecological communities may be the focal point of a landscape plan, and high quality communities, in general, require minimum effort to achieve multiple objectives for aesthetics, wildlife, and economics. Plantings of ornamental native species with value as wildlife food and cover may be desired to enhance the aesthetics of a high quality community. More disturbed or degraded communities may require more aggressive programs of weed eradication combined with extensive plantings.

Many of the principles outlined in the chapter on ecological restoration (Chapter 5) may be applied toward the enhancement of an existing natural community to satisfy natural landscaping objectives. Where natural communities are lacking, design options should reflect the objectives as stated in the landscape plan.

Principles for Designing With Native Plants

Using native plants in natural landscaping presents unique design opportunities and challenges. Unlike most cultivars, the adaptive quality and natural character of native plants has not been sacrificed to produce larger flowers or prolonged blooming periods. The aesthetic qualities of native plants are varied and often subtle. While some native plants produce large, showy blossoms, the most striking flower displays in nature often result from a tendency for a species to grow in groups or colonies. This clustering tendency can be recreated in the garden by imitating these natural patterns of arrangement. This clustering technique can also be used to display other attributes to their best advantage, such as attractive bark, twig, and foliage colors or textures.

With some exceptions, native plants tend to bloom for relatively brief periods of time. Designing a naturalized landscape with continuous bloom necessitates the use of a diversity of species having successive blooming periods. When a diversity of wildflowers is used, the naturalized landscape changes throughout the season. This dynamic quality is fascinating to observe, as is the variety of wildlife attracted to each successive production of flowers and seeds.

In eastern deciduous forests, many early-blooming wildflowers go completely dormant by summer. Inter-plantings of such species among other species that emerge later and persist well into the season is an efficient use of available space and keeps the planting interesting. For example, ferns are suitable for inter-planting among early bloomers with early dormancy, such as Dutchman's breeches, Virginia bluebells, shooting star, and dwarf larkspur. It should be kept in mind that a designed landscape of native plants will evolve over time as the plants self-propagate, filling in spaces, and rearranging their positions in the spirit of competition. We feel that this is a desirable progression, but in confined spaces it is often desirable to control this rearrangement process, either by heavy mulching which discourages self-propagation, or by hand pulling seedlings that appear in undesired locations.

Wildflowers often display a general progression of plant height corresponding to season of bloom. Early spring-blooming plants are often low to medium in height, while later blooming species are generally medium to tall. In the design of an island or border planting, early-blooming plants are placed in the forefront and middleground, with later-blooming plants constituting middle and background areas. Most native plant nurseries provide information on plant height and period of bloom for species they offer.

In addition to the plant component, a naturalized landscape is composed of other natural materials, both organic and inorganic. The addition of materials such as rocks and logs in a design can serve both as substrates for plants to grow on and as interesting features in themselves. There are a great variety of woodland mosses that colonize rocks and woody debris, many of which are extremely attractive and delicately textured. Their bright greens contrast pleasingly with the darker fronds of Christmas and leatherwood ferns, and lend a sense of age and establishment to a landscape. Rocks can form the basis of a rocky glade landscape, or be arranged in linear fashion to emulate a dry stream bed, with some boulders buried to one-third of their mass to appear more natural than just scattered (Beikmann pers. com.). Large and small boulders arranged along a stream bank can create an illusion of swiftly flowing whitewater, or become the structural framework for designed waterfalls. One large boulder with a concave center filled with water can serve as a birdbath or drinking hole.

Natural materials can serve effectively as pathways through the naturalized landscape. Stone pathways made of native bedrock slabs blend well with naturalized plantings and are virtually indestructible. On wet sites, they should be set into a bed of gravel at least four inches deep (Diekelmann and Schuster 1982). Other materials that make satisfactory pathways are gravel, wood chips, and mosses on moist, shady sites. The use of path rush or poverty rush *(Juncus tenuis)*, a small plant that often becomes established naturally on foot trails, as a self-sustaining pathway material for low traffic areas deserves investigation.

Landscape Models

Designing a naturalized landscape is an attempt to capture the character of the ecological community serving as the model, whether it is a dry (xeric) forest of stunted, gnarled trees, or an alpine meadow with sweeping wildflower vistas. Even on a small scale, naturalized landscapes can suggest the patterns of light, colors, shapes, and textures reminiscent of their natural counterparts. The tranquil, reflective quality of a southern swamp can be captured in a pond garden. A patch of prairie wildflowers and grasses recalls the expansive vistas of the midwestern tallgrass prairies; a rocky xeriscape of cactus and other succulents mimics the textures and hues of the southwestern deserts.

The organization of the naturalized landscape may appear to be random, but it should reflect an order imposed by natural forces such as gravity, sunlight, wind, freezing, and thawing (Cox 1991). Knowing how these forces operate within ecological systems leads to more natural–appearing designs. The contours of a naturalized landscape should not be defined by straight lines or right angles, but should flow in response to a natural or planned scheme that harmonizes with the character of the surrounding landscape. Contours may follow the irregular patterns of soil, water, bedrock, topography, or other natural features, or be laid out to camouflage or create a harmony with rigid features imposed by property boundaries, buildings, and other human–made intrusions.

Naturalized landscapes can be divided into two general categories to assist the landscaper in developing broad design criteria: woodland (shady) landscapes and meadow (sunny) landscapes. Shady landscapes are modeled after forest and woodland communities, while sunny landscapes are based on prairie and meadow communities. Woodland or meadow landscapes can be dry, wet, or gradients in between; desert communities occur on the dry extreme while wetlands occur on the wet extreme. Theme gardens may be considered as variations in either category. For example, a water garden may be modeled after a wet forest or an open bog; a butterfly garden may be modeled after a dry, mesic, or wet prairie community with special attention given to selecting plants used for food and cover by a diversity (or selected species) of butterflies.

Using the ecological community as a model takes much of the guesswork out of selecting compatible species adapted to site–specific conditions. Plants should be selected first for their fitness for the total planting, and only then for color, shape, and texture (Diekelmann and Schuster 1982). A well–planned landscape is self–perpetuating with minimal maintenance. Perennials, which return each year from the original rootstock, often comprise the bulk of a planting. Annuals, which produce flowers and seeds and die in one season, provide quick cover and color, and usually contribute an abundance of seed for wildlife.

Woodland Landscapes

Forest communities serve as models for shady landscapes, landscapes dominated by trees and shrubs. Forest communities are complex environments with a great diversity of colors, forms, textures, odors, and sounds that appeal to all of our senses. Visitors travel great distances to experience the breathtaking spring wildflowers in the Great Smoky Mountains, the blazing autumn colors in New England, the languid mystery of the southern swamp, and the towering majesty of the giant Sequoias. On a more functional level, such landscapes offer shelter from the hot summer sun and cold winter wind, as well as a psychological sense of solitude and privacy. A desire to duplicate these qualities in our designed landscapes is a strong incentive for choosing the forest community as a landscape model.

The character of the forest is shaped largely by the trees and shrubs, which, by virtue of their numbers and size, influence localized environmental factors such as light, moisture, and wind. The trees in a healthy forest appear randomly spaced and exhibit many shapes and sizes. Unlike the spreading habit or growth pattern of open–grown trees, competition for light causes forest trees to grow straight upward before branching. In a mature forest, the overstory trees form a nearly continuous canopy of foliage, beneath which are several layers of foliage (at different levels) created by the understory trees (many of which are younger age classes of the overstory species), shrubs, and climbing vines. The amount of sunlight reaching the ground is filtered through the many layers of foliage and can be quite subdued. Near the ground is another layer of vegetation comprised of herbaceous plants such as grasses, wildflowers, and ferns, as well as mushrooms, liverworts, and mosses which may also grow part–way up tree trunks and branches. The forest floor is frequently littered with pieces of wood and bark, leaves, and other organic debris in varying stages of decomposition. This debris and humus provides sustenance for plants as well as many kinds of insects and other organisms, and makes a major contribution to the rich, loamy soil characteristic of many forest environments.

Existing site conditions, the size of the planting, and overall objectives for the site largely influence the design process. Where a woodland already exists, the objective of the design may simply be to enhance the aesthetic and wildlife qualities by removing undesirable plants and adding desirable species of trees, shrubs, and wildflowers. Trees and shrubs add vertical diversity to the woodland garden and form a structural framework for the wildflowers, ferns, and grasses. Flowering trees and shrubs and wildflowers can be concentrated along access routes and resting areas for maximum visual impact.

An area containing tall shade trees with a grassy groundcover presents greater design opportunities. The bright shade found beneath such trees can be ideal for growing a diversity of woodland plants. The entire area of trees may be developed into a woodland garden, or plantings may be established as "islands" or borders centered around clustered groups of trees, with existing grass maintained as mowed pathways between the plantings. Designing a woodland landscape on open, unshaded sites, requires the greatest amount of time and effort, but offers the greatest opportunities for expression. Establishing a tree cover is the first priority. The types and numbers of species should reflect the model community, but may be reduced on small sites to one or two species with an underplanting of wildflowers.

Woodland wildflowers and grasses add seasonal color and textural interest to the woodland garden. Most woodland wildflowers bloom in the spring and can be naturalized in large numbers beneath trees to create masses of solid color. Many wildflowers are grown not only for their spring flowers, but for their attractive foliage or colorful berries. Others, such as shooting star and Virginia bluebells, go completely dormant after setting seed and disappear from the landscape until the following spring.

Ferns are often used as the matrix or background of a woodland garden. Ferns make a handsome ground cover, and the more aggressive species, such as the hay–scented, fragile, sensitive, and bracken ferns, quickly form a dense cover in mesic forest, even in heavy shade. The shallow rooted species are especially compatible beneath deep–rooted trees and shrubs because they do not compete for moisture and nutrients (Cobb 1963). Pleasing effects may be created by choosing ferns with fronds of a shape, form, and texture that contrast with the growth forms of woody plants. An underplanting of fine–leaved maidenhair or beech ferns, for example, contrasts nicely with the solid formality of native evergreen rhododendrons and laurel (Cobb 1963). The taller species make an excellent backdrop for the colorful spring display of woodland wildflowers, and their many shades of green provide a cool respite from the intense light and heat of summer. Like most woodland wildflowers, ferns prefer a light, well–drained soil high in organic content. Cinnamon and royal ferns prefer a constantly moist soil in sun or very bright shade, and will even grow in saturated soils.

Meadow Landscapes

Prairie communities serve as the models for meadow landscapes, sunny herbaceous landscapes dominated by grasses and forbs. The name "prairie" brings to mind expansive vistas of tall grasses and brightly colored flowers waving in the summer breeze. The prairie community is best characterized in the great plains and midwestern regions, where it formerly occupied vast areas. In the predominantly forested eastern regions, such communities often occurred as openings of various sizes in the forest, sometimes called meadows or glades.

A prairie community achieves its most dramatic appeal when recreated or restored on a scale that emulates the expansive quality so characteristic of the prairie regions. Even on a smaller scale, a well–designed wildflower meadow or garden possesses all the elements that make the prairie such a desirable landscape system: an open visual field, a diversity of colors, shapes, and textures that change throughout the seasons, and from year to year, low maintenance requirements, and high wildlife value.

A prairie or meadow landscape is quicker to establish than a woodland landscape, but requires just as much attention to planning, site preparation, establishment, and maintenance. The prairie community develops under conditions of maximum sunlight. Although many species of prairie plants tolerate shade for part of the day, they may produce fewer flowers and not compete successfully with more shade–tolerant species on sites receiving less than six hours of sun each day. Within forested regions, prairies are more common on southern and western slopes, which are hotter and drier. However, like forest communities, prairies occupy all moisture gradients from wet to dry. Differences in moisture influence species composition.

Bird and Butterfly Gardens

Designing a garden to attract and feed wildlife is similar to other kinds of naturalizing, except that the plants are selected as much for their food and cover value as for their aesthetic appeal. The key to attracting the greatest variety of wildlife is to supply a diverse complement of food and cover plants in all seasons, as well as water. In a small garden, an understory tree or shrub and three or more herbaceous species may be adequate; nest boxes and feeding structures can be used to supply additional niches for wildlife to use. Small gardens will rarely satisfy the life requirements of feeding, nesting, and resting for numerous wildlife species, but they can serve as feeding oases in the midst of developed landscapes to attract and benefit the more mobile species that venture a distance from their forest or grassland homes.

Providing a reliable source of food benefits wildlife since they expend less energy searching for food; this can be especially critical for parents feeding young. The nesting and reproductive success of wildlife is greatest when dependable, season–long sources of food and cover are available. Many species of birds will return to the same locale each year where these requirements are consistently met.

Many wildflowers provide nectar sources for a variety of birds and insects, while others are adapted to only certain species of either group. Of the nectar feeders, hummingbirds are more attracted to tubular flowers in the warm color ranges of red, orange–red, and pink; bees prefer flowers that are blue, yellow, violet, or in the ultraviolet range; butterfly flowers may be purple, lavender, yellow, orange, white, or red and are usually tubular and fragrant.

Hummingbird Gardens

There are twenty–one species of hummingbirds that reach North America, sixteen of which breed here. They are present during some portion of the year in every region except the far north and treeless plains (Arbuckle and Crocker 1991). The ruby–throated and a number of western species winter along the Gulf coast in ever–increasing numbers. A number of hummingbird species are year–round residents in the west.

Gardens designed to attract hummingbirds can be of any size, including patio or porch gardens in pots or window boxes. No matter the size, the hummingbird garden should have a combination of food or nectar plants as well as plants that provide cover for resting and nesting. Certain "hummingbird flowers" are specifically adapted for pollination by hummingbirds. Such flowers are generally tubular, produce abundant nectar, have warm colors (often red, orange, or pink), lack fragrance, and are more accessible to hummingbirds than insects. The flowers are often pendant or positioned towards the outside of the plant where hummingbirds can feed without touching the foliage. In addition to nectar, hummingbirds obtain protein food by eating small insects such as beetles, flies, mosquitoes, aphids, and spiders (Terres 1980).

Hummingbirds spend about four–fifths of each day perched on branches near their preferred food sources. At night they roost in dense cover, and select trees or shrubs, often in or near the edge of woodland, as nest sites. Water can be an added attraction for drinking and bathing. Water can be supplied in the form of nectar or tree sap, but like other birds, hummingbirds will drink water from a variety of sources. They will bathe in shallow water, but the water in most birdbaths is too deep. Often, they bathe while flying through a fine spray of water from a waterfall or fountain. After bathing, the birds typically perch on a nearby branch to shake off the water and preen their feathers.

Plants should be chosen to provide nectar sources in the garden in all seasons that hummingbirds are present. Wildflowers generally offer more nectar than the cultivars derived from them and should constitute the bulk of a hummingbird planting. Cultivars and bulbs may be used to extend the season of bloom, and annuals such as impatiens and petunia can brighten up the forefront of a border garden. Hanging baskets of begonia, annual phlox or fuschia can be hung outdoors on warm spring days to provide nectar for early migrants, and brought inside during inclement weather.

Food can be provided entirely by growing preferred food plants, or by the addition of an artificial feeding structure filled with a sugar solution of one part white (sucrose) sugar to four parts water. The latter can be especially important when drought or other factors reduce natural food supplies.

Some of the best native plants that attract hummingbirds in each season are listed below. Non–native plants and cultivars can be incorporated as needed to assure continuous bloom.

Early spring: red columbine, wild blue phlox, fire pink, red buckeye, scarlet larkspur

Mid–late spring: beardtongues, New Jersey–tea, coralbells, azalea, and evening primrose, Canadian lousewort, ocotillo, black locust, hawthorns

Summer: bee balm, scarlet sage, blazing star, gilia, summer phlox, trumpet honeysuckle, trumpet–creeper, crossvine, rose mallow, royal catchfly, coral berry, wild jewelweeds, wild lilies, bushbean, Indian paintbrush, agave, lupine, crimson monkeyflower, currant, bouvardia, scarlet figwort, butterfly milkweed, scarlet penstemon

Late summer–fall: cardinal–flower, California fuschia,

Year–round (southern regions): lantana

Songbird Gardens

Songbirds delight us with their songs, brilliant colors, and playful antics. Because of their aerial habits, they tend to be more visible than other kinds of wildlife, and we are able to observe much of their daily activities. While some species of birds, most of them not indigenous, are troublesome pests in our cropland and orchards, songbirds are generally pleasant and interesting, and we find their presence in our gardens desirable.

Most birds require a variety of insect food as well as seeds. During the breeding season, songbird diets are often higher in protein–rich animal foods. A garden that attracts insects will often attract a variety of birds that feed on them. In fall and winter, berries and seeds become important in the bird diet.

In winter, birds often feed on the "cones" of alder, birch, and sweetgum (Wilson 1987). Good sources of seed are the native sunflowers, which are very attractive to goldfinch, sparrows, and other finches. Other good sources of seed which are also attractive garden plants include asters, coneflowers, blazing stars, tickseeds, partridge pea, coreopsis, blanket flower, ox–eye sunflower, clovers, wild bergamot, beardtongues, phlox, black–eyed susans, Juneberry, serviceberry, and native blueberry. Some good berry–producing shrubs and small trees that make attractive additions to the garden include dogwoods, red mulberry, black cherry, wild plums, elderberry, sumacs, red cedar, winterberry, deciduous holly, wild roses, red chokeberry, viburnums, and hawthorns. Some shrubs which have been touted for their berry production but which are extremely invasive into natural habitats and should be avoided include the non–native honeysuckles, multiflora rose, autumn and Russian olive, buckthorn, and barberry (see Chapter 5 for more information on non–native pests).

Butterfly Gardens

Humans are naturally attracted to the brilliant kaleidoscope of colors and patterns of butterflies, and to their delicate flight which captures the imagination. They inspire curiosity rather than revulsion because they are without the means to sting, bite, or otherwise inflict human injury (Schneck 1990). Many butterfly species have wide ranges while others are found only in certain regions. As a first step in designing a butterfly garden, the landscaper should learn which species occur in the planting region, then attempt to provide plant species which afford food and cover for all life stages.

Butterflies need food plants in all stages of life; the larval, or caterpillar stage feeds on specific plant hosts, and the adult butterfly feeds on nectar and other materials (Arbuckle and Crocker 1991, Newsom–Brighton 1987, Schneck 1990). Planting many kinds of nectar–producing flowers provides continuous bloom and attracts a diversity of butterflies all season. Since caterpillars are often very specific in the plant species they use for food and cover, it is possible to attract particular butterfly species by planting their preferred food plants.

Since they are cold blooded, butterflies require sunshine to warm up and become active. They also require protection from wind. A background planting or border of trees, shrubs, taller herbaceous plants, or dense vines over a wall, fence, or trellis, can help create a sheltered feeding area and warmer conditions favorable to butterfly movement. The planting should be located on the upwind side of the garden for best protection. Some suitable cover plants include passion flower and pipevine for vine cover; New Jersey tea and leadplant for low shrub cover; hydrangea and sweetshrub for taller shrub cover; and black cherry, mulberry, and hackberry for tree cover.

Butterflies cannot drink directly from open water, but make regular visits to and even congregate in large numbers at puddles of wet sand or earth (Schneck 1990). In addition to water, they imbibe salts and trace minerals. Scattered depressions in the ground with stones and sticks placed on top will further enhance a garden's attractiveness to butterflies.

Water Gardens

Water in the garden has a particular fascination, adding dimensions of light, depth, and movement to the naturalized landscape. Water gardens are often used as an added attraction within other types of landscapes and can become a visual focal point for other garden themes such as bird and butterfly and rock gardens. Larger ponds may attract a variety of wildlife, including waterfowl, shorebirds, muskrat, and beaver. Even small ponds can support an abundance of life such as fish, frogs, and snails.

Wetland (palustrine) communities serve as models for water gardens and landscapes characterized by emergent aquatic plants. These landscapes can be designed as part of a natural wetland, in ponds or pools constructed for this purpose, or even in water–holding containers of varying sizes. The relatively new innovations in pool liners and preformed pools combined with a greater understanding of how to maintain the balance of life in a pool, has caused a revolution in water gardening.

Methods of constructing a water garden are varied and depend on the type of materials used. Construction techniques are beyond the scope of this book, but there are many references on the subject, and mail–order nurseries and garden centers often have valuable expertise to offer. Existing ponds and lakes can be visually enhanced by planting emergent aquatic plants along the shores. Abrupt or steep shorelines may need to be graded to reduce the slope before plants are installed. Gradual or graduated shorelines are ideally suited to many plant species and allow better accessibility for wildlife.

Any container capable of holding water is a potential water garden. Vinegar and wine barrels cut in half are popular, but wood containers that contained oil, tar, or wood preservative should not be used as an unsightly scum may form on the water surface, and the high concentration of arsenic used in most pressure treated materials can be highly toxic to people and wildlife (Beikmann, pers. com.). Any container should be thoroughly scrubbed before use, but soaps and detergents should be avoided. Fountains, waterfalls, and other structures help move water through the garden. A good filtration system, including mechanical, bacterial, and plant components, is essential for maintaining clean water in constructed gardens.

Newly constructed water gardens should be carefully sited. Most aquatic plants prefer a good deal of sun but should be given protection from wind. A natural water garden may be located in the lowest part of the landscape as would occur in nature, or at least made to appear lower than the adjacent land (Xerces Society 1990). This effect can be achieved by mounding soil behind the pool, which creates a nice stage for a backdrop planting of wildflowers and ferns to reflect in the pool's surface. The mound can be sited so as to provide protection from wind. If placed in a low–lying area, run–off from adjacent land should be diverted around the pool to prevent contamination by fertilizers, pesticides, silt, and decaying matter (Roth 1988). Low–lying areas should be avoided when locating a pool that is artificially lined. The soil should be well–drained to prevent heaving, cracking and breaking, and the pooling of run–off which can displace a plastic liner. Soil which is very sandy or crumbly may require a retaining wall to prevent soil from caving in.

Most aquatic plants prefer six or more hours of sunlight each day for extensive blooms (Roth 1988), so water gardens should be located in open areas away from trees, if the objective is to grow water lilies and other open water plants. A water garden may be located in the shade and a variety of plants can be used around the margins, but smaller pools may have to be cleaned of fallen leaves frequently during the autumn to maintain ecological balance.

The selection of plant species depends on the size and depth of the water garden. Certain emergent plants, such as cattails and water lotus, can become aggressive in shallow water, and in time may cover the entire water surface. Such plants should be used only around the margins of deep, (three feet or deeper) pools if maintaining open water is desired. Around smaller pools, overhanging vegetation should be avoided; leaves, fruits, and other plant parts can accumulate in the water and become toxic to fish. All sizes of water gardens benefit from the inclusion of oxygenating plants. These are usually submerged plants whose function is to maintain healthy, well–oxygenated water for fish, snails, and other aquatic life. By consuming mineral salts, they compete with the green algae which can otherwise become overly abundant, unsightly, and deplete the oxygen supply. Some excellent oxygenator plants include pondweeds, cabomba, coontail, and water celery.

Water plants may be planted directly into the natural substrate of lakes and ponds, or into a substrate of gravel, soil, or mulch placed in the bottom of artificial ponds or pools. Water plants can also be grown in containers placed at the appropriate water depth, usually six to twelve inches below the water surface, in either natural or artificial ponds. Use of containers is often preferred for more aggressive water plants which spread rapidly if planted in substrate (e.g., cattail, lotus). Containerized plants will need to be divided periodically. In regions with cold winters, potted plants can be removed before pools freeze over and stored in a protected location.

Containerized water plants should be planted in good, clean, heavy soil topped off with a generous layer of pea gravel to hold the soil in place. Commercial potting soils are not recommended since they can become "hot" when saturated for extended times. Slow release fertilizer tablets designed for water plants can be inserted directly into the pot (caution: some fertilizers may release ammonia into the water, which can be toxic to fish).

Different plant species have different requirements for water depth, and should be placed at the appropriate depth recommended by the nursery source. Water gardens are often constructed with shelves at different depths to accommodate varying depth requirements. Pots can also be placed on variously–sized rocks or other materials set within the water garden.

Artificial Animal Structures

The wildlife value of a landscape can often be improved with the addition of artificial shelters such as bird and bat houses. In a natural forest, there are normally numerous dead and dying, standing trees that provide cavities used by woodpeckers and other bird species. Artificial cavities placed within or along the transition zones of young woodlands will attract cavity–nesters such as wren, chickadee, screech owl, woodpeckers, raccoon, flying squirrel, and tree squirrel. Wood ducks will use nest boxes placed in woods along streams and swamps, and artificial houses provide shelter for beneficial insect–eating bats. Recent information indicates that larger, colonial houses are more likely to attract bats. Bluebirds and kestrels prefer nest boxes placed in or near an open meadow. A roost box, which usually has the opening near the bottom of the box, provides shelter and warmth for smaller birds in winter. Warmer air is trapped at the upper end of the box. Nesting platforms are used by the robin, barn swallow, and other "edge nesters". Many kinds of nesting and roosting structures are available at garden centers, and companies which offer restoration services often have specifications for making many kinds of wildlife structures.

Establishment and Maintenance

Establishment Techniques

A naturalized landscape may be established using seed, nursery stock, or a combination of both. No matter how a natural landscape is established, special attention must be given to site preparation, installation, and maintenance during the establishment period. Design considerations, the type of community being established, availability of the desired species of seed or stock, budget constraints, and establishment time influence the technique used.

Establishing a naturalized landscape from seed can be more economical on larger sites (usually 1,000 square feet or larger), but normally requires a longer establishment time than when nursery stock is used. Seed mixes are often used to establish meadow landscapes on larger sites, and although it can take several years to mature, observing the successional process can be rewarding. Establishment using nursery stock is often preferable on smaller sites. While initially more expensive, this technique has the shortest establishment time and allows for complete control over the placement of species by height, color, and other design specifications. Nursery stock may also be preferred where weeds are a problem because it is easier to control weeds by mulching around established plants than among unevenly distributed seedlings. Another option is to establish a meadow planting by seed, supplemented with nursery stock to fill in gaps in the planting or to highlight visually sensitive areas with flowers of a preferred color or height. Using a wildflower seed mix can be a cost effective way to establish a meadow landscape on larger sites. It is a common misconception, however, that it is easy to grow a lush meadow of beautiful wildflowers simply by throwing a seed mixture on unprepared ground.

Site Preparation

Site preparation begins with delineating the boundaries of the planting site on the ground, followed by eliminating competing vegetation and preparing the planting bed for seeds or nursery stock. Selecting appropriate plant species for existing site conditions reduces the amount of effort and cost associated with preparing the planting site.

Soil Improvement

Selecting a natural community adapted to existing site conditions will in most instances eliminate the need for extensive soil improvement. Soils with naturally poor drainage will often support a wetland or bog community, while dry, excessively drained sites may support xeric forest, glade, or dry prairie or desert communities. The need for improving the soil will be indicated by survey data or may be ascertained from the condition of the vegetation growing on the site. A site which presently supports a lush growth of vegetation probably does not need much improvement. Sites which do not presently support a healthy stand of vegetation will probably require soil improvement before planting or seeding. Sites disturbed by construction may be compacted and have little or no topsoil. Amending severely degraded soils requires the application of large amounts of topsoil and other organic matter and may take several years to prepare. Subsoiling may be necessary on soil compacted by heavy equipment.

Organic matter may need to be increased if the site has been under cultivation and is being restored to woodland. Woodland plants generally prefer a soil high in organic content. Woodland herbs adapted to a mesic site, for example, may require soil organic content ranging anywhere from 10 to 33 percent of volume, or even more in clay or sandy soils (Diekelmann and Schuster 1982). Many prairie plants will tolerate a well–drained soil with average fertility, and tend to become "leggy" and topple in a very rich soil. Fertile soils with poor drainage can be improved with the addition of coarse, quarried sand or gravel.

A variety of soil amendments may be used to improve the organic content, fertility, aeration, water retention, drainage, and structure of a substandard soil. Composted materials such as leaves, grass clippings, manure, yard waste, and kitchen waste can be used. Commercial products such as packaged topsoil, compost, humus, peat, and shredded bark can also be used, and are sometimes available by the truck–load; keep in mind that unpackaged materials sometimes contain many weed seeds.

Most native plants have a broad tolerance for soil pH (e.g., the degree of acidity or alkalinity of a soil). Soil pH may be lowered (more acidic) using copper sulfate, peat, shredded pine bark or needles, or other available materials, or raised using lime, which also helps break up heavy clay soil into more friable particles (Beikmann, pers. com.) (follow label directions for appropriate application rates).

Weed Elimination and Control

Whether the planting area is to be established by seed or nursery stock, the soil needs to be loosened and cleared of sod, weeds, and other competing vegetation. When establishing an area from seed, it is particularly important to eliminate weeds prior to seeding, as post–emergent weed control is difficult and marginally effective. Even with effective weed control prior to seeding, a variety of annual, biennial, and perennial weeds can be expected to appear in the planting. Thorough pre–planting weed control gives native plant seedlings a head start on competing with weeds during the establishment process.

Sod can be removed manually with a sod cutter (available at most rental centers) and stockpiled for up to several weeks for use at another location. Sod can be killed under a thick layer of grass clippings or other kind of mulch, but this usually requires a period of several months to be effective. Or, sod can be killed with a tilling/herbicide program as described below for perennial weeds.

Weeds exist in the form of actively growing vegetation and seeds. Weed seeds often remain dormant in the soil until favorable conditions of light and moisture promote their germination. Tilling and other removal of surface vegetation can expose weed seeds to improved light conditions and promote germination of new weed crops. A deep tilling often exposes even more weed seeds and compounds weed problems. A single, shallow tilling (to a maximum depth of one to four inches) may be expected to expose fewer weed seeds than repeated or deep tillings, but tilling alone is often insufficient to kill perennial weeds. If use of chemicals is not desired, repeated tilling, often for a full year, is required to eliminate weeds. Planting seeds with a seed drill eliminates the need to till, and is an excellent method of seeding on slopes and other erosion–prone sites.

An effective weed control program for sites with actively growing weeds combines shallow tilling with use of a powerful broad–spectrum herbicide such as a glyphosate. Many of the most persistent perennial weeds and grasses such as Johnson grass, Bermuda grass, and fescue have strong root systems which will resprout vigorously if the plants are simply cut or tilled under. While tilling may be used to break up sod and kill shallow rooted plants, it may need to be followed by one or more herbicide treatments to kill resprouting perennial weeds. After the first herbicide treatment, a waiting period of ten days will allow for the re–sprouting of weeds, and keeping the soil moist will hasten the process. Raking treated vegetation away from the planting site will help prevent re–sprouting. If new growth appears, a second herbicide treatment is warranted, followed by another ten–day waiting period.

Herbicides are most effective on actively growing vegetation. After mowing, new growth should be well underway before treatment. Herbicides are potentially toxic to fish and wildlife and should be used only in accordance with the manufacturer's instructions, and under conditions of no wind or precipitation. Oil or ester based herbicides should be avoided near streams and wetlands. Using large spray droplets and low pressure in the sprayer helps prevent wind drift. Wick application of herbicides is one way to prevent drift, which often occurs with spraying. Herbicides which break down quickly in the soil will minimize environmental hazards. Seed can generally be planted seven to ten days after using such products. Areas previously in cropland that were treated with long–term residuals such as atrazine should not be seeded for one or two years following treatment; a soil test can be taken to identify residue levels, or a small test plot can be seeded to test for germination success.

If weeds are not actively growing on a site, a fumigant can be used. Fumigants are very toxic chemicals that sterilize the soil, killing roots, seeds, and even soil fauna, and generally require a special license for use. Pre–emergent herbicides, also fairly toxic, can be used on tilled soil to prevent weed seeds from germinating, but should not be used in areas to be established from seed. An effective program for the control of actively growing weeds will usually control successive weed seed crops and eliminate the need for using highly toxic herbicides.

On smaller planting sites, it may be practical to use solarization to kill weeds. After tilling, the site is covered with clear plastic which is well–anchored to the ground. With the heat of the sun, moisture trapped beneath the plastic turns to steam, and the heat and steam act to kill both weeds and weed seeds. The process requires from one to two months, but usually eliminates the need for herbicides.

The common horticultural practice of mulching, using various materials to prevent weeds and conserve soil moisture, can be used to prevent weeds around planted nursery stock, and is effective in preventing frost heaving in fall plantings. Mulch should be applied after the ground freezes to prevent rodents from feeding on plant parts over winter. But mulching, if applied too heavily, can also discourage natural propagation. Mulch should be used sparingly, or not at all, if self–propagation is desired, or used heavily to discourage natural spreading. Annual native plants, which live only a single season, typically produce large numbers of seed to assure their perpetuation in the wild. The seed must make good contact with the soil to germinate. Biennials usually spend their first season in a vegetative condition, dying the second season after producing flowers and seed. Similar to the annuals, biennials rely primarily on seed production for perpetuation in the wild. Heavy mulching can prevent seeds from germinating. Perennial plants are typically long–lived from a perennial root system, and may not bloom until the second or third season. Many perennial species multiply by sending out rhizomes or stolons from the parent plant, with new plants produced along their lengths. Heavy mulching will reduce light availability and discourage the production of new plants.

Establishment from Seed

Many native species can be established from seed, but it can take several years for a planting from seed to become well established. Wildflowers often have complex seed dormancy mechanisms that prevent germination of seed during unfavorable conditions. Some species must be subjected to a period of moist cold, called moist stratification. Such species should be sown before winter for spring germination, or can be stored in a sealed container with moist sand, vermiculite or other inert material for one to two months to simulate a natural winter chilling; containers should be examined weekly to adjust moisture levels and to prevent molding. Seed with hard coats may require scarification to promote germination. This consists of breaking down the seed coat by soaking in water or acid, nicking with a knife, or by abrasion with sandpaper. Seed of some species (e.g., bloodroot, celandine poppy), must be sown fresh or germination can take years or may never occur. Legume seeds benefit from inoculation with a species–specific bacterium. Most seed companies provide directions for the best germination methods for each wildflower species. Wildflowers require specific soil, temperature, and moisture conditions for successful seed germination and seedling growth. Attention must be given to site selection, species selection, seedbed preparation, maintaining favorable soil moisture, and controlling weeds throughout the establishment process.

The development of a meadow planting can be an interesting and educational process when expectations are realistic and informed. Many environmental factors can affect the success of a wildflower seeding. Adverse weather conditions such as drought, hail, or excessive winds may seriously affect successful germination and seedling growth. Over–wintering seeds may be subject to animal predation, rot, and erosional forces which can displace seeds from the site. Use of a cover crop or erosion netting can help reduce seed loss. Vinyl netting can capture and kill both birds and snakes and should be avoided. Jute or other material that quickly biodegrades is a good substitute.

Possibly the most important factor in a successful seeding is patience. Many wildflower plantings from seed have been plowed under because the growers were uninformed about the establishment process. It is unreasonable to expect to produce in one or two years what nature has taken hundreds of years to achieve. Establishing a wildflower meadow from seed requires several years, and during the establishment period, a wildflower planting might appear weedy. The creation of a sustainable landscape necessitates the use of perennial species, many of which are slow to establish and mature to blooming size. Many perennial species will not germinate until exposed to a period of moist cold; such species may not bloom until the third season following a spring planting. During the first growing season, 75 percent of the growth of native warm season grasses can be devoted to the development of an extensive root system. A diversity of native species should be apparent by the second season.

Many factors must be considered when formulating a wildflower seed mix, including flower color, number of blooms per plant, period of bloom, seed availability and price, regional adaptivity, and number of seeds per pound. While it may be tempting to custom formulate a seed mix to satisfy certain design objectives, it is often easier, less costly, and more successful to purchase a commercial wildflower seed mix. Commercial mixes vary considerably as to quality, and care should be taken to choose a mix with the greatest potential for successful establishment in the planting area. Researchers at the National Wildflower Research Center (1989) offer the following guidelines for selecting wildflower seed mixes:

- ■ Select a mix with a high percentage of species native to the region where the seed will be planted. The Center warns against the "shotgun approach" to seed mix formulation, in which a mix contains a variety of species adapted to different regions in an attempt to cover a wide geographic area. A high percentage of the species in such a mix will not establish in one region or another, the result being money spent on thousands of seeds that will not germinate or on non–native annuals that fail to persist after the first year or two. Shotgun mixes may also include inexpensive, bulky filler seed of common cultivated flowers (not wildflowers) or cool season grasses such as fescue. Often this filler seed is present in such large amounts that it competes with the native wildflowers! The Center instead recommends using a regionally adapted mix containing a high percentage of species native to the marketing area. Such mixes are usually produced by small, local nurseries which obtain seed through local field collection and propagation. The advantage of such mixes, when used in the appropriate area, is a much greater establishment rate. While some larger seed companies are now marketing "regionalized" wildflower seed mixes, they generally include a high percentage of non native, annual wildflowers which fail to re seed, and are therefore not true regional mixes. When used to provide temporary cover and color, annuals should not be so abundant in a mix as to impair the successful establishment of the perennials in the mix.

- Wildflower mixes should be comprised of species which bloom in the spring, summer, and fall to produce a long season of flower display. Commercial mixes often fail to include asters, goldenrods, and sunflowers which extend the blooming period well into the fall months.

- Indigenous native grasses, which are a dominant feature of the natural prairie or meadow community, should comprise 50 to 80 percent of the volume of a seed mix. Native grasses lend structural support to tall wildflowers, stabilize the soils and minimize erosion with their extensive root systems, help prevent invasion by weeds, add late season color and texture to the landscape, and provide valuable food and cover for wildlife. In contrast to sod–forming grasses such as many of the fescues, bunch–forming native grasses provide adequate spaces in which wildflowers can become established.

Seeding Rates

The seeding rate for wildflowers and grasses will vary depending on the species or type of seed mix used and the sowing method. The National Wildflower Research Center (1989) suggests seeding rates for establishing pure stands for a number of wildflower species; the rates will change when species are combined. For landscapes that are to be viewed up close, a seeding rate of six to ten seeds per square foot is recommended; for distance viewing four to five seeds per square foot may be adequate. Seed mixes are often sold in bags of four to six ounces to cover about 1,000 square feet, or in pounds for larger sites. A rate of eight to ten pounds of grass/forb seed mix per acre is often used, but this rate may be reduced or as much as doubled depending on site conditions and species used. Hydromulching can require a rate three time greater than normal. Seed companies will often recommend a suitable rate for selected species based on a description of site conditions. Quick–growing, bunch forming grasses are often included in a mix for temporary cover or as a 'nurse crop' while the perennial grasses are becoming established. Canada ryegrass is often used in northern states, while sheep fescue and hard fescue are used in the west. Annual cover crops such a spring oats and annual rye have been used successfully, but aggressive perennials such as perennial ryegrass and Kentucky 31 fescue should be avoided.

Timing

Most reputable seed companies will recommend the best time to sow wildflower seeds in their marketing region. In the northern and northeastern regions where harsh winters occur, an early spring seeding will promote fast germination of the native grasses, tender annuals, and many species of perennials. A late fall seeding, however, can improve germination rates for many perennial wildflower species which require a period of moist cold to break seed dormancy (e.g., including many kinds of asters, goldenrods, coneflowers, and blazing stars). In the southern and far western regions, fall (September through December) is a favorable time for seeding. This timing takes advantage of warm soil temperatures and soil moisture to promote rapid germination and root growth prior to dormancy. An early spring seeding is also possible, but the early onset of hot, dry weather may necessitate supplemental watering.

Sowing Methods

Prior to sowing, wildflower seed should be mixed with a carrier to increase volume and promote more even seed distribution over the site; sand, sawdust, vermiculite, perlite, and commercial potting soil have all been used successfully. Wildflower seed mixes contain a variety of seed sizes and shapes, and uneven seed distribution can result from the settling of smaller, heavier or smoother seeds during sowing. Continuous agitation of the mix during sowing, either by hand or mechanically, keeps seed more evenly distributed in the mix and on the ground.

Wildflower seed may be sown by any of the normal seeding methods, but on smaller areas hand broadcasting is often most effective. Walking two sets of transects across the planting area results in more even coverage. Half of the seed is sown walking a set of parallel transects; the second half is sown while walking a set of transects perpendicular to the first, resulting in a grid pattern of seeding (Fig. 4.1).

Mechanical seed broadcasters and seed drills are often used on larger planting sites. Use of a seed drill adapted to handle warm season grasses can be

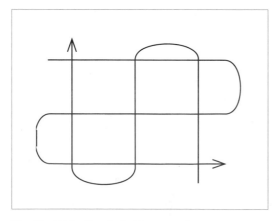

Fig. 4.1. Grid pattern for hand sown seeds.

especially effective on slopes and other erosion–prone sites where tilling is not practical; such drills are not readily available in the east but are more common in the west. Hydroseeding, a process where seed is mixed with a liquid slurry and sprayed on a site, is often used on sloping or otherwise difficult to seed sites. A tacky or sticky material can be added to the slurry which helps the seed adhere to the ground surface and may eliminate the need for mulching. A disadvantage is that it is difficult to adjust for an accurate seeding rate when using a wildflower seed mix and the seeding rate may need to be tripled to compensate. Hydromulching can be used after broadcast seeding to spray a tacky material on seeded ground in place of mulch.

Good soil contact is essential to anchor seeds and promote successful germination and seedling growth. To achieve good soil contact, surface sown seed can be lightly raked, pressed, or rolled into the soil. Walking on a seeded site is often sufficient to achieve good soil contact. Care should be taken to avoid covering the seed more than one–eighth inch deep; some seed should remain visible on the surface. Small seeds may require light to germinate and do not have enough food stored for a lengthy period of below–surface growth.

Establishment From Nursery Stock

Seed of many wildflower species is commercially available, but seed of woodland species is often available only in limited quantities. Establishing a woodland from seed can be a very rewarding process, but can take generations to achieve results. Woodland community types and smaller meadow gardens are more commonly established using nursery stock.

When examining nursery sources of native plants, be sure the stock is nursery–propagated rather than collected from the wild. The increasing market demand for wildflowers has resulted in a profitable industry involving collection of plants from the wild. Collection of most wild plants, by individuals as well as by nurseries, is essentially unregulated and has the potential to result in the depletion of local populations, and possibly of certain species throughout their range. Part of the incentive behind landscaping with native plants is the preservation of the natural heritage unique to each region of the country. With so many nurseries now offering a wide selection of nursery–propagated natives at affordable prices, strong conservation ethics do not support the use of wild–collected plants in our designed landscapes.

A wide variety of native species are available from mail order nurseries. Perennials can be purchased as bare–root or containerized material. Bare–root material is often less expensive but more difficult to transplant successfully. Container–grown plants should have well–developed root systems that make transplanting into the landscape easy and generally more successful. Many species of native trees and shrubs are available as bare–root stock up to six feet in height. Such stock generally has high transplant success and is often preferred for larger woodland landscapes to hold down initial and replacement costs. Bare–root stock used in northern growing zones (U.S.D.A. hardiness zones six and up) is usually planted during dormancy for greater transplant success. Some species of trees and shrubs are available in larger landscaping sizes and are usually balled and burlapped. Such material can be planted almost anytime and generally has high survivability.

Planting Density

The spacing of nursery stock should in most cases follow the suggestions provided by the nursery where the plants were obtained. One outstanding feature of native plants is their ability to self propagate both sexually (seed production) and asexually (vegetatively). This ability can be used to advantage in certain situations to reduce plant material and installation costs. The initial planting density can be lower than natural to allow for dispersal by seed or other means. Species which spread by rhizomes or stolons will often form colonies around each parent plant; those which spread by seed can produce hundreds of new plants each season. Within a few years, the intervening spaces will be filled, the rate depending on the species used and on soil and other characteristics of the planting site. On erosion–prone sites, it may be necessary to install plants at a relatively high density to quickly stabilize soils.

Trees appear randomly spaced in a natural forest. The trees in a woodland design should be spaced close enough to encourage upright growth rather than the spreading habit characteristic of open–grown trees. State forestry offices can often provide guidelines as to suitable planting density

for local forest conditions. Keep in mind, however, that commercial timber plantings are often established at denser rates than those designed for aesthetic and wildlife purposes, and a dense planting may require successive thinnings as it matures.

Timing

Planting should be timed so as to take advantage of natural patterns of precipitation. If supplemental irrigation is possible, plants may be installed anytime except during the hottest months. In the eastern regions, rainfall is most reliable during late winter and spring, and thereafter occurs mostly in the form of short, sporadic, often heavy thundershowers. Nursery stock can be planted in early spring as soon as the ground is workable, but young plants should be mulched if danger of hard frost has not passed. An early fall planting in warm soil allows plant roots time to grow and provide an anchoring system which prevents frost–heaving during winter.

Bare–root materials are normally planted during dormancy, i.e., before new growth is initiated in the spring. Bare–root material may be removed from the growing fields during winter and stored under refrigeration, and shipped later in the season before the weather gets hot. Balled and burlapped material can be planted almost anytime, but will require irrigation if natural rainfall is inadequate to sustain soil moisture during the establishment period.

Establishing Tree Cover

Tree cover may be established using larger, landscape size material for quicker results, but this can be cost–prohibitive on large sites, and the diversity of species available as large material may be limited. Bare–root material is often used to establish tree cover on large sites, advantages being less initial expense and the availability of a greater variety of species. Larger materials (five or six feet in height) may need staking the first year to prevent root damage from wind (Beikmann, pers. com.).

Trees may be planted into an existing groundcover of grass or other cover, but an area the diameter of the tree crown should be cleared of vegetation around each tree planted. This area should be mulched after planting. On dry sites a raised border of mulch should be made around each tree to trap water. A greater increase in trunk diameter will be attained if seedlings are not pruned, particularly the lower branches of balled and burlapped and containerized trees (Beikmann, pers. com.). Understory plants should not be installed until the tree cover is sufficient to provide protective shade.

Natural Landscape Maintenance

Maintenance of a naturalized landscape initially focuses on maintaining adequate soil moisture and controlling weeds. It is important to keep soil evenly moist, not wet, during the establishment period. During extended dry periods in the first year, water may be necessary in response to wilting leaves. Once established, and if species are sited appropriately, irrigation should not be necessary except in cases of extreme environmental stress.

Post–germination weed control in a landscape established from seed is often difficult because weed seedlings may be hard to identify before they grow large, and herbicides are usually not selective enough to use on weeds growing among young wildflower and grass seedlings. On smaller plantings, manual removal of weeds is the most effective technique but is relatively labor–intensive. Weed control on larger areas is usually accomplished by mowing, spot–spraying with narrow spectrum herbicides, and prescribed burning.

Mowing weeds early in the spring before the natives emerge benefits native plantings by improving sun exposure and reducing weed vigor. Mowing, to a height of six inches, can only be used until the native plants attain this height. Wick application of herbicides is effective on weeds such as thistle when they are taller than the native plants. Spot spraying of herbicides is usually reserved for areas where weed growth is so heavy as to prevent effective establishment of native plants. Such areas may have to be re–seeded when the weed problem is under control. Prescribed burning is often used to control weeds and improve vigor in an established planting. The burn should be conducted when cool season weeds have initiated new growth, which is in early spring throughout much of the midwestern and eastern regions. Burning has the advantage of quickly returning nutrients to the soil as well as reducing weed vigor.

Fertilizing a planting is not normally part of maintenance requirements when the planting site is properly prepared. Fertilizer often promotes weed growth at the expense of the native species. In cases where severe nutrient deficiency is suspected of inhibiting a planting, an all–purpose fertilizer can be used at half the strength recommended on the label. Acidifying fertilizers can be used on azaleas and other acid–loving plants.

Water Garden Maintenance

An ecologically balanced water garden will stay healthy and attractive with minimum maintenance (Atkinson 1991). Regular maintenance will be needed to keep the garden clean, but usually a few minutes a week is all that is needed (Roth 1988). During summer, water lost to evaporation will need to be replaced, and regular maintenance of pump and filter systems will assure constantly clean water. Like most gardens, some weeding, thinning, and hand pruning of vegetation may be required, and potted plants may need dividing or transplanting into larger containers. Plants should be inspected each week for insect damage; most pests can be washed off or removed by hand; pesticides should be avoided because they can harm the ecological balance of pond life. Water lilies can be fertilized through December in warmer climates; other plants will not need fertilizer after September. Fish will need to be fed until water temperatures fall below forty–five degrees (F). In autumn, falling leaves and other debris should be removed with a siphon or plastic rake to prevent build up of decaying matter which can be toxic to aquatic animals.

Winter preparation can include a thorough cleaning after leaves have fallen, and pumps and filters are removed and stored. Water lilies should be stored in a location that will not freeze, but other plants can over–winter in the bottom of in–ground pools; a sheet of white plastic secured over the top will moderate temperatures. Most plastic pots and pond materials will not crack or become damaged during freezing and thawing.

Fish should be over–wintered in an indoor aquarium if the pool is likely to freeze completely or remain covered with ice for an extended period. Ice can be prevented in milder winters by placing a circulating pump on the pond bottom. Small pools can be protected by placing a PVC–covered frame over part of the water. In more severe climates, a thermostatically controlled de–icer may be needed. For occasional ice, slowly melt a section using a pan of hot water (Roth 1988).

Algae Control

One of the main concerns in water gardening is controlling the growth of algae, a green plant that can affect the health and beauty of a water garden. A combination of sunlight, warm temperatures, and excessive amounts of nutrients such as nitrates and phosphorous promote algae growth. The green 'bloom' of algae common in natural ponds and small lakes in spring is often the result of an influx of nutrients transported via runoff from nearby land containing fertilizer or animal waste. These nutrients, combined with ample sunlight and warm water temperatures, cause an algae population explosion which turns the water an unattractive, murky green. In addition to its appearance, too much algae depletes the oxygen in the water, which adversely affects fish and other aquatic creatures. The result is an imbalance in the pond's ecology.

Several practices can help minimize algae growth in a pond or pool garden by helping establish and maintain ecological balance:

- Floating plants such as water lilies can be installed to shade the water surface, thus reducing sunlight and water temperature. A single mature water lily can cover an area of eight square feet or more, and smaller–leaved species can be used in small pools or tub gardens. Planting overhanging vegetation along pond margins can have the same effect.

- The amount of oxygen in the water can be increased by using oxygenating plants such as water celery and coontail or by installing fountains, waterfalls or cascades which aerate the water. This promotes healthy fish populations which will feed on algae and insect larvae and help control mosquitos.

- Fish produce ammonia which can be toxic. In an artificial fish pond, a biological filter will promote the growth of bacteria that break down the ammonia into nitrates which promote the growth of algae, which in turn is eaten by fish.

- Avoid using copper salts and other chemicals or algicides, some of which can kill aquatic wildlife if used at high concentrations. There are some new products on the market which are advertised as safe for fish, but use of chemicals should be a last resort.

- Pond filters help rid the water of algae and debris, thus promoting a cleaner pond environment.

CHAPTER 5

Ecological Restoration

Introduction

Restoration as a general term means returning some degraded portion of landscape to an improved and more natural pre–existing condition. John Berger (1990), author of *Restoring the Earth*, called restoration "an effort to imitate nature in all its artistry and complexity by taking a degraded system and making it more diverse and productive." It can involve the reestablishment of an ecosystem, the control of air pollution, the prevention of acid rain, or the protection of habitat for animals where they nest, rest, and spend the winter. Restoration can mean making something grow on bare soil or on damaged inverted soils (e.g., mine spoil). Restoration also means replanting a forest in a field. Sometimes it is the practice of an art (things work for reasons not known) and sometimes it is science (things work and we know why). Because this book deals broadly with the restoration of landscapes and managed lands, we decided to use the term ecological restoration to mean returning a specific area to its pre–disturbance condition, including both functional and structural characteristics. In reality some of the projects and goals outlined in this book are habitat creations. The uncertainty about the extent and composition of the original community may make habitat creation both practical and necessary for overall ecological restoration. In the limited areas available for golf course construction, for example, restoration of a hydrologically altered wetland may not be possible, but creation of a fully functioning marsh or swamp may be possible and desirable.

What is the difference between ecological restoration and natural landscaping? To some extent, restoration encompasses all plantings designed to improve a site. Natural landscaping can be considered a form of restoration. For the purposes of this book, ecological restoration is distinguished from

natural landscaping. If the goal is to restore a native plant community, and a complement of native species from that community has been used in a planting scheme, then it is ecological restoration. Natural landscaping is the planting of a group of native species to meet some specific aesthetic, management, or design goals. There is generally a difference of intent and scale between these two actions. Ecological restoration is large and allows a community to evolve and natural succession to occur. Natural landscaping is conducted on a smaller scale and tends to remain at a particular managed level or state.

The natural world without human intervention is the cumulative, dynamic response to millions of years of reacting to itself and the physical world around it. Humans do not understand all of the intricacies of ecosystems. We channelize a stream to drain a wetland and in the simplicity of our desires and understanding, destroy what the wetland is to the stream—a source of water in summer, a filter of chemicals and sediment, a refuge for young fish, and a sponge to soak up and hold heavy rains. Destroying that million years of nature's work is infinitely easier than restoring it.

Ecological restoration is the art and science of recreating viable natural or ecological communities. It goes beyond just doing plantings for the purpose of stabilizing areas that are eroding. It goes beyond the idea of landscaping with native plants. It is an attempt to recreate nature. Nature, of course, is a lot of things. It is weather and climate, soils, water, slope, aspect, and altitude. It is also a squirrel that buries an acorn and a bird that eats a seed. Nature is mushrooms, lichens, wildflowers, and trees. To restore a truly natural system is beyond the capacity and knowledge of humans. We can, however, bring together the basic components and characteristic plants and animals of an area (Table

Habitat Characteristic	Habitat elements	No. of species
1. Forest Cover 0–9 Years Old	Forage, open areas, high stem densities, dense cover	49
2. Old Growth–Forest Cover >100 Years Old	Large diameter, mast, snags, dens, logs, layered vegetation	270
3. Oak and Oak–Pine Forest >50 Years Old	Mast, cavity trees, and snags	80
4. Pole and Sawtimber with Crown Closure over 80%	Forest cover with closed canopies	41
5. Sawtimber with 20–30% Ground Cover	Sawtimber with moderate to open understory	61
6. Oak forest >50 Years Old With a Dense Understory	Sawtimber with moderate to dense understory	74
7. Open and Semi–Open (nonforested) Habitats	Forage, dense cover, some mast, cavities	200
8. Permanent Water Sources	Water for drinking, breeding, feeding, roosting sites	——
9./10. Den Trees/Snags	Cavities for nesting, roosting, song and observation perches, feeding, shelter, and eventually fallen woody material	155

Table 5.1. Representative habitat characteristics identified for the Mark Twain National Forest (Putnam 1988).

5.1). Nature is assisted and directed by ecological restoration. Natural processes will take over and other components of the natural system will naturally invade the restored system. Of course, some systems are so devastated and the sources of plants and animals available for reinvasion are so remote that nearly everything must be provided by the restorationist.

Don Falk (1990) of the Center for Plant Conservation says in ecological restoration we seek not to "preserve" a static entity but to protect and nurture its capacity for change. "Restoration thus uses the past not as a goal but as a reference point for the future. If we seek to recreate the temperate forests, tallgrass savannas, or desert communities of centuries past, it is not to turn back the evolutionary clock but to set it ticking again."

John Cairns (1988) questions whether restoration of ecological communities to their original condition may be practical or possible. He offers the following observations:

■ Information about the original system may be inadequate. For example, there is no adequate description of the pre–industrial Ohio River that includes a detailed species inventory, along with detailed descriptions of the spatial relationships, trophic dynamics, and functional attributes of the system.

■ An adequate source of species for recolonization may not be available because of the uniqueness of the damaged community or because the remaining communities of this type would be damaged by removing organisms for recolonization elsewhere.

■ It may be impossible to put a halt to some of the factors causing the damage. The notorious example is acid rain, which may originate many miles away in a political jurisdiction over which the restorationist has no influence.

■ The original ecosystem may have developed as a result of a sequence of meteorological events that are unlikely to be repeated and may be difficult or impossible to reproduce.

■ The sheer complexity of duplicating the sequencing of species introductions is overwhelming. To recreate the original community, it is not only necessary that species colonize at the appropriate time, but also that some decolonize (disappear) at the appropriate time.

The restoration efforts envisioned by this book can be considered only partial restorations of natural communities, designed to set the "evolutionary clock ticking again." A repertoire of target ecological communities is compiled as Appendix A. They represent over 200 different dominant communities found in thirty natural regions of the continental United States (see Chapter 6). These communities can be targets for more restoration research as well as starting points for initiating restoration efforts. The species lists will, we hope, encourage nurseries to propagate these plant materials for restoring these basic ecological communities.

The type of restoration program undertaken depends upon the goals for a site or landscape. Goals can include aesthetics, reestablishment of natural conditions, maintenance of a diversity of plant and animal species, protection of the local gene pool of particular species, reduction of grounds maintenance costs and environmental impacts, and creation of representative local ecosystems.

Ecological Restoration Planning

Many steps are required to conduct a successful restoration project. The most important component for success is understanding that restoration takes time. Actually, restoration, like other aspects of looking after the earth, is an eternal vigil. As part of that vigil, planting trees is an act of hope and optimism. If one plants small trees and waits for a canopy to plant understory shrubs, many years will pass. Even a restored prairie of grasses and forbs will take years before it resembles a natural community. The level of maintenance required to look after a forest while it is developing is, however, relatively low compared to the meticulous, incessant care of a golf green or a lawn. The long–term maintenance of a restored natural ecosystem is negligible. Following are some of the basic steps in a restoration project:

- **Seek help from experts and use a multidisciplinary team in planning**. This is especially true of wetland projects that need hydrologic information. Biologists, ecologists, horticulturalists, foresters, agronomists, engineers, geologists, soil scientists, and hydrogeologists all have expertise to offer restorationists.

- **Clearly define objectives, goals, and measurements**. An ecosystem is complex. A successful restoration will evolve through many stages before the end result is achieved. Therefore it is important to establish site–specific goals for each project. These goals can relate to the number and composition of plant species restored, size of area, structure of vegetation, reinvasion or establishment of animal species, density of exotics, functions restored to the site, and aesthetics. Both short– and long–term goals are needed to ensure that the various stages result in the desired final goal.

- **Conduct a site specific analysis of the hydrological, geological, and biological variables at the site**. This can include soil types, basic geology, disturbance history, biological inventory, and natural seed sources of desirable and undesirable species. The county soil survey, published by the U.S.D.A. Soil Conservation Service, is available at no cost from the District Conservationists in most county seats in the nation. It is an excellent source of information on soils, hydrology, and potential vegetation. Also identify sources and connections to water supplies.

- **Develop a detailed site plan**. The plan should include specific information about the characteristics of that site and which areas of a site will be restored to what type of community. Clearly outline the boundaries of the site and different communities on a site plan map.

- **Reflect the local biota in species, composition, and source of material**. Every regional population of plants and animals has a local gene pool that has evolved. Success of restoration is enhanced when local sources of material are used.

- **Select species for the site carefully**. Use this book, literature sources, local experts, and an analysis of similar communities in the selection of species for use in the restoration project.

- **Create a detailed design for each differ-**

ent community including a spatial and temporal planting plan. Experts can provide valuable information concerning species specific requirements that impact both the location and sequence of plantings. The design should minimize maintenance requirements.

■ **Identify sources for the species to be used in the project**. This may include seed or nursery stock, plants grown in one's own greenhouse, or stock taken from other sites. Taking plants from the wild is viewed as destructive and unethical except in certain circumstances (e.g., road construction site where the plants will otherwise be destroyed).

■ **Prepare the site**. This can include physical changes such as grading. More often, it will involve decisions concerning whether to add fertilizer, water, and other soil treatments. It can also involve management decisions concerning existing vegetation on the site.

■ **Supervise project implementation**. Bulldozer operators and workers removing vegetation or applying chemicals or fertilizer need guidance to ensure that the work done is consistent with the plan. Be sure planting either with seeds or plants, is conducted correctly and with the guidance and supervision of someone familiar with the site plan and planting techniques.

■ **Control exotic and undesirable species**. Monitoring for exotics that may be problems in your area is crucial. Control of exotics may include manual removal or the use of chemicals.

■ **Establish a plan for feedback and mid–course corrections**. Many things can change throughout a restoration. There must be a process for making assessments of conditions and responding at any time. Plants or seed availability, replanting needs, water level changes, substrate differences, and exotic invasions can necessitate mid–course corrections in order to achieve success.

■ **Develop a plan for long–term monitoring, management, and maintenance**. This plan should very specifically address the goals of the project and measure the success of reaching those goals. A restored ecosystem should be similar in both structure and function to the original ecosystem. To restore a natural tallgrass prairie with at least fifty native species from the local gene pool is an example of a measurable goal.

Forest Restoration

When we think of recreating a forest, large trees come to mind. But a forest is more than large trees. A forest contains an understory of trees and shrubs, a ground layer of herbaceous plants, and leaf litter. Birds, squirrels, bugs, mushrooms, and a list of living organisms too long to name inhabit the forest. "Forests are remarkably complex, with great differences in composition and character, even within the same region" (Horowitz 1990). Site specific strategies must be developed for a restoration project. How do we know when we have restored a forest? The recreation of an upland forest can be evaluated in at least two ways. Evelyn Howell (1986) describes it this way.

"One emphasizes community structure and species composition, and judges the success of a restoration effort by asking how closely the resulting community resembles the natural, or `model,' community with respect to characteristics such as the relative abundances, age–class structure, spacing, and distribution of particular species. An assumption underlying this 'compositional' approach is that if these species groupings are fairly accurately reproduced, then the dynamics and functions of the communities will also resemble those of the model community.

The second way of establishing goals and evaluating the success of restoration projects emphasizes ecosystem functions, often with little or no reference to species composition. From this point of view, for example, the presence or absence of a particular species is less important than the provision of functions and processes such as nutrient cycling, erosion control, or biomass production."

Many techniques for restoring a forest have been tried and new procedures are regularly being introduced. The creation of canopy is the most critical issue because of its influence on the microclimate of the community. Starting from a treeless situation, restorations use at least six approaches (Howell 1986).

■ Plant canopy trees in ultimately desired densities and proportions; mulch the ground beneath and around the trees; plant desired midstory and understory species immediately.

■ Plant and mulch canopy trees as in the above approach, but plant light–loving ground cover initially (or let "weeds" grow), and add (or encourage natural invasion by) woodland understory and midstory later as shade develops.

■ Plant trees in savanna distribution patterns (less than ultimately desired densities), with savanna understory (prairie plants). Then, as shade develops, gradually plant additional trees; and finally plant (and/or manage for the natural invasion of) desired understory and midstory species.

■ Plant trees in greater than ultimately desired densities and either thin or allow self–thinning as the canopy develops. Add midstory and understory species later and/or manage for natural invasion.

■ Plant short–lived, fast–growing trees (aspen) or tall shrubs (pagoda dogwood, alder) as a cover crop and as this canopy develops underplant with slow–growing, shade–tolerant, long–lived trees that will become the site dominants. Upgrade the understory as the canopy progresses, thinning the cover crop species as necessary to reduce competition with the eventual dominants.

■ Do no planting; allow woody species to invade, and selectively remove those which are not desired; treat understory and midstory in a similar fashion.

In most of these methods, the herbaceous layer is added after the formation of canopy. Transplants and potted seedlings are recommended; however, seeds have been used successfully. "In general, success is closely related to the care the plantings receive during the first year, watering at regular intervals being especially important. Habitat matches are also especially important, factors most likely to be crucial being light, humidity, and depth of litter" (Howell 1986). In some situations acorn planting can be used to establish forests at lower costs than tree planting. They can be collected locally with minimal impact upon natural ecosystems. About 1000 per acre is a desired stocking rate.

A combination of stresses including drought, low soil fertility, excessive salinity, and herbivory impact desert systems (Virginia 1990). Many woody, legume species of desert trees develop deep root systems and therefore can serve to provide moisture and nutrients (especially by nitrogen fixation) for an herbaceous layer. Techniques used to improve establishment of plants in arid regions include deep ripping, augering holes to improve water infiltration, soil imprinting, careful seed and plant selection, and appropriate symbiont inoculation (Virginia 1990, Dixon 1990, Bainbridge 1990).

The important role of ectomycorrhizal fungi in the establishment of forest is now widely recognized. Donald Marx (1991) reports that ectomycorrhizae occur on about 10 percent of the world flora, and that 2,100 species of fungi form ectomycorrhizae with forest trees in North America. The most common fungus and one now used extensively for inoculating tree roots is *Pisolithus tinctorius*. The fruiting body of this fungus is the familiar puffball. Ectomycorrhizae of *P. tinctorius,* or Pt for short, have formed in many species of *Abies*, *Carya*, *Picea*, *Pinus*, *Pseudosuga*, *Quercus*, *Castanea*, *Fagus*, and *Salix*. Because trees with ectomycorrhizae have a more active area for nutrient and water absorption, they are able to absorb and accumulate nitrogen, phosphorus, potassium, and calcium more rapidly and for longer periods than trees without ectomycorrhizae (Marx 1991). Marx further reports that "ectomycorrhizae also appear to increase the tree's tolerance to drought, high soil temperatures, organic and inorganic soil toxins, and extremes of soil acidity caused by high levels of sulfur, manganese, or aluminum." Private and government nurseries are now inoculating tree stock. Restorationists should look for and use inoculated nursery stock. Three methods have been suggested (Perry and Amaranthus 1990) for inoculating seedlings 1) using whole soil from established plant communities, 2) using pieces of chopped up root, and 3) using spores of the fungi. The duff inoculation method that has been used in nursery beds can be used in the field. Forest duff, collected from mature stands of target species can be broadcast and plowed in at a particular site (St. John 1990). "Because of the important role of mycorrhizal fungi and other rhizoshpere organisms in creating favorable soil structure, sites with very sandy or very clayey soils may be especially susceptible to improvement" (Perry and Amaranthus 1990).

Grassland Restoration

Modern ecological restoration began in the 1930's at the University of Wisconsin Arboretum when Aldo Leopold began restoring a site to native prairie. Prairie may now be the community type restorationists know best. The recreation of prairie has been accomplished many times over. Also the management technique of using fire is understood. Fire is so widely used as a management tool that conservation organizations like The Nature Conservancy conduct fire schools for staff.

The restoration of grasslands follows the basic steps outlined for all restoration projects. In addition, the following should be considered:

- Planting can be accomplished from either seeds or greenhouse grown seedlings.
- Many prairie forb seeds require stratification (cold treatment); some (i.e. those with hard seed coats) also require scarification (nicking or roughing up the seed coat). Stratification should occur soon after collection to prevent drying and dormancy.
- Controlled burning after the third year is the most effective management option. Early spring mowing inhibits weeds and woody species.
- Collecting prairie seeds takes considerable effort. The seeds of prairie species mature at different seasons of the year, at different times at different locations, or a few at a time throughout the season. This means that collecting must be done a number of times at the same site.
- Legumes need to be inoculated with appropriate rhizobia bacteria for the nitrogen fixing capability to develop. Other mycorrhizal fungi need to be evaluated for improving specific species functioning.

Wetland Restoration

Wetlands are America's most maligned environment. This is ironic because of the many essential functions of wetlands. Wetlands serve as wildlife habitat, fish propagation and nursery areas, flood storage, groundwater recharge, and filters that prevent sediment and chemicals from entering streams (Mitsch and Gosselink 1986). Wetland restoration is a very active field today. This is primarily due to federal regulations promulgated as a result of extensive wetland losses suffered in the United States. Overall, the United States has lost over 50 percent of its wetlands, and in some states the loss is 90 percent (National Research Council 1992). Wetland restorations are undertaken for a variety of reasons, and fall short of restoring all the values of original wetlands. Some of the reasons for restoration projects include creation of wildlife habitat, improvement of water quality, storage of water, and reduction of flooding.

The success of restoring wetlands is higher for sites that were wetlands but modified for some reason such as agriculture. If the hydrologic regime has been destroyed on a site, then it must be restored if the wetland is to survive. Success has occurred most often with the revegetation of coastal, estuarine, and freshwater marshes (Kusler and Kentula 1990). Prior to modification of a site it is very important to conduct an investigation for jurisdictional wetlands. The U. S. Army Corps of Engineers (ACE) has to concur with any wetland delineation to make it official. It is important to remember that wetlands may not be disturbed without a permit from at least the ACE and often local or state agencies. It may require wetland replacement or mitigation to obtain a permit, but often the best and cheapest mitigation is avoidance of any jurisdictional wetlands. These natural wetlands can often be incorporated into your site plan and increase habitat diversity.

Wetland communities include riparian forests, swamps, bogs, wet meadows, and bottomland hardwood forests. Mitigation of wetland losses, while required by law, is not the only motivating factor for recommending restoration. Because of the value of wetlands and the significant loss of this community type, we recommend restoring these communities whenever appropriate sites are available. If a golf course is going to be developed from an old farm, we would encourage close examination to determine the existence of suitable areas that can be restored to wetland. In many cases there are sites, such as along an intermittent stream, where a small wetland may be created that never existed before.

In addition to all of the general steps that must be followed for any restoration project, there are a few specific minimum requirements that wetland restorationist Hal Bryan (pers. com.) recommends when considering a wetland creation or restoration plan. Three main areas must be addressed—hydrology, soils, and vegetation.

Hydrology

- If you get hydrology right, you will get the wetland right. Evaluate the hydrologic conditions for a site, such as water level elevations, velocity, hydroperiod, salinity, nutrient and chemical levels, and sedimentation rates.
- Source of water can be surface flooding from streams, groundwater, or rainwater.
- Watershed/wetland size ratio should be considered. Usually the larger, the better. Smaller ratios are possible to restore with more poorly drained soils.
- Periodicity of inundation or saturation determines the type of community restored or created. For example, a bottomland hardwood forest may require twenty to thirty days of continuous inundation in the growing season and a period of drydown in the late summer. A shrub swamp may need twice as much inundation with little drydown.
- Restoration of hydrology may require the removal of berms, the plugging of human-made ditches, the renovation of stream meanders and flood regimes, or the destruction of sub-surface drainage tiles.
- Creation of shallow ponds for habitat diversity will increase the number of kinds of plants and animals. Use clay subsoil from ponds for ditch plugs or berms.
- The use of water control structures, where possible, will provide some ability to manipulate water levels, which is especially important during the early periods of plant establishment.

Soils

- Select areas of hydric soils for restoration. A list and soil maps can be obtained from the U.S. Soil Conservation Service. Be sure you are not restoring in an existing jurisdictional wetland without a permit.
- Store and replace topsoil during the construction phase.
- Use topsoil or muck from impacted wetlands if possible. Muck is a seed source and also provides many microorganisms characteristic of the wetland but not commercially available.
- Be concerned with erosion possibilities.

Slopes should be very gentle and stable even without vegetative cover.
- Use small equipment on-site; large machinery can compact subsoil and restrict root penetration.

Vegetation

- When possible, select potential restoration locations adjacent to existing wetlands to allow natural regeneration.
- Trees can often be reestablished using bare-root seedlings (usually on ten foot centers) or acorns (1000 per acre).
- Container-grown stock is often the most successful for the price.
- Adjacent wetlands can be used as a seed source.
- Herbaceous wetland plants can be installed in small wetlands, or in those wetlands where quick establishment is essential.
- In some cases seeds of wetland plants are used in a temporary matrix of grass like red-top or rye (non-natives that will die out in standing water), or switchgrass. Fescue should be avoided except in the most difficult to establish areas.
- Select species carefully according to targeted depth of water.

Additional Suggestions

- Use nest boxes for wood ducks, bats, or other animals if appropriate. Put in perches (dead snags) for birds to use.
- Money should be set aside to monitor and maintain the restored wetland. Be prepared to respond quickly to problems such as erosion or trees dying.
- Plan for buffer areas to protect the wetland from sedimentation, pollution, and other human impacts.

Managing Natural Plant Succession and Pest Species

Plant communities change over time. They go through a process known as succession. This process creates a temporal series of plant communities known as "seres." This basic ecological concept is complex in nature and even though it has been studied since the early 1900's, it is far from understood. Robert McIntosh (1980) calls it "one of the oldest, most basic, yet in some ways, most confounded of ecological concepts." Plant community changes involve "species replacements, shifts in population structure, and changes in availability of resources such as light and soil nutrients" (Luken 1990). Succession must be mentioned in the context of restoration because one option for a particular site is to leave it alone and allow the natural course of plant and animal invasions and extinctions to occur. Succession can also be managed to achieve desired results. James Luken has dealt with this subject in considerable depth in his book *Directing Ecological Succession*. Table 5.2 from Luken offers a list of management problems where managing succession can achieve management goals.

A number of principles can be gleaned from Luken's book. They include the following:

- All plant communities show some form of succession at all times.
- Management activities modify the rate and direction of succession rather than the state of vegetation.
- The initial or early pool of plants on a site is critical to the succession of that site.
- The "vital attributes" of particular species will determine the course of succession. This involves shade tolerance, pH tolerance, and moisture requirements.
- The depth and duration of standing water is the most critical determining factor for vegetation succession in wetlands.
- Soil nutrient availability can be an important determinant of species composition. In old fields and disturbed soil the primary limiting element is nitrogen. This can affect which species can invade and grow.
- Grasses are usually favored by fertilization. Woody plants and forbs are more competitive in nutrient–limited situations.

Luken writes that "succession will continue to function as a repair process following human disturbance just as it has done for the last 5000 years. In many situations this may be adequate resource management. In the majority of situations, however, we need to refine and augment this repair process to better preserve and use our dwindling natural resources."

Luken proposes a three–component succession management model. The three components are designed disturbance, controlled colonization, and controlled species performance. "Designed disturbance includes activities initiated to create or eliminate site availability. Controlled colonization includes methods used to decrease or enhance availability and establishment of specific plant species." Colonization is controlled by two factors "the propagule pool (seeds, spores, rootstocks, bulbs, stumps, rhizomes, plant fragments and entire plants) and the initial floristics of a site." Controlled species performance includes methods used to decrease or enhance growth and reproduction of specific plant species. When

Conserving rare or endangered species
Conserving and restoring communities
Manipulating the diversity of plant and animal communities
Creating relatively stable plant communities on rights–of–way
Revegetating drastically disturbed lands
Minimizing the impact and spread of introduced species
Maximizing wood production from forests
Minimizing adverse environmental effects of forestry
Predicting fuel buildup and fire hazards
Increasing animal populations for recreation and aesthetics
Developing multiple use plans for parks and nature reserves
Determining the minimum size of nature reserves
Minimizing the impact of roads, parking areas, trails and campsites
Preserving scenic vistas in parks
Minimizing the cost of grounds maintenance on public lands
Controlling water pollution
Minimizing erosion
Maintaining high quality forage production
Minimizing the cost of crop production in agricultural communities
Developing vegetation in wetlands or on the edges of reservoirs

Table 5.2. Some resource management problems where succession can be manipulated to achieve management goals (Luken 1990).

removing undesirable species, care should be taken to avoid harm to the rest of the community. Techniques include mulching, burning, cutting, managing grazing animals, and adjusting water levels. Selective use of herbicides is also used to remove species.

In several places in this book we refer to the need to control *pest* species. West (1984) defines a *pest* species as any species not native to a site or management unit that poses a threat to the integrity of natural communities within the site. In addition, native species can sometimes become pests by occurring in large numbers or out–competing desired species.

Controlling pest plants can take a variety of forms.

- **Prevention**—This includes such measures as removing livestock from prairies and not introducing exotics (such as autumn olive) through wildlife enhancement programs.
- **Monitoring**—Sites being restored must be monitored for exotic invaders.
- **Integrated Pest Management (IPM)**— Using biological controls and minimum pesticides is highly desirable.
- **Herbicides**—Foliar application of certain short–lived herbicides can be effective.
- **Mowing**—This practice inhibits woody plants and agricultural weeds.
- **Cutting**—This practice inhibits woody plants from maturing.
- **Burning**—This practice inhibits woody plants and kills some herbaceous pests (usually annual exotics).
- **Hand pulling**—This practice is especially useful in wetlands.
- **Water level manipulation**—Controlling pests in wetlands can be achieved with this method.

The introduction of exotic or non–native species is still encouraged by a variety of government and private agencies. These exotics are recommended for wildlife purposes, erosion control, ease of establishment, disease resistance, reduced susceptibility to insect damage, and tradition. Recent examples of intentional introductions for the purpose of marsh restoration that are now of urgent concern include the spread of three *Spartina* species (*Spartina alterniflora*, *S. patens*, and *S. townsendii/anglica*) along the West coast of North America (National Research Council 1992). *Cornus mas*, Cornelian cherry dogwood, is recommended by the Soil Conservation Service even though there are "at least eleven species of shrubby dogwoods native to the eastern United States that could be substituted instead, with no ecological risks" (Harty 1992). An exotic is not just a species from Europe or Asia. It is any species introduced outside of its natural range. The planting of exotic pest species should be discouraged if not eliminated.

The concept of substituting native species for exotic species is compelling. Bratton (1982) reports that exotic plants have a variety of impacts. For example, in arid regions, the deep–rooted tamarisk (*Tamarix* spp.) can lower the water table which displaces native plants and eliminates water for wildlife. Exotic species can also change the nutrient balance in the soil, acidify soils, change soil structure, serve as reservoirs for parasites, and produce allelopathic chemicals which retard the growth of other species. In many urban woodlands exotic shrubs such as privet and honeysuckle are displacing natural tree and shrub regeneration. The overstory trees are not replacing themselves and the forests will be completely gone when these canopy residents succumb to old age (Hal Bryan per. comm.).

It is possible for agencies and organizations to begin making these substitutions. Harty (1991) reports that the Illinois Department of Conservation nurseries now produce sixty–seven species of native trees and shrubs to use in wildlife habitat, reclamation projects, and community restorations. They also produce seven species of prairie grasses and thirty–seven species of prairie forbs for prairie restoration projects.

It is impossible to list all known pest species. John Randall of The Nature Conservancy polled many managers from their preserves and came up with a list of 177 egregious plant species (Cheater 1992). Table 5.3 is a list of pest species compiled from Bratton (1982), Cole (1991), Ebinger (1983, 1991), Ebinger, et al. (1984), Glass (1992), Harrington and Howell (1990), Harty (1991), Heidorn (1991), Hester (1991), Hutchison (1992), Kennay and Fell (1992), Myers and Ewel (1990), National Research Council (1992), Szafoni (1991), and West (1984). Restorationists and natural landscapers should avoid using these plants outside of their natural ranges. Some species, such as cattails, should be used carefully even within their natural range.

Table 5.3. Pest Plants
(Scientific names are as they appeared in publications)

Scientific Name	Common Name	Natural Range
Acer ginnula	Amur maple	E. Asia
Acer platanoides	Norway maple	Europe
Ailanthus altissima	tree–of–heaven	Asia
Albizzia julibrissin	mimosa	Asia/Africa
Alliaria petiolata	garlic mustard	Europe
Ammophila arenaria	European beach grass	Europe
Bromus inermis	Hungarian brome	Europe
Carduus nutans	musk thistle	Europe
Casuarina equisetifolia	Australian pine	Australia
Celastrus orbiculata	Asian bittersweet	E. Asia
Cirsium arvense	"Canada" thistle	Europe
Coronilla varia	crown vetch	Europe
Daucus carota	Queen Anne's lace	Europe
Dipsacus laciniatus	cut–leaved teasel	Europe
Dipsacus sylvestris	wild teasel	Europe
Eichhornia crassipes	water hyacinth	S. America
Elaeagnus umbellata	autumn olive	E. Asia
Elymus arenarius	European lyme grass	Eurasian
Euonymus alata	winged wahoo	E. Asia
Euonymus fortunei	none given	Asia
Euphorbia esula	leafy spurge	Europe
Festuca pratensis	tall fescue	Europe
Hedera helix	English ivy	Europe
Imperata cylindria	cogon grass	Pantropical
Juniperus virginiana	red cedar	United States
Lespedeza cuneata	sericea lespedeza	E. Asia
Ligustrum obtusifolium	blunt–leaved privet	Japan
Ligustrum vulgare	privet	Europe
Lonicera japonica	Japanese honeysuckle	Asia
Lonicera maackii	amur honeysuckle	Eurasia
Lonicera tatarica	tartarian honeysuckle	Eurasia
Lysimachia vulgaris	garden loosestrife	Europe
Lythrum salicaria	purple loosestrife	Europe
Maclura pomifera	osage orange	United States
Melaleuca quinquenervia	cajeput tree	Australia
Melia azedarach	chinaberry	Asia
Melilotus alba	white sweet clover	Europe
Melilotus officinalis	yellow sweet clover	Europe
Mesembryanthemum ssp.	ice plant	Africa
Myriophyllum brasiliense	water–feather	S. America
Nasturtium officinale	watercress	Europe
Pastinaca sativa	wild parsnip	Europe
Paulownia tomentosa	princess tree	E. Asia
Phalaris arundinacea	reed canary grass	Eurasia

Phragmites communis	reed	Eurasia/N. America
Pinus nigra	Austrian pine	Europe
Pinus sylvestris	Scotch pine	Europe
Pinus thunbergii	Japanese black pine	East Asia
Poa compressa	"Canada" bluegrass	Eurasia
Poa pratensis	"Kentucky" bluegrass	Eurasia
Polygonum cuspidatum	Japanese knotweed	E. Asia
Populus alba	white poplar	Europe
Potamogeton crispus	pondweed	Europe
Pueraria lobata	kudzu–vine	E. Asia
Rhamnus cathartica	common buckthorn	Europe
Rhamnus davurica	Dahurian buckthorn	E. Asia
Rhamnus frangula	alder buckthorn	Europe
Rhodomyrtus tomentosus	downy myrtle	E. Asia
Robinia pseudoacacia	black locust	United States
Rosa multiflora	multiflora rose	E. Asia
Schinus terebinthifolius	peppertree	S. America
Sorghum halepense	Johnson–grass	Eurasia
Tamarix gallica	tamarisk	S. Europe
Tamarix spp.	tamarisk	S. Europe
Typha angustifolia	narrow–leaved cattail	United States/Eurasia
Ulmus procera	English elm	Europe
Ulmus pumila	dwarf elm	Asia
Verbascum thapsis	common mullein	Europe
Viburnum lantana	wayfaringtree	Europe
Viburnum opulus	guelder–rose	Europe
Vinca major	large periwinkle	Europe
Vinca minor	common periwinkle	Europe

Ecological Communities

An important step in any restoration project is determining which natural or ecological community is the appropriate model for restoration. The ecological community descriptions (Appendix A) may be used as a general guide to the species composition for these communities. They are not meant to define the specific species composition at a point on the ground. For that level of detail one should consult local experts in the state Natural Heritage Programs, native plant societies, environmental organizations, and universities, as well as restorationists and native plant consultants.

For example, suppose individuals in Elizabethtown, Kentucky wanted to restore or create a natural community on their property, but had no idea what types of communities occurred there or which ones would do well. First, they would locate their property on the natural regions map in this book. They find they are located in the Ozark/

Interior Plateaus Natural Region. Turning to that section of Appendix A, they will find a list of Dominant Ecological Communities which occur (or occurred) within that region.

They will then need to determine which of those communities occurred or could be restored on their particular site. To do this, a detailed site analysis will be required to find out certain base–line data such as soil type, geologic substrate, topography, aspect, current vegetation, and land use. Once this is accomplished a community type or types can be selected. For example, the site may be a gently rolling upland with well drained and moderately fertile soil over limestone bedrock. This eliminates the wetland communities and a selection can be made from the terrestrial communities.

At this point local expertise is needed. Since the Elizabethtown area contained forest, woodland, wetland, and prairie communities at the time of settlement, any of these could be selected for restoration or creation purposes. However, a local expert knows that the oak–pine community did not occur in the area and that mesophytic forest, which does occur in the area, probably did not occur on the site because it is too dry. Therefore the selection comes down to oak/oak–hickory forest, oak barrens, or bluestem prairie as appropriate for this site.

Even though detailed site planning is beyond the scope of this book, two worksheets are provided (Figs. 5.1 and 5.2) to help organize the ecological community information. The site planning checklist can be used for each specific planning unit on the site. The checklist provides the opportunity to assess the basic conditions of each planning unit, the relationship among planning units, and the overall regional situation. An aerial photo, soil maps, topographic map, or good knowledge of the regional landscape will be needed to address some of the questions.

The second worksheet is for compiling a species list for a restoration project on a specific planning unit. It contains four categories of information in addition to the species name. The categories are as follows:

■ **Range of species**—The first category to complete is range information about the species. All species used in a restoration should naturally occur in the region. In the space provided a "yes" or "no" can be written. The reference from which range information was obtained can be listed or other qualifiers can be used such as marginal, unknown, probable, or county record only.

■ **Environmental tolerance**—The information for this category can be obtained from the matrices in Appendix B. If other information is available such as requirements for certain pH ranges, that can be noted in this column.

■ **Wildlife**—The wildlife values also come from the matrices in Appendix B. These values relate to animal use of particular species of plants. This is not critical to restoration, but if certain animal species are targeted then the plant species to support them must be present.

■ **Nursery**—This category is to identify the nursery or nurseries selling this species. Many nurseries will also contract to grow particular species. Appendix C is a list of nurseries that carry native plants.

Restoration in Practice

Fernwood Prairie

In 1975, Don and Kay Harker, working with Stan Beikmann and Max Medley, conceived and planned a prairie restoration project at Fernwood (a botanic garden and nature center near Niles, Michigan). The early planning was inspired and guided by Ray Schulenberg from the Morton Arboretum. The Fernwood prairie project is now fifteen years old and considered complete (Photos 5.1–5.4). Six botanists and scores of weeders and other workers have contributed to the prairie restoration over the years.

The original goals of the project were the following:

■ create a five–acre natural tallgrass prairie representative of southwestern Michigan. High diversity was desired.

■ use the restored prairie to help preserve the local gene pool by collecting seeds from local remnant prairies as close to Fernwood as possible.

■ use the prairie as a focus for educational and interpretive programs about this disappearing ecosystem.

The actual planting plan took several different directions over the years. Initially seeds were collected in the late summer and early fall from the surrounding remnant prairies (Fig. 5.3). These prairie remnants include wet, mesic, and dry tallgrass prairies. Most of the Fernwood site was planted in mesic species. A small portion was planted in wet species and a small sandy knoll was created for dry species.

The original site was a fescue–covered field. Soil preparation began with a late summer plowing and then a disking. In the spring the soil was deep plowed (not recommended), then disked and raked prior to planting. Initially all weed control was through hand weeding. It was very labor intensive.

The seeds were scarified and stratified where appropriate, and planted in flats in the Fernwood greenhouse. Both greenhouse plants and the treated seeds were planted in the prepared soil. The prairie was hand weeded throughout the year.

The largest percentage of species planted were the warm season grasses, big bluestem (*Andropogon gerardii*), Indian grass (*Sorghastrum nutans*), and little bluestem (*Schizachyrium scoparium*). The

Site Planning Check List

Site name: _____

Natural region: _____

Size of the site: _____acres. Sketch the site and identify the planning units.

Planning unit name or number and size: _____

Planning unit type and conditions:

    Upland   wet _____   mesic _____   dry _____

    Wetland   standing water ___   depth _____   saturated soils _____

    Estuarine   depth _____   salinity _____

Desired vegetation type:

    closed forest   open forest   grassland   shrubland

Ecological community chosen: _____

Local ecological community survey completed?   yes   no

Location: _____

Results:

Proximity to natural communities in the region:

Proximity to natural communities on the site:

Do corridors currently exist between patches of natural communities?

Fig. 5.1 Site Planning Check List

Preferred Species List for Restoration				
Plant Name	**Range**	**Env. Tol.**	**Wildlife**	**Nursery**

Fig. 5.2 Preferred Species List For Restoration

forbs were planted randomly. Approximately one–half acre of prairie was added each year.

The final restored prairie has a very high diversity of species. The initial planting included ninety species and the final prairie has 150 native prairie species. The species are not all conservative prairie species, meaning some also grow places other than prairies.

Ecological restoration takes considerable time and effort. Educating the public about the project, especially in the early stages, is important. If the public shares the vision, they will support the long effort necessary for restoration. The Fernwood prairie is now a major attraction for visitors.

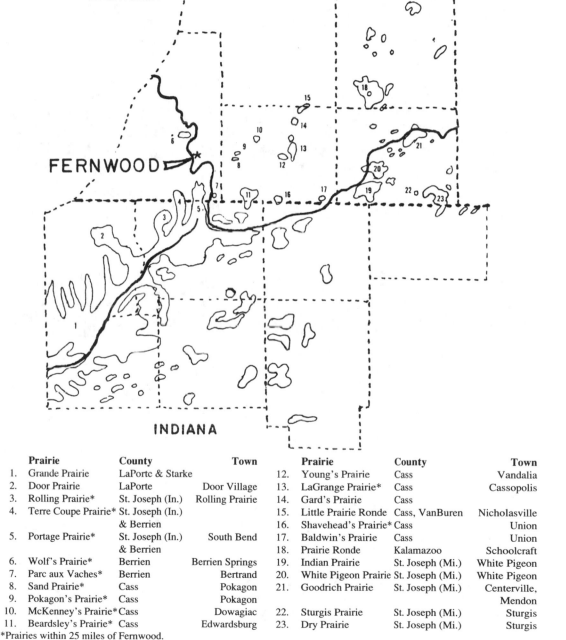

	Prairie	County	Town		Prairie	County	Town
1.	Grande Prairie	LaPorte & Starke		12.	Young's Prairie	Cass	Vandalia
2.	Door Prairie	LaPorte	Door Village	13.	LaGrange Prairie*	Cass	Cassopolis
3.	Rolling Prairie*	St. Joseph (In.)	Rolling Prairie	14.	Gard's Prairie	Cass	
4.	Terre Coupe Prairie*	St. Joseph (In.) & Berrien		15.	Little Prairie Ronde	Cass, VanBuren	Nicholasville
				16.	Shavehead's Prairie*	Cass	Union
5.	Portage Prairie*	St. Joseph (In.) & Berrien	South Bend	17.	Baldwin's Prairie	Cass	Union
				18.	Prairie Ronde	Kalamazoo	Schoolcraft
6.	Wolf's Prairie*	Berrien	Berrien Springs	19.	Indian Prairie	St. Joseph (Mi.)	White Pigeon
7.	Parc aux Vaches*	Berrien	Bertrand	20.	White Pigeon Prairie	St. Joseph (Mi.)	White Pigeon
8.	Sand Prairie*	Cass	Pokagon	21.	Goodrich Prairie	St. Joseph (Mi.)	Centerville,
9.	Pokagon's Prairie*	Cass	Pokagon				Mendon
10.	McKenney's Prairie*	Cass	Dowagiac	22.	Sturgis Prairie	St. Joseph (Mi.)	Sturgis
11.	Beardsley's Prairie*	Cass	Edwardsburg	23.	Dry Prairie	St. Joseph (Mi.)	Sturgis

*Prairies within 25 miles of Fernwood.

Fig. 5.3. Remnant natural prairies near Fernwood. Many remnants were used as seed sources (Medley 1976).

Photo 5.1. Restored prairie and a new area being prepared for spring planting with a fall plowing.

Photo 5.2. Newly planted section of prairie.

Photo 5.3. Restored tallgrass prairie.

Photo 5.4. Fire is used to maintain prairies.

CHAPTER 6

Natural Regions of the United States and Their Dominant Ecological Communities

Introduction

Appendix A lists the dominant ecological communities within each ecological system and class for the thirty natural regions outlined for this book. This chapter explains how we developed the classification system for the natural regions, ecological systems, and classes. This classification was developed to make it possible for someone anywhere in the country to determine what general types of ecological communities could occur at a particular site.

Classification of the landscape and its natural vegetation has been approached from many different views and levels of detail, depending upon the purpose. It is fairly naive and simplistic to write down a series of categories and definitions and assume that nature has been neatly classified. It is uncommon in nature for regions or communities to be clearly delineated. Rather, they tend to grade into one another or form a mosaic, making it difficult to distinguish entities. However, classifying the landscape is the only way for us to study and comprehend an incredibly complex system. It is certainly necessary to provide a basis for what to restore and where.

Natural Regions

In the pocket of this book you will find a map showing thirty natural regions. This natural regions classification system was developed using numerous sources. Because the level of detail in any single source was not thought to be adequate for our purposes, multiple sources of information were used to delineate the natural regions at the appropriate scale. The primary sources used to develop the natural regions were *Potential Natural Vegetation of the Conterminous United States* (Küchler 1964, 1975) (see Appendix A and map in pocket), *Ecoregions of the United States* (Bailey 1978) (Fig. 6.1 and 6.2), *Ecoregions of the Conterminous United States* (Omernik 1986), and *North American Terrestrial Vegetation* (Barbour and Billings 1988).

Using the Küchler (1964) and Bailey (1978) maps combined as a base, the country was divided into thirty natural regions. These natural regions generally follow Bailey's regions and subregions as laid over Küchler's potential natural vegetation map. The lines dividing regions generally follow a Küchler vegetation type. Figure 6.3 lists the specific ecoregions of Bailey's that occur in each of the thirty natural regions. These natural regions are areas of the country that have certain natural features in common. These features include soils, geologic history, landforms, topography, vegetation types, plant and animal distributions, and climate. These natural regions are broad, or coarse, divisions which make it easier to subdivide and define the landscape and its vegetation. Appendix A provides descriptions of each natural region.

Fig. 6.1. Bailey's Ecoregions of the United States.

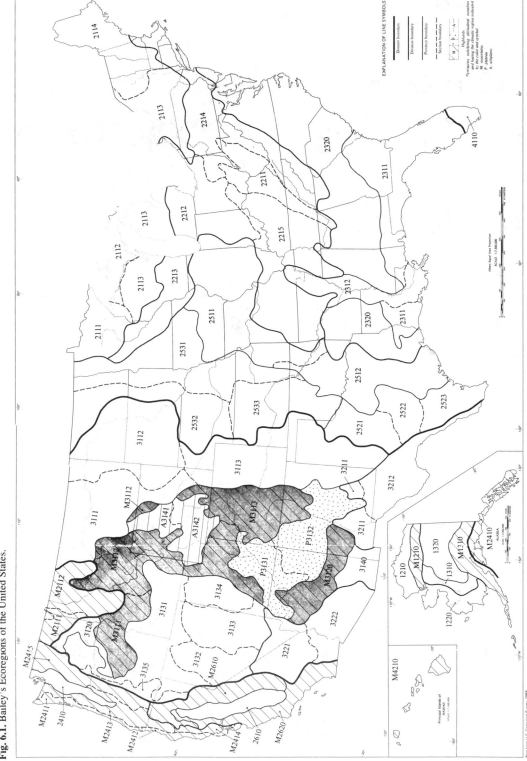

Base from U.S. Geological Survey, 1984

Lowland Ecoregions		Highland Ecoregions*	
Province	**Section**	**Province**	**Section**
2110 Laurentian Mixed Forest	2111 Spruce–fir Forest 2112 Northern Hardwoods-Fir Forest 2113 Northern Hardwoods Forest 2114 Northern Hardwoods-Spruce Forest	M2110 Columbia Forest (Dry Summer)	M2111 Douglas-fir Forest M2112 Cedar–Hemlock–Douglas-fir Forest
2210 Eastern Deciduous Forest	2211 Mixed Mesophytic Forest 2212 Beech–Maple Forest 2213 Maple–Basswood Forest + Oak Savanna 2214 Appalachian Oak Forest 2215 Oak–Hickory Forest		
2310 Outer Coastal Plain Forest	2311 Beech-Sweetgum-Magnolia–Pine–Oak Forest 2312 Southern Floodplain Forest		
2320 Southeastern Mixed Forest			
2410 Willamette-Puget Forest		M2410 Pacific Forest	M2411 Sitka Spruce–Cedar Hemlock Forest M2412 Redwood Forest M2413 Cedar–Hemlock–Douglas-fir Forest M2414 California Mixed Evergreen Forest M2415 Silver Fir–Douglas-fir Forest
2510 Prairie Parkland	2511 Oak–Hickory–Bluestem Parkland 2512 Oak + Bluestem Parkland		
2520 Prairie Brushland	2521 Mesquite–Buffalo Grass 2522 Juniper–Oak–Mesquite 2523 Mesquite–Acacia		
2530 Tall-grass Prairie	2531 Bluestem Prairie 2532 Wheatgrass–Bluestem–Needlegrass 2533 Bluestem–Grama Prairie		
2610 California Grassland		M2610 Sierran Forest M2620 California Chaparral	
3110 Great Plains Short-grass Prairie	3111 Grama–Needlegrass–Wheatgrass 3112 Wheatgrass Needlegrass 3113 Grama–Buffalo Grass	M3110 Rocky Mountain Forest	M3111 Grand Fir–Douglas-fir Forest M3112 Douglas-fir Forest M3113 Ponderosa Pine–Douglas-fir Forest
3120 Palouse Grassland		M3120 Upper Gila Mountains Forest	
3130 Intermountain Sagebrush	3131 Sagebrush-Wheatgrass 3132 Lahontan Saltbush-Greasewood 3133 Great Basin Sagebrush 3134 Bonneville Saltbush-Greasewood 3135 Ponderosa Shrub Forest	P3130 Colorado Plateau	P3131 Juniper–Pinyon Woodland + Sagebrush–Saltbush Mosaic P3132 Grama–Galleta Steppe + Juniper–Pinyon Woodland Mosaic
3140 Mexican Highlands Shrub Steppe		A3140 Wyoming Basin	A3141 Wheatgrass–Needlegrass–Sagebrush
3210 Chihuanhuan Dexert	3211 Grama-Tobosa 3212 Tarbush-Creosote Bush		
3220 American Desert (Mojave-Colorado-Sonoran)	3221 Creosote Bush 3222 Creosote Bush-Bur Sage		
4110 Everglades			*M–mountains, P–plateaus, A–altiplano

Fig. 6.2. Codes for Bailey's Ecoregion Map

Natural Regions	Bailey's Ecoregions	Natural Regions	Bailey's Ecoregions
West Coast Mountains	M2411	Southern Deserts	3211
	M2412		3212
	M2413		3140
	M2414		
	M2415	Northern Great Plains	3111
	2410		3112
Sierra Nevada Mountains	M2610 partial	Western High Plains	3113
Central/		Great Plains	2531
Southern California	M2620		2532
	2610		2533
	M2610		
		Central Plains	2511
High Desert	3131		
	3120	Texas/Oklahoma Plains	2512
	3135		
		Central Texas Plateau	2521
Northern Basin and Range	3132		2522
	3133		
	3134	South Texas Plains	2523
Southern Basin and Range	3221	Western Gulf Coastal Plain	2523 partial
	3222		2512 partial
			2320 partial
Northern Rocky Mountains	M2112		2311 partial
	M2111		
	M3111	Northern Great Lakes	2111
	M3112		2112
			2113
Wyoming Basin	A3141		
	A3142	Southern Great Lakes	2213
			2212
Wasatch/Uinta Mountains	M3112		
		Eastern Great Lakes	2113
Colorado Plateaus	P3131		
	M3112 partial	Ozark/Interior Plateaus	2251
Southern Rocky Mountains	M3113	Southeastern Plains	2320
Arizona/		Southern Coastal Plain	2311
New Mexico Plateaus	P3132		2312
			4110
Arizona/			
New Mexico Mountains	M3120	Appalachian Plateaus	2214
		and Mountains	2211
		New England	2214

Fig. 6.3. Bailey's Ecoregions comprising the natural regions used in this book.

Ecological Systems and Classes

Ecological systems are categories which describe general ecological functions and processes. Upland (terrestrial), wetland (palustrine), and estuarine systems are included in this classification. The wetland definitions mainly follow the classification of Cowardin et al. (1979). True aquatic systems such as lakes, oceans, and rivers (called lacustrine, marine and riverine systems, respectively) are not included in this book.

The upland, wetland, and estuarine systems are further subdivided into more specific classes. The classes are defined by the dominant life form of the vegetation which reflects the basic physiognomy, or appearance of the habitat. Forest, woodland–barrens, shrub, and herbaceous are the classes used in this classification. The systems and classes are combined in the following definitions. These definitions are necessary because they help us distinguish between a wetland and an upland—or a forest and a woodland. The differences between systems or classes are often technical and difficult to recognize in the field. Again, nature is not so neatly classified. In order to analyze a site and determine the appropriate ecological community, it is necessary to be familiar with the systems and classes. The species lists for ecological communities in Appendix A are organized by regions and according to the following systems and classes.

Upland Systems

The upland systems include all areas that are typically found on dry land and have soil that is rarely saturated with water or is saturated only briefly, such as after prolonged rains. The upland systems are dominated by plants that cannot withstand prolonged flooding or saturated soils.

Upland Forests occur in areas where sufficient moisture and soil is available to support relatively dense stands of trees. Upland forests are dominated by medium to tall trees which form a closed to mostly closed canopy which restricts most direct sunlight from reaching the forest floor during the growing season. These forests can be either evergreen or deciduous or a combination of both. Beneath the canopy, shade–tolerant species of small trees, shrubs, and forbs can occur. Because of their closed canopy, forests often modify the local environment creating cooler, more humid conditions.

Upland Woodlands and Barrens, sometimes called savannas, are intermediate between forested and non–forested habitats. Woodlands and barrens generally have a canopy cover ranging from 10 percent to 60 percent which allows variable amounts of sunlight to reach the ground. The understory may vary considerably from prairie grass dominated to interspersed forest and prairie herb dominated. Often this habitat is "park–like" with open–grown trees with wide spreading branches and an open grassy understory with few shrubs. Most woodland–barrens are fire maintained and require periodic fires to exist. Some woodland–barrens are edaphically maintained (i.e., have poor, thin or doughy soil which retards dense tree growth) and exist without the benefit of fire.

Upland shrub, sometimes called scrub or shrub, occurs in areas that are dominated by dense to open stands of shrubs with few to no trees present. Generally shrubs are considered to be woody plants less than twenty feet tall. This can include true shrubs, small trees, and trees stunted due to environmental conditions. This type of community class is most common in the western United States where more arid conditions prevail. Most deserts are considered shrub communities. Herbaceous vegetation of grasses and forbs is often present but depends upon the density of the shrub cover and degree of available moisture. Some shrublands result from fire, a lack of fire, or overgrazing, depending upon the local situation and are thus considered successional or disturbance communities.

Upland herbaceous communities are those that are dominated by herbaceous vegetation with woody trees or shrubs absent, or restricted to scattered individuals or groves. Natural herbaceous dominated communities occur throughout the United States but are extensive only in the western and some mid–western states. Prairies and meadows, dominated by grasses, are the most widespread upland herbaceous communities. Other communities such as tundra can be dominated by herbaceous vegetation. Many upland herbaceous communities are maintained by fire and/or grazing. Fire also controls the invasion of woody species, except in the western states where climatic conditions (lack of rainfall) control.

Wetland Systems

Wetland systems include freshwater areas that are transitional between upland and aquatic systems. They typically have a high water table with saturated soil or shallow, standing water during all or a significant part of the growing season. They are dominated by emergent hydrophytic plants that can tolerate prolonged flooding or saturated soils. Wetland systems can grade into deep, open water (aquatic) systems.

Wetland forests are dominated by trees that form a closed to partly closed canopy. They occur in areas where water is not too deep to support trees and favorable environmental conditions exist, at least periodically, for the germination of tree seeds. Wetland forests range from deep water swamps to periodically flooded bottomland forests. They can be evergreen, deciduous, or a combination of both.

Wetland shrub communities occur in areas dominated by a shrub layer with few or no trees. Also called shrub swamps, these communities are often a successional stage of forested wetland. Some shrub swamps do appear to be relatively stable.

Wetland herbaceous communities are wetlands dominated by emergent herbaceous vegetation with little or no woody vegetation present. Wet prairie, marsh, sedge meadow, fen, and open bog are some of the different names applied to herbaceous wetlands.

Estuarine Systems

These systems include coastal wetlands that occupy intertidal zones where sea water is diluted by freshwater run–off from the land. Plants that grow in this community can tolerate salty or brackish water and fluctuating water levels caused by tidal activity or land runoff.

Estuarine forests occur primarily on shallow flats in the intertidal zone of coastal areas such as along tidal rivers and embayments. They are of limited occurrence in the United States, being primarily restricted to the more tropical climate of Florida. They are broadleaf, evergreen forests dominated exclusively by three species of mangrove trees, thus called mangrove forests or mangrove swamps.

Estuarine shrub communities occupy shallow flats in the intertidal zone of coastal areas. They are dominated by sometimes dense stands of shrubs or stunted trees usually less than twenty feet tall.

Estuarine herbaceous communities, often referred to as salt marshes, are the most common or typical estuarine communities in the United States. They are dominated by non–woody, salt–tolerant plants and often cover large areas where the intertidal zone is extensive due to low relief and high tidal range.

Ecological Communities

The ecological communities used in this classification are interrelated assemblages of flora, fauna, and other biotic and abiotic features. A particular ecological community tends to occur repeatedly under a similar set of environmental conditions (i.e., soils, geologic substrate, hydrology, climate, microclimate, topography, and aspect). These communities are delineated based on the potential natural vegetation and the dominant or characteristic plant species that occur (or occurred) naturally in a given region of the country.

In today's landscape, very little undisturbed natural vegetation remains. Almost all areas of the country have either been converted to other uses (i.e., cropland, pasture, urbanization, and roads) or have been severely modified through logging, grazing, mining, or flooding. The term "potential natural vegetation" is used to indicate the vegetation which did or would occur naturally without the influence of modern civilization. Natural vegetation is considered from the time frame of the natural conditions which greeted the first Euro–American settlers. Because most of the landscape has been modified, determining the potential natural vegetation for a specific site may be difficult; however, it should be one of the first steps in choosing the appropriate ecological communities for your site.

In Appendix A, the dominant ecological communities in each natural region are briefly described and lists of dominant and characteristic plant species are provided. The information available from published literature on different communities varies considerably. Some community types are well documented while others have very little information available. The community descriptions reflect this availability of data. Ecological communities considered rare, or of very limited extent within a region, are not included in the community descriptions although they may be mentioned in the regional description. For example, glades are mentioned in the New England Region but a description and species list are not given because they are extremely rare and are of very limited extent. However, in the Ozark/Interior Plateaus Region glades are described as a dominant ecological community because they are more common and occupy considerable acreage.

The ecological community descriptions and accompanying lists of species were also compiled from many sources. State and regional floras, state Natural Heritage Program data, and many other books and articles were used. Because of this variety of sources, all plant names, both common and scientific, have been standardized with Kartesz (1990 and 1991). Although locally important, subspecies and varieties have not been used because of the large areas covered by the dominant ecological communities in each natural region.

Many judgements were made in deciding which lesser or smaller communities to combine and which larger communities to divide in creating the ecological communities described in this book. Communities can be identified and described at many levels from the largest, the earth, to the smallest, a drop of pond water. This classification falls somewhere in between. We attempted to define the ecological communities at a useful level for national reference without losing too much of the detail of smaller community divisions. The references used in this effort can be found in the bibliography.

The ecological community descriptions in Appendix A are to be used as a guide to the species composition of the dominant vegetation types as they occur in a particular region. They cannot be used to define the specific species composition of a point on the ground. It must be realized that individual species, although a component of a community in a particular area, may not occur over the entire geographical range of the community. For that level of detail one should consult local experts in the state Natural Heritage Programs, native plant societies, environmental groups, or universities.

The authors recognize that this list of communities and species is a first effort. Attempting to accurately delineate the ecological communities of the United States is a huge undertaking and was not the primary purpose of this book. Organizations, such as The Nature Conservancy through its nationwide network of Natural Heritage Programs, have been working to develop detailed community descriptions of the United States for many years. These lists of communities and species in this book are, in part, a way of both asking and partially answering the questions—what are the dominant ecological communities and what are their characteristic species?

The authors invite and encourage comments, suggestions, additions, and deletions. Please send any comments to Donald Harker, 311 Wilkinson St., Frankfort, Kentucky 40601.

Bibliography

Aaseng, N. E., et al. 1992. Minnesota's native vegetation. Minnesota Natural Heritage Program.

Abrahamson, W. G., and D. C. Hartnett. 1990. Pine flatwoods and dry prairies. In Ecosystems of Florida, eds., R. L. Myers and J. J. Ewel. Orlando: University of Central Florida.

Adams, L. W., and L. E. Dove. 1989. Wildlife reserves and corridors in the urban environment. Columbia: National Institute for Urban Wildlife.

Adkinson, S., ed. 1991. Garden pools, fountains, and waterfalls. Menlo Park: Sunset Publishing Company.

Ahlgren, C. E. 1966. Small mammals and reforestation following prescribed burning. Journal of Forestry (September): 614-618.

Ajilvsgi, G. 1979. Wild flowers of the big thicket. Number Four: The W. L. Moody, Jr., Natural History Series. College Station: Texas A and M University Press.

Ambuel, B., and S. A. Temple. 1983. Area- dependent changes in the bird communities and vegetation of southern Wisconsin forests. Ecology 65(5): 1057-1068.

Amos, B. B., and F. R. Gehlback, eds. 1988. Edwards Plateau vegetation: plant ecological studies in central Texas. Waco: Baylor University Press.

Anderson, S. H., K. Mann, and H. H. Shugart, Jr. 1977. The effect of transmission-line corridors on bird populations. American Midland Naturalist 97: 216-22.

Anderson, S. H., and H. H. Shugart, Jr. 1974. Habitat selection of breeding birds in an east Tennessee deciduous forest. Ecology 55: 828-837.

Anonymous. no date. Guide to the natural communities of Florida. Tallahassee: Florida Natural Areas Inventory and Florida Department of Natural Resources.

Anonymous. 1987. We don't move until the baby hawks fly. Golf Course Management 55(2): 145-147.

Anonymous. 1991. Natural landscapes of Maine: a classification of ecosystems and natural communities. Augusta: Maine Natural Heritage Program.

Anonymous. 1991. Plant communities of Texas. Austin: Texas Natural Heritage Program.

Anonymous. 1991. Wyoming plant community classification. Larami: Wyoming Natural Heritage Program.

Aplet, G. H., R. D. Laven, and P. L. Fiedler. 1992. The relevance of conservation biology to natural resource management. Conservation Biology 6(2): 298-300.

Arbuckle, N., and C. Crocker, eds. 1991. How to attract hummingbirds and butterflies. San Ramon: Ortho Books.

Armitage, A. M. 1989. Herbaceous perennial plants. Athens: Varsity Press, Inc.

Asher, S. C., and V. G. Thomas. 1985. Analysis of temporal variation in the diversity of a small mammal community. Canadian Journal of Zoology 63: 1106-1109.

Ashton, P. S. 1988. Conservation of biological diversity in botanical gardens. In Biodiversity, ed. E. O. Wilson. Washington: National Academy Press.

Askins, R. A., and M. J. Philbrick. 1987. Effects of changes in regional forest abundance on the decline and recovery of a forest bird community. Wilson Bulletin 99(1): 7-21.

Atwood, W. W. 1940. The physiographic provinces of North America. New York: Ginn and Company.

Ault, E. B. 1983. Charting the course going "natural". Golf Course Management 51(8): 59-60.

Bailey, R. G. 1978. Ecoregions of the United States. Ogden: Forest Service, U. S. Department of Agriculture.

Bainbridge, D. A. 1990. The restoration of agricultural lands and drylands. In Environmental restoration, ed., J. J. Berger. Washington: Island Press.

Balogh, J. C., and W. J. Walker, eds. 1992. Golf course management and construction. Chelsea: Lewis Publishers.

Balser, D., A. Bielak, G. De Boer, T. Tobias, G. Adindu, and R. S. Dorney. 1981. Nature reserve designation in a cultural landscape, incorporating island biogeography theory. Landscape Planning 8: 329-347.

Barbour, M. G. 1988. Californian upland forests and woodlands. In North American terrestrial vegetation, eds., M. G. Barbour and W. D. Billings. Cambridge: Cambridge University Press.

Barbour, M. G., and W. D. Billings, eds. 1988. North American terrestrial vegetation. Cambridge: Cambridge University Press.

Barbour M. G., J. H. Burk, and W. D. Pitts. 1987. Terrestrial plant ecology. Menlo Park: The Benjamin Cummings Publishing Company, Inc.

Barbour, M. G., and J. Major, eds. 1988. Terrestrial vegetation of California. Sacramento: California Native Plant Society.

Bare, J. E. 1979. Wildflowers and weeds of Kansas. Lawrence: The Regents Press of Kansas.

Barry, J. M. 1980. Natural vegetation of South Carolina. Columbia: University of South Carolina Press.

Begon, M., J. L. Harper, and C. R. Townsend. 1986. Ecology: individuals, populations, and communities Oxford: Blackwell Scientific Publications.

Benson, L. 1969. The cacti of Arizona, 3rd ed. Tucson: The University of Arizona Press.

Benson, L., and R. A. Darrow. 1981. Trees and shrubs of the southwestern deserts, 3rd ed. Tucson: The University of Arizona Press.

Berger, J. J. 1985. Restoring the earth. New York: Alfred A. Knopf.

Berger, J. J., ed. 1990. Environmental restoration. Washington: Island Press.

Beikmann, S. 1992. Personal communication during review.

Blake, J. G. 1983. Trophic structure of bird communities in forest patches in east-central Illinois. Wilson Bulletin 95(3): 416-430.

Blake, J. G. 1987. Species-area relationships of winter residents in isolated woodlots. Wilson Bulletin 99(2): 243-252.

Blake, J. G., and J. R. Karr. 1984. Species composition of bird communities and the conservation benefit of large versus small forests. Biological Conservation 30: 173-187.

Blake, J. G., and J. R. Karr. 1987. Breeding birds of isolated woodlots: area and habitat relationships. Ecology 68(6): 1724-1734.

Blouin, M. S., and E. F. Connor. 1985. Is there a best shape for nature reserves? Biological Conservation 32: 277-288.

Boecklen, W. J., and D. Simberloff. 1986. Area-based extinction models in conservation. In Dynamics of extinctions, ed., D. K. Elliott. New York: John Wiley and Sons.

Boon, W., and H. Groe. 1990. Nature's heartland, native plant communities of the Great Plains. Ames: Iowa State University Press.

Bratton, S. P. 1982. The effects of exotic plant and animal species on nature preserves. Natural Areas Journal 2(3): 3-13.

Bratton, S. P. 1986. Manager reflects on new environmental ethics program at University of Georgia. Restoration and Management Notes 4(1): 3-4.

Braun, L. F. [1950] 1967. Deciduous forests of eastern North America. Reprint. New York: Hafner Publishing Company.

Brinson, M. M., B. L. Swift, R. C. Plantico, and J. S. Barclay. 1981. Riparian ecosystems: their ecology and status. U.S. Fish and Wildlife Service, FWS OBS-81/17.

Brothers, T. S., and A. Spingarn. 1992. Forest fragmentation and alien plant invasion of central Indiana old-growth forests. Conservation Biology 6(1): 91-100.

Brown, C. A. [1945] 1972. Louisiana trees and shrubs. Reprint. Baton Rouge: Claitor's Publishing Division.

Brown, D. E., ed. 1982. Desert plants. In Biotic communities of the American southwest - United States and Mexico, ed., F. S. Crosswhite, Vol. 4 (Vols. 1-4). Superior: University of Arizona for the Boyce Thompson Southwestern Arboretum.

Brown, L. 1995. Grasslands. New York: Alfred A. Knopf.

Bryan, H. D. 1987. Important habitats and quantitative environmental assessment. In Proceedings of the Fourth Symposium on Environmental Concerns in Rights-of-Way Management, eds., W. R. Byrnes and H. A. Holt. Indianapolis, Indiana. October 15-28.

Bryan, H. D. 1991. The distribution, habitat, and ecology of shrews (Soricidae: *Blarina*, *Sorex*, an *Cryptotis*) in Kentucky. Journal of the Tennessee Academy of Science 66(4): 187-189.

Bryan, Hal. 1992. Personal communication during review.

Burk, J. H. 1988. Sonoran desert vegetation. In Terrestrial vegetation of California, eds., M. G. Barbour and J. Major. Davis: California Native Plant Society.

Burns, R. M., and B. H. Honkala. 1990. Silvics of North America. Vols 1-2, Hardwoods. Agriculture Handbook 654. Washington: Forest Service, United States Department of Agriculture.

Butcher, G. S., W. A. Niering, W. J. Barry, and R. H. Goodwin. 1981. Equilibrium biogeography and the size of nature preserves: an avian case study. Oecologia 49: 29-37.

Cairns, J. 1988. Restoration and the alternative: a research strategy. Restoration and Management Notes 6(2): 65-67.

Cairns, J., Jr., K. L. Dickson, and E. E. Herricks, eds. 1977. Recovery and restoration of damaged ecosystems. Charlottesville: University Press of Virginia.

Carr, Bill. 1992. Personal communication during review.

Cathey, H. M. 1990. U. S. D. A. plant hardiness zone map. Agricultural Research Service Miscellaneous Publication Number 1475. Washington: United States Department of Agriculture

Chapman, K. A. 1986. Draft descriptions of Michigan natural community types. Lansing: Michigan Natural Features Inventory.

Cheater, M. 1992. Alien invasion. Nature Conservancy: (September/October): 24-29.

Christensen, N. L. 1988. Vegetation of the southeastern coastal plains. In North American terrestrial vegetation, eds., M. G. Barbour and W. D. Billings. Cambridge: Cambridge University Press.

Clark, K., D. Euler, and E. Armstrong. 1983. Habitat associations of breeding birds in cottage and natural areas of central Ontario. Wilson Bulletin 95(1): 77-96.

Clewell, A. F. 1985. Guide to the vascular plants of the Florida panhandle. Tallahassee: Florida State University Press.

Cobb, B.1963. A field guide to the ferns and their related families. Boston: The Peterson Field Guide Series, Houghton Mifflin Company.

Cody, M. L. 1985. Habitat selection in grassland and open-country birds. In Habitat selection in birds, ed., M. L. Cody. Orlando: Academic Press Inc.

Cody, M. L., ed. 1985. Habitat selection in birds. Orlando: Academic Press Inc.

Cody, M. L., and J. M. Diamond, eds. 1975. Ecology and evolution of communities. Cambridge: The Belknap Press of Harvard University Press.

Cole, M. A. R. 1991, Vegetation management guideline: leafy spurge (*Euphorbia esula* L.). Natural Areas Journal 11(3): 271.

Collins, S. L., and S. M. Glenn. 1991. Importance of spatial and temporal dynamics in species regional abundance and distribution. Ecology 72(2): 654-664.

Constant, P., E. M.-C. Eybert, and R. Maheo. 1973. Recherches sur les oiseaux nicheurs dans les plantations des resineaux de la foret de Paimpont (Bertagne). Ardea 41: 371-384.

Core, E. L. 1966. Vegetation of West Virginia. Parsons: McClain Printing Company.

Corley, W. L. 1989. Wildflower establishment and cultivation for roadsides, meadows and beauty spots. Research News, Georgia Department of Transportation, Office of Materials and Research.

Correll, D. S., and M. C. Johnston. 1970. Manual of the vascular plants of Texas. Renner: Texas Research Foundation.

Cox, J. 1991. Landscaping with nature. Emmaus: Rodale Press.

Cowardin, L. M., V. Carter, F. C. Golet, and E. T. LaRoe. 1979. Classification of wetlands and deepwater habitats of the United States. U.S. Fish Wildlife Serv. Biol. Service Program, FMS/OBS.79/31.

Craig, R. M. 1984. Plants for coastal dunes of the gulf and south Atlantic coasts and Puerto Rico. Washington: U.S. Government Printing Office.

Craighead, J. J., F. C. Craighead, Jr., and R. J. Davis. 1963. A field guide to Rocky Mountain wildflowers from northern Arizona and New Mexico to British Columbia. Boston: Houghton Mifflin company.

Cronquist, A., A. H. Holmgren, N. H. Holmgren, J. L. Reveal, and P. K. Holmgren. 1972. Intermountain flora: vascular plants of the intermountain west, U.S.A. (Vols. 1, 3, 4, 6). New York: Hafner Publishing Company.

Crum H. A., and L. E. Anderson. 1981. Mosses of eastern North America. Vols. 1-2. New York: Columbia University Press.

Currie, D. J. 1991. Energy and large-scale patterns of animal- and plant-species richness. American Naturalist 137: 27-49.

Curtis, J. T. 1959. The vegetation of Wisconsin. Madison: The University of Wisconsin Press.

Dasmann, R. F. 1976. Environmental conservation. 4th ed. New York: John Wiley and Sons, Inc.

Daubenmire, R. 1978. Plant geography. New York: Academic Press.

Davis, A. M., and T. F. Glick. 1978. Urban ecosystems and island biogeography. Environmental Conservation 5: 299-304.

Davis, R. J. 1952. Flora of Idaho. Dubuque: Wm. C. Brown Company.

Diamond, J. M. 1978. Critical areas for maintaining viable populations of species. In The breakdown and restoration of ecosystems, eds., M. W. Holdgate and M. J. Woodman. New York: Plenum Press.

Diamond, J. M., and M. E. Gilpin. 1982. Examination of the "null" model of Connor and Simberloff for species co-occurrences on islands. Oecologia 52: 64-74.

Diamond, J. M., and R. M. May. 1981. Island biogeography and the design of natural reserves. In Theoretical ecology: principles and applications, ed., R. M. May. Sunderland: Sinauor Associates, Inc.

Dick-Peddie, W. A. 1992. New Mexico vgetation: past, present and future. Albuquerque: University of New Mexico Press.

Diekelmann, J., and R. Schuster. 1982. Natural landscaping: designing with native plant communities. New York: McGraw-Hill Book Company.

Dirr, M. A. 1990. Manual of woody landscape plants their identification, ornamental characteristics, culture, propagation and uses. Champaign: Stipes Publishing Company.

Disney, H. J. S., and A. Stokes. 1976. Birds in pine and native forests. Emu 78: 133-138.

Dixon, R. M. 1990. Land imprinting for dryland revegetation and restoration. In Environmental restoration, ed., J. J. Berger. Washington: Island Press.

Dorn, R. D. 1988. Vascular plants of Wyoming. Cheyenne: Mountain West Publishing.

Duncan, W. H., and L. E. Foote. 1975. Wildflowers of the southeastern United States. Athens: The University of Georgia Press.

Dunn, C. D., and C. Loehle. 1988. Species-area parameter estimation: testing the null model of lack of relationship. Journal of Biogeography 15: 721-728.

Ebinger, J. E. 1983. Exotic shrubs (*Elaeagnus umbellata*, *Ligustrum obtusifolium*) a potential problem in natural area management in Illinois. Natural Areas Journal 3(1): 3-6.

Ebinger, J. E. 1991. Naturalized amur maple (*Acer ginnala* Maxim.) in Illinois. Natural Areas Journal 11(3): 170-171.

Ebinger, J. E., J. Newman, and R. Nyboer. 1984. Naturalized winged wahoo (*Euonymus alatus*) in Illinois. Natural Areas Journal 4(2): 26-29.

Evans, J. E., and M. Heitlinger. 1984. IPM: a review for natural area managers. Restoration and Management Notes 11(1): 18-24.

Ewel, J. J. 1990. Introduction. In Ecosystems of Florida, eds., R. L. Myers and J. J. Ewel. Orlando: University of Central Florida.

Ewel, K. C. 1990. Swamps. In Ecosystems of Florida, eds., R. L. Myers and J. J. Ewel. Orlando: University of Central Florida.

Eyre, F. H. ed. 1980. Forest cover types of the United States and Canada. Washington: Society of American Foresters.

Falk, D. 1990. Discovering the future, creating the past: some reflections on restoration. Restoration and Management Notes 8(2): 71-72.

Fernald, M. L. 1970. Gray's manual of botany. 8th ed., corrected printing. New York: Van Nostrand Reinhold Company.

Finch, D. M. 1991. Population ecology, habitat requirements, and conservation of neotropical migratory birds. General Technical Report RM-205. Fort Collins: Forest Service, United States Department of Agriculture.

Forman, R. T. T. ed. 1979. Pine barrens: ecosystem and landscape. New York: Academic Press.

Forman, R. T. T., A. Galli, and C. Leck. 1976. Forest size and avian diversity in New Jersey woodlots with some land use implications. Oecologia 26: 1-8.

Forman, R. T. T., and M. Godron. 1986. Landscape ecology. New York: John Wiley and Sons.

Frankel, O. H., and M. E. Soule. 1981. Conservation and evolution. New York: Cambridge University Press.

Franklin, J. F., and C. T. Dyrness. 1973. Natural vegetation of Oregon and Washington. Salem: Oregon State University Press.

Franklin, J. F., W. H. Moir, M. A. Hemstrom, S. E. Greene, and B. G. Smith. 1988. The forest communities of Mount Rainier National Park. Scientific Monograph Series No. 19. Washington: U. S. Department of the Interior.

Freemark, K. E., and H. G. Merriam. 1986. Importance of area and habitat heterogeneity to bird assemblages in temperate forest fragments. Biological Conservation 36: 115-141.

Gilkey, H. M., and L. J. Dennis. 1967. Handbook of northwestern plants. Corvallis: Oregon State University Bookstores, Inc.

Galli, A. E., C. F. Leck, and R. T. Forman. 1976. Avian distribution patterns in forest islands of different sizes in central New Jersey. Auk 93: 356-364.

Gill, J. D., and W. M. Healy, eds. 1974. Shrubs and vines for northeastern wildlife. Forest Service General Technical Report NE-9. Upper Darby: U. S. Department of Agriculture.

Giller, P. S. 1984. Community structure and the niche. London: Chapman and Hall.

Glass, W. D. 1991. Vegetation management guideline: cut-leaved teasel (*Dipsacus laciniatus* L.) and common teasel (*D. sylvestris* Huds.). Natural Areas Journal 11(4): 213-214.

Glass, W. D. 1992. Vegetation management guideline: white poplar (*Populus alba* L.). Natural Areas Journal 12(1): 39-40.

Gleason, H. A., and A. Cronquist. 1963. Manual of vascular plants of northeastern United States and adjacent Canada. New York: D. Van Nostrand company.

Gleason, H. A., and A. Cronquist. 1964. The natural geography of plants. New York: Columbia University Press.

Gleason, H. A., and A. Cronquist. 1991. Manual of vascular plants of northeastern United States and adjacent Canada. 2nd ed. Bronx: New York Botanical Garden.

Godfrey, R. K. 1988. Trees, shrubs, and woody vines of northern Florida and adjacent Georgia and Alabama. Athens: The University of Georgia Press.

Goodall, D. W., and R. A. Perry, eds. 1979. Aridland ecosystems: structure, functioning and management. Vol 1. Cambridge: Cambridge University Press.

Goodwin, R. H., and W. A. Niering. 1975. Inland wetlands of the United States. National Park Service Natural History Theme Studies Number 2. New London: Connecticut College.

Grant, J. A., and C. L. Grant. 1990. Trees and shrubs for Pacific northwest gardens. Portland: Timber Press.

Green, A. W., and R. C. Conner. 1989. Forests in Wyoming. Resource Bulletin INT-61. Ogden: Forest Service, United States Department of Agriculture.

Green, B. H., and I. C. Marshall. 1987. An assessment of the role of golf courses in Kent, England, in protecting wildlife and landscapes. Landscape and Urban Planning 14: 143-154.

Griffin, J. R. 1988. Oak woodland. In Terrestrial vegetation of California, eds., M. G. Barbour and J. Major. Davis: California Native Plant Society.

Grigg, G. T. 1990. Seeking a fresh vision of environmental responsibility. Golf Course Management 58(9): 38-46.

Grumbine, E. 1990. Protecting biological diversity through the greater ecosystem concept. Natural Areas Journal 10(3): 114-120.

Guinon, M., and D. Allen. 1990. Restoration of dune habitat at Spanish Bay. In Environmental restoration, ed., J. J. Berger. Washington: Island Press.

Hanes, T. L. 1988. Chaparral. In Terrestrial vegetation of California, eds., M. G. Barbour and J. Major. Davis: California Native Plant Society.

Hansson, L., and P. Angelstam. 1991. Landscape ecology as a theoretical basis for nature conservation. Landscape Ecology 5(4): 191-201.

Harrington, J., and E. Howell. 1990. Pest plants in woodland restorations. In Environmental restoration, ed., J. J. Berger. Washington: Island Press.

Harris, L. D. 1984. The fragmented forest. Chicago: University of Chicago Press.

Harrison, R. L. 1992. Toward a theory of interrefuge corridor design. Conservation Biology 6(2): 293-295.

Harty, F. M. 1991. How Illinois kicked the exotic habit. Conference on Biological Pollution: The control and Impact of Invasive Exotic Species. Sponsored by the Indiana Academy of Science, October 25-26, Indianapolis, Indiana.

Hazen, W. E. ed. [1964] 1975. Readings in population and community ecology. 3rd ed. Philadelphia: W. B. Saunders Company.

Heady, H. F. 1988. Valley grassland. In Terrestrial vegetation of California, eds., M. G. Barbour and J. Major. Davis: California Native Plant Society.

Henderson, C. L. 1987. Landscaping for wildlife. St. Paul: Minnesota's Bookstore, State of Minnesota Department of Administration Print Communications Division.

Hester, F. E. 1991. The U. S. National Park Service experience with exotic species. Natural Areas Journal 11(3): 127-128.

Heidorn, R. 1992. Vegetation management guideline: exotic buckthorns common buckthorn (*Rhamnus cathartica* L.), glossy buckthorn (*Rhamnus frangula* L.), dahurian buckthorn (*Rhamnus davurica* Pall.). Natural Areas Journal 11(4): 216-217.

Hitchcock, A. S. [1950] 1971. Manual of the grasses of the United States. 2 vols. 2nd ed., ed. Agnes Chase. New York: Dover Publications, Inc.

Hitchcock, C. L., and A. Cronquist. 1973. Flora of the Pacific northwest. Seattle: University of Washington Press.

Holdgate, M. W., and M. J. Woodman, eds. 1978. The breakdown and restoration of ecosystems. New York: Plenum Press.

Holland, M. M., P. G. Risser, and R. J. Naiman, eds. 1991. Ecotones: the role of landscape boundaries in the management and restoration of changing environments. New York: Chapman and Hall.

Holland, R. F. 1986. Preliminary descriptions of the terrestrial natural communities of California. Sacramento: State of California, Department of Fish and Game.

Holland, R., and S. Jain. 1988. Vernal pools. In Terrestrial vegetation of California, eds., M. G. Barbour and J. Major. Davis: California Native Plant Society.

Howell, E. A. 1986. Woodland restoration: an overview. Restoration and Management Notes 4(1): 13-17.

Hunter, M. L., Jr. 1990. Wildlife, forests, and forestry. Engelwood Cliffs: Prentice Hall.

Hutchison, M. 1992. Vegetation management guideline: reed canary grass (*Phalaris arundinacea* L.). Natural Areas Journal 12(3): 159-160.

Irwin, H. S. 1961. Roadside flowers of Texas. Austin: University of Texas Press.

Jepson, W. L. 1951. A manual of the flowering plants of California. Berkeley: University of California Press.

Johnson, A. F., and M. G. Barbour. 1990. Dunes and maritime forests. In Ecosystems of Florida, eds. R. L. Myers and J. J. Ewel, 429-480. Orlando: University of Central Florida.

Johnston, D. W., and E. P. Odum. 1956. Breeding bird populations in relation to plant succession of the piedmont of Georgia. Ecology 37(1): 50-62.

Jones, F. B. 1977. Flora of the Texas coastal bend. Sinton: Rob and Bessie Welder Wildlife Foundation.

Jordan, W. R., III, M. E. Gilpin, and J. D. Aber, eds. 1987. Restoration ecology: a synthetic approach to ecological research. New York: Cambridge University Press.

Kartesz, J. T. 1990. Common names for the North American flora. Portland: Timber press.

Kartesz, J. T. 1991. Synonymized checklist of the vascular flora of the United States. Chapel Hill: North Carolina Botanical Garden, The University of North Carolina.

Kearney, T. H., and R. H. Peebles, and collaborators. 1960. Arizona flora, 2nd ed. Supplement by J. T. Howell and E. McClintock and collaborators. Berkeley: University of California Press.

Keator, G. 1990. Complete garden guide to the native perennials of California. San Francisco: Chronicle Books.

Keeley J. E., and S. C. Keeley. 1988. Chaparral. In North American terrestrial vegetation, eds., M. G. Barbour and W. D. Billings. Cambridge: Cambridge University Press.

Kennay, J., and G. Fell. 1992. Vegetation management guideline: siberian elm (*Ulmus pumila* L.). Natural Areas Journal 12(1): 40-41.

Knight, D. H., R. J. Hill, and T. A. Harrison. 1976. Potential natural landmarks in the Wyoming Basin. Laramie: University of Wyoming, Department of Botany.

Kruckeberg, A. R. 1982. Gardening with native plants of the Pacific Northwest: an illustrated guide. Seattle: University of Washington Press.

Küchler, A. W. 1964. Manual to accompany the map potential natural vegetation of the conterminous United States. American Geographical Society Special Publication No. 36. New York: American Geographical Society.

Küchler, A. W. 1967. Vegetation mapping. New York: The Ronald Press Company.

Küchler, A. W. [1964] 1975. Potential natural vegetation of the conterminous United States. 2nd ed. New York: American Geographical Society.

Kushlan, J. A. 1990. Freshwater marshes. In Ecosystems of Florida, eds., R. L. Myers and J. J. Ewel. Orlando: University of Central Florida.

Kusler, J. A., and M. E. Kentula. 1990. Wetland creation and restoration: the status of the science. Washington: Island Press.

Latting, J., ed. 1976. Plant communities of southern California. Symposium Proceedings. No place. Special Publication Number 2 California Native Plant Society.

Lauver, C. L. 1989. Preliminary classification of the natural communities of Kansas. Kansas Biological Survey Report No. 50. Lawrence: Kansas Natural Heritage Program.

Little, C. E. 1990. Greenways for America. Baltimore: The Johns Hopkins University Press. Loughmiller, C., and L. Loughmiller. 1984. Texas wildflowers. Austin: University of Texas Press.

Lowe, C. H., 1964. Arizona's natural environment. Tucson: University of Arizona Press.

Luken, J. O. 1990. Directing ecological succession. New York: Chapman and Hall.

Luken, J. O., and D. T. Mattimiro. 1991. Habitat-specific resilience of the invasive shrub amur honeysuckle (*Lonicera maackii*) during repeated clipping. Ecological Applications 1(1): 104-109.

Lynch, J. F., and D. F. Whigham. 1984. Effects of forest fragmentation on breeding bird communities in Maryland, USA. Biological Conservation 28: 287-324.

Marble, A. D. 1992. A guide to wetland functional design. Boca Raton: Lewis Publishers.

MacArthur, R. H. 1972. Geographical ecology. New York: Harper and Row.

MacArthur, R. H., and J. MacArthur. 1961. On bird species diversity. Ecology 42(3): 594-599.

MacArthur, R. H., and E. O. Wilson. 1967. The theory of island biogeography. Princeton: Princeton University Press.

Macdonald, K. B. 1988. Coastal salt marsh. In Terrestrial vegetation of California, eds., M. G. Barbour and J. Major. Davis: California NativePlant Society.

Mackintosh, G. 1989. Preserving communities and corridors. Washington: Defenders of Wildlife.

Martin, A. C., H. S. Zim, and A. L. Nelson. 1951. American wildlife and plants a guide to wildlife food habits. New York: Dover Publications.

Martin, W. H., S. G. Boyce, and A. S. Echternacht, eds. In press. Biodiversity of the southeastern United States. 2 Vols. New York: John Wiley and Sons.

Marx, D. H. 1991. The practical significance of ectomycorrhizae in forest establishment. Symposium at the Marcus Wallenberg Prize Ceremonies. September 27, 1991. Stockholm, Sweden.

Marx, D. H. 1991. Forest application of the ectomychorrhizal fungus *Pisolithus tinctorius*. The Marcus Wallenburg Prize lecture. September 26, 1991, Stockholm, Sweden.

Maser, C. 1988. The redesigned forest. San Pedro: R. and E. Miles.

Mauk, R. L., and J. A. Henderson. 1984. Coniferous forest habitat types of northern Utah. General Technical Report INT-170. Ogden: Forest Service, United States Department of Agriculture.

McGregor R. L., T. M. Barkley, R. E. Brooks, and E. K. Schofield. 1986. Flora of the Great Plains. Lawrence: University Press of Kansas.

McIntyre, S., and G. W. Barrett. 1992. Habitat variegation, an alternative to fragmentation. Conservation Biology 6(1): 146-147.

McMahan, C. A. , R. G. Frye, and K. L. Brown. 1984. The vegetation types of Texas including cropland. Austin: Wildlife Division, Texas Parks and Wildlife Department.

Medley, Max. 1976. The prairie, a historical perspective. Fernwood Notes: No. 111.

Merriam, G. 1984. Connectivity: a fundamental ecological characteristic of landscape pattern. In Methodology in landscape ecological research and planning, eds., J. Brandt and P. Agger. Denmark: Roskilde University Centre.

Miller, R. M. 1985. Mycorrhizae. Restoration and Management Notes 3(1): 14-20.

Mitsch, W. J., and J. G. Gosselink. 1986. Wetlands. New York: Van Nostrand Reinhold Company.

Morrison, M. L., B. G. Marcot, and R. W. Mannan. 1992. Wildlife-habitat relationships. Madison: University of Wisconsin Press.

Montague, C. L., and R. G. Wiegert. 1990. Salt marshes. In Ecosystems of Florida, eds., R. L. Myers and J. J. Ewel. Orlando: University of Central Florida Press.

Myers, R. L. 1990. Scrub and high pine. In Ecosystems of Florida, eds., R. L. Myers and J. J. Ewel. Orlando: University of Central Florida Press.

Myers, R. L., and J. J. Ewel, eds. 1990. Ecosystems of Florida. Orlando: University of Central Florida Press.

National Research Council. 1992. Restoration of aquatic ecosystems. Washington: National Academy Press.

National Wildflower Research Center. 1992. Wildflower handbook. Stillwater: Voyageur Press.

Nelson, J. B. 1986. The natural communities of South Carolina. No place. South Carolina Wildlife and Marine Resources Department.

Norton, B., ed. 1986. The preservation of species. Princeton: Princeton University Press.

Noss, R. F. 1983. A regional landscape approach to maintain diversity. Bioscience 33(11): 700-706.

Odum, W. E., and C. C. McIvor. 1990. Mangroves. In Ecosystems of Florida, eds., R. L. Myers and J. J. Ewel. Orlando: University of Central Florida Press.

Omernik, J. M. 1986. Ecoregions of the conterminous United States. Corvallis: Corvallis Environmental Research Laboratory, U. S. Environmental Protection Agency.

Opdam, P., G. Rijsdijk, and F. Hustings. 1985. Bird communities in small woods in an agricultural landscape: effects of area and isolation. Biological Conservation 34: 333-352.

Oosting, H. J. [1948] 1956. The study of plant communities. 2nd ed. San Francisco: W. H. Freeman and Company.

Parker, K. F. 1972. An illustrated guide to Arizona weeds. Tucson: The University of Arizona Press.

Patterson, J., and G. Stevenson. 1977. Native trees of the Bahamas. Hope Town: Jack Patterson.

Peattie, D. C. 1981. A natural history of western trees. Boston: Houghton Mifflin Company.

Peet, R. K. 1988. Forests of the Rocky Mountains. In North American terrestrial vegetation, eds., M. G. Barbour and W. D. Billings. Cambridge: Cambridge University Press.

Perry, D. A., and M. P. Amaranthus. 1990. The plant-soil bootstrap: microorganisms and reclamation of degraded ecosystems. In Environmental restoration, ed., J. J. Berger. Washington: Island Press.

Petrides, G. A. 1992. A field guide to western trees. New York: Houghton Mifflin Company.

Pfister, R. D., B. L. Kovalchik, S. F. Arno, and R.C. Presby. 1977. Forest habitat types of Montana. Ogden: USDA Forest Service.

Phillip, H. R. 1985. Growing and propagating wildflowers. Chapel Hill: The University of North Carolina Press.

Platt, W. J., and M. W. Schwartz. 1990. Temperate hardwood forests. In Ecosystems of Florida, eds., R. L. Myers and J. J. Ewel. Orlando: University of Central Florida Press.

Pool, J. R. 1913. A study of the vegetation of the Sandhills of Nebraska. Ph.D. diss., University of Nebraska, Lincoln.

Preston, R. J., Jr. 1948. North American trees. Ames: Iowa University Press. Putnam, C. 1988. The Development and application of habitat standards for maintaining vertebrate species diversity on a national forest. Natural Areas Journal 8(4): 256-266.

Radford, A. E., H. E. Ahles, and C. R. Bell. 1968. Manual of the vascular flora of the Carolinas. Chapel Hill: The University of North Carolina Press.

Reschke, C. 1990. Ecological communities of New York State. Latham: New York Natural Heritage Program.

Riskind, D. H., and D. O. Diamond. 1988. An introduction to environments and vegetation. In Edwards Plateau vegetation: plant ecological studies in Central Texas, eds., B. B. Amos and F. R. Gehlbach. Waco: Baylor University Press.

Risser, P. G., E. C. Birney, H. D. Blocker, S. W. May, W. J. Parton, and J. A. Wiens. 1981. The true prairie ecosystem. Stroudsburg: Hutchinson Ross Publishing Company.

Robinette, G. O. ed. [1977] 1983. Landscape planning for energy conservation. New York: Van Nostrand Reinhold Company.

Rodiek, J. E., and E. G. Bolen, eds. 1991. Wildlife and habitats in managed landscapes. Washington: Island Press.

Roth, S. A., ed. 1988. Garden pools and fountains. San Ramon: Ortho Books.

Rundel, P. W., D. J. Parsons, and D. T. Gordon. 1988. Montane and subalpine vegetation of the Sierra Nevada and Cascade Ranges. In Terrestrial vegetation of California, eds., M. G. Barbour and J. Major. Davis: California Native Plant Society,

Rydberg, P. A. [1922] 1954. Flora of the Rocky Mountains and adjacent plains. 2nd ed. Reprint. New York: Hafner Publishing Company.

Sampson, F. B., and F. L. Knopf. 1982. In search of a diversity ethic for wildlife management. Transactions of the North American Wildlife Natural Resources Conference 47: 421-431.

Saunders, D. A., G. W. Arnold, A. A. Burbidge, and A. J. M. Hopkins. 1987. Nature conservation: the role of remnants of native vegetation. Australia: Surrey Beatty and Sons Pty Limited.

Sawyer, J. O., D. A. Thornburgh, and J. R. Griffin. 1988. Mixed evergreen forest. In Terrestrial vegetation of California, eds., M. G. Barbour and J. Major. Davis: California Native Plant Society.

Schafer, C. L. 1990. Nature Preserves. Washington: Smithsonian Institution Press.

Schaid, T. A., D. W. Ureska, W. L. Tucker, and R. L. Linder. 1983. Effects of surface mining on the vesper sparrow in the northern Great Plains. Journal of Range Management 36: 500-503.

Schmidt, M. G. 1980. Growing California native plants. California Natural History Guides 45. Berkeley: University of California Press.

Schneck, M. 1990. Butterflies: how to identify and attract them to your garden. Emmaus: Rodale Press.

Schneegas, E. R. 1975. National forest nongame bird management. Symposium on Management of Forest and Range Habitats for Nongame Birds, May 6-9, 1975. Tucson, Arizona.

Schroeder, R. L. 1986. Habitat suitability index models: wildlife species richness in shelterbelts. U.S. Fish Wildlife Service Biological Report 82(10.128).

Schwartz, O. A., and P. D. Whitson. 1987. A 12-year study of vegetation and mammal succession on a reconstructed tallgrass prairie in Iowa. The American Midland Naturalist 117(2): 240-249.

Sedenko, J. 1991. The butterfly garden: creating beautiful gardens to attract butterflies. New York: Villard Books.

Shafer, C. L. 1990. Nature preserves. Washington: Smithsonian Institution Press.

Shaffer, M. L., and F. B. Sampson. 1985. Population size and extinction: a note on determining critical population size. American Naturalist 125: 144-152.

Shealy, S. 1989. Environment by design: landscaping the highways. Drive (Spring).

Shelford, V. E. 1974. The ecology of North America. Chicago: University of Illinois Press.

Simberloff, D. S., and L. G. Abele. 1982. Refuge design and island biogeographic theory: effects of fragmentation. American Naturalist 120: 41-50.

Simberloff, D. S., and L. G. Abele. 1984. Conservation and obfuscation: subdivision of reserves. Oikos 42: 399-401.

Simberloff, D. and N. Gotelli. 1984. Effects of insularization on plant species richness in the prairie-forest ecotone. Biological Conservation 29: 27-46.

Simpson, G. G. 1964. Species density of North American recent mammals. Systematic Zoology 13: 75-73.

Sims, P. L. 1988. Grasslands. In North American terrestrial vegetation, eds., M. G. Barbour and W. D. Billings. Cambridge: Cambridge University Press.

Smith, K. D. 1974. The utilization of gum trees by birds in Africa. Ibis 116: 155-164.

Smith, R. L. 1966. Ecology and field biology. New York: Harper and Row, Publishers.

Smith, T. L. no date. Natural ecological communities of Pennsylvania.

Smith, T. M., and H. H. Shugart. 1987. Territory size variation in the ovenbird: the role of habitat structure. Ecology 68(3): 695-704.

Snyder, J. R., A. Herndon, and W. B. Robertson, Jr. 1990. South Florida rockland. In Ecosystems of Florida, eds., R. L. Myers and J. J. Ewel. Orlando: University of Central Florida Press.

Soule, M. E. and B. A. Wilcox, eds. 1980. Conservation biology an evolutionary-ecological perspective. Sunderland: Sinauer Associates, Inc.

Spellenberg, R. 1979. The Audubon Society field guide to North American wildflowers: western region. New York: Alfred A. Knopf.

Sperka, M. 1973. Growing wildflowers. New York: Charles Scribner's Sons.

Sprunt, A. 1975. Habitat management implications of migration. Symposium on Management of Forest and Range Habitats for Nongame Birds, May 6-9, 1975. Tucson, Arizona.

Stamps, J. A., M. Buechner, and V. V. Krishnan. 1987. The effects of edge permeability and habitat geometry on emigration from patches of habitat. The American Naturalist 129(4): 533-552.

Stauffer, D. F., and L. Best. 1980. Habitat selection by birds of riparian communities: evaluating effects of habitat alterations. Journal of Wildlife Management 44(1): 1-15.

Steele, R., R. D. Pfister, R. A. Ryker, and J. A. Kittams. 1981. Forest habitat types of central Idaho. General Technical Report INT-114. Ogden: Forest Service, United States Department of Agriculture.

Stokes, D., and L. Stokes. 1989. The hummingbird book. Boston: Little, Brown and Company.

Stokes, D., and L. Stokes. 1991. The bluebird book. Boston: Little, Brown and Company.

Stokes, D., L. Stokes, and E. Williams. 1991. The butterfly book. Boston: Little, Brown and Company.

Stritch, L. R. 1990. Barrens restoration in the cretaceous hills of Pope and Massac Counties, Illinois. In Environmental restoration, ed., J. J. Berger. Washington: Island Press.

St. John, T. V. 1990. Mycorrhizal inoculation of container stock for restoration of self-sufficient vegetation. In Environmental restoration, ed., J.J. Berger. Washington: Island Press.

Swindells, P. 1985. The water garden. London: Ward Lock Limited.

Swink, F. 1974. Plants of the Chicago region: a check list of the vascular flora of the Chicago region with notes on local distribution and ecology. 2nd edition. Lisle: The Morton Arboretum.

Szafoni, R. E. 1992. Vegetation management guideline: autumn olive, *Elaeagnus umbellata* Thunb. Natural Areas Journal 11(2): 121-122.

Temple, S. A. 1986. Predicting impacts of habitat fragmentation on forest birds: a comparison of two models. In Wildlife 2000, eds., J. Verner, M.L. Morrison, and C. J. Ralph. Madison: The University of Wisconsin Press.

Temple, S. A. 1992. Conservation biologists and wildlife managers getting together. Conservation Biology 6(1): 4.

Terres, J. K. 1980. The Audubon encyclopedia of North American birds. New York: Alfred A. Knopf, Inc.

Tharp, B. C. 1926. Structure of Texas vegetation east of the 98th meridian. University of Texas Bulletin No. 2606. Austin: University of Texas Press.

Tharp, B. C. 1939. The vegetation of Texas. Houston: Anson Jones Press.

Thomas, J. W. ed. 1979. Wildlife habitats in managed forests. Agriculture Handbook No. 553. Washington: Forest Service, United States Department of Agriculture.

Thompson, J. R. 1992. Prairies, forests, and wetlands. Iowa City: University of Iowa Press.

Thorne, R. F. 1976. The vascular plant communities of southern California. In Plant communities of southern California, ed., J. Latting. CNPS Special Publication Number 2. Berkeley: CNPS.

Thorne, R. F. 1988. Montane and subalpine forests of the transverse and peninsular ranges. In Terrestrial vegetation of California, eds., M. J. Barbour and J. Major. Davis: California Native Plant Society.

Tilghman, N. G. 1987. Characteristics of urban woodlands affecting breeding bird diversity and abundance. Landscape and Urban Planning 14: 481-495.

Trimble, G. R. 1959. Logging roads in northeastern municipal watersheds. Journal of the American Water Works Assocociation 51: 407-410.

Trimble, G. R., Jr., and R. S. Sartz. 1957. How far from a stream should a logging road be located. Journal of Forestry 55: 339-341.

Turner, M. G., ed. 1987. Landscape heterogeneity and disturbance. New York: Springer-Verlag.

Turner, M. G., and R. H. Gardner, eds. 1991. Quantitative methods in landscape ecology. New York: Springer-Verlag.

Vasek, F. C., and M. G. Barbour. 1988. Mojave desert scrub vegetation. In Terrestrial vegetation of California, eds., M. G. Barbour and J. Major. D a v i s : California Native Plant Society.

Vasek, F. C., and R. F. Thorne. 1988. Transmontane coniferous vegetation. In Terrestrial vegetation of California, eds., M. G. Barbour and J. Major. Davis: California Native Plant Society.

Verner, J. 1975. Avian behavior and habitat management. The Symposium on Management of Forest and Range Habitats for Nongame Birds. May 6-9, 1975. Tucson, Arizona.

Verner, J., M. L. Morrison, and C. J. Ralph. 1986. Wildlife 2000. Madison: The University of Wisconsin Press.

Vines, R. A. 1960. Trees, shrubs, and woody vines of the southwest. Austin: University of Texas Press.

Virginia, R. A. 1990. Desert restoration: the role of woody legumes. In Environmental restoration, ed., J. J. Berger. Washington: Island Press.

Vogl, R. J., W. P. Armstrong, K. L. White, and K. L. Cole. 1988. The closed-cone pines and cypress. In Terrestrial vegetation of California, eds., M.G Barbour and J. Major. Davis: California Native Plant Society.

Waggoner, G. S. 1975. Eastern Deciduous Forest. 2 Vols. Washington: U.S. Government Printing Office.

Ward, G. B. and O. M. Ward. No data. Wild flowers of the southwest deserts in natural color. Palm Desert: Best-West Publications.

Wasowski, S. with A. Wasowski. 1991. Native Texas plants: landscaping region by region. Houston: Gulf Publishing Company.

Weathers, L. A., and M. Hunter. 1990. Flowers wild and wonderful. Southern Living April: 90-95.

Weaver, J. E. 1954. North American prairie. Lincoln: Johnsen Publishing Company.

Weaver, J. E. 1965. Native vegetation of Nebraska. Lincoln: University of Nebraska Press.

Weaver. J. E. 1968. Prairie plants and their environment. Lincoln: University of Nebraska Press.

Weber, W. A. 1976. Rocky Mountain flora. Boulder: Colorado Associated University Press.

Weber, W. A. 1987. Colorado flora: western slope. Boulder: Colorado Associated University Press.

Weber, W. A. 1990. Colorado flora: eastern slope. Boulder: University Press of Colorado.

Weddell, B. J. 1991. Distribution and movements of Columbian ground squirrels (*Spermophilus columbianus* (Ord)): are habitat patches like islands? Journal of Biogeography 18: 285-294.

Weddle, A. E., ed. 1983. Landscape techniques. New York: Van Rostrand Reinhold Co.

Welsh, S. L., N. D. Atwood, S. Goodrich, and L. C. Higgins, eds. 1987. A Utah flora. Great Basin Naturalist Memoirs Number 9. Provo: Brigham Young University.

West, K. A. 1984. Major pest species listed, control measures summarized at natural areas workshop. Restoration and Management Note II(1): 34-35.

West, N. E. 1988. Intermountain deserts, shrub steppes, and woodlands. In North American terrestrial vegetation, eds., M. G. Barbour and W. D. Billings. Cambridge: Cambridge University Press.

Wharton, C. H. 1989. The natural environments of Georgia. Bulletin 114. Atlanta: Geologic and Water Resources Division and Resource Planning Section, Georgia Department of Natural Resources.

Wherry, E. T. 1948. Wild flower guide: northeastern and midland United States. New York: Doubleday and Company, Inc.

Whitcomb, R. F. 1977. Island biogeography and "habitat islands" of eastern forests. American Birds 31: 3-5.

Whitcomb, R. F., C. S. Robbins, J. F. Lynch, B. L. Klimkiewicz, B. L. Whitcomb, and D. Bystrak. 1981. Effects of forest fragmentation on avifauna of the eastern deciduous forest. In Forest island dynamics in man-dominated landscapes, eds., R. L. Burgess and D. M. Sharpe. New York: Springer-Verlag.

Whitcomb, B. L., R. Whitcomb, and D. Bystrak. 1977. Long-term turnover and effects of selective logging on the avifauna of forest fragments. American Birds 31(1): 17-23.

Wilcox. B. A. 1980. Insular ecology and conservation. In Conservation biology: an evolutionary-ecological perspective, eds., M. E. Soule and B. A. Wilcox. Sunderland: Sinauer

Willson, M. F. 1974. Avian community organization and habitat structure. Ecology 55: 1017-1029.

Xerces Society. 1990. Butterfly gardening: creating summer magic in your garden. San Francisco: Sierra Club Books.

Zinke, P. J. 1988. The redwood forest and associated north coast forests. In Terrestrial vegetation of California, eds., M. G. Barbour and J. Major. Davis: California Native Plant Society.

Zonneveld, I. S., and R. T. T. Forman, eds. 1990. Changing landscapes: an ecological perspective. New York: Springer-Verlag.

APPENDIX A

Natural Regions and Dominant Ecological Communities*

See Chapter 6 for a description of ecological systems, dominant ecological communities, and background information on how they were developed.

Table of Contents*

*Regional maps are on the facing page to each region

Natural Regions of the United States

The color map of the natural regions of the United States and the Küchler codes will appear following page A-20.

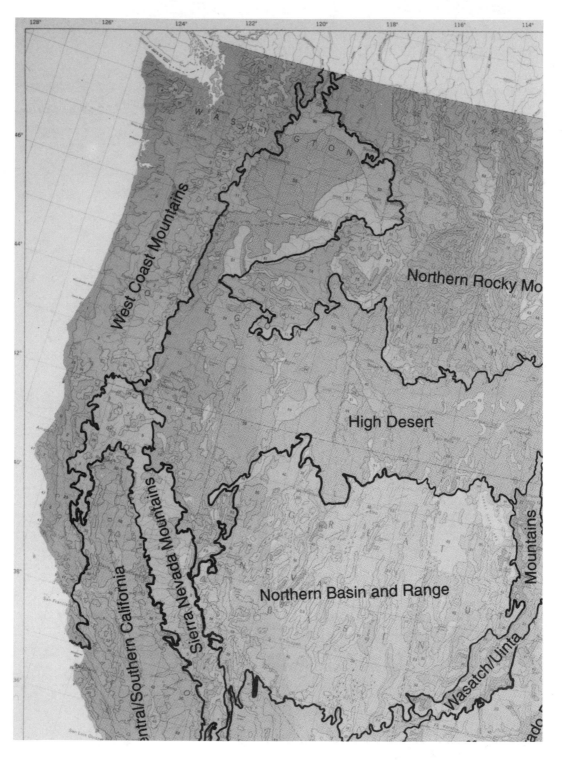

West Coast Mountains

West Coast Mountains

Introduction

The West Coast Mountain region includes the coastal mountains and the west slopes of the Cascade Mountains in Washington and Oregon, and the north coastal region of California. The region also includes the Klamath Mountains of northwestern California and southwestern Oregon. This region is often referred to as the temperate rainforest region because rain or fog are part of the daily climate for most of the year. A number of climatic and geographic variables cause these forests to support some of the largest and tallest species in the world. Important factors in the success of the trees are the winter rains and the summer fog which provide moisture throughout the year. This prevents extensive moisture stress and temperature change and creates optimal growing conditions.

Many factors determine the composition of forest types, however, an elevational gradient is the most useful for describing changes in species composition. Douglas-fir is the most extensive species in this region occupying low- to mid-elevations in the Cascade and Olympic Mountains. At higher elevations Pacific silver fir and mountain hemlock become dominant. Sitka spruce and redwood forests are the most common along the coast. Deciduous forest, scrub, and grassland communities also occur in the region. The Klamath Mountains support a complex and unique assemblage of plant communities because of their location between the mesic coastal forests and the dry interior valleys. The floodplains of the Willamette and Columbia Rivers support Riparian Forests which are frequently dominated by deciduous trees. The interior valleys of the Umpqua, Rogue, and Willamette Rivers, which are in the rainshadow of the coast mountains, support communities such as oak woodlands, chaparral, and dry grasslands. Grasslands and shrub communities also occur along the coast.

Minor but unique communities to this region include: the prairies in the Willamette Valley and Puget Sound; alpine meadows and parklands occurring above treeline in the Cascade Mountains; and lava, mud flow, and serpentine areas associated with the geology of the Cascade Mountains.

The primary sources used to develop descriptions and species lists are: Barbour and Billings 1988; Barbour and Major 1988; Franklin and Dyrness 1973; Holland 1986.

Dominant Ecological Communities

Upland Systems
Sitka Spruce–Hemlock Coastal Forest
Redwood Forest
Douglas-fir–Hemlock Forest
Silver Fir–Mountain Hemlock Forest
Mixed Evergreen Forest
Oregon Oak Woodland
Pine–Cypress Forest
Montane Chaparral
Coastal Mountain Grassland

Wetland Systems
Riparian Forest
Cedar–Alder Swamp

Estuarine Systems
Salt Marsh

UPLAND SYSTEMS
Sitka Spruce–Hemlock Coastal Forest

Sitka spruce characterizes the forest that occurs along the length of Washington's and Oregon's coasts. Sitka spruce forests are most often found below elevations of 495 feet but may reach elevations up to 1980 feet in the mountains closest to the coast. The climate in the area near the ocean is mild. Even in the characteristic dry northwest summers, frequent fog and fog drip protect the forest from extreme moisture stress. The understory of Sitka Spruce—Hemlock Coastal Forest is lush with dense growth of shrubs, herbs, and ferns. Unique in this community are the epiphyte-draped big-leaf maples in the understory. This community corresponds to Küchler #1.

Canopy
Characteristic Species
Picea sitchensis	sitka spruce
Thuja plicata	western arborvitae
Tsuga heterophylla	western hemlock

Associates
Abies amabilis	Pacific silver fir
Abies grandis	grand fir
Alnus rubra	red alder
Chamaecyparis lawsoniana	Port Orford cedar
Pinus contorta	lodgepole pine
Pseudotsuga menziesii	Douglas-fir
Sequoia sempervirens	redwood

Woody Understory
Acer circinatum	vine maple
Acer macrophyllum	big-leaf maple
Frangula purshiana	cacsara sagrada
Gaultheria shallon	salal
Menziesia ferruginea	fool's-huckleberry
Myrica californica	Pacific bayberry
Oplopanax horridum	devil's-club
Rhododendron macrophyllum	California rhododendron
Rubus spectabilis	salmon raspberry
Umbellularia californica	California-laurel
Vaccinium ovalifolium	oval-leaf blueberry
Vaccinium ovatum	evergreen blueberry
Vaccinium parvifolium	red blueberry

Herbaceous Understory
Athyrium filix-femina	subarctic lady fern
Blechnum spicant	deerfern
Claytonia sibirica	Siberian springbeauty
Disporum smithii	large-flower fairybells
Dryopteris campylpotera	mountain wood fern
Hylocomium splendens	feathermoss
Hypnum circinale	moss
Maianthemum dilatatim	two-leaf false Solomon's-seal

Oxalis oregana	redwood-sorrel
Polystichum munitum	pineland sword fern
Tiarella trifoliata	three-leaf foamflower
Viola glabella	pioneer violet
Viola sempervirens	redwood violet

Redwood Forest

Redwood Forest extends from southern Oregon into California along the coast and interior along streams or rivers. This community may occur just inland of sitka spruce and Douglas-fir-dominated forests. Although dependant on the summer fogs that are characteristic of the marine environment, redwoods do not tolerate salt spray as successfully as sitka spruce or Douglas-fir. This community corresponds to Küchler #6.

Canopy
Characteristic Species

Pseudotsuga menziesii	Douglas-fir
Sequoia sempervirens	redwood

Associates

Abies grandis	grand fir
Lithocarpus densiflorus	tan-oak
Tsuga heterophylla	western hemlock

Woody Understory

Acer macrophyllum	big-leaf maple
Gaultheria shallon	salal
Myrica californica	Pacific bayberry
Rhododendron macrophyllum	California rhododendron
Torreya californica	California-nutmeg
Umbellularia californica	California-laurel
Vaccinium ovatum	evergreen blueberry

Herbaceous Understory

Oxalis oregona	redwood-sorrel
Polystichum munitum	pineland sword fern
Vancouveria hexandra	white inside-out-flower
Whipplea modesta	modesty

Douglas-fir–Hemlock Forest

Large areas from sea level up to 3300 feet in the West Coast Mountains region are dominated by Douglas-fir trees. Douglas-fir trees need an open canopy and exposure to the sun to become established. Periodic forest fires are important in creating openings for regeneration. Western hemlock trees are also common within this community and may dominate on sites protected from windfall and fire. Unlike Douglas-fir, hemlock is successful in regenerating in the shade. Red cedar or western arborvitae, a common characteristic species throughout this region, is found along streams and in more mesic sites. This community corresponds to Küchler #2 and #12.

Canopy
Characteristic Species

Pseudotsuga menziesii	Douglas-fir
Thuja plicata	western arborvitae
Tsuga heterophylla	western hemlock

Associates

Abies amabilis	Pacific silver fir
Abies concolor	white fir
Abies grandis	grand fir
Arbutus menziesii	Pacific madrone
Calocedrus decurrens	incense-cedar
Chamaecyparis lawsoniana	Port Orford-cedar
Larix occidentalis	western larch
Lithocarpus densiflorus	tan-oak
Picea glauca	white spruce
Picea pungens	blue spruce
Picea sitchensis	sitka spruce
Pinus contorta	lodgepole pine
Pinus lambertiana	sugar pine
Pinus monticola	western white pine
Pinus ponderosa	ponderosa pine
Quercus garryana	Oregon white oak

Woody Understory

Acer circinatum	vine maple
Acer macrophyllum	big-leaf maple
Alnus rubra	red alder
Castanopsis chrysophylla	golden chinkapin
Cornus nuttallii	Pacific flowering dogwood
Corylus cornuta	western beaked hazelnut
Frangula purshiana	cassara sagrada
Fraxinus latifolia	Oregon ash
Gaultheria shallon	salal
Holodiscus discolor	hillside oceanspray
Linnaea borealis	American twinflower
Mahonia nervosa	Cascate Oregon-grape
Populus balsamifera	balsam poplar
Populus tremuloides	quaking aspen
Rhododendron macrophyllum	California rhododendron
Rubus spectabilis	salmon raspberry
Rubus ursinus	California dewberry
Symphoricarpos mollis	creeping snowberry
Taxus brevifolia	Pacific yew
Umbellularia californica	California-laurel
Vaccinium parvifolium	red blueberry

Herbaceous Understory

Achlys triphylla	sweet-after-death

Asarum caudatum	wildginger long-tail
Athyrium filix-femina	subarctic lady fern
Blechnum spicant	deerfern
Chimaphila umbellata	pipsissewa
Collomia heterophylla	variable-leaf mountain-trumpet
Coptis laciniata	Oregon goldthread
Disporum hookeri	drops-of-gold
Festuca occidentalis	western fescue
Galium triflorum	fragrant bedstraw
Hieracium albiflorum	white flower hawkweed
Iris tenax	tough-leaf iris
Lathyrus polyphyllus	leafy vetchling
Lysichitum americanum	yellow skunk-cabbage
Madia gracilis	grassy tarplant
Oxalis oregana	redwood-sorrel
Polystichum munitum	pineland sword fern
Synthyris reniformis	snowqueen
Tiarella trifoliata	three-leaf foamflower
Trientalis borealis	American starflower
Trillium ovatum	western wakerobin
Vancouveria hexandra	white inside-out-flower
Viola sempervirens	redwood violet
Whipplea modesta	modesty
Xerophyllum tenax	western turkeybeard

Silver Fir–Mountain Hemlock Forest

Silver Fir–Mountain Hemlock Forest occurs on the western slopes of the Cascade Range generally at elevations from 2600 to 6100 feet. Often referred to as "subalpine forests", silver fir is common between 2600 and 4200 feet and mountain hemlock common between 4200 and 6000 feet. Areas dominated by silver fir and mountain hemlock are wetter, cooler, and receive considerably more precipitation in the form of snow than areas dominated by Douglas-fir–Hemlock Forest. Much of the snow accumulates in snow packs of 3 to 10 feet in silver fir areas and to nearly 25 feet in higher mountain hemlock areas. In the highest elevations the mountain hemlock canopy opens into alpine "parklands" and meadows. The parklands consist of patches of forest and tree groups interspersed with shrubby or herbaceous sub-alpine communities. This community corresponds to Küchler #3, #4, and #15.

Canopy
Characteristic Species
Abies amabilis	Pacific silver fir
Abies lasiocarpa	subalpine fir
Abies procera	noble fir
Pseudotsuga menziesii	Douglas-fir
Tsuga mertensiana	mountain hemlock

Associates
Abies grandis	grand fir
Chamaecyparis nootkatensis	Alaska-cedar
Larix occidentalis	western larch
Picea engelmannii	Engelmann's spruce
Pinus contorta	lodgepole pine

Pinus monticola	western white pine
Thuja plicata	western arborvitae
Tsuga heterophylla	western hemlock

Woody Understory

Acer circinatum	vine maple
Arctostaphylos nevadensis	pinemat manzanita
Gaultheria shallon	salal
Linnaea borealis	American twinflower
Mahonia nervosa	Cascade Oregon-grape
Menziesia ferruginea	fool's-huckleberry
Oplopanax horridus	devil's-club
Phyllodoce empetriformis	pink mountain-heath
Rhododendron albiflorum	cascade azalea
Rubus lasiococcus	hairy-fruit smooth dewberry
Rubus pedatus	strawberry-leaf raspberry
Vaccinium deliciosum	ranier blueberry
Vaccinium membranaceum	square-twig blueberry
Vaccinium ovalifolium	oval-leaf blueberry
Vaccinium parvifolium	red blueberry
Vaccinium scoparium	grouseberry

Herbaceous Understory

Achlys triphylla	sweet-after-death
Athyrium filix-femina	subarctic lady fern
Chimaphila umbellata	pipsissewa
Clintonia uniflora	bride's bonnet
Coptis asplenifolia	fern-leaf goldthread
Cornus canadensis	Canadian bunchberry
Erythronium montanum	white avalanche-lily
Gymnocarpium dryopteris	western oak fern
Listera caurina	north western twayblade
Lysichitum americanum	yellow skunk-cabbage
Maianthemum stellata	starry false Solomon's-seal
Orthilia secunda	sidebells
Tiarella trifoliata	three-leaf foamflower
Trillium ovatum	western wakerobin
Valeriana stichensis	sitka valerian
Viola sempervirens	redwood violet
Xerophyllum tenax	western turkeybeard

Mixed Evergreen Forest

In the western Siskiyou and Klamath Mountains of southern Oregon and northern California evergreen needle-leaved and sclerophyllous broad-leaved trees occur in Mixed Evergreen Forest. Mixed Evergreen Forest is geographically and biologically transitional between the dense coniferous forests of northwestern California and the open woodlands and savannas of the interior. Dominant species are Douglas-fir and tan-oak. This community corresponds to Küchler #29.

Canopy
Characteristic Species
Arbutus menziesii	Pacific madrone
Lithocarpus densiflorus	tan-oak
Pseudotsuga menziesii	Douglas-fir
Quercus chrysolepis	canyon live oak

Associates
Acer circinatum	vine maple
Acer macrophyllum	big-leaf maple
Aesculus californica	California buckeye
Calocedrus decurrens	incense-cedar
Castanopsis chrysophylla	golden chinkapin
Chamaecyparis lawsoniana	Port Orford-cedar
Pinus jeffreyi	Jeffrey pine
Pinus lambertiana	sugar pine
Pinus ponderosa	ponderosa pine
Quercus douglasii	blue oak
Quercus garryana	Oregon white oak
Quercus kelloggii	California black oak
Quercus wislizenii	interior live oak

Woody Understory
Arctosaphylos manzanita	big manzanita
Ceanothus parryi	ladybloom
Ceanothus thyrsiflorus	bluebrush
Cornus nuttallii	Pacific flowering dogwood
Corylus cornuta	beaked hazelnut
Gaultheria shallon	salal
Holodiscus discolor	hillside oceanspray
Lonicera hispidula	pink honeysuckle
Mahonia nervosa	cascade Oregon-grape
Philadelphus lewisii	Lewis' mock orange
Quercus sadleriana	deer oak
Quercus vaccinifolia	huckleberry oak
Rhododendron macrophyllum	California rhododendron
Rosa gymnocarpa	wood rose
Rubus ursinus	California dewberry
Taxus brevifolia	Pacific yew
Toxicodendron diversilobum	Pacific poison-oak
Umbellularia californica	California-laurel

Herbaceous Understory
Achlys triphylla	sweet-after-death
Apocynum androsaemifolium	spreading dogbane
Disporum hookeri	drops-of-gold
Festuca occidentalis	western fescue
Goodyera oblongifolia	green-leaf rattlesnake-plantain
Hieracium alboflorum	white-flower hawkweed

Linnaea borealis	American twinflower
Melica harfordii	Harford's melic grass
Polystichum munitum	pineland sword fern
Pteridium aquilinum	northern bracken fern
Trientalis borealis	American starflower
Wipplea mosesta	modesty
Xerophyllum tenax	western turkeybeard

Oregon Oak Woodland

Oregon Oak Woodland occupies very dry habitats and often occurs in the areas referred to as the "interior" valleys of Oregon and California. These areas include the valley bottoms and lowlands of the Umpqua, Rogue, and Willammette River valleys which occur between the Cascade mountain range to the east and the Coast or Siskiyou ranges to the west. The understory of the oak woodlands is often dominated by grasses and as a consequence the areas are often subject to heavy grazing. Other plant communities associated with these dry valleys include grasslands and "chaparral". This community corresponds to Küchler #26.

Canopy
Characteristic Species
Acer macrophyllum	big-leaf maple
Pseudotsuga menziesii	Douglas-fir
Quercus garryana	Oregon white oak

Associates
Abies grandis	grand fir
Arbutus menziesii	Pacific madrone
Calocedrus decurrens	incense-cedar
Pinus ponderosa	ponderosa pine
Quercus chrysolepis	canyon live oak
Quercus kelloggii	California black oak

Woody Understory
Amelanchier alnifolia	Saskatoon service-berry
Corylus cornuta	beaked hazelnut
Crataegus douglassii	black hawthorn
Holodiscus discolor	hillside oceanspray
Oemleria cerasiformis	oso-berry
Rosa gymnocarpa	wood rose
Rosa nutkana	Nootka rose
Rubus parviflorus	western thimble-berry
Rubus ursinus	California dewberry
Symphoricarpos albus	common snowberry
Toxicodendron diversilobum	Pacific poison-oak

Herbaceous Understory
Bromus laevipes	woodland brome
Danthonia californica	California wild oat grass
Elymus glaucus	blue wild rye

Festuca californica	California fescue
Festuca rubra	red fescue
Fragaria virginiana	Virginia strawberry
Melica bulbosa	onion grass
Osmorhiza chilensis	mountain sweet cicely
Polystichum munitum	pineland sword fern
Pteridium aquilium	northern bracken fern
Satureja douglasii	Oregon-tea
Tellima grandiflora	fragrant fringecup

Pine–Cypress Forest

Pine–Cypress Forest occurs on coastal headlands, bluffs, and islands along the length of the California coast. These forests are subject to nearly constant onshore winds. Areas where they occur have well drained sandy soils and experience the typical coastal summer fog. The dominant species in these forests have closed or "serotinous" cones. The cones remain closed after maturity and accumulate on the tree until opened by fire. Periodic fires are essential to the reproduction of the dominant species which characterize this plant community. This community corresponds to Küchler #9.

Canopy
Characteristic Species

Cupressus goveniana	Gowen cypress
Cupressus macrocarpa	Monterey cypress
Pinus contorta	lodgepole pine
Pinus muricata	Bishop pine
Pinus radiata	Monterey pine

Associates

Cupressus bakeri	Modoc cypress
Cupressus forbesii	Tecate cypress
Cupressus macnabiana	MacNab's cypress
Cupressus nevadensis	Paiute cypress
Cupressus pygmaea	Mendocino cypress
Cupressus sargentii	Sargent's cypress
Cupressus stephensonii	Cuyamaca cypress
Pinus attenuata	knob-cone pine
Pinus torreyana	Torrey pine
Quercus agrifolia	coastal live oak

Woody Understory

Arctostaphylos nummularia	Fort Braff manzanita
Arctostaphylos tomentosa	hairy manzanita
Artemisia californica	coastal sagebrush
Baccharis pilularis	coyotebrush
Ceanothus thyrsiflorus	bluebrush
Frangula californica	California coffee berry
Heteromeles arbutifolia	California-Christmas-berry
Ledum glandulosum	glandular Labrador tea
Rubus ursinus	California dewberry
Symphoricarpos mollis	creeping snowberry

Toxicodendron diversilobum	Pacific poison-oak
Vaccinium ovatum	evergreen blueberry

Herbaceous Understory

Agrostis dieogensis	leafy bent
Dudleya farinosa	powdery live-forever
Elymus glaucus	blue wild rye
Erigeron glaucus	seaside fleabane
Eriophyllum staechidifolium	seaside woolly-flower
Galium californicum	California bedstraw
Iris douglasiana	mountain iris
Pteridium aquilinum	northern bracken fern
Xerophyllum tenax	western turkeybeard

Montane Chaparral

Montane Chaparral is most widely distributed from the foothills of the Sierra Nevada Mountains of California to the Pacific Ocean. The northern limits of chaparral communities occur in the West Coast Mountain Region in the drier parts of the Rogue River watershed in Oregon. Chaparral consists of a continuous cover of closely spaced shrubs three to thirteen feet tall with intertwining branches. Herbaceous vegetation is sparse except immediately after fires, which can be frequent in the Chaparral. This community corresponds to Küchler #34.

Characteristic Woody Species

Arctostaphylos canescens	hoary manzanita
Arctostaphylos viscida	white-leaf manzanita
Ceanothus cuneatus	sedge-leaf buckbrush

Associates

Adenocaulon fasciculatum	American trailplant
Aesculus californica	California buckeye
Amelanchier pallida	pale service-berry
Arctostaphylos glandulosa	Eastwood's manzanita
Arctostaphylos glauca	big-berry manzanita
Ceanothus cordulatus	mountain whitethorn
Ceanothus greggii	Mojave buckbrush
Ceanothus integerrimus	deerbrush
Ceanothus leucodermis	jackbrush
Ceanothus velutinus	tobacco-brush
Cercis canadensis	redbud
Cercocarpus montanus	alder-leaf mountain-mahogany
Chrysothamnus nauseosus	rubber rabbitbrush
Cornus glabrata	smooth-leaf dogwood
Eriodictyon californicum	California yerba-santa
Frangula californica	California coffee berry
Fraxinus dipetala	two-petal ash
Fremontodendron californicum	California flannelbush
Garrya fremontii	bearbush
Heteromeles arbutifolia	California-Christmas-berry
Lithocarpus densiflorus	tan-oak

Lonicera involucrata	four-line honeysuckle
Pickeringia montana	stingaree-bush
Prunus ilicifolia	holly-leaf cherry
Quercus chrysolepis	canyon live oak
Quercus dumosa	California scrub oak
Quercus wislizenii	interior live oak
Rhus ovata	sugar sumac
Rhus trilobata	ill-scented sumac
Toxicodendron diversilobum	Pacific poison-oak

Coastal Mountain Grassland

Coastal Mountain Grassland occurs along the coast on the peaks of coast range mountains. These areas, often called "grass balds," are incapable of supporting tree growth because of shallow soils. Grasslands also occur in the interior valleys. Examples of native grass communities are rare because of extensive grazing and the introduction of alien species into grassland areas. Forests have encroached on much of the natural prairie areas as a result of the suppression of natural fires. This community corresponds to Küchler #47.

Characteristic Species

Carex tumulicola	foothill sedge
Danthonia californica	California wild oat grass
Deschampsia cespitosa	tufted hair grass
Festuca idahoensis	bluebunch fescus

Associates

Agrostis hallii	Hall's bent
Armeria maritima	sea thrift
Calamagrostis nutkaensis	nootka reed grass
Calochortus luteus	yellow mariposa-lily
Danthonia intermedia	timber wild oat grass
Dichelostemma pulchellum	bluedicks
Elymus elymoides	western bottle-brush grass
Elymus glaucus	blue wild rye
Eriophyllum lanatum	common wooly-sunflower
Festuca rubra	red fescue
Frageria chiloensis	beach strawberry
Grindelia hirsutula	hairy gumweed
Heterotheca bolanderi	Bolander's false golden-aster
Iris douglasiana	mountain iris
Koeleria macrantha	prairie Koeler's grass
Lupinus formosus	summer lupine
Lupinus versicolor	Lindley's varied lupine
Nassella lepida	tussock grass
Nassella pulchra	tussock grass
Pteridium aquilinum	northern bracken fern
Ranunculus californicus	California buttercup
Sanicula arctopoides	footsteps-of-spring
Sanicula bipinnatifida	purple black-snakeroot
Sisyrinchium bellum	California blue-eyed-grass

Stipa nelsonii	Nelson's needle grass
Veronica peregrina	neckweed
Vicia americana	American purple vetch

WETLAND SYSTEMS

Riparian Forest

Hardwood forests are not typical in the West Coast Mountain Region. However, hardwood forests do occur in this region along the floodplains of the Willamette and Columbia Rivers and other major rivers and on poorly drained sites subject to flooding. Black cottonwood (balsam poplar) is the most common species along the major rivers. Stands of black cottonwood occur on islands and along the shoreline. This community corresponds to Küchler #25.

Canopy
Characteristic Species

Alnus rubra	red alder
Fraxinus latifolia	Oregon ash
Populus balsamifera	balsam poplar

Associates

Acer macrophyllum	big-leaf maple
Alnus rhombifolia	white alder
Pinus ponderosa	ponderosa pine
Quercus garryana	Oregon white oak

Woody Understory

Salix eriocephala	Missouri willow
Salix lucida	shining willow
Salix melanopsis	dusky willow
Salix scouleriana	Scouler's willow
Salix sessilifolia	sessile-leaf willow
Umbellularia californica	California-laurel

Herbaceous Understory

Aralia californica	California spikenard
Deschampsia caespitosa	tufted hair grass

Cedar–Alder Swamp

Red alder and western red cedar (western arborvitae) are characteristic of swamps in and on the coastal plain of the West Coast Mountain Region. The best developed swamps can be found in the coastal plain of the Olympic Peninsula. Cedar–Alder Swamp often occurs along the mouths of rivers or around margins of lakes and springs. These swamps occur where there is a high water table, or even standing surface water, for all or a portion of the year.

Canopy
Characteristic Species

Alnus rubra	red alder
Thuja plicata	western arborvitae

Associates

Abies amabilis	Pacific silver fir
Picea sitchensis	sitka spruce
Pinus contorta	lodgepole pine
Pinus monticola	western white pine
Tsuga heterophylla	western hemlock

Woody Understory

Gaultheria shallon	salal
Menziesia ferruginea	fool's-huckleberry
Rubus spectabilis	salmon raspberry
Salix hookeriana	coastal willow
Spiraea douglasii	Douglas' meadowsweet
Vaccinium ovalifolium	oval-leaf blueberry
Vaccinium ovatum	evergreen blueberry
Vaccinium parvifolium	red blueberry

Herbaceous Understory

Athyrium filix-femina	subarctic lady fern
Blechnum spicant	deerfern
Carex obnupta	slough sedge
Cornus canadensis	Canadian bunchberry
Lysichitum americanum	yellow skunk-cabbage
Maianthemum dilatatum	two-leaf false Solomon's-seal
Oenanthe sarmentosa	Pacific water-dropwort
Stachys mexicana	Mexican hedge-nettle
Tolmiea menziesii	piggyback-plant

ESTUARINE SYSTEMS

Salt Marsh

There are many tideland communities associated with estuaries along the Oregon, Washington, and California coasts. The predominant tideland communities are marshes on tidal flats. Salt Marsh is found along sheltered inland margins of bays, lagoons, and estuaries. The soils of these marshes are subject to regular tidal inundation for at least part of the year. Tidal influences are especially prevalent on islands in the lower Columbia basin.

Characteristic Species

Distichlis spicata	coastal salt grass
Jaumea carnosa	marsh Jaumea

Spartina foliosa	California cord grass
Associates	
Argentina egedii	Pacific silverweed
Atriplex patula	halberd-leaf orache
Carex lyngbyei	Lyngbye's sedge
Cotula coronopifolia	common brassbuttons
Cressa truxillensis	spreading alkali-weed
Deschampsia cespitosa	tufted hair grass
Eleocharis parvula	little-head spike-rush
Frankenia salina	alkali sea-heath
Glaux maritima	sea-milkwort
Grindelia integrifolia	Pudget Sound gumweed
Grindelia paludosa	Suisun Marsh gumweed
Hainardia cylindrica	barb grass
Juncus balticus	Baltic rush
Juncus effusus	lamp rush
Juncus lesueurii	salt rush
Lasthenia minor	coastal goldfields
Limonium californicum	marsh-rosemary
Plantago maritima	goosetongue
Puccinellia kurilensis	dwarf alkali grass
Salicornia maritima	sea saltwort
Salicornia virginica	woody saltwort
Scirpus americanus	chairmaker's bulrush
Scirpus maritimus	saltmarsh bulrush
Spergularia salina	sandspurrey
Suaeda californica	broom seepweed
Triglochin concinnam	slender arrow-grass
Triglochin maritimum	seaside arrow-grass

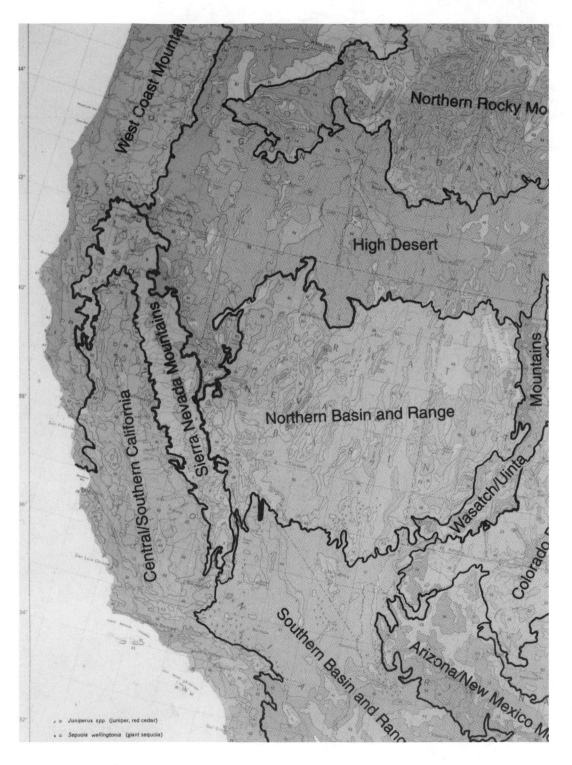

Sierra Nevada Mountains

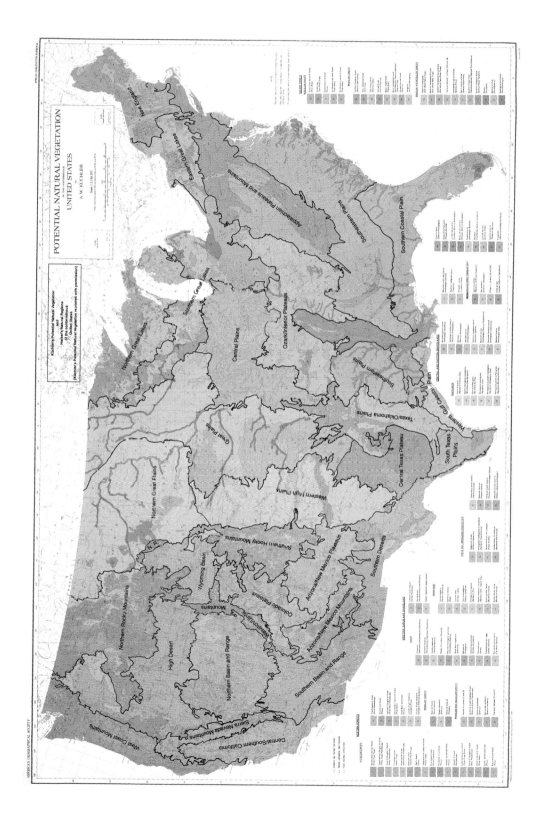

POTENTIAL NATURAL VEGETATION
UNITED STATES
A. W. KÜCHLER

Küchler's Potential Natural Vegetation
and
Harber's Natural Regions
of the nonhumitrous
United States
(Küchler's Potential Natural Vegetation re-printed with permission)

New England
Eastern Great Lakes
Appalachian Plateaus and Mountains
Southeastern Plains
Southern Coastal Plain
Southern Great Lakes
Northern Great Lakes
Central Plains
Ozark/Interior Plateaus
Southeastern Plains
Western Gulf Coastal Plain
Texas/Oklahoma Plains
South Texas Plains
Great Plains
Central Texas Plateau
Northern Great Plains
Western High Plains
Southern Rocky Mountains
N. R.
Wyoming Basin
Southern Desert
Arizona/New Mexico Mountains
Colorado Plateaus
Wasatch Uinta Mountains
Northern Rocky Mountains
High Desert
Northern Basin and Range
Sierra Nevada Mountains
Southern Basin and Range
Central/Southern California
West Coast Mountains

WESTERN FORESTS

NEEDLELEAF FORESTS

1 — Spruce-cedar hemlock forest
(Picea-Thuja-Tsuga)

2 — Cedar-hemlock-Douglas fir forest
(Thuja-Tsuga-Pseudotsuga)

3 — Silver fir-Douglas fir forest
(Abies-Pseudotsuga)

4 — Fir-hemlock forest
(Abies-Tsuga)

5 — Mixed conifer forest
(Abies-Pinus-Pseudotsuga)

6 — Redwood forest
(Sequoia-Pseudotsuga)

7 — Red fir forest
(Abies)

8 — Lodgepole pine-subalpine forest
(Pinus-Tsuga)

9 — Pine-cypress forest
(Pinus-Cupressus)

10 — Ponderosa shrub forest
(Pinus)

11 — Western ponderosa forest
(Pinus)

12 — Douglas fir forest
(Pseudotsuga)

13 — Cedar-hemlock-pine forest
(Thuja-Tsuga-Pinus)

14 — Grand fir-Douglas fir forest
(Abies-Pseudotsuga)

15 — Western spruce-fir forest
(Picea-Abies)

16 — Eastern ponderosa forest
(Pinus)

17 — Black Hills pine forest
(Pinus)

18 — Pine-Douglas fir forest
(Pinus-Pseudotsuga)

19 — Arizona pine forest
(Pinus)

20 — Spruce-fir-Douglas fir forest
(Picea-Abies-Pseudotsuga)

21 — Southwestern spruce-fir forest
(Picea-Abies)

22 — Great Basin pine forest
(Pinus)

23 — Juniper-pinyon woodland
(Juniperus-Pinus)

24 — Juniper steppe woodland
(Juniperus-Artemisia-Agropyron)

BROADLEAF FORESTS

25 — Alder-ash forest
(Alnus-Fraxinus)

26 — Oregon oakwoods
(Quercus)

27 — Mesquite bosques
(Prosopis)

BROADLEAF AND NEEDLELEAF FORESTS

28 — Mosaic of numbers 2 and 26

29 — California mixed evergreen forest
(Quercus-Arbutus-Pseudotsuga)

30 — California oakwoods
(Quercus)

31 — Oak-juniper woodland
(Quercus-Juniperus)

32 — Transition between 31 and 37

WESTERN SHRUB AND GRASSLAND

SHRUB

33 — Chaparral
(Adenostoma-Arctostaphylos-Ceanothus)

34 — Montane chaparral
(Arctostaphylos-Castanopsis-Ceanothus)

35 — Coastal sagebrush
(Salvia-Eriogonum)

36 — Mosaic of numbers 30 and 35

37 — Mountain mahogany-oak scrub
(Cercocarpus-Quercus)

38 — Great Basin sagebrush
(Artemisia)

39 — Blackbrush
(Coleogyne)

40	Saltbush-greasewood *(Atriplex-Sarcobatus)*
41	Creosote bush *(Larrea)*
42	Creosote bush-bur sage *(Larrea-Franseria)*
43	Palo verde-cactus shrub *(Cercidium-Opuntia)*
44	Creosote bush-tarbush *(Larrea-Flourensia)*
45	Ceniza shrub *(Leucophyllum-Larrea-Prosopis)*
46	Desert: vegetation largely absent

GRASSLANDS

47	Fescue-oatgrass *(Festuca-Danthonia)*
48	California steppe *(Stipa)*
49	Tule marshes *(Scirpus-Typha)*
50	Fescue-wheatgrass *(Festuca-Agropyron)*
51	Wheatgrass-bluegrass *(Agropyron-Poa)*

52	Alpine meadows and barren *(Agrostis, Carex, Festuca, Poa)*
53	Grama-galleta steppe *(Bouteloua-Hilaria)*
54	Grama-tobosa prairie *(Bouteloua-Hilaria)*

SHRUB AND GRASSLANDS COMBINATIONS

55	Sagebrush steppe *(Artemisia-Agropyron)*
56	Wheatgrass-needlegrass shrubsteppe *(Agropyron-Stipa-Artemisia)*
57	Galleta-three awn shrubsteppe *(Hilaria-Aristida)*
58	Grama-tobosa shrubsteppe *(Bouteloua-Hilaria-Larrea)*
59	Trans-Pecos shrub savanna *(Flourensia-Larrea)*
60	Mesquite savanna *(Prosopis-Hilaria)*
61	Mesquite-acacia savanna *(Prosopis-Acacia-Andropogon-Setaria)*
62	Mesquite-live oak savanna *(Prosopis-Quercus-Andropogon)*

CENTRAL AND EASTERN GRASSLANDS

GRASSLANDS

63	Foothills prairie *(Agropyron-Festuca-Stipa)*
64	Grama-needlegrass-wheatgrass *(Bouteloua-Stipa-Agropyron)*
65	Grama-buffalo grass *(Bouteloua-Buchloë)*
66	Wheatgrass-needlegrass *(Agropyron-Stipa)*
67	Wheatgrass-bluestem-needlegrass *(Agropyron-Andropogon-Stipa)*
68	Wheatgrass-grama-buffalo grass *(Agropyron-Bouteloua-Buchloë)*
69	Bluestem-grama prairie *(Andropogon-Bouteloua)*
70	Sandsage-bluestem prairie *(Artemisia-Andropogon)*

71	Shinnery *(Quercus-Andropogon)*
72	Sea oats prairie *(Uniola-Andropogon)*
73	Northern cordgrass prairie *(Distichlis-Spartina)*
74	Bluestem prairie *(Andropogon-Panicum-Sorghastrum)*
75	Nebraska Sandhills prairie *(Andropogon-Calamovilfa)*
76	Blackland prairie *(Andropogon-Stipa)*
77	Bluestem-sacahuista prairie *(Andropogon-Spartina)*
78	Southern cordgrass prairie *(Spartina)*
79	Palmetto prairie *(Serenoa-Aristida)*

GRASSLAND AND FOREST COMBINATIONS

80 Marl-Everglades
(*Mariscus* and *Persea-Taxodium*)

81 Oak savanna
(*Quercus-Andropogon*)

82 Mosaic of numbers 74 and 100

83 Cedar glades
(*Juniperus-Quercus-Sporobolus*)

84 Cross timbers
(*Quercus-Andropogon*)

85 Mesquite-buffalo grass
(*Prosopis-Buchloë*)

86 Juniper-oak savanna
(*Juniperus-Quercus-Andropogon*)

87 Mesquite-oak savanna
(*Prosopis-Quercus-Andropogon*)

88 Fayette prairie
(*Andropogon-Buchloë*)

89 Blackbelt
(*Liquidambar-Quercus-Juniperus*)

90 Live oak-sea oats
(*Quercus-Uniola*)

91 Cypress savanna
(*Taxodium-Mariscus*)

92 Everglades
(*Mariscus* and *Magnolia-Persea*)

EASTERN FORESTS

NEEDLELEAF FORESTS

98 Great Lakes spruce-fir forest
(*Picea-Abies*)

99 Conifer bog
(*Larix-Picea-Thuja*)

100 Great Lakes pine forest
(*Pinus*)

101 Northeastern spruce-fir forest
(*Picea-Abies*)

102 Southeastern spruce-fir forest
(*Picea-Abies*)

BROADLEAF FORESTS

98 Northern floodplain forest
(*Populus-Salix-Ulmus*)

99 Maple-basswood forest
(*Acer-Tilia*)

100 Oak-hickory forest
(*Quercus-Carya*)

101 Elm-ash forest
(*Ulmus-Fraxinus*)

102 Beech-maple forest
(*Fagus-Acer*)

103 Mixed mesophytic forest
(*Acer-Aesculus-Fagus-Liriodendron-Quercus-Tilia*)

104 Appalachian oak forest
(*Quercus*)

105 Mangrove
(*Avicennia-Rhizophora*)

BROADLEAF AND NEEDLELEAF FORESTS

106 Northern hardwoods
(*Acer-Betula-Fagus-Tsuga*)

107 Northern hardwoods-fir forest
(*Acer-Betula-Abies-Tsuga*)

108 Northern hardwoods-spruce forest
(*Acer-Betula-Fagus-Picea-Tsuga*)

109 Transition between numbers 104 and 106

110 Northeastern oak-pine forest
(*Quercus-Pinus*)

111 Oak-hickory-pine forest
(*Quercus-Carya-Pinus*)

112 Southern mixed forest
(*Fagus-Liquidambar-Magnolia-Pinus-Quercus*)

113 Southern floodplain forest
(*Quercus-Nyssa-Taxodium*)

114 Pocosin
(*Pinus-Ilex*)

115 Sand pine scrub
(*Pinus-Quercus*)

116 Subtropical pine forest
(*Pinus-Tetrazygia*)

J = *Juniperus spp.* (juniper, red cedar)

s = *Sequoia wellingtonia* (giant sequoia)

Y = *Yucca brevifolia* (Joshua tree)

Sierra Nevada Mountains

Introduction

The Sierra Nevada Mountains region is characterized by steep slopes and rough terrain. The region's vegetation is diverse, but conifer forests are the most prevalent vegetation type. This region includes both the east and west slopes of the Sierra Nevada Mountains. The southern portion of the Cascade Mountain Range and the Trinity Mountains, which extend along the northwestern rim of the Great Valley, are also included. The Klamath and Siskiyou Mountains of southern Oregon and northern California are not part of this region (see West Coast Mountains region for descriptions of the vegetation in these mountain areas).

The most extensive forest type is the Ponderosa Pine Forest. The forest composition changes on an altitudinal gradient. Altitude affects the length of the growing season, available moisture, and soil depth, therefore affecting species' dominance, abundance, and diversity. There are vegetation differences between the western slopes and the eastern desert-facing slopes of the Sierra Nevada Mountains. The eastern slopes are in a rain shadow and forest cover is less continuous with soils more "skeletal" than on western slopes. Although there are differences, the vegetative types described in this region are relevant to both sides of the mountains unless specifically noted.

Periodic fires are extremely common and help maintain the structure of the vegetation. It is estimated that prior to 1875, fire frequency averaged about one fire every eight years in pine-dominated sites and about one per sixteen years in more mesic fir-dominated sites. Fire suppression and control has significantly changed many of the plant communities.

In the Sierra Nevada Mountains region, unique groves of the celebrated giant sequoia are found in areas that support sierran white fir (see Sierran White Fir Forest description). Hardwood trees, primarily of oak and aspen species, are present in this region as successional phases or as isolated stands in particular sites such as canyons or steep slopes. Within pine communities, oak species tend to occur in openings in ponderosa pine areas and quaking aspens occur in areas with higher moisture availability. Although there is no riparian forest described in this region, aspen woodlands often occur along mountain streams. Forest types found in subalpine and treeline areas include: mountain hemlock, western white pine, whitebark pine, foxtail pine, and limber pine.

The primary sources used to develop descriptions and species lists are: Barbour and Billings 1988; Barbour and Major 1988; Thorne 1976.

Dominant Ecological Communities

Upland Systems
Ponderosa Pine Forest
Sierran White Fir Forest
Red Fir Forest
Lodgepole Pine Forest
Montane Chaparral

Wetland Systems
Mountain Meadow

UPLAND SYSTEMS
Ponderosa Pine Forest

Ponderosa Pine Forest is the most extensive forest type in California. The forest has been called, "mid-montane conifer forest," "yellow pine forest," "white fir forest," and "big tree forest." Although each type listed may have dominants other than ponderosa pine, ponderosa pine occurs throughout each forest type. Generally, ponderosa pine occurs on dry sites at elevations between 1000 and 6000 feet in the north and 4000 and 7000 feet in the south. Where soil moisture increases, white fir may become dominant. Where soils are too poor for ponderosa pine, California black oak will become dominant. On the east side of the Sierras where conditions are generally drier and colder, Jeffrey pine is likely to share dominance with ponderosa pine. Ponderosa pine forests depend on periodic fires for regeneration. Fires create openings where young trees can establish in full sunlight. This community corresponds to Küchler #5.

Canopy
Characteristic Species
Pinus ponderosa	ponderosa pine

Associates
Abies concolor	white fir
Calocedrus decurrens	incense-cedar
Pinus attenuata	knob-cone pine
Pinus coulteri	Coulter's pine
Pinus jeffreyi	Jeffrey pine
Pinus lambertiana	sugar pine
Pseudotsuga macrocarpa	big-cone Douglas-fir
Quercus chrysolepis	canyon live oak
Quercus kelloggii	California black oak

Woody Understory
Arctostaphylos glandulosa	Eastwood's manzanita
Arctostaphylos patula	green-leaf manzanita
Ceanothus cordulatus	mountain whitethorn
Ceanothus integerrimus	deerbrush
Chamaebatia foliolosa	Sierran mountain-misery
Cornus nuttallii	Pacific flowering dogwood
Eriastrum densifolium	giant woolstar
Eriodictyon trichocalyx	hairy yerba-santa
Frangula californica	California coffee berry
Garrya flavescens	ashy silktassel
Lithocarpus densiflorus	tan-oak
Ribes roezlii	Sierran gooseberry

Herbaceous Understory
Gilia splendens	splendid gily-flower
Iris hartwegii	rainbow iris
Lupinus excubitus	interior bush lupine
Lupinus formosus	summer lupine
Solanum xantii	chaparral nightshade
Streptanthus bernardinus	laguna mountain jewelflower

Sierran White Fir Forest

Sierran White Fir Forest occurs on relatively moist sites on the lower slopes of the Sierra Nevada Mountains. They generally occur from 4100 to 7300 feet. Giant sequoia (*Sequoiadendron giganteum*) groves occur within the Sierran White Fir Forest on west-side slopes. Giant sequoias are restricted to sites that have sufficient soil moisture throughout the summer drought months. Reproduction within sequoia groves depends on periodic fire. Without regular fire the accumulation of litter on the forest floor inhibits germination and establishment of sequoia seedlings and white fir will invade and eventually dominate sequoia groves. This community corresponds to Küchler #5. Sequoia groves are marked on the Küchler map with an "S".

Canopy
Characteristic Species
Abies concolor	white fir
Calocedrus decurrens	incense-cedar
Pinus lambertiana	sugar pine

Associates
Arbutus menziesii	Pacific madrone
Pseudotsuga menziesii	Douglas-fir

Woody Understory
Acer macrophyllum	big-leaf maple
Arctostaphylos patula	green-leaf manzanita
Castanopsis sempervirens	Sierran chinkapin
Ceanothus cordulatus	mountain whitethorn
Ceanothus integerrimus	deerbrush
Ceanothus parvifolius	cattlebush
Chamaebatia foliolosa	Sierran mountain-misery
Cornus nuttallii	Pacific flowering dogwood
Prunus emarginata	bitter cherry
Quercus chrysolepis	canyon live oak
Quercus kelloggii	California black oak
Ribes roezlii	Sierran gooseberry
Ribes viscosissimum	sticky currant
Rosa gymnocarpa	wood rose
Salix scouleriana	Scouler's willow
Symphoricarpos oreophilus	mountain snowberry
Taxus brevifolia	Pacific yew

Herbaceous Understory
Adenocaulon bicolor	American trailplant
Asarum hartwegii	Hartweg's wild ginger
Chimaphila menziesii	little prince's-pine
Clintonia uniflora	bride's-bonnet
Disporum hookeri	drops-of-gold
Fragaria vesca	woodland strawberry
Galium sparsiflorum	Sequoia bedstraw
Goodyera oblongifolia	green-leaf rattlesnake-plantain
Hieracium albiflorum	white-flower hawkweed

Iris hartwegii	rainbow iris
Lupinus latifolius	broad-leaf lupine
Osmorhiza chilensis	mountain sweet-cicely
Pteridium aquilinum	northern bracken fern
Pyrola picta	white-vein wintergreen
Viola glabella	pioneer violet
Viola lobata	moose-horn violet

Red Fir Forest

Red Fir Forest occurs between 6000 and 9000 feet in the Sierra Nevada Mountains. In these high elevations, snow is the major form of precipitation. Red Fir Forest is very dense, often limiting the understory growth. Red fir seedlings do, however, prefer shade to open areas for regeneration. Where fires or other disturbances cause breaks in the canopy, lodgepole pine is likely to be dominant at these altitudes. This community corresponds to Küchler #7.

Canopy
Characteristic Species
Abies concolor	white fir
Abies magnifica	California red fir

Associates
Calocedrus decurrens	incense-cedar
Pinus contorta	lodgepole pine
Pinus jeffreyi	Jeffrey pine
Pinus lambertiana	sugar pine
Pinus monticola	western white pine
Tsuga mertensiana	mountain hemlock

Woody Understory
Acer glabrum	Rocky Mountain maple
Arctostaphylos patula	green-leaf manzanita
Castanopsis sempervirens	Sierran chinkapin
Ceanothus cordulatus	mountain white-thorn
Ceanothus velutinus	tobacco-brush
Lonicera conjugialis	purple-flower honeysuckle
Prunus emarginata	bitter cherry
Quercus vacciniifolia	huckleberry oak
Ribes roezlii	Sierran gooseberry
Ribes viscosissimum	sticky currant
Salix scouleriana	Scouler's willow
Symphoricarpos oreophilus	mountain snowberry

Herbaceous Understory
Arabis platysperma	pioneer rockcress
Aster breweri	Brewer's aster
Chimaphila umbellata	pipsissewa
Cistanthe umbellata	Mt. Hood pussypaws

Corallorrhiza maculata	summer coralroot
Elymus elymoides	western bottle-brush grass
Eriogonum nudum	naked wild buckwheat
Gayophytum humile	dwarf groundsmoke
Hieracium albiflorum	white-flower hawkweed
Monardella odoratissima	alpine mountainbalm
Orthilia secunda	sidebells
Pedicularis semibarbata	pinewoods lousewort
Poa bolanderi	Bolander's blue grass
Pterospora andromedea	pine drops
Pyrola picta	white-vein wintergreen
Sarcodes sanguinea	snowplant
Viola purpurea	goose-foot yellow violet
Wyethia mollis	woolly mule's-ears

Lodgepole Pine Forest

Lodgepole Pine Forest generally occurs above Red Fir Forest in the Sierra Nevada Mountains. Lodgepole pine is common between 6000 and 8000 feet in the north and between 7400 and 11000 feet in the south. The growing season in these high elevations is relatively short (two to three months) and the snow accumulation is heavy. Due to the short growing season and harsh environment, trees are shorter than those growing at lower elevations and in less severe environments. Limber pine is an associate at high elevations. Suppression of naturally occurring fires in the forests over the years has resulted in increased density and cover in Lodgepole Pine Forest. Although fire may occur periodically in these pine forests and influence community structure, other significant environmental influences in Lodgepole Pine Forest and higher elevation communities are the lower mean annual temperature and precipitation in the form of persistent snow. These factors have been used to distinguish subalpine forests that are here included within the Lodgepole Pine Forest type. This community corresponds to Küchler #8.

Canopy
Characteristic Species
Pinus contorta	lodgepole pine

Associates
Pinus flexilis	limber pine
Populus tremuloides	quaking aspen
Tsuga mertensiana	mountain hemlock

Woody Understory
Arctostaphylos nevadensis	pinemat manzanita
Phyllodoce breweri	red mountain-heath
Ribes montigenum	western prickly gooseberry
Salix arctica	stout arctic willow

Herbaceous Understory
Potentilla breweri	Sierran cinquefoil

Montane Chaparral

In the Sierra Nevada Mountains region, Montane Chaparral occurs on hills and lower mountain slopes that are dry. Although Montane Chaparral reaches maximum development in southern California, it is common in the foothills along the eastern side of the Great Central Valley and in the foothills and higher regions of the Sierra Nevada Mountains. Several different types of chaparral, identified by associations and geographical location, have been identified in the literature. Montane Chaparral is the most common type in the Sierra Nevada Mountains. Montane Chaparral is lower and more "compact" than other chaparral types. The development of Montane Chaparral is slowed by cold temperatures, snow, and a short growing season. Many of the shrub species in the Montane Chaparral also occur as understory or gap colonizers in conifer forests. The interface of the Montane Chaparral and adjacent forests is strongly influenced by fire frequency. This community corresponds to Küchler #34.

Characteristic Woody Species

Arctostaphylos nevadensis	pinemat manzanita
Arctostaphylos parryana	pineland manzanita
Arctostaphylos patula	green-leaf manzanita
Castanopsis sempervirens	Sierran chinkapin
Ceanothus cordulatus	mountain whitethorn
Ceanothus diversifolius	pinemat
Ceanothus integerrimus	deerbrush
Ceanothus pinetorum	Kern River buckbrush
Ceanothus sanguineus	Oregon teatree

Associates

Arctostaphylos canescens	hairy manzanita
Arctostaphylos viscida	white-leaf manzanita
Ceanothus fresnensis	fresnomat
Ceanothus parvifolius	cattlebush
Ceanothus prostratus	squawcarpet
Ceanothus tomentosus	ionebush
Ceanothus velutinus	tobacco-brush
Cercocarpus ledifolius	curl-leaf mountain-mahogany
Cercocarpus montanus	alder-leaf mountain-mahogany
Chrysothamnus nauseosus	rubber rabbitbush
Eriodictyon californicum	California yerba-santa
Frangula californica	California coffee berry
Frangula purshiana	cascara sagrada
Garrya buxifolia	dwarf silktassel
Garrya flavescens	ashy silktassel
Garrya fremontii	bearbush
Heteromeles arbutifolia	California-Christmas-berry
Prunus emarginata	bitter cherry
Prunus virginiana	western choke cherry
Symphoricarpos oreophilus	mountain snowberry

WETLAND SYSTEMS

Mountain Meadow

Throughout the Sierra Nevada Mountains there are many meadows. Meadows are common above the treeline. In lower areas meadows may be created by conditions too wet to support trees or may be the result of avalanche or fire activity. A shallow water table is the most important factor in explaining the occurrence and distribution of meadows. Although most of the species listed relate to wet site conditions, the woodland and upper elevation meadows also occur under drier conditions, the latter even in dry gravelly soils.

Characteristic Species

Artemisia rothrockii	timberline sagebrush
Aster alpigenus	tundra aster
Calamagrostis breweri	short-hair reed grass
Camassia quamash	small camass
Cardamine breweri	Sierran bittercress
Carex bolanderi	Bolander's sedge
Carex exserta	short-hair sedge
Carex macloviana	Falkland Island sedge
Carex nebrascensis	Nebraska sedge
Carex rostrata	swollen beaked sedge
Carex scopulorum	Holm's Rocky Mountain sedge
Carex teneriformis	Sierran slender sedge
Cistanthe umbellata	Mt. Hood pussypaws
Deschampsia cespitosa	tufted hair grass
Dodecatheon jeffreyi	tall mountain shootingstar
Eleocharis bella	delicate spike-rush
Eleocharis quinqueflora	few-flower spike-rush
Eriogonum incanum	frosted wild buckwheat
Eriogonum ovalifolium	cushion wild buckwheat
Eriophorum cringerum	fringed cotton-grass
Festuca brachyphylla	short-leaf fescue
Gentiana newberryi	alpine gentian
Glyceria elata	tall manna grass
Heracleum maximum	cow-parsnip
Ivesia purpurascens	summit mousetail
Juncus nevadensis	Sierran rush
Juncus orthophyllus	straight-leaf rush
Lupinus breweri	matted lupine
Lupinus polyphyllus	blue-pod lupine
Mimulus primuloides	yellow creeping monkey-flower
Muhlenbergia filiformis	pullup muhly
Penstemon davidsonii	timberline beardtongue
Pteridium aquilinum	northern bracken fern
Ptilagrostis kingii	Sierran false needle grass
Scirpus congdonii	Congdon's bulrush
Senecio scorzonella	Sierran ragwort
Solidago multiradiata	Rocky Mountain goldenrod
Stipa occidentalis	western needle grass

Triglochin palustre	marsh arrow-grass
Trisetum spicatum	narrow false oat
Vaccinium cespitosum	dwarf blueberry
Veratrum californicum	California false hellebore
Veratrum fimbriatum	fringed false hellebore

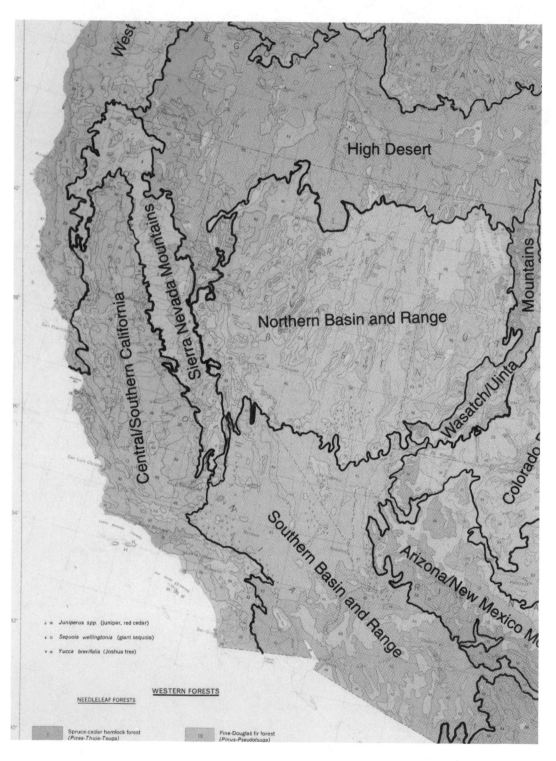

West

High Desert

Central/Southern California

Sierra Nevada Mountains

Northern Basin and Range

Wasatch/Uinta Mountains

Colorado

Southern Basin and Range

Arizona/New Mexico M

J = *Juniperus spp.* (juniper, red cedar)

s = *Sequoia wellingtonia* (giant sequoia)

v = *Yucca brevifolia* (Joshua tree)

WESTERN FORESTS

NEEDLELEAF FORESTS

Spruce-cedar hemlock forest
(*Picea-Thuja-Tsuga*)

Pine-Douglas fir forest
(*Pinus-Pseudotsuga*)

Central/Southern California

Central/Southern California

Introduction

The Central/Southern California region includes the Sacramento and San Joaquin Valleys (also known as the Central Valley), the Transverse and Peninsular Mountain Ranges, and the Central Coast Ranges. The islands off the coast of southern California are also included in the region. The region includes the salt marshes in the lowest areas near the coast to the alpine meadows in the highest elevations of the San Bernardino and San Gabriel Mountains. A wide diversity of vegetation types is represented within the region.

Oak woodlands are the most extensive vegetation type in the region. Oak woodlands occur around the Central Valley and throughout the Coast Ranges. The woodlands occur on mountain slopes and foothills where sufficient moisture exists to support an open canopy of trees. Within the oak woodland, chaparral and prairie species are common understory components. Native prairies were originally quite extensive in this region, especially in the Sacramento and San Joaquin Valleys. Nearly all native prairie has been drained and converted to agriculture.

The Transverse Mountain Range, at the southwest edge of the state, supports several forest communities similar to Sierra Nevada Mountain communities. In fact, these mountains have been described as "islands of Sierran vegetation".

Unique to this region are the numerous freshwater wetlands. Unfortunately, much of the freshwater wetland has been drained and converted for agricultural purposes. The Vernal Pools are among the most unique vegetation features in this region.

The primary sources used to develop descriptions and species lists are: Barbour and Billings 1988; Barbour and Major 1988; Holland 1986; Holland and Jain 1988; Thorne 1976.

Dominant Ecological Communities

Upland Systems
Yellow Pine Forest
White Fir–Sugar Pine Forest
Lodgepole Pine Forest
Coulter Pine Woodland
California Oak Woodland
Juniper–Pinyon Woodland
Chaparral
Coastal Sagebrush
San Joaquin Saltbush
California Prairie

Wetland Systems
Riparian Forest
Vernal Pools
Tule Marsh
Mountain Meadow

Estuarine Systems
Coastal Salt Marsh

UPLAND SYSTEMS

Yellow Pine Forest

Yellow Pine Forest is a mid-montane conifer forest type that occurs in the Transverse mountains between 4500 and 9000 feet. Both dominant canopy species, Jeffrey and ponderosa pine, are often referred to as "yellow pine" and share dominance in this region. Ponderosa pine is more common on lower, more mesic slopes. Jeffrey pine is more common in higher areas. The two yellow pines are closely related and have many associated species in common. This community corresponds to Küchler #5.

Canopy
Characteristic Species
Pinus jeffreyi	Jeffrey pine
Pinus ponderosa	ponderosa pine

Associates
Abies concolor	white fir
Calocedrus decurrens	incense-cedar
Pinus coulteri	Coulter's pine
Pinus lambertiana	sugar pine
Pseudotsuga macrocarpa	big-cone Douglas-fir
Quercus chrysolepis	canyon live oak
Quercus kelloggii	California black oak

Woody Understory
Arctostaphylos glandulosa	Eastwood's manzanita
Arctostaphylos patula	green-leaf manzanita
Arctostaphylos pringlei	pink-bract manzanita
Castanopsis sempervirens	Sierran chinkapin
Ceanothus integerrimus	deerbrush
Cornus nuttallii	Pacific flowering dogwood
Eriodictyon trichocalyx	hairy yerba-santa
Eriogonum wrightii	bastard-sage
Frangula californica	coffee berry
Garrya flavescens	ashy silktassel
Ribes roezlii	Sierran gooseberry
Symphoricarpos oreophilus	mountain snowberry

Herbaceous Understory
Arabis repanda	Yosemite rockcress
Asclepias eriocarpa	Indian milkweed
Bromus marginatus	large mountain brome
Bromus orcuttianus	Chinook brome
Calystegia occidentalis	chaparral false bindweed
Carex multicaulis	many-stem sedge
Castilleja martinii	Martin's Indian-paintbrush
Chaenactis santolinoides	Santolina pincushion
Chimaphila menziesii	little prince's-pine
Clarkia rhomboidea	diamond fairyfan
Collinsia childii	child's blue-eyed Mary

Cordylanthus nevinii	Nevin's bird's-beak
Cordylanthus rigidus	stiff-branch bird's beak
Elymus elymoides	western bottle-brush grass
Eriastrum densifolium	giant woolstar
Eriogonum parishii	mountainmist
Fritillaria pinetorum	pinewoods missionbells
Galium johnstonii	Johnston's bedstraw
Gayophytum diffusum	spreading groundsmoke
Gayophytum heterozygum	zigzag groundsmoke
Gilia splendens	spendid gily-flower
Iris hartwegii	rainbow iris
Ivesia santolinoides	Sierran mousetail
Koeleria macrantha	prairie Koeler's grass
Linanthus ciliatus	whiskerbrush
Lotus nevadensis	Nevada bird's-foot-trefoil
Lupinus elatus	tall silky lupine
Lupinus excubitus	interior bush lupine
Lupinus formosus	summer lupine
Lupinus peirsonii	long lupine
Melica imperfecta	coast range melic grass
Melica stricta	rock melic grass
Penstemon caesius	San Bernardino beardtongue
Penstemon grinnellii	Grinnell's beardtongue
Penstemon labrosus	San Gabriel beardtongue
Penstemon rostriflorus	beaked beardtongue
Phacelia imbricata	imbricate scorpion-weed
Poa secunda	curly blue grass
Sarcodes sanguinea	snowplant
Silene lemmonii	Lemmon's catchfly
Solanum xantii	chaparral nightshade
Stipa coronata	giant needle grass
Streptanthus bernardinus	Laguna Mountain jewelflower
Viola purpurea	goose-foot yellow violet

White Fir–Sugar Pine Forest

White Fir–Sugar Pine Forest occurs at higher elevations (5500-8500 feet) than Yellow Pine Forest. White and sugar pine dominated areas are usually moist, steep, and on north and east facing slopes. This forest type grades into Lodgepole Pine Forest at higher elevations and Yellow Pine Forest at lower elevations. Cover contribution from each forest layer varies with site condition but four layers are usually present.

Canopy
Characteristic Species

Abies concolor	white fir
Calocedrus decurrens	incense-cedar
Pinus lambertiana	sugar pine

Associates

Arbutus menziesii	Pacific madrone
Castanopsis chrysophylla	golden chinkapin
Juniperus occidentalis	western juniper
Pinus contorta	lodgepole pine
Pinus flexilis	limber pine
Pinus jeffreyi	Jeffrey pine
Pinus monophylla	single-leaf pinyon
Pseudotsuga menziesii	Douglas-fir
Quercus chrysolepis	canyon live oak
Quercus kelloggii	California black oak
Taxus brevifolia	Pacific yew

Woody Understory

Acer macrophyllum	big-leaf maple
Arctostaphylos patula	green-leaf manzanita
Castanopsis sempervirens	Sierran chinkapin
Ceanothus cordulatus	mountain whitethorn
Ceanothus greggii	Mojave buckbrush
Ceanothus integerrimus	deerbrush
Ceanothus parvifolius	cattlebush
Cerocarpus ledifolius	curl-leaf mountain-mahogany
Chamaebatia foliolosa	Sierran mountain-misery
Cornus nuttallii	Pacific flowering dogwood
Eriogonum umbellatum	sulphur-flower wild buckwheat
Eriogonum wrightii	bastard-sage
Fremontodendron californicum	California flannelbush
Holodiscus boursieri	Boursier's oceanspray
Leptodactylon pungens	granite prickly-phlox
Prunus emarginata	bitter cherry
Prunus virginiana	western choke cherry
Ribes roezlii	Sierran gooseberry
Ribes viscosissimum	sticky currant
Rosa gymnocarpa	wood rose
Rubus parviflorus	western thimble-berry
Salix sitchensis	sitka willow
Sambucus cerulea	blue elder
Symphoricarpos oreophilus	mountain snowberry

Herbaceous Understory

Adenocaulon bicolor	American trailplant
Asarum hartwegii	Hartweg's wild ginger
Chimaphila menziesii	little prince's-pine
Clintonia uniflora	bride's bonnet
Disporum hookeri	drops-of-gold
Eriogonum kennedyi	Kennedy's wild buckwheat
Fragaria vesca	woodland strawberry
Galium sparsiflorum	Sequoia bedstraw
Goodyera oblongifolia	green-leaf rattlesnake-plantain

Hieracium albiflorum	white-flower hawkweed
Iris hartwegii	rainbow iris
Lupinus latifolius	broad-leaf lupine
Osmorhiza chilensis	mountain sweet-cicely
Pteridium aquilinum	northern bracken fern
Pyrola picta	white-vein wintergreen
Viola glabella	pioneer violet
Viola lobata	moose-horn violet

Lodgepole Pine Forest

Lodgepole Pine Forest, an upper montane forest type, occurs in the Transverse Mountain Ranges between 8000 and 10700 feet. Lodgepole Pine Forest is often a very dense forest, but in higher elevations the canopy may open and trees may take a "krummholz form". Precipitation is primarily in the form of snow at this elevation. Soils are very shallow and rocky.

Canopy
Characteristic Species

Pinus contorta	lodgepole pine

Associates

Pinus flexilis	limber pine

Woody Understory

Castanopsis sempervirens	Sierran chinkapin
Ceanothus cordulatus	mountain whitethorn
Eriogonum umbellatum	sulphur-flower wild buckwheat
Holodiscus boursieri	Boursier's oceanspray
Leptodactylon pungens	granite prickly-phlox
Phyllodoce breweri	red mountain heath
Ribes cereum	white squaw currant
Ribes montigenum	western prickly gooseberry

Herbaceous Understory

Antennaria rosea	rosy pussytoes
Arabis breweri	Brewer's rockcress
Arabis platysperma	pioneer rockcress
Calochortus invenustus	plain mariposa-lily
Carex macloviana	Falkland Island sedge
Carex rossii	Ross' sedge
Chimaphila umbellata	pipsissewa
Collinsia torreyi	Torrey's blue-eyed Mary
Corallorrhiza maculata	summer coralroot
Cryptogramma acrostichoides	American rockbrake
Draba corrugata	southern California whitlow-grass
Elymus elymoides	western bottle-brush grass
Erigeron breweri	Brewer's fleabane
Eriogonum saxatile	hoary wild buckwheat
Galium parishii	Parish's bedstraw
Heuchera abramsii	San Gabriel alumroot

Minuartia nuttallii	brittle stitchwort
Monardella cinerea	gray mountainbalm
Oreonana vestita	woolly mountain-parsley
Polypodium hesperium	western polypody
Pterospora andromedea	pine drops
Sarcodes sanguinea	snowplant
Sedum niveum	Davidson's stonecrop
Sibbaldia procumbens	creeping-glow-wort
Silene verecunda	San Francisco catchfly
Viola purpurea	goose-foot yellow violet
Woodsia oregana	Oregon cliff fern
Woodsia scopulina	Rocky Mountain cliff fern

Coulter Pine Woodland

This mixed evergreen forest community occurs in the southern and western Coast range and the Transverse and Peninsular ranges. Coulter Pine Woodland is best developed between 4000 and 6000 feet and may occur within the range of the Yellow Pine Forest and chaparral communities. Associates vary between sites, and particularly between different mountain ranges in the region.

Canopy
Characteristic Species

Pinus coulteri	coulter pine

Associates

Pinus ponderosa	ponderosa pine
Quercus chrysolepis	canyon live oak
Quercus kelloggii	California black oak

Woody Understory

Arctostaphylos canescens	hoary manzanita
Arctostaphylos viscida	white-leaf manzanita
Arctostaphylos glandulosa	Eastwood's manzanita
Rhamnus spp.	buckthorn
Ribes spp.	currant
Ceanothus integerrimus	deerbrush

Herbaceous Understory

Carex spp.	sedge
Galium spp.	bedstraw
Gayophytum spp.	groundsmoke
Lupinus spp.	lupine
Pyrola spp.	wintergreen

California Oak Woodland

California Oak Woodland occurs as a belt around the Central Valley of California generally at elevations between 250 to 3000 feet. Oak woodlands occur between grassland or scrub at lower elevations and montane forests at higher elevations. Several distinct oak "phases" are recognized such as "valley oak phase" and "blue oak phase". The phases can differ in canopy composition but, they all have a partial deciduous oak canopy and a grassy ground cover. Shrubs are usually present but contribute very little cover. The ground cover in the California Oak Woodland may include many grassland species listed in the California Prairie community. This community corresponds to Küchler #30.

Canopy
Characteristic Species
Pinus sabiniana	digger pine
Quercus douglasii	blue oak
Quercus lobata	valley oak

Associates
Aesculus californica	California buckeye
Juglans californica	southern California walnut
Quercus agrifolia	coastal live oak
Quercus engelmannii	Englemann's oak
Quercus kelloggii	California black oak
Quercus wislizeni	interior live oak

Woody Understory
Arctostaphylos manzanita	big manzanita
Arctostaphylos viscida	white-leaf manzanita
Ceanothus cuneatus	sedge-leaf buckbrush
Frangula californica	coffee berry
Heteromeles arbutifolia	California-Christmas-berry
Prunus ilicifolia	holly-leaf cherry
Rhamnus crocea	holly-leaf buckthorn
Toxicodendron diversilobum	Pacific poison-oak

Herbaceous Understory
Bromus diandrus	ripgut brome
Hordeum murinum	wall barley

Juniper–Pinyon Woodland

Juniper–Pinyon Woodland occurs along the slopes of the Transverse Mountain ranges. This community is especially common on the north side of the San Gabriel and San Bernardino mountains. Junipers generally occur on the lower slopes and Pinyon on the upper slopes in this area. Chaparral type shrubs may occur in the understory, especially on sites where these woodlands intergrade with chaparral.

Canopy
Characteristic Species
Juniperus californica	California juniper
Pinus monophylla	single-leaf pinyon

Associates
Juniperus osteosperma	Utah juniper
Pinus quadrifolia	four-leaf pinyon
Quercus dumosa	California scrub oak
Quercus turbinella	shrub live oak

Woody Understory

Arctostaphylos glauca	big-berry manzanita
Artemisia tridentata	big sagebrush
Cercocarpus montanus	alder-leaf mountain-mahogany
Chrysothamnus nauseosus	rubber rabbitbrush
Chrysothamnus teretifolius	needle-leaf rabbitbrush
Coleogyne ramosissima	blackbrush
Crossosoma bigelovii	ragged rockflower
Diplacus longiflorus	southern bush-monkey-flower
Echinocereus engelmannii	saints cactus
Encelia virginensis	Virgin River brittlebush
Ephedra nevadensis	Nevada joint-fir
Ericameria cuneata	cliff heath-goldenrod
Ericameria linearifolius	narrow-leaf heath-goldenrod
Eriogonum elongatum	long-stem wild buckwheat
Eriogonum fasciculatum	eastern Mojave wild buckwheat
Gutierrezia sarothrae	kindlingweed
Krameria grayi	white ratany
Leptodactylon pungens	granite prickly-phlox
Nolina bigelovii	Bigelow's bear-grass
Opuntia basilaris	beaver-tail cactus
Oreonana vestita	wooly mountain-parsley
Prunus fasciculata	desert almond
Purshia glandulosa	antelope-brush
Salazaria mexicana	Mexican bladder-sage
Salvia dorrii	gray ball sage
Tetradymia axillaris	cottonhorn
Viguiera deltoidea	triangle goldeneye
Yucca brevifolia	Joshua-tree
Yucca schidigera	Mojave yucca

Herbaceous Understory

Anisocoma acaulis	scalebud
Caulanthus amplexicaulis	clasping-leaf wild cabbage
Erigeron parishii	Parish's fleabane
Eriogonum ovalifolium	cushion wild buckwheat
Eriophyllum confertiflorum	yellow-yarrow
Hilaria rigida	big galleta
Layia glandulosa	white tidytips
Lotus rigidus	broom bird's-foot-trefoil
Mirabilis bigelovii	desert wishbonebush
Monardella linoides	flax-leaf mountainbalm
Pellaea mucronata	bird-foot cliffbrake
Penstemon grinnellii	Grinnell's beardtongue
Phacelia austromontana	southern Sierran scorpion-weed
Plagiobothrys kingii	Great Basin popcorn-flower
Poa secunda	curly blue grass
Silene parishii	Parish's catchfly
Stipa coronata	giant needle grass
Stipa speciosa	desert needle grass

Chaparral

In central and southern California, Chaparral occurs on most of the hills and lower mountain slopes from the Sierra Nevada Mountains to the coast. The characteristic species in chaparral communities are evergreen, woody shrubs. More than 100 evergreen shrub species are a part of chaparral communities. These species, however, do not occur together, but in the many different chaparral associations in the various climatic and geographic areas. The chaparral species are adapted to fire, drought, and nutrient poor soils and grow best on rocky, steep slopes. Chaparral occurs in many areas but is best developed in southern California. Periodic fires occur frequently and are an important aspect of nutrient cycling in chaparral communities. This community corresponds to Küchler #33.

Characteristic Species

Adenostoma fasciculatum	common chamise
Adenostoma sparsifolium	redshank
Arctostaphylos spp.	manzanita
Ceanothus thyrsiflorus	bluebrush

Associates

Arctostaphylos glandulosa	Eastwood's manzanita
Arctostaphylos glauca	big-berry manzanita
Arctostaphylos manzanita	big manzanita
Arctostaphylos myrtifolia	lone manzanita
Arctostaphylos parryana	pineland manzanita
Arctostaphylos stanfordiana	Stanford's manzanita
Arctostaphylos viscida	white-leaf manzanita
Artemisia californica	coastal sagebrush
Ceanothus crassifolius	snowball
Ceanothus cuneatus	buckbrush
Ceanothus dentatus	sandscrub
Ceanothus impressus	Santa Barbara buckbrush
Ceanothus jepsonii	muskbush
Ceanothus oliganthus	explorer's bush
Ceanothus palmeri	cuyamaca-bush
Ceanothus parryi	ladybloom
Ceanothus spinosus	redheart
Ceanothus tomentosus	ionebush
Ceanothus verrucosus	barranca-bush
Cercocarpus montanus	alder-leaf mountain-mahogany
Eriogonum fasciculatum	eastern Mojave wild buckwheat
Fraxinus dipetala	two-petal ash
Garrya elliptica	wavy-leaf silktassel
Garrya flavescens	ashy silktassel
Garrya veatchii	canyon silktassel
Heteromeles arbutifolia	California-Christmas-berry
Leymus condensatus	giant lyme grass
Lonicera interrupta	chaparral honeysuckle
Lonicera subspicata	Santa Barbara honeysuckle
Malosma laurina	laurel-sumac
Prunus ilicifolia	holly-leaf cherry
Quercus dumosa	California scrub oak
Quercus durata	leather oak

Quercus wislizeni	interior live oak
Rhamnus crocea	holly-leaf buckthorn
Rhus integrifolia	lemonade sumac
Rhus ovata	sugar sumac
Ribes amarum	bitter gooseberry
Ribes californicum	California gooseberry
Ribes indecorum	white-flower currant
Ribes malvaceum	chaparral currant
Ribes viburnifolium	Santa Catalina currant
Salvia apiana	California white sage
Salvia mellifera	California black sage
Salvia spathacea	hummingbird sage
Yucca whipplei	Our-Lord's-candle

Coastal Sagebrush

Coastal Sagebrush occurs on the southern California coastal mountains on sites with lower moisture availability than sites which support chaparral. It generally occurs on the lower slopes of the California coastal mountains facing the ocean, or in the interior coastal range in the rain shadow. This community corresponds to Küchler #35.

Characteristic Species
Artemisia californica	coastal sagebrush
Eriogonum fasciculatum	eastern Mojave wild buckwheat
Salvia apiana	California white sage
Salvia mellifera	California black sage

Associates
Baccharis pilularis	coyote brush
Carpobrotus aequilateralus	baby sun-rose
Encelia californica	California brittlebush
Encelia farinosa	goldenhills
Eriophyllum confertiflorum	yellow-yarrow
Grindelia hirsutula	hairy gumweed
Hazardia squarrosa	saw-tooth bristleweed
Horkelia cuneata	wedge-leaf honeydew
Isocoma menziesii	jimmyweed
Malosma laurina	laurel-sumac
Opuntia littoralis	coastal prickly-pear
Rhus integrifolia	lemonade sumac
Salvia leucophylla	San Luis purple sage
Yucca whipplei	Our-Lord's-candle

San Joaquin Saltbush

Saltbush shrub communities may occur where the soil and available groundwater have high degrees of either salt or alkali. In the San Joaquin Valley, saltbush communities occur on wet sites near playas, sinks, and seeps that are fed with groundwater high in mineral content. Much of the area supporting saltbush communities has been lost to flood control, agricultural development, and groundwater pumping.

Characteristic Species
Atriplex polycarpa	cattle-spinach

Associates
Allenrolfea occidentalis	iodinebush
Artemisia tridentata	big sagebrush
Arthrocnemum subterminale	Parish's glasswort
Atriplex fruticulosa	ball saltbush
Atriplex lentiformis	quailbush
Atriplex phyllostegia	arrow saltbush
Atriplex spinifera	spinescale
Distichlis spicata	coastal salt grass
Ephedra californica	California joint-fir
Kochia californica	California summer-cypress
Lycium cooperi	peachthorn
Nitrophila occidentalis	boraxweed
Pyrrocoma racemosa	clustered goldenweed
Sarcobatus vermiculatus	greasewood
Sporobolus airoides	alkali sacaton
Suaeda moquinii	shrubby seepweed

California Prairie

California Prairie once occurred throughout the Central Valley and in the surrounding mountains from sea level to 4000 feet. Today the grasslands occur as a ring around the Central Valley and the species composition of these grasslands are dramatically different than the original prairie. The original prairie was a mixture of annuals and perennials. Since European settlement, the prairies have become dominated by annuals, many of which are non-native to the area. The prairie communities have been changed by the invasion of exotic species, changes in grazing patterns, cultivation, and fire. This community corresponds to Küchler #48.

Characteristic Species
Nassella cernua	tussock grass
Nassella pulchra	tussock grass

Associates
Aristida divaricata	poverty three-awn
Aristida oligantha	prairie three-awn
Aristida ternipes	spider grass
Deschampsia danthonioides	annual hair grass
Elymus glaucus	blue wild rye
Eschscholzia californica	California-poppy
Festuca idahoensis	bluebunch fescue
Gilia clivorum	purple-spot gily-flower
Gilia interior	inland gily-flower
Gilia minor	little gily-flower
Gilia tricolor	bird's-eyes
Koeleria macrantha	prairie Koeler's grass
Lasthenia californica	California goldfields
Leymus triticoides	beardless lyme grass
Lupinus bicolor	miniature annual lupine
Lupinus luteolus	butter lupine

Melica californica	California melic grass
Melica imperfecta	coast range melic grass
Nassella lepida	tussock grass
Orthocarpus attenuatus	valley-tassels
Orthocarpus campestris	field owl-clover
Orthocarpus erianthus	Johnnytuck
Orthocarpus linearilobus	pale owl-clover
Orthocarpus purpurascens	red owl-clover
Plagiobothrys nothofulvus	rusty popcorn-flower
Poa secunda	curly blue grass
Sisyrinchium bellum	Calfornia blue-eyed-grass
Stipa coronata	giant needle grass
Trifolium albopurpureum	rancheria clover
Trifolium depauperatum	balloon sack clover
Trifolium gracilentum	pin-point clover
Trifolium microdon	valparaiso clover
Trifolium olivaceum	olive clover
Vulpia microstachys	small six-weeks grass
Vulpia myuros	rat-tail six-weeks grass

WETLAND SYSTEMS

Riparian Forest

Riparian Forest in the Central Valley previously formed extensive stands along major streams. Due to flood control, water diversion, agricultural development, and urban expansion, these forest are now reduced and scattered or present as isolated young stands. Riparian Forest occurs on soils near streams that provide subsurface water even when the streams or rivers are dry.

Canopy
Characteristic Species
Populus fremontii	Fremont's cottonwood
Salix gooddingii	Goodding's willow

Associates
Acer negundo	ash-leaf maple
Alnus rhombifolia	white alder
Fraxinus latifolia	Oregon ash
Platanus racemosa	California sycamore
Quercus lobata	valley oak

Woody Understory
Cephalanthus occidentalis	common buttonbush
Clematis ligusticifolia	deciduous traveler's-joy
Rubus vitifolius	Pacific dewberry
Salix bonplandiana	Bonpland's willow
Salix hindsiana	sandbar willow
Salix lasiolepis	arroyo willow

Salix lucida	shining willow
Vitis californica	California grape

Herbaceous Understory

Leymus triticoides	beardless lyme grass
Urtica dioica	stinging nettle

Vernal Pools

Vernal pools are small depressions in valley grasslands that fill with water during the winter and become dry during the spring and summer. As they dry, various annual plants flower in concentric rings. The pools most commonly border the east side of the Central Valley at the base of the Sierran Foothills. The vegetation of these pools is commonly described in terms of "zones". The zones are usually organized from pool bottom to mound top. The pools support alkali or salt-associated plants. No trees, shrubs, or succulents are known to occur in vernal pools.

Characteristic Species

Alopecurus saccatus	Pacific meadow-foxtail
Astragalus tener	alkali milk-vetch
Blennosperma nanum	common stickyseed
Boisduvalia glabella	smooth spike-primrose
Bromus hordeaceus	soft brome
Cressa truxillensis	spreading alkali-weed
Deschampsia danthonioides	annual hair grass
Distichlis spicata	coastal salt grass
Downingia bella	Hoover's calico-flower
Evax caulescens	involucrate pygmy-cudweed
Gratiola ebracteata	bractless hedge-hyssop
Grindelia camporum	great valley gumweed
Isoetes howellii	Howell's quillwort
Juncus bufonius	toad rush
Layia chrysanthemoides	smooth tidytips
Lepidium latipes	San Diego pepperwort
Lilaea scilloides	flowering-quillwort
Limnanthes douglasii	Douglas' meadowfoam
Machaerocarpus californicus	fringed-water-plantain
Marsilea vestita	hairy water-clover
Mimulus tricolor	tricolor monkey-flower
Minuartia californica	California stitchwort
Myosurus minimus	tiny mousetail
Navarretia intertexta	needle-leaf pincushion-plant
Navarretia leucocephala	white-flower pincushion-plant
Neostapfia colusana	colusa grass
Orthocarpus campestris	field owl-clover
Pilularia americana	American pillwort
Plagiobothrys acanthocarpus	adobe popcorn-flower
Plagiobothrys distantiforus	Calfornia popcorn-flower
Plagiobothrys humistratus	dwarf popcorn-flower
Plagiobothrys hystriculus	bearded popcorn-flower

Plagiobothrys leptocladus	alkali popcorn-flower
Plagiobothrys stipitatus	stalked popcorn-flower
Pogogyne ziziphoroides	Sacramento mesa-mint
Trifolium barbigerum	bearded clover
Trifolium cyathiferum	bowl clover
Trifolium depauperatum	ballon sack clover
Trifolium fucatum	sour clover
Trifolium variegatum	white-tip clover
Veronica peregrina	neckweed
Vulpia myuros	rat-tail six-weeks grass

Tule Marsh

Tule Marsh is a community type consisting of "freshwater marshes" that occur along the coast in river deltas and in coastal valleys near lakes and springs. Freshwater marshes use to be common throughout the Sacramento and San Joaquin Valleys, but have been reduced due to development pressures. Although the marshes may occur in areas near the coast, they are not influenced by tidal currents and are permanently flooded with fresh water.

Characteristic Species

Scirpus acutus	hard-stem bulrush
Typha latifolia	broad-leaf cat-tail

Associates

Carex lanuginosa	woolly sedge
Carex obnupta	slough sedge
Carex senta	western rough sedge
Cyperus eragrostis	tall flat sedge
Cyperus esculentus	chufa
Eleocharis palustris	pale spike-rush
Hydrocotyle verticillata	whorled marsh-pennywort
Juncus balticus	Baltic rush
Juncus effusus	lamp rush
Limosella aquatica	awl-leaf mudwort
Phragmites australis	common reed
Scirpus americanus	chairmaker's bulrush
Scirpus californicus	California bulrush
Scirpus robustus	seaside bulrush
Scirpus tabernaemontani	soft-stem bulrush
Sparganium eurycarpum	broad-fruit burr-reed
Typha angustifolia	narrow-leaf cat-tail
Typha domingensis	southern cat-tail
Verbena bonariensis	purple-top vervain

Mountain Meadow

Mountain Meadow occurs in the Transverse Mountain ranges where the water table is just below the surface of the soil. Often meadows occur along streams or snowmelt gullies.

Characteristic Species

Agrostis idahoensis	Idaho bent
Barbarea orthoceras	American yellow-rocket
Carex hassei	Hasse's sedge
Carex heteroneura	different-nerve sedge
Carex jonesii	Jones' sedge
Carex schottii	Schott's sedge
Carex senta	western rough sedge
Castilleja miniata	great red Indian-paintbrush
Cystopteris fragilis	brittle bladder fern
Dodecatheon redolens	scented shootingstar
Draba albertina	slender whitlow-grass
Epilobium angustifolium	fireweed
Epilobium ciliatum	fringed willowherb
Epilobium glaberrimum	glaucous willowherb
Galium bifolium	twin-leaf bedstraw
Helenium bigelovii	Bigelow's sneezeweed
Heracleum sphondylium	eltrot
Hoita orbicularis	round-leaf leather-root
Hypericum anagalloides	tinker's penny
Iris missouriensis	Rocky Mountain iris
Juncus covillei	Coville's rush
Juncus nevadensis	Sierran rush
Lewisia nevadensis	Nevada bitter-root
Lilium parryi	lemon lily
Lithophragma tenellum	slender woodlandstar
Lotus oblongifolius	streambank bird's-foot-trefoil
Lupinus latifolius	broad-leaf lupine
Luzula congesta	heath wood-rush
Maianthemum stellatum	starry false Solomon's-seal
Mimulus moschatus	muskflower
Mimulus suksdorfii	minature monkey-flower
Oenothera elata	Hooker's evening-primrose
Perideridia parishii	Parish's yampah
Platanthera leucostachys	Sierra rein orchid
Platanthera sparsiflora	canyon bog orchid
Potentilla glandulosa	sticky cinquefoil
Pycnanthemum californicum	California mountain-mint
Ribes cereum	white squaw currant
Ribes montigenum	western prickly gooseberry
Ribes roezlii	Sierran gooseberry
Rubus leucodermis	white-stem raspberry
Salix lasiolepis	arroyo willow
Senecio triangularis	arrow-leaf ragwort
Sisyrinchium bellum	California blue-eyed-grass
Solidago californica	northern California goldenrod
Sphenosciadium capitellatum	swamp whiteheads
Trifolium monanthum	mountain carpet clover
Trisetum spicatum	narrow false oat
Veratrum californicum	California false hellebore
Viola blanda	sweet white violet

ESTUARINE SYSTEMS

Coastal Salt Marsh

Coastal Salt Marsh occurs along the southern California coast in bays, lagoons, and estuaries. Salt marshes are not as extensive in southern California as they are in northern California. Salt marshes may be broken into two categories: deep water sites and smaller, shallower sites. These two types have different tidal and flooding regimes which influence the community composition.

Characteristic species
Salicornia virginica   woody saltwort

Associates
Amblyopappus pusillus   dwarf coastweed
Anemopsis californica   yerba-mansa
Arthrocnemum subterminale   Parish's glasswort
Atriplex patula   halberd-leaf orache
Atriplex watsonii   Watson's saltbush
Batis maritima   turtleweed
Carpobrotus aequilateralus   baby sun-rose
Cotula coronopifolia   common brassbuttons
Cressa truxillensis   spreading alkali-weed
Distichlis spicata   coastal salt grass
Frankenia salina   alkali sea-heath
Heliotropium convolvulaceum   wide-flower heliotrope
Heliotropium curassavicum   seaside heliotrope
Jaumea carnosa   marsh jaumea
Juncus acutus   spiny rush
Juncus mexicanus   Mexican rush
Lasthenia glabrata   yellow-ray goldfields
Limonium californicum   marsh-rosemary
Monanthochloe littoralis   shore grass
Salicornia bigelovii   dwarf saltwort
Scirpus californicus   California bulrush
Spartina foliosa   California cord grass
Spergularia salina   sandspurrey
Suaeda californica   broom seepweed
Triglochin maritimum   seaside arrow-grass
Typha latifolia   broad-leaf cat-tail

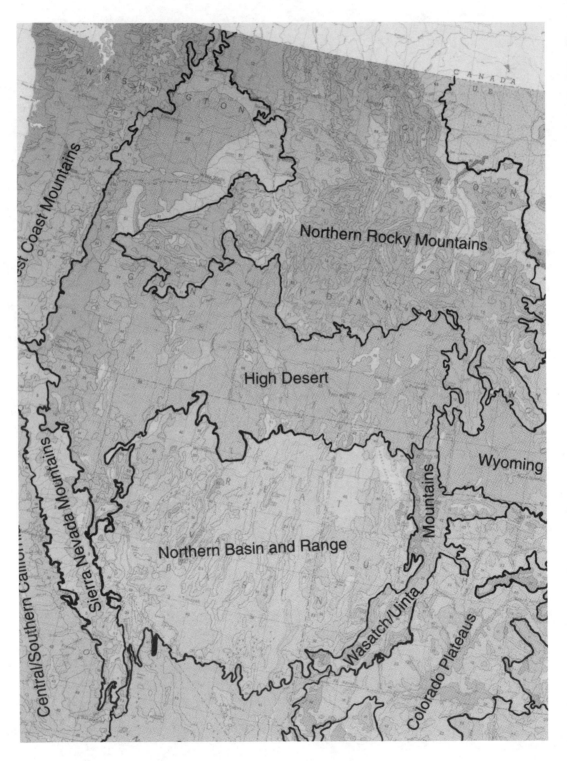

High Desert

High Desert

Introduction

The High Desert region occurs in the rain shadow of the Cascade Mountain Range. The region includes most of central and southeastern Washington, much of eastern Oregon (excluding the Blue Mountains), southern Idaho, and parts of northern California, Nevada and Colorado. This region is arid to semi-arid with warm-to-hot, dry summers and relatively cold winters. Sagebrush and dry grassland communities are common in this region, with woodland and forest communities in the mountains.

The vegetation of this region is related to the distribution of precipitation. Beginning in the dry Columbia Basin, extending eastward to the foothills of the Rocky Mountains, and westward to the east side of the Cascades, the vegetation changes from shrub-steppe dominated by sagebrush, to steppe dominated by bunchgrass. It then changes to meadow-steppe which supports grasses and forbs common to more mesic areas.

The High Desert Region has undergone many vegetational changes in the past century. Before European settlement, grazing animals were not an integral part of this region. Since the 1860's, however, cattle and sheep grazing have impacted much of the steppe and many exotic or nonnative species have been introduced into the ecosystem. One of the more aggressive weeds is cheatgrass (*Bromus tectorum*), which out competes the native grasses by its ability to grow through the fall and the winter. Cheatgrass has also made this region more susceptible to earlier and more frequent fires.

Unique communities in this area include vegetation of the sand dunes near the Columbia River and marshes around the numerous ponds in the Columbia basin. Several other plant communities found in this region, but not included in the descriptions, are Juniper–Pinyon Woodland and Western Spruce–Fir Forest. These types are more widely represented in the adjacent regions and will be discussed at length in the Northern Basin and Range region or the Northern Rocky Mountain region.

The primary sources used to develop descriptions and species lists are: Barbour and Billings 1988; Cronquist et al. 1972; Franklin and Dyrness 1973.

Dominant Ecological Communities

Upland Systems

Ponderosa Pine Forest
Juniper Woodland
Sagebrush Steppe
Saltbush–Greasewood Shrub
Palouse Prairie
Meadow Steppe

UPLAND SYSTEMS

Ponderosa Pine Forest

Within this region, Ponderosa Pine Forest occupies a narrow band on the eastern slopes of the Cascade Range. This area is very dry with a short growing season and very little summer precipitation. Much of the annual precipitation occurs in winter as snow. Ponderosa pine grows best on coarse-textured, sandy soils, often forming a mosaic with steppe or shrub-steppe communities. Ponderosa Pine Forest extends beyond the eastern slopes of the Cascades into the Ochoca, Blue, and Wallowa Mountains and into the Northern Rockies. In all of these areas Idaho fescue (bluebunch fescue) and bitterbrush are understory species. This community corresponds to Küchler #10 and #11.

Canopy
Characteristic Species
Pinus ponderosa	ponderosa pine

Associates
Juniperus occidentalis	western juniper
Pinus contorta	lodgepole pine
Populus tremuloides	quaking aspen
Quercus garryana	Oregon white oak

Woody Understory
Amelanchier alnifolia	Saskatoon service-berry
Crataegus douglasii	black hawthorn
Eriogonum niveum	snow erigonum
Holodiscus discolor	hillside oceanspray
Mahonia repens	creeping Oregon-grape
Physocarpus malvaceus	mallow-leaf ninebark
Prunus virginiana	choke cherry
Purshia tridentata	bitterbrush
Symphoricarpos albus	common snowberry

Herbaceous Understory
Antennaria dimorpha	cushion pussytoes
Apocynum androsaemifolium	spreading dogbane
Arabis holboellii	Holboell's rockcress
Balsamorhiza sagittata	arrow-leaf balsamroot
Bromus vulgaris	Columbian brome
Calamagrostis rubenscens	pinegrass
Carex geyeri	Geyer's sedge
Claytonia perfoliata	miner's-lettuce
Collinsia parviflora	small-flower blue-eyed Mary
Elymus glaucus	blue wild rye
Epilobium brachycarpum	tall annual willowherb
Erigeron compositus	dwarf mountain fleabane
Eriogonum heracleoides	parsnip buckwheat
Erythronium grandiflorum	yellow avalanche-lily
Festuca idahoensis	bluebunch fescue
Festuca occidentalis	western fescue
Frasera albicaulis	white-stem elkweed
Galium aparine	sticky-willy
Galium boreale	northern bedstraw
Koeleria macrantha	prairie Koeler's grass
Lithophragma glabrum	bulbous woodlandstar
Lithospermum ruderale	Columbian puccoon
Lotus nevadensis	Nevada bird's-foot-trefoil
Madia exigua	little tarplant

Osmorhiza chilensis	mountain sweet-cicely
Phlox gracilis	slender phlox
Poa secunda	curly bluegrass
Potentilla gracilis	graceful cinquefoil
Pseudoroegneria spicata	bluebunch-wheat grass
Ranunculus glaberrimus	sagebrush buttercup
Sisyrinchium douglasii	grass windows
Stellaria nitens	shining starwort
Stipa occidentalis	western needle grass
Vicia americana	American purple vetch
Vulpia microstachys	small six-weeks grass

Juniper Woodland

Juniper Woodland is the most xeric of the tree-dominated vegetation types in the Pacific Northwest. Juniper Woodland occupies habitats of intermediate moisture between the Ponderosa Pine Forest and the steppe or shrub-steppe vegetation. It is primarily in central Oregon around the Deschutes, Crooked, and John Day Rivers. Juniper is the dominant species, however, ponderosa pine may be found in canyon bottoms or on north slopes where soil moisture is greater. This community corresponds to Küchler #24.

Canopy
Characteristic Species

Juniperus occidentalis	western juniper

Associates

Pinus ponderosa	ponderosa pine

Woody Understory

Artemisia tridentata	big sagebrush
Chrysothamnus nauseosus	rubber rabbitbrush
Chrysothamnus viscidiflorus	green rabbitbrush
Eriogonum umbellatum	sulfur-flower wild buckwheat
Purshia tridentata	bitterbrush

Herbaceous Understory

Astragalus purshii	Pursh's milk-vetch
Claytonia perfoliata	miner's lettuce
Collinsia parviflora	small-flower blue eyed Mary
Collomia grandiflora	large-flowered mountain-trumpet
Cryptantha ambigua	basin cat's-eye
Elymus elymoides	western bottle-brushgrass
Erigeron linearis	desert yellow fleabane
Eriogonum baileyi	Bailey's wild buckwheat
Eriophyllum lanatum	common wooly-sunflower
Festuca idahoensis	bluebunch fescue
Gayophytum humile	dwarf groundsmoke
Koeleria macrantha	prairie Koeler's grass
Lomatium triternatum	nineleaf desert-parsley
Mentzelia albicaulis	white-stem blazingstar
Penstemon humilis	low beardtongue
Phlox caespitosa	clustered phlox

Poa secunda	curly blue grass
Pseudoroegneria spicata	bluebunch-wheat grass
Stipa thurberiana	Thurber's needle grass

Sagebrush Steppe

Sagebrush Steppe is the driest and the most widespread community in this region. Sagebrush occupies the center of the Columbia river basin and extends west into the foothills of the Cascades and southeast into Oregon. Big sagebrush (*Artemisia tridentata*) is the most characteristic species. Fire within the Sagebrush Steppe community has increased since an exotic, cheatgrass (*Bromus tectorum*), has become dominant. Cheatgrass grows fast and then dries up creating perfect tinder for fires ignited by lightening. This community corresponds to Küchler #55.

Characteristic Woody Species
Artemisia tridentata	big sagebrush

Associates
Artemisia tripartita	three-tip sagebrush
Chrysothamnus nauseosus	rubber rabbitbrush
Chrysothamnus viscidiflorus	green rabbitbrush
Grayia spinosa	spiny hop-sage
Juniperus occidentalis	western juniper
Tetradymia canescens	spineless horsebrush

Herbaceous Understory
Elymus elymoides	western bottle-brush grass
Lappula occidentalis	flat-spine sheepburr
Poa fendleriana	mutton grass
Poa secunda	curly blue grass
Pseudoroegneria spicata	bluebunch-wheat grass
Stipa comata	needle-and-thread
Stipa thurberiana	Thurber's needle grass
Tortula brevipes	moss
Tortula princeps	moss
Tortula ruralis	moss

Saltbush–Greasewood Shrub

Saltbush–Greasewood Shrub is a desert-shrub community which occurs on saline soils and old lakebeds. Few plants can survive in this dry, salty habitat. A sizable representation of this community type occurs in southeast Oregon and southern Idaho. Saltbush–Greasewood Shrub, however, is more widely represented in the Southern and Northern Basin and Range regions. This community corresponds to Küchler #40.

Characteristic Woody Species
Artiplex confertifolia	shadscale
Artiplex nuttallii	Nuttall's saltbush sage
Sarcobatus vermiculatus	greasewood

Associates
Allenrolfea occidentalis	iodinebush
Artemisia spinescens	bud sagebrush

Artemisia tridentata	big sagebrush
Grayia spinosa	spiny hop-sage
Krascheninnikovia lantata	winterfat
Lycium cooperi	peachthorn
Menodora spinescens	spiny menodora
Suaeda moquinii	shrubby seepweed

Herbaceous Understory

Distichlis spicata	coastal salt grass
Elymus elymoides	western bottle-brush grass
Kochia americana	greenmolly
Leymus cinereus	Great Basin lyme grass
Leymus triticoides	beardless lyme grass
Oryzopsis hymenoides	Indian mountain-rice grass
Poa secunda	curly blue grass

Palouse Prairie

Palouse Prairie depends on a greater degree of moisture than Sagebrush Steppe and usually occurs at higher altitudes than sagebrush communities. Most native Palouse Prairie has been destroyed by excessive grazing and cultivation which has resulted in the replacement of native perennial bunchgrasses with sagebrush, cheatgrass, or agricultural crops. This community corresponds to Küchler #50.

Characteristic Species

Festuca idahoensis	blue bunch fescue
Leymus condensatus	giant lyme grass
Poa secunda	curly blue grass
Pseudoroegneria spicata	bluebunch-wheat grass

Associates

Astragalus spaldingii	Spalding's milk-vetch
Chrysothamnus nauseosus	rubber rabbitbrush
Festuca campestris	prairie fescue
Koeleria macrantha	prairie Koeler's grass
Lappula occidentalis	flat-spine sheepburr
Montia linearis	linear-leaf candy-flower
Pascopyrum smithii	western-wheat grass
Phlox gracilis	slender phlox
Phlox longifolia	long-leaf phlox
Plantago patagonica	woolly plantain
Stellaria nitens	shiny starwort
Stipa comata	needle-and-thread

Meadow Steppe

Meadow Steppe is the most mesic of the steppe communities. This vegetation type encircles the Columbia Basin Province of Oregon and Washington. The dominant species are herbaceous, however, dwarfed shrubs may occur with the grasses forming shrubby islands or thickets. Where heavy grazing and fire have impacted community composition and structure, exotics such as Kentucky Bluegrass (*Poa pratensis*) may dominate.

Characteristic Species

Festuca idahoensis	bluebunch fescue
Koeleria macrantha	prairie Koeler's grass
Poa secunda	curly blue grass
Pseudoroegneria spicata	bluebunch-wheat grass
Symphoricarpos albus	common snowberry

Associates

Astragalus arrectus	palouse milk-vetch
Balsamorhiza sagittata	arrow-leaf balsamroot
Castilleja lutescens	stiff yellow Indian-paintbrush
Geranium viscosissimum	sticky purple crane's-bill
Geum triflorum	old-man's-whiskers
Helianthella uniflora	Rocky Mountain dwarf-sunflower
Hieracium cynoglossoides	hound-tongue hawkweed
Iris missouriensis	Rocky Mountain iris
Lupinus sericeus	Pursh's silky lupine
Potentilla gracilis	graceful cinquefoil
Rosa nutkana	Nootka rose
Rosa woodsii	woods' rose

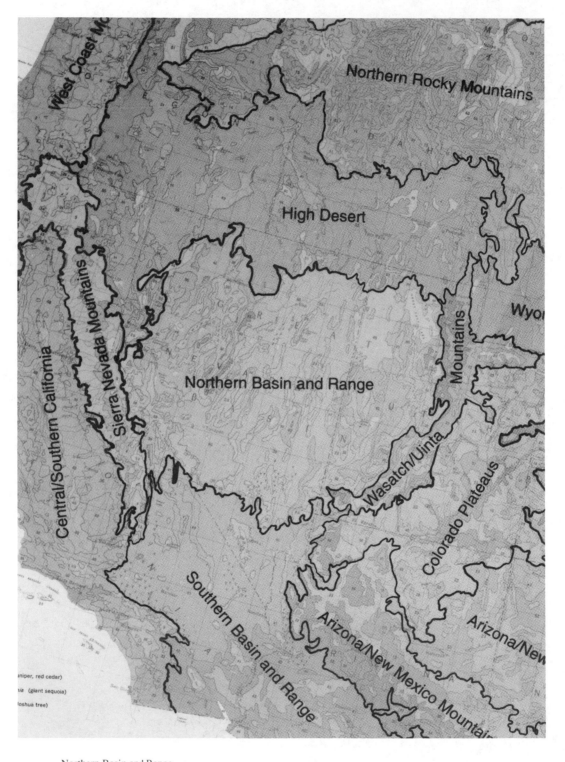

Northern Basin and Range

Northern Basin and Range

Introduction

The Northern Basin and Range region is also referred to as the intermountain region and the cold desert biome because of its cool climate and location between the Rocky Mountains to the east and the Sierra Nevada and Cascade Mountains to the west. The region encompasses most of Nevada and western Utah. The Snake River lava flows are the northern boundary with the Wasatch and Uinta Mountains to the west.

The Northern Basin and Range region, as its name implies, is characterized by numerous flat basins which occur between the many small mountain ranges. The soils are generally rocky, thin, low in organic matter, and high in minerals. The region is very arid with the mountains capturing more moisture than the basins. The moisture that does make its way into the basins most often flows into low, flat playa lakes where the water evaporates leaving salt and mineral deposits. Because of this moisture regime a large part of the vegetation is adapted to soils with a high mineral and salt content.

The primary sources used to develop descriptions and species lists are: Barbour and Billings 1988; Cronquist et al. 1972.

Dominant Ecological Communities

Upland Systems
Great Basin Pine Forest
Juniper–Pinyon Woodland
Mountain-Mahogany–Scrub Oak
Great Basin Sagebrush
Saltbush Scrub
Greasewood Scrub

Wetland Systems
Salt Marsh

UPLAND SYSTEMS

Great Basin Pine Forest

Great Basin Pine Forest occurs on several of the higher mountain ranges in the Northern Basin and Range region. The White Mountains, the Shoshone Mountains and the Stillwater Range are among the ranges where the pine forest, dominated by limber pine and bristle-cone pine, can be found. These forests are best developed between 9500 feet and timberline (about 10500 feet). The trees are relatively short (between thirty and forty feet). Bristle-cone pine is dominant is the southern half of the region and limber pine is dominant in the north. This community corresponds to Küchler #22.

Canopy
Characteristic Species

Pinus aristata	bristle-cone pine
Pinus flexilis	limber pine

Associates

Pinus ponderosa	ponderosa pine

Woody Understory

Artemisia tridentata	big sagebrush
Astragalus platytropis	broad-keel milk-vetch
Cercocarpus ledifolius	curl-leaf mountain-mahogany
Cryptantha hoffmannii	Hoffman's cat's-eye
Cryptantha roosiorum	bristle-cone cat's-eye
Cymopterus cinerarius	gray spring-parsley
Ericameria gilmanii	white-flower heath-goldenrod
Holodiscus dumosus	glandular oceanspray

Herbaceous Understory

Festuca idahoensis	bluebunch fescue
Poa secunda	curly blue grass
Pseudoroegneria spicata	bluebunch-wheat grass
Stipa pinetorum	pine-forest needle grass

Juniper–Pinyon Woodland

Juniper–Pinyon Woodland occurs on the slopes of the mountains throughout the Northern Basin and Range region. Pinyon and juniper are generally found at elevations between 5000 and 8000 feet. Pinyon tends to dominate at upper elevations and juniper at lower elevations. Much of the woodland area has been heavily grazed which has disrupted the natural fire cycles. Historically these communities were more likely open with a grass-dominated understory. These changes have resulted in the loss of understory species and an increase in erosion. This community corresponds to Küchler #23.

Canopy
Characteristic Species

Juniperus monosperma	one-seed juniper
Juniperus osteosperma	Utah juniper
Pinus edulis	two-needle pinyon
Pinus monophylla	single-leaf pine

Associates

Acer glabrum	Rocky Mountain maple
Amelanchier alnifolia	Saskatoon service-berry
Juniperus deppeana	alligator juniper
Juniperus occidentalis	western juniper
Quercus emoryi	Emory's oak
Quercus gambelii	Gambel's oak
Quercus grisea	gray oak

Woody Understory

Artemisia arbuscula	dwarf sagebrush
Artemisia tridentata	big sagebrush
Ceanothus velutinus	tobacco-brush
Cercocarpus ledifolius	curl-leaf mountain-mahogany
Chrysothamnus nauseosus	rubber rabbitbrush
Chrysothamnus viscidiflorus	green rabbitbrush
Ephedra viridis	Mormon-tea
Eriogonum umbellatum	sulphur-flower wild buckwheat

Fallugia paradoxa	Apache-plume
Gutierrezia sarothrae	kindlingweed
Holodiscus dumosus	glandular oceanspray
Purshia mexicana	Mexican cliff-rose
Purshia tridentata	bitterbrush
Ribes cereum	white squaw currant
Ribes velutinum	desert gooseberry
Symphoricarpos oreophilus	mountain snowberry
Tetradymia canescens	spineless horsebrush

Herbaceous Understory

Balsamorhiza sagittata	arrow-leaf balsamroot
Bouteloua curtipendula	side-oats grama
Bouteloua gracilis	blue grama
Elymus elymoides	western bottle-brush grass
Eriogonum heracleoides	parsnip-flower wild buckwheat
Eriophyllum lanatum	common wooly-sunflower
Festuca idahoensis	bluebunch fescue
Festuca kingii	King's fescue
Frasera albomarginata	desert elkweed
Grindelia squarrosa	curly-cup gumweed
Heterotheca villosa	hairy false golden-aster
Hymneoxys richardsonii	Colorado rubberweed
Ipomopsis aggregata	scarlet skyrocket
Koeleria macrantha	prairie Koeler's grass
Lithospermum ruderale	Columbian puccoon
Lupinus sericeus	Pursh's silky lupine
Oryzopsis hymenoides	Indian mountain-rice grass
Pascopyrum smithii	western-wheat grass
Pentstemon speciosus	royal beardtongue
Pentstemon watsonii	Watson's beardtongue
Poa fendleriana	mutton grass
Poa secunda	curly blue grass
Pseudoroegneria spicatum	bluebunch-wheat grass
Sporbolus cryptandrus	sand dropseed
Stipa comata	needle-and-thread
Stipa nelsonii	Nelson's needle grass
Stipa thurberiana	Thurber's needle grass

Mountain-Mahogany–Scrub Oak

Mountain-Mahogany–Scrub Oak occurs in the Northern Basin and Range region in the foothills of several mountain ranges including the Toiyabee and Shoshone Mountains. This community is more widely represented in the Uinta mountains at the northeast boundary of this region. Community dominants vary throughout the region and even locally with elevations and other factors. Within the Mountain-Mahogany–Scrub Oak community type there has been a decrease in herbaceous understory species due to extensive livestock grazing. This community corresponds to Küchler #37.

Canopy
Characteristic Species
Cercocarpus ledifolius	curl-leaf mountain-mahogany
Quercus gambelii	Gambel's oak

Associates
Acer glabrum	Rocky Mountain maple
Acer grandidentatum	canyon maple
Acer negundo	ash-leaf maple
Amelanchier alnifolia	Saskatoon service-berry
Amelanchier utahensis	Utah service-berry
Cercocarpus montanus	alder-leaf mountain-mahogany
Quercus havardii	Harvard's oak
Quercus turbinella	shrub live oak

Woody Understory
Arctostaphylos spp.	manzanita
Artemisia arbuscula	dwarf sagebrush
Artemisia tridentata	big sagebrush
Betula occidentalis	water birch
Ceanothus fendleri	Fendler's buckbrush
Ceanothus velutinus	tobacco-brush
Chrysothamnus viscidiflorus	green rabbitbrush
Fallugia paradoxa	Apache-plume
Gutierrezia sarothrae	kindlingweed
Pachystima myrsinites	Oregon boxwood
Physocarpus malvaceus	mallow-leaf ninebark
Populus angustifolia	narrow-leaf cottonwood
Prunus virginiana	choke cherry
Purshia mexicana	Mexican cliff-rose
Purshia tridentata	bitterbrush
Rhamnus crocea	holly-leaf buckthorn
Rhus trilobata	ill-scented sumac
Ribes cereum	white squaw currant
Rosa woodsii	Arizona rose
Sambucus cerulea	blue elder
Symphoricarpos oreophilus	mountain snowberry

Herbaceous Understory
Claytonia lanceolata	lance-leaf springbeauty
Collinsia parviflora	small-flower blue-eyed Mary
Delphinium nuttallianum	two-lobe larkspur
Erigeron flagellaris	trailing fleabane
Erythronium grandiflorum	yellow avalanche-lily
Gayophytum ramosissimum	pinyon groundsmoke
Geranium caespitosum	purple cluster crane's-bill
Heliomeris multiflora	Nevada showy false goldeneye
Hydrophyllum capitatum	cat's-breeches
Leymus cinereus	great basin lyme grass
Lithophragma parviflorum	prairie woodlandstar

Nemophila breviflora	Great Basin baby-blue-eyes
Orthocarous luteus	golden-tongue owl-clover
Stipa comata	needle-and-thread
Stipa lettermanii	Letterman's needle grass
Wyethia amplexicaulis	northern mule's-ears

Great Basin Sagebrush

Sagebrush vegetation occurs in desert areas within the Northern Basin and Range region where annual precipitation is at least seven inches. The sagebrush communities are usually located in the foothills and mountainsides above 5000 feet, some sagebrush communities may extend up to 10000 feet. Great Basin Sagebrush communities are very arid and desert-like. The sagebrush seldom grows over one foot in height and the grasses are sparse. In the northern part of the region the sagebrush communities are similar to the Sagebrush Steppe of the High Desert region. Much of the sagebrush area has been converted into farmland. This community corresponds to Küchler #38.

Characteristic Woody Species

Artemisia tridentata	big sagebrush

Associates

Artemisia nova	black sagebrush
Atriplex confertifolia	shadscale
Chrysothamnus nauseosus	rubber rabbitbrush
Chrysothamnus viscidiflorus	green rabbitbrush
Coleogyne ramosissima	blackbrush
Ephedra torreyana	Torrey's joint-fir
Ephedra viridis	Mormon-tea
Grayia spinosa	spiny hop-sage
Purshia tridentata	bitterbrush
Ribes velutinum	desert gooseberry
Tetradymia glabrata	little-leaf horsebrush

Herbaceous Understory

Allium acuminatum	taper-tip onion
Aristida purpurea	purple three-awn
Balsamorhiza sagittata	arrow-leaf balsamroot
Calochortus nuttallii	sego-lily
Castilleja angustifolia	northwestern Indian-paintbrush
Crepis acuminata	long-leaf hawk's-beard
Delphinium andersonii	desert larkspur
Elymus elymoides	western bottle-brush grass
Elymus lanceolatus	streamside wild rye
Festuca idahoensis	bluebunch fescue
Heterotheca villosa	hairy false golden-aster
Hymenoxys richardsonii	Colorado rubberweed
Koeleria macrantha	prairie Koeler's grass
Leptodactylon pungens	granite prickly-phlox
Leymus cinereus	great basin lyme grass
Lupinus caudatus	Kellogg's spurred lupine
Lupinus sericeus	Pursh's silky lupine

Oryzopsis hymnoides	Indian mountain-rice grass
Pascopyrum smithii	western-wheat grass
Phlox hoodii	carpet phlox
Phlox longifolia	long-leaf phlox
Poa fendleriana	mutton grass
Poa secunda	curly blue grass
Pseudoroegneria spicata	bluebunch-wheat grass
Sporobolus airoides	alkali-sacaton
Stipa comata	needle-and-thread
Viola beckwithii	western pansy
Wyethia amplexicaulis	northern mule's-ears
Zigadenus paniculatus	sand-corn

Saltbush Scrub

Saltbush Scrub occurs in areas with little moisture and on saline valley soils. Structurally, this community is predominantly low, widely-spaced shrubs. This community type is also often referred to as the "shadscale community." This community corresponds, in part, to Küchler #40.

Characteristic Woody Species
Atriplex confertifolia	shadscale

Associates
Artemisia spinescens	bud sagebrush
Atriplex canescens	four-wing saltbush
Atriplex gardneri	Gardner's saltbush
Atriplex nuttallii	Nuttall's saltbush
Chrysothamnus viscidiflorus	green rabbitbrush
Ephedra nevadensis	Nevada joint-fir
Grayia spinosa	spiny hop-sage
Gutierrezia sarothrae	kindlingweed
Krascheninnikovia lanata	winterfat
Lycium cooperi	peachthorn
Sarcobatus vermiculatus	greasewood
Tetradymia glabrata	little-leaf horsebrush

Herbaceous Understory
Camissonia boothii	shredding suncup
Camissonia claviformis	browneyes
Camissonia scapoidea	Paiute suncup
Cardaria draba	heart-pod hoary cress
Cryptantha circumscissa	cushion cat's-eye
Eriogonum ovalifolium	cushion wild buckwheat
Halogeton glomeratus	saltlover
Iva nevadensis	Nevada marsh-elder
Kochia americana	greenmolly
Mirabilis alipes	winged four-o'clock
Sphaeralcea grossulariaefolia	currant-leaf globe-mallow
Vulpia octoflora	eight-flower six-weeks grass
Xylorhiza glabriuscula	smooth woody-aster

Greasewood Scrub

Greasewood Scrub is the most salt tolerant community in the Northern Basin and Range region. This vegetation type occurs in the valley bottoms where the water table is relatively close to the surface. This community corresponds, in part, to Küchler #40.

Characteristic Woody Species
Sarcobatus vermiculatus	greasewood

Associates
Allenrolfea occidentalis	iodinebush
Artemisia spinescens	bud sagebrush
Atriplex confertifolia	shadscale
Atriplex lentiformis	quailbush
Suaeda monquinii	shrubby seepweed
Thelypodium sagittatum	arrowhead thelypody

Herbaceous Understory
Cordylanthus maritimus	saltmarsh bird's-beak
Glaux maritima	sea-milkwort
Halogeton glomeratus	saltlover
Hutchinsia procumbens	ovalpurse
Iva axillaris	deer-root
Juncus balticus	Baltic rush
Kochia americana	red sage
Pyrrocoma lanceolata	lance-leaf goldenweed
Salicornia rubra	red saltwort
Sarcocornia pacifica	Pacific swampfire
Sporobolus airoides	alkali-sacaton

WETLAND SYSTEMS

Salt Marsh

Salt Marsh develops in areas with high salinity and poor drainage. This vegetation develops around shallow lake shores and across areas of standing shallow water. This community corresponds to Küchler #49.

Characteristic Species
Allenrolfea occidentalis	iodinebush
Berula erecta	cut-leaf-water-parsnip
Castilleja exilis	small-flower annual indian-paintbrush
Centaurium exaltatum	desert centaury
Ceratophyllum demersum	coontail
Distichlis spicata	coastal salt grass
Eleocharis rostellata	beaked spike-rush
Juncus balticusi	Baltic rush
Najas marina	holly-leaf waternymph
Phragmites australis	common reed

Ruppia maritima	beaked ditch-grass
Sarcocornia pacifica	Pacific swampfire
Scirpus acutus	hard-stem bulrush
Scirpus americanus	chairmaker's bulrush
Scirpus maritimus	saltmarsh bulrush
Sporobolus airoides	alkail-sacaton
Triglochin maritimum	seaside arrow-grass
Typha latifolia	broad-leaf cat-tail

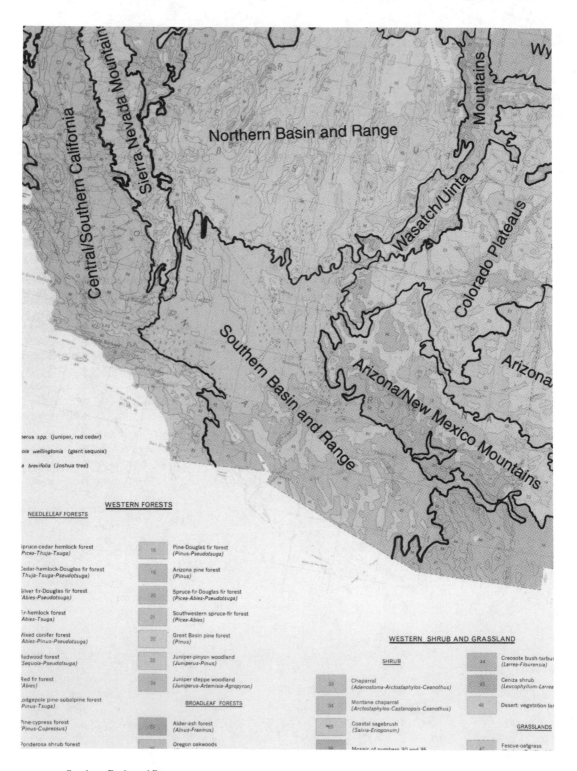

Within the map image, labeled regions include: Central/Southern California, Sierra Nevada Mountains, Northern Basin and Range, Wasatch/Uinta Mountains, Colorado Plateaus, Wy[oming], Arizona, Southern Basin and Range, Arizona/New Mexico Mountains.

Legend text:

...perus spp. (juniper, red cedar)

...oia wellingtonia (giant sequoia)

...a brevifolia (Joshua tree)

WESTERN FORESTS

NEEDLELEAF FORESTS

Spruce-cedar hemlock forest (*Picea-Thuja-Tsuga*)	18 Pine-Douglas fir forest (*Pinus-Pseudotsuga*)
Cedar-hemlock-Douglas fir forest (*Thuja-Tsuga-Pseudotsuga*)	19 Arizona pine forest (*Pinus*)
Silver fir-Douglas fir forest (*Abies-Pseudotsuga*)	20 Spruce-fir-Douglas fir forest (*Picea-Abies-Pseudotsuga*)
Fir-hemlock forest (*Abies-Tsuga*)	21 Southwestern spruce-fir forest (*Picea-Abies*)
Mixed conifer forest (*Abies-Pinus-Pseudotsuga*)	22 Great Basin pine forest (*Pinus*)
Redwood forest (*Sequoia-Pseudotsuga*)	23 Juniper-pinyon woodland (*Juniperus-Pinus*)
Red fir forest (*Abies*)	24 Juniper steppe woodland (*Juniperus-Artemisia-Agropyron*)
Lodgepole pine-subalpine forest (*Pinus-Tsuga*)	BROADLEAF FORESTS
Pine-cypress forest (*Pinus-Cupressus*)	Alder-ash forest (*Alnus-Fraxinus*)
Ponderosa shrub forest	Oregon oakwoods

WESTERN SHRUB AND GRASSLAND

SHRUB

33 Chaparral (*Adenostoma-Arctostaphylos-Ceanothus*)	44 Creosote bush-tarbus (*Larrea-Flourensia*)
34 Montane chaparral (*Arctostaphylos-Castanopsis-Ceanothus*)	45 Ceniza shrub (*Leucophyllum-Larrea*
35 Coastal sagebrush (*Salvia-Eriogonum*)	46 Desert: vegetation lar
Mosaic of numbers 30 and 35	GRASSLANDS
	47 Fescue-oatgrass

Southern Basin and Range

Southern Basin and Range

Introduction

The Southern Basin and Range region includes portions of southeast Arizona, southwestern California and southern Nevada. This is a very dry area with desert scrub the dominant vegetation in the basins and flats. The scattered mountain ranges support woodlands and pine and juniper forests at higher elevations.

The primary sources used to develop descriptions and species lists are: Barbour and Billings 1988; Barbour and Major 1988; Brown 1982; Thorne 1976.

Dominant Ecological Communities

Upland Systems
Mojave Montane Forest
Great Basin Pine Woodland
Juniper–Pinyon Woodland
Mojave Desert Scrub
Sonoran Desert Scrub

Wetland Systems
Desert Oasis Woodland
Riparian Woodland

UPLAND SYSTEMS

Mojave Montane Forest

Mojave Montane Forest is found on Clark, Kingston, and New York Mountains in southern California and on the Charleston Mountains in southern Nevada at elevations from 5700 to 7100 feet. These open forests often contain pinyon and are found on north-facing slopes or other mesic areas.

Canopy
Characteristic Species
Abies concolor	white fir

Associates
Acer glabrum	Rocky Mountain maple
Juniperus osteosperma	Utah juniper
Pinus monophylla	single-leaf pinyon
Quercus chrysolepis	canyon live oak
Quercus turbinella	shrub live oak

Woody Understory
Amelanchier utahensis	Utah service-berry
Fraxinus anomala	single-leaf ash
Holodiscus boursieri	Boursier's oceanspray
Leptodactylon pungens	granite prickly-phlox
Petrophyton caespitosum	Rocky Mountain rockmat

Philadelphus microphyllus	little-leaf mock orange
Ribes cereum	white squaw currant
Ribes velutinum	desert goose berry
Sambucus cerulea	blue elder

Great Basin Pine Woodland

This woodland community is characterized by widely spaced limber pines and is the timberline woodland of eastern California. It is frequently found on granitic soils above 7,000 feet. The trees are short and widely spaced. The woodlands are similar to the pine forests of the Great Basin and may contain pure stands of bristle-cone pines. This community corresponds to Küchler # 22.

Canopy
Characteristic Species
Pinus flexilis	limber pine
Pinus longaeva	Intermountain bristle-cone pine

Associates
Acer glabrum	Rocky Mountain maple
Pinus ponderosa	ponderosa pine
Populus tremuloides	quaking aspen

Woody Understory
Artemisia tridentata	big sagebrush
Cerococarpus ledifolius	cutleaf mountain-mahogany
Chamaebatiaria millefolium	fernbush
Chrysothamnus viscidiflorus	green rabbitbrush
Ericameria gilmanii	white-flower heath-goldenrod
Holodiscus dumosus	glandular oceanspray
Leptodactylon pungens	granite prickly-phlox
Ribes cereum	white squaw currant
Ribes montigenum	western prickly gooseberry
Sphaeromeria cana	gray chicken-sage
Stenotus acaulis	stemless mock goldenweed
Symphoricarpos longiflorus	desert snowberry

Herbaceous Understory
Antennaria rosea	rosy pussytoes
Arenaria kingii	King's sandwort
Artemisia dracunculus	dragon wormwood
Astragalus kentrophyta	spiny milk-vetch
Astragalus platytropis	broad-keel milk-vetch
Cryptantha hoffmannii	Hoffmann's cat's-eye
Cryptantha roosiorum	bristle-cone cat's-eye
Cymopterus cinerarius	gray spring-parsley
Elymus elymoides	western bottle-brush grass
Erigeron spp.	fleabane
Festuca brachyphylla	short-leaf fescue
Festuca idahoensis	bluebunch fescue
Galium hypotrichium	alpine bedstraw

Heuchera rubescens	pink alumroot
Hymenoxys cooperi	Cooper's rubberweed
Koeleria macrantha	prairie Koeler's grass
Linanthus nuttallii	Nuttall's desert-trumpets
Mimulus bigelovii	yellow-throat monkey-flower
Muhlenbergia richardsonis	matted muhly
Oenothera cespitosa	tufted evening-primrose
Oxytropis parryi	Parry's locoweed
Pellaea breweri	Brewer's cliffbrake
Phlox covillei	Coville's phlox
Poa glauca	white blue grass
Poa secunda	curly blue grass
Pseudoroegneria spicata	bluebunch-wheat grass
Senecio spartioides	broom-like ragwort
Stipa pinetorum	pine-forest needle grass

Juniper–Pinyon Woodland

Juniper–Pinyon Woodland of southern California, southern Nevada, and southwestern Arizona occurs on dry, rocky mountain slopes or other areas at elevations from 5000 to 8000 feet. These woodlands represent the western most extension of similar woodlands in the Northern Basin and Range and the Colorado Plateau regions. The pinyon and juniper components of this community may be somewhat distinct forming a mosaic of pinyon or juniper areas. This community corresponds to Küchler #23.

Canopy
Characteristic Species

Juniperus californica	California juniper
Juniperus monosperma	one-seed juniper
Juniperus osteosperma	Utah juniper
Pinus edulis	two-needle pinyon
Pinus monophylla	single-leaf pinyon

Associates

Juniperus deppeana	alligator juniper
Juniperus occidentalis	western juniper
Pinus quadrifolia	four-leaf pinyon
Quercus chrysolepis	canyon live oak
Quercus emoryi	Emory's oak
Quercus gambelii	Gambel's oak
Quercus grisea	gray oak
Quercus turbinella	shrub live oak

Woody Understory

Arctostaphylos glauca	big-berry manzanita
Arctostaphylos pungens	Mexican manzanita
Artemisia arbuscula	dwarf sagebrush
Artemisia biglovii	flat sagebrush
Artemisia tridentata	big sagebrush
Baccharis sergiloides	squaw's false willow
Brickellia californica	California brickellbush

Ceanothus greggii	Mojave buckbrush
Cerocarpus intricatus	little-leaf mountain-mahogany
Cerocarpus ledifolius	cut-leaf mountain-mahogany
Cerocarpus montanus	alder-leaf mountain mahogany
Chrysothamnus depressus	long-flower rabbitbrush
Chrysothamnus nauseosus	rubber rabbitbrush
Chrysothamnus teretifolius	needle-leaf rabbitbrush
Chrysothamnus viscidiflorus	green rabbitbrush
Coleogyne ramosissima	blackbrush
Crossosoma bigelovii	ragged rockflower
Echinocereus engelmannii	saints cactus
Echinocereus triglochidiatus	king-cup cactus
Ephedra nevadensis	Nevada joint-fir
Ephedra viridis	Mormon-tea
Ericameria cuneata	cliff heath-goldenrod
Ericameria cooperi	Cooper's heath-goldenrod
Ericameria linearifolius	narrow-leaf heath-goldenrod
Eriodictyon angustifolia	marrow-leaf yerba-santa
Eriogonum fasciculatum	eastern Mojave wild buckwheat
Eriogonum heermannii	Heerman's wild buckwheat
Eriogonum umbellatum	sulphur-flower wild buckwheat
Eriogonum wrightii	bastard-sage
Fallugia paradoxa	Apache-plume
Forestieria pubescens	swamp-privet
Frangula californica	California coffee berry
Fraxinus anomala	single-leaf ash
Garrya flavescens	ashy silktassel
Glossopetalon spinescens	spiny greasebush
Gutierrezia sarothrae	Kindlingweed
Holodiscus boursieri	Boursier's oceanspray
Mahonia haematocarpa	red Oregon-grape
Menodora spinescens	spiny menodora
Opuntia erinacea	oldman cactus
Opuntia phaeacantha	tulip prickly-pear
Petradoria pumila	grassy rock-goldenrod
Petrophyton caespitosum	Rocky Mountain rockmat
Philadelphus microphyllus	little-leaf mock orange
Prunus fasciculata	desert almond
Purshia glandulosa	antelope-brush
Purshia mexicana	Mexican cliff-rose
Purshia tridentata	bitterbrush
Rhamnus crocea	holly-leaf buckthorn
Rhus trilobata	ill-scented sumac
Ribes cereum	white squaw currant
Ribes velutinum	desert gooseberry
Salazaria mexicana	Mexican bladder-sage
Symphoricarpos longiflorus	desert snowberry
Yucca baccata	banana yucca
Yucca brevifolia	Joshua-tree
Yucca schidigera	Mojave yucca

Herbaceous Understory

Anisocoma acaulis	scalebud
Arabis spp.	rockcress
Bouteloua curtipendula	side-oats grama
Bouteloua gracilis	blue grama
Caulanthus amplexicaulis	clasping-leaf wild cabbage
Elymus elymoides	western bottle-brush grass
Eriophyllum confertiflorum	yellow-yarrow
Hilaria rigida	big galleta
Layia glandulosa	white tidytips
Monardella linoides	flax-leaf mountainbalm
Oreonana vestita	woolly mountain-parsley
Oryzopsis hymenoides	Indian mountain-rice grass
Pascopyrum smithii	western-wheat grass
Pellaea mucronata	bird-foot cliffbrake
Penstemon grinnellii	Grinnell's beardtongue
Phacelia austromontana	southern Sierran scorpion-weed
Poa secunda	curly blue grass
Salvia dorii	gray ball sage
Salvia pachyphylla	rose sage
Sporobolus cryptandrus	sand dropseed
Stipa coronata	giant needle grass
Stipa speciosa	desert needle grass

Mojave Desert Scrub

Mojave Desert Scrub is found in southeastern California, southern Nevada, extreme southwestern Utah, and western and northwestern Arizona between the Great Basin Desert to the north and the Sonoran Desert to the south. Different shrubs form the dominant vegetation in different areas. The San Bernardino, Little San Bernardino, Cottonwood, and Eagle Mountains form a fairly definite southern boundary. At its northern limits it gives way to Great Basin Scrub at elevations of 2700 to 3150 feet. The desert scrub occurs on elevations below the coniferous woodlands in the Mojave Desert and is composed mainly of low shrubs. Creosote bush frequently occurs alone or with a single associate, most commonly white burrobush. Saltbush, creosote bush, blackbrush, shadscale, and Joshua tree associations are typical vegetation types. Mojave Desert Scrub is unlike Sonoran Desert Scrub in that few trees occur even along arroyos and other drainage ways. Mojave Desert Scrub has lower diversity and contains fewer perennial plants than Sonoran Desert Scrub. Many ephemeral plants are endemic in this region. The Mojave desert rarely has summer rain. Considerable variation in the vegetation occurs regionally, locally, seasonally, and annually. This community corresponds to Küchler #40 and #41.

Characteristic Woody Species

Ambrosia dumosa	white burrobush
Atriplex canescens	four-wing saltbush
Atriplex confertifolia	shadscale
Baccharis sergiloides	squaw's false willow
Coleogyne ramosissima	blackbrush
Encelia farinosa	goldenhills
Grayia spinosa	spiny hop-sage
Larrea tridentata	creosote-bush

Lycium andersonii	red-berry desert-thorn
Salazaria mexicana	Mexican bladder-sage
Sarcobatus vermiculatus	greasewood
Sphaeralcea ambigua	apricot globe-mallow
Tetradymia axillaris	cottonthorn
Yucca brevifolla	Joshua-tree

Associates

Acacia greggii	long-flower catclaw
Acamptopappus shockleyi	Shockley's goldenhead
Agave utahensis	Utah century-plant
Allenrolfea occidentalis	iodinebush
Artemisia spinescens	bud sagebrush
Artemisia tridentata	big sagebrush
Atriplex hymenolytra	desert-holly
Atriplex polycarpa	cattle-spinach
Atriplex spinifera	spinescale
Chrysothamnus paniculatus	dotted rabbitbrush
Echinocactus polycephalus	cotton-top cactus
Echinocereus engelmannii	saints cactus
Ephedra california	California joint-fir
Ephedra nevadensis	Nevada joint-fir
Eriogonum fasciculatum	eastern Mojave wild buckwheat
Eriogonum wrighti	bastard-sage
Escobaria vivipara	desert pincushion
Ferocactus cylindraceus	barrel cactus
Fouquiera splendens	ocotillo
Hibiscus denudatus	paleface
Hymenoclea salsola	white cheesebush
Krameria grayi	white ratany
Krameria eracta	small-flower ratany
Krascheninnikovia lanata	winterfat
Lepidospartum latisquamum	Nevada scalebroom
Lycium andersonii	red-berry desert-thorn
Lycium cooperi	peachthorn
Lycium fremontii	Fremont's desert-thorn
Menadora spinescens	spiny menodora
Opuntia acanthocarpa	buck-horn cholla
Opuntia basilaris	beaver-tail cactus
Opuntia bigelovii	teddy-bear cholla
Opuntia echinocarpa	golden cholla
Opuntia erinacea	oldman cactus
Opuntia parishii	matted cholla
Opuntia ramosissima	darning-needle cactus
Peucephyllum schottii	Scott's pygmy-cedar
Psorothamus arborescens	Mojave smokebush
Psorothamus emoryi	Emory's smokebush
Psorothamus fremontii	Fremont's smokebush
Psorothamus spinosus	smokethorn
Purshia gladulosa	antelope-brush

Salvia dorrii	gray ball sage
Salvia funerea	death valley sage
Salvia mohavensis	Mojave sage
Senna armata	desert wild sensitive-plant
Suaeda moquinii	shrubby seepweed
Thamnosma montana	turpentine-broom
Yucca baccata	banana yucca
Yucca schidigera	Mojave yucca

Herbaceous Understory

Asclepias subulata	rush milkweed
Atrichoseris platyphylla	parachute-plant
Bouteloua spp.	grama
Calycoseris parryi	yellow tackstem
Camissonia brevipes	golden suncup
Camissonia chamaenerioides	long-capsule suncup
Chaenactis carphoclinia	pebble pincushion
Chorizanthe brevicornu	brittle spineflower
Chorizanthe rigida	devil's spineflower
Cryptantha maritima	guadalupe cat's-eye
Distichlis spicata	coastal salt grass
Encelia farinosa	goldenhills
Eriogonum inflatum	Indian-pipeweed
Eriogonum trichopes	little desert trumpet
Gilia scopulorum	rock gily-flower
Hilaria mutica	tobosa grass
Hilaria rigida	big galleta
Kochia americana	greenmolly
Langloisia setosissima	bristly-calico
Lepidium lasiocarpum	hairy-pod pepperwort
Lotus salsuginosus	coastal bird's-foot-trefoil
Lupinus arizonicus	Arizona lupine
Mentzelia involucrata	white-bract blazingstar
Mirabilis bigelovii	desert wishbonebush
Nitrophila spp.	niterwort
Oenothera deltoides	devil's-lantern
Oryzopsis hymenoides	Indian mountain-rice grass
Perityle emoryi	Emory's rockdaisy
Phacelia crenulata	notch-leaf scorpion-weed
Phacelia distans	distant scorpion-weed
Plagiobothrys jonesii	Mojave popcorn-flower
Plantago ovata	blond plantain
Prenanthella exigua	brightwhite
Salicornia spp.	saltwort
Salvia columbariae	California sage
Stipa speciosa	desert needle grass
Stylocline micropoides	woolly-head neststraw
Trichoptilium incisum	yellowdome

Riparian trees only

Acacia greggii	long-flower catclaw
Chilopsis linearis	desert-willow
Prosopis glandulosa	honey mesquite

Sonoran Desert Scrub

Sonoran Desert Scrub covers most of southwestern Arizona and southeastern California extending into Sonora, Mexico. This region is commonly called the Colorado Desert in California. Trees and large succulents differentiate the Sonoran from the Mojave and Chihuahuan Deserts. The understory may be composed of one to several species of shrubs which form several layers. It is the hottest of the desert scrubs of the southwest. It is found from 100 to 4000 feet in elevation depending on slope and exposure. Rainfall is distinctly bi-seasonal and occurs primarily during the winter. In Arizona the desert scrub has two distinct communities, the creosote bush community and the palo-verde–saguaro community. The palo-verde–saguaro community contains small-leaved desert trees, cacti, and shrubs and is best developed on rocky bajadas or coarse-soiled slopes. This community corresponds to Küchler #42 and #43.

Characteristic Woody Species

Ambrosia dumosa	white burrobush
Bursera microphylla	elephant-tree
Canotia holacantha	crucifixion-thorn
Carnegia gigantea	saguaro
Celtis pallida	shiny hackberry
Holocantha emoryi	thorn-of-Christ
Larrea tridentata	creosote-bush
Olneya tesota	desert-ironwood
Opuntia fulgida	jumping cholla
Pachycereus schottii	senita
Parkinsonia microphylla	yellow palo-verde
Stenocereus thurberi	organ-pipe cactus

Associates

Acacia constricta	mescat wattle
Acacia greggii	long-flower catclaw
Ambrosia deltoidea	triangle burr-ragweed
Atriplex polycarpa	cattle-spinach
Calliandra eriophylla	fairy-duster
Cleome isomeris	bladder-pod spider-flower
Condalia spathulata	squawbush
Echinocereus engelmanii	saints catcus
Encelia farinosa	goldenhills
Ephedra trifurca	long-leaf joint-fir
Eriogonum fasiculatum	eastern Mojave wild buckwheat
Ferocactus cylindraceus	California barrel cactus
Ferocactus wislezenii	candy barrel cactus
Fouguiera splendens	ocotillo
Jatropha cardiophylla	sangre-de-cristo
Krameria grayi	white ratany
Lycium richii	Santa Catalina desert-thorn
Mammillaria grahamii	Graham's nipple cactus
Mammillaria tetrancistra	corkseed catcus

Opuntia bigelovii	teddy-bear cholla
Opuntia echinocarpa	golden cholla
Opuntia engelmannii	catcus-apple
Opuntia kunzei	devil's cholla
Opuntia ramosissima	darning-needle cactus
Opuntia spinosior	walkingstick cactus
Opuntia versicolor	stag-horn cholla
Parkinsonia florida	blue palo-verde
Peucephyllum schottii	Schott's pygmy-cedar
Prosopis velutina	velvet mesquite
Psorothamnus arborescens	Mojave smokebush
Psorothamnus schottii	Schott's smokebush
Psorothamnus spinosus	smokethorn
Salvia vaseyi	bristle sage
Senna armata	desert wild sensitive-plant
Simmondsia chinensis	jojoba
Thamnosma montana	turpentine-broom

Herbaceous Understory

Chaenactis fremontii	morningbride
Emmenanthe penduliflora	yellow whispering-bells
Hilaria rigida	big galleta
Malacothrix glabrata	smooth desert-dandelion
Phacelia distans	distant scorpion-weed
Rafinesquia neomexicana	New Mexico plumseed
Zinnia acerosa	white zinnia

Riparian Trees of Dry Arroyos

Acacia greggi	long-flower catclaw
Baccharis sarothroides	rosinbush
Celtis laevigata	sugar-berry
Chilopsis linearis	desert-willow
Lycium andersonii	red-berry desert-thorn
Olneya tesota	desert-ironwood
Parkinsonia florida	blue palo-verde
Prosopis gladulosa	honey mesqutie
Psorothamnus spinosus	smokethorn
Sapium biloculare	Mexican jumping-bean
Ziziphus obtusifolia	lotebush

WETLAND SYSTEMS

Desert Oasis Woodland

These palm-dominated woodlands are found at the heads or in the bottoms of canyons and arroyos where permanent springs or seeps occur. Oases are found in and around the Salton Basin in the United States and extend into Mexico. The palms are fire tolerant but the understory species are not. Periodic fire opens the understory allowing seedlings to establish. The reduced understory also removes competition for water.

Canopy
Characteristic Species

Washingtonia filifera	California fan palm

Associates

Fraxinus velutina	velvct ash
Platanus racemosa	California sycamore
Populus fremontii	Fremont's cottonwood

Woody Understory

Baccharis sergiloides	squaw's false willow
Isocoma acradenia	alkali jimmyweed
Pluchea sericea	arrow-weed
Prosopis pubescens	American screw-bean
Salix bonplandiana	Bonpland's willow
Salix gooddingii	Goodding's willow

Herbaceous Understory

Distichlis spicata	coastal salt grass
Juncus acutus	spiny rush
Juncus cooperi	Copper's rush
Sporobolus airoides	alkali-sacaton
Typha domingensis	southern cat-tail

Riparian Woodland

Riparian Woodland occurs along perennial streams throughout this region. It is composed of deciduous trees which grow in a relatively narrow band along riparian floodplains.

Canopy
Characteristic Species

Populus fremontii	Fremont's cottonwood

Associates

Acer glabrum	Rocky Mountain maple
Acer negundo	ash-leaf maple
Alnus rhombifolia	white alder
Betula occidentalis	water birch
Fraxinus velutina	velvet ash
Platanus racemosa	California sycamore
Populus balsamifera	balsam popular
Populus tremuloides	quaking aspen
Quercus chrysolepis	canyon live oak
Rubus vitifolius	Pacific dewberry
Salix bonplandiana	Bonpland's willow
Salix geyeriana	Geyer's willow
Salix lasiolepis	arroyo willow
Sambucus cerulea	blue elder

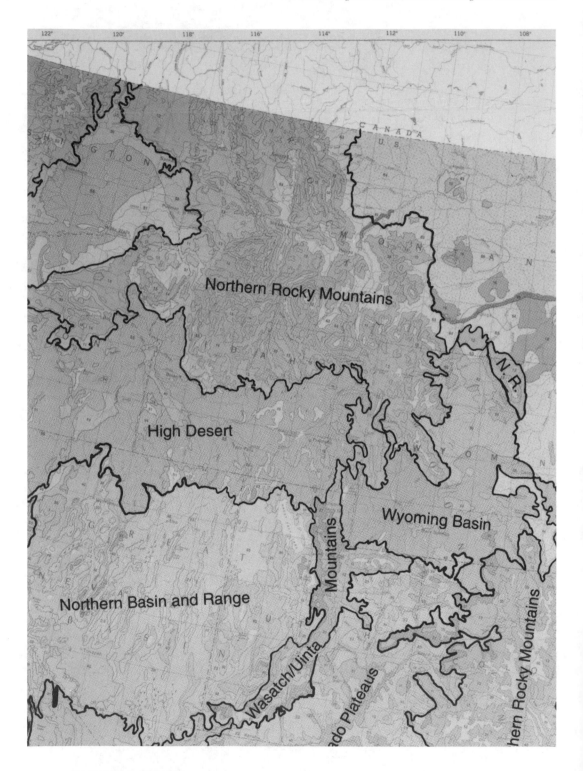

Northern Rocky Mountains

Northern Rocky Mountains

Introduction

The Northern Rocky Mountain region includes mountain ranges in Eastern Washington, Oregon, Idaho, Montana and Wyoming. This region is bounded by the Northern Great Plains to the east, the High Desert to the west and the Wyoming Basin to the south.

The characteristic vegetation of the Northern Rocky Mountain region is conifer forest. There are many conifer forest types in the region. Other vegetation types such as Sagebrush Steppe, Mountain Meadow, and Riparian Forest occur less commonly than the conifer forests.

In this very mountainous region the forest composition changes along environmental gradients often related to altitude. Generally, as the elevation gets higher the temperature drops, precipitation increases, solar and ultraviolet radiations increase, and snow depth and duration increase. Other considerations in mountainous areas include the topographical position. For example, south-facing slopes and ridge tops will generally be warmer and drier than north-facing slopes and sheltered valley bottoms. Soil texture is also an important factor in the type of vegetation that will grow on mountain slopes and in valleys.

The high elevation grassland communities are not included in the descriptions. Groves of aspen trees are also notable in the region but are more common in the Southern Rocky Mountain region (see that region for descriptions).

Intensive livestock grazing and fire management have altered the vegetation throughout the Rocky Mountains.

The primary sources used to develop descriptions and species lists are: Barbour and Billings 1988; Franklin and Dyreness 1973; Green and Conner 1989.

Dominant Ecological Communities

Upland Systems
Western Ponderosa Forest
Douglas-fir Forest
Grand Fir Forest
Hemlock–Pine–Cedar Forest
Western Spruce–Fir Forest
Sagebrush Steppe
Foothills Prairie
Mountain Meadow
Wetland Systems
Riparian Forest

UPLAND SYSTEMS

Western Ponderosa Forest

Western Ponderosa Forest occurs on the lower mountain slopes. At its upper limits Western Ponderosa Forest may grade into Douglas-fir or grand fir dominated forests and at its lower limit it may grade into Sagebrush Steppe. Ponderosa pine occupies relatively dry sites and is subject to periodic fires which regulate the density of the community. Fire also favors the reproduction of grasses in the understory.

Intensive livestock grazing in some cases has slowed the growth of the herbaceous layer and encouraged a shrub layer to develop in the understory. The community corresponds to Küchler #11.

Canopy
Characteristic Species
Pinus ponderosa	ponderosa pine

Associates
Juniperus occidentalis	western juniper
Pinus contorta	lodgepole pine
Populus tremuloides	quaking aspen

Woody Understory
Amelanchier alnifolia	Saskatoon service-berry
Arctostaphylos uva-ursi	red bearberry
Crataegus douglasii	black hawthorn
Eriogonum heracleoides	parsnip-flower wild buckwheat
Holodiscus discolor	hillside oceanspray
Physocarpus malvaceus	mallow-leaf ninebark
Prunus virginiana	choke cherry
Purshia tridentata	bitterbrush
Rosa nutkana	Nootka rose
Rosa woodsii	Woods' rose
Symphoricarpos albus	common snowberry

Herbaceous Understory
Antennaria dimorpha	cushion pussytoes
Arabis holboellii	Holboell's rockcress
Balsamorhiza sagittata	arrow-leaf balsamroot
Calamagrostis rubescens	pinegrass
Carex geyeri	Geyer's sedge
Carex rossii	Ross's sedge
Claytonia perfoliata	miner's-lettuce
Collinsia parviflora	small-flower blue-eyed Mary
Draba cinerea	gray-leaf whitlow-grass
Epilobium brachycarpum	tall annual willowherb
Erigeron compositus	dwarf mountain fleabane
Festuca idahoensis	bluebunch fescue
Frasera albicaulis	white-stemmed elkwood
Galium aparine	sticky-willy
Koeleria macrantha	prairie Koeler's grass
Lithophragma glabrum	bulbous woodlandstar
Lithospermum ruderal	Columbian puccoon
Lotus nevadensis	Nevada bird's-foot-trefoil
Madia exigua	little tar plant
Montia linearis	linear-leaf candy-flower
Poa secunda	curly blue grass
Pseudoroegneria spicata	bluebunch-wheat grass
Ranunculus glaberrimus	sagebrush buttercup
Sisyrinchium douglasii	grasswidows

Stellaria nitens	shining chickweed
Stipa occidentalis	western needle grass
Triteleia grandiflora	large-flower triplet-lily
Vulpia microstachys	small six-weeks grass

Douglas-fir Forest

Douglas-fir Forest occurs in areas higher than Western Ponderosa Forest. These higher areas are more mesic with cooler temperatures and higher annual precipitation. This community corresponds to Küchler #12.

Canopy
Characteristic Species
Pseudotsuga menziesii	Douglas-fir

Associates
Abies concolor	white fir
Larix occidentalis	western larch
Picea glauca	white spruce
Picea pungens	blue spruce
Pinus contorta	lodgepole pine
Pinus ponderosa	ponderosa pine
Populus tremuloides	quaking aspen

Woody Understory
Arctostaphylos uva-ursi	red bearberry
Physocarpus malvaceus	mallow-leaf ninebark
Rosa nutkana	Nootka rose
Rosa woodsii	Woods' rose
Symphoricarpos albus	common snowberry

Herbaceous Understory
Arnica latifolia	daffodil leopard-bane
Calamagrostis rubescens	pinegrass
Carex concinnoides	northwestern sedge
Carex geyeri	Geyer's sedge

Grand Fir Forest

Grand Fir Forest typically occurs at higher elevations than Western Ponderosa and Douglas- fir Forest. They also occur at lower elevations than the subalpine Spruce–Fir Forest. The precipitation in Grand Fir Forest is higher and the temperature is lower than lower elevation forests, which often experience summer dryness and drought. These forests require higher temperatures and lesser accumulations of snow than subalpine forests. This community corresponds to Küchler #14.

Canopy
Characteristic Species
Abies grandis	grand fir
Larix occidentalis	western larch
Pinus contorta	lodgepole pine

Pinus ponderosa	ponderosa pine
Pseudotsuga menziesii	Douglas-fir

Associates

Abies lasiocarpa	subalpine fir
Abies magnifica	California red fir
Calocedrus decurrens	incense-cedar
Picea engelmannii	Engelmann's spruce
Pinus lambertiana	sugar pine
Pinus monticola	western white pine
Tsuga mertensiana	mountain hemlock

Woody Understory

Arctostaphylos nevadensis	pinemat manzanita
Arctostaphylos patula	green-leaf manzanita
Ceanothus velutinus	tobacco-brush
Linnaea borealis	American twinflower
Pachystima myrsinites	myrtle boxleaf
Ribes lacustre	bristly black gooseberry
Rosa gymnocarpa	wood rose
Rubus lasiococcus	hairy-fruit smooth dewberry
Symphoricarpos albus	common snowberry
Vaccinium membranaceum	square-twig blueberry

Herbaceous Understory

Adenocaulon bicolor	American trailplant
Anemone lyallii	little mountain thimbleweed
Anemone piperi	Piper's windflower
Apocynum androsaemifolium	spreading dogbane
Arnica cordifolia	heart-leaf leopard-bane
Asarum caudatum	long-tail wildginger
Bromus vulgaris	Columbian brome
Calamagrostis rubescens	pinegrass
Carex concinnoides	northwestern sedge
Carex geyeri	Geyer's sedge
Carex occidentalis	western sedge
Carex rossii	Ross' sedge
Chimaphila menziesii	little prince's-pine
Chimaphila umbellata	pipsissewa
Clintonia uniflora	bride's bonnet
Corallorhiza maculata	summer coralroot
Cryptantha affinis	quill cat's-eye
Epilobium angustifolium	fireweed
Festuca idahoensis	bluebunch fescue
Fragaria chilosensis	beach strawberry
Fragaria virginiana	Virginia strawberry
Galium triflorum	fragrant bedstraw
Gayophytum humile	dwarf groundsmoke
Hieracium albiflorum	white-flower hawkweed

Listera convallariodes	broad-tip twayblade
Lupinus caudatus	Kellogg's spurred lupine
Lupinus latifolius	broad-leaf lupine
Maianthemum stellatum	starry Solomon's-seal
Mitella stauropetala	side-flower bishop's-cap
Moehringia macrophylla	big-leaf grove-sandwort
Monotropa hypopithys	many-flower Indian-pipe
Orthilia secunda	sidebells
Poa nervosa	Hooker's blue grass
Pyrola asariflia	pink wintergreen
Pyrola picta	white-vein wintergreen
Elymus elymoides	western bottle-brush grass
Stipa occidentalis	western needle grass
Thalictrum occidentale	western meadow-rue
Trillium ovatum	western wakerobin
Viola glabella	pioneer violet

Hemlock–Pine–Cedar Forest

Hemlock–Pine–Cedar Forest occurs throughout the Northern Rocky Mountain region. This community corresponds to Küchler #13.

Canopy
Characteristic Species
Pinus monticola	western white pine
Thuja plicata	western arborvitae (cedar)
Tsuga heterophylla	western hemlock

Associates
Abies grandis	grand fir
Larix occidentalis	western larch
Pinus ponderosa	ponderosa pine
Pseudotsuga menziesii	Douglas-fir

Woody Understory
Oplopanax horridus	devil's-club
Pachystima myrsinites	myrtle boxleaf
Vaccinium membranaceum	square-twig blueberry

Herbaceous Understory
Athyrium filix-femina	subarctic lady fern
Clintonia uniflora	bride's bonnet
Dryopteris campyloptera	mountain wood fern
Gymnocarpium dryopteris	western oak-fern
Tiarella trifoliata	three-leaf foam flower

Western Spruce–Fir Forest

Western Spruce–Fir Forest may be bounded at its lower limits by hemlock, western red cedar, grand fir, or Douglas-fir. This Spruce–Fir Forest reaches its upper limit in a subalpine environment where the trees thin out and become a forest-meadow parkland. This community corresponds to Küchler #15.

Canopy
Characteristic Species
Abies lasiocarpa	subalpine fir
Picea engelmannii	Engelmann's spruce
Pinus contorta	lodgepole pine

Associates
Abies grandis	grand fir
Larix lyallii	subalpine larch
Larix occidentalis	western larch
Pinus albicaulis	white-bark pine
Pinus monticola	western white pine
Populus tremuloides	quaking aspen
Pseudotsuga menziesii	Douglas-fir
Tsuga mertensiana	mountain hemlock

Woody Understory
Acer glabrum	Rocky Mountain maple
Amelachier alnifolia	Saskatoon service-berry
Arctostaphylos uva-ursi	red bearberry
Juniperus communis	common juniper
Ledum glandulosum	glandular Labrador tea
Menziesia ferruginea	fool's-huckleberry
Rhododendron albiflorum	cascade azalea
Rubus parviflorus	western thimble-berry
Shepherdia canadensis	russet buffalo-berry
Symphoricarpos albus	common snowberry
Vaccinium cespitosum	dwarf blueberry
Vaccinium membranaceum	square-twig blueberry
Vaccinium scoparium	grouseberry

Herbaceous Understory
Actaea rubra	red baneberry
Adenocaulon bicolor	American trailplant
Arnica cordifolia	heart-leaf leopard-bane
Aster conspicuus	eastern showy aster
Calamagrostis canadensis	blue joint
Clintonia uniflora	bride's bonnet
Coptis occidentalis	Idaho goldthread
Galium triflorum	fragrant bedstraw
Hieracium albiflorum	white-flower hawkweed
Mitella stauropetala	side-flower bishop's-cap
Moehringia macrophylla	big-leaf grove-sandwort
Viola glabella	pioneer violet
Xerophyllum tenax	western turkeybeard

Sagebrush Steppe

Sagebrush Steppe is the driest community in this region. Big sagebrush is the most characteristic species. Changes in dominance are probably a result of grazing, fire, or cultivation. Fire within the Sagebrush Steppe community has increased since an exotic, cheatgrass (*Bromus tectorum*), has become dominant. This community corresponds to Küchler #55.

Characteristic Woody Species
Artemisia tridentata	big sagebrush

Associates
Artemisia arbuscula	dwarf sagebrush
Artemisia nova	black sagebrush
Artemisia tripartita	three-tip sagebrush
Chrysothamnus nauseosus	rubber rabbitbrush
Chrysothamnus viscidiflorus	green rabbitbrush
Grayia spinosa	spiny hop-sage
Juniperus occidentalis	western juniper
Purshia tridentata	bitterbrush
Tetradymia canescens	spineless horsebrush

Herbaceous Understory
Balsamorrhiza sagittata	arrow-leaf balsamroot
Elymus elymoides	western bottle-brush grass
Festuca idahoensis	bluebunch fescue
Lappula occidentalis	flat-spine sheepburr
Lithospermum ruderale	Columbian puccoon
Lupinus sericeus	Pursh's silky lupine
Oryzopsis hymenoides	Indian mountain rice grass
Poa fendleriana	mutton grass
Poa secunda	curly blue grass
Pseudoroegneria spicata	bluebunch-wheat grass
Stipa comata	needle-and-thread
Stipa thurberiana	Thurber's needle grass

Foothills Prairie

Foothills Prairie is characterized by perennial bunchgrasses. This community depends on a greater degree of moisture than Sagebrush Steppe and usually occurs at higher altitudes than the sagebrush communities. Excessive grazing in the area has resulted in a replacement of the native perennial bunchgrasses with *Artemisia* and *Bromus* species. This community corresponds to Küchler #63.

Characteristic Species
Festuca campestris	prairie fescue
Festuca idahoensis	bluebunch fescue
Leymus condensatus	giant lyme grass
Poa secunda	curly blue grass
Pseudoroegneria spicata	bluebunch-wheat grass
Stipa comata	needle-and-thread grass

Associates
Artemisa frigida	prairie sagebrush
Astragalus spaldingii	Spalding's milk-vetch
Bouteloua gracilis	blue grama
Carex filifolia	thread-leaf sedge
Chrysothamnus nauseosus	rubber rabbitbrush
Koeleria macrantha	prairie Koeler's grass
Lappula occidentalis	flat-spine sheepburr
Lithophragma glabrum	bulbous woodlandstar
Lupinus sericeus	Pursh's silky lupine
Montia linearis	linear-leaf candy-flower
Pascopyrum smithii	western-wheat grass
Phlox gracilis	slender phlox
Phlox longifolia	long-leaf phlox
Plantago patagonica	woolly plantain
Stellaria nitens	shiny starwort
Vulpia microstachys	small six-weeks grass

Mountain Meadow

Mountain Meadow is a permanent herbaceous community type found on relatively gentle topography along and near the heads of stream courses. In many areas grazing pressure has deteriorated the meadow communities from a perennial grass climax into a weedy annual community.

Characteristic Species
Deschampsia cespitosa	tufted hair grass

Associates
Aster occidentalis	western mountain aster
Festuca rubra	red fescue
Juncus balticus	Baltic rush
Polygonum bistortoides	American bistort

WETLAND SYSTEMS

Riparian Forest

Riparian Forest occurs at low elevations in canyons and along streams in the Northern Rocky Mountains region. This is the least typical forest type of the region.

Canopy
Characteristic Species
Populus angustifolia	narrow-leaf cottonwood
Populus balsamifera	balsam poplar

Herbaceous Understory
Aralia nudicaulis	wild sarsaparilla

Carex sprengelii	long-beak sedge
Ranunculus abortivus	kidney-leaf buttercup
Ratibida pinnata	gray-head Mexican-hat

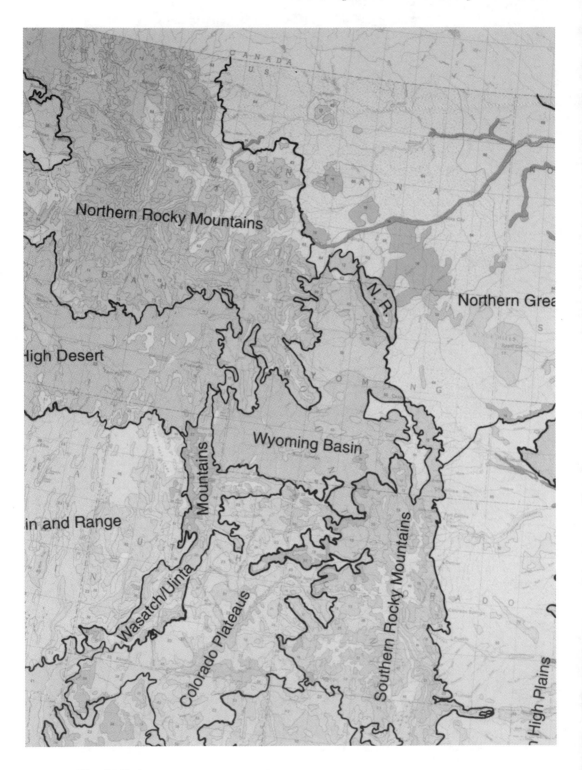

Wyoming Basin

Wyoming Basin

Introduction

The Wyoming Basin region occurs between the northern and southern Rocky Mountains. This region encompasses several major basins including the Big Horn, Wind River, Bridger, and Shirley Basins. The altitudes of the Wyoming Basin region are mostly between 6000 and 8000 feet above sea level. The basins are interrupted by mountains, buttes, river valleys, and badlands.

The characteristic vegetation is sagebrush and short grasses. Saltbush, greasewood, and mountain-mahogany are also common in specific sites. River floodplains support vegetation characterized by cottonwood, willow, and alder. Although shrub and grasslands are the most common vegetation types, there are also islands of forests in the mountains. A large portion of the region's floodplains has been converted to agriculture uses. Throughout the Wyoming Basin natural areas have been altered by livestock grazing and the introduction of exotic species.

The primary sources used to develop descriptions and species lists are: Barbour and Billings 1988; Knight et al. 1976; Wyoming Nature Conservancy 1991.

Dominant Ecological Communities

Upland Systems
Sagebrush Steppe
Greasewood Scrub
Saltbush Scrub
Mountain-Mahogany Shrub
Shrub Grassland
Wetland Systems
Floodplain Forest

UPLAND SYSTEMS

Sagebrush Steppe

Sagebrush Steppe is widespread throughout the Wyoming Basin. On drier sites the sagebrush may be dwarfed, while on more mesic sites, it may be tall. Sagebrush Steppe may be separated based on plant height. This community corresponds to Küchler #55.

Characteristic Woody Species
Artemisia arbuscula	dwarf sagebrush
Artemisia tridentata	big sagebrush

Associates
Amelanchier alnifolia	Saskatoon service-berry
Artemisia cana	hoary sagebrush
Artemisia frigida	prairie sagebrush
Artemisia nova	black sagebrush
Artemisia pedatifida	bird-foot sagebrush
Artemisia tripartita	three-tip sagebrush

Atriplex canescens	four-wing saltbush
Atriplex confertifolia	shadscale
Atriplex gardneri	Gardner's saltbush
Chrysothamnus nauseosus	rubber rabbitbrush
Chrysothamnus viscidiflorus	green rabbitbrush
Eriogonum microthecum	slender wild buckwheat
Grayia spinosa	spiny hop-sage
Gutierrezia sarothrae	kindlingweed
Krascheninnikovia lanata	winterfat
Opuntia polyacantha	hair-spine prickly-pear
Ribes cereum	white squaw currant
Tetradymia canescens	spineless horsebrush
Tetradymia spinosa	short-spine horsebrush

Herbaceous Understory

Agoseris glauca	pale goat-chicory
Allium acuminatum	taper-tip onion
Allium textile	wild white onion
Alyssum desertorum	desert madwort
Antennaria dimorpha	cushion pussytoes
Antennaria rosea	rosy pussytoes
Arabis holboellii	Holboell's rockcress
Arabis lignifera	Owens valley rockcress
Arabis sparsiflora	elegant rockcress
Arenaria hookeri	Hooker's sandwort
Artemisia ludoviciana	white sagebrush
Astragalus miser	timber milk-vetch
Astragalus pectinatus	narrow-leaf milk-vetch
Astragalus purshii	Pursh's milk-vetch
Astragalus spatulatus	tufted milk-vetch
Atriplex powellii	Powell's orache
Balsamorhiza incana	hoary balsamroot
Balsamorhiza sagittata	arrow-leaf balsamroot
Calochortus nuttallii	sego-lily
Carex duriuscula	spike-rush sedge
Carex filifolia	thread-leaf sedge
Carex obtusata	blunt sedge
Castilleja angustifolia	northwestern Indian-paintbrush
Chenopodium leptophyllum	narrow-leaf goosefoot
Comandra umbellata	bastard-toadflax
Cordylanthus ramosus	bushy bird's-beak
Crepis modocensis	siskiyou hawk's-beard
Cryptantha watsonii	Watson's cat's-eye
Delphinium bicolor	flat-head larkspur
Delphinium geyeri	Geyer's larkspur
Descurainia incana	mountain tansy-mustard
Distichilis spicta	coastal salt grass
Elymus elymoides	western bottle-brush grass
Elymus lanceolatus	streamside wild rye
Elymus trachycaulus	slender rye grass

Erigeron caespitosus	tufted fleabane
Erigeron engelmanni	Engelmann's fleabane
Eriogonum caespitosum	matted wild buckwheat
Eriogonum cernuum	nodding wild buckwheat
Eriogonum compositum	arrow-leaf wild buckwheat
Eriogonum ovalifolium	cushion wild buckwheat
Festuca idahoensis	bluebunch fescue
Gayophytum ramosissimum	pinyon groundsmoke
Halogeton glomeratus	saltlover
Hilaria jamesii	Jame's galleta
Hordeum jubatum	fox-tail barley
Hymenoxys richardsonii	Colorado rubberweed
Iva axillaris	deer-root
Juncus balticus	Baltic rush
Koeleria macrantha	prairie Koeler's grass
Lappula occidentalis	flat-spine sheepburr
Leptodactylon pungens	granite prickly-phlox
Lesquerella ludoviciana	Louisiana bladderpod
Leymus cinereus	Great Basin lyme grass
Lithospermum incisum	fringed gromwell
Lomatium foeniculaceum	carrot-leaf desert-parsley
Lupinus argenteus	silver-stem lupine
Machaeranthera canescens	hoary tansy-aster
Mertensia oblongifolia	languid-lady
Monolepis nuttalliana	Nuttall's poverty-weed
Musineon divaricatum	leafy wild parsley
Oryzopsis hymenoides	Indian mountain-rice grass
Pascopyrum smithii	western-wheat grass
Penstemon arenicola	red desert beardtongue
Penstemon fremontii	Fremont's beardtongue
Phlox hoodii	carpet phlox
Phlox longifolia	long-leaf phlox
Phlox multiflora	Rocky Mountain phlox
Poa fendleriana	mutton grass
Poa secunda	curly bluegrass
Polygonum douglasii	Douglas' knotweed
Pseudocymopterus montanus	alpine false mountain-parsley
Pseudoroegneria spicata	bluebunch-wheat grass
Sphaeralcea coccinea	scarlet globe-mallow
Stenotus acaulis	stemless mock goldenweed
Stipa comata	needle-and-thread
Stipa lettermani	Letterman's needle-grass
Stipa nelsonii	Nelson's needle grass
Thelypodiopsis elegans	westwater tumble-mustard
Thermopsis rhombifolia	prairie golden-banner
Trifolium gymnocarpon	holly-leaf clover
Vulpia octoflora	eight-flower six-weeks grass
Xylorhiza glabriuscula	smooth woody-aster
Zigadenus paniculatus	sand-corn
Zigadenus venenosus	meadow deathcamas

Greasewood Scrub

Greasewood Shrub is found throughout the Wyoming Basin in moist depressions frequently associated with floodplains and ponds. These flatlands are characterized by poor drainage and salt accumulations. Because Greasewood Scrub occurs near sources of water, many of these areas have been damaged by livestock as they find their way to the ponds associated with this vegetation type. This community corresponds in part to Küchler #40.

Characteristic Woody Species

Atriplex confertifolia	shadscale
Sarcobatus vermiculatus	greasewood

Associates

Artemisia spinescens	bud sagebrush
Artemisia tridentata	big sagebrush
Atriplex gardneri	Gardner's saltbush
Chrysothamnus nauseosus	rubber rabbitbrush
Grayia spinosa	spiny hop-sage
Krascheninnikovia lanata	winterfat
Opuntia polyacantha	hair-spine prickly-pear
Suaeda moquinii	shrubby seepweed
Tetradymia spinosa	short-spine horsebrush

Herbaceous Understory

Allium textile	wild white onion
Atriplex patula	halberd-leaf orache
Atriplex argentea	silverscale
Bouteloua gracilis	blue grama
Chamaesyce serphyllifolia	thyme-leaf sandmat
Chenopodium dessicatum	arid-land goosefoot
Crepis occidentalis	large-flower hawk's-beard
Descurainia pinnata	western tansy mustard
Dodecatheon pulchellum	dark-throated shootingstar
Elymus elymoides	western bottle-brush grass
Erigeron pumilus	shaggy fleabane
Festuca brachyphylla	short-leaf fescue
Halogeton glomeratus	saltlover
Helianthus petilolaris	prairie sunflower
Hordeum jubatum	foxtail barley
Hordeum pusillum	little barley
Hymenoxys richardsonii	Colorado rubberweed
Ipomopsis pumila	spike skyrocket
Iris missouriensis	Rocky Mountain iris
Iva axillaris	deer-root
Juncus balticus	Baltic rush
Lappula occidentalis	flat-spine sheepburr
Lepidium desiflorum	miner's pepperwort
Machaeranthera canescens	hoary tansy-aster
Machaeranthera tanacetifolia	takhoka-daisy
Monolepis nuttalliana	Nuttall's poverty-weed

Monroa squarrosa	false buffalo grass
Nassella viridula	green tussock
Oenothera pallida	white-pole evening-primrose
Pascopyrum smithii	western-wheat grass
Plantago eriopoda	red-woolly plantain
Plantago patagonica	woolly plantain
Poa secunda	curly blue grass
Puccinellia nuttalliana	Nuttall's alkali grass
Salicornia rubra	red saltwort
Schoenocrambe linifolium	Solomn River plains-mustard
Scirpus acutus	hard-stem bulrush
Spartina gracilis	alkali cord-grass
Sporobolus airoides	alkali-sacaton
Triglochin maritimum	seaside arrow-grass
Triglochin palustris	marsh arrow-grass
Vulpia octoflora	cight-flowered six-weeks grass

Saltbush Scrub

Saltbush Scrub occurs in the drier parts of the Wyoming Basin on old lake beds that are only wet in the spring. They are the most desert-like of all the plant communities in this region. Soils are characteristically dry and alkaline. This community corresponds in part to Küchler #40.

Characteristic Woody Species
Atriplex confertifolia	shadscale
Atriplex gardneri	Gardner's saltbush

Associates
Artemisia spinescens	bud sagebrush
Opuntia polyacantha	hair-spine prickly-pear
Sarcobatus vermiculatus	greasewood

Herbaceous Understory
Chenopodium atrovirens	pinyon goosefoot
Cymopterus bulbosus	bulbous spring-parsley
Elymus elymoides	western bottle-brush grass
Eriogonum cernuum	nodding buckwheat
Halogeton glomeratus	saltlover
Hordeum jubatum	foxtail barley
Oxyzopsis hymenoides	Indian mountain-rice grass
Pascopyrum smithii	western-wheat grass
Poa secunda	curly blue grass
Thelypodiopsis elegans	westwater tumble-mustard

Mountain-Mahogany Shrub

Mountain-Mahogany Shrub occurs in the foothills of most mountain ranges in and adjacent to the Wyoming Basin. This community corresponds to Küchler #37.

Characteristic Woody Species

Cercocarpus montanus	alder-leaf mountain-mahogany
Cercocarpus ledifolius	curl-leaf mountain-mahogany
Quercus gambelii	Gambel's oak

Associates

Acer grandidentatum	canyon maple
Amelanchier alnifolia	Saskatoon service-berry
Amelanchier utahensis	Utah service-berry
Artemisia frigida	prairie sagebrush
Artemisia tridentata	big sagebrush
Ceanothus velutinus	tobacco-brush
Chrysothamnus nauseosus	rubber rabbitbrush
Chrysothamnus parryi	Parry's rabbitbrush
Chrysothamnus viscidiflorus	green rabbitbrush
Erigonum umbellatum	sulphur-flower wild buckwheat
Fallugia paradoxa	Apache-plume
Gutierrezia sarothrae	kindlingweed
Juniperus scopulorum	Rocky Mountain juniper
Juniperus osteosperma	Utah juniper
Krascheninnikovia lanata	winterfat
Pachystima myrsinites	myrtle boxleaf
Physocarpus malvaceus	mallow-leaf ninebark
Purshia mexicana	Mexican cliff-rose
Purshia tridentata	bitterbrush
Quercus havardii	Harvard's oak
Quercus turbinella	shrub live oak
Rhus trilobata	ill-scented sumac
Symphoricarpos albus	common snowberry

Herbaceous Understory

Antennaria rosea	rosy pussytoes
Besseya wyomingensis	Wyoming coraldrops
Carex duriuscula	spike-rush sedge
Cerastium arvense	field mouse-ear chickweed
Chenopodium leptophyllum	narrow-leaf goosefoot
Delphinium nuttallianum	two-love larkspur
Descurainia pinnata	western tansy-mustard
Elymus lanceolatus	streamside wild rye
Elymus trachycaulis	slender rye grass
Erigeron poliospermus	purple cushion fleabane
Festuca idahoensis	bluebunch fescue
Festuca kingii	King's fescue
Galium boreale	northern bedstraw
Grindelia squarrosa	curly-cup gumweed
Harbouria trachypleura	whiskybroom-parsley
Hedeoma drummondii	Drummond's false pennyroyal
Heuchera parvifolia	little-flower alumroot
Koeleria macrantha	prairie Koeler's grass
Lesquerella argentea	bladderpod
Linum lewisii	prairie flax

Mertensia lanceolata	prairie bluebells
Muhlenbergia filiculmis	slim-stem muhly
Orobanche ludoviciana	Louisiana broom-rape
Oryzopsis hymenoides	Indian mountain-rice grass
Pascopyrum smithii	western-wheat grass
Phlox multiflora	Rocky Mountain phlox
Pseudoroegneria spicatum	bluebunch-wheat grass
Stipa comata	needle-and-thread

Shrub Grassland

Shrub Grassland occurs in the foothills of the mountains above 7000 feet. Shrub Grassland requires a more moist environment than the shrublands in the lower areas. It is a community of short grasses and scattered small shrubs. This community corresponds to Küchler #56.

Characteristic Woody Species
Artemisia frigida	prairie sagebrush

Associates
Atriplex gardneri	Gardner's saltbush
Chrysothamnus vaseyi	Vasey's rabbitbrush
Chrysothamnus viscidiflorus	green rabbitbrush
Gutierrezia sarothrae	kindlingweed
Krascheninnikovia lanata	winterfat
Opuntia polyacantha	hair-spine prickly-pear
Pediocactus simpsonii	snowball cactus
Tetradymia canescens	spineless horsebrush

Herbaceous Understory
Allium textile	white wild onion
Arabis holboellii	Holboell's rockcress
Arenaria hookeri	Hooker's sandwort
Astragalus adsurgens	standing milk-vetch
Astragalus purshii	Pursh's milk-vetch
Astragalus spatulatus	tufted milk-vetch
Bouteloua gracilis	blue grama
Calamovilfa longifolia	prairie sand-reed
Carex duriuscula	spike-rush sedge
Carex filifolia	thread-leaf sedge
Cymopterus montanus	mountain spring-parsley
Erigeron nematophyllus	needle-leaf fleabane
Eriogonum flavum	alpine golden wild buckwheat
Eriogonum ovalifolium	cushion wild buckwheat
Ipomopsis spicata	spiked skyrocket
Koeleria macrantha	prairie Koeler's grass
Lesquerella ludoviciana	Lousisana bladderpod
Lygodesmia juncea	rushn skeleton-plant
Machaeranthera canescens	hoary tansy-aster
Orobanche fasciculata	clustered broom rape
Oryzopsis hymenoides	Indian mountain-rice grass

Oxytropis lagopus	hare-foot locoweed
Paronychia sessiliflora	low nailwort
Pascopyrum smithii	western-wheat grass
Penstemon angustifolius	broad-beard beardtongue
Poa secunda	curly blue grass
Polygonum douglasii	Douglas' knotweed
Pseudoroegneria spicata	bluebunch-wheat grass
Senecio canus	silver-woolly ratwort
Sphaeralcea coccinea	scarlet globe-mallow
Stenotus acaulis	stemless mock goldenweed
Trifolium gymnocarpon	holly-leaf clover

WETLAND SYSTEMS

Floodplain Forest

Floodplain Forest is commonly associated with rivers throughout the Wyoming Basin. Cottonwood is the most common tree species although blue spruce may be found at higher elevations. Alder thickets and meadows occur where the canopy is more open.

Canopy
Characteristic Species

Betula occidentalis	water birch
Populus angustifolia	narrow-leaf cottonwood

Associates

Alnus incana	speckled alder
Juniperus osteosperma	Utah juniper
Picea pungens	blue spruce

Woody Understory

Cornus stolonifera	redosier
Elaeagnus commutata	American silver-berry
Prunus virginiana	choke cherry
Salix drummondiana	Drummond's willow
Salix exigua	sandbar willow
Salix geyeriana	Geyer's willow
Salix monticola	mountain willow

Herbaceous Understory

Agrostis scabra	rough bent
Artemisia ludoviciana	white sagebrush
Glycyrrhiza lepidota	American licorice
Hordeum jubatum	fox-tail barley
Juncus balticus	Baltic rush
Mentha arvensis	American wild mint
Oryzopsis hymenoides	Indian mountain-rice grass
Rumex maritimus	golden dock
Sporobolus airoides	alkali-sacaton

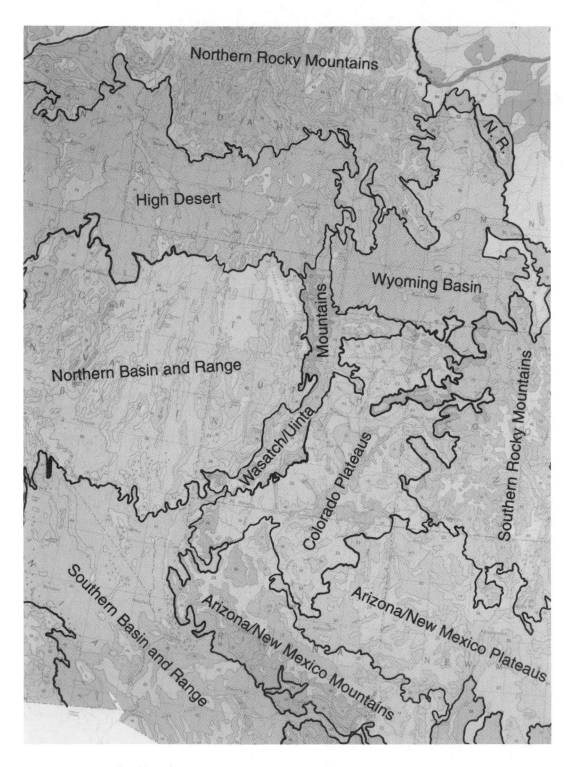

Wasatch/Uinta Mountains

Wasatch/Uinta Mountains

Introduction

The Wasatch and Uinta Mountains form a north/south ridge of high mountains between the Northern Basin and Range and the Colorado Plateau. The high elevation of these mountains creates a mesic environment supporting forests similar to the forests in the Northern Rocky Mountains. The southern part of the region supports communities that are closely related to the vegetation of the Colorado Plateaus and the Arizona and New Mexico mountains to the south.

The primary sources used to develop descriptions and species lists are: Barbour and Billings 1988; Cronquist et al. 1972.

Dominant Ecological Communities

Upland Systems
Douglas-fir Forest
Western Spruce–Fir Forest
Spruce–Fir–Douglas-fir Forest
Ponderosa Pine Forest
Aspen–Lodgepole Pine Forest
Mountain-Mahogany–Oak Scrub
Juniper–Pinyon Woodland
Mountain Sagebrush
Dry Mountain Meadow
Wheat grass–Blue grass Prairie
Wetland Systems
Wet Mountain Meadow

UPLAND SYSTEMS

Douglas-fir Forest

Douglas-fir Forest occurs in the Wasatch and Uinta Mountains in high areas on mesic sites. This forest type is very similar to Douglas-fir Forest in the Northern Rocky Mountains and in the Front Range of the Southern Rocky Mountains. This community corresponds to Küchler #12.

Canopy
Characteristic Species

Pseudotsuga menziesii	Douglas-fir

Associates

Abies concolor	white fir
Larix occidentalis	western larch
Picea glauca	white spruce
Picea pungens	blue spruce
Pinus contorta	lodgepole pine

Pinus ponderosa	ponderosa pine
Populus tremuloides	quaking aspen

Woody Understory

Arctostaphylos uva-ursi	red bearberry
Physocarpus malvaceus	mallow-leaf ninebark
Rosa nutkana	Nootka rose
Rosa woodsii	Woods' rose
Symphoricarpos albus	common snowberry

Herbaceous Understory

Arnica latifolia	daffodil leopard-bane
Calamagrostis rubescens	pinegrass
Carex concinnoides	northwestern sedge
Carex geyeri	Geyer's sedge

Western Spruce–Fir Forest

Western Spruce–Fir Forest, dominated by subalpine fir and Englemann spruce, occurs throughout the Wasatch and Uinta Mountains and throughout the entire Rocky Mountain area at high altitudes. Aspen is also abundant within the areas supporting spruce–fir forests. This community corresponds to Küchler #15.

Canopy

Characteristic Species

Abies lasiocarpa	subalpine fir
Picea engelmannii	Engelmann's spruce

Associates

Pinus albicaulis	white-bark pine
Pinus contorta	lodgepole pine
Pinus flexilis	limber pine
Pinus longaeva	Intermountain bristle-cone pine
Populus tremuloides	quaking aspen
Pseudotsuga menziesii	Douglas-fir

Woody Understory

Arctostaphylos uva-ursi	red bearberry
Shepherdia canadensis	russet buffalo-berry
Symphoricarpos albus	common snowberry
Vaccinium myrtillus	whortle-berry
Vaccinium scoparium	grouseberry
Viburnum edule	squashberry

Herbaceous Understory

Arnica cordifolia	heart-leaf leopard-bane
Calamagrostis canadensis	blue joint
Orthilia secunda	sidebells
Polemonium pulcherrimum	beautiful Jacob's ladder
Xerophyllum tenax	western turkeybeard

Spruce–Fir–Douglas-fir Forest

In the southern part of the region, Douglas-fir becomes mixed, and shares dominance with white fir and blue spruce. This forest type occurs at elevations between 8000 and 10000 feet. Within these communities, there may be areas dominated by aspen. This community corresponds to Küchler #20.

Canopy
Characteristic Species

Abies concolor	white fir
Picea pungens	blue spruce
Pseudotsuga menziesii	Douglas-fir

Associates

Populus angustifolia	narrow-leaf cottonwood
Populus tremuloides	quaking aspen

Woody Understory

Acer glabrum	Rocky Mountain maple
Amelanchier alnifolia	Saskatoon service-berry
Betula occidentalis	water birch
Ceanothus fendleri	Fendler's buckbrush
Cornus sericea	redosier
Holodiscus dumosa	glandular oceanspray
Juniperus communis	common juniper
Mahonia repens	creeping Oregon-grape
Pachystima myrsinites	myrtle boxleaf
Physocarpus malvaceus	mallow-leaf ninebark
Prunus virginiana	choke cherry
Ribes cereum	white squaw currant
Ribes montigenum	western prickly gooseberry
Salix lutea	yellow willow
Salix scouleriana	Scouler's willow
Sambucus cerulea	blue elder
Shepherdia canadensis	russet buffalo-berry
Sorbus scopulina	Cascade Mountain-ash
Symphoricarpos oreophilus	mountain snowberry

Herbaceous Understory

Aconitum columbianum	Columbian monkshood
Angelica pinnata	small-leaf angelica
Aquilegia coerulea	Colorado blue columbine
Aquilegia formosa	crimson columbine
Arnica cordifolia	heart-leaf leopard-bane
Bromus marginatus	large mountain brome
Cardamine cordifolia	large mountain bittercress
Castilleja miniata	great red Indian-paintbrush
Corallorrhiza maculata	summer coralroot
Delphinium occidentale	dunce-cap larkspur
Dracocephalum parvifolium	American dragonhead
Elymus glaucus	blue wild rye

Frageria vesca	woodland strawberry
Ipomopsis aggregata	scarlet skyrocket
Mimulus guttatus	seep monkey-flower
Mitella stauropetala	side-flower bishop's cap
Monardella odoratissima	alpine mountainbalm
Osmorhiza depauperata	blunt-fruit sweet-cicely
Polemonium foliosissimum	towering Jacob's ladder
Pseudoroegneria spicata	bluebunch-wheat grass
Pseudostellaria jamesiana	sticky-starwort
Rudbeckia occidentalis	western coneflower
Scrophularia lanceolata	lance-leaf figwort
Silene douglasii	seabluff catchfly
Stipa lettermanii	Letterman's needle grass
Stipa nelsonii	Nelson's needle grass
Thalictrum fendleri	Fendler's meadow-rue
Veronica americana	American-brooklime

Ponderosa Pine Forest

Ponderosa Pine Forest occurs at low elevations in the Wasatch and Uinta Mountains. Ponderosa Pine Forest is often similar to woodlands, with an open canopy and a grassy understory. In higher areas ponderosa pine may form dense stands. The characteristic grassy understory of Ponderosa Pine Forest is highly flammable during dry summers. Suppression of wildfires and the introduction of cattle onto Ponderosa Pine Forest changed the species composition and the forest structure by increasing the shrub and understory species.

Canopy
Characteristic Species
Pinus ponderosa	ponderosa pine

Associates
Pinus cembroides	Mexican pinyon
Pinus flexilis	limber pine
Pinus leiophylla	Chihuahuan pine
Populus tremuloides	quaking aspen
Pseudotsuga menziesii	Douglas-fir
Quercus gambelii	Gambel's oak

Woody Understory
Arctostaphylos patula	green-leaf manzanita
Artemisia nova	black sagebrush
Artemisia tridentata	big sagebrush
Ceanothus fendleri	Fendler's buckbrush
Chamaebatiaria millefolium	fernbush
Chrysothamnus parryi	Parry's rabbitbrush
Fallugia paradoxa	Apache-plume
Fendlerella utahensis	Utah-fendlerbush
Holodiscus boursieri	Boursier's oceanspray
Holodiscus dumosus	glandular oceanspray
Jamesia americana	five-petal cliffbush

Juniperus communis	common juniper
Mahonia repens	creeping Oregon-grape
Pachystima myrsinites	myrtle boxleaf
Philadelphus microphyllus	little-leaf mock orange
Physocarpus monogynus	mountain ninebark
Purshia mexicana	Mexican cliff-rose
Ribes cereum	white squaw currant
Robinia neomexicana	New Mexico locust
Rubus idaeus	common red raspberry

Herbaceous Understory

Artemisia ludoviciana	white sagebrush
Blepharoneuron tricholepis	pine-dropseed
Bothriochloa barbinodis	cane beard grass
Bouteloua gracilis	blue grama
Bromus spp.	brome
Comandra umbellata	bastard toadflax
Elymus elymoides	western bottle-brush grass
Festuca arizonica	Arizona fescue
Hedeoma dentatum	Arizona false pennyroyal
Iris missouriensis	Rocky Mountain iris
Koeleria macrantha	prairie Koeler's grass
Lupinus palmeri	Palmer's lupine
Monarda fistulosa	Oswego-tea
Muhlenbergia montana	mountain muhly
Muhlenbergia wrightii	Wright's muhly
Oxytropis lamberti	stemless locoweed
Pteridium aquilinum	northern bracken fern
Sphaeralcea fendleri	thicket globe-mallow
Thalictrum fendleri	Fendler's meadow-rue
Thermopsis rhombifolia	prairie golden-banner
Vicia americana	American purple vetch

Aspen–Lodgepole Pine Forest

Aspen–Lodgepole Pine Forest occurs on mountain slopes, generally between 8000 and 10000 feet. Aspen is common in both the Wasatch and Uinta Mountains, but only small areas of lodgepole pine are represented in the Wasatch Range. Aspen and lodgepole pine establish and grow well in areas that have burned although they are not exclusive to burned areas.

Canopy
Characteristic Species

Pinus contorta	lodgepole pine
Populus tremuloides	quaking aspen

Associates

Pinus flexilis	limber pine
Pseudotsuga menziesii	Douglas-fir

Woody Understory

Acer grandidentatum	canyon maple
Arctostaphylos uva-ursi	red bearberry
Arnica cordifolia	heart-leaf leopard-bane
Ceanothus velutinus	tobacco-brush
Mahonia repens	creeping Oregon grape
Pachystima myrsinites	myrtle boxleaf
Rubus parviflorus	western thimble-berry
Sambucus cerulea	blue elder
Shepherdia canadensis	russet buffalo-berry

Herbaceous Understory

Hydrophyllum capitatum	cat's breeches
Nemophila breviflora	Great Basin baby-blue-eyes
Penstemon subglaber	Utah smooth beardtongue
Phacelia sericea	purplefringe
Poa fendleriana	mutton grass
Pyrola asarifolia	pink wintergreen
Scrophularia lanceolata	lance-leaf figwort
Solidago spathulata	coastal-dune goldenrod
Thalictrum fendleri	Fendler's meadow rue
Wyethia amplexicaulis	northern mule's-ears

Mountain-Mahogany–Oak Scrub

Mountain-Mahogany–Oak Scrub occurs in the Wasatch and Uinta Mountains at elevations between 5000 and 9000 feet. Mountain-mahogany, Gambel's oak, and canyon maple are the dominant species. Unlike most upland forest types in this region, the dominants are deciduous. On some sites, understory shrubs form dense thickets. This community corresponds to Küchler #37.

Characteristic Woody Species

Acer grandidentatum	canyon maple
Cercocarpus ledifolius	curl-leaf mountain-mahogany
Quercus gambelii	Gambel's oak

Associates

Acer glabrum	Rocky Mountain maple
Acer negundo	ash-leaf maple
Amelanchier alnifolia	Saskatoon service-berry
Amelanchier utahensis	Utah service-berry
Arctostaphylos spp.	manzanita
Artemisia nova	black sagebrush
Artemisia tridentata	big sagebrush
Betula occidentalis	water birch
Ceanothus fendleri	Fendler's buckbrush
Ceanothus velutinus	tobacco-brush
Cercocarpus montanus	alder-leaf mountain-mahogany
Chrysothamnus viscidiflorus	green rabbitbrush
Fallugia paradoxa	Apache-plume
Gutierrezia sarothrae	kindlingweed

Physocarpus malvaceus	mallow-leaf ninebark
Populus angustifolia	narrow-leaf cottonwood
Prunus virginiana	choke cherry
Purshia mexicana	Mexican cliff-rose
Purshia tridentata	bitterbrush
Quercus havardii	Harvard's oak
Quercus turbinella	shrub live oak
Rhamnus crocea	holly-leaf buckthorn
Rhus trilobata	ill-scented sumac
Ribes cereum	white squaw currant
Rosa woodsii	Arizona rose
Sambucus cerulea	blue elder
Symphoricarpos oreophilis	mountain snowberry

Herbaceous Understory

Claytonia lanceolata	lance-leaf springbeauty
Collinsia parviflora ·	small-flower blue-eyed Mary
Delphinium nuttallianum	two-lobe larkspur
Erigeron flagellaris	trailing fleabane
Erythronium grandiflorum	yellow avalanche-lily
Gayophytum ramosissimum	pinyon groundsmoke
Geranium caespitosum	purple cluster crane's-bill
Heliomeris multiflora	Nevada showy false goldeneye
Hydrophyllum capitatum	cat's-breeches
Leymus cinereus	Great Basin lyme grass
Lithophragma parviflora	prairie woodlandstar
Nemophila breviflora	Great Basin baby-blue-eyes
Orthocarpus luteus	golden-tongue owl-clover
Stipa comata	needle-and-thread
Stipa lettermanii	Letterman's needle grass
Wyethia amplexicaulis	northern mule's-ears

Juniper–Pinyon Woodland

Juniper–Pinyon Woodland occurs on the slopes of the Wasatch and Uinta Mountains at elevations between 5000 and 8000 feet. In lower areas, there is usually not enough precipitation to support these trees. The trees in the Juniper–Pinyon Woodland rarely grow over 20 feet in height. Much of the area has been heavily grazed resulting in the loss of understory species. There has also been an increase in erosion on the mountain slopes. This community corresponds to Küchler #23.

Canopy
Characteristic Species

Juniperus monosperma	one-seed juniper
Juniperus osteosperma	Utah juniper
Pinus edulis	two-needle pinyon
Pinus monophylla	single-leaf pinyon

Associates

Juniperus occidentalis	western juniper
Juniperus deppeana	alligator juniper

Quercus emoryi	Emory's oak
Quercus gambelii	Gambel's oak
Quercus grisea	gray oak

Woody Understory

Acer glabrum	Rocky Mountain maple
Amelanchier alnifolia	Saskatoon service-berry
Artemisia arbuscula	dwarf sagebrush
Artemisia tridentata	big sagebrush
Ceanothus velutinus	tobacco-brush
Cercocarpus ledifolius	curl-leaf mountain-mahogany
Chrysothamnus nauseosus	rubber rabbitbrush
Chrysothamnus viscidiflorus	green rabbitbrush
Ephedra viridis	Mormon-tea
Eriogonum microthecum	slender wild buckwheat
Eriogonum umbellatum	sulphur-flower wild buckwheat
Fallugia paradoxa	Apache-plume
Gutierrezia sarothrae	kindlingweed
Holodiscus dumosus	glandular oceanspray
Purshia mexicana	Mexican cliff-rose
Purshia tridentata	bitterbrush
Ribes cereum	white squaw currant
Ribes velutinum	desert gooseberry
Symphoricarpos oreophilus	mountain snowberry
Tetradymia canescens	spineless horsebrush

Herbaceous Understory

Balsamorhiza sagittata	arrow-leaf balsamroot
Bouteloua curtipendula	side-oats grama
Bouteloua gracilis	blue grama
Elymus elymoides	western bottle-brush grass
Eriogonum heracleoides	parsnip-flower wild buckwheat
Eriophyllum lanatum	common wooly-sunflower
Festuca idahoensis	bluebunch fescue
Festuca kingii	King's fescue
Frasera albomarginata	desert elkweed
Grindelia squarrosa	curly-cup gumweed
Heterotheca villosa	hairy false golden-aster
Hymenoxys richardsonii	Colorado rubberweed
Ipomopsis aggregata	scarlet skyrocket
Koeleria macrantha	prairie Koeler's grass
Lithospermum ruderale	Columbian puccoon
Lupinus sericeus	Pursh's silky lupine
Oryzopsis hymenoides	Indian mountain-rice grass
Pascopyrum smithii	western-wheat grass
Penstemon speciosus	royal beardtongue
Penstemon watsonii	Watson's beardtongue
Poa fendleriana	mutton grass
Poa secunda	curly blue grass
Pseudoroegneria spicata	bluebunch-wheat grass

Sporobolus cryptandrus	sand dropseed
Stipa comata	needle-and-thread
Stipa nelsonii	Nelson's needle grass
Stipa thurberiana	Thurber's needle grass

Mountain Sagebrush

Mountain Sagebrush occurs on mountain slopes between 7000 and 8000 feet. Big sagebrush is the most common species, although in areas of more moisture, silver sagebrush may dominate. Where the soil is rocky, black sagebrush may be dominant. This community corresponds to Küchler #38.

Characteristic Woody Species

Artemisia cana	silver sagebrush
Artemisia nova	black sagebrush
Artemisia tridentata	big sagebrush

Associates

Amelanchier alnifolia	Saskatoon service-berry
Amelanchier utahensis	Utah service-berry
Cercocarpus montanus	alder-leaf mountain-mahogany
Eriogonum umbellatum	sulphur-flower wild buckwheat
Juniperus scopulorum	Rocky Mountain juniper
Purshia tridentata	bitterbrush
Symphoricarpos oreophilus	mountain snowberry

Herbaceous Understory

Arabis drummondii	Canadian rockcress
Balsamorhiza sagittata	arrow-leaf balsamroot
Castilleja flava	lemon-yellow Indian-paintbrush
Castilleja linariaefolia	Wyoming Indian-paintbrush
Collomia linearis	narrow-leaf mountain-trumpet
Cymopterus longipes	long-stalk spring-parsley
Elymus elymoides	western bottle-brush grass
Eriogonum heracleoides	parsnip-flower wild buckwheat
Erysimum asperum	plains wallflower
Frasera speciosa	monument plant
Hackelia patens	spotted stickseed
Heterotheca villosa	hairy false golden-aster
Hymenoxys richardsonii	Colorado rubberweed
Koeleria macrantha	prairie Koeler's grass
Leymus salinus	salinas lyme grass
Ligusticum porteri	Porter's wild lovage
Linum lewisii	prairie flay
Oenothera cespitosa	evening-primrose
Orthocarpus tolmiei	Tolmie's owl-clover
Phacelia sericea	purplefringe
Phlox longifolia	long-leaf phlox
Poa fendleriana	mutton grass
Sedum stenopetalum	worm-leaf stonecrop
Senecio multilobatus	lobe-leaf ragwort
Stipa lettermanii	Letterman's needle grass

Dry Mountain Meadow

Within the higher elevations there are many dry meadows. These meadows may be the result of the slow filling-in of former glacial lakes or the results of past burns. These areas are usually dominated by grasses and forbs, but many rocky areas and forest interfaces support shrubs.

Characteristic Species

Agastache urticifolia	nettle-leaf giant-hyssop
Aquilegia coerulea	Colorado blue columbine
Artemisia frigida	prairie sagebrush
Artemisia michauxiana	Michaux's wormwood
Calamagrostis canadensis	bluejoint
Carex microptera	small-wing sedge
Castilleja applegatei	wavy-leaf Indian-paintbrush
Castilleja rhexiifolia	rosy Indian-paintbrush
Castilleja sulphurea	sulphur Indian-paintbrush
Cerastium beeringianum	Bering Sea mouse-ear chickweed
Clematis columbiana	Columbian virgin's-bower
Danthonia intermedia	timber wild oat grass
Delphinium barbeyi	subalpine larkspur
Delphinium occidentale	dunce-cap larkspur
Deschampsia cespitosa	tufted hair grass
Elymus trachycaulum	slender wild rye
Festuca kingii	King's fescue
Frasera speciosa	monument plant
Geranium richardsonii	white crane's-bill
Heliomeris multiflora	Nevada showy false goldeneye
Heuchera parvifolia	little-flower alumroot
Ligusticum filicinum	fern-leaf wild lovage
Mertensia arizonica	aspen bluebells
Osmorhiza occidentalis	Sierran sweet-cicely
Penstemon rydbergii	meadow beardtongue
Penstemon whippleanus	dark beardtongue
Polemonium foliosissimum	towering Jacob's ladder
Sedum stenopetalum	worm-leaf stonecrop
Solidago multiradiata	Rocky Mountain goldenrod
Stipa lettermanii	Letterman's needle grass
Stipa nelsonii	Nelson's needle grass
Thalictrum fendleri	Fendler's meadow-rue
Trisetum spicatum	narrow false oat
Valeriana occidentalis	small-flower valerian

Wheat grass–Blue grass Prairie

There is only a very small representation of this community in the Wasatch and Uinta Mountain region. This community corresponds to Küchler #51.

Characteristic Species

Festuca idahoensis	bluebunch fescue
Poa secunda	curly blue grass
Pseudoroegneria spicata	bluebunch-wheat grass

Associates

Chrysothamnus nauseosus	rubber rabbitbrush
Lithophragma glabrum	bulbous woodlandstar
Lupinus sericeus	Pursh's silky lupine
Plantago patagonica	woolly plantain
Stellaria nitens	shiny starwort
Vulpia microstachys	small six-weeks grass

WETLAND SYSTEMS

Wet Mountain Meadow

In the Wasatch and Uinta mountains there are many formerly glaciated areas with small lakes and wet meadows. The wet meadows develop in depressional areas of former small lakes. Grasses, sedges, and rushes predominate in these meadows but a mix of emergent plants occur in deeper water, including both shrubs and forbs.

Characteristic Species

Aconitum columbianum	Columbian monkshood
Alopecurus borealis	meadow-foxtail
Arnica chamissonis	leafy leopard-bane
Calamagrostis canadensis	bluejoint
Caltha leptosepala	white marsh-marigold
Cardamine cordifolia	large mountain bittercress
Carex aurea	golden-fruit sedge
Carex microptera	small-wing sedge
Castilleja rhexiifolia	rosy Indian-paintbrush
Deschampsia cespitosa	tufted hair grass
Eleocharis quinqueflora	few-flower spike-rush
Erigeron ursinus	Bear River fleabane
Hordeum brachyantherum	meadow barley
Mertensia ciliata	tall fringe bluebells
Muhlenbergia richardsonis	matted muhly
Pedicularis groenlandica	bull elephant's-head
Phleum alpinum	mountain timothy
Poa alpina	alpine blue grass
Poa reflexa	nodding blue grass
Polygonum bistortoides	American bistort
Primula parryi	brook primrose
Rorippa teres	southern marsh yellowcress
Saxifraga odontoloma	streambank saxifrage
Sedum rhodanthum	queen's-crown
Trisetum spicatum	narrow false oat
Veratrum californicum	California false hellebore
Zigadenus elegans	mountain deathcamas

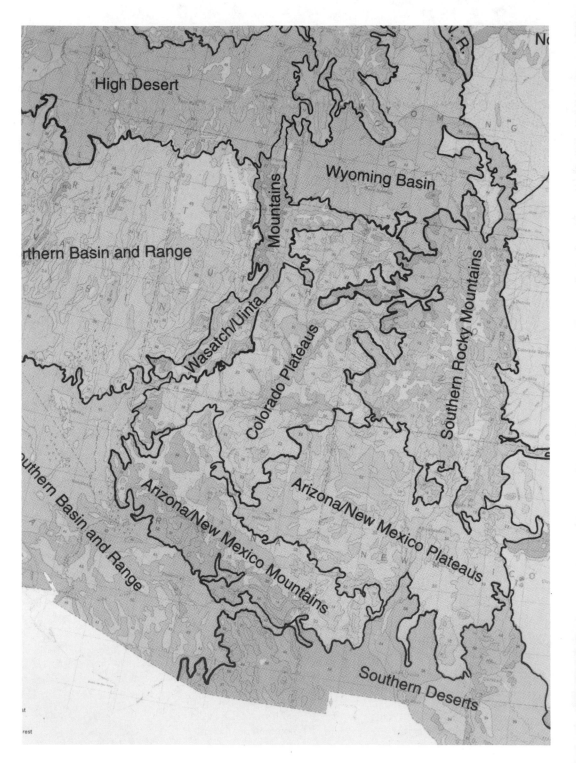

Colorado Plateaus

Colorado Plateaus

Introduction

The Colorado Plateaus region consists of plateaus, valleys, and canyons bordered by high mountains. The area is relatively high in elevation, between 5000 and 12000 feet, and arid. Some of the plateau areas are higher than the surrounding mountains. The region is in the rain shadow of the Rocky Mountains to east, the Wasatch and Uinta mountains to the north and west, and the Arizona and New Mexico Mountains to the South. There are only two major gaps in the mountainous rim that surrounds the region. One gap is a low divide between the San Juan and Rio Grande Rivers. The other gap is called the "Dixie Corridor" which connects this region to the Mojave desert to the southwest.

Canyons are a characteristic feature throughout the region. The Colorado, Green, and San Juan are the major rivers. These rivers and their tributaries dissect this region and have created numerous canyons. Beyond the spectacular geological formations, this region is of interest to botanists because it supports a large number of endemic species.

The vegetation in the region is predominantly Juniper–Pinyon Woodland and scrub. Forests are found only in a few locations where there is sufficient moisture. Two vegetation types which do not develop extensively elsewhere are the Blackbrush Shrub and the Galleta–Three–Awn Shrubsteppe.

The primary sources used to develop descriptions and species lists are: Barbour and Billings 1988; Cronquist et al. 1972.

Dominant Ecological Communities

Upland Systems
Southwestern Spruce–Fir Forest
Pine–Douglas-fir Forest
Juniper–Pinyon Woodland
Blackbrush Scrub
Great Basin Sagebrush
Saltbush Scrub
Greasewood Scrub
Galleta–Three-Awn Shrubsteppe
Grama–Tobosa Shrubsteppe
Grama–Galleta Steppe

UPLAND SYSTEMS

Southwestern Spruce–Fir Forest

Southwestern Spruce–Fir Forest is most common in the Southern Rocky Mountain region, but extends into this region. This community corresponds to Küchler #21.

Canopy
Characteristic Species
Abies lasiocarpa   subalpine fir
Picea engelmannii   Englemann's spruce

Associates

Picea glauca	white spruce
Pinus aristata	bristle-cone pine
Pinus flexilis	limber pine
Populus tremuloides	quaking aspen

Woody Understory

Acer glabrum	Rocky Mountain maple
Alnus incana	speckled alder
Juniperus communis	common juniper
Lonicera involucrata	four-line honeysuckle
Mahonia repens	creeping Oregon-grape
Pachystima myrsinites	myrtle boxleaf
Pentaphylloides floribunda	golden-hardhack
Prunus emarginata	bitter cherry
Salix bebbiana	long-beak willow
Salix scouleriana	Scouler's willow
Symphoricarpos oreophilus	mountain snowberry
Vaccinium myrtillus	whortle-berry

Herbaceous Understory

Actaea rubra	red baneberry
Aquilegia chrysantha	golden columbine
Carex spp.	sedge
Dugaldia hoopesii	owl's-claws
Festuca rubra	red fescue
Gentiana spp.	gentian
Juncus spp.	rush
Pedicularis procera	giant lousewort
Pedicularis racemosa	parrot's-beak
Phleum alpinum	mountain timothy
Primula spp.	primrose
Trisetum spicatum	narrow false oat
Veratum californicum	California false hellebore
Viola canadensis	Canadian white violet
Viola nephrophylla	northern bog violet

Pine–Douglas-fir Forest

Pine–Douglas-fir Forest is found on high plateaus and mountains, extending southward from the Rocky Mountains to the Colorado Plateau. This forest type is also found in parts of Utah, New Mexico, and Arizona. This community responds to Küchler #18.

Canopy
Characteristic Species

Pinus ponderosa	ponderosa pine
Pseudotsuga menziesii	Douglas-fir

Associates

Picea pungens	blue spruce
Pinus flexilis	limber pine

Woody Understory

Acer glabrum	Rocky Mountain maple
Alnus incana	speckled alder
Ceanothus fendleri	Fendler's buckbrush
Chamaebatiaria millifolium	fernbush
Holodiscus dumosus	glandular oceanspray
Jamesia americana	five-petal cliffbush
Juniperus communis	common juniper
Prunus emarginata	bitter cherry

Herbaceous Understory

Blepharoneuron tricholepis	pine-dropseed
Festuca arizonica	Arizona fescue

Juniper–Pinyon Woodland

Juniper–Pinyon Woodland is best developed at elevations of 5000 to 8000 feet under conditions of annual precipitation of 12 inches or more. The canopy of this community type is widely spaced and the woody species are low, evergreen trees. This community corresponds to Küchler #23.

Canopy

Characteristic Species

Juniperus monosperma	one-seed juniper
Juniperus osteosperma	Utah juniper
Pinus edulis	two-needle pinyon

Associates

Juniperus deppeana	alligator juniper
Juniperus occidentalis	western juniper
Pinus monophylla	single-leaf pinyon
Quercus emoryi	Emory's oak
Quercus gambelii	Gambel's oak
Quercus grisea	gray oak
Quercus turbinella	shrub live oak

Woody Understory

Amelanchier alnifolia	Saskatoon service-berry
Atriplex confertifolia	shadscale
Artemisia nova	black sagebrush
Artemisia tridentata	big sagebrush
Ceanothus fendleri	Fendler's buckbrush
Ceanothus integerrimus	deerbrush
Cercocarpus intricatus	little-leaf mountain-mahogany
Cercocarpus ledifolius	curl-leaf mountain-mahogany
Cercocarpus montanus	alder-leaf mountain-mahogany
Chamaebatiaria millifolium	fernbush
Chrysothamnus depressus	long-flower rabbitbrush
Chrysothamnus nauseosus	rubber rabbitbrush
Coleogyne ramosissima	blackbrush
Echinocereus coccineus	scarlet hedgehog cactus

Ephedra viridis	Mormon-tea
Fallugia paradoxa	Apache-plume
Garrya wrightii	Wright's silktassel
Krashcheninnikovia lanata	winterfat
Mahonia fremonti	desert Oregon-grape
Opuntia basilaris	beaver-tail cactus
Opuntia erinacea	oldman cactus
Opuntia fragilis	pygmy prickly-pear
Opuntia polyacantha	hair-spine prickly-pear
Opuntia whipplei	rat-tail cholla
Purshia mexicana	Mexican cliff-rose
Purshia tridentata	bitterbrush
Yucca baccata	banana yucca

Herbaceous Understory

Bouteloua curtipendula	side-oats grama
Bouteloua eriopoda	black grama
Bouteloua gracilis	blue grama
Calochortus ambiguus	doubting mariposa-lily
Castelleja integra	squawfeather
Elymus elymoides	western bottle-brush grass
Festuca arizonica	Arizona fescue
Keckiella antirrhinoides	chaparral bush-beardtongue
Koeleria macrantha	prairie Koeler's grass
Muhlenbergia torreyi	ringed muhly
Oryzopsis hymenoides	Indian mountain-rice grass
Pascopyrum smithii	western-wheat grass
Piptochaetium fimbriatum	pinyon spear grass
Sphaeralcea emoryi	Emory's globe-mallow
Sporobolus cryptandrus	sand dropseed
Stipa nelsonii	Nelson's needle grass

Blackbrush Scrub

Blackbrush Scrub occurs in lower parts of the Colorado Plateaus in areas with low rainfall and non-saline, sandy soil. Blackbrush occurs in an environment that is too harsh for many plants. Blackbrush occurs widely in an area between the cold deserts to the north and the warm deserts to the south. Other shrubs are rare in the area and very few herbaceous species can survive the climate. This community corresponds to Küchler #39.

Characteristic Woody Species

Coleogyne ramosissima	blackbrush
Associates	
Artemisia filifolia	silver sagebrush
Artemisia tridentata	big sagebrush
Atriplex confertifolia	shadscale
Ephedra nevadensis	Nevada joint-fir
Ephedra torreyana	Torrey's joint-fir
Ericameria linearifolius	narrow-leaf heath-goldenrod

Erigonum fasciculatum	eastern Mojave wild buckwheat
Gutierrezia sarothrae	kindlingweed
Opuntia ramosissima	darning-needle cholla
Prunus fasciculata	desert almond
Psorothamnus fremontii	Fremont's smokebush
Salazaria mexicana	Mexican bladder sage
Thamnosa montana	turpentine-broom
Yucca baccata	banana yucca
Yucca brevifolia	Joshua-tree

Herbaceous Understory

Bouteloua eriopoda	black grama
Brickellia oblongifolia	narrow-leaf brickellbush
Hilaria jamesii	James' galleta
Hilaria rigida	big galleta
Muhlenbergia porteri	bush muhly
Oryzopsis hymenoides	Indian mountain-rice grass

Great Basin Sagebrush

Great Basin Sagebrush is a desert-like mix of shrubs, primarily sagebrush, and perennial grasses. Great Basin Sagebrush occurs above 5000 feet and may extend up to 10000 feet. This community corresponds to Küchler #38 and #55.

Characteristic Woody Species

Artemisia tridentata	big sagebrush

Associates

Artemisia arbuscula	dwarf sagebrush
Artemisia nova	black sagebrush
Atriplex confertifolia	shadscale
Chrysothamnus nauseosus	rubber rabbitbrush
Chrysothamnus viscidiflorus	green rabbitbrush
Coleogyne ramosissima	blackbrush
Ephedra torreyana	Torrey's joint-fir
Ephedra viridis	Mormon-tea
Grayia spinosa	spiny hop-sage
Leptodactylon pungens	granite prickly-pear
Purshia tridentata	bitterbrush
Ribes velutinum	desert gooseberry
Tetradymia glabrata	little-leaf horsebrush

Herbaceous Understory

Allium acuminatum	taper-tip onion
Aristida pupurea	purple three-awn
Balsamorhiza sagittata	arrow-leaf balsamroot
Calochortus nuttallii	sego-lily
Castilleja angustifolia	northwestern Indian-paintbrush
Crepis acuminata	long-leaf hawk's-beard
Delphinium andersonii	desert larkspur

Elymus elymoides	western bottle-brush grass
Elymus lanceolatus	streamside wild rye
Festuca idahoensis	bluebunch fescue
Heterotheca villosa	hairy false golden-aster
Hymenoxys richardsonii	Colorado rubberweed
Koeleria macrantha	prairie Koeler's grass
Leymus cinereus	Great basin lyme grass
Lupinus caudatus	Kellogg's spurred lupine
Lupinus sericeus	Pursh's silky lupine
Oryzopsis hymnoides	Indian mountain-rice grass
Pascopyrum smithii	western-wheat grass
Phlox hoodii	carpet phlox
Phlox longifolia	long-leaf phlox
Poa fendleriana	mutton grass
Poa secunda	curly blue grass
Pseudoroegneria spicata	bluebunch-wheat grass
Sporobolus airoides	alkali-sacaton
Stipa comata	needle-and-thread
Viola beckwithii	western pansy
Wyethia amplexicaulis	northern mule's-ears
Zigadenus paniculatus	sand-corn

Saltbush Scrub

Saltbush Scrub occurs in areas with little moisture and on saline valley soils. This community type is often referred to as the "shadscale community." Structurally, this desert community is made up of low, widely-spaced shrubs, typically covering about 10 percent of the ground. Vegetation is characteristically grayish, spiney, and very small leaved. This community corresponds to Küchler #40.

Characteristic Woody Species

Atriplex confertifolia	shadscale

Associates

Artemisia spinescens	bud sagebrush
Atriplex canescens	four-wing saltbush
Atriplex gardneri	Gardner's saltbush
Atriplex nuttallii	Nuttall's saltbush
Chrysothamnus viscidiflorus	green rabbitbrush
Ephedra nevadensis	Nevada joint-fir
Grayia spinosa	spiny hop-sage
Gutierrezia sarothrae	kindlingweed
Krascheninnikovia lanata	winterfat
Lycium cooperi	peachthorn
Sacrobatus vermiculatus	greasewood
Tetradymia glabrata	little-leaf horsebrush

Herbaceous Understory

Camissonia boothii	shredding suncup
Camissonia claviformis	browneyes
Camissonia scapoidea	Paiute suncup

Cardaria draba	heart-pod hoarycress
Cryptantha circumscissa	cushion cat's-eye
Eriogonum ovalifolium	cushion wild buckwheat
Halogeton glomeratus	saltlover
Iva nevadensis	Nevada marsh-elder
Kochia americana	greenmolly
Mirabilis alipes	winged four-o'clock
Sphaeraliea grossulariifolia	currant-leaf globe-mallow
Vulpia octoflora	eight-flower six-weeks grass
Xylorhiza glabriuscula	smooth woody-aster

Greasewood Scrub

Greasewood Scrub is a salt tolerant community that occurs in valley bottoms where the water table is relatively close to the surface. This community corresponds to Küchler #40.

Characteristic Woody Species
Sarcobatus vermiculatus	greasewood

Associates
Allenrolfea occidentalis	iodinebush
Artemisia spinescens	bud sagebrush
Atriplex confertifolia	shadscale
Atriplex lentiformis	quailbrush
Suaeda moquinii	shrubby seepweed

Herbaceous Understory
Cordylanthus maritimus	saltmarsh bird's-beak
Distichlis spicata	coastal salt grass
Glaux maritima	sea-milkwort
Halogeton glomeratus	saltlover
Hutchinsia procumbens	ovalpurse
Iva axillaris	deer-root
Juncus balticus	Baltic rush
Kochia americana	greenmolly
Pyrrocoma lanceolatus	lance-leaf goldenweed
Salicornia rubra	red saltwort
Sarcocornia pacifica	Pacific swampfire
Sporobolus airoides	alkali-sacoton
Thelypodium sagittatum	arrowhead thelypody

Galleta–Three-Awn Shrubsteppe

Galleta–Three-Awn Shrubsteppe is an arid grassland interspersed with shrubs. One of the community dominants, galleta, is a sod forming grass and three-awn is a weedy bunchgrass. The sandy soils in these areas are covered by a microphytic crust. Grazing breaks up the crust causing dunes to form and allowing shrubs to invade and increase. This community corresponds to Küchler #57.

Characteristic Species

Aristida purpurea	purple three-awn
Artemisia filifolia	silver sagebrush
Ephedra viridis	Mormon tea
Hilaria jamesii	James' galleta

Associates

Ambrosia acanthicarpa	flat-spine burr-ragweed
Bouteloua gracilis	blue grama
Chrysothamnus nauseosus	rubber rabbitbrush
Chrysothamnus viscidiflorus	green rabbitbrush
Encelia farinosa	goldenhills
Ephedra torryana	Torrey's joint-fir
Helianthus anomalus	western sunflower
Heliotropium convolvulaceum	wide-flower heliotrope
Heterotheca villosa	hairy false golden-aster
Lepidium fremontii	bush pepperwort
Machaeranthera canescens	hoary tansy-aster
Mahonia fremontii	desert Oregon-grape
Mentzelia pumila	golden blazingstar
Monroa squarrosa	false buffalo grass
Muhlenbergia pungens	sandhill muhly
Oenothera albicaulis	white-stem evening-primrose
Oryzopsis hymenoides	Indian mountain-rice grass
Poliomintha incana	hoary rosemary-mint
Sphaeralcea grossulariifolia	currant-leaf globe-mallow
Sphaeralcea leptophylla	scaly globe-mallow
Sporobolus cryptandrus	sand dropseed
Stephanomeria pauciflora	brown-plume wire-lettuce

Grama–Tobosa Shrubsteppe

Grama–Tobosa Shrubsteppe is a mosaic of short grasses and shrubs that vary from open to dense. This community corresponds to Küchler #58.

Characteristic Species

Bouteloua eriopoda	black grama
Hilaria mutica	tobosa grass
Larrea tridentata	creosote-bush

Associates

Acacia constricta	mescat wattle
Aristida californica	California three-awn
Aristida divaricata	poverty three-awn
Aristida purpurea	purple three-awn
Aristida ternipes	spider grass
Baileya multiradiata	showy desert-marigold
Bothriocholoa barbinodis	cane beard grass
Bouteloua curtipendula	side-oats grama
Bouteloua gracilis	blue grama
Gutierrezia sarothrae	kindlingweed

Hilaria belangeri	curly-mesquite
Hilaria jamessii	James' galleta
Muhlenbergia porteri	bush muhly
Prosopis glandulosa	honey mesquite
Sporobolus airoides	alkali-sacoton
Sporobolus cryptandrus	sand dropseed
Sporobolus flexuosus	mesa dropseed
Yucca baccata	banana yucca
Yucca elata	soaptree yucca
Zinnia acerosa	white zinnia
Zinnia grandiflora	little golden zinnia

Grama–Galleta Steppe

Grama–Galleta Steppe is characterized by low to medium tall grasslands with few woody plants. This community corresponds to Küchler #53.

Characteristic Species

Bouteloua gracilis	blue grama
Hilaria jamesii	James' galleta

Associates

Andropogon hallii	sand bluestem
Artemisia tridentata	big sagebrush
Atriplex canescens	four-wing saltbush
Bouteloua curtipendula	side-oats grama
Bouteloua hirsuta	hairy grama
Ephedra viridis	Mormon-tea
Optuntia whipplei	rat-tail cholla
Oryzopsis hymenoides	Indian mountain-rice grass
Schizachyrium scoparium	little false bluestem
Yucca glauca	soapweed yucca

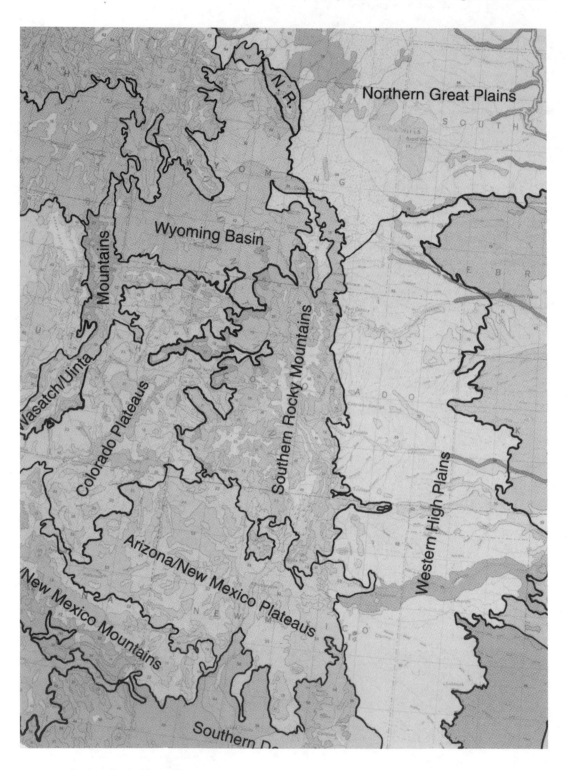

Southern Rocky Mountains

Southern Rocky Mountains

Introduction

The Southern Rocky Mountains region occupies most of central and western Colorado. The mountain ranges of this region also extend north into Wyoming and south into New Mexico. The mountains begin at approximately 4950 feet and rise to 14520 feet. Major ranges within the Southern Rockies include the San Juan Mountains, the Sangre de Cristo Mountains, the Front Ranges, and the Medicine Bow Mountains.

The predominant vegetation type of the region is conifer forest. Environmental gradients associated with elevation influence the vegetation types occurring in an area. The lowest elevation forests are dominated by ponderosa pine. As elevation increases, Douglas-fir and then subalpine fir and Engelmann's spruce become common species. The lower mountain slopes and basins support shrub communities of Sagebrush Steppe, Juniper-Pinyon Woodland, and Mountain Mahogany-Oak Scrub.

Frequent fire is characteristic of the Southern Rocky Mountains, as it is in the Northern Rockies. Other disturbances caused by wind, insects, avalanches, and browsing are also natural factors which periodically change the vegetation. Humans, however, have caused major changes in the region's natural vegetation by suppressing natural fires and introducing intensive domestic livestock grazing.

A unique feature of the Southern Rocky Mountain region is the "park." Parks are low elevation valley bottoms on fine textured soils, dominated by grasses, sedges, and forbs. Although not covered by this book, many interesting alpine communities exist in extreme conditions in the highest altitudes of the Rocky Mountains.

The primary sources used to develop descriptions and species lists are: Barbour and Billings 1988; Brown 1982.

Dominant Ecological Communities

Upland Systems
    Ponderosa Pine Forest
    Douglas-fir Forest
    Spruce–Fir Forest
    Juniper–Pinyon Woodland
    Mountain-Mahogany–Oak Scrub
    Sagebrush Steppe
    Saltbush–Greasewood Shrub
    Shortgrass Prairie
Wetland Systems
    Riparian Forest

UPLAND SYSTEMS

Ponderosa Pine Forest

Ponderosa Pine Forest is more open at lower elevations. It closes, becomes mixed with Douglas-fir, and grades to Douglas-fir Forest at higher elevations. This community corresponds, in part, to Küchler #18.

Canopy
Characteristic Species
Pinus ponderosa	ponderosa pine
Pseudotsuga menziesii	Douglas-fir

Associates
Picea pungens	blue spruce
Pinus flexilis	limber pine
Pinus strobliformis	southwestern white pine
Quercus gambelii	Gambel's oak

Woody Understory
Acer glabrum	Rocky Mountain maple
Alnus incana	speckled alder
Ceanothus fendleri	Fendler's buckbrush
Chamaebatiaria millifolium	fernbush
Holodiscus dumosus	glandular oceanspray
Jamesia americana	five-petal cliffbush
Juniperus communis	common juniper
Mahonia repens	creeping Oregon-grape
Physocarpus monogynus	mountain ninebark
Prunus emarginata	bitter cherry
Rhus glabra	smooth sumac
Ribes aureum	golden currant
Ribes pinetorum	orange gooseberry
Ribes viscosissimum	sticky currant
Robinia neomexicana	New Mexico locust
Rosa woodsii	Arizona rose
Sambucus cerulea	blue elder
Symphoricarpos longiflorus	desert snowberry
Symphoricarpos oreophilus	mountain snowberry
Symphoricarpos rotundifolius	round-leaf snowberry

Herbaceous Understory
Blepharoneuron tricholepis	pine-dropseed
Bromus anomalus	nodding brome
Bromus ciliatus	fringed brome
Carex geophila	white mountain sedge
Cyperus fendlerianus	Fendler's flat sedge
Elymus elymoides	western botttle-brush grass
Festuca arizonica	Arizona fescue
Koeleria macrantha	prairie Koeler's grass
Muhlenbergia minutissima	least muhly
Muhlenbergia montana	mountain muhly
Muhlenbergia virescens	screw leaf muhly
Panicum bulbosum	bulb panic grass
Piptochaetium pringlei	Pringle's spear grass
Poa fendleriana	mutton grass

Douglas-fir Forest

Douglas-fir Forest occurs between Ponderosa Pine Forest and the colder Spruce–Fir Forest of higher elevations and is predominant on north-facing slopes and ravines. Douglas-fir and associated canopy species, *Pinus contorta* and *Pinus ponderosa* are tolerant of fire. Frequent low-intensity fires favor regeneration of this forest type. This community corresponds to Küchler #12 and #18.

Canopy
Characteristic Species

Pseudotsuga menziesii	Douglas-fir

Associates

Abies concolor	white fir
Larix occidentalis	western larch
Picea pungens	blue spruce
Pinus contorta	lodgepole pine
Pinus ponderosa	ponderosa pine
Populus tremuloides	quaking aspen

Woody Understory

Acer glabrum	Rocky Mountain maple
Alnus incana	speckled alder
Ceanothus fendleri	Fendler's buckbrush
Chamaebatiaria millefolium	fernbush
Holodiscus dumosus	glandular oceanspray
Jamesia americana	five-petal cliffbush
Juniperus communis	common juniper
Physocarpus malvaceus	mallow-leaf ninebark
Prunus emarginata	bitter cherry

Herbaceous Understory

Arnica latifolia	daffodil leopard-bane
Blepharoneuron tricholepis	pine-dropseed
Calamagrostis rubescens	pinegrass
Carex concinnoides	northwestern sedge
Carex geyeri	Geyer's sedge
Festuca arizonica	Arizona fescue

Spruce–Fir Forest

Spruce–Fir Forest occurs at higher elevations than Douglas-fir and Ponderosa Pine Forest, and is predominant in the sub-alpine portion of the Rocky Mountains. Spruce–Fir Forest occurs at high elevations throughout the Rocky Mountains, however, changes in species will occur along a north-south gradient. Shrubs and herbaceous species are sparse in this forest where the canopy is closed. In areas that are open due to past disturbances, species diversity and abundance increase in the herbaceous and shrub understory. This community corresponds to Küchler #15 and #21.

Canopy
Characteristic Species

Abies lasiocarpa	subalpine fir
Picea engelmannii	Engelmann's spruce

Associates

Picea pungens	blue spruce
Pinus aristata	bristle-cone pine
Pinus flexilis	limber pine
Populus tremuloides	quaking aspen

Woody Understory

Acer glabrum	Rocky Mountain maple
Alnus incana	speckled alder
Arctostaphylos uva-ursi	red bearberry
Juniperus communis	common juniper
Lonicera involucrata	four-line honeysuckle
Mahonia repens	creeping Oregon-grape
Pachystima myrsinites	myrtle boxleaf
Pentaphylloides floribunda	golden-hardhack
Prunus emarginata	bitter cherry
Salix bebbiana	long-beak willow
Salix scouleriana	Scouler's willow
Sambucus cerulea	blue elder
Symphoricarpos oreophilus	mountain snowberry
Vaccinium myrtillus	whortle-berry

Herbaceous Understory

Arnica cordifolia	heart-leaf leopard-bane
Epilobium spp.	willowherb
Erigeron formosissimus	beautiful fleabane
Fragaria virginiana	Virginia strawberry
Lathyrus lanszwertii	Nevada vetchling
Pseudocymopterus montanus	alpine false mountain-parsley
Trisetum spicatum	narrow false oat
Veratrum californicum	California false hellebore
Vicia spp.	vetch

Juniper–Pinyon Woodland

Juniper–Pinyon Woodland is predominant in the foothills of eastern slopes in this region. This community corresponds to Küchler #23.

Canopy
Characteristic Species

Juniperus monosperma	one-seed juniper
Pinus edulis	Colorado juniper

Associates

Juniperus occidentalis	western juniper
Quercus emoryi	Emory's oak
Quercus gambelii	Gambel's oak
Quercus grisea	gray oak

Woody Understory

Artemisia tridentata	big sagebrush
Fallugia paradoxa	Apache-plume

Purshia mexicana	Mexican cliff-rose
Purshia tridentata	bitterbrush

Herbaceous Understory

Bouteloua curtipendula	side-oats grama
Bouteloua gracilis	blue grama
Oryzopsis hymenoides	Indian mountain-rice grass
Pascopyrum smithii	western-wheat grass
Sporobolus cryptandrus	sand dropseed

Mountain-Mahogany–Oak Scrub

Mountain-Mahogany–Oak Scrub occupies a transition zone between coniferous forests and treeless plains and plateaus at margins of the Rocky Mountains. This community corresponds to Küchler #37.

Characteristic Woody Species

Cercocarpus ledifolius	curl-leaf mountain-mahogany
Quercus gambelii	Gambel's oak

Associates

Acer grandidentatum	canyon maple
Amelanchier utahensis	Utah service-berry
Arctostaphylos pringlei	pink-bract manzanita
Arctostaphylos pungens	Mexican manzanita
Artemisia tridentata	big sagebrush
Ceanothus greggii	Mojave buckbrush
Ceanothus velutinus	tobacco-brush
Cercocarpus montanus	alder-leaf mountain-mahogany
Eriodictyon angustifolium	narrow-leaf yerba-santa
Fallugia paradoxa	Apache-plume
Garrya flavescens	ashy silktassel
Garrya wrightii	Wright's silktassel
Pachystima myrsinites	myrtle boxleaf
Physocarpus malvaceus	mallow-leaf ninebark
Purshia mexicana	Mexican cliff-rose
Purshia tridentata	bitterbrush
Quercus chrysolepis	canyon live oak
Quercus dumosa	California scrub oak
Quercus emoryi	Emory's oak
Quercus havardii	Harvard's oak
Quercus turbinella	shrub live oak
Rhamnus crocea	holly-leaf buckthorn
Rhus trilobata	ill-scented sumac

Sagebrush Steppe

Sagebrush Steppe is a mix of scattered shrubs, primarily sagebrush, and perennial grasses. However, the structure and floristic diversity of the sagebrush community is variable depending on moisture availability, grazing, fire frequency, and other factors. Grazing pressure in the sagebrush community has resulted in an increase in shrubs over perennial grasses. This community corresponds to Küchler #55 and #38.

Characteristic Woody Species

Artemisia tridentata	big sagebrush

Associates

Artemisia nova	black sagebrush
Atriplex confertifolia	shadscale
Balsamorrhiza sagittata	arrow-leaf balsamroot
Purshia tridentata	bitterbrush

Herbaceous Understory

Festuca idahoensis	bluebunch fescue
Lithospermum ruderale	Columbian puccoon
Lupinus sericeus	Pursh's silky lupine
Oryzopsis hymenoides	Indian mountain-rice grass
Pascopyrum smithii	western-wheat grass
Poa secunda	curly blue grass
Pseudoroegneria spicata	bluebunch-wheat grass

Saltbush–Greasewood Shrub

Saltbush–Greasewood Shrub occurs primarily on highly saline soils, although it can be found on other dry, hard desert soils. In some areas, vegetation is entirely lacking due to extreme conditions. Water availability can also vary from standing water much of the year to xeric. This community corresponds to Küchler #40.

Characteristic Species

Atriplex confertifolia	shadscale
Sacrobatus vermiculatus	greasewood

Associates

Allenrolfea occidentalis	iodinebush
Artemisia spinescens	bud sagebrush
Distichlis spicata	coastal salt grass
Grayia spinosa	spiny hop-sage
Kochia americana	greenmolly
Krascheninnikovia lanata	winterfat
Lycium cooperi	peachthorn
Mendora spinescens	spiny mendora
Suaeda moquinii	shrubby seepweed

Shortgrass Prairie

This grassland community is found in dry, arid conditions within the Southern Rocky Mountains region. Although some ecologists believe this community is a result of grazing, primarily by buffalo, most believe it is the unique environmental conditions that have influenced the development of these grasslands. This community corresponds to Küchler #66.

Characteristic Species

Bouteloua gracilis	blue grama
Pascopyrum smithii	western-wheat grass
Stipa comata	needle-and-thread

Associates

Artemisia frigida	prairie sagebrush
Chrysothamnus viscidiflorus	green rabbitbrush
Elymus trachycaulus	slender wild rye
Festuca arizonica	Arizona fescue
Koeleria macrantha	prairie Koeler's grass
Muhlenbergia montana	mountain muhly
Oryzopsis hymenoides	Indian mountain-rice grass
Tetradymia canescens	spineless horsebrush

WETLAND SYSTEMS

Riparian Forest

Riparian Forest, dominated by the deciduous cottonwood tree, *Populus angustifolia*, is the least common forest type in the Southern Rocky Mountain Region. The riparian forest, however, occurs throughout the region in canyons and along streams. Riparian Forest occurs from elevations as low as 4450 to 7600 feet. On some sites within the riparian zone, the forest canopy is absent and willow thickets are well developed.

Canopy
Characteristic Species

Populus angustifolia	narrow-leaf cottonwood

Associates

Abies concolor	white fir
Acer glabrum	Rocky Mountain maple
Acer grandidentatum	canyon maple
Alnus incana	speckled alder
Alnus oblongifolia	Arizona alder
Betula occidentalis	water birch
Pinus ponderosa	ponderosa pine
Populus deltoides	eastern cottonwood
Populus fremontii	Fremont's cottonwood
Populus tremuloides	quaking aspen
Prunus americanus	American plum
Quercus gambelii	Gambel's oak
Robinia neomexicana	New Mexico locust

Woody Understory

Acer negundo	ash-leaf maple
Cornus stolonlifera	redosier
Parthenocissus vitacea	thicket-creeper
Prunus emarginata	bitter cherry
Rhus glabra	smooth sumac
Salix spp.	willow
Sambucus cerulea	blue elder

Herbaceous Understory

Aralia nudicaulis	wild sarsaparilla
Blepharoneuron tricholepsis	pine-dropseed
Carex sprengelii	long-beak sedge
Ranunculus abortivus	kidney-leaf buttercup
Ratibida pinnata	gray-head Mexican-hat

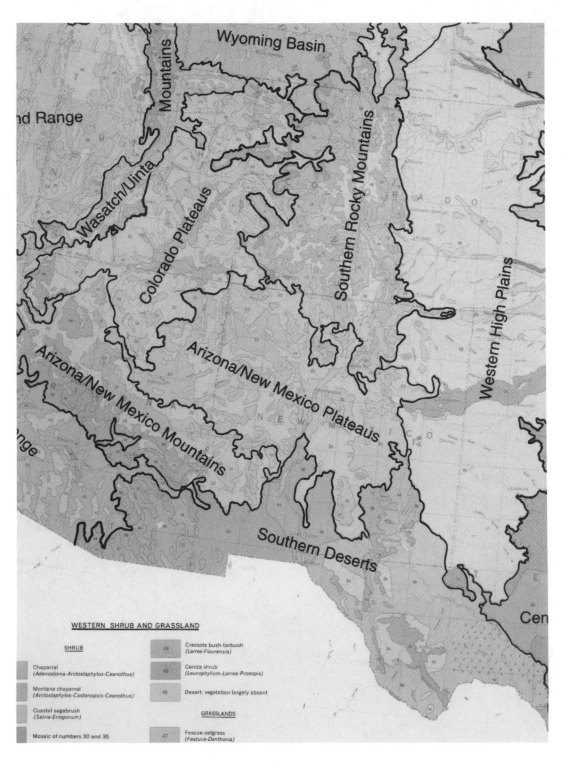

WESTERN SHRUB AND GRASSLAND

SHRUB

Chaparral
(Adenostoma-Arctostaphylos-Ceanothus)

Montane chaparral
(Arctostaphylos-Castanopsis-Ceanothus)

Coastal sagebrush
(Salvia-Eriogonum)

Mosaic of numbers 30 and 35

44   Creosote bush-tarbush
(Larrea-Flourensia)

45   Ceniza shrub
(Leucophyllum-Larrea-Prosopis)

46   Desert: vegetation largely absent

GRASSLANDS

47   Fescue-oatgrass
(Festuca-Danthonia)

Arizona/New Mexico Plateaus

Arizona/New Mexico Plateaus

Introduction

The Arizona/New Mexico Plateau Region is located in northeastern Arizona and northwestern and central New Mexico. This region encompasses several large plateaus and scattered mountain ranges. Evergreen forests of pines and areas of fir with spruce dominate the higher elevations. Evergreen woodland generally occupies areas below the forests while grasslands and desert scrub occur in the driest areas.

The primary sources used to develop descriptions and species lists are: Barbour and Billings 1988; Dick-Peddie 1992; Lowe 1964.

Dominant Ecological Communities

Upland Systems
Pine–Douglas-fir Forest
Ponderosa Pine Forest
Juniper–Pinyon Woodland
High Desert Scrub
Desert Grassland

Wetland Systems
Riparian Woodland

UPLAND SYSTEMS

Pine–Douglas-fir Forest

Pine–Douglas-fir Forest is found on high plateaus and mountains and extends southward from the Rocky Mountains to the southwest in Colorado, Utah, New Mexico, and Arizona. The forests range from open to dense with tall evergreen trees. In the southern mountains there is often much undergrowth. This community corresponds to Kuchler #18.

Canopy
Characteristic Species
Pinus ponderosa	ponderosa pine
Pseudotsuga menziesii	Douglas-fir

Associates
Picea pungens	blue spruce
Pinus flexilis	limber pine

Woody Understory
Acer glabrum	Rocky Mountain maple
Alnus incana	speckled alder
Ceanothus fendleri	Fendler's buckbrush
Chamaebatiaria millefolium	fernbush
Holodiscus dumosus	glandular oceanspray
Jamesia americana	five-petal cliffbush

Juniperus communis	common juniper
Prunus emarginata	bitter cherry

Herbaceous Understory

Blepharoneuron tricholepis	pine-dropseed
Festuca arizonica	Arizona fescue

Ponderosa Pine Forest

Ponderosa Pine Forest is similar to and shares many species with the Ponderosa Pine Forest of the Arizona/New Mexico Mountains and the Southern Deserts regions. The Ponderosa Pine Forest of this region, however, occurs on large flat mesas and plateaus. The forests are, as in the Southern Deserts region, found below the fir forests. The trees form an open to dense canopy. The shrubs are few, rarely dense and not especially common. In the open canopy Ponderosa Pine Forest, the principle groundcovers are often grasses. There are fewer tree species than in the southern Arizona Ponderosa Pine Forest. This community corresponds to Küchler #19.

Canopy
Characteristic Species

Pinus ponderosa	ponderosa pine

Associates

Pinus cembroides	Mexican pinyon
Pinus flexilis	limber pine
Pinus leiophylla	Chihuahuan pine
Populus tremuloides	quaking aspen
Pseudotsuga menziesii	Douglas-fir
Quercus gambelii	Gambel's oak

Woody Understory

Arctostaphylos patula	green-leaf manzanita
Artemisia nova	black sagebrush
Artemisia tridentata	big sagebrush
Ceanothus fendleri	Fendler's buckbrush
Chamaebatiaria millefolium	fernbush
Chrysothamnus parryi	Parry's rabbitbrush
Fallugia paradoxa	Apache-plume
Fendlerella utahensis	Utah-fendlerbush
Holodiscus boursieri	Boursier's oceanspray
Holodiscus dumosus	glandular oceanspray
Jamesia americana	five-petal cliffbush
Juniperus communis	common juniper
Mahonia repens	creeping Oregon-grape
Pachystima myrsinites	myrtle boxleaf
Philadelphus microphyllus	little-leaf mock orange
Physocarpus monogynus	mountain ninebark
Purshia mexicana	Mexican cliff-rose
Ribes cereum	white squaw currant
Robinia neomexicana	New Mexico locust
Rubus idaeus	common red raspberry

Herbaceous Understory

Artemisia ludoviciana	white sagebrush
Blepharoneuron tricholepis	pine-dropseed
Bothriochloa barbinodis	cane beard grass
Bouteloua gracilis	blue grama
Comandra umbellata	bastard-toadflax
Elymus elymoides	western bottle-brush grass
Festuca arizonica	Arizona fescue
Hedeoma dentatum	Arizona false pennyroyal
Iris missouriensis	Rocky Mountain iris
Koeleria macrantha	prairie Koeler's grass
Lupinus palmeri	Palmer's lupine
Monarda fistulosa	Oswego-tea
Muhlenbergia montana	mountain muhly
Muhlenbergia wrightii	Wright's muhly
Oxytropis lamberti	stemless locoweed
Pteridium aquilinum	northern bracken fern
Sphaeralcea fendleri	thicket globe-mallow
Thalictrum fendleri	Fendler's meadow-rue
Thermopsis rhombifolia	prairie golden-banner
Vicia americana	American purple vetch

Juniper–Pinyon Woodland

Juniper–Pinyon Woodland covers large areas below Ponderosa Pine Forest on the Mogollon, Coconino, and Kaibab plateaus. It usually occurs between 5500 and 7000 feet on flat-topped mesas and plateaus. The woodlands are an open mixture of shrubs with herbaceous plants forming the understory. The oaks may be in tree or shrub form. This community corresponds to Küchler #23.

Canopy
Characteristic Species

Juniperus monosperma	one-seed juniper
Juniperus osteosperma	Utah juniper
Pinus edulis	two-needle pinyon
Pinus monophylla	single-leaf pinyon

Associates

Juniperus occidentalis	western juniper
Juniperus scopulorum	Rocky Mountain juniper
Quercus emoryi	Emory's oak
Quercus gambelii	Gambel's oak
Quercus grisea	gray oak
Quercus turbinella	shrub live oak

Woody Understory

Amelachier alnifolia	Saskatoon service-berry
Artemisia nova	black sagebrush
Artemisia tridentata	big sagebrush
Ceanothus fendleri	Fendler's buckbrush
Ceanothus integerrimus	deerbrush
Cercocarpus ledifolius	curl-leaf mountain-mahogany

Cerocarpus intricatus	little-leaf mountain-mahogany
Cerocarpus montanus	alder-leaf mountain-mahogany
Chamaebatiaria millifolium	fernbush
Chrysothamnus depressus	long-flower rabbitbrush
Chrysothamnus nauseosus	rubber rabbitbrush
Coleogyne ramosissima	blackbrush
Echinocereus coccineus	scarlet hedgehog cactus
Ephedra viridis	Mormon-tea
Fallugia paradoxa	Apache-plume
Garrya wrightii	Wright's silktassel
Krascheninnikovia lanata	winterfat
Mahonia fremonti	desert Oregon-grape
Opuntia basilaris	beaver-tail cactus
Opuntia erinacea	oldman cactus
Opuntia fragilis	pygmy prickly-pear
Opuntia polyacantha	hair-spine prickly-pear
Opuntia whipplei	rat-tail cholla
Purshia mexicana	Mexican cliff-rose
Purshia tridentata	bitterbrush
Yucca baccata	banana yucca

Herbaceous Understory

Bouteloua curtipendula	side-oats grama
Bouteloua eriopoda	black grama
Bouteloua gracilis	blue grama
Calochortus ambiguus	doubting mariposa-lily
Castilleja integra	squawfeather
Elymus elymoides	western bottle-brush grass
Festuca arizonica	Arizona fescue
Keckiella antirrhinoides	chapparral bush-beardtongue
Koeleria macrantha	prairie Koeler's grass
Muhlenbergia torreyi	ringed muhly
Oryzopsis hymenoides	Indian mountain-rice grass
Pascoyprum smithii	western-wheat grass
Piptochaetium fimbriatum	pinyon spear grass
Sphaeralcea emoryi	Emory's globe-mallow
Sporobolus cryptandrus	sand dropseed
Stipa nelsonii	Nelson's needle grass

High Desert Scrub

High Desert Scrub occurs in areas ranging in elevation from 3000 to 6500 feet and is sometimes referred to as cool or cold desert. It is the southeastern limit of the Great Basin desert system. Rainfall averages from seven to twelve inches per year and is more evenly distributed throughout the year than in the desert types to the south. Dominance within this community may vary from area to area with one or two species of shrub often forming pure stands. This community corresponds, in part, to Küchler #38 and #40.

Characteristic Woody Species

Artemisia tridentata	big sagebrush
Atriplex canescens	four-wing saltbush
Atriplex confertifolia	shadscale
Coleogyne ramosissima	blackbrush
Sarcobatus vermiculatus	greasewood

Associates

Allenrolfea occidentalis	iodinebush
Artemisia bigelovii	flat sagebrush
Artemisia filifolia	silver sagebrush
Artemisia nova	black sagebrush
Artemisia spinescens	bud sagebrush
Chrysothamnus nauseosus	rubber rabbitbrush
Ephedra nevadensis	Nevada joint-fir
Ephedra viridis	Mormon-tea
Grayia spinosa	spiny hop-sage
Gutierrezia sarothrae	kindlingweed
Krascheninnikovia lanata	winterfat
Lycium cooperi	peachthorn
Lycium pallidum	pale desert-thorn
Menodora spinescens	spiny menodora
Opuntia erinacea	oldman cactus
Opuntia polyacantha	hair-spine prickly-pear
Opuntia whipplei	rat-tail cholla
Purshia tridentata	bitterbrush
Yucca angustissima	fine-leaf yucca

Herbaceous Understory

Balsamorhiza sagittata	arrow-leaf balsamroot
Bouteloua gracilis	blue grama
Camissonia boothii	shredding suncup
Camissonia claviformis	browneyes
Camissonia scapoidea	Paiute suncup
Cardaria draba	heart-pod hoarycress
Cryptantha circumscissa	cushion cat's-eye
Distichlis spicata	coastal salt grass
Eriogonum ovalifolium	cushion wild buckwheat
Festuca idahoensis	bluebunch grass
Halogeton glomeratus	saltlover
Iva nevadensis	Nevada marsh-elder
Kochia americana	greenmolly
Lupinus sericeus	Pursh's silky lupine
Mirabilis alipes	winged four-o'clock
Oryzopsis hymenoides	Indian mountain-rice grass
Pascopyrum smithii	western-wheat grass
Poa secunda	curly blue grass
Sphaeralcea grossulariifolia	currant-leaf globe-mallow
Sporobolus airoides	alkali-sacaton
Vulpia octoflora	eight-flower six-weeks grass
Xylorhiza glabriuscula	smooth woody-aster

Desert Grassland

The short grasses vary from dense to open cover and are very similar to the grasslands of the Southern Deserts region. See the Southern Deserts region for a species list of this community.

WETLAND SYSTEMS

Riparian Woodland

Riparian Woodland occurs along permanent or semi-permanent streams. See the Southern Deserts region for a species list of this community.

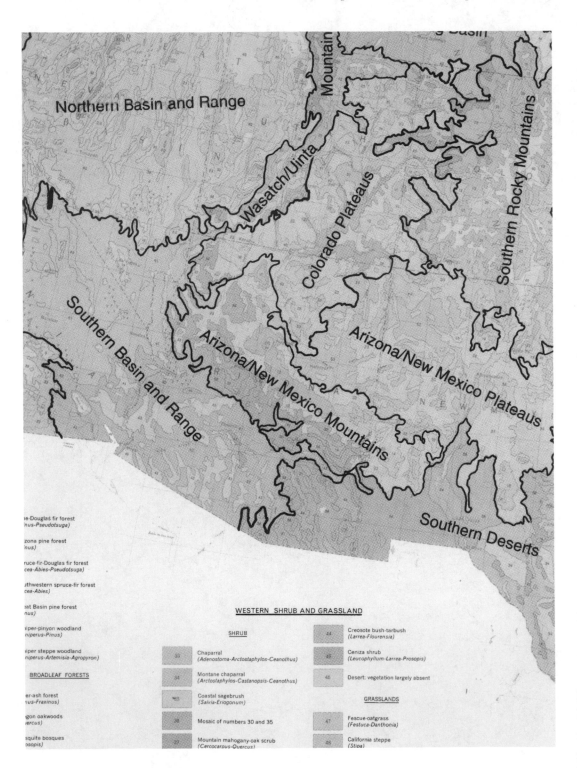

WESTERN SHRUB AND GRASSLAND

e-Douglas fir forest
(inus-Pseudotsuga)

zona pine forest
(nus)

ruce-fir-Douglas fir forest
(cea-Abies-Pseudotsuga)

uthwestern spruce-fir forest
(cea-Abies)

eat Basin pine forest
(nus)

iper-pinyon woodland
(niperus-Pinus)

iper steppe woodland
(niperus-Artemisia-Agropyron)

BROADLEAF FORESTS

er-ash forest
(nus-Fraxinus)

gon oakwoods
(ercus)

squite bosques
(osopis)

SHRUB

33	Chaparral *(Adenostoma-Arctostaphylos-Ceanothus)*
34	Montane chaparral *(Arctostaphylos-Castanopsis-Ceanothus)*
35	Coastal sagebrush *(Salvia-Eriogonum)*
36	Mosaic of numbers 30 and 35
37	Mountain mahogany-oak scrub *(Cercocarpus-Quercus)*

44	Creosote bush-tarbush *(Larrea-Flourensia)*
45	Ceniza shrub *(Leucophyllum-Larrea-Prosopis)*
46	Desert: vegetation largely absent

GRASSLANDS

47	Fescue-oatgrass *(Festuca-Danthonia)*
48	California steppe *(Stipa)*

Arizona/New Mexico Mountains

Arizona/New Mexico Mountains

Introduction

The ecological communities of the Arizona and New Mexico Mountains region are similar to communities of the Southern Deserts region. Many of the plant species are shared by the two regions. The ecological communities change in response to the temperature and precipitation changes of increased elevation. The bi-seasonal rain pattern of widespread, gentle rains in the winter and localized, heavy rains accompanying thunderstorms in the summer is found in both regions and significantly impacts plant communities.

Aspen occurs throughout the region in burned or disturbed areas. Riparian Woodland occurs along streams that flow for at least several months during winter and spring each year.

The primary sources used to develop descriptions and species lists are: Barbour and Billings 1988; Dick-Peddie 1992; Lowe 1964.

Dominant Ecological Communities

Upland Systems
Southwestern Spruce–Fir Forest
Spruce–Fir–Douglas-fir Forest
Ponderosa Pine Forest
Pine–Douglas-fir Forest
Juniper–Pinyon Woodland
Montane Scrub
Desert Grassland
Wetland Systems
Riparian Woodland

UPLAND SYSTEMS

Southwestern Spruce–Fir Forest

Southwestern Spruce–Fir Forest contains dense to open stands of low to medium tall needleleaf evergreen trees. Spruce–fir forests are found throughout the southern Rocky Mountains with the southern most extensions found on mountain peaks in the Arizona/New Mexico Mountains region between 8500 and 9000 feet. Because of the accumulation of litter and the often dense canopy, the herbaceous layer is not well developed in these forests. This community corresponds to Küchler #21.

Canopy
Characteristic Species
Abies lasiocarpa	subalpine fir
Picea engelmannii	Englemann's spruce

Associates
Abies concolor	white fir
Picea glauca	white spruce
Pinus aristata	bristle-cone pine

| *Pinus flexilis* | limber pine |
| *Populus tremuloides* | quaking aspen |

Woody Understory

Acer glabrum	Rocky Mountain maple
Alnus incana	speckled alder
Juniperus communis	common juniper
Lonicera involucrata	four-line honeysuckle
Mahonia repens	creeping Oregon-grape
Pachystima myrsinites	myrtle boxleaf
Pentaphylloides floribunda	golden-hardhack
Prunus emarginata	bitter cherry
Salix bebbiana	long-beak willow
Salix scouleriana	Scouler's willow
Symphoricarpos oreophilus	mountain snowberry
Vaccinium myrtillus	whortle-berry

Herbaceous Understory

Actaea rubra	red baneberry
Aquilegia chrysantha	golden columbine
Carex spp.	sedge
Dugaldia hoopesii	owl's-claws
Festuca rubra	red fescue
Gentiana spp.	gentian
Juncus spp.	rush
Pedicularis procera	giant lousewort
Pedicularis racemosa	parrot's-beak
Phleum alpinum	mountain timothy
Primula spp.	primrose
Trisetum spicatum	narrow false oat
Veratum californicum	California false hellebore
Viola canadensis	Canadian white violet
Viola nephrophylla	northern bog violet

Spruce–Fir–Douglas-fir Forest

Spruce Fir–Douglas-fir Forest is found at lower elevations than Southwestern Spruce–Fir Forest and is composed of large to medium trees. The forest has an open to dense canopy. If the canopy is open, broadleaf deciduous trees and shrubs are found in the understory. This community corresponds to Küchler #20.

Canopy
Characteristic Species

Abies concolor	white fir
Picea pungens	blue spruce
Pseudotsuga menziesii	Douglas-fir

Associates

| *Pinus ponderosa* | ponderosa pine |
| *Populus tremuloides* | quaking aspen |

Woody Understory

Acer glabrum	Rocky Mountain maple
Amelanchier alnifolia	Saskatoon service-berry
Chamaebatiaria millefolium	fernbush
Pachystima myrsinites	myrtle boxleaf
Physocarpus malvaceus	mallow-leaf ninebark
Prunus virginiana	choke cherry
Sambucus cerulea	blue elder
Symphoricarpos oreophilus	mountain snowberry
Vaccinium myrtillus	whortle-berry

Herbaceous Understory

Adiantum pedatum	northern maidenhair
Dugaldia hoopesii	owl's-claws
Erigeron eximius	spruce-fir fleabane
Festuca arizonica	Arizona fescue
Leymus triticoides	beardless lyme grass
Muhlenbergia virescens	screw leaf muhly

Ponderosa Pine Forest

Ponderosa Pine Forest of this region is similar to and shares many species with Ponderosa Pine Forest of the Arizona/New Mexico Plateaus and Southern Deserts regions. The Ponderosa Pine Forest of this region, however, occurs on large flat mesas and plateaus. The forests are found below the spruce-fir forests. The trees form an open to dense canopy; however, the open canopy with grass understories are not found on the steep slopes in southern Arizona. The shrubs are few, rarely dense, and not especially common. In the open canopy Ponderosa Pine Forest, the principle groundcovers are often grasses. There are fewer tree species than in the southern Arizona Ponderosa Pine Forest. This community corresponds to Küchler #19.

Canopy
Characteristic Species

Pinus ponderosa	ponderosa pine

Associates

Pinus cembroides	Mexican pinyon
Pinus flexilis	limber pine
Pinus leiophylla	Chihuahuan pine
Populus tremuloides	quaking aspen
Pseudotsuga menziesii	Douglas-fir
Quercus gambelii	Gambel's oak

Woody Understory

Arctostaphylos patula	green-leaf manzanita
Artemisia nova	black sagebrush
Artemisia tridentata	big sagebrush
Ceanothus fendleri	Fendler's buckbrush
Chamaebatiaria millefolium	fernbush
Chrysothamnus parryi	Parry's rabbitbrush
Fallugia paradoxa	Apache-plume
Fendlerella utahensis	Utah-fendlerbush

Holodiscus boursieri	Boursier's oceanspray
Holodiscus dumosus	glandular oceanspray
Jamesia americana	five-petal cliffbush
Juniperus communis	common juniper
Mahonia repens	creeping Oregon-grape
Pachystima myrsinites	myrtle boxleaf
Philadelphus microphyllus	little-leaf mock orange
Physocarpus monogynus	mountain ninebark
Purshia mexicana	Mexican cliff-rose
Ribes cereum	white squaw currant
Robinia neomexicana	New Mexico locust
Rubus idaeus	common red raspberry

Herbaceous Understory

Artemisia ludoviciana	white sagebrush
Blepharoneuron tricholepis	pine-dropseed
Bothriochloa barbinodis	cane beard grass
Bouteloua gracilis	blue grama
Comandra umbellata	bastard-toadflax
Elymus elymoides	western bottle-brush grass
Festuca arizonica	Arizona fescue
Hedeoma dentatum	Arizona false pennyroyal
Iris missouriensis	Rocky Mountain iris
Koeleria macrantha	prairie Koeler's grass
Lupinus palmeri	Palmer's lupine
Monarda fistulosa	Oswego-tea
Muhlenbergia montana	mountain muhly
Muhlenbergia wrightii	Wright's muhly
Oxytropis lamberti	stemless locoweed
Pteridium aquilinum	northern bracken fern
Sphaeralcea fendleri	thicket globe-mallow
Thalictrum fendleri	Fendler's meadow-rue
Thermopsis rhombifolia	prairie golden-banner
Vicia americana	American purple vetch

Pine–Douglas-fir Forest

Pine–Douglas-fir Forest is found on high plateaus and mountains and extends southward from the Rocky Mountains southwest to Colorado, Utah, New Mexico, and Arizona. The forests range from open to dense with tall, evergreen trees. In the southern mountains there is often much undergrowth. This community type corresponds to Küchler #18.

Canopy
Characteristic Species

Pinus ponderosa	ponderosa pine
Pseudotsuga menziesii	Douglas-fir

Associates

Picea pungens	blue spruce
Pinus flexilis	limber pine

Woody Understory

Acer glabrum	Rocky Mountain maple
Alnus incana	speckled alder
Ceanothus fendleri	Fendler's buckbrush
Chamaebatiaria millefolium	fernbush
Holodiscus dumosus	glandular oceanspray
Jamesia americana	five-petal cliffbush
Juniperus communis	common juniper
Prunus emarginata	bitter cherry

Herbaceous Understory

Blepharoneuron tricholepis	pine-dropseed
Festuca arizonica	Arizona fescue

Juniper–Pinyon Woodland

Juniper–Pinyon Woodland covers large areas below Ponderosa Pine Forest on the Mogollon, Coconino, and Kaibab plateaus. It is usually between 5500 and 7000 feet on flat-topped mesas and plateaus. The woodlands are open with a mixture of shrubs and herbaceous plants forming the understory. The oaks may be in tree or shrub form. This community corresponds to Küchler #23 and, in part, #32.

Canopy
Characteristic Species

Juniperus monosperma	one-seed juniper
Juniperus osteosperma	Utah juniper
Pinus edulis	two-needle pinyon

Associates

Juniperus deppeana	alligator juniper
Juniperus occidentalis	western juniper
Pinus monophylla	single-leaf pinyon
Quercus emoryi	Emory's oak
Quercus gambelii	Gambel's oak
Quercus grisea	gray oak
Quercus turbinella	shrub live oak

Woody Understory

Amelanchier alnifolia	Saskatoon service-berry
Amelanchier utahensis	Utah service-berry
Artemisia nova	black sagebrush
Artemisia tridentata	big sagebrush
Atriplex canescens	four-wing saltbush
Ceanothus fendleri	Fendler's buckbrush
Ceanothus integerrimus	deerbrush
Cercocarpus intricatus	little-leaf mountain-mahogany
Cercocarpus ledifolius	curl-leaf mountain-mahogany
Cerocarpus montanus	alder-leaf mountain-mahogany
Chamaebatiaria millifolium	fernbush
Chrysothamnus depressus	long-flower rabbitbrush
Chrysothamnus nauseosus	rubber rabbitbrush

Coleogyne ramosissima	blackbrush
Echinocereus coccineus	scarlet hedgehog cactus
Ephedra viridis	Mormon-tea
Fallugia paradoxa	Apache-plume
Garrya wrightii	Wright's silktassel
Gutierrezia sarothrae	kindlingweed
Krascheninnikovia lanata	winterfat
Mahonia fremonti	desert Oregon-grape
Opuntia basilaris	beaver-tail cactus
Opuntia erinacea	oldman cactus
Opuntia fragilis	pygmy prickly-pear
Opuntia polyacantha	hair-spine prickly-pear
Opuntia whipplei	rat-tail cholla
Purshia mexicana	Mexican cliff-rose
Purshia tridentata	bitterbrush
Robinia neomexicana	New Mexico locust
Symphoricarpos oreophilus	Mountain snowberry
Yucca baccata	banana yucca

Herbaceous Understory

Bouteloua curtipendula	side-oats grama
Bouteloua eriopoda	black grama
Bouteloua gracilis	blue grama
Calochortus ambiguus	doubting mariposa-lily
Castelleja integra	squawfeather
Elymus elymoides	western bottle-brush grass
Festuca arizonica	Arizona fescue
Hilaria jamesii	James' galleta
Keckiella antirrhinoides	chaparral bush-beardtongue
Koeleria macrantha	prairie Koeler's grass
Muhlenbergia torreyi	ringed muhly
Oryzopsis hymenoides	Indian Mountain-rice grass
Pascopyrum smithii	western-wheat grass
Piptochaetium fimbriatum	pinyon spear grass
Schizachyrium scoparium	little false bluestem
Sphaeralcea emoryi	Emory's globe-mallow
Sporobolus cryptandrus	sand dropseed
Stipa nelsonii	Nelson's needle grass
Stipa neomexicana	New Mexico needle grass

Montane Scrub

Montane Scrub is found at elevations of 3500 to 7000 feet in Arizona from the foothills of the Mogollon Rim to south of the Gila River. The precipitation varies from thirteen to twenty-three inches per year and occurs during two periods of the year. The shrubs have small, evergreen leaves and regenerate rapidly from root crowns after fires. Natural fires occur every 50 to 100 years. The surface vegetation dates from the last fire, the root systems are much older. The shrub cover varies from dense to somewhat open and exhibits a uniform height varying from three to seven feet. Because of grazing, the native grasses are limited to rocky areas. This community corresponds, in part, to Küchler #58.

Characteristic Woody Species
Quercus turbinella　　　　　　　　　　shrub live oak
Associates
Arctostaphylos pringlei	pink-bract manzanita
Arctostaphylos pungens	Mexican manzanita
Brickellia californica	California brickellbrush
Ceanothus greggi	Mojave buckbrush
Ceanothus intergerrimus	deerbrush
Cercocarpus ledifolius	curl-leaf mountain-mahogany
Cercocarpus montanus	alder-leaf mountain-mahogany
Eriodictyon angustifolium	narrow-leaf yerba-santa
Fallugia paradoxa	Apache-plume
Forestiera pubescens	stretchberry
Frangula betulifolia	birch-leaf buckthorn
Frangula californica	California coffee berry
Fraxinus anomala	single-leaf ash
Garrya flavescens	ashy silktassel
Garrya wrightii	Wright's silktassel
Juniperus monosperma	one-seed juniper
Mahonia haematocarpa	red Oregon-grape
Mimosa biuncifera	cat-claw mimosa
Prunus virginiana	choke cherry
Purshia mexicana	Mexican cliff-rose
Quercus chrysolepis	canyon live oak
Quercus emoryi	Emory's oak
Rhamnus crocea	holly-leaf buckthorn
Rhus glabra	smooth sumac
Rhus ovata	sugar sumac
Rhus trilobata	ill-scented sumac
Toxicodendron diversilobum	Pacific poison-oak
Vauquelinia californica	Arizona-rosewood

Herbaceous Understory
Aristida orcuttiana	single-awn three-awn
Aristida purpurea	purple three-awn
Aristida ternipes	spider grass
Bothriochloa barbinodis	cane beard grass
Bouteloua curtipendula	side-oats grama
Bouteloua eriopoda	black grama
Bouteloua hirsuta	hairy grama
Dalea albiflora	white-flower prairie-clover
Eragrostis intermedia	plains love grass
Glandularia wrightii	Davis Mountain mock vervain
Lycurus phleoides	common wolf's-tail
Penstemon eatoni	Eaton's beardtongue
Penstemon linarioides	toadflax beardtongue
Penstemon palmeri	scented beardtongue
Solanum xantii	chaparral nightshade
Solidago velutina	three-nerve goldenrod

Desert Grassland

The short grasses of this community type vary from dense to open cover and are very similar to the grasslands of the Southern Deserts region. See Southern Deserts region for a species list of this community.

WETLAND SYSTEMS

Riparian Woodland

Riparian Woodland occurs along permanent or semi-permanent streams. See the Southern Deserts region for a species list of this community.

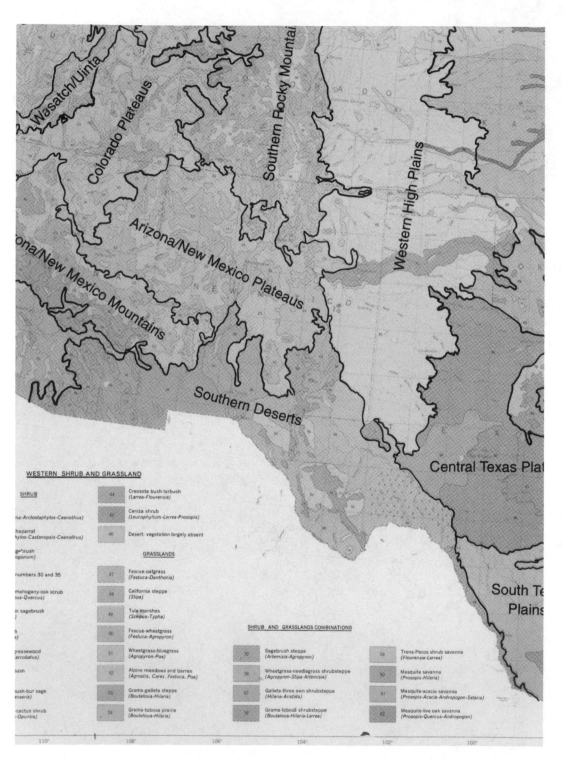

Southern Deserts

Introduction

The Southern Deserts region encompasses southeastern Arizona, Southern New Mexico, and Transpecos Texas extending in a narrow band along the Rio Grande River. The vegetation varies from Desert Scrub at low elevations to spruce-fir forests in the mountains. Desert Grassland, Evergreen Woodland, and Ponderosa Pine Forest are found at middle elevations. Broad ecotones exist where slope, soil, and topographic changes create a mosaic of vegetation types. The forests and woodlands vary from sparsely spaced trees to dense forests. The vegetation of the Southern Deserts region contains plants associated with the vegetation of Mexico as well as the Rocky Mountains.

The climate is characterized by bi-seasonal rains. Widespread, gentle rains occur in winter. The summer precipitation, beginning in July and continuing through October, occurs as intense local thunderstorms. As elevation increases, so does precipitation and thus changes in vegetation. Additionally, exposure and soils influence the distribution of vegetation types.

The riparian communities that occur along perennial streams vary with altitude. The deciduous trees of the riparian community often extend far into the Desert Scrub along streams. Trees found along dry washes and arroyos are distinct and characterized by small deciduous leaves.

The primary sources used to develop descriptions and species lists are: Barbour and Billings 1988; Dick-Peddie 1992; Lowe 1964.

Dominant Ecological Communities

Upland Systems
Southwestern Spruce–Fir Forest
Ponderosa Pine Forest
Evergreen Woodland
Desert Scrub
Desert Grassland

Wetland Systems
Riparian Woodland

UPLAND SYSTEMS

Southwestern Spruce–Fir Forest

Southwestern Spruce–Fir Forest is found at elevations of 7500 to 11500 feet on the highest peaks in the Southern Deserts region. Precipitation, mostly as snow, averages from thirty to twenty-five inches per year. Frequent afternoon thunderstorms occur during the summer. Where the conifers do not form a closed canopy, a few broadleaf, deciduous trees occur. Aspen is the most common tree in areas of fire or disturbances. Shrubs are more common on sites where the canopy is open. Sedges, mosses, lichens, and liverworts occur under dense canopies. In some areas stands of fir dominate exclusively. Where fir is dominate there is often little understory due to the considerable duff which accumulates on the forest floor. This community corresponds to Küchler #21.

Canopy
Characteristic Species
Abies concolor	white fir
Abies lasiocarpa	subalpine fir
Picea engelmannii	Englemann's spruce
Picea pungens	blue spruce
Pinus aristata	bristle-cone pine
Pinus flexilis	limber pine
Pseudotsuga menziesii	Douglas-fir

Associates
Acer negundo	ash-leaf maple
Pinus ponderosa	ponderosa pine
Pinus strobiformis	southwestern white pine
Populus tremuloides	quaking aspen
Quercus gambelii	Gambel's oak

Woody Understory
Acer glabrum	Rocky Mountain maple
Alnus incana	speckled alder
Arctostaphylos uva-ursi	red bearberry
Betula occidentalis	water birch
Juniperus communis	common juniper
Lonicera involucrata	four-line honeysuckle
Mahonia repens	creeping Oregon-grape
Pachystima myrsinites	myrtle boxleaf
Pentaphylloides floribunda	golden-hardhack
Prunus emarginata	bitter cherry
Ribes wolfii	winaha currant
Robinia neomexicana	New Mexican locust
Rubus spp.	raspberry
Salix bebbiana	long-beak willow
Salix scouleriana	Scouler's willow
Sambucus cerulea	blue elder
Vaccinium myrtillus	whortle-berry

Herbaceous Understory
Actaea spp.	baneberry
Adiantum pedatum	Northern maidenhair
Agrostis scabra	rough bent
Aquilegia spp.	columbine
Balsamorhiza spp.	balsamroot
Bromus anomalus	nodding brome
Bromus ciliatus	fringed brome
Bromus marginatus	large mountain brome
Carex spp.	sedge
Chimaphila umbellata	pipsissewa
Danthonia spp.	wild oat grass
Deschampsia cespitosa	tufted hair grass
Dugaldia hoopesii	owl's-claws

Epilobium spp.	willowherb
Erigeron formosissimus	beautiful fleabane
Festuca rubra	red fescue
Fragaria virginiana	Virginia strawberry
Frasera speciosa	monument plant
Gentiana spp.	gentian
Goodyera oblongifolia	green-leaf rattlesnake-plantain
Helenium spp.	sneezeweed
Heuchera rubescens	pink alumroot
Juncus spp.	rush
Lathyrus lanszwertii	Nevada vetchling
Maianthemum racemosum	feathery false Solomon's-seal
Oxalis spp.	wood-sorrel
Pedicularis spp.	lousewort
Phleum alpinum	mountain timothy
Poa spp.	blue grass
Primula spp.	primrose
Pseudocymopterus montanus	alpine false mountain-parsley
Pyrola chlorantha	green-flower wintergreen
Scrophularia parviflora	pineland figwort
Senecio spp.	ragwort
Trifolium spp.	clover
Trisetum spicatum	narrow false oat
Valeriana arizonica	Arizona valerian
Veratrum californicum	California false hellebore
Vicia americana	American purple vetch
Viola adunca	hook-spur violet
Viola canadensis	Canadian white violet

Ponderosa Pine Forest

Ponderosa Pine Forest is found between 6000 and 9000 feet. The development of ponderosa pine is controlled by precipitation which must be between eighteen and twenty-six inches annually. These pines, which may occur in pure stands, are isolated from the Ponderosa Pine Forest that occurs further north and have some different understory species. Because of the steep topography, with few level areas, grasslands and parks are uncommon in the southern Arizona pine forests. Such parks are more common in northern Arizona. Few well-developed riparian areas exist because of the steep topography. The importance and distribution of the associated trees, shrubs, and herbaceous vegetation vary across the Southern Deserts region. This community corresponds to Küchler #19.

Canopy
Characteristic Species

Pinus ponderosa	ponderosa pine

Associates

Acer grandidentatum	canyon maple
Alnus oblongifolia	Arizona alder
Arbutus arizonica	Arizona madrone
Cupressus arizonica	Arizona cypress
Juniperus deppeana	alligator juniper
Juniperus flaccida	drooping juniper

Pinus leiophylla	Chihuahuan pine
Pinus strobiformis	southwestern white pine
Populus tremuloides	quaking aspen
Pseudotsuga menziesii	Douglas-fir
Quercus emoryi	Emory's oak
Quercus gambelii	Gambel's oak
Quercus gravesii	Graves' oak
Quercus grisea	gray oak
Quercus hypoleucoides	silver-leaf oak
Quercus muehlenbergii	chinkapin oak

Woody Understory

Arctostaphylos pringlei	pink-bract manzanita
Arctostaphylos pungens	Mexican manzanita
Ceanothus fendleri	Fendler's buckbrush
Ceanothus integerrimus	deerbrush
Echinocereus triglochidiatus	king-cup cactus
Frangula betulifolia	birch-leaf buckthorn
Frangula californica	California coffee berry
Garrya wrightii	Wright's silktassel
Holodiscus dumosus	glandular oceanspray
Mahonia repens	creeping Oregon-grape
Morus microphylla	Texas mulberry
Pachystima myrsinites	myrtle boxleaf
Prunus serotina	black cherry
Quercus rugosa	net-leaf oak
Rhamnus crocea	holly-leaf buckthorn
Rhus glabra	smooth sumac
Rhus trilobata	ill-scented sumac
Ribes aureum	golden currant
Ribes pinetorum	orange gooseberry
Ribes viscosissimum	sticky currant
Robinia neomexicana	New Mexico locust
Rosa woodsii	Wood's rose
Sambucus cerulea	blue elder
Symphoricarpos longiflorus	desert snowberry
Symphoricarpos oreophilus	mountain snowberry
Yucca schottii	hoary yucca

Herbaceous Understory

Astragalus amphioxys	Aladdin's-slippers
Astragalus castaneiformis	chestnut milk-vetch
Astragalus tephrodes	ashen milk-vetch
Astragalus troglodytus	creeping milk-vetch
Blepharoneuron tricholepis	pine-dropseed
Bothriochloa barbinodis	cane beard grass
Bouteloua curtipendula	side-oats grama
Bouteloua gracilis	blue grama
Castilleja integra	squawfeather

Castilleja linarifolia	Wyoming Indian-paintbrush
Castilleja minor	alkali Indian-paint
Comandra umbellata	bastard-toadflax
Elyonurus barbiculmis	wool-spike grass
Erigeron arizonicus	Arizona fleabane
Erigeron concinnus	Navajo fleabane
Erigeron divergens	spreading fleabane
Erigeron lemmonii	Lemmon's fleabane
Erigeron neomexicanus	New Mexico fleabane
Erigeron oreophilus	chaparral fleabane
Erigeron platyphyllus	broad-leaf fleabane
Festuca arizonica	Arizona fescue
Hedeoma costatum	ribbed false pennyroyal
Hedeoma dentata	Arizona false pennyroyal
Hedeoma drummondii	Drummond's false pennyroyal
Hedeoma hyssopifolium	aromatic false pennyroyal
Hedeoma oblongifolium	oblong-leaf false pennyroyal
Hymenoxys bigelovii	Bigelow's rubberweed
Hymenoxys quinquesquamata	Rincon rubberweed
Iris missouriensis	Rocky Mountain iris
Laennecia schiedeana	pineland marshtail
Lathyrus graminifolius	grass-leaf vetchling
Lathyrus lanszwertii	Nevada vetchling
Lotus pleblus	long-bract bird's-foot-trefoil
Lotus unifoliolatus	American bird's-foot-trefoil
Lotus wrightii	scrub bird's-foot-trefoil
Lupinus brevicaulis	short-stem lupine
Lupinus huachucanus	Huachuca Mountain lupine
Lupinus neomexicanus	New Mexico lupine
Lupinus palmeri	Palmer's lupine
Monarda fistulosa	Oswego-tea
Muhlenbergia emersleyi	bull grass
Muhlenbergia montana	mountain muhly
Muhlenbergia virescens	screw-leaf muhly
Panicum bulbosum	bulb panic grass
Penstemon barbatus	beard-lip beardtongue
Penstemon virgatus	upright blue beardtongue
Piptochaetium fimbriatum	pinyon spear grass
Piptochaetium pringlei	Pringle's spear grass
Potentilla crinita	bearded cinquefoil
Potentilla hippiana	woolly cinquefoil
Potentilla thurberi	scarlet cinquefoil
Pteridium aquilinum	northern bracken fern
Schizachyrium cirratum	Texas false bluestem
Schizachyrium scoparium	little false bluestem
Senecio cynthioides	white mountain ragwort
Senecio eremophilus	desert ragwort
Senecio parryi	mountain ragwort
Solidago missouriensis	Missouri goldenrod

Solidago velutina	three-nerve goldenrod
Solidago wrightii	Wright's goldenrod
Sphaeralcea fendleri	thicket globe-mallow
Tetraneuris acaulis	stemless four-nerve-daisy
Thermopsis rhombifolia	pairie golden-banner
Viola canadensis	Canadian white violet
Viola nephrophylla	northern bog violet
Viola umbraticola	ponderosa violet

Evergreen Woodland

Evergreen Woodland is dominated by evergreen oaks on hill and mountain slopes between 4000 and 6500 feet. Evergreen Woodland varies from open to very dense with numerous associated species of grasses, dry tropic shrubs, succulents, and some cacti. The center of the Evergreen Woodland is the Sierra Madre of Mexico but it extends northward to the mountains of southeastern Arizona, southwestern New Mexico, and Transpecos Texas. Evergreen Woodland is typically very open. On the upper elevations the evergreen oaks are mixed with pine and juniper, and on the lower elevations grassland species are frequent in the open areas. This community corresponds, in part, to Küchler #31 and #71.

Canopy
Characteristic Species

Pinus engelmannii	Apache pine
Pinus leiophylla	Chihuahuan pine
Quercus arizonica	Arizona white oak
Quercus emoryi	Emory's oak
Quercus grisea	gray oak
Quercus hypoleucoides	silver-leaf oak
Quercus oblongifolia	Mexican blue oak
Quercus rugosa	net-leaf oak

Associates

Cupressus arizonica	Arizona cypress
Juniperus deppeana	alligator juniper
Juniperus erythrocarpa	red-berry juniper
Juniperus monosperma	one-seed juniper
Juniperus pinchotii	Pinchot's juniper
Pinus cembroides	Mexican pinyon
Pinus edulis	two-needle pinyon
Pinus remota	paper-shell pinyon

Woody Understory

Agave palmeri	Palmer's century-plant
Agave parryi	Parry's century-plant
Aplopappus laricifolius	turpentine bush
Arctostaphylos pungens	Mexican manzanita
Ceanothus fendleri	Fendler's buckbrush
Cercocarpus montanus	alder-leaf mountain-mahogany
Coryphantha recurvata	Santa Cruz beehive cactus
Dalea formosa	featherplume
Dasylirion wheeleri	common sotol

Echinocereus fendleri	pink-flower hedgehog cactus
Echinocereus rigidissimus	rainbow hedgehog cactus
Echinocereus triglochidiatus	king-cup cactus
Erythrina flabelliformis	coral-bean
Escobaria vivipara	spinystar
Eysenhardtia orthocarpa	Tahitian kidneywood
Fouquieria splendens	ocotillo
Mahonia haematocarpa	red Oregon-grape
Mammillaria heyderi	little nipple cactus
Mammillaria viridiflora	green-flower nipple cactus
Mimosa biuncifera	cat-claw mimosa
Mimosa dysocarpa	velvet-pod mimosa
Nolina microcarpa	sacahuista bear-grass
Opuntia phaeacantha	tulip prickly-pear
Opuntia santa-rita	Santa Rita prickly-pear
Opuntia spinosior	walkingstick cactus
Opuntia versicolor	stag-horn cholla
Prosopis glandulosa	honey mesquite
Purshia mexicana	Mexican cliff-rose
Quercus mohriana	Mohr's oak
Quercus toumeyi	Toumey's oak
Rhus virens	evergreen sumac
Robinia neomexicana	New Mexico locust
Vauquelinia californica	Arizona-rosewood
Yucca baccata	banana yucca
Yucca schottii	hoary yucca

Herbaceous Understory

Artemisia ludoviciana	white sagebrush
Bothriochloa barbinodis	cane beard grass
Bouteloua curtipendula	side-oats grama
Bouteloua eriopoda	black grama
Bouteloua gracilis	blue grama
Bouteloua hirsuta	hairy grama
Brickellia spp.	brickellbush
Calochortus spp.	mariposa lily
Cyperus spp.	flatsedge
Dalea versicolor	oakwoods prairie-clover
Elyonurus barbiculmis	wool-spike grass
Eragrostis intermedia	plains love grass
Eriogonum spp.	wild buckwheat
Heteropogon contortus	twisted tanglehead
Hibiscus spp.	rose-mallow
Leptochloa dubia	green sprangletop
Lupinus spp.	lupine
Lycurus phleoides	common wolf's-tail
Muhlenbergia emersleyi	bull grass
Muhlenbergia porteri	bush muhly
Muhlenbergia torreyi	ringed muhly

Oxalis spp.	wood sorrel
Penstemon spp.	beardtongue
Phaseolus spp.	bean
Salvia spp.	sage
Schizachyrium scoparium	little false bluestem
Senna hirsuta	woolly wild sensitive-plant
Sphaeralcea spp.	globe mallow
Verbena spp.	vervain

Desert Scrub

Desert Scrub is part of the Chihuahuan Desert and lies between 1800 feet in Transpecos Texas to above 3500 feet in Arizona. It covers southwest Texas, southern New Mexico, smaller portions of southeast Arizona, and extends into Mexico. Many shrub complexes occur throughout the Desert Scrub. It is a complex transition community between the grassland plains and Sonoran Desert. The dominant shrubs can change over short distances in response to changes in soil conditions. Some ecologists believe that this was once desert grassland but as it was degraded by grazing and fire control, shrubs were favored and the community structure changed. This community corresponds to Küchler #44, #45, and #59.

Characteristic Woody Species

Flourensia cernua	American tarwort
Larrea tridentata	creosote-bush

Associates

Acacia berlandieri	guajillo
Acacia constricta	mescat wattle
Acacia greggii	long-flower catclaw
Acacia neovernicosa	trans-pecos wattle
Agave lechuguilla	lechuguilla
Agave neomexicana	New Mexico century-plant
Agave parryi	Parry's century-plant
Agave scabra	rough century-plant
Aloysia gratissima	whitebrush
Aloysia wrightii	Wright's beebrush
Artemisia filifolia	silver sagebrush
Atriplex canescens	four-wing saltbush
Castela erecta	goatbush
Condalia ericoides	javelin-bush
Coryphantha cornifera	rhinoceros cactus
Coryphantha macromeris	nipple beehive cactus
Coryphantha ramillosa	whiskerbush
Coryphantha scheeri	long-tubercle beehive cactus
Dasylirion leiophyllum	green sotol
Dasylirion wheeleri	common sotol
Echinocactus horizonthalonius	devil's-head
Echinocactus texensis	horse-crippler
Echinocereus chloranthus	brown-spine hedgehog cactus
Echinocereus enneacanthus	pitaya
Echinocereus pectinatus	Texas rainbow cactus

Echinocereus rigidissimus	rainbow hedgehog cactus
Echinocereus stramineus	strawberry hedgehog cactus
Echinocereus triglochidiatus	king-cup cactus
Ephedra trifurca	long-leaf joint-fir
Epithelantha micromeris	ping-pong-ball cactus
Escobaria tuberculosa	white-column fox-tail cactus
Escobaria vivipara	spinystar
Euphorbia antisyphilitica	candelilla
Eysenhardtia texana	Texas kidneywood
Ferocactus hamatacanthus	turk's head
Forestiera pubescens	stretchberry
Fouquieria splendens	ocotillo
Garrya ovata	lindheimer silktassel
Guajacum angustifolium	Texas lignumvitae
Gutierrezia microcephala	small-head snakeweed
Gutierrezia sarothrae	kindlingweed
Haploesthes greggii	false broomweed
Hechtia texensis	Texas false agave
Isocoma pluriflora	southern jimmyweed
Jatropha dioica	leatherstem
Koeberlinia spinosa	crown-of-thorns
Leucophyllum frutescens	Texas barometer-bush
Leucophyllum minus	Big Bend barometer-bush
Mahonia trifoliata	Laredo Oregon-grape
Mammillaria heyderi	little nipple cactus
Mammillaria pottsii	rat tail nipple cactus
Menodora scabra	rough menadora
Mortonia sempervirens	Rio Grande saddlebush
Nolina erumpens	foothill bear-grass
Nolina microcarpa	sacahuista bear-grass
Nolina texana	Texas bear-grass
Opuntia engelmannii	cactus-apple
Opuntia imbricata	tree cholla
Opuntia kleiniae	candle cholla
Opuntia leptocaulis	Christmas cholla
Opuntia macrocentra	purple prickly-pear
Opuntia phaeacantha	tulip prickly-pear
Opuntia polyacantha	hair-spine prickly-pear
Opuntia schottii	dog cholla
Opuntia tunicata	thistle cholla
Parkinsonia texana	Texas palo-verde
Parthenium argentatum	guayule
Parthenium incanum	mariola
Peniocereus greggii	night-blooming-cereus
Prosopis glandulosa	honey mesquite
Quercus sinuata	bastard oak
Rhus aromatica	fragrant sumac
Rhus microphylla	little-leaf sumac

Schaefferia cuneifolia	desert-yaupon
Sclerocactus intertextus	white fish-hook cactus
Sclerocactus scheeri	Scheer's fish-hook cactus
Sclerocactus uncinatus	Chihuahuan fish-hook cactus
Senna wislizeni	Wislizenus' wild sensitive-plant
Thelocactus bicolor	glory-of-Texas
Tiquilia canescens	woody crinklemat
Tiquilia greggii	plumed crinklemat
Viguiera stenoloba	resinbush
Yucca baccata	banana yucca
Yucca elata	soaptree yucca
Yucca faxoniana	Eve's-needle
Yucca thompsoniana	Thompson's yucca
Yucca torreyi	Torrey's yucca
Ziziphus obtusifolia	lotebush

Herbaceous Understory

Aristida californica	California three-awn
Aristida divaricata	poverty three-awn
Aristida purpurea	purple three-awn
Aristida ternipes	spider grass
Baileya multiradiata	showy desert-marigold
Bothriochloa barbinodis	cane beard grass
Bothriochloa saccharoides	plumed beard grass
Bouteloua breviseta	gypsum grass
Bouteloua curtipendula	side-oats grama
Bouteloua eriopoda	black grama
Bouteloua gracilis	blue grama
Bouteloua hirsuta	hairy grama
Bouteloua ramosa	chino grama
Bouteloua rigidiseta	Texas grama
Bouteloua trifida	red grama
Buchloë dactyloides	buffalo grass
Chamaesaracha sordida	hairy five-eyes
Croton dioicus	grassland croton
Distichlis spicata	coastal salt grass
Engelmannia pinnatifida	Englemann's daisy
Erioneuron pulchellum	low woolly grass
Helianthus spp.	sunflower
Hilaria belangeri	curly-mesquite
Hilaria jamesii	James' galleta
Hilaria mutica	tobosa grass
Hymenoxys spp.	rubberweed
Mentzelia spp.	blazingstar
Muhlenbergia porteri	bush muhly
Nassella leucotricha	Texas wintergrass
Oryzopsis hymenoides	Indian mountain-rice grass
Pappophorum bicolor	pink pappus grass
Proboscidea louisianica	ram's horn

Schizachyrium scoparium	little false bluestem
Scleropogon brevifolius	burro grass
Senna roemeriana	two-leaved wild sensitive-plant
Setaria macrostachya	plains bristle grass
Sporobolus airoides	alkali-sacaton
Sporobolus contractus	narrow-spike dropseed
Sporobolus cryptandrus	sand dropseed
Sporobolus flexuosus	mesa dropseed
Sporobolus giganteus	giant dropseed
Sporobolus wrightii	Wright's dropseed
Thymophylla acerosa	American prickyleaf
Thymophylla pentachaeta	five-needle prickleleaf
Tidestromia spp.	honeysweet
Tridens muticus	awnless fluff grass
Xanthocephalum spp.	matchweed
Zinnia acerosa	white zinnia
Zinnia grandiflora	little golden zinnia

Desert Grassland

Desert Grassland is found throughout this region from Transpecos Texas through southern New Mexico to southeast Arizona and extends south into Mexico. These grasslands form extensive mosaics over large ecotones between the Desert Scrub and Evergreen Woodland. The two characteristic species are tobosa grass (on heavy soils subject to flooding) and black grama (gravelly uplands). The desert grasslands occur from 3500 to 7000 feet and receive approximately ten to fifteen inches of rain annually. Originally the grasses were perennial bunch grasses. In many areas these grasses have been replaced with low growing sod grasses or desert scrublands as a result of grazing and the suppression of natural fire. Trees and shrubs occur but vary in size, composition, and density from site to site. The compositional mix of the most prevalent grasses varies across the grassland depending on site specific characteristics. Desert grasslands vary from very open with bare ground between the bunches of grass to areas which have continuous to nearly uninterrupted cover. Tobosa grass may form dense stands in sites that receive excess run-off from the surrounding landscape and hence represent small, internally drained basins. Alkali-sacaton dominates in saline areas. This community corresponds, in part, to Küchler #53, #54, and #58

Characteristic Herbaceous Species

Bouteloua eriopoda	black grama
Bouteloua gracilis	blue grama
Hilaria jamesii	James' galleta
Hilaria mutica	tobosa grass

Associates

Ageratina wrightii	Wright's snakeroot
Allionia incarnata	trailing windmills
Amaranthus palmeri	Palmer's amaranth
Andropogon hallii	sand bluestem
Aristida californica	California three-awn
Aristida divaricata	poverty three-awn
Aristida purpurea	purple three-awn
Aristida ternipes	spider grass
Artemisia ludoviciana	white sagebrush
Astragalus mollissimus	woolly milk-vetch

Astragalus wootonii	Wooton's milk-vetch
Baileya multiradiata	showy desert-marigold
Bothriochloa barbinodis	cane beard grass
Bouteloua breviseta	gypsum grama
Bouteloua chondrosioides	spruce-top grama
Bouteloua curtipendula	side-oats grama
Bouteloua hirsuta	hairy grama
Bouteloua repens	slender grama
Buchloë dactyloides	buffalo grass
Calcohortus ambiguus	doubting mariposa-lily
Cryptantha micrantha	red-root cat's-eye
Dalea candida	white prairie-clover
Dalea purpurea	violet prairie-clover
Digitaria californica	California crab grass
Eragrostis intermedia	plains love grass
Erioneuron pulchellum	low woolly grass
Froelichia gracilis	slender snakecotton
Gaillardia pulchella	firewheel
Gaura coccinea	scarlet beeblossom
Glandularia bipinnatifida	Dakota mock vervain
Gossypium thurberi	Thurber's cotton
Grindelia squarrosa	curly-cup gumweed
Heteropogon contortus	twisted tanglehead
Hilaria belangeri	curly-mesquite
Leptochloa spp.	sprangletop
Lesquerella gordonii	Gordon's bladderpod
Lycurus phleoides	common wolf's-tail
Mentzelia albicaulis	white-stem blazingstar
Mentzelia multiflora	Adonia blazingstar
Muhlenbergia porteri	bush muhly
Muhlenbergia torreyi	ringed muhly
Oryzopsis hymenoides	Indian mountain-rice grass
Pacopyrum smithii	western-wheat grass
Panicum obtusum	blunt panic grass
Pappophorum vaginatum	whiplash pappus grass
Schizachyrium scoparium	little false bluestem
Scleropogon brevifolius	burro grass
Senecio flaccidus	thread-leaf ragwort
Senna bauhinioides	shrubby wild sensitive-plant
Setaria macrostachya	plains bristle grass
Sphaeralcea angustifolia	copper globe-mallow
Sphaeralcea coccinea	scalet globe-mallow
Sphaeralcea incana	soft globe-mallow
Sporobolus airoides	alkali-sacaton
Sporobolus cryptandrus	sand dropseed
Sporobolus flexuosus	mesa dropseed
Sporobolus wrightii	Wright's dropseed
Stipa comata	needle-and-thread
Tridens muticus	awnless fluff grass

Verbesina encelioides	golden crownbeard
Xanthocephalum spp.	matchweeds
Zinnia acerosa	white zinnia
Zinnia grandiflora	little golden zinnia

Woody Associates

Acacia constricta	mescat wattle
Acacia greggii	long-flower catclaw
Acacia neovernicosa	trans-pecos wattle
Agave lechuguilla	lechuguilla
Agave palmeri	Palmer's century-plant
Agave parryi	Parry's century-plant
Agave parviflora	small-flower century-plant
Agave scabra	rough century-plant
Agave schottii	Schott's century-plant
Aloysia wrightii	Wright's beebrush
Anisacanthus thurberi	Thurber's desert-honeysuckle
Artemisia bigelovii	flat sagebrush
Artemisia frigida	prairie sagebrush
Artemisia tridentata	big sagebrush
Atriplex canescens	four-wing saltbush
Buddleja scordioides	escobilla butterfly-bush
Calliandra eriophylla	fairy-duster
Celtis laevigata	sugar-berry
Celtis pallida	shiny hackberry
Condalia ericoides	javelin-bush
Condalia spathulata	squawbush
Coryphantha recurvata	Santa Cruz beehive cactus
Coryphantha scheeri	long-tubercle beehive cactus
Coursetia glandulosa	rosary baby-bonnets
Dalea formosa	featherplume
Dasylirion leiophyllum	green sotol
Dasylirion wheeleri	common sotol
Dodonaea viscosa	Florida hopbush
Echinocactus horizonthalonius	devil's-head
Echinocereus fendleri	pink-flower hedgehog cactus
Echinocereus rigidissimus	rainbow hedgehog cactus
Ephedra antisyphilitica	clapweed
Ephedra torreyana	Torrey's joint-fir
Ephedra trifurca	long-leaf joint-fir
Ephedra viridis	Mormon-tea
Ericameria laricifolia	turpentine-bush
Eriogonum abertianum	Abert's wild buckwheat
Eriogonum rotundifolium	round-leaf wild buckwheat
Eriogonum wrightii	bastard-sage
Erythrina flabelliformis	coral-bean
Escobaria orcuttii	Orcutt's fox-tail cactus
Escobaria tuberculosa	white-column fox-tail cactus
Escobaria vivipara	spinystar

Eysenhardtia orthocarpa	Tahitian kidneywood
Ferocactus wislizeni	candy barrel cactus
Flourensia cernua	American tarwort
Fouquieria splendens	ocotillo
Gutierrezia sarothrae	kindlingweed
Isocoma pluriflora	southern jimmyweed
Isocoma tenuisecta	shrine jimmyweed
Juniperus monosperma	one-seed juniper
Koeberlinia spinosa	crown-of-thorns
Larrea tridentata	creosote-bush
Lysiloma watsonii	little-leaf false tamarind
Mahonia trifoliata	Laredo Oregon-grape
Mammillaria grahamii	Graham's nipple cactus
Mammillaria heyderi	little nipple cactus
Mammillaria mainiae	counter-clockwise nipple cactus
Mammillaria wrightii	Wright's nipple cactus
Menodora scabra	rough menodora
Mimosa biuncifera	cat-claw mimosa
Mimosa dysocarpa	velvet-pod mimosa
Nolina erumpens	foothill bear-grass
Nolina microcarpa	sacahuista bear-grass
Nolina texana	Texas bear-grass
Opuntia chlorotica	clock-face prickly-pear
Opuntia engelmannii	cactus-apple
Opuntia gosseliniana	violet prickly-pear
Opuntia imbricata	tree cholla
Opuntia kunzei	devil's cholla
Opuntia leptocaulis	Christmas cholla
Opuntia macrocentra	purple prickly-pear
Opuntia phaeacantha	tulip prickly-pear
Opuntia polyacantha	hair-spine prickly-pear
Opuntia santa-rita	Santa Rita prickly-pear
Opuntia spinosior	walkingstick cactus
Opuntia tetracantha	Tucson prickly-pear
Parthenium incanum	mariola
Prosopis glandulosa	honey mesquite
Prosopis velutina	velvet mesquite
Rhus microphylla	little-leaf sumac
Rhus virens	evergreen sumac
Sageretia wrightii	Wright's mock buckthorn
Sclerocactus erectocentrus	red-spine fish-hook cactus
Sclerocactus intertextus	white fish-hook cactus
Senecio flaccidus	thread-leaf ragwort
Sideroxylon lanuginosum	gum bully
Yucca baccata	banana yucca
Yucca elata	soaptree yucca
Yucca faxoniana	Eve's-needle
Yucca glauca	soapweed yucca
Yucca thompsoniana	Thompson's yucca

Yucca torreyi	Torrey's yucca
Yucca treculeana	Don Quixote's-lace
Ziziphus obtusifolia	lotebush

WETLAND SYSTEMS

Riparian Woodland

Very little riparian vegetation remains in the deserts of the southwest. The riparian vegetation of the southwest varies from large deciduous trees forming a full canopy to riparian scrublands and changes with altitude. Cottonwood and willows can still be found in some areas forming a canopy immediately adjacent to perennial streams. Large thickets of mesquite called bosques were once found on floodplains, but few representatives remain. The understory of mature bosques historically contained annual and perennial grasses and young trees. Mesquite also forms the understory on stream banks. Some trees and shrubs of the riparian habitat are found along dry washes far into Desert Scrub regions.

Canopy
Characteristic Species

Fraxinus velutina	velvet ash
Juglans major	Arizona walnut
Platanus wrightii	Arizona sycamore
Populus deltoides	eastern cottonwood
Populus fremontii	Fremont's cottonwood
Salix bonplandiana	Bonpland's willow
Salix gooddingii	Goodding's willow

Associates

Acer grandidentatum	canyon maple
Celtis laevigata	sugar-berry
Populus angustifolia	narrow-leaf cottonwood
Prunus serotina	black cherry

Woody Understory

Acacia constricta	mescat wattle
Acacia farnesiana	mealy wattle
Acacia greggii	long-flower catclaw
Acacia rigidula	chaparro-prieto
Acer glabrum	Rocky Mountain maple
Acer negundo	ash-leaf maple
Alnus oblongifolia	Arizona alder
Atriplex lentiformis	quailbush
Atriplex polycarpa	cattle-spinach
Baccharis sarothroides	rosinbush
Brickellia laciniata	split-leaf brickellbush
Cephalanthus occidentalis	common buttonbush
Chilopsis linearis	desert-willow
Clematis ligusticifolia	deciduous traveler's-joy
Fallugia paradoxa	Apache-plume

Fraxinus berlandieriana	Mexican ash
Hymenoclea monogyra	single-whorl cheesebush
Lycium andersonii	red-berry desert-thorn
Lycium berlandieri	silver desert-thorn
Lycium fremontii	Freemont's desert-thorn
Morus microphylla	Texas mulberry
Olneya tesota	desert-ironwood
Parkinsonia florida	blue palo-verde
Parkinsonia texana	Texas palo-verde
Pluchea camphorata	plowman's wort
Pluchea sericea	arrow-weed
Prosopis glandulosa	honey mesquite
Prosopis pubescens	American screw-bean
Rhus microphylla	little-leaf sumac
Salix amygdaloides	peach-leaf willow
Salix interior	sandbar willow
Salix lasiolepis	arroyo willow
Salix lucida	shining willow
Salix nigra	black willow
Salix scouleriana	Scouler's willow
Sambucus cerulea	blue elder
Sapindus saponaria	wing-leaf soapberry
Suaeda moquinii	shrubby seepweed
Vitis arizonica	canyon grape
Ziziphus obtusifolia	lotebush

Herbaceous Understory

Amaranthus palmeri	Palmer's amaranth
Chloracantha spinosa	Mexican devilwood
Cucurbita spp.	gourd
Heliotropium curassavicum	seaside heliotrope
Panicum obtusum	blunt panic grass
Phragmites australis	common reed
Pteridium aquilinum	northern bracken fern
Sarcostemma spp.	twinevine
Verbesina encelioides	golden crownbeard

Riparian Woody Species of Dry Arroyos and Washes
Arizona

Acacia greggii	long-flower catclaw
Celtis laevigata	sugar-berry
Chilopsis linearis	desert willow
Juniperus monosperma	one-seed juniper
Parkinsonia florida	blue paloverde
Prosopis glandulosa	mesquite
Psorothamnus spinosus	smoketree
Sapindus saponaria	wing-leaf soapberry
Sapium biloculare	Mexican jumping bean

Transpecos Texas

Acacia farnesiana	mealy wattle
Acacia greggii	long-flower catclaw
Brickellia laciniata	split-leaf brickellbush
Celtis laevigata	sugar-berry
Celtis pallida	shiny hackberry
Chilopsis linearis	desert willow
Fraxinus velutina	velvet ash
Juglans microcarpa	little walnut
Populus fremontii	Fremont's cottonwood
Prosopis glandulosa	honey mesquite
Quercus pungens	scrub oak
Rhus microphylla	little-leaf sumac
Rhus virens	evergreen sumac
Sapindus saponaria	wing-leaf soapberry
Ungnadia speciosa	Mexican-buckeye

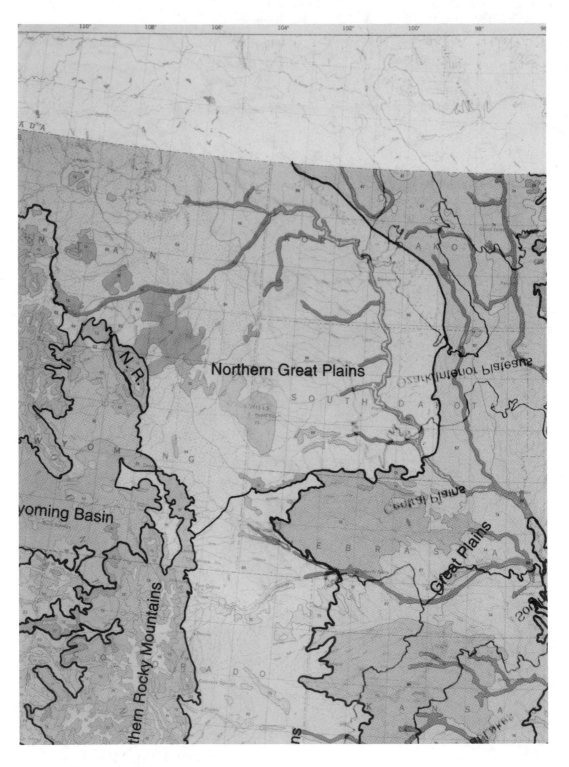

Northern Great Plains

Northern Great Plains

Introduction

The Northern Great Plains region includes western North and South Dakota, central and eastern Montana, and eastern Wyoming. The region is characterized by mixed and shortgrass prairies with forest communities more common at higher elevations. The region's boundaries are the tallgrass prairie to the east, the Rocky Mountains with conifer forests to the west, the blue grama and buffalo grass dominated shortgrass prairie to the south, and to the north grasslands extend into Canada.

Mixed Grass Prairie is characteristic of the eastern half of this region. In areas with sufficient moisture, the Mixed Grass Prairie community type may be dominated by tallgrass prairie species; shortgrass prairie species may dominate in drier situations. This area is an ecotone between the tallgrass and shortgrass prairies. Moving west into Wyoming and Montana, the short grasses become more dominant.

The Blackhills of South Dakota and Wyoming support ponderosa pine forests. The Bighorn, Little Belt, Bear Paw, and Little Rocky Mountains also occur within the region. These mountains support vegetation similar to that found in the Rocky Mountains to the West, including Douglas-fir Forest which is described in the Rocky Mountain region.

The primary sources used to develop descriptions and species lists are: Barbour and Billings 1988; Boon and Groe 1990; Pfister et al. 1977.

Dominant Ecological Communities

Upland Systems
   Blackhills Pine Forest
   Eastern Ponderosa Forest
   Sagebrush Steppe
   Foothills Prairie
   Mixed Grass Prairie
   Northern Shortgrass Prairie
Wetland Systems
   Northern Floodplain Forest
   Wet Meadow
   Pothole Marsh

UPLAND SYSTEMS

Blackhills Pine Forest

The Blackhills of South Dakota and eastern Montana support ponderosa pine forest communities. On the east side of the Blackhills, ponderosa pine forests may have broadleaf deciduous trees as a component of the canopy. On the west side of the Blackhills, shrubs are more likely to become important components of the community structure. Along streams within the Blackhills Pine Forest, hackberry, burr oak, and American elm are important community components. This community corresponds to Küchler #17.

Canopy
Characteristic Species
Pinus ponderosa	ponderosa pine

Associates
Acer negundo	ash-leaf maple
Betula papyrifera	paper birch
Picea glauca	white spruce
Prunus virginiana	choke cherry
Quercus macrocarpa	burr oak
Ulmus americana	American elm

Woody Understory
Amelanchier alnifolia	Saskatoon service-berry
Arctostaphylos uva-ursi	red bearberry
Artemisia tridentata	big sagebrush
Celtis occidentalis	common hackberry
Chrysothamnus nauseosus	rubber rabbitbrush
Gutierrezia sarothrae	kindlingweed
Juniperus communis	common juniper
Mahonia repens	creeping Oregon-grape
Opuntia polyacantha	hair-spine prickly-pear
Ostrya virginiana	eastern hop-hornbeam
Physocarpus opulifolius	Atlantic ninebark
Rosa woodsii	Woods' rose
Symphoriocarpos albus	common snowberry
Symphoriocarpos occidentalis	western snowberry

Herbaceous Understory
Antennaria plantaginifolia	woman's-tobacco
Aristida purpurea	purple three-awn
Bouteloua gracilis	blue grama
Buchloë dactyloides	buffalo grass
Carex concinna	low northern sedge
Carex duriuscula	spike-rush sedge
Carex filifolia	thread-leaf sedge
Carex foenea	dry-spike sedge
Carex inops	long-stolon sedge
Danthonia spicata	poverty wild oat grass
Fragaria virginiana	Virginia strawberry
Galium boreale	northern bedstraw
Koeleria macrantha	prairie Koeler's grass
Lathyrus ochroleucus	cream vetchling
Lupinus argenteus	silver-stem lupine
Oryzopsis asperifolia	white-grain mountain-rice grass
Pascopyrum smithii	western-wheat grass
Plantago patagonica	woolly plantain
Pseudoroegneria spicatum	bluebunch-wheat grass
Schizachyrium scoparium	little false bluestem
Stipa comata	needle-and-thread

Eastern Ponderosa Forest

Eastern Ponderosa Forest occurs in central Montana in the Bighorn, Snowy, Little Belt, Bear Paw, and Little Rocky Mountains. This community corresponds to Küchler #16.

Canopy
Characteristic Species
Pinus ponderosa	ponderosa pine

Associates
Juniperus scopulorum	Rocky Mountain juniper
Prunus virginiana	choke cherry

Woody Understory
Amelanchior alnifolia	Saskatoon service-berry
Mahonia repens	creeping Oregon-grape
Opuntia spp.	prickly-pear
Purshia tridentata	bitterbrush
Rhus trilobata	ill-scented sumac
Symphoricarpos albus	common snowberry
Toxicodendron radicans	eastern poison-ivy
Yucca glauca	soapweed yucca

Herbaceous Understory
Andropogon gerardii	big bluestem
Antennaria rosea	rosy pussytoes
Arnica cordifolia	heart-leaf leopard-bane
Balsamorhiza sagittata	arrow-leaf balsamroot
Bouteloua gracilis	blue grama
Carex pensylvanica	Pennsylvania sedge
Cystopteris fragilis	brittle bladder fern
Danthonia unispicata	few-flower wild oat grass
Festuca campestris	prairie fescue
Festuca idahoensis	bluebunch fescue
Galium boreale	northern bedstraw
Lithospermum ruderale	Columbian puccoon
Pascopyrum smithii	western-wheat grass
Pseudoroegneria spicata	bluebunch-wheat grass
Schizachne purpurascens	false melic grass
Schizachyrium scoparium	little false bluestem
Stipa comata	needle-and-thread

Sagebrush Steppe

Sagebrush Steppe occurs in the Northern Great Plains region, in the northeastern corner of Wyoming. This community corresponds to Küchler #55.

Characteristic Species
Artemisia tridentata	big sagebrush
Pseudoroegneria spicatum	bluebunch-wheat grass

Associates

Agoseris glauca	pale goat-chicory
Allium acuminatum	taper-tip onion
Allium textile	wild white onion
Alyssum desertorum	desert madwort
Amelanchier alnifolia	Saskatoon service-berry
Antennaria dimorpha	cushion pussytoes
Antennaria rosea	rosy pussytoes
Arabis holboellii	Holboell's rockcress
Arabis lignifera	Owen's valley rockcress
Arabis sparsiflora	elegant rockcress
Arenaria hookeri	Hooker's sandwort
Artemisia cana	hoary sagebrush
Artemisia ludoviciana	white sagebrush
Artemisia nova	black sagebrush
Artemisia pedatifida	bird-foot sagebrush
Artemisia tripartita	three-tip sagebrush
Artimisia frigida	prairie sagebrush
Astragalus miser	timber milk-vetch
Astragalus pectinatus	narrow-leaf milk-vetch
Astragalus purshii	Pursh's milk-vetch
Astragalus spatulatus	tufted milk-vetch
Atriplex canescens	four-wing saltbush
Atriplex confertifolia	shadscale
Atriplex gardneri	Gardner's saltbush
Balsamorhiza incana	hoary balsamroot
Balsamorhiza sagittata	arrow-leaf balsamroot
Calochortus nuttallii	sego-lily
Carex duriuscula	spike-rush sedge
Carex filifolia	threadleaf sedge
Carex obtusata	blunt sedge
Castilleja angustifolia	northwestern Indian-paintbrush
Chenopodium leptophyllum	narrow-leaf goosefoot
Chrysothamnus nauseosus	rubber rabbitbrush
Chrysothamnus viscidiflorus	green rabbitbrush
Comandra umbellata	bastard-toadflax
Cordylanthus ramosus	bushy bird's-beak
Crepis modocensis	siskiyou hawk's-beard
Cryptantha watsonii	Watson's cat's-eye
Delphinium bicolor	flat-head larkspur
Delphinium geyeri	Geyer's larkspur
Descurainia incana	mountain tansy-mustard
Distichilis spicata	coastal salt grass
Elymus elymoides	western bottle-brush grass
Elymus macrourus	thick-spike wild rye
Elymus trachycaulus	slender rye grass
Erigeron caespitosus	tufted fleabane
Erigeron engelmannii	Englemann's fleabane
Eriogonum caespitosum	matted wild buckwheat

Eriogonum cernuum	nodding wild buckwheat
Eriogonum compositum	arrow-leaf wild buckwheat
Eriogonum microthecum	slender wild buckwheat
Eriogonum ovalifolium	cushion wild buckwheat
Festuca idahoensis	bluebunch fescue
Gayophytum ramosissimum	pinyon groundsmoke
Grayia spinosa	spiny hop-sage
Gutierrezia sarothrae	kindlingweed
Hilaria jamesii	James' galleta
Hordeum jubatum	fox-tail barley
Hymenoxys richardsonii	Colorado rubberweed
Iva axillaris	deer-root
Juncus balticus	Baltic rush
Koeleria macrantha	prairie Koeler's grass
Krascheninnikovia lanata	winterfat
Lappula occidentalis	flat-spine sheepburr
Leptodactylon pungens	granite prickly-phlox
Lesquerella ludoviciana	Louisiana bladderpod
Leymus cinereus	Great Basin lyme grass
Lithospermum incisum	fringed gromwell
Lithospermum ruderale	Columbian puccoon
Lomatium foeniculaceum	carrot-leaf desert-parsley
Lupinus argenteus	silver-stem lupine
Lupinus sericeus	Pursh's silky lupine
Machaeranthera canescens	hoary tansy-aster
Mertensia oblongifolia	languid-lady
Monolepis nuttalliana	Nuttall's poverty-weed
Musineon divaricatum	leafy wild parsley
Opuntia polyacantha	hair-spine prickly-pear
Oryzopsis hymenoides	Indian mountain-rice grass
Pascopyrum smithii	western-wheat grass
Penstemon arenicola	red desert beardtongue
Penstemon fremontii	Fremont's beardtongue
Phlox hoodii	carpet phlox
Phlox longifolia	long-leaf phlox
Phlox multiflora	Rocky Mountain phlox
Poa fendleriana	mutton grass
Poa secunda	curly blue grass
Polygonum douglasii	Douglas' knotweed
Pseudocymopterus montanus	alpine false mountain-parsley
Pseudoroegneria spicatum	bluebunch-wheat grass
Purshia tridentata	bitterbrush
Ribes cereum	white squaw currant
Sphaeralcea coccinea	scarlet globe-mallow
Stenotus acaulis	stemless mock goldenweed
Stipa comata	needle-and-thread
Stipa lettermani	Letterman's needle grass
Stipa nelsonii	Nelson's needle grass
Tetradymia canescens	spineless horsebrush

Tetradymia spinosa	short-spine horsebrush
Thermopsis rhombifolia	prairie golden-banner
Trifolium gymnocarpon	holly-leaf clover
Vulpia octoflora	eight-flower six-weeks grass
Xylorhiza glabriuscula	smooth woody-aster
Ziadenus venosus	meadow deathcamas
Zigadenus paniculatus	sand-corn

Foothills Prairie

Foothills Prairie occurs in the foothills of the few mountain ranges within the region and along the western boundary of the region in the foothills of the Rocky Mountains. This prairie type is dominated by short grasses. This community corresponds to Küchler #63.

Characteristic Species

Festuca campestris	prairie fescue
Festuca idahoensis	bluebunch fescue
Pseudoroegneria spicatum	bluebunch-wheat grass
Stipa comata	needle-and-thread

Associates

Artemisia frigida	prairie sagebrush
Bouteloua gracilis	blue grama
Carex filifolia	threadleaf sedge
Koeleria macrantha	prairie Koeler's grass
Pascopyrum smithii	western-wheat grass
Poa secunda	curly blue grass

Mixed Grass Prairie

Mixed Grass Prairie occurs in the eastern half of the Northern Great Plains region. Along with a mixture of short and tall grasses, this community supports scattered needle-leaf evergreen shrubs and small trees. This prairie community is found throughout North and South Dakota. This community corresponds to Küchler #66 and #68.

Characteristic Species

Bouteloua gracilis	blue grama
Buchloë dactyloides	buffalo grass
Nassella viridula	green tussock
Pascopyrum smithii	western-wheat grass
Stipa comata	needle-and-thread

Associates

Artemisia drancunculus	dragon wormwood
Artemisia frigida	prairie sagebrush
Artemisia ludoviciana	white sagebrush
Aster ericoides	white heath aster
Bouteloua curtipendula	side-oats grama
Carex duriuscula	spike rush sedge
Carex filifolia	threadleaf sedge
Carex inops	long-stolon sedge
Echinacea angustifolia	blacksamson

Elymus trachycaulus	slender rye grass
Juniperus scopulorum	Rocky Mountain juniper
Koeleria macrantha	prairie Koeler's grass
Liatris punctata	dotted gay feather
Oryzopsis hymenoides	Indian mountain-rice grass
Pediomelum argophyllum	silver-leaf Indian-breadroot
Schizachyrium scoparium	little false bluestem
Stipa spartea	porcupine grass

Northern Shortgrass Prairie

Northern Shortgrass Prairie occurs in western North and South Dakota, eastern Montana, Wyoming, and Colorado. This prairie, a short-medium tall grassland, is the dominant vegetation type in this region. This community correspond to Küchler #64.

Characteristic Species

Bouteloua gracilis	blue grama
Pascopyrum smithii	western-wheat grass
Stipa comata	needle-and-thread

Associates

Artemisia frigida	prairie sagebrush
Carex filifolia	threadleaf sedge
Gutierrezia sarothrae	kindlingwood
Heterotheca villosa	hairy false golden-aster
Koeleria macrantha	prairie Koeler's grass
Liatris punctata	dotted gay feather
Muhlenbergia cuspidata	stony-hills muhly
Nassella viridula	green tussock
Poa secunda	curly blue grass
Pseudoroegneria spicatum	bluebunch-wheat grass
Schizachyrium scoparium	little false bluestem
Sporobolus cryptandrus	sand dropseed
Stipa spartea	porcupine grass

WETLAND SYSTEMS

Northern Floodplain Forest

Northern Floodplain Forest occurs along major rivers and streams from North Dakota south to Oklahoma. This community corresponds to Küchler #98.

Canopy

Characteristic Species

Populus deltoides	eastern cottonwood
Salix nigra	black willow
Ulmus americana	American elm

Associates

Acer negundo	ash-leaf maple
Acer rubrum	red maple
Acer saccharinum	silver maple
Betula nigra	river birch
Celtis occidentalis	common hackberry
Fraxinus americana	white ash
Fraxinus pennsylvanica	green ash
Gleditsia triacanthos	honey-locust
Juglans nigra	black walnut
Platanus occidentalis	American sycamore
Prunus virginiana	choke cherry
Quercus macrocarpa	burr oak
Ulmus rubra	slippery elm

Woody Understory

Amorpha fruticosa	false Indigo-bush
Celastrus scandens	American bittersweet
Clematis virginiana	devil's-darning-needles
Parthenocissus quinquefolia	Virgina creeper
Rhus glabra	smooth sumac
Ribes missouriense	Missouri gooseberry
Salix amygdaloides	peach-leaf willow
Salix interior	sandbar willow
Smilax tamnoides	chinaroot
Symphoricarpos occidentalis	western snowberry
Symphoricarpos orbiculatus	coral-berry
Vitis riparia	river-bank grape
Vitis vulpina	frost grape

Herbaceous Understory

Elymus virginicus	Virginia wild rye
Galium aparine	sticky-willy
Laportea canadensis	Canadian wood-nettle

Wet Meadow

Wet Meadow occurs scattered throughout the eastern Great Plains region. Wet Meadow occupies areas slightly higher than the Pothole Marshes. The soils of the Wet Meadow are usually wet and soggy for most of the year.

Characteristic Species

Carex trichocarpa	hairyfruit sedge
Eleocharis acicularis	needle spike-rush
Eleocharis compressa	flat-stem spike-rush
Eleocharis palustris	pale spike-rush
Juncus balticus	Baltic rush
Juncus marginatus	grass-leaf rush
Juncus nodosus	knotted rush

Juncus tenuis	poverty rush
Juncus torreyi	Torrey's rush
Scirpus americanus	chairmaker's bulrush

Associates

Agalinis tenuifolia	slender-leaf false foxglove
Agrostis gigantea	black bent
Agrostis hyemalis	winter bent
Alopecurus aequalis	short-awn meadow foxtail
Aureolaria virginica	downy yellow false-foxglove
Calamagrostis stricta	slim-stem reedgrass
Caltha palustris	yellow marsh-marigold
Campanula aparinoides	marsh bellflower
Carex festucacea	fescue sedge
Carex gravida	heavy sedge
Carex hystericina	porcupine sedge
Carex lanuginosa	woolly sedge
Carex nebrascensis	Nebraska sedge
Carex scoparia	pointed broom sedge
Carex stricta	uptight sedge
Catabrosa aquatica	water whorl grass
Cicuta maculata	spotted water-hemlock
Crepis runcinata	fiddle-leaf hawk's-beard
Cyperus squarrosus	awned flat sedge
Distichlis spicata	coastal salt grass
Dodecatheon meadia	eastern shootingstar
Epilobium palustre	marsh willowherb
Eriophorum gracile	slender cotton-grass
Galium trifidum	three-petal bedstraw
Galium triflorum	fragrant bedstraw
Gentiana andrewsii	closed bottle gentian
Gentiana saponaria	harvestbells
Glyceria striata	fowl manna grass
Helianthus tuberosus	Jerusalem-artichoke
Hordeum jubatum	fox-tail barley
Hypericum majus	greater Canadian St. John's-wort
Hypoxis hirsuta	eastern yellow star-grass
Juncus longistylis	long-style rush
Lilium philadelphicum	wood lily
Liparis loeselii	yellow wide-lip orchid
Lobelia siphilitica	great blue lobelia
Lotus unifoliolatus	American bird's-foot-trefoil
Lycopus asper	rough water-horehound
Lysimachia ciliata	fringed yellow-loosestrife
Lysimachia thyrsiflora	tufted yellow-loosestrife
Lythrum alatum	wide-angle loosestrife
Mentha arvensis	American wild mint
Menyanthes trifoliata	buck-bean
Plantago eriopoda	red-woolly plantain
Platanthera leucophaea	prairie white fringed orchid

Potentilla paradoxa	bushy cinquefoil
Ranunculus cymbalaria	alkali buttercup
Ranunculus sceleratus	cursed crowfoot
Scirpus pallidus	pale bulrush
Scutellaria galericulata	hooded skullcap
Spartina cynosuroides	big cord grass
Spiranthes cernua	white nodding ladies'-tresses
Spiranthes romanzoffiana	hooded ladies'-tresses
Stachys palustris	woundwort
Strophostyles leiosperma	slick-seed fuzzy-bean
Teucrium canadense	American germander
Triadenum virginicum	Virginia marsh-St. John's-wort
Triglochin maritimum	seaside arrow-grass

Pothole Marsh

Pothole Marsh occurs around the Minnesota-South Dakota border and northward into Canada. Pothole Marsh is a very important nesting habitat for ducks in North America. It is found on poorly drained soils of lowland and backwater bays or pothole depressions of mesic prairie. The outer margins of the pothole depressions are dominated by cord grass mixed with other species such as swamp milkweed and ironweed. The centers are typically dominated by smartweed which may be mixed with duck-potato and cat-tail. This is a community in transition, eventually filling up with organic matter and becoming fertile prairie soils. Draining activities have greatly diminished the extent of these valuable wetlands.

Characteristic Species

Phragmites australis	common reed
Scirpus americanus	chairmaker's bulrush
Scirpus tabernaemontani	soft-stem bulrush
Typha latifolia	broad-leaf cat-tail
Zizania aquatica	Indian wild rice

Associates

Alisma subcordatum	American water-plantain
Asclepias incarnata	swamp milkweed
Berula erecta	cut-leaf water-parsnip
Bidens frondosa	devil's pitchfork
Eleocharis acicularis	needle spike-rush
Eleocharis palustris	pale spike-rush
Equisetum hyemale	tall scouring-rush
Lobelia siphilitica	great blue lobelia
Polygonum amphibium	water smartweed
Sagitarria latfolia	duck-potato
Scirpus fluviatilis	river bulrush
Scirpus pallidus	pale bulrush
Spartina cynosuroides	big cord grass
Spartina pectinata	salt-meadow cord grass
Verbena hastata	simpler's-joy
Vernonia fasciculata	prairie ironweed

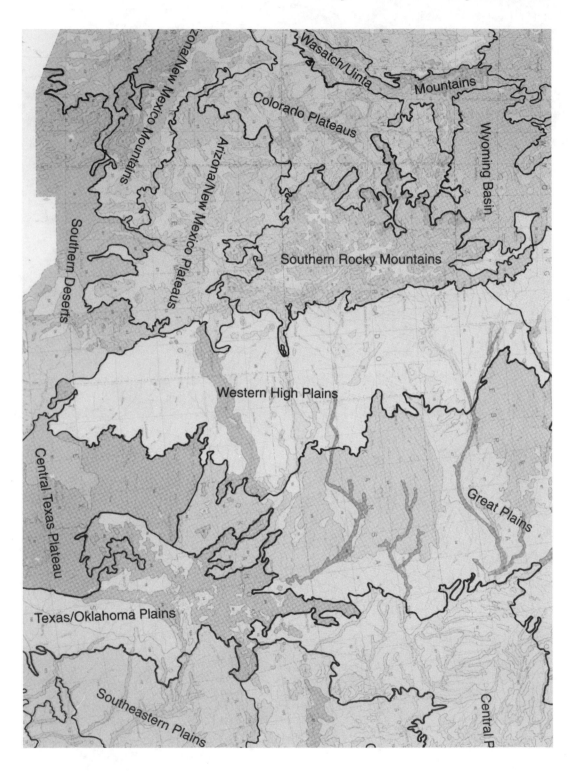

Western High Plains

Western High Plains

Introduction

The Western High Plains region extends from the eastern boundary of the southern Rocky Mountains in Wyoming through the panhandle of Nebraska into western Kansas and south into the panhandle of Oklahoma, Texas, and eastern New Mexico. The characteristic vegetation of the region is Shortgrass Prairie. The most common Shortgrass Prairie species include blue grama and buffalo grass. Unsuccessful attempts to farm large areas of shortgrass prairie have resulted in an increase of annual and perennial weeds to the detriment of the native grasses.

Although the region is mainly Shortgrass Prairie, mixedgrass and tallgrass communities may be found in moist areas and in areas along the eastern boundary where there is greater precipitation. The Nebraska panhandle contains ponderosa pine forests. Since this community is more typical of the area north and west of the high plains, it is described in the Northern Great Plains region. The Canadian River in the panhandle of Texas provides habitat for several uncommon species of oaks and tall grasses.

The primary sources used to develop descriptions and species lists are: Barbour and Billings 1988; Dick-Peddie 1992; McMahan et al. 1984.

Dominant Ecological Communities

Upland Systems
> Juniper–Pinyon Woodland
> Shinnery
> Sagebrush–Bluestem Prairie
> Shortgrass Prairie
> Sandhill Prairie

Wetland Systems
> Floodplain Forest

UPLAND SYSTEMS

Juniper–Pinyon Woodland

Juniper–Pinyon Woodland is the southwestern-most community in this region occurring in the foothills of the Rocky Mountains. This community corresponds to Küchler #23.

Canopy
Characteristic Species

Juniperus monosperma	one-seed juniper
Juniperus osteosperma	Utah juniper
Pinus edulis	two-needle pinyon

Associates

Juniperus occidentalis	western juniper
Quercus emoryi	Emory's oak
Quercus gambelii	Gambel's oak
Quercus grisea	gray oak

Woody Understory

Artemisia tridentata	big sagebrush
Fallugia paradoxa	Apache-plume
Purshia mexicana	Mexican cliff-rose
Purshia tridentata	bitterbrush

Herbaceous Understory

Bouteloua curtipendula	side-oats grama
Bouteloua gracilis	blue grama
Oryzopsis hymenoides	Indian mountain-rice grass
Pascopyrum smithii	western-wheat grass
Sporobolus cryptandrus	sand dropseed

Shinnery

Shinnery is a savanna community of midgrass prairie species with evergreen trees and shrubs. This community occurs on sandy soils and dunes in the panhandle of Texas and eastern New Mexico in close proximity to the Canadian River which runs through the western High Plains region of these states. Areas along the Canadian River may also support tallgrass prairie species where there is sufficient water. This community corresponds in part to Küchler #65.

Characteristic Species

Quercus mohriana	Mohr's oak
Schizachyrium scoparium	little false bluestem

Associates

Andropogon gerardii	big bluestem
Andropogon hallii	sand bluestem
Artemisia filifolia	silver sagebrush
Bouteloua curtipendula	side-oats grama
Bouteloua gracilis	blue grama
Buchloë dactyloides	buffalo grass
Calamovilfa gigantea	giant sand-reed
Celtis laevigata	sugar-berry
Eriogonum annuum	annual wild buckwheat
Juniperus pinchotii	Pinchot's juniper
Panicum virgatum	wand panic grass
Prosopis glandulosa	honey mesquite
Prunus angustifolia	chickasaw plum
Quercus havardii	Harvard's oak
Quercus pungens	sandpaper oak
Rhus trilobata	ill-scented sumac
Sorghastrum nutans	yellow Indian grass
Sporobolus cryptandrus	sand dropseed
Sporobolus giganteus	giant dropseed
Yucca campestris	plains yucca
Yucca glauca	soapweed yucca

Sagebrush–Bluestem Prairie

Sagebrush–Bluestem Prairie occurs throughout eastern Colorado in the panhandle of Oklahoma and in western Kansas. The community is characterized by medium-tall grasses and the dwarf shrub, silver sagebrush (sandsage). Sagebrush-Bluestem Prairie is considered a mixed prairie of both tall and short grasses. This community corresponds to Küchler #70.

Characteristic Species
Andropogon hallii	sand bluestem
Artemisia filifolia	silver sagebrush
Bouteloua hirsuta	hairy grama
Schizachyrium scoparium	little false bluestem

Associates
Bouteloua gracilis	blue grama
Buchloë dactyloides	buffalo grass
Calamovilfa longifolia	prairie sand-reed
Eragrostis trichodes	sand love grass
Helianthus petiolaris	prairie sunflower
Hordeum jubatum	fox-tail barley
Panicum virgatum	wand panic grass
Redfieldia flexuosa	blowout grass
Sporobolus cryptandrus	sand dropseed
Stipa comata	needle-and-thread
Yucca glauca	soapweed yucca

Shortgrass Prairie

Shortgrass Prairie is the most common community in the High Plains region. Blue grama is the most abundant grass and shares dominance with buffalo grass. The extensive shortgrass prairie was once home to herds of buffalo and pronghorn antelope. Much of the area has been converted to agricultural and livestock purposes which has caused irreparable changes in the community structure. This community corresponds in part to Küchler #65.

Characteristic Species
Bouteloua gracilis	blue grama
Buchloë dactyloides	buffalo grass

Associates
Aristida purpurea	purple three-awn
Bouteloua curtipendula	side-oats grama
Bouteloua hirsuta	hairy grama
Elymus elymoides	western bottle-brush grass
Gaura coccinea	scarlet beeblossom
Grindelia squarrosa	curly-cup gumweed
Lycurus phleoides	common wolf's-tail
Machaeranthera pinnatifida	lacy tansy-aster
Muhlenbergia torreyi	ringed muhly
Pascopyrum smithii	western-wheat grass
Plantago patagonica	woolly plantain
Psoralidium tenuiflorum	slender-flower lemonweed
Ratibida columnifera	red-spike Mexican-hat

Sphaeralcea coccinea	scarlet globe-mallow
Sporobolus cryptandrus	sand dropseed
Yucca glauca	soapweed yucca
Zinnia grandiflora	little golden zinnia

Sandhill Prairie

Sandhill Prairie is more characteristic of the Nebraska Sandhills in the Great Plains Region. It is of limited extent in this region, confined to several isolated locations near the Platte River valley. This community corresponds to Küchler #75.

Characteristic Species

Andropogon gerardii	big bluestem
Andropogon hallii	sand bluestem
Calamovilfa longifolia	prairie sand-reed
Schizachyrium scoparium	little false bluestem
Stipa comata	needle-and-thread

Associates

Androsace occidentalis	western rock-jasmine
Anemone caroliniana	Carolina thimbleweed
Aristida longespica	red three-awn
Artemisia campestris	pacific wormwood
Asclepias arenaria	sand milkweed
Asclepias lanuginosa	side-cluster milkweed
Asclepias latifolia	broad-leaf milkweed
Asclepias stenophylla	slim-leaved milkweed
Asclepias viridiflora	green comet milkweed
Aster ericoides	white heath aster
Astragalus crassicarpus	ground-plum
Bouteloua curtipendula	side-oats grama
Bouteloua hirsuta	hairy grama
Calylophus serrulatus	yellow sundrops
Carex duriuscula	spike-rush sedge
Carex filifolia	thread-leaf sedge
Carex inops	long-stolon sedge
Chamaesyce geyeri	Geyer's sandmat
Chamaesyce missurica	prairie sandmat
Cirsium canescens	prairie thistle
Collomia linearis	narrow-leaf mountain-trumpet
Commelina virginica	Virginia dayflower
Cymopteris montanus	mountain spring-parsley
Cyperus schweinitzii	sand flat sedge
Dalea candida	white prairie-clover
Dalea purpurea	violet prairie-clover
Dalea villosa	silky prairie-clover
Eragrostis trichodes	sand love grass
Erigeron bellidiastrum	western daisy fleabane
Eriogonum annuum	annual wild buckwheat
Erysimum asperum	plains wallflower
Euphorbia hexagona	six-angle spurge

Froelichia floridana	plains snake-cotton
Heterotheca villosa	hairy false golden-aster
Hymenopappus filifolius	fine-leaf woollywhite
Ipomopsis longiflora	white-flower skyrocket
Koeleria macrantha	prairie Koeler's grass
Lespedeza capitata	round-head bush-clover
Leucocrinum montanum	star-lily
Liatris squarrosa	scaly gayfeather
Linum rigidum	large-flower yellow flax
Lithospermum caroliniense	hairy puccoon
Lithospermum incisum	fringed gromwell
Machaeranthera canescens	hoary tansy-aster
Machaeranthera pinnatifida	lacy tansy-aster
Mirabilis hirsuta	hairy four-o'clock
Mirabilis linearis	narrow-leaf four-o'clock
Oenothera pallida	white-pole evening-primrose
Oenothera rhombipetala	greater four-point evening-primrose
Opuntia humifusa	eastern prickly-pear
Orobanche fasciculata	clustered broom-rape
Oryzopsis hymenoides	Indian mountain-rice grass
Oxytropis lamberti	stemless locoweed
Panicum virgatum	wand panic grass
Paspalum setaceum	slender crown grass
Pediomelum cuspidatum	large-bract Indian-breadroot
Pediomelum esculentum	large Indian-breadroot
Penstemon albidus	red-line beardtongue
Penstemon angustifolius	broad-beard beardtongue
Penstemon gracilis	lilac beardtongue
Phlox caespitosa	clustered phlox
Polygala alba	white milkwort
Polygala verticillata	whorled milkwort
Senecio plattensis	prairie ragwort
Sisyrinchium angustifolium	narrow-leaf blue-eyed-grass
Sorghastrum nutans	yellow Indian grass
Sporobolus asper	tall dropseed
Sporobolus cryptandrus	sand dropseed
Talinum teretifolium	quill fameflower
Thelesperma megapotamicum	hopi-tea
Tradescantia occidentalis	prairie spiderwort

Wetland Systems

Floodplain Forest

Floodplain Forest occurs along major rivers including the Missouri, Little Missouri, Yellowstone, and White Rivers.

Canopy
Characteristic Species
Populus deltoides	eastern cottonwood
Salix nigra	black willow
Ulmus americana	American elm

Associates
Acer negundo	ash-leaf maple
Acer rubrum	red maple
Acer saccharinum	silver maple
Betula nigra	river birch
Celtis occidentalis	common hackberry
Fraxinus americana	white ash
Fraxinus pennsylvanica	green ash
Gleditsia triacanthos	honey-locust
Juglans nigra	black walnut
Platanus occidentalis	American sycamore
Prunus virginiana	choke cherry
Quercus macrocarpa	burr oak
Ulmus rubra	slippery elm

Woody Understory
Amorpha fruticosa	false Indigo-bush
Celastrus scandens	American bittersweet
Clematis virginiana	devil's-darning-needles
Parthenocissus quinquefolia	Virginia-creeper
Rhus glabra	smooth sumac
Ribes missouriense	Missouri gooseberry
Salix amygdaloides	peach-leaf willow
Salix interior	sandbar willow
Smilax tamnoides	chinaroot
Symphoricarpos occidentalis	western snowberry
Symphoricarpos orbiculatus	coral-berry
Toxicodendron radicans	eastern poison-ivy
Vitis riparia	river-bank grape
Vitis vulpina	frost grape

Herbaceous Understory
Elymus virginicus	Virginia wild rye

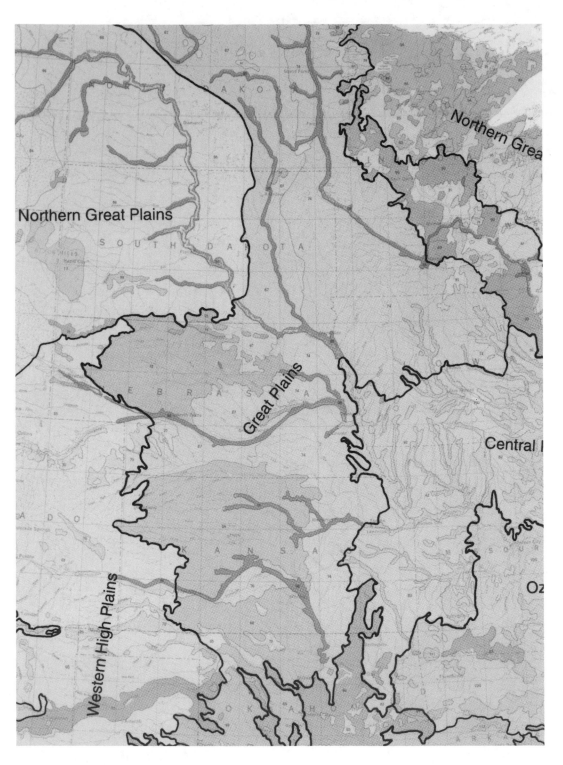

Great Plains

Great Plains

Introduction

The Great Plains extend from southern Manitoba, Canada, through the eastern Dakotas, western Minnesota, northern Iowa, Nebraska, Kansas, and western Oklahoma. This region is characterized by tallgrass and mixed grass prairie communities on flat and rolling plains. The boundaries of the region are the forested areas to the east and the shortgrass plains to the west.

The Great Plains support several kinds of prairie communities. Big bluestem, Indian grass, and wand panic grass (switchgrass) are characteristic throughout the region in relatively moist areas. In the areas of the tall grasses, big bluestem sometimes reaches heights of eight feet above the ground with roots extending equally deep into the soil. As one moves west across the grasslands precipitation tends to decrease, evaporation tends to increase, and the grasses become shorter and less dense. Where moisture is less abundant and evaporation greater, little false bluestem, dropseed, and side-oats grama are characteristic. These mid-height grasses generally grow in bunches or clumps two to four feet tall. The prairie soils in this region are very dark and rich with humus topsoil.

Other communities in the region include: Northern Floodplain Forest along major rivers and streams, Oak-Hickory Forest and Oak Barrens along the eastern prairie border, and the Cross Timbers Woodland to the south. Oak-Hickory Forest and Oak Barrens are described in the Central Plains and Southern Great Lakes regions. Throughout the area, marsh and wet meadow communities occur in depressions. The area around the Minnesota-South Dakota border is notable because of the numerous small marshes called "marsh or prairie pot-holes".

Prairies were once widespread throughout the region but today only small patches of prairie remain. Wild grazing animals such as the bison and pronghorn antelope were an integral component of the native prairie ecosystem. Natural fires were also very important in the maintenance of the prairie. Most of the region today has been converted to agriculture.

The primary sources used to develop descriptions and species lists are: Barbour and Billings 1988, Boon and Groe 1990; Pool 1913; Weaver 1954.

Dominant Ecological Communities

Upland Systems
Bluestem Prairie
Western Bluestem Prairie
Sand Prairie
Mixed Grass Prairie
Mixed Grass–Shrub Prairie

Wetland Systems
Northern Floodplain Forest
Wet Meadow
Pothole Marsh

UPLAND SYSTEMS

Bluestem Prairie

Bluestem Prairie occurs from North Dakota and Minnesota south to Iowa, Nebraska, Kansas, and Oklahoma. It is often referred to as the "True Prairie" and is one of three recognized "tallgrass" prairie types. Bluestem Prairie is dominated by big bluestem, wand panic grass, and yellow Indian grass. Bluestem Prairie has largely been converted to agricultural purposes. Suppression of fire has also encouraged the invasion of shrubs and trees into the prairie. This community corresponds to Küchler #74.

Characteristic Species

Andropogon gerardii	big bluestem
Panicum virgatum	wand panic grass
Sorghastrum nutans	yellow Indian grass

Associates

Amorpha canescens	leadplant
Antennaria neglecta	field pussytoes
Artemisia ludoviciana	white sagebrush
Asclepias ovalifolia	oval-leaf milkweed
Asclepias speciosa	showy milkweed
Aster ericoides	white heath aster
Aster laevis	smooth blue aster
Astragalus crassicarpus	ground-plum
Baptisia alba	white wild indigo
Baptisia bracteata	long-bract wild indigo
Bouteloua curtipendula	side-oats grama
Cirsium flodmanii	Flodman's thistle
Dalea candida	white prairie-clover
Dalea purpurea	violet prairie-clover
Delphinium carolinianum	Carolina larkspur
Dichanthelium leibergii	Leiberg's rosette grass
Dichanthelium oligosanthes	Heller's rosette grass
Echinacea angustifolia	blacksamson
Erigeron strigosus	prairie fleabane
Galium boreale	northern bedstraw
Galium tinctorium	stiff marsh bedstraw
Helianthus grosseserratus	saw-tooth sunflower
Helianthus maximiliani	Michaelmas-daisy
Helianthus pauciflorus	stiff sunflower
Heuchera richardsonii	Richardson's alumroot
Koeleria macrantha	prairie Koeler's grass
Liatris aspera	tall gayfeather
Liatris punctata	dotted gayfeather
Liatris scariosa	devil's-bite
Lilium philadelphicum	wood lily
Lithospermum canescens	hoary puccoon
Pedicularis canadensis	Canadian lousewort
Pediomelum argophyllum	silver-leaf Indian-breadroot
Pediomelum esculentum	large Indian-breadroot

Phlox pilosa	downy phlox
Potentilla arguta	tall cinquefoil
Prenanthes racemosa	purple rattlesnake-root
Psoralidium tenuiflorum	slender-flower lemonweed
Ratibida columnifera	red-spike Mexican-hat
Ratibida pinnata	gray-head Mexican-hat
Rosa arkansana	prairie rose
Schizachyrium scoparium	little false bluestem
Silphium laciniatum	compassplant
Solidago canadensis	Canadian goldenrod
Solidago missouriensis	Missouri goldenrod
Solidago rigida	hard-leaf goldenrod
Spartina pectinata	freshwater cord grass
Sporobolus heterolepis	prairie dropseed
Stipa spartea	porcupine grass
Viola pedatifida	crow-foot violet
Zigadenus elegans	mountain deathcamas
Zizia aptera	heart-leaf alexanders

Western Bluestem Prairie

The western edge of the "true prairie" is indicated by the abundance of western-wheat grass and porcupine grass (needle grass). This tallgrass prairie community originally covered an area approximately thirty-five to forty-five miles wide extending north from North Dakota into South Dakota and Nebraska. This community corresponds to Küchler #67.

Characteristic Species

Andropogon gerardii	big bluestem
Pascopyrum smithii	western-wheat grass
Stipa spartea	porcupine grass

Associates

Artemisia frigida	prairie sagebrush
Artemisia ludoviciana	white sagebrush
Aster ericoides	white heath aster
Bouteloua curtipendula	side-oats grama
Bouteloua gracilis	blue grama
Echinacea angustifolia	blacksamson
Elymus trachycaulus	slender wild rye
Koeleria macrantha	prairie Koeler's grass
Liatris punctata	dotted gayfeather
Nassella viridula	green tussock grass
Pediomelum argophyllum	silver-leaf Indian-breadroot
Rosa arkansana	prairie rose
Schizachyrium scoparium	little false bluestem
Solidago missouriensis	Missouri goldenrod
Solidago mollis	velvet goldenrod
Stipa comata	needle-and-thread

Sand Prairie

Sand Prairie occurs in areas in central and south-central Kansas and widely in the Sandhills region in Nebraska. Sand Prairie is the third recognized tallgrass prairie type. Unique in the Nebraska Sandhills are formations on the hillsides referred to as "blow-outs". Plants associated with dune stabilization can be found in "blow-out" areas.

Characteristic Species

Andropogon gerardii	big bluestem
Andropogon hallii	sand bluestem
Calamovilfa longifolia	prairie sand-reed
Schizachyrium scoparium	little false bluestem
Stipa comata	needle-and-thread

Associates

Androsace occidentalis	western rock-jasmine
Anemone caroliniana	Carolina thimbleweed
Aristida longespica	red three-awn
Artemisia campestris	Pacific wormwood
Asclepias arenaria	sand milkweed
Asclepias lanuginosa	side-cluster milkweed
Asclepias latifolia	broad-leaf milkweed
Asclepias stenophylla	slim-leaf milkweed
Asclepias viridiflora	green comet milkweed
Aster ericoides	white heath aster
Astragalus crassicarpus	ground-plum
Bouteloua curtipendula	side-oats grama
Bouteloua hirsuta	hairy grama
Calylophus serrulatus	yellow sundrops
Carex duriuscula	spike-rush sedge
Carex filifolia	thread-leaf sedge
Carex inops	long-stolon sedge
Chamaesyce geyeri	Geyer's sandmat
Chamaesyce missurica	prairie sandmat
Cirsium canescens	prairie thistle
Collomia linearis	narrow-leaf mountain-trumpet
Commelina virginica	Virginia dayflower
Cymopterus montanus	mountain spring-parsley
Cyperus schweinitzii	sand flat sedge
Dalea candida	white prairie-clover
Dalea purpurea	violet prairie-clover
Dalea villosa	silky prairie-clover
Eragrostis trichodes	sand lover grass
Erigeron bellidiastrum	western daisy fleabane
Eriogonum annuum	annual wild buckwheat
Erysimum asperum	plains wallflower
Euphorbia hexagona	six-angle spurge
Froelichia floridana	plains snake-cotton
Heterotheca villosa	hairy false golden-aster
Hymenopappus filifolius	fine-leaf woollywhite
Ipomopsis longiflora	white-flower skyrocket

Koeleria macrantha	prairie Koeler's grass
Lespedeza capitata	round-head bush-clover
Leucocrinum montanum	star-lily
Liatris squarrosa	scaly gayfeather
Linum rigidum	large-flower yellow flax
Lithospermum caroliniense	hairy puccoon
Lithospermum incisum	fringed gromwell
Machaeranthera canescens	hoary tansy-aster
Machaeranthera pinnatifida	lacy tansy-aster
Mirabilis hirsuta	hairy four-o'clock
Mirabilis linearis	narrow-leaf four-o'clock
Oenothera pallida	white-pole evening-primrose
Oenothera rhombipetala	greater four-point evening-primrose
Opuntia humifusa	eastern prickly-pear
Orobanche fasciculata	clustered broom-rape
Oryzopsis hymenoides	Indian mountain-rice grass
Oxytropis lamberti	stemless locoweed
Panicum virgatum	wand panic grass
Paspalum setaceum	slender crown grass
Pediomelum cuspidatum	large-bract Indian-breadroot
Pediomelum esculentum	large Indian-breadroot
Penstemon albidus	red-line beardtongue
Penstemon angustifolius	broad-beard beardtongue
Penstemon gracilis	lilac beardtongue
Phlox caespitosa	clustered phlox
Polygala alba	white milkwort
Polygala verticillata	whorled milkwort
Senecio plattensis	prairie ragwort
Sisyrinchium angustifolium	narrow-leaf blue-eyed-grass
Sorghastrum nutans	yellow Indian grass
Sporobolus asper	tall dropseed
Sporobolus cryptandrus	sand dropseed
Talinum teretifolium	quill fameflower
Thelesperma megapotamicum	Hopi-tea
Tradescantia occidentalis	prairie spiderwort

Mixed Grass Prairie

Mixed Grass Prairie occurs in Kansas and Oklahoma west of the more mesic Bluestem and Western Bluestem Prairies. Mixed Grass Prairie is considered a "mixed prairie" due to the occurrence of both tall and short grasses. Because mixed grass prairies occur as a transition zone between the short and tall grass types they support a very diverse mix of species. The transitional nature of mixed prairies makes them the most floristically rich of all the grasslands. Grazing pressure and drought have caused many changes in the original vegetation. This community corresponds to Küchler #69.

Characteristic Species

Bouteloua curtipendula	side-oats grama
Bouteloua gracilis	blue grama
Schizachyrium scoparium	little false bluestem

Associates

Ambrosia psilostachya	western ragwort
Amorpha canescens	leadplant
Andropogon gerardii	big bluestem
Buchloë dactyloides	buffalo grass
Calylophus serrulatus	yellow sundrops
Clematis fremontii	Fremont's leather-flower
Dalea enneandra	nine-anther prairie-clover
Echinacea angustifolia	blacksamson
Erysimum asperum	plains wallflower
Hedeoma hispidum	rough false pennyroyal
Liatris punctata	dotted gayfeather
Panicum virgatum	wand panic grass
Paronychia jamesii	James' nailwort
Pascopyrum smithii	western-wheat grass
Psoralidium tenuiflorum	slender-flower lemonweed
Scutellaria resinosa	resin-dot skullcap
Sorghastrum nutans	yellow Indian grass
Sporobolus asper	tall dropseed
Stenosiphon linifolius	false gaura

Mixed Grass–Shrub Prairie

Mixed Grass–Shrub Prairie occurs in southcentral Nebraska, Kansas, and northwestern Oklahoma. The community is characterized by medium-tall grasses and the dwarf shrub, silver sagebrush (sandsage). This prairie community is considered a mixed prairie, having both tall and short grasses. This community corresponds to Küchler #70.

Characteristic Species

Andropogon hallii	sand bluestem
Artemisia filifolia	silver sagebrush
Bouteloua hirsuta	hairy grama
Schizachyrium scoparium	little false bluestem

Associates

Bouteloua gracilis	blue grama
Buchloë dactyloides	buffalo grass
Calamovilfa longifolia	prairie sand-reed
Eragrostis trichodes	sand lover grass
Helianthus petiolaris	prairie sunflower
Hordeum jubatum	fox-tail barley
Panicum virgatum	wand panic grass
Redfieldia flexuosa	blowout grass
Sporobolus cryptandrus	sand dropseed
Stipa comata	needle-and-thread
Yucca glauca	soapweed yucca

WETLAND SYSTEMS

Northern Floodplain Forest

Many rivers dissect the eastern Great Plains region. The Red, James, Platt, Kansas, and Arkansas Rivers are among the largest streams that support Northern Floodplain Forest. Floodplain species tolerate both flooding and drought. This community corresponds to Küchler #98.

Canopy
Characteristic Species
Populus deltoides	eastern cottonwood
Salix nigra	black willow
Ulmus americana	American elm

Associates
Acer negundo	ash-leaf maple
Acer rubrum	red maple
Acer saccharinum	silver maple
Betula nigra	river birch
Celtis occidentalis	common hackberry
Fraxinus americana	white ash
Fraxinus pennsylvanica	green ash
Gleditsia triacanthos	honey-locust
Juglans nigra	black walnut
Platanus occidentalis	American sycamore
Prunus virginiana	choke cherry
Quercus macrocarpa	burr oak
Ulmus rubra	slippery elm

Woody Understory
Amorpha fruticosa	false indigo-bush
Celastrus scandens	American bittersweet
Clematis virginiana	devil's-darning-needles
Parthenocissus quinquefolia	Virgina-creeper
Rhus glabra	smooth sumac
Ribes missouriense	Missouri gooseberry
Salix amygdaloides	peach-leaf willow
Salix interior	sandbar willow
Smilax tamnoides	chinaroot
Symphoricarpos occidentalis	western snowberry
Symphoricarpos orbiculatus	coral-berry
Toxicodendron radicans	eastern poison-ivy
Vitis riparia	river-bank grape
Vitis vulpina	frost grape

Herbaceous Understory
Elymus virginicus	Virginia wild rye
Galium aparine	sticky-willy
Laportea canadensis	Canadian wood-nettle

Wet Meadow

Wet Meadow occurs scattered throughout the eastern Great Plains region. Wet Meadow occupies areas slightly higher than Pothole Marsh. The soils of Wet Meadow are usually wet and soggy for most of the year.

Characteristic Species

Carex trichocarpa	hairy-fruit sedge
Eleocharis acicularis	needle spike-rush
Eleocharis compressa	flat-stem spike-rush
Eleocharis palustris	pale spike-rush
Juncus balticus	Baltic rush
Juncus marginatus	grass-leaf rush
Juncus nodosus	knotted rush
Juncus tenuis	poverty rush
Juncus torreyi	Torrey's rush
Scirpus americanus	chairmaker's bulrush

Associates

Agalinis tenuifolia	slender-leaf false foxglove
Agrostis gigantea	black bent
Agrostis hyemalis	winter bent
Alopecurus aequalis	short-awn meadow foxtail
Aureolaria virginica	downy yellow false-foxglove
Calamagrostis stricta	slim-stem reedgrass
Caltha palustris	yellow marsh-marigold
Campanula aparinoides	marsh bellflower
Carex festucacea	fescue sedge
Carex gravida	heavy sedge
Carex hystericina	porcupine sedge
Carex lanuginosa	woolly sedge
Carex nebrascensis	Nebraska sedge
Carex praegracilis	clustered field sedge
Carex scoparia	pointed broom sedge
Carex stricta	uptight sedge
Catabrosa aquatica	water whorl grass
Cicuta maculata	spotted water-hemlock
Crepis runcinata	fiddle-leaf hawk's-beard
Cyperus squarrosus	awned flat sedge
Distichlis spicata	coastal salt grass
Dodecatheon meadia	eastern shootingstar
Epilobium palustre	marsh willowherb
Eriophorum gracile	slender cotton-grass
Galium trifidum	three-petal bedstraw
Galium triflorum	fragrant bedstraw
Gentiana andrewsii	closed bottle gentian
Gentiana saponaria	harvestbells
Glyceria striata	fowl manna grass
Helianthus tuberosus	Jerusalem-artichoke
Hordeum jubatum	fox-tail barley

Hypericum majus	greater Canadian St. John's-wort
Hypoxis hirsuta	eastern yellow star-grass
Juncus longistylis	long-style rush
Lilium philadelphicum	wood lily
Liparis loeselii	yellow wide-lip orchid
Lobelia siphilitica	great blue lobelia
Lotus unifoliolatus	American bird's-foot-trefoil
Lycopus asper	rough water-horehound
Lysimachia ciliata	fringed yellow-loosestrife
Lysimachia thyrsiflora	tufted yellow-loosestrife
Lythrum alatum	wing-angle loosestrife
Mentha arvensis	American wild mint
Menyanthes trifoliata	buck-bean
Plantago eriopoda	red-woolly plantain
Platanthera leucophaea	prairie white fringed orchid
Potentilla paradoxa	bushy cinquefoil
Ranunculus cymbalaria	alkali buttercup
Ranunculus sceleratus	cursed crowfoot
Scirpus pallidus	pale bulrush
Scutellaria galericulata	hooded skullcap
Spartina cynosuroides	big cord grass
Spiranthes cernua	white nodding ladies'-tresses
Spiranthes romanzoffiana	hooded ladies'-tresses
Stachys palustris	woundwort
Strophostyles leiosperma	slick-seed fuzzy-bean
Teucrium canadense	American germander
Triadenum virginicum	Virginia marsh-St. John's-wort
Triglochin maritimum	seaside arrow-grass

Pothole Marsh

Pothole Marsh occurs around the Minnesota-South Dakota Boarder and northward into Canada. Pothole Marsh is a very important nesting habitat for ducks in North America. It is found on poorly drained soils of lowland and backwater bays or pothole depressions of mesic prairie. The outer margins of the pothole depressions are dominated by cord grass mixed with other species such as swamp milkweed and ironweed. The centers are typically dominated by smartweed which may be mixed with duck-potato and cat-tail. This is a community in transition, eventually filling up with organic matter and becoming fertile prairie soils. Draining activities have greatly diminished the extent of these valuable wetlands.

Characteristic Species

Phragmites australis	common reed
Scirpus americanus	chairmaker's bulrush
Scirpus tabernaemontani	soft-stem bulrush
Typha latifolia	broad-leaf cat-tail
Zizania aquatica	Indian wild rice

Associates

Alisma subcordatum	American water-plantain
Asclepias incarnata	swamp milkweed
Berula erecta	cut-leaf water-parsnip
Bidens frondosa	devil's pitchfork

Eleocharis acicularis	needle spike-rush
Eleocharis palustris	pale spike-rush
Equisetum hyemale	tall scouring-rush
Lobelia siphilitica	great blue lobelia
Polygonum amphibium	water smartweed
Sagittaria latifolia	duck-potato
Scirpus fluviatilis	river bulrush
Scirpus pallidus	pale bulrush
Spartina cynosuroides	big cord grass
Spartina pectinata	freshwater cord grass
Verbena hastata	simpler's-joy
Vernonia fasciculata	prairie ironweed

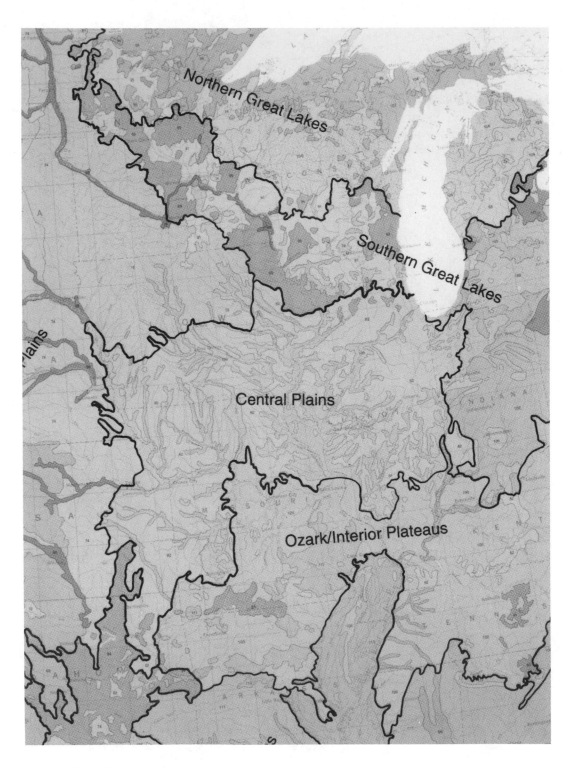

Central Plains

Central Plains

Introduction

The Central Plains region extends from extreme western Indiana west to southwestern Iowa and eastern Kansas. The region encompasses most of Illinois, southern Iowa, northern and western Missouri, parts of eastern Kansas and northern Oklahoma.

At the time of settlement most of this region was covered in a mosaic of Bluestem Prairie, Oak Barrens (savanna) and Oak-Hickory Forest. Floodplain Forest, Wet Prairie, and Marsh occupied the broad river floodplains. Periodic fires were important in maintaining the prairie and barrens.

Today, very little of the natural vegetation remains. Almost all of the prairie and forest have been destroyed, primarily for agricultural purposes.

The primary sources used to develop descriptions and species lists are: Barbour and Billings 1988; Braun 1950.

Dominant Ecological Communities

Upland Systems
Bluestem Prairie
Oak–Hickory Forest
Oak Barrens
Wetland Systems
Floodplain Forest
Marsh
Wet Prairie

UPLAND SYSTEMS

Bluestem Prairie

Bluestem Prairie dominated this region at the time of settlement. Vast tracts of grassland covered much of the uplands between drainages. Most of these prairies were rich and mesic but drier prairies occurred on sandy or gravelly soil. The dominant grasses were big bluestem, yellow Indian grass and wand panic grass (switchgrass). This community corresponds to Küchler #74.

Characteristic Species

Andropogon gerardii	big bluestem
Panicum virgatum	wand panic grass
Schizachyrium scoparium	little false bluestem
Sorghastrum nutans	yellow Indian grass

Associates

Allium cernuum	nodding onion
Amorpha canescens	leadplant
Asclepias tuberosa	butterfly milkweed
Asclepias viridiflora	green coment milkweed
Aster ericoides	white heath aster

Aster laevis	smooth blue aster
Aster sericeus	western silver aster
Baptisia alba	white wild indigo
Baptisia leucophaea	long-bract wild indigo
Bouteloua curtipendula	side-oats grama
Ceanothus americanus	New Jersey-tea
Dalea candida	white prairie-clover
Dalea purpurea	violet prairie-clover
Desmanthus illinoensis	prairie bundle-flower
Dodecatheon meadia	eastern shootingstar
Echinacea pallida	pale purple-coneflower
Elymus canadensis	nodding wild rye
Eryngium yuccifolium	button eryngo
Gaura parviflora	velvetweed
Gentiana puberulenta	downy gentian
Helianthus grosseserratus	saw-tooth sunflower
Helianthus mollis	neglected sunflower
Heliopsis helianthoides	smooth oxeye
Lespedeza capitata	round-head bush-clover
Liatris aspera	tall gayfeather
Liatris pycnostachya	cat-tail gayfeather
Lobelia spicata	pale-spike lobelia
Parthenium integrifolium	wild quinine
Phlox pilosa	downy phlox
Potentilla arguta	tall cinquefoil
Ratibida pinnata	gray-head Mexican-hat
Rudbeckia hirta	black-eyed-susan
Silphium laciniatum	compass plant
Silphium terebinthinaceum	prairie rosinweed
Solidago missouriensis	Missouri goldenrod
Solidago rigida	hard-leaf goldenrod
Sporobolus asper	tall dropseed
Sporobolus heterolepis	prairie dropseed
Stipa spartea	porcupine grass
Veronicastrum virginicum	culver's-root
Zizia aptera	heart-leaf alexanders

Oak–Hickory Forest

Oak–Hickory Forest occurs scattered throughout the region on dry to dry-mesic uplands. Dominance and species composition varies in response to topography, soils, geology and disturbance history. This community corresponds to Küchler #100.

Canopy
Characteristic Species

Carya glabra	pignut hickory
Carya ovata	shag-bark hickory
Quercus alba	northern white oak
Quercus rubra	northern red oak
Quercus velutina	black oak

Associates

Acer rubrum	red maple
Acer sacharum	sugar maple
Carya ovalis	red hickory
Carya texana	black hickory
Diospyros virginiana	common persimmon
Fraxinus americana	white ash
Fraxinus quadrangulata	blue ash
Nyssa sylvatica	black tupelo
Pinus echinata	short-leaf pine
Quercus coccinea	scarlet oak
Quercus falcata	southern red oak
Quercus marlandica	blackjack oak
Quercus muhlenbergia	chinkapin oak
Quercus prinoides	dwarf chinkapin oak
Quercus shumardii	Shumard's oak
Quercus stellata	post oak
Ulmus rubra	slippery elm

Woody Understory

Amelanchier arborea	downy service-berry
Ceanothus americanus	New Jersey tea
Cercis canadensis	redbud
Cornus drummondi	rough-leaf dogwood
Cornus florida	flowering dogwood
Cornus racemosa	gray dogwood
Parthenocissus quinquefolia	Virginia-creeper
Rhus aromatica	fragrant sumac
Ulmus alata	winged elm
Vaccinium arboreum	tree sparkle-berry
Vaccinium pallidum	early lowbush blueberry
Vitis aestivalis	summer grape

Herbaceous Understory

Brachyelytrum erectum	bearded shorthusk
Carex pensylvanica	Pennsylvania sedge
Cunila marina	common dittany
Danthonia spicata	poverty wild oat grass
Desmodium nudiflorum	naked-flower tick-trefoil
Frasera caroliniensis	American-columbo
Galium concinnum	shining bedstraw
Galium pilosum	hairy bedstraw
Hieracium gronovii	queendevil
Podophyllum peltatum	may-apple
Prenanthes alba	white rattlesnake-root
Prenanthes altissima	tall rattlesnake-root
Solidago hispida	hairy goldenrod
Tradescantia virginiana	Virginia spiderwort

Oak Barrens

Oak Barrens was a widespread woodland community in this region. This community type is often considered a transition zone between prairie and forest. The herbaceous understory is made up primarily of prairie grasses and forbs. Periodic fires are important in maintaining the savanna-like conditions of this community.

Canopy

Characteristic Species

Quercus alba	northern white oak
Quercus macrocarpa	burr oak
Quercus marilandica	blackjack oak
Quercus stellata	post oak

Associates

Carya laciniosa	shell-bark hickory
Carya ovata	shag-bark hickory
Carya texana	black hickory
Juniperus virginiana	eastern red cedar
Quercus imbricaria	shingle oak
Quercus velutina	black oak

Woody Understory

Amorpha canescens	leadplant
Ceanothus americanus	New Jersey-tea
Ceanothus herbaceus	prairie redroot
Cornus drummondii	rough-leaf dogwood
Cornus racemosa	gray dogwood
Corylus americana	American hazelnut
Crataegus spp.	hawthorn
Malus ioensis	prairie crabapple
Rhus aromatica	fragrant sumac
Rosa carolina	Carolina rose
Salix humilis	small pussy willow

Herbaceous Understory

Andropogon gerardii	big bluestem
Antennaria neglecta	field pussytoes
Asclepias verticillata	whorled milkweed
Aster drummondii	Drummond's aster
Aster ericoides	white heath aster
Aster laevis	smooth blue aster
Baptisia alba	white wild indigo
Cacalia atriplicifolia	pale Indian-plantain
Camassia scilloides	Atlantic camas
Carex bicknellii	Bicknell's sedge
Claytonia virginica	Virginia springbeauty
Comandra umbellata	bastard-toadflax
Coreopsis tripteris	tall tickseed
Cyperus filiformis	wiry flat sedge

Desmodium illinoense	Illinois tick-trefoil
Dichanthelium oligosanthes	Heller's rosette grass
Elymus canadensis	nodding wild rye
Eragrostis spectabilis	petticoat-climber
Eryngium yuccifolium	button eryngo
Euphorbia corollata	flowering spurge
Fragaria virginiana	Virginia strawberry
Gentiana puberulenta	downy gentian
Helianthus occidentalis	few-leaf sunflower
Lespedeza capitata	round-head bush-clover
Lespedeza violacea	violet bush-clover
Lobelia spicata	pale-spike lobelia
Monarda fistulosa	Oswego-tea
Parthenium integrifolium	wild quinine
Pycnanthemum virginianum	Virginia mountain-mint
Ranunculus fascicularis	early buttercup
Ratibida pinnata	gray-head Mexican-hat
Rudbeckia hirta	black-eyed-Susan
Schizachyrium scoparium	little false bluestem
Silene regia	royal catchfly
Silene stellata	widow's frill
Silphium integrifolium	entire-leaf rosinweed
Sisyrinchium albidum	white blue-eyed-grass
Solidago nemoralis	gray goldenrod
Solidago rigida	hard-leaf goldenrod
Sorghastrum nutans	Yellow Indian grass
Stipa spartea	porcupine grass
Tephrosia virginiana	goat's-rue
Tradescantia ohiensis	bluejacket
Verbena stricta	hoary vervain
Viola sororia	hooded blue violet

WETLAND SYSTEMS

Floodplain Forest

Floodplain Forest occurs throughout the region along large streams and rivers where floodplains have developed. The canopy is composed of a variety of large deciduous trees and the understory and herbaceous layer ranges from well developed to poorly developed depending upon the duration of annual flooding. This community corresponds to Küchler #98.

Canopy
Characteristic Species

Acer saccharinum	silver maple
Betula nigra	river birch
Carya laciniosa	shell-bark hickory
Celtis occidentalis	common hackberry

Liquidambar styracifula	sweet-gum
Populus deltoides	eastern cottonwood
Quercus bicolor	swamp white oak
Quercus lyrata	overcup oak
Quercus macrocarpa	burr oak
Quercus pagoda	cherry-bark oak
Quercus palustris	pin oak
Ulmus americana	American elm
Ulmus rubra	slippery elm

Associates

Acer negundo	ash-leaf maple
Acer rubrum	red maple
Carya cordiformis	bitter-nut hickory
Fraxinus pennsylvanica	green ash
Gleditsia triacanthos	honey locust
Juglans nigra	black walnut
Nyssa sylvatica	black tupelo
Platanus occidentalis	American sycamore
Quercus michauxii	swamp chestnut oak
Salix nigra	black willow

Woody Understory

Arundinaria gigantea	giant cane
Asimina triloba	common pawpaw
Campsis radicans	trumpet-creeper
Carpinus caroliniana	American hornbeam
Cornus foemina	stiff dogwood
Ilex decidua	deciduous holly
Lindera benzoin	northern spicebush
Toxicodendron radicans	eastern poison-ivy
Vitis spp.	grape

Herbaceous Understory

Boehmeria cylindrica	small-spike false nettle
Carex grayi	Gray's sedge
Carex tribuloides	blunt broom sedge
Cinna arundinacea	sweet wood-reed
Impatiens capensis	spotted touch-me-not
Laportea canadensis	Canadian wood-nettle
Mertensia virginica	Virginia bluebells
Onoclea sensibilis	sensitive fern
Phacelia purshii	Miami-mist
Sanicula canadensis	Canadian black-snakeroot
Viola cucullata	marsh blue violet

Marsh

Marsh is primarily associated with floodplains of larger streams and rivers although it also occurs in upland depressions.

Characteristic Species

Alisma subcordatum	American water-plantain
Boltonia asteroides	white doll's-daisy
Carex hyalinolepis	shoreline sedge
Carex lupulina	hop sedge
Carex tribuloides	blunt broom sedge
Carex vulpinoidea	common fox sedge
Eleocharis acicularis	needle spike-rush
Eleocharis obtusa	blunt spike-rush
Hibiscus laevis	halberd-leaf rose-mallow
Iris virginica	Virginia blueflag
Juncus effusus	lamp rush
Leersia oryzoides	rice cut grass
Leersia virginica	white grass
Nelumbo lutea	American lotus
Nuphar lutea	yellow pond-lily
Polygonum amphibium	water smartweed
Polygonum hydropiperoides	swamp smartweed
Polygonum pensylvanicum	pinkweed
Rumex verticillatus	swamp dock
Sagittaria latifolia	duck-potato
Scirpus americanus	chairmaker's bulrush
Scirpus atrovirens	dark-green bulrush
Scirpus cyperinus	cottongrass bulrush
Scirpus tabernaemontani	soft-stem bulrush
Sparganium eurycarpum	broad-fruit burr-reed
Typha latifolia	broad-leaf cat-tail

Wet Prairie

Wet prairie was often associated with marsh communities in floodplains of larger streams and in poorly drained depressions in the uplands. These grass dominated wetlands are essentially eradicated now with most areas converted to cropland.

Characteristic Species

Amsonia illustris	Ozark bluestar
Asclepias incarnata	swamp milkweed
Aster umbellatus	parasol flat-top white aster
Calamogrostis canadensis	bluejoint
Caltha palustris	yellow marsh-marigold
Carex arkansana	Arkansas sedge
Carex bicknellii	Bicknell's sedge
Carex lacustris	lakebank sedge
Carex vulpinoidea	common fox sedge
Cephalanthus occidentalis	common buttonbush

Cicuta maculata	spotted water-hemlock
Eupatorium maculatum	spotted joe-pye-weed
Helianthus angustifolius	swamp sunflower
Helianthus grosseserratus	saw-tooth sunflower
Juncus interior	inland rush
Leersia oryzoides	rice cut grass
Lysimachia quadrifolia	whorled yellow-loosestrife
Panicum virgatum	wand panic grass
Physostegia virginiana	obedient plant
Potentilla simplex	oldfield cinquefoil
Rhexia mariana	Maryland meadow-beauty
Sium suave	hemlock water-parsnip
Spartina pectinata	freshwater cord grass
Spiraea alba	white meadowsweet
Stachys palustris	woundwort
Tripsicum dactyloides	eastern mock grama

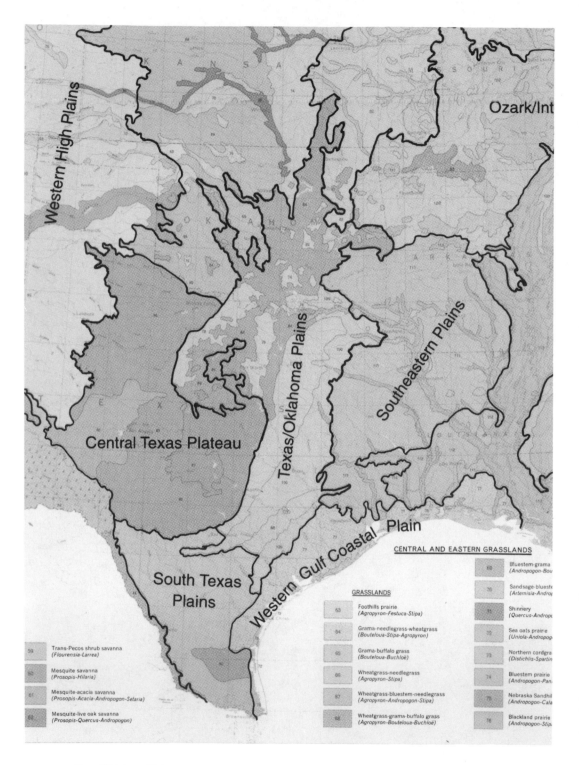

Texas/Oklahoma Plains

Texas/Oklahoma Plains

Introduction

The Texas/Oklahoma Plains region extends from southeastern Kansas into central Oklahoma and central Texas. This region is characterized by a mixture of both prairie and woodland vegetation. Major vegetation types include Blackland Prairie and Cross Timbers Woodland or Post Oak Savanna, as it is also known. Most species found in this area have ranges that extend northward into the Great Plains or eastward into the eastern deciduous forests.

The Blackland Prairie is a tallgrass prairie which extends from the Red River to the chaparral communities of south central Texas. Very few examples of the native vegetation of the Blackland Prairie remain because the rich soil in the area has either been converted to croplands or the prairie has been heavily grazed. In general, little false bluestem, yellow Indian grass and big bluestem were dominant grasses in the presettlement prairie. Much of this area has been invaded by silver bluestem, Texas wintergrass, and buffalo grass.

The Cross Timbers Woodland is dominated by post oak and blackjack oak in the canopy and prairie species in the understory. It is presumed that early Texas settlers named the region "Cross Timbers" because they found belts of oak forests crossing strips of prairie grasslands.

The primary sources used to develop descriptions and species lists are: Barbour and Billings 1988; Bill Carr (pers. com.); McMahan et al. 1984; Risser et al. 1981; Sims 1988; Texas Natural Heritage Program 1991.

Dominant Ecological Communities

Upland Systems
Oak–Hickory Forest
Cross Timbers Woodland
Bluestem Prairie
Fayette Prairie
Blackland Prairie
Wetland Systems
Floodplain Forest

UPLAND SYSTEMS

Oak–Hickory Forest

Oak–Hickory Forest extends along the eastern edge of the Texas/Oklahoma Plains region. This is the western-most range of the Oak–Hickory Forest and is generally much drier and more open than oak-hickory forests further east. This is reflected in the lower diversity of trees and greater diversity of prairie plants in the understory. This community corresponds to Küchler #100.

Canopy
Characteristic Species
Carya texana	black hickory
Quercus incana	bluejack oak
Quercus marilandica	blackjack oak
Quercus stellata	post oak

Associates
Juniperus virginiana	eastern red-cedar
Prosopis glandulosa	honey mesquite
Quercus virginiana	live oak
Ulmus crassifolia	cedar elm

Woody Understory
Ascyrum hypericoides	St. Andrew's cross
Berchemia scandens	Alabama supplejack
Callicarpa americana	American beauty-berry
Campsis radicans	trumpet-creeper
Ilex vomitoria	yaupon
Prunus texana	peachbush
Rhus aromatica	fragrant sumac
Rhus copallinum	winged sumac
Rubus trivialis	southern dewberry
Sideroxylon lanuginosa	gum bully
Smilax bona-nox	fringed greenbriar
Symphoricarpas orbiculatus	coral-berry
Toxicodendron pubescens	Atlantic poison-oak
Vaccinium arboreum	tree sparkle-berry
Viburnum rufidulum	rusty blackhaw
Vitis mustangensis	mustang grape
Yucca arkansana	Arkansas yucca
Zanthoxylum clava-herculis	Hercules'-club

Herbaceous Understory
Alophia drummondii	propeller-flower
Berlandiera texana	Texas greeneyes
Bothriochloa saccaroides	plumed beard grass
Bouteloua hirsuta	hairy grama
Brachiaria ciliatissima	fringed signal grass
Carex muhlenbergii	Muhlenberg's sedge
Cenchrus carolinianus	sandburr
Centrosema virginianum	spurred butterfly-pea
Chaetopappa asteroides	Arkansas leastdaisy
Chamaecrista fasciculata	sleepingplant
Chamaesyce cordifolia	heart-leaf sand-mat
Chasmanthium laxum	slender wood-oats
Chloris cucullata	hooded windmill grass
Cnidoscolus texanus	Texas bullnettle
Coreopsis basalis	golden-mane tickseed
Croton capitatus	hogwort

Croton glandulosus	vente-conmigo
Dichanthelium laxiflorum	open-flower rosette grass
Dichanthelium oligosanthes	Heller's rosette grass
Dichanthelium ravenelii	Ravenel's rosette grass
Eragrostis secundiflora	red love grass
Eragrostis trichodes	sand love grass
Froelichia floridana	plains snake-cotton
Gaillardia aestivalis	lance-leaf blanket-flower
Galactia canescens	hoary milk-pea
Helianthemum georgianum	Georgia frostweed
Helianthus debilis	cucumber-leaf sunflower
Hymenopappus artemisiifolius	old-plains-man
Lechea tenuifolia	narrow-leaf pinweed
Liatris elegans	pink-scale gayfeather
Lupinus subcarnosus	Texas bluebonnet
Mirabilis albida	white four-o'clock
Mirabilis linearis	narrow-leaf four-o'clock
Monarda punctata	spotted beebalm
Neptunia lutea	yellow puff
Nuttalanthus texanus	Texas-toadflax
Palafoxia rosea	rosy palafox
Panicum anceps	beaked panic grass
Panicum virgatum	wand panic grass
Paronychia drummondii	Drummond's nailwort
Phlox drummondii	annual phlox
Phyllanthus abnormix	Drummond's leaf-flower
Polypremum procumbens	juniper-leaf
Rhynchosia americana	American snout-bean
Rhynchospora harveyi	Harvey's beak sedge
Rudbeckia hirta	black-eyed-Susan
Schizachyrium scoparium	little false bluestem
Scleria triglomerata	whip nut-rush
Stillingia sylvatica	queen's-delight
Stylisma pickeringii	Pickering's dawnflower
Stylosanthes biflora	side-beak pencil-flower
Tephrosia virginiana	goat's-rue
Tetragonotheca ludoviciana	Louisiana nerveray

Cross Timbers Woodland

Cross Timbers Woodland is the most common woody vegetation type in the region. These woodlands are a combination of deciduous forest species and grassland species. The dominant species include post oak and blackjack oak which make up approximately 92 percent of the mostly open canopy. Little false bluestem is the most common understory species. This community corresponds to Küchler #84.

Canopy
Characteristic Species

Quercus marilandica	blackjack oak
Quercus stellata	post oak

Associates

Carya texana	black hickory
Celtis laevigata	sugar-berry
Fraxinus texensis	Texas ash
Juniperus virginiana	eastern red cedar
Prosopis glandulosa	honey mesquite
Quercus falcata	southern red oak
Quercus fusiformis	plateau oak
Quercus incana	bluejack oak
Quercus virginiana	live oak
Ulmus crassifolia	cedar elm

Woody Understory

Ascyrum hypericoides	St. Andrew's cross
Berchemia scandens	Alabama supplejack
Callicarpa americana	American beauty-berry
Campsis radicans	trumpet-creeper
Cercis canadensis	redbud
Cornus drummondii	rough-leaf dogwood
Coryphantha sulcata	pineapple cactus
Echinocereus reichenbachii	lace hedgehog cactus
Forestiera pubescens	stretchberry
Ilex decidua	deciduous holly
Ilex vomitoria	yaupon
Lonicera albiflora	white honeysuckle
Opuntia engelmanii	cactus-apple
Opuntia leptocaulis	Christmas cholla
Prunus mexicana	bigtree plum
Rhus aromatica	fragrant sumac
Rhus glabra	smooth sumac
Sideroxylon lanuginosum	gum bully
Smilax bona-nox	fringed greenbriar
Symphoricarpus orbiculatus	coral-berry
Toxicodendron pubescens	Atlantic poison-oak
Viburnum rudifulum	rusty blackhaw
Vitis mustangensis	mustang grape
Yucca constricta	Buckley's yucca
Zizyphus obtusifolia	lotebush

Herbaceous Understory

Acalypha gracilens	three-seed mercury
Allium canadense	meadow garlic
Ambrosia psilostachya	western ragweed
Andropogon gerardii	big bluestem
Andropogon ternarius	split-beard bluestem
Antennaria parlinii	Parlin's pussytoes
Asclepias asperula	spider antelope horns
Bothriochloa saccharoides	plumed beard grass
Bouteloua curtipendula	side-oats grama

Bouteloua hirsuta	hairy grama
Carex muhlenbergii	Muhlenberg's sedge
Carex planostachys	cedar sedge
Chaetopappa asteroides	Arkansas leastdaisy
Desmodium sessilifolium	sessil-leaf tick-trefoil
Dichanthelium acuminatum	tapered rosette grass
Dichanthelium linearifolium	slim-leaf rosette grass
Dichanthelium oligosanthes	Heller's rosette grass
Dyschoriste linearis	polkadots
Elymus canadensis	nodding wild rye
Elymus virginicus	Virginia wild rye
Eragrositis trichodes	sand love grass
Eragrostis spectabilis	petticoat-climber
Euphorbia dentata	toothed spurge
Euphorbia tetrapora	weak spurge
Gaillardia pulchella	firewheel
Houstonia pusilla	tiny bluet
Hymenopappus artemisiifolius	old-plains-man
Ipomopsis rubra	standing-cypress
Lotus unifoliolatus	American bird's-foot-trefoil
Matelea reticulata	netted milkvine
Monarda clinopodioides	basil beebalm
Myosotis verna	spring forget-me-not
Nassella leucotricha	Texas wintergrass
Nothoscordum bivalve	crow poison
Panicum virgatum	wand panic grass
Penstemon australis	Eustis Lake beardtongue
Psoralidium tenuiflorum	slender-flower lemonweed
Schizachyrium scoparium	little false bluestem
Sorghastrum nutans	yellow Indian grass
Sporobolus asper	tall dropseed
Sporobolus cryptandrus	sand dropseed
Tephrosia lindheimeri	Lindheimer's hoary-pea
Tradescantia ohiensis	bluejacket
Verbena halei	Texas vervain

Bluestem Prairie

Patches of Bluestem Prairie occur within the Cross Timbers Woodland in the northern part of this region. The Bluestem Prairie community in this region is very similar to the Bluestem Prairie in the Great Plains region. It is considered distinct, however, because it occurs on a different soil type. This community corresponds to Küchler #74.

Characteristic Species

Andropogon gerardii	big bluestem
Panicum virgatum	wand panic grass
Schizachyrium scoparium	little false bluestem
Sorghastrum nutans	yellow Indian grass

Associates

Amorpha canescens	leadplant
Antennaria neglecta	field pussytoes
Aster ericoides	white heath aster
Aster laevis	smooth blue aster
Baptisia alba	white wild indigo
Baptisia bracteata	long-bract wild indigo
Bouteloua curtipendula	side-oats grama
Dichanthelium leibergii	Leiberg's rosette grass
Dichanthelium oligosathes	Heller's rosette grass
Erigeron strigosus	prairie fleabane
Galium tinctorum	stiff marsh bedstraw
Helianthus grosseserratus	saw-tooth sunflower
Helianthus maximiliani	Michaelmas-daisy
Koeleria macrantha	prairie Koeler's grass
Liatrus aspera	tall gayfeather
Liatrus punctata	dotted gayfeather
Liatrus scariosa	devil's-bite
Pediomelum argophyllum	silver-leaf Indian-breadroot
Phlox pilosa	downy phlox
Psoralidium tenuiflorum	slender-flower lemonweed
Ratibida columnifera	red-spike Mexican-hat
Ratibida pinnata	gray-head Mexican-hat
Rosa arkansana	wild prairie rose
Silphium laciniatum	compassplant
Solidago canadensis	Canadian goldenrod
Solidago missouriensis	Missouri goldenrod
Solidago rigida	hard-leaf goldenrod
Sporobolus asper	tall dropseed
Stipa spartea	porcupine grass

Fayette Prairie

Fayette Prairie is a mixed grass prairie which occurs in the southern part of the region. Scattered oak and hickory trees occur throughout this prairie type. This community corresponds to Küchler #88.

Characteristic Species

Buchloë dactyloides	buffalo grass
Schizachyrium scopariuum	little false bluestem

Associates

Acacia angustissima	prairie wattle
Andropogon gerardii	big bluestem
Andropogon ternarius	split-beard bluestem
Aristida purpurascens	arrow-feather three-awn
Aster ericoides	white heath aster
Aster patens	late purple aster
Bifora americana	prairie bishop
Bothriochloa saccharoides	plumed beard grass

Bouteloua curtipendula	side-oats grama
Bouteloua rigidiseta	Texas grama
Brickellia eupatorioides	false boneset
Camassia scilloides	Atlantic camas
Carex microdonta	little-tooth sedge
Castilleja indivisa	entire leaf Indian-paintbrush
Coelorachis cylindrica	Carolina joint-tail grass
Dalea compacta	compact prairie-clover
Dalea multiflora	round-head prairie-clover
Echinacea angustifolia	blacksamson
Eragrostis intermedia	plains love grass
Helianthus maximilliani	Michaelmas-daisy
Houstonia pusilla	tiny bluet
Liatris squarrosa	scaly gayfeather
Lupinus subcarnosus	Texas bluebonnet
Marshallia caespitosa	puffballs
Monarda citriodora	lemon beebalm
Muhlenbergia capillaris	hair-awn muhly
Nassella leucotricha	Texas wintergrass
Nemastylis geminiflora	prairie pleatleaf
Panicum obtusum	blunt panic grass
Panicum virgatum	wand panic grass
Paspalum floridanum	Florida crown grass
Paspalum plicatulum	brown-seed crown grass
Paspalum setaceum	slender crown grass
Penstemon cobaea	cobaea breadtongue
Penstemon tubiflorus	white wand beardtongue
Polytaenia texana	Texas false-parsley
Rudbeckia hirta	black-eyed-Susan
Ruellia humilis	finge-leaf wild petunia
Sabatia campestris	Texas-star
Salvia azurea	azure-blue sage
Sorgastrum nutans	yellow Indian grass
Sporobolus asper	tall dropseed
Tripsacum dactyloides	eastern mock grama
Vernonia texana	Texas ironweed

Blackland Prairie

Blackland Prairie is also referred to as the "Grand Prairie". Most of the Blackland Prairie has been converted to agriculture or has been heavily grazed. The dominant grass of the Blackland Prairie was little false bluestem, however, heavy grazing and disturbance have caused buffalo grass and Texas grama to invade and increase. This community corresponds to Küchler #76.

Characteristic Species

Nassella leucotricha	Texas wintergrass
Schizachyrium scoparium	little false bluestem

Associates

Acacia angustissima	prairie wattle
Ambrosia psilostachya	western ragweed
Andropogon gerardii	big bluestem
Aristida purpurea	purple three-awn
Aster ericoides	white heath aster
Bifora americana	prairie bishop
Bothriochloa saccharoides	plumed beard grass
Bouteloua curtipendula	side-oats grama
Bouteloua hirsuta	hairy grama
Bouteloua rigidiseta	Texas grama
Brickellia eupatorioides	false boneset
Buchloë dactyloides	buffalo grass
Carex meadii	Mead's sedge
Carex microdonta	little-tooth sedge
Castilleja indivisa	entire-leaf Indian-paintbrush
Dalea candida	white priarie-clover
Dalea purpurea	violet prairie-clover
Desmanthus illinoensis	prairie bundle flower
Echinacea angustifolia	blacksamson
Elymus canadensis	nodding wild rye
Erioneuron pilosum	hairy woolly grass
Eryngium leavenworthii	Leavenworth's eryngo
Eryngium yuccifolium	button eryngo
Fimbristylis puberula	hairy fimbry
Hedyotis nigricans	diamond-flowers
Helianthus maximiliani	Michaelmas-daisy
Horedeum pusillum	little barley
Liatris punctata	dotted gayfeather
Limnodea arkansana	Ozark grass
Monarda citriodora	lemon beebalm
Nothoscordum bivalve	cowpoison
Oenothera speciosa	pinkladies
Panicum virgatum	wand panic grass
Paspalum floridanum	Florida crown grass
Penstemon cobaea	cobaea beardtongue
Polytaenia texana	Texas false-parsley
Ratibida columnifera	red-spike Mexican-hat
Rudbeckia hirta	black-eyed-Susan
Ruellia humilis	fringe-leaf wild petunia
Salvia azurea	azure-blue sage
Silphium laciniatum	compassplant
Silphium radula	rough stem rosinweed
Solidago missouriensis	Missouri goldenrod
Sorgastrum nutans	yellow Indian grass
Sporobolus asper	tall dropseed
Sporobolus silveanus	Silveus' dropseed
Tragia ramosa	branched noseburn
Tridens strictus	long-spike fluff grass

Tripsacum dactyloides	eastern mock grama
Vernonia texana	Texas ironweed
Vulpia octoflora	eight-flower six-weeks grass

WETLAND SYSTEMS

Floodplain Forest

Floodplain Forest in the Texas/Oklahoma Plains region occurs along the major rivers. The floodplains may be dominated by pecan, sugar-berry, and cedar elm. These forests have many similarities to the Southern Floodplain Forest of the Southeastern Coastal Plain.

Canopy
Characteristic Species

Carya illinoinensis	pecan
Celtis laevigata	sugar-berry
Ulmus americana	American elm
Ulmus crassifolia	cedar elm

Associates

Acer rubrum	red maple
Fraxinus pennslyvanica	green ash
Gleditsia triacanthos	honey-locust
Juglans nigra	black walnut
Liquidambar styraciflua	sweet-gum
Morus rubra	red mulberry
Plantanus occidentalis	American sycamore
Populus deltoides	eastern cottonwood
Quercus buckleyi	Buckley's oak
Quercus fusiformis	plateau oak
Quercus lyrata	overcup oak
Quercus macrocarpa	burr oak
Quercus nigra	water oak
Quercus pagoda	cherry-bark oak
Quercus virginiana	live oak
Sapindus saponaria	wing-leaf soapberry
Salix nigra	black willow
Taxodium distichum	southern bald-cypress

Woody Understory

Amorpha fruticosa	false indigo-bush
Ampelopsis cordata	heart-leaf peppervine
Cornus drummondii	rough-leaf dogwood
Forestiera pubescens	stretchberry
Fraxinus texensis	Texas ash
Ilex decidua	deciduous holly
Prosopis glandulosa	honey mesquite
Sideroxylon lanuginosa	gum bully

Smilax bona-nox	fringed greenbriar
Toxicodendron pubescens	Atlantic poison-oak
Vitis mustangensis	mustang grape

Herbaceous Understory

Ambrosia psilostachya	western ragweed
Aster drummondii	Drummond's aster
Carex amphibola	eastern narrow-leaf
Chasmanthium latifolium	Indian wood-oats
Clematis pitcheri	bluebill
Elephantopus carolinianus	Carolina elephant's foot
Elymus canadensis	nodding wild rye
Elymus virginicus	Virginia wild rye
Geum canadense	white avens
Paspalum pubiflorum	hairy-seed crown grass
Passiflora lutea	yellow passion-flower
Rivina humilis	rougeplant
Solidago canadensis	Canadian goldenrod
Teucrium canadense	American germander
Verbesina virginica	white crownbeard

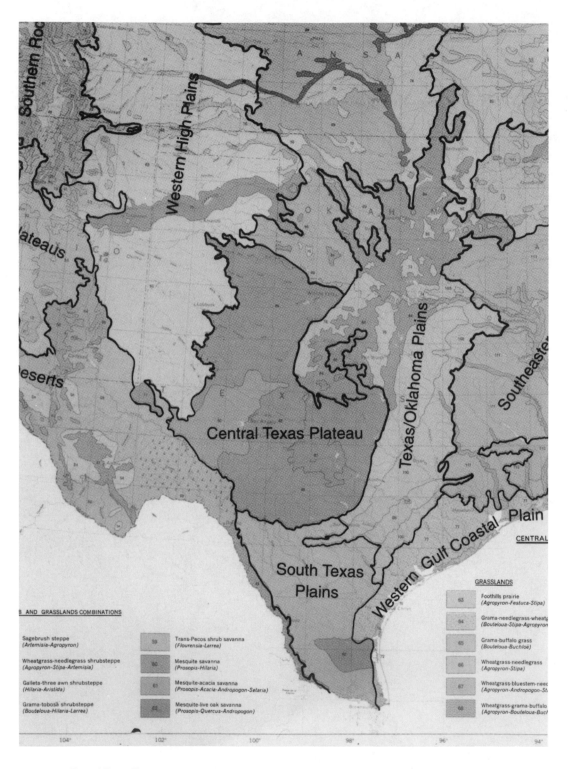

Central Texas Plateau

Central Texas Plateau

Introduction

The Central Texas Plateau region includes what is commonly known as the "Edwards Plateau" and "Rolling Plains". In its natural state the area is predominantly shortgrass and midgrass prairie with areas of savanna and woodland. The vegetation is more diverse toward the south and eastern boundaries of the region in an area known as the Balcones Escarpment. This area is characterized by numerous canyons with deciduous woodland and forest.

The vegetation throughout the region has been heavily impacted by overgrazing of livestock and other developments. The prairies in the rolling plains, once dominated by side-oats grama, little false bluestem, and blue grama have been converted to grain fields or have been cleared for oil well pads. Throughout the region shrub species have been spreading as the native grasses decline due to overgrazing.

The primary sources used to develop descriptions and species lists are: Barbour and Billings 1988; Bill Carr (pers. com.); Correll and Johnston 1970; McMahan et al. 1984; Riskin and Diamond 1988; Tharp 1939; Tharp 1991.

Dominant Ecological Communities

Upland Systems
Deciduous Woodland
Juniper–Oak Savanna
Mesquite–Oak Savanna
Mesquite Savanna
Midgrass Prairie
Wetland Systems
Floodplain Forest

UPLAND SYSTEMS

Deciduous Woodland

Along the southern boundary of the Central Texas region the Balcones Escarpment provides conditions for woodlands and forests. The north- and east-facing slopes in the canyons of the Balcones Escarpment generally have the mesic conditions required for woodlands to develop.

Canopy
Characteristic Species
Fraxinus texensis	Texas ash
Juniperus ashei	Ashe's juniper
Prunus serotina	black cherry
Quercus buckleyi	Buckley's oak
Quercus fusiformis	plateau oak

Associates
Celtis laevigata	sugar-berry
Juglans major	Arizona walnut

Morus rubra	red mulberry
Quercus laceyi	Lacey's oak
Quercus muehlenbergii	chinkapin oak
Quercus sinuata	bastard oak
Tilia americana	American basswood
Ulmus americana	American elm
Ulmus crassifolia	cedar elm

Woody Understory

Aesculus pavia	red buckeye
Buddleja racemosa	wand butterfly-bush
Callicarpa americana	American beauty-berry
Cercis canadensis	redbud
Cornus drummondii	rough-leaf dogwood
Forestiera pubescens	stretchberry
Frangula caroliniana	Carolina buckthorn
Ilex decidua	deciduous holly
Ilex vomitoria	yaupon
Lindera benzoin	northern spicebush
Parthenocissus quinquefolia	Virginia-creeper
Prunus mexicana	bigtree plum
Ptelea trifoliata	common hoptree
Rhus aromatica	fragrant sumac
Rhus virens	evergreen sumac
Rubus trivialis	southern dewberry
Sideroxylon lanuginosum	gum bully
Smilax bona-nox	fringed greenbriar
Sophora affinis	Eve's necklacepod
Sophora secundiflora	mescal-bean
Ungnadia speciosa	Mexican-buckeye
Viburnum rufidulum	rusty blackhaw
Vitis monticola	sweet mountain grape
Vitis mustangensis	mustang grape
Zanthoxylum hirsutum	Texas hercules'-club

Herbaceous Understory

Anemone edwardsiana	plateau thimbleweed
Aquilegia canadensis	red columbine
Arisaema dracontium	greendragon
Aristolochia serpentaria	Virginia-snakeroot
Brickellia cylindracea	gravel-bar brickellbush
Carex edwardsiana	Edwards plateau sedge
Carex planostachys	cedar sedge
Chaetopappa effusa	spreading leastdaisy
Chasmanthium latifolium	Indian wood-oats
Desmodium psilophyllum	simple-leaf tick-trefoil
Dichanthelium acuminatum	tapered rosette grass
Dichanthelium oligosanthes	Heller's rosette grass
Dichanthelium pedicellatum	cedar rosette grass

Elymus virginicus	Virginia wild rye
Euphorbia roemeriana	Roemer's spurge
Galium texense	Texas bedstraw
Geum canadense	white avens
Hedeoma acinoides	slender false pennyroyal
Lespedeza texana	Texas bush-clover
Matelea edwardsensis	plateau milkvine
Matelea reticulata	netted milkvine
Muhlenbergia lindheimeri	Lindheimer's muhly
Muhlenbergia reverchonii	seep muhly
Muhlenbergia schreberi	nimblewill
Parietaria pensylvanica	Pennsylvania pellitory
Passiflora affinis	bracted passion-flower
Passiflora tenuiloba	bird-wing passion-flower
Polygala lindheimeri	shrubby milkwort
Salvia roemeriana	cedar sage
Schizachyrium scoparium	little false bluestem
Scutellaria drummondii	Drummond's skullcap
Scutellaria ovata	heart-leaf skullcap
Sporobolus asper	tall dropseed
Stipa leucotricha	Texas needle grass
Tinantia anomala	widow's-tears
Tradescantia edwardsiana	plateau spiderwort
Tragia ramosa	branched noseburn
Tridens spp.	fluff grass
Urtica chamidryoides	heart-leaf nettle
Verbesina virginica	white crownbeard
Viola missouriensis	Missouri violet

Juniper–Oak Savanna

Juniper–Oak Savanna occurs in the Edwards Plateau area where it occupies sloping sites with dry, shallow soil. It is composed of dense to very open stands of low trees and shrubs. The trees and shrubs are deciduous or broadleaf evergreen and needleleaf evergreens. This community corresponds to Küchler #86.

Canopy
Characteristic Species

Juniperus ashei	Ashe's juniper
Quercus fusiformis	plateau oak

Associates

Fraxinus texensis	Texas ash
Prosopis glandulosa	honey mesquite
Quercus buckleyi	Buckley's oak
Quercus sinuata	bastard oak

Woody Understory

Cercis canadensis	redbud
Diospyros texana	Texas persimmon

Echinocereus reichenbachii	lace hedgehog cactus
Echinocereus triglochidiatus	king-cup cactus
Mahonia trifoliata	Laredo Oregon-grape
Mimosa borealis	fragrant mimosa
Opuntia engelmannii	cactus-apple
Rhus aromatica	fragrant sumac
Rhus virens	evergreen sumac
Yucca rupicola	Texas yucca

Herbaceous Understory

Andropogon gerardii	big bluestem
Anemone berlandieri	ten-petal thimbleweed
Artistida longespica	red three-awn
Artistida purpurea	purple three-awn
Bouteloua curtipendula	side-oats grama
Bouteloua hirsuta	hairy grama
Bouteloua pectinata	tall grama
Buchloë dactyloides	buffalo grass
Carex planostachys	cedar sedge
Chaetopappa bellidifolia	white-ray leastdaisy
Chamaesyce angusta	black-foot sandmat
Chamaesyce fendleri	Fendler's sandmat
Dichanthelium oligosanthes	Heller's rosette grass
Dichanthelium pedicellatum	cedar rosette grass
Elymus canadensis	nodding wild rye
Eragrostis intermedia	plains love grass
Erioneuron pilosum	hairy woolly grass
Hedeoma acinoides	slender false pennyroyal
Hedeoma drummondii	Drummond's false pennyroyal
Hilaria belangeri	curly-mesquite
Leptochloa dubia	green spangletop
Lespedeza texana	Texas bush-clover
Marshallia cespitosa	puffballs
Melampodium leucanthum	plains blackfoot
Muhlenbergia reverchonii	seep muhly
Nassella leucotricha	Texas wintergrass
Panicum obtusum	blunt panic grass
Phyllanthus polygonoides	smartweed leaf-flower
Polygala alba	white milkwort
Schizachyrium scoparium	little false bluestem
Simsia calva	awnless bush-sunflower
Sorghastrum nutans	yellow Indian grass
Sporobolus asper	tall dropseed
Stillingia texana	Texas toothleaf
Tetraneuris linearifolia	fine-leaf four-nerve-daisy
Tetraneuris scaposa	stemmed four-nerve-daisy
Thelesperma filifolium	stiff greenthread
Thelesperma simplicifolium	slender greenthread
Tridens muticus	awnless fluff grass
Wedelia hispida	hairy creeping-oxeye

Mesquite–Oak Savanna

This is an open canopy community with a groundcover of tall to medium grasses. Tree density varies with local conditions. This community is common in the Llano uplift area. This community corresponds to Küchler #87.

Canopy
Characteristic Species
Prosopis glandulosa	honey mesquite
Quercus marilandica	blackjack oak
Quercus stellata	post oak

Associates
Aloysia ligustrina	beebrush
Celtis laevigata	sugar-berry
Diospyros texana	Texas persimmon
Juniperus ashei	Ashe's juniper
Quercus fusiformis	plateau oak
Ulmus crassifolia	cedar elm

Woody Understory
Aloysia gratissima	whitebrush
Mahonia trifoliata	Laredo Oregon-grape
Opuntia engelmannii	cactus-apple
Opuntia leptocaulis	Christmas cholla
Opuntia macrorhiza	twist-spine prickly-pear
Rhus aromatica	fragrant sumac
Rhus virens	evergreen sumac
Yucca constricta	Buckley's yucca
Yucca torreyi	Torrey's yucca
Zanthoxylum hirsutum	Texas hercules'-club

Herbaceous Understory
Agrostis elliottiana	Elliott's bent
Aphanostephus skirrhobasis	Arkansas dozedaisy
Aristida longespica	red three-awn
Aristida purpurea	purple three-awn
Astragalus nuttallianus	turkey-pea
Bothriochloa saccharoides	plumed beard grass
Bouteloua curtipendula	side-oats grama
Bouteloua hirsuta	hairy grama
Bouteloua rigidiseta	Texas grama
Buchloë dactyloides	buffalo grass
Callirhoe involucrata	purple poppy-mallow
Carex muhlenbergii	Muhlenberg's sedge
Carex planostachys	cedar sedge
Castilleja indivisa	entire-leaf Indian-paintbrush
Chaetopappa asteroides	Arkansas leastdaisy
Cnidoscolus texanus	Texas bull-nettle
Dichanthelium oligosanthes	Heller's rosette grass

Eragrostis intermedia	plains love grass
Eriogonum tenellum	tall wild buckwheat
Gaillardia pulchella	firewheel
Helenium amarum	yellowdicks
Helianthemum georgianum	Georgia frostweed
Hypericum drummondii	nits-and-lice
Lechea san-sabeana	San Saba pinweed
Linum hudsonioides	Texas flax
Lotus unifoliolatus	American bird's-foot-trefoil
Lupinus texensis	Texas lupine
Nassella leucotricha	Texas wintergrass
Nuttalanthus texana	Texas-toadflax
Panicum virgatum	wand panic grass
Phacelia patuliflora	sand scorpion-weed
Phlox drummondii	annual phlox
Schizachyrium scoparium	little false bluestem
Sedum nuttallianum	yellow stonecrop
Senecio ampullaceus	Texas ragwort
Sorghastrum nutans	yellow Indian grass
Spermolepis echinata	bristly scaleseed
Sporobolus asper	tall dropseed
Tripogon spicatus	American five-minute grass
Valerianella texana	Edwards plateau cornsalad
Xanthisma texanum	Texas sleepy-daisy

Mesquite Savanna

This is an open canopy community dominated by scattered broadleaf evergreen or deciduous shrubs and low trees with a dense to open grass groundcover. This community corresponds to Küchler #60 and #85.

Characteristic Species

Prosopis glandulosa	honey mesquite

Associates

Acacia greggii	long-flower catclaw
Juniperus ashei	Ashe's juniper
Juniperus pinchotii	Pinchot's juniper
Opuntia spp.	prickly-pear
Quercus fusiformis	plateau oak

Herbaceous Understory

Aphanostephus skirrhobasis	Arkansas dozedaisy
Aristida purpurea	purple three-awn
Astragalus nuttallianus	turkey-pea
Bothriochloa barbinodis	cane beard grass
Bouteloua curtipendula	side-oats grama
Bouteloua rigidiseta	Texas grama
Buchloë dactyloides	buffalo grass
Chaetopappa asteroides	Arkansas leastdaisy
Gaillardia pulchella	firewheel

Helenium amarum	yellowdicks
Hilaria belangeri	curly-mesquite
Hilaria mutica	Tobosa grass
Nuttalanthes texanus	Texas-toadflax

Midgrass Prairie

Midgrass Prairie occurs on upland areas in the Rolling Plains and Edwards Plateau.

Characteristic Species

Bouteloua curtipendula	side-oats grama
Schizachyrium scoparium	little false bluestem

Associates

Artemisia ludoviciana	white sagebrush
Asclepias latifolia	broad-leaf milkweed
Astragalus missouriensis	Missouri milkvetch
Bothriochloa barbinodis	cane beard grass
Bouteloua gracilis	blue grama
Bouteloua hirsuta	hairy grama
Buchloë dactyloides	buffalo grass
Calylophus berlandieri	Berlandier's sundrops
Calylophus hartwegii	Hartweg's sundrops
Chamaesyce lata	hoary sandmat
Dalea aurea	golden prairie-clover
Dalea candida	white prairie-clover
Dalea enneandra	nine-anther prairie-clover
Dalea formosa	featherplume
Dalea frutescens	black prairie-clover
Digitaria californica	California crab grass
Elymus canadensis	nodding wild rye
Eriogonum alatum	winged wild buckwheat
Gaura villosa	woolly beeblossom
Hedyotis nigricans	diamond-flower
Helianthus maximiliani	Michaelmas-daisy
Hilaria belangeri	curly-mesquite
Juniperus ashei	Ashe's juniper
Juniperus pinchotii	Pinchot's juniper
Liatris punctata	dotted gayfeather
Machaeranthera pinnatifida	lacy tansy-aster
Melampodium leucanthum	plains blackfoot
Mirabilis albida	white four-o'clock
Monarda citriodora	lemon beebalm
Nassella leucotricha	Texas wintergrass
Panicum obtusum	blunt panic grass
Polygala alba	white milkwort
Prosopis glandulosa	honey msequite
Psoralidium tenuiflorum	slender-flower lemonweed
Quercus mohriana	Mohr's oak
Ratibida columnaris	red-spike Mexican-hat
Rhus microphylla	little-leaf sumac

Sorghastrum nutans	yellow Indian grass
Sphaeralcea angustifolia	copper globe-mallow
Sphaeralcea coccinea	scarlet globe-mallow
Sporobolus cryptandrus	sand dropseed
Thelesperma megapotamicum	Hopi-tea
Tridens muticus	awnless tuft grass
Tragia ramosa	branched noseburn
Ziziphus obtusifolia	lotebush

WETLAND SYSTEMS

Floodplain Forest

Floodplain Forest in this region occurs along perennial streams and in terraces of the Balcones Escarpment. Species composition varies from east to west with baldcypress, sycamore, pecan, ,chinkapin oak, and Arizona walnut more important in the east, and live oak and sugar-berry dominant in the west.

Canopy
Characteristic Species

Carya illinoinensis	pecan
Celtis laevigata	sugar-berry
Fraxinus pennsylvanica	green ash
Platanus occidentalis	American sycamore
Quercus fusiformis	plateau oak
Taxodium distichum	southern baldcypress
Ulmus americana	American elm
Ulmus crassifolia	cedar elm

Associates

Acer negundo	ash-leaf maple
Fraxinus berlandieriana	Mexican ash
Juglans major	Arizona walnut
Quercus buckeyi	Buckley's oak
Quercus macrocarpa	burr oak
Quercus muehlenbergi	chinkapin oak
Quercus virginiana	live oak
Salix nigra	black willow
Sapindus saponaria	wing-leaf soapberry
Tillia americana	American basswood

Woody Understory

Amorpha fruticosa	false indigo-bush
Ampelopsis arborea	peppervine
Cephalanthus occidentalis	common buttonbush
Cornus drummondii	rough-leaf dogwood
Ilex decidua	deciduous holly
Juglans microcarpa	little walnut
Parthenocissus quinquefolia	Virginia-creeper

Rhus trivialis	southern dewberry
Viburnum rufidulum	rusty blackhaw
Vitis mustangensis	mustang grape

Herbaceous Understory

Andropogon glomeratus	bushy bluestem
Aster drummondii	Drummond's aster
Boehmeria cylindrica	small-spike false nettle
Carex amphibola	eastern narrow-leaf sedge
Carex blanda	white sedge
Carex cephalophora	oval-leaf sedge
Carex emoryi	Emory's sedge
Carex microdonta	little-tooth sedge
Carex planostachys	cedar sedge
Chasmanthium latifolium	Indian wood-oats
Clematis pitcheri	bluebill
Dicliptera brachiata	branched foldwing
Elymus virginicus	Virginia wild rye
Eupatorium serotinum	late-flowering thoroughwort
Galium aparine	sticky-willy
Geum canadense	white avens
Malvaviscus drummondii	Texas wax-mallow
Melothria pendula	Guadeloupe-cucumber
Muhlenbergia lindheimeri	Lendheimer's muhly
Muhlenbergia schreberi	nimblewill
Muhlenbergia utilis	aparejo grass
Panicum virgatum	wand panic grass
Paspalum pubiflorum	hairy-seed crown grass
Poa arachnifera	Texas blue grass
Ranunculus macranthus	large buttercup
Ruellia drummondiana	Drummond's wild petunia
Sanicula canadensis	Canadian black-snakeroot
Setaria scheelei	southwestern bristle grass
Tinantia anomala	widow's-tears
Tradescantia gigantea	giant spiderwort
Valerianella stenocarpa	narrow-cell cornsalad
Verbesina virginica	white crownbeard
Viola missouriensis	Missouri violet

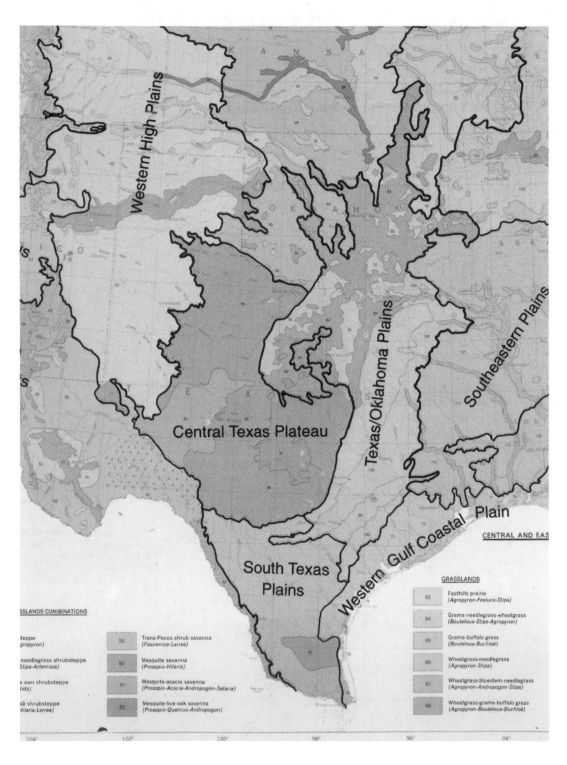

South Texas Plains

South Texas Plains

Introduction

The South Texas Plains region encompasses most of the southern tip of Texas. The northern boundary is the Balcones Escarpment. The region extends south to the tip of Texas at the mouth of the Rio Grande River near Brownsville. This region does not include the vegetation of the arid plains bordering the Rio Grande River to the west. A description of the vegetation found along the Rio Grande can be found in the Southern Deserts region. The vegetation of the Gulf Coast and barrier islands to the east is found in the Western Gulf Coastal Plains region.

The natural vegetation is characterized by grasslands and savanna-woodland communities. Before changes in the region, such as excessive grazing, conversion to cropland, and suppression of natural fires, the area was predominantly open grasslands with scattered trees and shrubs. Today the area is increasingly dominated with the thorny scrub vegetation which was once limited to rocky upland areas.

Unique in this region are small groves of native palm which occur in southern-most Texas near Brownsville.

The primary sources used to develop descriptions and species lists are: Barbour and Billings 1988; Bill Carr (pers. com.); Correll and Johnston 1970; McMahan et al. 1984; Texas Natural Heritage Program 1991; Thasp 1926.

Dominant Ecological Communities

Upland Systems
Mesquite–Granjeno Woodland
Mesquite–Blackbrush Shrub
Rio Grande Shrubland
Live Oak Savanna
South Texas Prairie

Wetland Systems
Floodplain Forest

UPLAND SYSTEMS

Mesquite–Granjeno Woodland

Mesquite–Granjeno Woodland occurs throughout the South Texas Plains. This woodland may occur within shrub dominated areas where there is little or no distinction between canopy and understory layers. This community corresponds, in part, to Küchler #61.

Canopy
Characteristic Species
Celtis pallida	shiny hackberry (granjeno)
Prosopis glandulosa	honey mesquite

Associates
Acacia berlandieri	guajillo
Acacia greggii	long-flower catclaw

Acacia minuta	coastal scrub wattle
Acacia rigidula	chaparro-prieto
Aloysia gratissima	whitebrush
Colubrina texensis	hog-plum
Condalia hookeri	Brazilian bluewood
Eysenhardtia texana	Texas kidneywood
Forestiera angustifolia	Texas swamp-privet
Guajacum angustifolium	Texas lignumvitae
Karwinskia humboldtiana	coyotillo
Lycium berlandieri	silver desert-thorn
Opuntia engelmannii	cactus-apple
Opuntia leptocaulis	Christmas cholla
Opuntia macrorhiza	twist-spine prickly-pear
Parkinsonia aculeata	Jerusalem-thorn
Schaefferia cuneifolia	desert-yaupon
Sideroxylon lanuginosum	gum bully
Zanthoxylum fagara	lime prickly-ash
Ziziphus obtusifolia	lotebush

Herbaceous Understory

Acleisanthes anisophylla	oblique-leaf trumpets
Ambrosia confertiflora	weak-leaf burr-ragweed
Aphanostephus ramosissimus	plains dozedaisy
Aristida purpurea	purple three-awn
Bothriochoa saccharoides	plumed beard grass
Bouteloua rigidiseta	Texas grama
Bouteloua trifida	red grama
Cardiospermum corindum	faux-persil
Chloris ciliata	fringed windmill grass
Chloris cucullata	hooded windmill grass
Cnidoscolus texanus	Texas bull-nettle
Cocculus diverisifolius	snailseed
Croton dioicus	grassland croton
Florestina tripteris	sticky florestina
Gaillardia suavis	perfumeballs
Helianthus annuus	common sunflower
Helianthus ciliaris	Texas-blueweed
Heteropogon contortus	twisted tanglehead
Hilaria berlangeri	curly-mesquite
Isocoma drummondii	Drummond's jimmyweed
Liatris mucronata	cusp gayfeather
Machaeranthera pinnatifida	lacy tansy-aster
Nassella leucotricha	Texas wintergrass
Nyctaginia capitata	devil's-bouquet
Palafoxia texana	Texas palafox
Panicum hallii	Hall's panic grass
Pappophorum bicolor	pink pappus grass
Parthenium hysterophorus	Santa Maria feverfew

Passiflora foetida	scarlet-fruit
Salvia coccinea	blood sage
Schizachyrium scoparium	little false bluestem
Setaria macrostachya	plains bristle grass
Simsia calva	awnless bush-sunflower
Siphonoglossa pilosella	hairy tubetongue
Solanum elaeagnifolium	silver-leaf nightshade
Sporobolus pyramidatus	whorled dropseed
Tiquilia canescens	woody crinklemat
Tridens eragrostoides	love fluff grass
Tridens muticus	awnless fluff grass

Mesquite–Blackbrush Scrub

Mesquite–Blackbrush Scrub is widely represented in the region. It occurs in rocky, broken uplands and may grade into other shrub communities depending on soil, slope, and moisture. This community corresponds, in part, to Küchler #61.

Characteristic Woody Species

Acacia rigidula	chaparro-prieto (blackbrush)
Prosopis glandulosa	honey mesquite

Associates

Acacia berlandieri	guajillo
Acacia greggii	long-flower catclaw
Acacia schaffneri	Schaffner's wattle
Aloysia gratissima	whitebrush
Castela erecta	goatbush
Celtis pallida	shiny hackberry
Condalia hookeri	Brazilian bluewood
Diospyros texana	Texas persimmon
Ephedra antisyphilitica	clapweed
Eysenhardtia texana	Texas kidneywood
Forestiera angustifolia	Texas swamp-privet
Guajacum angustifolium	Texas lignumvitae
Jatropha dioica	leatherstem
Koeberlinia spinosa	crown-of-thorns
Leucophyllum frutescens	Texas barometer-bush
Lycium berlandieri	silver desert-thorn
Mahonia trifoliata	Laredo Oregon-grape
Mammillaria heyderi	little nipple cactus
Opuntia engelmannii	cactus-apple
Opuntia leptocaulis	Christmas cholla
Rhus microphylla	little-leaf sumac
Schaefferia cuneifolia	desert-yaupon
Thelocactus setispinus	miniature-barrel cactus
Yucca treculeana	Don Quixote's-lace
Ziziphus obtusifolia	lotebush

Herbaceous Understory

Acleisanthes anisophylla	oblique-leaf trumpets
Acleisanthes longiflora	angel's trumpets
Acourtia runcinata	feather-leaf desert-peony
Amblyolepis setigera	huisache-daisy
Aphanostephus ramosissimus	plains dozedaisy
Aristida purpurea	purple three-awn
Bouteloua curtipendula	side-oats grama
Bouteloua gracilis	blue grama
Bouteloua hirsuta	hairy grama
Carex planostachys	cedar sedge
Centaurea americana	American star-thistle
Chamaesyce serpens	matted sandmat
Chloris ciliata	fringed windmill grass
Chloris cucullata	hooded windmill grass
Chloris verticillata	tumble windmill grass
Clematis drummondii	Texas virgin's-bower
Cordia podocephala	Texas manjack
Croton dioicus	grassland croton
Florestina tripteris	sticky florestina
Hedyotis nigricans	diamond-flower
Hymenopappus scabiosaeus	Carolina woolywhite
Isocoma drummondii	Drummond's jimmyweed
Liatris mucronata	cusp gayfeather
Oxalis dichondraefolia	peony-leaf wood-sorrel
Panicum hallii	Hall's panic grass
Pappophorum bicolor	pink pappus grass
Parthenium hysterophorus	Santa Maria feverfew
Phyllanthus polygonoides	smartweed leaf-flower
Pinaropappus roseus	white rock-lettuce
Polygala ovatifolia	egg-leaf milkwort
Ruellia nudiflora	violet wild petunia
Schizachyrium scoparium	little false bluestem
Senna roemeriana	two-leaved wild sensitive-plant
Setaria macrostachya	plains bristle grass
Setaria ramiseta	Rio Grande bristle grass
Siphonoglossa pilosella	hairy tubetongue
Thamnosma texanum	rue-of-the-mountains
Thymophylla pentachaeta	five-needle pricklyleaf
Tiquilia canescens	woody crinklemat
Tridens muticus	awnless fluff grass
Wedelia hispida	hairy creeping-oxeye

Rio Grande Shrubland

Most of the vegetation in the area around the mouth of the Rio Grande River has been altered through development or conversion to cropland. Some areas remain in the native subtropical evergreen shrubland or forest. This area, generally characterized by ebony blackbead (Texas ebony) also supports groves of Rio Grande palmetto.

Characteristic Woody Species
Ehretia anacua	knockaway
Pithecellobium ebano	ebony blackbead

Associates
Acacia greggii	long-flower catclaw
Celtis pallida	shiny hackberry
Condalia hookeri	Brazilian bluewood
Harvardia pallens	haujillo
Leucaena pulverulenta	great leadtree
Opuntia leptocaulis	Christmas cholla
Phaulothamnus spinescens	devilqueen
Prosopis glandulosa	honey mesquite
Sabal mexicana	Rio Grande palmetto
Sideroxylon celastrinum	saffron-plum
Ulmus crassifolia	cedar elm
Yucca torreyi	Torrey's yucca
Zanthoxylum fagara	lime prickly-ash
Zizphus obtusifolia	lotebush

Herbaceous Understory
Bothriochloa barbinodis	cane beard grass
Buchloë dactyloides	buffalo grass
Cardiospermum corindum	faux-persil
Chloris pluriflora	multi-flower windmill grass
Cocculus diversifolius	snailseed
Eupatorium azureum	blue boneset
Malpighia glabra	wild crape-myrtle
Ruellia drummondiana	Drummond's wild petunia
Salvia coccinea	blood sage
Serjania brachycarpa	little-fruit slipplejack
Setaria leucopila	streambed bristle grass
Stachys drummondii	Drummond's hedge-nettle
Stellaria prostrata	prostrate starwort
Urtica chamidryoides	heart-leaf nettle
Verbesina microptera	Texas crownbeard

Live Oak Savanna

The trees of Live Oak Savanna are either evergreen or deciduous broadleaf and occur scattered or in groves. This community corresponds to Küchler #62.

Canopy
Characteristic Species
Prosopis glandulosa	honey mesquite
Quercus virginiana	live oak

Associates
Acacia rigidula	chaparro-prieto
Aloysia gratissima	whitebrush
Diospyros texana	Texas persimmon
Lycium berlandieri	silver desert-thorn

Maclura pomifera	osage-orange
Opuntia engelmannii	cactus-apple
Opuntia leptocaulis	Christmas cholla
Oxalis frutescens	shrubby wood-sorrel
Sideroxylon lanuginosum	gum bully
Zanthoxylum fagara	lime prickly-ash
Ziziphus obtusifolia	lotebush

Herbaceous Understory

Andropogon gerardii	big bluestem
Aristida purpurea	purple three-awn
Bouteloua gracilis	blue grama
Brachiaria ciliatissima	fringed signal grass
Callirhoe involucrata	purple poppy-mallow
Chamaecrista fasciculata	sleepingplant
Chamaesyce serpens	matted sandmat
Cnidoscolus texanus	Texas bull-nettle
Croton capitatus	hogwort
Elyonurus tripsacoides	pan-American balsamscale
Gaillardia aestivalis	lance-leaf blanket-flower
Helianthus argophyllus	silver-leaf sunflower
Heteropogon contortus	twisted tanglehead
Heterotheca subaxillaris	camphorweed
Muhlenbergia capillaris	hairy awn muhly
Panicum hallii	Hall's panic grass
Panicum virgatum	wand panic grass
Pappophorum bicolor	pink pappus grass
Paspalum monostachyum	gulf dune crown grass
Paspalum plicatulum	brown-seed crown grass
Schizachyrium scoparium	little false bluestem
Schrankia microphylla	little-leaf sensitive-briar
Senna roemeriana	two-leaved wild sensitive-plant
Solanum elaeagnifolium	silver-leaf nightshade
Sorghastrum nutans	yellow Indian grass
Sporobolus cryptandrus	sand dropseed
Tephrosia lindheimeri	Lindheimer's hoary-pea
Thelesperma nuecense	Rio Grande greenthread
Trachypogon secundus	one-sided crinkle-awn grass
Tridens elegans	Silveus' grass
Tridens flavus	tall redtop

South Texas Prairie

The South Texas Plains formerly supported a large area dominated by mid-height grasslands. The prairies, however, have been overgrazed resulting in an over-abundance of shrubs in this once grass-dominated area. Other factors in the elimination of grassland habitat include conversion to cropland and suppression of natural fires.

Characteristic Species

Bothriochloa barbinodis	cane beard grass
Chloris pluriflora	multi-flower windmill grass

Associates

Ambrosia confertiflora	weak-leaf burr-ragweed
Aristida purpurea	purple three-awn
Bouteloua gracilis	blue grama
Buchloë dactyloides	buffalo grass
Chamaesyce serpens	matted sandmat
Chloris cucullata	hooded windmill grass
Cnidoscolus texanus	Texas bull-nettle
Hilaria belangeri	curly-mesquite
Pappophorum bicolor	pink pappus grass
Phyllanthus polygonoides	smartweed leaf-flower
Schizachyrium scoparium	little false bluestem
Senna roemeriana	two-leaved wild sensitive-plant
Setaria macrostachya	plains bristle grass
Thymophylla pentachaeta	five-needle pricklyleaf
Tridens muticus	awnless fluff grass

WETLAND SYSTEMS

Floodplain Forest

Floodplain Forest in the South Texas Plains is a deciduous forest which occurs along the major rivers.

Canopy

Characteristic Species

Carya illinoinensis	pecan
Celtis pallida	shiny hackberry
Morus rubra	red mulberry
Prosopis glandulosa	honey mesquite
Ulmus americana	American elm
Ulmus crassifolia	cedar elm

Associates

Acer negundo	ash-leaf maple
Celtis laevigata	sugar-berry
Fraxinus berlandieriana	Mexican ash
Juglans nigra	black walnut
Platanus occidentalis	American sycamore
Quercus fusiformis	plateau oak
Quercus macrocarpa	burr oak
Salix nigra	black willow
Sapindus saponaria	wing-leaf soapberry

Woody Understory

Acacia minuta	coastal-scrub wattle
Ampelopsis arborea	peppervine
Baccharis neglecta	Roosevelt-weed
Diospyros texana	Texas persimmon
Mimosa pigra	black mimosa
Parkinsonia aculeata	Jerusalem-thorn
Rubus trivialis	southern dewberry
Sideroxylon lanuginosum	gum bully
Smilax bona-nox	fringed greenbriar
Toxicodendron pubescens	atlantic poison-oak
Vitis mustangensis	mustang grape

Herbaceous Understory

Ambrosia psilostachya	western ragweed
Carex brittoniana	Britton's sedge
Chasmanthium latifolium	Indian wood-oats
Chloracantha spinosus	Mexican devilweed
Clematis drummondii	Texas virgin's-bower
Cocculus diversifolius	snailseed
Dicliptera brachiata	branched foldwing
Elymus virginicus	Virginia wild rye
Malvaviscus drummondii	Texas wax-mallow
Nassella leucotricha	Texas wintergrass
Panicum virgatum	wand panic grass
Rivina humilis	rougeplant
Ruellia nudiflora	violet wild petunia
Salvia coccinea	blood sage
Urtica chamaedryoides	heart-leaf nettle
Verbesina virginica	white crownbeard

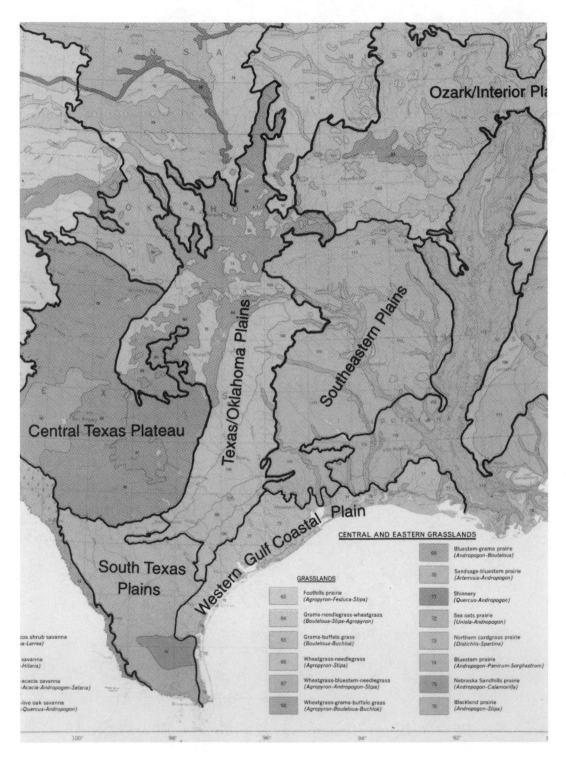

Western Gulf Coastal Plain

Western Gulf Coastal Plain

Introduction

The Western Gulf Coastal Plain is a long narrow grassy plain bordering the Gulf of Mexico along the Texas coast. The barrier islands off the coast are also included. The region supports both upland and lowland grasslands, evergreen woodlands, freshwater marshes, and salt marshes. Grasslands were once the characteristic vegetation of this region. The area is now mostly cultivated, or heavily grazed, with natural vegetation occurring as fragmented remnants. Excessive grazing and other human disturbances have caused much of the area to be invaded by trees and brush such as mesquite, oaks, prickly pear, and acacias.

The primary sources used to develop descriptions and species lists are: Barbour and Billings 1988; Bill Carr 1992 (pers. com.); Correll and Johnston 1970; Jones 1977; McMahan et al. 1984; Texas Natural Heritage program 1991; Tharp 1926.

Dominant Ecological Communities

Upland Systems
Coastal Woodland
Coastal Prairie
Island Prairie

Wetland Systems
Floodplain Forest
Fresh Water Marsh

Estuarine System
Salt Marsh

UPLAND SYSTEMS

Coastal Woodland

Coastal Woodland occurs throughout the Coastal Prairie. The composition of Coastal Woodland varies according to geographical distribution. The proximity of the woodland to Floodplain Forest, prairies, and other woodland communities such as Cross Timbers Woodland at the northeastern boundary of the region are important factors.

Canopy
Characteristic Species
Carya illinoinensis	pecan
Quercus stellata	post oak
Quercus virginiana	live oak

Associates
Celtis laevigata	sugar-berry
Persea borbonia	red bay
Quercus hemisphaerica	Darlington's oak
Quercus laurifolia	laurel oak
Quercus marilandica	blackjack oak
Ulmus alata	winged elm

Woody Understory
Crateagus spp.	hawthorn
Ilex vomitoria	yaupon

Herbaceous Understory
Paspalum plicatulam	brown-seed crown grass
Schizachyrium scoparium	little false bluestem

Coastal Prairie

The Western Gulf Coastal Plain Region was once characterized by the tallgrass upland prairies. Woodlands of live oak may be mixed with the prairie. Most of the prairie today has been converted into farmland or heavily grazed. This community corresponds to Küchler #77.

Characteristic Species
Andropogon gerardii	big bluestem
Schizachyrium scoparium	little false bluestem
Spartina spartinae	gulf cord grass
Sorghastrum nutans	yellow Indian grass

Associates
Andropogon glomeratus	bushy bluestem
Andropogon virginicus	broom-sedge
Aristida purpurea	purple three-awn
Bouteloua curtipendula	side-oats grama
Buchloë dactyloides	buffalo grass
Fimbristylis puberula	hairy fimbry
Muhlenbergia capillaris	hairy-awn muhly
Paspalum monostachyum	gulf dune crown grass
Paspalum plicatulum	brown-seed crown grass
Schizachyrium tenerum	slender false bluestem
Sporobolus indicus	smut grass

Island Prairie

Island Prairie is a midgrass to tallgrass prairie occurring on the partially stabilized dunes of the coastal barrier islands. This community corresponds to Küchler #72.

Characteristic Species
Panicum amarum	bitter panic grass
Schizachyrium scoparium	little false bluestem
Uniola paniculata	sea-oats

Associates
Agalinis maritima	saltmarsh false foxglove
Ambrosia psilostachya	western ragweed
Aphanostephus skirrhobasis	Arkansas dozedaisy
Buchnera americana	American bluehearts
Chamaecrista fasciculata	sleepingplant
Chamaesyce bombensis	dixie sandmat
Croton capitatus	hogwort
Croton punctatus	gulf croton

Digitaria texana	Texas crab grass
Erythrina herbacea	red cardinal
Eupatorium betonicifolium	betony-leaf thoroughwort
Fimbristylis caroliniana	Carolina fimbry
Fimbristylis castanea	marsh fimbry
Helianthus argophyllus	silver-leaf sunflower
Hypericum hypericoides	St. Andrew's-cross
Ipomaea imperati	beach morning-glory
Ipomaea pes-caprae	bay-hops
Juncus spp.	rush
Limonium carolinianum	Carolina sea-lavendar
Machaeranthera phyllocephala	camphor-daisy
Muhlenbergia capillaris	hairy-awn muhly
Myrica cerifera	southern bayberry
Oenothera drummondii	beach evening-primrose
Opuntia engelmannii	cactus-apple
Panicum amarum	bitter panic grass
Panicum virgatum	wand panic grass
Paspalum monostachyum	gulf dune crown grass
Paspalum vaginatum	talquezal
Persea borbonia	red bay
Quercus hemisphaerica	Darlington's oak
Quercus virginiana	live oak
Sabal minor	dwarf palmetto
Sabatia arenicola	sand rose-gentian
Samolus ebracteatus	limewater brookweed
Senecio riddellii	Riddell's ragwort
Sesuvium portulacastrum	shoreline sea-purslane
Solidago sempervirens	seaside goldenrod
Spartina patens	salt-meadow cord grass
Trichoneura elegans	Siveus' grass
Vasevochloa multinervosa	Texas grass
Vigna luteola	piedmont cow-pea

WETLAND SYSTEMS

Floodplain Forest

Floodplain Forest occurs on floodplains and along bayous in the Western Gulf Coastal Plain. Evergreen Woodland and grassland species from adjacent communities contribute to the diversity of the floodplain forest.

Canopy
Characteristic Species

Carya illinoinensis	pecan
Carya texana	black hickory
Fraxinus pennsylvanica	green ash

Platanus occidentalis	American sycamore
Populus deltoides	eastern cottonwood
Quercus nigra	water oak
Quercus phellos	willow oak
Quercus shumardii	Shumard's oak
Quercus virginiana	live oak
Salix nigra	black willow
Sapindus saponaria	wing-leaf soapberry
Ulmus americana	American elm

Associates

Celtis laevigata	sugar-berry
Liquidambar styraciflua	sweet-gum
Quercus lyrata	overcup oak
Quercus pagoda	cherry-bark oak
Ulmus crassifolia	cedar elm

Woody Understory

Aesculus pavia	red buckeye
Ampelopsis arborea	peppervine
Bignonia capreolata	crossvine
Campsis radicans	trumpet-creeper
Carpinus caroliniana	American hornbeam
Cornus drummondii	rough-leaf dogwood
Diospyros virginiana	common persimmon
Forestiera acuminata	eastern swamp-privet
Ilex decidua	deciduous holly
Ilex vomitoria	yaupon
Lonicera sempervirens	trumpet honeysuckle
Maclura pomifera	osage-orange
Ostrya virginiana	eastern hop-hornbeam
Parthenocissus quinquefolia	Virginia-creeper
Sambucus canadensis	American elder
Toxicodendron pubescens	Atlantic poison-ivy
Viburnum dentatum	southern arrow-wood

Herbaceous Understory

Arisaema dracontium	greendragon
Carex amphibola	eastern narrow-leaf sedge
Carex cephalophora	oval-leaf sedge
Carex cherokeensis	Cherokee sedge
Chasmanthium latifolium	Indian wood-oats
Chasmanthium laxum	Slender wood-oats
Corydalis micrantha	small-flower fumewort
Dicliptera brachiata	branched foldwing
Elephantopus carolinianus	Carolina elephant's-foot
Elymus virginicus	Virginia wild rye
Nassella leucotricha	Texas wintergrass
Nemophila phacelioides	large-flower baby-blue-eyes
Ruellia caroliniensis	Carolina wild petunia

Senecio glabellus	cress-leaf ragwort
Stellaria media	common chickweed
Verbesina virginica	white crownbeard

Fresh Water Marsh

Fresh Water Marsh occurs in low, poorly drained areas where water is near or at the surface for prolonged periods of time. In this region, Fresh Water Marsh is usually found landward of Salt Marsh and Coastal Prairie. Emergent herbaceous plants which dominate the marsh are alligator weed and maiden-cane. Woody vegetation is almost completely lacking.

Characteristic Species

Panicum hemitomon	maiden-cane

Associates

Cabomba caroliniana	Carolina fanwort
Ceratophyllum demersum	coontail
Hydrocotyle verticillata	whorled marsh-pennywort
Lemna aequinoctialis	lesser duckweed
Nymphaea odorata	American white water-lily
Pontederia cordata	pickerelweed
Sagittaria papillosa	nipple-bract arrowhead
Typha latifolia	broad-leaf cat-tail

ESTUARINE SYSTEMS

Salt Marsh

Salt Marsh occurs along the Gulf coast and is influenced by tidal activity. The marshes that are subject to the daily ebb and flow of the tides will have *Juncus* species. This community corresponds to Küchler #78.

Characteristic Species

Distichlis spicata	coastal salt grass
Spartina alterniflora	saltwater cord grass
Spartina patens	salt-meadow cord grass
Spartina spartinae	gulf cord grass

Associates

Avicennia germinans	black mangrove
Batis maritima	turtleweed
Halodule beaudettei	shoalweed
Juncus effusus	lamp rush
Juncus roemerianus	Roemer's rush
Panicum hemitomon	maiden-cane
Panicum repens	torpedo grass
Panicum virgatum	wand panic grass
Paspalum vaginatum	talquezal
Phragmites australis	common reed
Ruppia maritima	beaked ditch-grass

Sagittaria lancifolia	bull-tongue arrowhead
Salicornia virginica	woody saltwort
Scirpus americanus	chairmaker's bulrush
Scirpus californicus	California bulrush
Spartina cynosuroides	big cord grass
Sporobolus virginicus	seashore dropseed
Typha domingensis	southern cat-tail
Zizaniopsis miliacea	marsh-millet

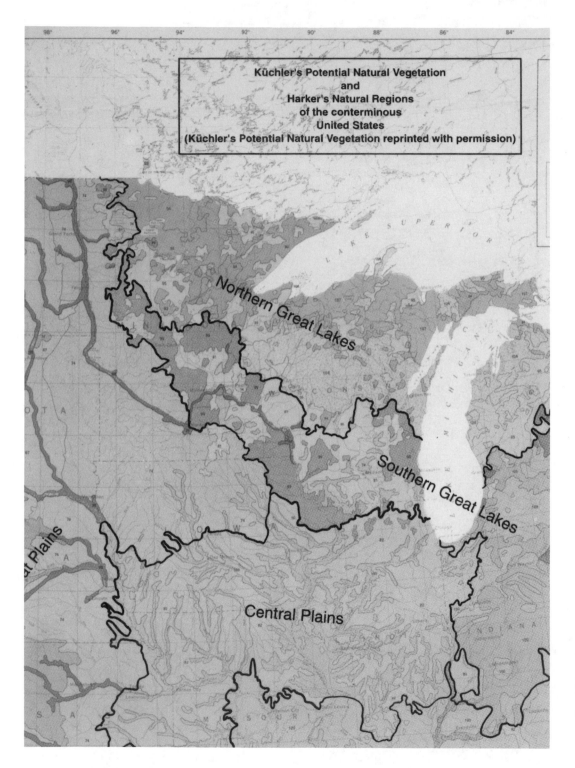

Northern Great Lakes

Northern Great Lakes

Introduction

The Northern Great Lakes region encompasses northern and upper peninsula Michigan, northern Wisconsin, and northeastern Minnesota. This region contains a narrow strip that crosses Michigan, Wisconsin, and Minnesota, known as the tension zone, that splits these states into northern and southern provinces. The northern and the southern zones in these states support distinctive flora, however, species overlap in the tension zone.

Spruce–fir forests dominate in northern Minnesota and the upper peninsula of Michigan. Northern Hardwoods–Conifer, and Great Lakes Pine Forest dominate in Wisconsin and Michigan. Open canopy forests and barrens are also notable, especially the Pine Barrens. This vegetation type is becoming less common due to fire suppression. Wetland areas are important as habitat for migrating waterfowl. Forested bogs, shrub swamps, and wet meadows are common.

The primary sources used to develop descriptions and species lists are: Aaseng et al. 1992; Barbour and Billings 1988; Chapman 1986; Curtis 1959.

Dominant Ecological Communities

Upland Systems
Northern Hardwoods–Conifer Forest
Great Lakes Spruce–Fir Forest
Great Lakes Pine Forest
Pine Barrens

Wetland Systems
Conifer Bog
Hardwood–Conifer Swamp
Northern Shrub Swamp
Open Bog
Northern Wet Meadow

UPLAND SYSTEMS

Northern Hardwoods–Conifer Forest

Northern Hardwoods–Conifer Forest occurs on dry to mesic sites and is frequently found on sandy-deep loam soils, but may also be found on coarser soils and on slopes. Species diversity is greater in southern portions of this system. This community corresponds to Küchler #106 and #107.

Canopy
Characteristic Species

Abies balsamea	balsam fir
Acer rubrum	red maple
Acer saccharum	sugar maple
Betula alleghaniensis	yellow birch
Betula papyrifera	paper birch

Fagus grandifolia	American beech
Pinus strobus	eastern white pine
Quercus rubra	northern red oak
Tilia americana	American basswood
Tsuga canadensis	eastern hemlock

Associates

Acer pensylvanicum	striped maple
Carya ovata	shag-bark hickory
Fraxinus americana	white ash
Fraxinus nigra	black ash
Juglans cinerea	white walnut
Ostrya virginiana	eastern hop-hornbeam
Picea glauca	white spruce
Pinus resinosa	red pine
Populus grandidentata	big-tooth aspen
Prunus pensylvanica	fire cherry
Prunus serotina	black cherry
Quercus alba	northern white oak
Quercus ellipsoidalis	northern pin oak
Thuja occidentalis	eastern arborvitae
Ulmus americana	American elm
Ulmus rubra	slippery elm

Woody Understory

Acer spicatum	mountain maple
Corylus cornuta	beaked hazelnut
Dirca palustris	eastern leatherwood
Kalmia latifolia	mountain-laurel
Linnaea borealis	American twinflower
Lonicera canadensis	American fly-honeysuckle
Lonicera oblongifolia	swamp fly-honeysuckle
Prunus virginiana	choke cherry
Ribes lacustre	bristly black gooseberry
Taxus canadensis	American yew
Viburnum acerifolium	maple-leaf arrow-wood

Herbaceous Understory

Actaea pachypoda	white baneberry
Adiantum pedatum	northern maidenhair
Anemone quinquefolia	nightcaps
Aralia nudicaulis	wild sarsaparilla
Aralia racemosa	American spikenard
Aster macrophyllus	large-leaf aster
Athyrium filix-femina	subarctic lady fern
Botrychium virginianum	rattlesnake fern
Cardamine diphylla	crinkleroot
Circaea alpina	small enchanter's-nightshade
Claytonia caroliniana	Carolina springbeauty
Clintonia borealis	yellow bluebead-lily

Conopholis americana	American squawroot
Cornus canadensis	Canadian bunchberry
Dicentra canadensis	squirrel-corn
Dryopteris campyloptera	mountain wood fern
Epifagus virginiana	beechdrops
Erythronium americanum	American trout-lily
Galium triflorum	fragrant bedstraw
Gymnocarpium dryopteris	western oak fern
Hepatica nobilis	liverwort
Huperzia lucidula	shining club-moss
Lycopodium obscurum	prince-pine
Maianthemum canadense	false lily-of-the-valley
Maianthemum racemosum	feathery false Solomon's-seal
Mitchella repens	partridge-berry
Mitella nuda	bare-stem bishop's-cap
Oryzopsis asperifolia	white-grain mountain-rice grass
Osmorhiza claytonii	hairy sweet-cicely
Panax trifolius	dwarf ginseng
Polygonatum pubescens	hairy Solomon's-seal
Streptopus roseus	rosy twistedstalk
Trientalis borealis	American starflower
Trillium cernuum	whip-poor-will-flower
Trillium grandiflorum	large-flower wakerobin
Uvularia grandiflora	large-flower bellwort
Uvularia sessilifolia	sessile-leaf bellwort
Viola cucullata	marsh blue violet
Viola pubescens	downy yellow violet

Great Lakes Spruce–Fir Forest

Great Lakes Spruce–Fir Forest occurs in northern Minnesota, the upper peninsula of Michigan, on islands in the northern Great Lakes, and scattered in extreme northern areas of Wisconsin. The dominant species are balsam fir and white spruce. The spruce–fir forest is also known as the boreal forest due to its northern affinities. Cool temperatures, short growing season, abundant available moisture during the growing season, and deep snows in winter are the dominant climatic forces in the spruce-fir zone. Soils are generally sand and sandy loam. This community corresponds to Küchler #93.

Canopy
Characteristic Species

Abies balsamea	balsam fir
Betula papyrifera	paper birch
Picea glauca	white spruce
Picea mariana	black spruce
Pinus strobus	eastern white pine
Thuja occidentalis	eastern arborvitae

Associates

Acer rubrum	red maple
Acer saccharum	sugar maple
Betula alleghaniensis	yellow birch

Carya cordiformis	bitter-nut hickory
Fraxinus americana	white ash
Fraxinus nigra	black ash
Fraxinus pennsylvanica	green ash
Larix laricina	American larch
Pinus banksiana	jack pine
Pinus resinosa	red pine
Populus balsamifera	balsam poplar
Populus grandidentata	big-tooth aspen
Populus tremuloides	quaking aspen
Prunus pensylvanica	fire cherry
Prunus serotina	black cherry
Quercus alba	northern white oak
Quercus ellipsoidalis	northern pin oak
Quercus rubra	northern red oak
Tilia americana	American basswood
Tsuga canadensis	eastern hemlock
Ulmus americana	American elm
Ulmus rubra	slippery elm

Woody Understory

Acer spicatum	mountain maple
Alnus incana	speckled alder
Carpinus caroliniana	American hornbeam
Cornus rugosa	round-leaf dogwood
Corylus cornuta	beaked hazelnut
Diervilla lonicera	northern bush-honeysuckle
Gaultheria hispidula	creeping-snowberry
Gaultheria procumbens	eastern teaberry
Ledum groenlandicum	rusty Labrador-tea
Linnaea borealis	American twinflower
Lonicera canadensis	American fly-honeysuckle
Lonicera hirsuta	hairy honeysuckle
Ostrya virginiana	eastern hop-hornbeam
Ribes cynosbati	eastern prickly gooseberry
Rubus idaeus	common red raspberry
Rubus parviflorus	western thimble-berry
Rubus pubescens	dwarf red raspberry
Sorbus americana	American mountain-ash
Sorbus decora	northern mountain-ash
Vaccinium angustifolium	late lowbush blueberry
Vaccinium myrtilloides	velvet-leaf blueberry

Herbaceous Understory

Actaea rubra	red baneberry
Anemone quinquefolia	nightcaps
Apocynum androsaemifolium	spreading dogbane
Aralia nudicaulis	wild sarsaparilla
Aster macrophyllus	large-leaf aster

Athyrium filix-femina	subarctic lady fern
Brachyelytrum erectum	bearded shorthusk
Carex arctata	drooping woodland sedge
Carex eburnea	bristle-leaf sedge
Carex pedunculata	long-stalk sedge
Carex pensylvanica	Pennsylvania sedge
Circaea alpina	small enchanter's-nightshade
Clintonia borealis	yellow bluebead-lily
Coptis trifolia	three-leaf goldthread
Cornus canadensis	Canadian bunchberry
Cypripedium arietinum	ram-head lady's-slipper
Dryopteris campyloptera	mountain wood fern
Equisetum arvense	field horsetail
Fragaria virginiana	Virginia strawberry
Galium triflorum	fragrant bedstraw
Goodyera oblongifolia	green-leaf rattlesnake-plantain
Gymnocarpium dryopteris	western oak fern
Hepatica nobilis	liverwort
Impatiens capensis	spotted touch-me-not
Iris lacustris	dwarf lake iris
Lycopodium clavatum	running ground-pine
Lycopodium obscurum	princess pine
Maianthemum canadense	false lily-of-the-valley
Maianthemum racemosum	feathery false Solomon's-seal
Mitchella repens	partridge-berry
Mitella nuda	bare-stem bishop's-cap
Orthilia secunda	sidebells
Oryzopsis asperifolia	white-grain mountain rice grass
Osmorhiza claytoni	hairy sweet-cicely
Phegopteris connectilis	narrow beech fern
Polygala paucifolia	gaywings
Polygonatum pubescens	hairy Solomon's-seal
Prenanthes alba	white rattlesnake-root
Pteridium aquilinum	northern bracken fern
Pyrola elliptica	shinleaf
Sanicula marilandica	Maryland black-snakeroot
Streptopus roseus	rosy twistedstalk
Trientalis borealis	American starflower
Trillium cernuum	whip-poor-will-flower
Viola blanda	sweet white violet
Viola conspersa	American dog violet
Viola pubescens	downy yellow violet

Great Lakes Pine Forest

Great Lakes Pine Forest occurs throughout the Northern Great Lakes region, mainly on dry sites. The dominant species are white pine, jack pine, and red pine. Pine forests, however, may have a mixture of hardwoods in the canopy especially red maple, quaking aspen, and oak. These forests are dependent on periodic fires which help maintain the pines as dominants. This community corresponds to Küchler #95.

Canopy
Characteristic Species
Pinus banksiana	jack pine
Pinus resinosa	red pine
Pinus strobus	eastern white pine

Associates
Abies balsamea	balsam fir
Acer rubrum	red maple
Betula papyrifera	paper birch
Picea glauca	white spruce
Picea mariana	black spruce
Populus grandidentata	big-tooth aspen
Populus tremuloides	quaking aspen
Prunus serotina	black cherry
Quercus alba	northern white oak
Quercus coccinea	scarlet oak
Quercus ellipsoidalis	northern pin oak
Quercus rubra	northern red oak
Quercus velutina	black oak
Thuja occidentalis	eastern arborvitae

Woody Understory
Acer spicatum	mountain maple
Amelanchier stolonifera	running service-berry
Arctostaphylos uva-ursi	red bearberry
Comptonia peregrina	sweet-fern
Cornus rugosa	round-leaf dogwood
Corylus americana	American hazelnut
Corylus cornuta	beaked hazelnut
Diervilla lonicera	northern bush-honeysuckle
Gaultheria procumbens	eastern teaberry
Gaylussacia baccata	black huckleberry
Kalmia angustifolia	sheep-laurel
Lonicera canadensis	American fly-honeysuckle
Prunus pumila	sand cherry
Rubus flagellaris	whiplash dewberry
Vaccinium angustifolium	late lowbush blueberry
Vaccinium myrtilloides	velvet-leaf blueberry
Viburnum rafinesquianum	downy arrow-wood

Herbaceous Understory
Apocynum androsaemifolium	spreading dogbane
Aralia nudicaulis	wild sarsaparilla
Aster ciliolatus	Lindley's aster
Aster macrophyllus	large-leaf aster
Carex pensylvanica	Pennsylvania sedge
Cornus canadensis	Canadian bunchberry
Danthonia spicata	poverty wild oat grass
Deschampsia flexuosa	wavy hair grass
Fragaria virginiana	Virginia strawberry

Hieracium venosum	rattlesnake-weed
Lycopodium obscurum	princess-pine
Maianthemum canadense	false lily-of-the-valley
Melampyrum lineare	American cow-wheat
Oryzopsis pungens	short-awn mountain-rice grass
Pteridium aquilinum	northern bracken fern

Pine Barrens

Pine Barrens is open pine forests with a grassland type understory. It occurs in areas of very sandy or rocky soil. Historically, there were large areas in the northern Great Lakes covered with woodland/barren communities. Communities such as these are now rare due to the suppression of natural fires. Fires maintain the open canopy structure of such a community through the occasional killing and scarring of young trees.

Canopy
Characteristic Species
Pinus banksiana	jack pine
Pinus resinosa	red pine
Populus grandidentata	big-tooth aspen
Quercus ellipsoidalis	northern pin oak

Associates
Picea mariana	black spruce
Populus tremuloides	quaking aspen
Quercus macrocarpa	burr oak
Quercus palustris	pin oak
Quercus rubra	northern red oak

Woody Understory
Amelanchier stolonifera	running service-berry
Arctostaphylos uva-ursi	red bearberry
Ceanothus ovatus	redroot
Comptonia peregrina	sweet-fern
Corylus americana	American hazelnut
Corylus cornuta	beaked hazelnut
Diervilla lonicera	northern bush-honeysuckle
Gaylussacia baccata	black huckleberry
Salix bebbiana	long-beak willow
Salix humilis	small pussy willow
Vaccinium angustifolium	late lowbush blueberry
Viburnum rafinesquianum	downy arrow-wood

Herbaceous Understory
Andropogon gerardii	big bluestem
Carex pensylvanica	Pennsylvania sedge
Danthonia spicata	poverty wild oat grass
Lithospermum canescens	hoary puccoon
Lupinus perennis	sundial lupine
Pteridium aquilinum	northern bracken fern
Pulsatilla patens	American pasqueflower
Schizachyrium scoparium	little false bluestem

WETLAND SYSTEMS

Conifer Bog

Conifer Bog occurs throughout the Northern Great Lakes region but is most common in northern Minnesota. Black spruce is the most common tree species due to its ability to reproduce in the layers of sphagnum mosses which cover the forest floor. Conifer Bog develops on peatlands where the surface substrate becomes isolated from groundwater flow because of peat accumulation. The wetter areas in bog complexes are dominated by mosses and shrubs (see Open Bog) while the trees occur on drier sites such as crests and upper slopes of raised bogs. Most of the water and nutrients in the bogs come from rainfall. This results in low concentrations of dissolved nutrients which affect the growth rate of the vegetation. This community corresponds to Küchler #94.

Canopy
Characteristic Species
Abies balsamea	balsam fir
Larix laricina	American larch
Picea mariana	black spruce
Thuja occidentalis	eastern arborvitae

Associates
Acer rubrum	red maple
Betula alleghaniensis	yellow birch
Betula papyrifera	paper birch
Fraxinus nigra	black ash
Picea glauca	white spruce
Pinus banksiana	jack pine
Pinus strobus	eastern white pine
Populus tremuloides	quaking aspen
Ulmus rubra	slippery elm

Woody Understory
Alnus incana	speckled alder
Andromeda polifera	bog-rosemary
Chamaedaphne calyculata	leatherleaf
Gaultheria hispidula	creeping-snowberry
Gaultheria procumbens	eastern teaberry
Ilex verticillata	common winterberry
Kalmia polifolia	bog laurel
Ledum groenlandicum	rusty Labrador-tea
Linnaea borealis	American twinflower
Nemopanthus mucronatus	catberry
Parthenocissus vitacea	thicket-creeper
Rubus pubescens	dwarf red raspberry
Vaccinium angustifolium	late lowbush blueberry
Vaccinium myrtilloides	velvet-leaf blueberry
Vaccinium oxycoccus	small cranberry
Vaccinium vitis-idaea	lingonberry

Herbaceous Understory

Aralia nudicaulis	wild sarsaparilla
Carex disperma	soft-leaf sedge
Carex trisperma	three-seed sedge
Clintonia borealis	yellow bluebead-lily
Coptis trifolia	three-leaf goldthread
Cypripedium acaule	pink lady's-slipper
Dicranum undulatum	feather moss
Dryopteris campyloptera	mountain wood fern
Dryopteris cristata	crested wood fern
Equisetum fluviatile	water horsetail
Eriophorum vaginatum	tussock cotton-grass
Eriophorum virginicum	tawny cotton-grass
Maianthemum trifolium	three-leaf false Solomon's-seal
Osmunda cinnamomea	cinnamon fern
Pleurozium schreberi	feather moss
Polytrichum strictum	feather moss
Sarracenia purpurea	purple pitcherplant
Sphagnum fuscum	moss
Sphagnum nemoreum	moss
Sphagnum rubellum	moss
Trientalis borealis	American starflower

Hardwood–Conifer Swamp

Hardwood–Conifer Swamp occurs on moist mineral soil or muck along floodplains, or as transitional communities between bogs and upland forests. This wetland type is similar to Hardwood Floodplain Forest but beaver dams and wind-thrown logs rather than the annual or seasonal rise of the water determine the particular structure and composition of the forest. The most common characteristic species are black spruce, American larch (tamarack), and eastern arborvitae (white cedar), however, ash, birch, maple, and elm species are also common.

Canopy
Characteristic Species

Abies balsamea	balsam fir
Acer rubrum	red maple
Betula alleghaniensis	yellow birch
Fraxinus nigra	black ash
Larix laricina	American larch
Picea mariana	black spruce
Populus tremuloides	quaking aspen
Sorbus americana	American mountain-ash
Thuja occidentalis	eastern arborvitae

Associates

Betula papyrifera	paper birch
Fraxinus pennsylvanica	green ash
Pinus strobus	eastern white pine
Quercus macrocarpa	burr oak
Quercus rubra	northern red oak
Tsuga canadensis	eastern hemlock
Ulmus americana	American elm

Woody Understory

Alnus incana	speckled alder
Andromeda polifera	bog-rosemary
Chamaedaphne calyculata	leatherleaf
Gaultheria hispidula	creeping-snowberry
Gaultheria procumbens	eastern teaberry
Ledum groenlandicum	rusty Labrador-tea
Linnaea borealis	American twinflower
Nemopanthus mucronatus	catberry
Parthenocissus vitacea	thicket-creeper
Rubus pubescens	dwarf red raspberry
Toxicodendron vernix	poison sumac
Vaccinium angustifolium	late lowbush blueberry
Vaccinium myrtilloides	velvet-leaf blueberry
Vaccinium oxycoccus	small cranberry

Herbaceous Understory

Aralia nudicaulis	wild sarsaparilla
Athyrium filix-femina	subarctic lady fern
Caltha palustris	yellow marsh-marigold
Carex bromoides	brome-like sedge
Carex disperma	soft-leaf sedge
Carex leptalea	bristly-stalk sedge
Carex trisperma	three-seed sedge
Clintonia borealis	yellow bluebead-lily
Coptis trifolia	three-leaf goldthread
Cypripedium acaule	pink lady's-slipper
Dryopteris campyloptera	mountain wood fern
Dryopteris cristata	crested wood fern
Equisetum fluviatile	water horsetail
Eriophorum vaginatum	tussock cotton-grass
Eriophorum virginicum	tawny cotton-grass
Lycopus uniflorus	northern water-horehound
Maianthemum canadense	false lily-of-the-valley
Maianthemum trifolium	three-leaf false Solomon's-seal
Mentha arvensis	American wild mint
Mitella nuda	bare-stem bishop's cap
Onoclea sensibilis	sensitive fern
Osmunda cinnamomea	cinnamon fern
Osmunda claytoniana	interrupted fern
Pilea pumila	Canadian clearweed
Sarracenia purpurea	purple pitcher-plant
Scutellaria galericulata	hooded scullcap
Scutellaria lateriflora	mad dog scullcap
Symplocarpus foetidus	skunk-cabbage
Trientalis borealis	American starflower
Viola macloskeyi	smooth white violet

Northern Shrub Swamp

Northern Shrub Swamp is a common community along streams and around lakes where the soil is muck or peat. This community type is dominated by alder and is often referred to as alder thicket. Often shrub dominated communities are considered a successional stage toward a forest community. Shrub swamps in this area, however, are relatively stable due to limiting conditions associated with stream or lakeside habitat that are unsuitable for tree growth. The Northern Shrub Swamp may also be caused by prior fires.

Characteristic Woody Species
Alnus incana	speckled alder
Betula pumila	bog birch
Cornus stolonifera	redosier
Myrica gale	sweet gale
Ribes americanum	wild black currant
Spiraea alba	white meadowsweet
Viburnum nudum	possumhaw

Associates
Betula papyrifera	paper birch
Frangula alnus	alder-buckthorn
Fraxinus nigra	black ash
Larix laricina	American larch
Thuja occidentalis	eastern arborvitae
Toxicodendron vernix	poison sumac

Herbaceous Understory
Asclepias incarnata	swamp milkweed
Aster lanceolatus	white panicle aster
Aster puniceus	purple-stem aster
Bromus ciliatus	fringed brome
Calamagrostis canadensis	bluejoint
Campanula aparinoides	marsh bellflower
Carex lacustris	lakebank sedge
Carex prairea	prairie sedge
Carex stricta	uptight sedge
Chelone glabra	white turtlehead
Comarum palustre	purple marshlocks
Dryopteris cristata	crested woodfern
Eupatorium maculatum	spotted joe-pye-weed
Eupatorium perfoliatum	common boneset
Galium asprellum	rough bedstraw
Glyceria grandis	American manna grass
Impatiens capensis	spotted touch-me-not
Iris virginica	Virginia blueflag
Lycopus uniflorius	northern water-horehound
Mentha arvensis	American wild mint
Onoclea sensibilis	sensitive fern
Poa palustris	fowl blue grass
Polygonum sagittatum	arrow-leaf tearthumb
Rumex orbiculatus	greater water dock
Scirpus atrovirens	dark-green bulrush

Solidago canadensis	Canadian goldenrod
Solidago gigantea	late goldenrod
Thalictrum dasycarpum	purple meadow-rue
Thelypteris palustris	eastern marsh fern
Typha latifolia	broad-leaf cat-tail

Open Bog

Open Bog is one stage in the succession from open-water lakes to conifer swamps. A typical open bog has a surface layer of sphagnum mosses over a layer of dead and loosely compacted peat. The vegetation is dominated by shrubs, sedges, or cotton grass. Open Bog remains open due to periodic fluctuations in the water table correlated with weather cycles. Stunted black spruce, American larch (tamarack), and shrubs may be scattered over the area, but cover no more than 30 percent of the area. Surface layers in the bog may become dry enough to support fires which will destroy the advancing shrubs and forest. Pitcher-plants and sundews are some of the insectivorous species that are unique to Open Bog. Many areas that were once open bogs have been converted to cranberry marshes. Other disturbances, such as peat mining, have contributed to the decline of bogs and the habitat which supports bog species.

Characteristic Species

Andromeda polifolia	bog-rosemary
Betula glandulosa	scrub birch
Carex oligosperma	few-seed sedge
Carex trisperma	three-seed sedge
Chamaedaphne calyculata	leatherleaf
Drosera rotundifolia	round-leaf sundew
Eriophorum vaginatum	tussock cotton-grass
Kalmia polifolia	bog-laurel
Ledum groenlandicum	rusty Labrador-tea
Sarracenia purpurea	purple pitcherplant
Sphagnum cuspidatum	moss
Sphagnum magellanicum	moss
Vaccinium angustifolium	late lowbush blueberry

Associates

Calla palustris	water-dragon
Carex magellanica	boreal-bog sedge
Comarum palustre	purple marshlocks
Cypripedium acaule	pink lady's-slipper
Dryopteris cristata	crested wood fern
Gaultheria hispidula	creeping-snowberry
Gaultheria procumbens	eastern teaberry
Iris versicolor	harlequin blueflag
Maianthemum trifolium	three-leaf false-Solomon's-seal
Menyanthes trifoliata	buck-bean
Nemopanthus mucronatus	catberry
Rhynchospora alba	white beak sedge
Sphagnum capillifolium	moss
Sphagnum fuscum	moss
Sphagnum papillosum	moss
Sphagnum recurvum	moss

Sphagnum russowii	moss
Sphagnum teres	moss
Thelypteris palustris	eastern marsh fern
Trientalis borealis	American starflower
Vaccinium macrocarpon	large cranberry
Vaccinium myrtilloides	velvet-leaf blueberry
Vaccinium oxycoccos	small cranberry

Northern Wet Meadow

Northern Wet Meadow typically borders streams but can also be found on pond and lake margins and above beaver dams. The dominant species, depending on the level of moisture, are sedges, bulrushes, or cattails. The soil is characteristically raw peat or muck and water is always plentiful. The stability of the meadow communities depends on the degree of saturation. Periodically, fire burns the dryer areas inhibiting the invasion of shrub and tree species.

Characteristics Species

Asclepias incarnata	swamp milkweed
Calamagrostis canadensis	bluejoint
Carex aquatilis	leafy tussock sedge
Carex haydenii	cloud sedge
Carex lacustris	lakebank sedge
Carex rostrata	swollen beaked sedge
Carex stricta	uptight sedge
Cicuta bulbifera	bulbet-bearing water-hemlock
Glyceria canadensis	rattlesnake manna grass
Phragmites australis	common reed
Poa palustris	fowl blue grass
Sagittaria latifolia	duck-potato
Scirpus acutus	hard-stem bulrush
Scirpus americanus	chairmaker's bulrush
Scirpus atrovirens	dark-green bulrush
Scirpus cyperinus	cottongrass bulrush
Scirpus fluviatilis	river bulrush
Scirpus heterochaetus	pale great bulrush
Scirpus tabernaemontani	soft-stem bulrush
Typha angustifolia	narrow-leaf cat-tail
Typha latifolia	broad-leaf cat-tail

Associates

Aster lanceolatus	white panicle aster
Aster puniceus	purple-stem aster
Bromus ciliatus	fringed brome
Calamagrostis stricta	slim-stem reed grass
Campanula aparinoides	marsh bellflower
Carex lanuginosa	woolly sedge
Chelone glabra	white turtlehead
Cicuta maculata	spotted water-hemlock
Equisetum arvense	field horsetail
Eupatorium maculatum	spotted joe-pye-weed

Eupatorium perfoliatum	common boneset
Euthamia graminifolia	flat-top goldentop
Impatiens capensis	spotted touch-me-not
Lycopus americanus	cut-leaf water-horehound
Lycopus uniflorus	northern water-horehound
Mentha arvensis	American wild mint
Onoclea sensibilis	sensitive fern
Polygonum amphibium	water smartweed
Polygonum sagittatum	arrow-leaf tearthumb
Scutellaria galericulata	hooded skullcap
Scutellaria lateriflora	mad dog skullcap
Solidago gigantea	late goldenrod
Solidago uliginosa	bog goldenrod
Spartina pectinata	freshwater cord grass
Spiraea alba	white meadowsweet
Thalictrum dasycarpum	purple meadow-rue
Thelypteris palustris	eastern marsh fern
Verbena hastata	simpler's-joy

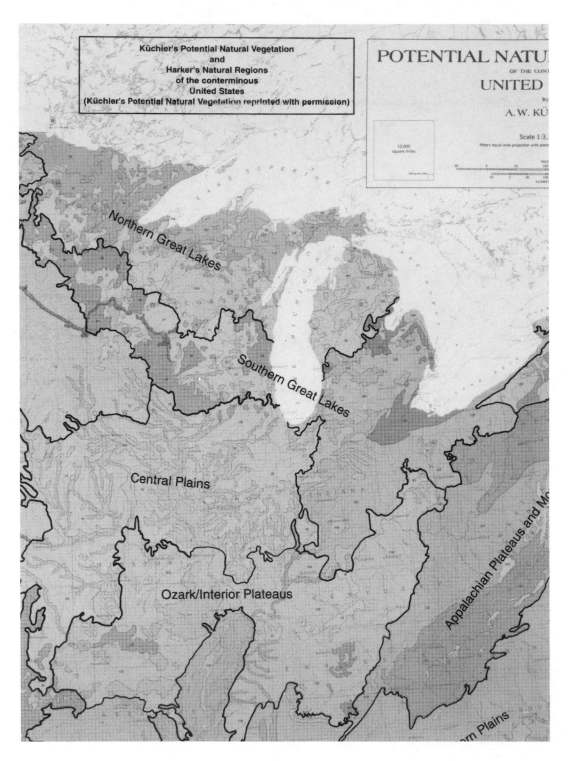

Southern Great Lakes

Southern Great Lakes

Introduction

The Southern Great Lakes region includes central Minnesota, the southern half of Wisconsin, Michigan, Indiana (excluding the very western portion), the northern half of Ohio, and a narrow band along Lake Erie which extends the region into a small area of Pennsylvania and eastern New York. The vegetation of the region is characterized by temperate deciduous forests. Maple–Basswood Forest is most common in Minnesota and Wisconsin. Beech–Maple and Oak–Hickory Forest are most common in Michigan, Indiana and Ohio. Oak Barrens is a major vegetation type in Minnesota and Wisconsin which marks the transition between the forests in the east and the prairies to the west. A small but important number of prairie communities occur in the region. The prairies are generally mesic prairies, however, some occur on both very dry and wet areas.

Wetland systems include floodplain forests, shrub swamps and wet meadows. Bogs occur but are not as prevalent as they are in the Northern Great Lakes Region.

Unique communities in the region include beech and dune communities associated with the Great Lakes. The beaches of the Great Lakes support a number of species which are rare on other lakes. The most important dune species along the Great Lakes is American beach grass (*Ammophila breviligulata*).

The primary sources used to develop descriptions and species lists are: Barbour and Billings 1988; Braun 1950; Curtis 1959.

Dominant Ecological Communities
Upland Systems
- Maple–Basswood Forest
- Oak Hickory Forest
- Beech–Maple Forest
- Oak Barrens
- Mesic Prairie

Wetland Systems
- Great Lakes Floodplain Forest
- Shrub Swamp
- Wet Meadow

UPLAND SYSTEMS

Maple–Basswood Forest

Maple–Basswood Forest extends from central Minnesota, which contains "Big Woods", the largest continuous area of Maple–Basswood Forest known, south into Wisconsin. The characteristic species are sugar maple, basswood, and beech. This forest occurs on fine textured and well drained loamy soils, also referred to as gray-brown forest soils. Maple–Basswood Forest is self-perpetuating in the absence of catastrophic disturbance and climate change. Natural stands of Maple–Basswood Forest are becoming rare because the soils on which the forest grows are suitable for cultivation and much of the area has been converted for crops. Grazing and lumbering has contributed to the loss of many of the ground layer species. This community corresponds to Küchler #99.

Canopy
Characteristic Species
Acer saccharum	sugar maple
Quercus rubra	northern red oak
Tilia americana	American basswood
Ulmus rubra	slippery elm

Associates
Betula papyrifera	paper birch
Carya cordiformis	bitter-nut hickory
Carya ovata	shag-bark hickory
Celtis occidentalis	common hackberry
Fagus grandifolia	American beech
Fraxinus americana	white ash
Fraxinus pennsylvanica	green ash
Fraxinus quadrangulata	blue ash
Gymnocladus dioicus	Kentucky coffeetree
Juglans cinerea	white walnut
Juglans nigra	black walnut
Populus grandidentata	big-toothed aspen
Prunus serotina	black cherry
Quercus alba	northern white oak
Quercus bicolor	swamp white oak
Quercus macrocarpa	burr oak
Quercus velutina	black oak
Ulmus americana	American elm
Ulmus thomasii	rock elm

Woody Understory
Acer negundo	ash-leaf maple
Carpinus caroliniana	American hornbeam
Celastrus scandens	American bittersweet
Cornus alternifolia	alternate-leaf dogwood
Corylus americana	American hazelnut
Dirca palustris	eastern leatherwood
Ostrya virginiana	eastern hop-hornbeam
Parthenocissus vitacea	thicket-creeper
Ribes cynosbati	eastern prickly gooseberry
Vitis vulpina	frost grape

Herbaceous Understory
Actaea pachypoda	white baneberry
Adiantum pedatum	northern maidenhair
Allium tricoccum	ramp
Amphicarpaea bracteata	American hog-peanut
Anemone quinquefolia	nightcaps
Arisaema triphyllum	jack-in-the-pulpit
Athyrium filix-femina	subarctic lady fern
Brachyelytrum erectum	bearded shorthusk
Cardamine concatenata	cut-leaf toothwort

Carex pedunculata	long-stalk sedge
Carex pensylvanica	Pennsylvania sedge
Caulophyllum thalictroides	blue cohosh
Circaea lutetiana	broad-leaf enchanter's-nightshade
Claytonia virginica	Virginia springbeauty
Cryptotaenia canadensis	Canadian honewort
Cystopteris fragilis	brittle bladder fern
Dicentra canadensis	squirrel-corn
Dicentra cucullaria	Dutchman's-breeches
Elymus hystrix	eastern bottle-brush grass
Enemion biternatum	eastern false rue-anemone
Erythronium americanum	American trout-lily
Galium aparine	sticky-willy
Galium concinnum	shining bedstraw
Galium triflorum	fragrant bedstraw
Geranium maculatum	spotted crane's-bill
Geum canadense	white avens
Hepatica nobilis	liverwort
Hydrophyllum virginianum	Shawnee-salad
Laportea canadensis	Canadian wood-nettle
Maianthemum racemosum	feathery false Solomon's-seal
Osmorhiza claytonii	hairy sweet-ciccly
Phryma leptostachya	American lopseed
Podophyllum peltatum	may-apple
Polygonatum pubescens	hairy Solomon's-seal
Prenanthes alba	white rattlesnake-root
Sanguinaria canadensis	bloodroot
Sanicula odorata	clustered black-snakeroot
Smilax ecirrata	upright carrion-flower
Thalictrum dioicum	early meadow-rue
Trillium grandiflorum	large-flower wakerobin
Uvularia grandiflora	large-flower bellwort
Vernonia baldwinii	western ironweed
Viola cucullata	marsh blue violet
Viola pubescens	downy yellow violet

Oak–Hickory Forest

Oak–Hickory Forest covers extensive areas from Texas to Canada. Oak Hickory Forest in the Southern Great Lakes Region is part of the northern division of the broader Oak–Hickory Forest association and occupies large areas across southern Michigan, Indiana, and central Ohio. Similar communities of predominantly oak species also occur in Minnesota and Wisconsin. White, red, and black oak and shagbark hickory are the most consistently occurring characteristic species. The Oak–Hickory Forest occurs on dry to dry-mesic sites. This community corresponds to Küchler #100.

Canopy
Characteristic Species

Carya alba	mockernut hickory
Carya glabra	pignut hickory
Carya ovata	shag-bark hickory

Quercus alba	northern white oak
Quercus macrocarpa	burr oak
Quercus rubra	northern red oak
Quercus shumardii	Shumard's oak
Quercus velutina	black oak

Associates

Acer rubrum	red maple
Acer saccharum	sugar maple
Carya cordiformis	bitter-nut hickory
Carya ovalis	red hickory
Fagus grandifolia	American beech
Fraxinus americana	white ash
Juglans nigra	black walnut
Pinus strobus	eastern white pine
Prunus serotina	black cherry
Quercus coccinea	scarlet oak
Quercus muehlenbergii	chinkapin oak
Tilia americana	American basswood
Tsuga canadensis	eastern hemlock
Ulmus americana	American elm

Woody Understory

Ceanothus americanus	New Jersey-tea
Corylus americana	American hazelnut
Hamamelis virginiana	American witch-hazel
Ostrya virginiana	eastern hop-hornbeam
Sassafras albidum	sassafras
Smilax tamnoides	chinaroot
Vitis aestivalis	summer grape

Herbaceous Understory

Actaea pachypoda	white baneberry
Adiantum pedatum	northern maidenhair
Brachyeletrum erectum	bearded shorthusk
Bromus pubescens	hairy woodland brome
Carex albursina	white bear sedge
Carex rosea	rosy sedge
Corallorrhiza maculata	summer coralroot
Galium triflorum	fragrant bedstraw
Hackelia virginiana	beggar's-lice
Lysimachia quadrifolia	whorled yellow loosestrife
Monotropa uniflora	one-flower Indian-pipe
Sanicula marilandica	Maryland black-snakeroot
Viola pubescens	downy yellow violet

Beech–Maple Forest

Beech–Maple Forest occurs throughout Indiana, Ohio, western Pennsylvania, and extends across the southern half of Michigan's lower peninsula. Beech–Maple occurs on rolling or slightly sloping topography in areas of medium moisture. On wetter sites, Beech–Maple grades into wet beech flats and on drier sites into oak-maple or oak-hickory. There may be conifers associated with Beech–Maple Forest but they are confined to soils and topography unfavorable to many of the hardwoods. This community corresponds to Küchler #102.

Canopy
Characteristic Species
Acer saccharum	sugar maple
Fagus grandifolia	American beech
Liriodendron tulipifera	tuliptree
Quercus rubra	northern red oak

Associates
Acer rubrum	red maple
Aesculus glabra	Ohio buckeye
Carya cordiformis	bitternut hickory
Carya ovata	shagbark hickory
Fraxinus americana	white ash
Juglans nigra	black walnut
Nyssa sylvatica	black tupelo
Prunus serotina	black cherry
Quercus alba	northern white oak
Quercus macocarpa	burr oak
Tilia americana	American basswood
Ulmus americana	American elm
Ulmus rubra	slippery elm

Woody Understory
Asimina triloba	common pawpaw
Cornus alternifolia	alternate-leaved dogwood
Cornus florida	flowering dogwood
Diervilla lonicera	northern bush honeysuckle
Dirca palustris	eastern leatherwood
Evonymus atropurpureus	eastern wahoo
Hamamelis virginiana	American witch-hazel
Lindera benzoin	northern spicebush
Lonicera canadensis	American fly-honeysuckle
Ostrya virginiana	eastern hop-hornbeam
Ribes cynosbati	eastern prickly gooseberry
Sambucus canadensis	American elder
Smilax rotundifolia	horsebrier
Staphlea trifolia	American bladdernut
Viburnum acerifolium	maple-leaf arrow-wood
Vitis spp.	grape

Herbaceous Understory

Allium tricoccum	ramp
Aralia nudicaulis	wild sarsaparilla
Arisaema triphyllum	jack-in-the-pulpit
Asarum canadense	Canadian wild ginger
Cardamine concatenata	cut-leaf toothwort
Carex pensylvanica	Pennsylvania sedge
Carex plantaginea	broad scale sedge
Circaea lutetiana	broad-leaf enchanter's-nightshade
Claytonia virginica	Virginia springbeauty
Dicentra canadensis	squirrel-corn
Dicentra cucullaria	Dutchman's-breeches
Dryopteris carthusiana	spinulose wood fern
Enemion biternatum	eastern false rue-anemone
Epifagus virginiana	beechdrops
Erythronium americanum	American trout-lily
Galium aparine	sticky-willy
Geranium maculatum	spotted crane's-bill
Hepatica nobilis	liverwort
Hydrophyllum virginianum	Shawnee-salad
Maianthemum canadense	false lily-of-the-valley
Maianthemum racemosum	feathery false Solomon's-seal
Osmorhiza claytonii	hairy sweet-cicely
Phlox divaricata	wild blue phlox
Podophyllum peltatum	may-apple
Polygonatum biflorum	King Solomon's-seal
Sanguinaria canadensis	bloodroot
Streptopus amplexifolius	clasping twistedstalk
Trillium grandiflorum	large-flower wakerobin
Viola sororia	hooded blue violet

Oak Barrens

Oak Barrens occurs as a transition between prairie and closed canopy oak forests and is common in central Minnesota and southern Wisconsin. The most common characteristic species is burr oak. Where the canopy is open, prairie species may dominate. Oak Barrens occurs on dry to mesic sites, on sandy soils and on bluffs or outwash terraces. Fires and grazing help maintain the canopy structure of woodlands, but on draughty sites with thin soil and steep slopes, they may persist without fire. This community corresponds to Küchler #81.

Canopy

Characteristic Species

Quercus alba	northern white oak
Quercus ellipsoidalis	northern pin oak
Quercus macrocarpa	burr oak
Quercus rubra	northern red oak
Quercus velutina	black oak

Associates

Acer negundo	ash-leaf maple

Betula papyrifera	paper birch
Carya ovata	shag-bark hickory
Fraxinus americana	white ash
Fraxinus pennsylvanica	green ash
Juglans nigra	black walnut
Juniperus viginiana	eastern red cedar
Populus balsamifera	balsam poplar
Populus grandidentata	big-tooth aspen
Populus tremuloides	quaking aspen
Prunus serotina	black cherry
Tilia americana	American basswood
Ulmus americana	American elm
Ulmus rubra	slippery elm

Woody Understory

Amelanchier spp.	service-berry
Amorpha canescens	leadplant
Ceanothus americanus	New Jersey tea
Cornus racemosa	gray dogwood
Corylus americana	American hazelnut
Parthenocissus vitacea	thicket-creeper
Prunus virginiana	choke cherry
Rhus glabra	smooth sumac
Ribes spp.	gooseberry
Rosa spp.	rose
Rubus spp.	raspberry
Salix humilis	small pussy willow
Toxicodendron radicans	eastern poison ivy
Vitis riparia	river-bank grape
Zanthoxylum americanum	toothachetree

Herbaceous Understory

Amphicarpaea bracteata	American hog-peanut
Andropogon gerardii	big bluestem
Anemone cylindrica	long-head thimbleweed
Antennaria neglecta	field pussytoes
Apocynum androsaemifolium	spreading dogbane
Aquilegia canadensis	red columbine
Arabis lyrata	lyre-leaf rockcress
Aralia nudicaulis	wild sarsaparilla
Artemisia campestris	Pacific wormwood
Asclepias syriaca	common milkweed
Aster cordifolius	common blue wood aster
Aster linariifolius	flax-leaf white-top aster
Carex pensylvanica	Pennsylvania sedge
Comandra umbellata	bastard-toadflax
Coreopsis palmata	stiff tickseed
Dalea purpurea	violet prairie-clover
Dalea villosus	silky prairie-clover
Desmodium glutinosum	pointed-leaf tick-trefoil

Dichanthelium leibergii	Leiberg's rosette grass
Euphorbia corollata	flowering spurge
Fragaria virginiana	Virginia strawberry
Galium boreale	northern bedstraw
Galium concinnum	shining bedstraw
Geranium maculatum	spotted crane's-bill
Helianthemum canadense	long-branch frostweed
Helianthus occidentalis	few-leaf sunflower
Helianthus pauciflorus	stiff sunflower
Helianthus strumosus	pale-leaf woodland sunflower
Heliopsis helianthoides	smooth oxeye
Heuchera richardsonii	Richardson's alumroot
Hudsonia tomentosa	sand golden-heather
Koeleria macrantha	prairie Koeler's grass
Krigia biflora	two-flowered dwarf-dandelion
Lathyrus venosus	veiny vetchling
Lespedeza capitata	round-head bush-clover
Liatris aspera	tall gayfeather
Lithospermum canescens	hoary puccoon
Lupinus perennis	sundial lupine
Maianthemum racemosum	feathery false Solomon's-seal
Monarda fistulosa	Oswego-tea
Oenothera biennis	king's-cureall
Phlox pilosa	downy phlox
Physalis virginiana	Virginia ground-cherry
Polygonatum biflorum	King Solomon's-seal
Polygonella articulata	coastal jointweed
Potentilla arguta	tall cinquefoil
Prenanthes alba	white rattlesnake-root
Pteridium aquilinum	northern bracken fern
Rudbeckia hirta	black-eyed-Susan
Schizachyrium scoparium	little false bluestem
Smilax herbacea	smooth carrion-flower
Solidago nemoralis	gray goldenrod
Sorghastrum nutans	yellow Indian grass
Sporobolus heterolepis	prairie dropseed
Stipa spartea	porcupine grass
Tephrosia virginiana	goat's-rue
Tradescantia ohiensis	bluejacket
Viola cucullata	marsh blue violet
Viola pedata	bird-foot violet

Mesic Prairie

Mesic Prairie is a grassland community characterized by a high species diversity on deep, fertile and well drained soils. Dominant grasses in the Mesic Prairie are big bluestem, little false bluestem, wand panic grass (switchgrass),yellow Indian grass and prairie drop-seed. Forbs are also abundant but usually subdominant to grasses. Mesic Prairie is a fire dependent community that succeeds to forest or woodland without periodic fires. This community corresponds to Küchler #74.

Characteristic Species

Andropogon gerardii	big bluestem
Dodecatheon meadia	eastern shootingstar
Galium tinctorium	stiff marsh bedstraw
Helianthus grosseserratus	saw-tooth sunflower
Liatris punctata	dotted gayfeather
Lithospermum canescens	hoary puccoon
Oxalis violacea	violet wood-sorrel
Panicum virgatum	wand panic grass
Phlox pilosa	downy phlox
Ratibida pinnata	gray-head Mexican-hat
Rudbeckia hirta	black-eyed-Susan
Schizachyrium scoparium	little false bluestem
Solidago rigida	hard-leaf goldenrod
Sorghastrum nutans	yellow Indian grass
Sporobolus heterolepis	prairie drop-seed
Stipa spartea	porcupine grass
Tradescantia ohiensis	bluejacket

Associates

Ambrosia artemisiifolia	annual ragweed
Amorpha canescens	leadplant
Anemone cylindrica	long-head thimbleweed
Antennaria neglecta	field pussytoes
Apocynum androsaemifolium	spreading dogbane
Artemisia ludoviciana	white sagebrush
Asclepias ovalifolia	oval-leaf milkweed
Asclepias speciosa	showy milkweed
Asclepias syriaca	common milkweed
Aster ericoides	white heath aster
Aster laevis	smooth blue aster
Aster oolentangiensis	sky blue aster
Astragalus crassicarpus	ground-plum
Baptisia alba	white wild indigo
Baptisia bracteata	long-bract wild indigo
Bouteloua curtipendula	side-oats grama
Calystegia sepium	hedge false bindweed
Ceanothus americanus	New Jersey-tea
Cirsium discolor	field thistle
Cirsium flodmanii	Flodman's thistle
Comandra umbellata	bastard-toadflax
Coreopsis palmata	stiff tickseed
Dalea candida	white prairie-clover
Dalea purpurea	violet prairie-clover
Delphinium carolinianum	Carolina larkspur
Desmodium canadense	showy tick-trefoil
Desmodium illinoense	Illinois tick-trefoil
Dichanthelium leibergii	Leiberg's rosette grass
Dichanthelium oligosanthes	Hellen's rosette grass

Echinacea angustifolia	blacksamson
Elymus canadensis	nodding wild rye
Erigeron strigosus	prairie fleabane
Eryngium yuccifolium	button eryngo
Euphorbia corollata	flowering spurge
Fragaria virginiana	Virginia strawberry
Galium boreale	northern bedstraw
Helianthus occidentalis	few-leaf sunflower
Helianthus pauciflorus	stiff sunflower
Heuchera richardsonii	Richardson's alumroot
Koeleria macrantha	prairie Koeler's grass
Lactuca canadensis	Florida blue lettuce
Lathyrus venosus	veiny vetchling
Lespedeza capitata	round-head bush-clover
Liatris aspera	tall gayfeather
Liatris scariosa	devil's-bite
Lilium philadelphicum	wood lily
Monarda fistulosa	Oswego-tea
Pedicularis canadensis	Canadian lousewort
Pediomelum argophyllum	silver-leaf Indian-breadroot
Pediomelum esculentum	large Indian-breadroot
Physalis virginiana	Virginia ground-cherry
Potentilla arguta	tall cinquefoil
Prenanthes racemosa	purple rattlesnake-root
Ratibida columnifera	red-spike Mexican-hat
Rhus glabra	smooth sumac
Rosa arkansana	prairie rose
Silphium integrifolium	entire-leaf rosinweed
Silphium laciniatum	compassplant
Solidago canadensis	Canadian goldenrod
Solidago missouriensis	Missouri goldenrod
Solidago speciosa	showy goldenrod
Stipa spartea	porcupine grass
Viola pedatifida	crow-foot violet
Zigadenus elegans	mountain deathcamas
Zizia aptera	heart-leaf alexanders

WETLAND SYSTEMS

Great Lakes Floodplain Forest

Great Lakes Floodplain Forest occurs on seasonally inundated soils along the Mississippi River and other major rivers and streams. Silver maple, cottonwood, black willow, and American elm are among the most common characteristic species. Species in this forest type are tolerant of periodic inundation and are adapted to soil disturbances caused by scouring during flooding and by deposition of alluvium when river currents are slow. This community corresponds, in part, to Küchler #98. This forest is also similar to Küchler's elm-ash forest (type #101) that covers low areas of ancient glacial lakebeds near Lakes Erie, Huron, and Michigan.

Canopy
Characteristic Species

Acer rubrum	red maple
Acer saccharinum	silver maple
Aesculus glabra	Ohio buckeye
Fraxinus pennsylvanica	green ash
Platanus occidentalis	American sycamore
Populus deltoides	eastern cottonwood
Salix nigra	black willow
Ulmus americana	American elm

Associates

Acer nigrum	black maple
Acer saccharum	sugar maple
Betula nigra	river birch
Carya cordiformis	bitter-nut hickory
Celtis occidentalis	common hackberry
Fagus grandifolia	American beech
Fraxinus americana	white ash
Fraxinus nigra	black ash
Fraxinus quadrangulata	blue ash
Gleditsia triacanthos	honey-locust
Gymnocladus dioica	Kentucky coffeetree
Juglans cinerea	white walnut
Juglans nigra	black walnut
Populus deltoides	eastern cottonwood
Populus tremuloides	quaking aspen
Prunus serotina	black cherry
Quercus alba	northern white oak
Quercus bicolor	swamp white oak
Quercus macrocarpa	burr oak
Quercus rubra	northern red oak
Tilia americana	American basswood
Ulmus rubra	slippery elm

Woody Understory

Aesculus glabra	Ohio buckeye
Asimina triloba	common pawpaw
Carpinus caroliniana	American hornbeam
Celastrus scandens	American bittersweet
Cephalanthus occidentalis	common buttonbush
Cercis canadensis	redbud
Clematis virginiana	devil's-darning-needles
Cornus alternifolia	alternate-leaf dogwood
Cornus amomum	silky dogwood
Crataegus spp.	hawthorn
Evonymus atropurpureus	eastern wahoo
Lindera benzoin	northern spicebush
Menispermum canadensis	Canadian moonseed

Morus rubra	red mulberry
Parthenocissus quinquefolia	Virginia-creeper
Parthenocissus vitacea	thicket-creeper
Salix amygdaloides	peach-leaf willow
Salix interior	sandbar willow
Sambucus canadensis	American elder
Smilax tamnoides	chinaroot
Symphoricarpos orbiculatus	coral-berry
Toxicodendron radicans	eastern poison-ivy
Vitis riparia	river-bank grape

Herbaceous Understory

Amphicarpaea bracteata	American hog-peanut
Apios americana	groundnut
Arisaema dracontium	greendragon
Aster lateriflorus	farewell-summer
Boehmeria cylindrica	small-spike false nettle
Camassia scilloides	Atlantic camas
Cardamine concatenata	cut-leaf toothwort
Carex typhina	cat-tail sedge
Chaerophyllum procumbens	spreading chevril
Cinna arundinacea	sweet wood-reed
Cryptotaenia canadensis	Canadian honewort
Diarrhena americana	American beakgrain
Echinocystis lobata	wild cucumber
Elymus virginicus	Virginia wild rye
Galium aparine	sticky-willy
Geum canadense	white avens
Impatiens capensis	spotted touch-me-not
Laportea canadensis	Canadian wood-nettle
Leersia virginica	white grass
Lycopus uniflorus	northern water-horehound
Lysimachia ciliata	fringed yellow-loosestrife
Mertensia virginica	Virginia bluebells
Muhlenbergia frondosa	wire-stem muhly
Onoclea sensibilis	sensitive fern
Osmorhiza claytoni	hairy sweet-cicely
Phlox divaricata	wild blue phlox
Pilea pumila	Canadian clearweed
Rudbeckia laciniata	green-head coneflower
Sanicula odorata	clustered black-snakeroot
Scutellaria lateriflora	mad dog skullcap
Sicyos angulatus	one-seed burr-cucumber
Solidago gigantea	late goldenrod
Stachys tenuifolia	smooth hedge-nettle
Teucrium canadense	American germander
Trillium nivale	dwarf white wakerobin
Trillium recurvatum	bloody-butcher
Trillium sessile	toadshade
Urtica dioica	stinging nettle

Shrub Swamp

Shrub Swamp occurs around lakes and ponds in the transition zone between sedge meadow and wet hardwood forests. Shrub Swamp is considered a successional community but may be quite stable when regularly fluctuating water levels retard forest development. The most important single species is the redosier, but willows collectively are of greater significance. Shrubs other than willows such as red raspberry, elderberry, and nanny-berry are common as well as numerous herbaceous species and woody vines. Shrub Swamp depends on saturated soil and fires to maintain community structure and composition.

Characteristic Woody Species
Cornus serica	redosier
Salix bebbiana	long-beak willow
Salix discolor	tall pussy willow
Salix interior	sandbar willow
Salix lucida	shining willow
Salix petiolaris	meadow willow
Sambucus canadensis	American elder

Associates
Acer rubrum	red maple
Alnus incana	speckled alder
Alnus serrulata	brookside alder
Aronia melanocarpa	black chokeberry
Cephalanthus occidentalis	common buttonbush
Clematis virginiana	devil's-darning-needles
Cornus amomum	silky dogwood
Cornus racemosa	gray dogwood
Ilex verticillata	common winterberry
Parthenocissus vitacea	thicket-creeper
Ribes americanum	wild black currant
Rosa palustris	swamp rose
Rubus idaeus	common red raspberry
Salix amygaloides	peach-leaf willow
Salix eriocephala	Missouri willow
Salix nigra	black willow
Salix sericea	silky willow
Sambucus canadensis	American elder
Spiraea alba	white meadowsweet
Toxicodendron radicans	eastern poison-ivy
Toxicodendron vernix	poison-sumac
Ulmus americana	American elm
Vaccinium corymbosum	highbush blueberry
Viburnum dentatum	southern arrow-wood
Viburnum lentago	nanny-berry

Herbaceous Understory
Asclepias incarnata	swamp milkweed
Aster lanceolatus	white panicle aster
Aster puniceus	purple-stem aster

Calamagrostis canadensis	bluejoint
Carex lacustris	lakebank sedge
Carex prairea	prairie sedge
Cicuta maculata	spotted water-hemlock
Cirsium muticum	swamp thistle
Echinocystis lobata	wild cucumber
Equisetum sylvaticum	woodland horsetail
Eupatorium maculatum	spotted joe-pye-weed
Eupatorium perfoliatum	common boneset
Glyceria striata	fowl manna grass
Impatiens capensis	spotted touch-me-not
Lycopus americanus	cut-leaf water-horehound
Lycopus uniflorus	northern water-horehound
Onoclea sensibilis	sensitive fern
Poa palustris	fowl blue grass
Rumex orbiculatus	greater water dock
Solidago canadensis	Canadian goldenrod
Solidago gigantea	late goldenrod
Stachys palustris	woundwort
Thalictrum dasycarpum	purple meadow-rue
Thelypteris palustris	eastern marsh fern
Typha latifolia	broad-leaf cat-tail
Viola cucullata	marsh blue violet

Wet Meadow

Wet Meadow occurs along streams, adjacent to lakes, and in depressions and channels in glacial outwash. Sedges and rushes are dominant, but, many other species are important in these meadows. Soils are wet mineral, muck, or shallow peat. Water in the meadows is abundant in the spring after heavy rains but, the water table is below the soil surface for much of the growing season. Wet meadows grade into wet prairies as moisture decreases. They grade into cattail and reed marshes in wetter conditions.

Characteristic Species

Asclepias incarnata	swamp milkweed
Calamagrostis canadensis	bluejoint
Carex aquatilis	leafy tussock sedge
Carex lacustris	lakebank sedge
Carex stricta	uptight sedge
Eleocharis acicularis	needle spike-rush
Eleocharis erythropoda	bald spike-rush
Eleocharis obtusa	blunt spike-rush
Eleocharis smallii	Small's spike-rush
Eupatorium maculatum	spotted joe-pye-weed
Juncus acuminatus	knotty-leaf rush
Juncus dudleyi	Dudley's rush
Juncus effusus	lamp rush
Juncus tenuis	poverty rush
Juncus torreyi	Torrey's rush
Peltandra virginica	green arrow-arum

Spartina pectinata	freshwater cord grass
Thalictrum dasycarpum	purple meadow-rue

Associates

Anemone canadensis	round-leaf thimbleweed
Angelica atropurpurea	purple-stem angelica
Aster lanceolatus	white panicle aster
Aster puniceus	purple-stem aster
Carex bebbii	Bebb's sedge
Carex cosmosa	bearded sedge
Carex crinita	fringed sedge
Carex frankii	Frank's sedge
Carex granularis	limestone-meadow sedge
Carex grayi	Gray's sedge
Carex haydenii	cloud sedge
Carex hystericina	porcupine sedge
Carex lanuginosa	woolly sedge
Carex lupulina	hop sedge
Carex rostrata	swollen beaked sedge
Carex scoparia	pointed broom sedge
Carex squarrosa	squarrose sedge
Carex tribuloides	blunt broom sedge
Carex vulpinoidea	common fox sedge
Chelone glabra	white turtlehead
Cicuta maculata	spotted water-hemlock
Cladium mariscoides	smooth saw-grass
Cyperus spp.	flat sedge
Dulichium arundinaceum	three-way sedge
Equisetum arvense	field horsetail
Eupatorium perfoliatum	common boneset
Galium obtusum	blunt-leaf bedstraw
Glyceria striata	fowl manna grass
Helianthus grosseserratus	saw-tooth sunflower
Impatiens capensis	spotted touch-me-not
Iris virginica	Virginia blueflag
Lathyrus palustris	marsh vetchling
Leersia oryzoides	rice cut grass
Lycopus americanus	cut-leaf water-horehound
Lycopus uniflorus	northern water-horehound
Mentha arvensis	American wild mint
Poa palustris	fowl blue grass
Sagittaria spp.	arrowhead
Salix bebbiana	long-beak willow
Salix discolor	tall pussy willow
Scirpus americanus	chairmaker's bulrush
Scirpus atrovirens	dark-green bulrush
Scirpus cyperinus	cottongrass bulrush
Scirpus fluviatilis	river bulrush
Scirpus lineatus	drooping bulrush
Solidago canadensis	Canadian goldenrod

Solidago gigantea	late goldenrod
Sparganium spp.	burr-reed
Stachys palustris	woundwort
Thelypteris palustris	eastern marsh fern
Typha angustifolia	narrow-leaf cat-tail
Typha latifolia	broad-leaf cat-tail
Viola cucullata	marsh blue violet

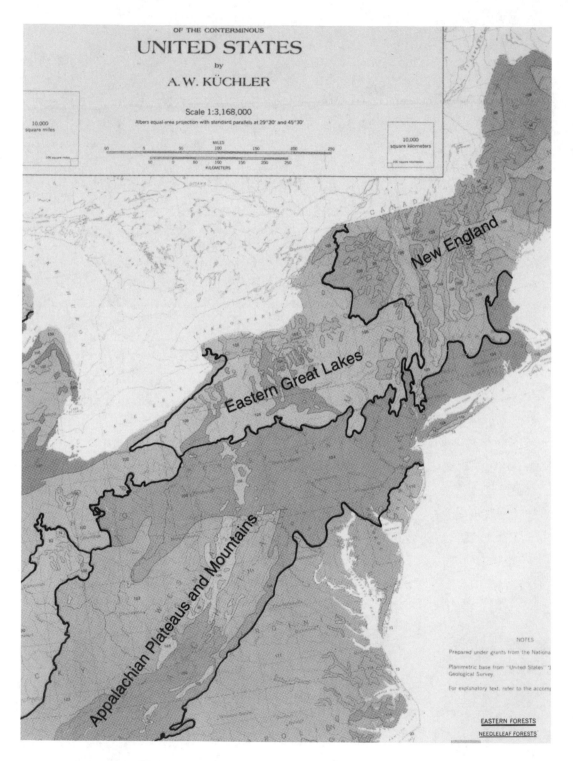

Eastern Great Lakes

Eastern Great Lakes

Introduction

The Eastern Great Lakes region encompasses northern Pennsylvania and most of New York state, except the Adirondack Mountain region and the coastal lowlands. The dominant forest communities in the Eastern Great Lakes are variants of northern hardwoods.

The primary sources used to develop descriptions and species lists are: Barbour and Billings 1988; Eyre 1980; Reschke 1990; Smith (no date).

Dominant Ecological Communities

Upland Systems
Northern Hardwoods–Conifer Forest
Northern Oak Forest
Mesophytic Forest
Coniferous Woodland
Deciduous Woodland

Wetland Systems
Floodplain Forest
Deciduous Swamp Forest
Coniferous Swamp Forest
Shrub Bog/Fen
Shrub Swamp
Herbaceous Peatland Fen/Wet Meadow
Mineral Soil Marsh

UPLAND SYSTEMS

Northern Hardwoods–Conifer Forest

Northern Hardwoods–Conifer Forest occurs throughout the eastern Great Lakes region as the major forest type. This broadly defined community has many regional and edaphic variants and plant associations within it. This community corresponds to Küchler #106.

Canopy
Characteristic Species

Acer rubrum	red maple
Acer saccharum	sugar maple
Betula papyrifera	paper birch
Fagus grandifolia	American beech
Picea rubens	red spruce
Pinus resinosa	red pine
Pinus strobus	eastern white pine
Populus tremuloides	quaking aspen
Tsuga canadensis	eastern hemlock

Associates

Abies balsamea	balsam fir
Betula alleghaniensis	yellow birch
Betula lenta	sweet birch
Prunus serotina	black cherry
Quercus rubra	northern red oak
Tilia americana	American basswood

Woody Understory

Acer pensylvanicum	striped maple
Acer spicatum	mountain maple
Amelanchier canadensis	Canadian service-berry
Epigaea repens	trailing-arbutus
Gaultheria procumbens	eastern teaberry
Kalmia angustifolia	sheep-laurel
Lonicera canadensis	American fly-honeysuckle
Rhododendron maximum	great-laurel
Taxus canadensis	American yew
Vaccinium angustifolium	late lowbush blueberry
Vaccinium myrtilloides	velvet-leaf blueberry
Viburnum acerifolium	maple-leaf arrow-wood
Viburnum lantanoides	hobblebush
Viburnum nudum	possumhaw

Herbaceous Understory

Aralia nudicaulis	wild sarsaparilla
Carex pensylvanica	Pennsylvania sedge
Clintonia borealis	yellow bluebead-lily
Coptis trifolia	three-leaf goldthread
Cornus canadensis	Canadian bunchberry
Dicranum polysetum	moss
Dryopteris campyloptera	mountain wood fern
Dryopteris intermedia	evergreen wood fern
Epifagus virginiana	beechdrops
Huperzia lucidula	shining club-moss
Leucobryum glaucum	white moss
Maianthemum canadense	false lily-of-the-valley
Medeola virginiana	Indian cucumber-root
Melampyrum lineare	American cow-wheat
Mitchella repens	partridge-berry
Oryzopsis asperifolia	white-grain mountain-rice grass
Oxalis montana	sleeping-beauty
Pleurozium schreberi	feather moss
Polystichum acrostichoides	Christmas fern
Pteridium aquilinum	northern bracken fern
Streptopus roseus	rosy twistedstalk
Tiarella cordifolia	heart-leaf foamflower
Trientalis borealis	American starflower
Trillium erectum	stinking-Benjamin

Trillium undulatum	painted wakerobin
Uvularia sessilifolia	sissile-leaf bellwort
Viola rotundifolia	round-leaf yellow violet

Northern Oak Forest

Northern Oak Forest occurs throughout the Eastern Great Lakes region on a diversity of mostly well-drained sites. White oak, red oak, and black oak are the most common canopy species. Several species of hickory consistently occur in the Northern Oak Forest but seldom make up more than ten percent of the canopy cover. This community corresponds to Küchler #104.

Canopy
Characteristic Species

Quercus alba	northern white oak
Quercus prinus	chestnut oak
Quercus rubra	northern red oak
Quercus velutina	black oak

Associates

Acer rubrum	red maple
Betula lenta	sweet birch
Carya glabra	pignut hickory
Carya ovalis	red hickory
Carya ovata	shag-bark hickory
Fagus grandifolia	American beech
Fraxinus americana	white ash
Nyssa sylvatica	black tupelo
Pinus rigida	pitch pine
Pinus strobus	eastern white pine
Pinus virginiana	Virginia pine
Populus grandidentata	big-tooth aspen
Prunus serotina	black cherry
Quercus coccinea	scarlet oak
Quercus stellata	post oak
Tsuga canadensis	eastern hemlock

Woody Understory

Amelanchier arborea	downy service-berry
Cornus florida	flowering dogwood
Cornus foemina	gray dogwood
Corylus cornuta	beaked hazelnut
Galussacia baccata	black huckleberry
Gaultheria procumbens	eastern teaberry
Hamamelis virginiana	American witch-hazel
Kalmia latifolia	mountain-laurel
Ostrya virginiana	eastern hop-hornbeam
Prunus pensylvanica	fire cherry
Prunus virginiana	choke cherry
Quercus ilicifolia	bear oak
Rhododendron periclymenoides	pink azalea
Rubus idaeus	common red raspberry

Sassafras albidum	sassafras
Vaccinium angustifolium	late lowbush blueberry
Vaccinium pallidum	early lowbush blueberry
Vaccinium stamineum	deerberry
Viburnum acerifolium	maple-leaf arrow-wood

Herbaceous Understory

Aralia nudicaulis	wild sarsaparilla
Carex pensylvanica	Pennsylvania sedge
Chimaphila maculata	striped prince's-pine
Cimicifuga racemosa	black bugbane
Clintonia umbellulata	white bluebead-lily
Desmodium glutinosum	pointed-leaf tick-trefoil
Desmodium paniculatum	panicled-leaf tick-trefoil
Hepatica nobilis	liverwort
Hieracium venosum	rattlesnake-weed
Leucobryum glaucum	white moss
Maianthemum racemosum	feathery false Solomon's-seal
Prenanthes alba	white rattlesnake-root
Pteridium aquilinum	northern bracken fern
Solidago palmata	white goldenrod
Viola triloba	early blue violet
Waldsteinia fragarioides	Appalachain barren-strawberry

Mesophytic Forest

Mesophytic Forest occurs on moist, well-drained soils. In the Eastern Great Lakes region this forest type is most commonly located at low elevations and on fertile, loamy soils. This is a diverse community with an abundance of spring wildflowers. This community corresponds to Küchler #102.

Canopy
Characteristic species

Acer rubrum	red maple
Acer saccharinum	silver maple
Betula lenta	sweet birch
Fagus grandifolia	American beech
Fraxinus americana	white ash

Associates

Carya cordiformis	bitter-nut hickory
Carya ovata	shag-bark hickory
Liriodendron tulipifera	tuliptree
Magnolia acuminanta	cucumber magnolia
Pinus strobus	eastern white pine
Prunus serotina	black cherry
Quercus alba	northern white oak
Quercus imbricaria	shingle oak
Quercus rubra	northern red oak
Tilia americana	American basswood
Tsuga canadensis	eastern hemlock
Ulmus americana	American elm
Ulmus rubra	slippery elm

Woody Understory

Acer pensylvanicum	striped maple
Amelanchier laevis	Allegheny service-berry
Asimina triloba	pawpaw
Carpinus caroliniana	American hornbeam
Cornus alternifolia	alternate-leaf dogwood
Cornus rugosa	round-leaf dogwood
Dievilla lonicera	northern bush-honeysuckle
Hamamelis virginiana	witch-hazel
Lonicera canadensis	American fly-honeysuckle
Ostrya virginiana	eastern hop-hornbeam
Rhododendron periclymenoides	pink azalea
Staphylea trifolia	American bladdernut
Vaccinium pallidum	early lowbush blueberry
Viburnum acerifolium	maple-leaf arrow-wood
Viburnum lantanoides	hobblebush

Herbaceous Understory

Actaea pachypoda	white baneberry
Allium tricoccum	ramp
Arisaema triphyllum	jack-in-the-pulpit
Asarum canadense	long-tail wildginger
Aster macrophyllus	large-leaf aster
Cardamine concantenata	cut-leaf toothwort
Cardamine diphylla	crinkleroot
Caulophyllum thalictroides	blue cohosh
Cimicifuga racemosa	black bugbane
Claytonia virginica	Virginia springbeauty
Clintonia umbellulata	white bluebead-lily
Collinsonia canadensis	richweed
Dicentra candensis	squirrel-corn
Dicentra cucullaria	Dutchman's-breeches
Disporum lanuginosum	yellow fairybells
Erythronium americanum	American trout-lily
Hepatica nobilis	liverwort
Maianthemum racemosum	feathery false Solomon's-seal
Mertensia virginica	Virginia bluebells
Mitchella repens	partridge-berry
Osmunda claytoniana	interrupted fern
Podophyllum peltatum	may-apple
Polystichum acrostichoides	Christmas fern
Prenanthes trifoliolata	gall-of-the-earth
Sanguinaria canadensis	bloodroot
Sanicula marilandica	Maryland black-snakeroot
Solidago caesia	wreath goldenrod
Thalictrum dioicum	early meadow-rue
Tiarella cordifolia	heart-leaf foamflower
Trillium erectum	stinking-Benjamin
Viola rotundifolia	round-leaf yellow violet

Coniferous Woodland

Coniferous Woodland occurs on flat summits and rocky ridges where the soil is well-drained and often rocky or sandy. The species composition of the woodland varies according to local conditions. For example, where the area is warm and dry, deciduous species may be associates but, where it is cool, balsam fir will be a likely addition to the community.

Canopy

Characteristic Species

Picea rubens	red spruce
Pinus banksiana	jack pine
Pinus rigida	pitch pine
Pinus strobus	eastern white pine
Quercus prinoides	dwarf chinkapin oak

Associates

Abies balsamea	balsam fir
Carya ovata	shag-bark hickory
Juniperus communis	common juniper
Juniperus virginiana	eastern red cedar
Populus grandidentata	big-tooth aspen
Quercus prinus	chestnut oak
Sorbus americana	American mountain-ash

Woody Understory

Aronia melanocarpa	black chokeberry
Betula populifolia	gray birch
Comptonia peregrina	sweet-fern
Gaylussacia baccata	black huckleberry
Kalmia angustifolia	sheep-laurel
Ostrya virginiana	eastern hop-hornbeam
Quercus ilicifolia	bear oak
Vaccinium angustifolium	late lowbush blueberry
Vaccinium myrtilloides	velvet-leaf blueberry
Vaccinium pallidum	early lowbush blueberry
Viburnum nudum	possumhaw

Herbaceous Understory

Andropogon gerardii	big bluestem
Antennaria plantaginifolia	woman's-tobacco
Aralia nudicaulis	wild sarsaparilla
Campanula rotundifolia	bluebell-of-Scotland
Carex eburnea	bristle-leaf sedge
Carex pensylvanica	Pennsylvania sedge
Cornus canadensis	Canadian bunchberry
Cypripedium acaule	pink lady's-slipper
Danthonia spicata	poverty wild oat grass
Deschampsia flexuosa	wavy hair grass
Fragaria virginiana	Virginia strawberry
Gaultheria procumbens	eastern teaberry
Lechea mucronata	hairy pinweed

Lespedeza capitata	round-head bush-clover
Lespedeza hirta	hairy bush-clover
Lespedeza procumbens	trailing bush-clover
Lespedeza stuevei	tall bush-clover
Lupinus perennis	sundial lupine
Maianthemum canadensis	false lily-of-the-valley
Melampyrum lineare	American cow-wheat
Oryzopsis pungens	short-awn mountain-rice grass
Polygala nuttallii	Nuttall's milkwort
Pteridium aquilinum	northern bracken fern
Schizachyrium scoparium	little false bluestem
Sibbaldiopsis tridentata	shrubby-fivefingers
Solidago spathulata	coastal-dune goldenrod
Sorghastrum nutans	yellow Indian grass
Tephrosia virginiana	goat's-rue

Deciduous Woodland

Deciduous Woodland occurs on well-drained, shallow soils where the bedrock is close to the surface and there are numerous rock outcrops. This community type may also cover slopes and sandy soils. There are many variants of community composition depending on soil fertility and moisture capacity. Tree species may occur in continuous stands with an open canopy or, as clusters of trees within savannas.

Canopy
Characteristic Species

Acer saccharum	sugar maple
Carya ovata	shag-bark hickory
Fraxinus americana	white ash
Juniperus virginiana	eastern red cedar
Picea glauca	white spruce
Pinus strobus	eastern white pine
Quercus alba	northern white oak
Quercus macrocarpa	burr oak
Quercus prinus	chestnut oak
Quercus rubra	northern red oak
Tilia americana	American basswood

Associates

Abies balsamea	balsam fir
Betula papyrifera	paper birch
Carya glabra	pignut hickory
Prunus pensylvanica	fire cherry
Quercus muhlenbergii	chinkapin oak
Quercus velutina	black oak
Thuja occidentalis	eastern arborvitae
Ulmus americana	American elm
Ulmus thomasii	rock elm

Woody Understory

Acer pensylvanicum	striped maple
Acer spicatum	mountain maple
Cornus foemina	gray dogwood
Cornus rugosa	round-leaf dogwood
Juniperus communis	common juniper
Lonicera dioica	limber honeysuckle
Ostrya virginiana	eastern hop-hornbeam
Prunus pumila	Great Lakes sand cherry
Quercus prinoides	dwarf chinkapin oak
Rhamnus alnifolia	alder-leaf buckthorn
Rhus aromatica	fragrant sumac
Rhus glabra	smooth sumac
Ribes cynosbati	eastern prickly gooseberry
Rosa blanda	smooth rose
Rubus flagellaris	whiplash dewberry
Rubus idaeus	common red raspberry
Rubus occidentalis	black raspberry
Shepherdia canadensis	russet buffalo-berry
Staphylea trifolia	American bladdernut
Symphoricarpos albus	common snowberry
Toxicodendron radicans	eastern poison-ivy
Vaccinium angustifolium	late lowbush blueberry
Viburnum rafinesquianum	downy arrow-wood
Zanthoxylum americanum	toothachetree

Herbaceous Understory

Actaea pachypoda	white baneberry
Adiantum pedatum	northern maidenhair
Andropogon gerardii	big bluestem
Anemone cylindracea	long-head thimbleweed
Aquilegia canadensis	red columbine
Asarum canadense	Canadian wild ginger
Asclepias tuberosa	butterfly milkweed
Asplenium rhizophyllum	walking fern
Asplenium trichomanes	maidenhair spleenwort
Aster ciliolatus	Lindley's aster
Aster divaricatus	white wood aster
Aster ericoides	white heath aster
Aster macrophyllus	large-leaf aster
Athyrium filix-femina	subarctic lady fern
Botrychium virginianum	rattlesnake fern
Campanula rotundifolia	bluebell-of-Scotland
Carex aurea	golden-fruit sedge
Carex eburnea	bristle-leaf sedge
Carex pensylvanica	Pennsylvania sedge
Carex platyphylla	plantain-leaf sedge
Caulophyllum thalictroides	blue cohosh
Comandra umbellata	bastard-toadflax

Cystoperis bulbifera	bulblet bladder fern
Cystoperis fragilis	brittle bladder fern
Danthonia compressa	flattened wild oat grass
Danthonia spicata	poverty wild oat grass
Deparia acrostichoides	silvery false spleenwort
Desmodium glabellum	Dillenius' tick-trefoil
Desmodium paniculatum	panicled-leaf tick-trefoil
Dryopteris marginalis	marginal wood fern
Eleocharis elliptica	elliptic spike-rush
Elmus hystrix	eastern bottle-brush grass
Fragaria virginiana	Virginia strawberry
Geranium robertianum	herbrobert
Houstonia longifolia	long-leaf summer bluet
Hypericum gentianoides	orange-grass
Maianthemum canadense	false lily-of-the-valley
Maianthemum racemosum	feathery false Solomon's-seal
Monarda fistulosa	Oswego-tea
Panax quinquefloius	American ginseng
Panicum flexile	wiry panic grass
Panicum philadelphicum	Philadelphia panic grass
Penstemon hirsutus	hairy beardtongue
Phlox divaricata	wild blue phlox
Polygonatum pubescens	hairy Solomon's seal
Polypodium virginianum	rock polypody
Polystichum acrostichoides	Christmas fern
Pteridium aquilinum	northern bracken fern
Rudbeckia hirta	black-eyed-Susan
Sanguinaria canadensis	bloodroot
Sanicula marilandica	Maryland black-snakeroot
Schizachyrium scoparium	little false bluestem
Senecio pauperculus	balsam ragwort
Solidago caesia	wreath goldenrod
Solidago flexicaulis	zigzag goldenrod
Solidago hispida	hairy goldenrod
Solidago juncea	early goldenrod
Solidago ptarmicoides	prairie goldenrod
Sorghastrum nutans	yellow Indian grass
Thalictrum dioicum	early meadow-rue
Trichostema dichotomum	forked bluecurls
Trillium grandiflorum	large-flower wakerobin
Waldsteinia fragaroides	Appalachian barren-strawberry

WETLAND SYSTEMS

Floodplain Forest

Floodplain Forest occurs on floodplain soils which are deep, fertile, and mesic. This community occurs along rivers throughout the region. Soils are seasonally saturated as a result of overflow from a nearby water body, groundwater, or drainage from adjacent uplands.

Canopy
Characteristic Species
Acer rubrum	red maple
Acer saccharum	sugar maple
Carya ovata	shagbark hickory
Fraxinus americana	white ash
Fraxinus nigra	black ash
Platanus occidentalis	American sycamore
Populus deltoides	eastern cottonwood
Quercus bicolor	swamp white oak
Salix nigra	black willow
Tilia americana	American basswood

Associates
Betula nigra	black birch
Carya cordiformis	bitter-nut hickory
Fraxinus pensylvanica	green ash
Juglans cinerea	butternut
Juglans nigra	black walnut
Quercus macrocarpa	burr oak
Ulmus americana	American elm

Woody Understory
Acer negundo	ash-leaf maple
Alnus serrulata	brookside alder
Cephalanthus occidentalis	common buttonbush
Clematis virginiana	devil's-darning-needles
Cornus amomum	silky dogwood
Lindera benzoin	northern spicebush
Parthenocissus quinquefolia	Virginia-creeper
Physocarpus opulifolius	Atlantic ninebark
Sambucus canadensis	American elder
Toxicodendron radicans	eastern poison-ivy

Herbaceous Understory
Ageratina altissima	white snakeroot
Arisaema dracontium	greendragon
Aster puniceus	purple-stem aster
Boehmeria cylindrica	small-spike false nettle
Impatiens capensis	spotted touch-me-not
Impatiens pallida	pale touch-me-not
Laportea canadensis	Canadian wood-nettle
Lobelia cardinalis	cardinal-flower
Lobelia siphilitica	great blue lobelia
Onoclea sensibilis	sensitive fern
Peltandra virginica	green arrow-arum
Polygonum virginianum	jumpseed
Saururus cernuus	lizard's-tail

Deciduous Swamp Forest

Deciduous Swamp Forest occurs in poorly drained depressions, along lakeshores, and rivers in inorganic (mineral) soils. These areas are usually uniformly wet with minimal seasonal fluctuations in water levels.

Canopy
Characteristic Species
Acer rubrum	red maple
Acer saccharinum	silver maple
Betula lenta	sweet birch
Fraxinus nigra	black ash
Nyssa sylvatica	black tupelo
Pinus strobus	eastern white pine
Quercus bicolor	swamp white oak
Quercus palustris	pin oak
Salix nigra	black willow
Tsuga canadensis	eastern hemlock
Ulmus americana	American elm

Associates
Betula alleghaniensis	yellow birch
Carya cordiformis	bitter-nut hickory
Fraxinus americana	white ash
Fraxinus pennsylvanica	green ash
Juglans cinerea	butternut
Picea mariana	black spruce
Pinus rigida	pitch pine
Quercus alba	northern white oak

Woody Understory
Alnus serrulata	brookside alder
Aronia melanocarpa	black chokeberry
Cephalanthus occidentalis	common buttonbush
Clethra alnifolia	coastal sweet-pepperbush
Cornus amomum	silky dogwood
Cornus sericea	redosier
Gaylussacia baccata	black huckleberry
Ilex verticillata	common winterberry
Lindera benzoin	northern spicebush
Parthenocissus quinquefolia	Virginia-creeper
Rhamnus alnifolia	alder-leaf buckthorn
Rhododendron periclymenoides	pink azalea
Rhododendron viscosum	clammy azalea
Toxicodendron radicans	eastern poison-ivy
Toxicodendron vernix	poison-sumac
Vaccinium angustifolium	late lowbush blueberry
Vaccinium corymbosum	highbush blueberry
Viburnum dentatum	southern arrow-wood

Herbaceous Understory

Carex intumenscens	great bladder sedge
Carex lacustris	lakebank sedge
Cinna arundinacea	sweet wood-reed
Cypripedium parviflorum	lesser yellow lady's-slipper
Dryopteris carthusiana	spinulose wood fern
Dryopteris cristata	crested wood fern
Glyceria striata	fowl manna grass
Impatiens capensis	spotted touch-me-not
Muhlenbergia racemosa	green muhly
Onoclea sensibilis	sensitive fern
Osmunda cinnamomea	cinnamon fern
Osmunda regalis	royal fern
Platanthera grandiflora	greater purple fringed orchid
Ranunculus recurvatus	blisterwort
Saururus cernuus	lizard's tail
Saxifraga pensylvanica	eastern swamp saxifrage
Scirpus cyperinus	cottongrass bulrush
Scutellaria galericulata	hooded skullcap
Symplocarpus foetidus	skunk-cabbage
Thelypteris palustris	eastern marsh fern
Trollius laxus	American globeflower

Coniferous Swamp Forest

Coniferous Swamp Forest occurs on sites with organic (peat) soils in poorly drained depressions. These areas are often spring fed and permanently or semi-permanently saturated. It is often dominated by boreal coniferous trees such as black spruce, balsam fir, and American larch (tamarack) and influenced by acidic water. It may have a nearly-closed to fairly-open canopy with scattered shrubs. The herbaceous layer has a diversity of mosses, sedges, and forbs.

Canopy
Characteristic Species

Abies balsamea	balsam fir
Chamaecyparis thyoides	Atlantic white-cedar
Larix laricina	American larch
Picea mariana	black spruce
Picea rubens	red spruce
Pinus rigida	pitch pine
Pinus strobus	eastern white pine
Tsuga canadensis	eastern hemlock
Thuja occidentalis	eastern arborvitae

Associates

Acer rubrum	red maple
Betula alleghaniensis	yellow birch
Betula populifolia	gray birch
Fraxinus nigra	black ash
Nyssa sylvatica	black tupelo

Woody Understory

Alnus incana	speckled alder
Alnus serrulata	brookside alder
Amelanchier arborea	smooth serviceberry
Aronia melanocarpa	black chokeberry
Betula pumila	bog birch
Chamaedaphne calyculata	leatherleaf
Clematis virginiana	devil's-darning-needles
Clethra alnifolia	coastal sweet-pepperbush
Cornus sericea	redosier
Gaultheria hispidula	creeping-snowberry
Gaultheria procumbens	eastern teaberry
Ilex laevigata	smooth winterberry
Ilex verticillata	common winterberry
Kalmia angustifolia	sheep-laurel
Kalmia polifolia	bog-laurel
Ledum groenlandicum	rusty Labrador-tea
Lonicera oblongifolia	swamp fly-honeysuckle
Nemopanthus mucronatus	catberry
Pentaphylloides floribunda	golden-hardhack
Rhamnus alnifolia	alder-leaf buckthorn
Rhododendron maximum	great-laurel
Rhododendron viscosum	clammy azalea
Ribes hirtellum	hairy-stem gooseberry
Rubus pubescens	dwarf red raspberry
Spiraea alba	white meadowsweet
Toxicodendron vernix	poison-sumac
Vaccinium corymbosum	highbush blueberry
Vaccinium myrtilloides	velvet-leaf blueberry
Vaccinium oxycoccos	small cranberry

Herbaceous Understory

Aulacomnium palustre	moss
Calla palustris	water-dragon
Caltha palustris	yellow marsh-marigold
Carex bromoides	brome-like sedges
Carex disperma	soft-leaf sedge
Carex eburnea	bristle-leaf sedge
Carex interior	inland sedge
Carex intumescens	great bladder sedge
Carex lacustris	lakebank sedge
Carex leptalea	bristly-stalk sedge
Carex scabrata	eastern rough sedge
Carex stricta	uptight sedge
Carex trisperma	three-seed sedge
Cirsium muticum	swamp thistle
Clintonia borealis	yellow bluebead-lily
Coptis trifolis	three-leaf goldthread

Cornus canadensis	Canadian bunchberry
Cypripedium parviflorum	lesser yellow lady's-slipper
Dryopteris cristata	crested wood fern
Eriophorum spp.	cotton-grass
Geum rivale	purple avens
Glyceria striata	fowl manna grass
Gymnocarpium dryopteris	western oak fern
Hylocomium splendens	feathermoss
Maianthemum canadense	false lily-of-the-valley
Maianthemum stellatum	starry false Solomon's-seal
Mitchella repens	partridge-berry
Mitella nuda	bare-stem bishop's-cap
Onoclea sensibilis	sensitive fern
Osmunda cinnamomea	cinnamon fern
Osmunda claytonia	interrupted fern
Osmunda regalis	royal fern
Platanthera blephariglottis	white fringed orchid
Pogonia ophioglossoides	snake-mouth orchid
Pteridium aquilinum	northern bracken fern
Ptilium crista-castrensis	feathermoss
Sarracenia purpurea	purple pitcherplant
Saxifraga pensylvanica	eastern swamp saxifrage
Senecio aureus	golden ragwort
Solidago patula	round-leaf goldenrod
Sphagnum centrale	moss
Sphagnum russowii	moss
Sphagnum warnstorifii	moss
Symplocarpus foetidus	skunk-cabbage
Thalictrum pubescens	king-of-the-meadow
Thelypteris palustris	eastern marsh fern
Trichocolea tomentella	leafy liverwort
Trientalis borealis	American starflower
Trollius laxus	globeflower
Typha latifolia	broad-leaf cat-tail
Veratrum viride	American false hellebore

Shrub Bog/Fen

The Shrub Bog/Fen community type occurs on peat substrate in continually wet areas fed by springs. The nutrient level of the water that feeds the bogs and fens strongly influences the diversity and type of vegetation that occurs. Some areas may have a high pH (6.0-7.9) and support a greater variety of species than areas that are fed by nutrient poor waters. Fen peatlands are influenced by calcareous water. In general, they are dominated by evergreen and deciduous shrubs although trees are often present.

Characteristic Woody Species

Betula pumila	bog birch
Chamaedaphne calyculata	leatherleaf
Gaylussacia baccata	black huckleberry
Kalmia angustifolia	sheep-laurel

Kalmia polifolia	bog-laurel
Vaccinium corymbosum	highbush blueberry
Vaccinium macrocarpon	large cranberry
Vaccinium oxycoccus	small cranberry

Associates

Abies balsamea	balsam fir
Acer rubrum	red maple
Alnus incana	speckled alder
Andromeda polifolia	bog-rosemary
Chamaedaphne calyculata	leatherleaf
Cornus sericea	redosier
Decodon verticillatus	swamp-loosestrife
Ilex verticillata	common winterberry
Juniperus virginiana	eastern red cedar
Larix laricina	American larch
Nemopanthus mucronatus	catberry
Pentaphylloides floribunda	golden-hardhack
Picea mariana	black spruce
Pinus rigida	pitch pine
Pinus strobus	eastern white pine
Rhamnus alnifolia	alder-leaf buckthorn
Rhododendron maximum	great-laurel
Rhododendron viscosum	clammy azalea
Salix candida	hoary willow
Salix discolor	tall pussy willow
Toxicodendron vernix	poison-sumac
Xyris montana	northern yellow-eyed-grass

Herbaceous Understory

Calla palustris	water-dragon
Calopogon tuberosus	tuberous grass-pink
Carex aquatilis	leafy tussock sedge
Carex atlantica	prickly bog sedge
Carex canescens	hoary sedge
Carex folliculata	northern long sedge
Carex lacustris	lakebank sedge
Carex rostrata	swollen beaked sedge
Carex stricta	uptight sedge
Carex trisperma	three-seed sedge
Drosera rotundifolia	round-leaf sundew
Eriophorum virginicum	tawny cotton-grass
Glyceria canadensis	rattlesnake manna grass
Iris versicolor	harlequin blueflag
Lobelia kalmii	brook lobelia
Maianthemum trifolia	three-flower false Solomon's-seal
Osmunda cinnamomea	cinnamon fern
Osmunda regalis	royal fern
Peltandra virginica	green arrow-arum
Platanthera blephariglottis	white fringed orchid

Pogonia ophioglossoides	snake-mouth orchid
Rhynchospora alba	white beak sedge
Sarracenia purpurea	purple pitcherplant
Scirpus acutus	hard-stem bulrush
Sphagnum angustifolium	moss
Sphagnum centrale	moss
Sphagnum fallax	moss
Sphagnum fimbriatum	moss
Sphagnum magellanicum	moss
Sphagnum nemoreum	moss
Sphagnum papillosum	moss
Sphagnum rubellum	moss
Thelypteris palustris	eastern marsh fern
Triandenum virginicum	Virginia marsh-St. John's-wort
Utricularia cornuta	horned bladderwort

Shrub Swamp

Shrub Swamp occurs scattered throughout the region in poorly drained areas. This community is dominated by shrubs (at least 50 percent) with less coverage in trees, on permanently flooded or saturated mineral soils. Species composition is influenced primarily by water depth and pH.

Characteristic Woody Species

Alnus incana	speckled alder
Alnus serrulata	brookside alder
Cephalanthus occidentalis	common buttonbush
Cornus amomum	silky dogwood
Cornus sericea	redosier
Decodon verticillatus	swamp-loosestrife
Rosa palustris	swamp rose
Sambucus canadensis	American elder
Vaccinium corymbosum	highbush blueberry

Associates

Aronia melanocarpa	black chokeberry
Betula populifolia	gray birch
Chamaedaphne calyculata	leatherleaf
Cornus foemina	gray dogwood
Gaylussacia baccata	black huckleberry
Ilex verticillata	common winterberry
Kalmia angustifolia	sheep-laurel
Lindera benzoin	northern spicebush
Lyonia ligustrina	maleberry
Physocarpus opulifolius	Atlantic ninebark
Rhododendron maximum	great-laurel
Rhododendron viscosum	clammy azalea
Salix bebbiana	long-beak willow
Salix discolor	tall pussy willow
Salix lucida	shining willow
Salix petiolaris	meadow willow

Spiraea alba	white meadowsweet
Spiraea tomentosa	steeplebush
Vaccinium macrocarpon	large cranberry
Vaccinium oxycoccos	small cranberry
Viburnum dentatum	southern arrow-wood

Herbaceous Understory

Caltha palustris	yellow marsh-marigold
Carex rostrata	swollen beaked sedge
Solanum dulcamara	climbing nightshade
Sphagnum spp.	moss
Symplocarpus foetidus	skunk-cabbage

Herbaceous Peatland Fen/Wet Meadow

Wet meadows and fens occur in peat soils that are fed by small springs or groundwater seepage. They have saturated soils and are seasonally or permanently flooded. Fens occur on higher or sloping ground and may contain trees and low shrubs.

Characteristic Species

Argentina anserina	common silverweed
Aster umbellatus	parasol flat-top white aster
Caltha palustris	yellow marsh-marigold
Carex aquatilis	leafy tussock sedge
Carex flava	yellow-green sedge
Carex hystericina	porcupine sedge
Carex interior	inland sedge
Carex lacustris	lakebank sedge
Carex lanuginosa	woolly sedge
Carex leptalea	bristly-stalk sedge
Carex prariea	prairie sedge
Carex sterilis	dioecious sedge
Carex stricta	uptight sedge
Carex viridula	little green sedge
Chelone glabra	white turtlehead
Cladium mariscoides	smooth sawgrass
Cyperus bipartitus	shining flat sedge
Deschampsia cespitosa	tufted hair grass
Drepanpcladus revolvens	moss
Drosera rotundifolia	round-leaf sundew
Dryopteris cristata	crested wood fern
Eleocharis palustris	pale spike-rush
Eleocharis rostellata	beaked spike-rush
Equisetum arvense	field horsetail
Equisetum variegatum	varigated scouring rush
Eriophorum viridicarinatum	tassel cotton-grass
Eupatorium perfoliatum	common boneset
Geum rivale	purple avens
Liparis loeselii	yellow wide-lip orchid

Lobelia cardinalis	cardinal-flower
Lobelia kalmii	brook lobelia
Lycopus uniflorus	northern water-horehound
Lycopus virginicus	Virginia water-horehound
Mentha arvensis	American wild mint
Muhlenbergia glomerata	spike muhly
Muhlenbergia racemosa	green muhly
Osmunda cinnamomea	cinnamon fern
Osmunda regalis	royal fern
Panicum flexile	wiry panic grass
Parnassia glauca	fen grass-of-Parnassus
Platanthera dilatata	scentbottle
Pogonia ophioglossoides	snake-mouth orchid
Polygonum amphibium	water smartweed
Rhynchospora alba	white beak sedge
Rhynchospora capillacaea	needle beak sedge
Rudbeckia laciniata	green-head coneflower
Sarracenia purpurea	purple pitcherplant
Scirpus acutus	hard-setm bulrush
Scleria verticillata	low nut-rush
Senecio aureus	golden ragwort
Solidago ohioensis	Ohio goldenrod
Solidago patula	round-leaf goldenrod
Solidago uliginosa	bog goldenrod
Spiranthes lucida	shining ladies'-tresses
Symplocarpus foetidus	skunk-cabbage
Thalictrum pubenscens	king-of-the-meadow
Thelypteris palustris	eastern marsh fern
Triglochin palustre	marsh arrow-grass
Trollius laxus	American globeflower
Typha angustifolia	narrow-leaf cat-tail
Typha latifolia	broad-leaf cat-tail
Utricularia minor	lesser blatterwort

Associates

Acer rubrum	red maple
Acorus americanus	sweetflag
Amelanchier arborea	smooth shadbush
Angelica atropurpurea	purple-stem angelica
Aronia melanocarpa	black chokeberry
Calamagrostis canadensis	bluejoint
Carex eburnea	bristle-leaf sedge
Clematis virginiana	devil's-darning-needles
Cornus foemina	gray dogwood
Cornus sericea	redosier
Eupatorium maculatum	spotted joe-pye-weed
Myrica gale	sweet-gale
Myrica pensylvanica	northern bayberry
Pentaphylloides floribunda	golden-hardhack
Rhamnus alnifolia	alder-leaf buckthorn

Ribes hirtellum	hairy-stem gooseberry
Rubus pubescens	dwarf red raspberry
Salix candida	hoary willow
Spiraea alba	white meadowsweet
Tsuga canadensis	eastern hemlock
Vaccinium corymbosum	highbush blueberry
Vaccinium macrocarpon	large cranberry

Mineral Soil Marsh

Mineral Soil Marsh often occurs along lake shores where the soil is gravelly, sandy, or muddy. These areas are permanently saturated and seasonally or periodically flooded. Where water is usually present and covering the soil, the community is known as an emergent marsh. Water depths in these areas may range from six inches to six feet. Woody species such as alder and willow may border the forb dominated marshes.

Characteristic Species

Alisma plantago-aquatica	water plantain
Bidens frondosa	devil's-pitchfork
Calamgrostis canadensis	bluejoint
Carex lurida	shallow sedge
Carex prairea	prairie sedge
Carex tetanica	rigid sedge
Eleocharis acicularis	needle spike-rush
Eleocharis obtusa	blunt spike-rush
Equisetum arvense	field horsetail
Glyceria melicaria	melic manna grass
Juncus effusus	lamp rush
Lathyrus palustris	marsh vetchling
Leersia oryzoides	rice cut grass
Onoclea sensibilis	sensitive fern
Polygonum pensylvanicum	pinkweed
Sagittaria latifolia	duck-potato
Scirpus americanus	chairmaker's bulrush
Scirpus atrovirens	dark-green bulrush
Symplocarpus foetidus	skunk-cabbage
Typha latifolia	broad-leaf cat-tail
Zizania aquatica	Indian wild rice

Associates

Acorus americanus	sweetflag
Argentina anserina	common silverweed
Armoracia lacustris	lakecress
Asclepias incarnata	swamp milkweed
Campanula aparinoides	marsh bellflower
Carex aurea	golden-fruit sedge
Carex flava	yellow-green sedge
Carex granularis	limestone-meadow sedge
Carex lacustris	lakebank sedge
Carex schweinitzii	Schweinitz's sedge
Carex stricta	uptight sedge
Carex viridula	little green sedge

Carex vulpinoidea	commmon fox sedge
Cyperus bipartitus	shining flat sedge
Cyperus squarrosus	awned flat sedge
Decodon verticillatus	swamp-loosestrife
Dulichium arundinaceum	three-way sedge
Eleocharis intermedia	matted spike-rush
Eleocharis palustris	pale spike-rush
Epilobium strictum	downy willowherb
Equisetum fluviatile	water horsetail
Equisetum variegatum	varigated scouring-rush
Eupatorium perfoliatum	common boneset
Fimbristylis autumnalis	slender fimbry
Fraxinus pennsylvanica	green ash
Glyceria canadensis	rattlesnake manna grass
Gratiloa neglecta	clammy hedge-hyssop
Heteranthera dubia	grass-leaf mud-plantain
Iris versicolor	Virginia blueflag
Juncus alpinoarticulatus	northern green rush
Juncus balticus	Baltic rush
Juncus canadensis	Canadian rush
Juncus nodosus	knotted rush
Juncus pelocarpus	brown-fruit rush
Juncus torreyi	Torrey's rush
Lobelia dortmanna	water lobelia
Lobelia kalmii	brook lobelia
Ludwigia palustris	marsh primrose-willow
Lythrum thrysiflora	thyme-leaf loosestrife
Nuphar lutea	yellow pond-lily
Nymphaea odorata	American white water-lily
Peltandra virginica	green arrow-arum
Polygonum amphibium	water smartweed
Ranunculus longirostris	long-beak water-crowfoot
Ranunculus reptans	lesser creeping spearwort
Rhynochospora capillacea	needle beak sedge
Salix petiolaris	meadow willow
Salix sericea	silky willow
Scirpus actus	hard-stem bulrush
Scirpus cyperinus	cottongrass bulrush
Scirpus tabernaemontani	soft-stem bulrush
Sium suave	water-parsnip
Sparganium americanum	American burr-reed
Sparganium eurycarpum	broad-fruit burr-reed
Thelypteris palustris	eastern marsh fern
Typha angustifolia	narrow-leaf cat-tail

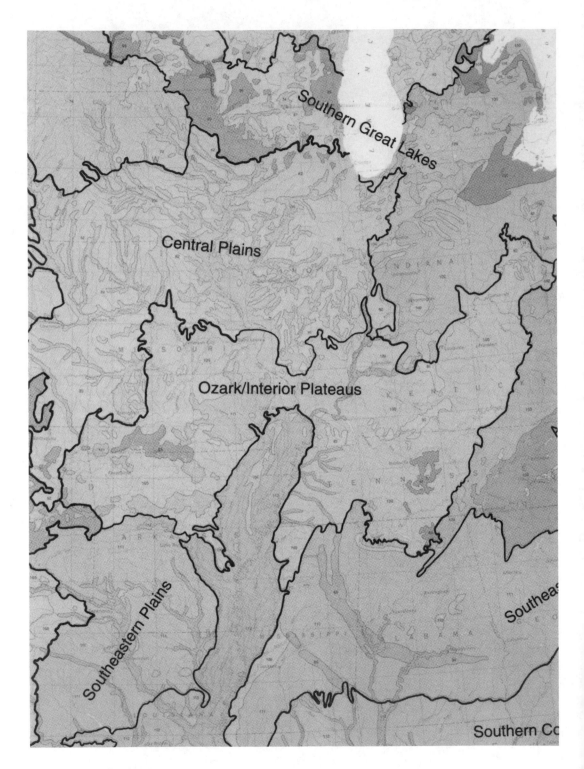

Ozark/Interior Plateaus

Ozark/Interior Plateaus

Introduction

This region encompasses most of Kentucky and Tennessee west of the Cumberland Plateau and portions of southwest Ohio, southern Indiana, extreme southern Illinois, southern Missouri, northern Arkansas and extreme northeastern Oklahoma. It does not include small portions of extreme western Kentucky and Tennessee and the southeastern part of Missouri known as the Bootheel region which are part of Southern Coastal Plain region.

At the time of settlement most of this region was covered with deciduous forest. Oak–Hickory Forest dominates the upland landscape and covers much of the region. Oak–Pine Forest becomes important west of the Mississippi River in the Ozark Plateaus. Rich, mesophytic forests are mainly restricted to protected north slopes and ravines and areas with fertile, well drained soils. Oak barrens, prairies, and glades are also important communities.

The primary sources used to develop descriptions and species lists are: Braun 1950; Nelson 1980; Solecki 1980; Styermark 1963.

Dominant Ecological Communities

Upland Systems
Oak–Hickory Forest
Oak–Pine Forest
Western Mesophytic Forest
Oak Barrens
Bluestem Prairie
Glade

Wetland Systems
Floodplain Forest
Swamp Forest
Marsh
Wet Prairie

UPLAND SYSTEMS

Oak–Hickory Forest

Oak–Hickory Forest occurs throughout the region on dry to dry-mesic uplands. Dominance and species composition varies in response to topography, soils, geology and disturbance history. This community corresponds to Küchler #100.

Canopy
Characteristic Species

Carya glabra	pignut hickory
Carya ovata	shag-bark hickory
Quercus rubra	northern red oak
Quercus velutina	black oak

Associates

Acer rubrum	red maple
Acer sacharrum	sugar maple
Carya ovalis	red hickory
Carya texana	black hickory
Diospyros virginiana	common persimmon
Fraxinus americana	white ash
Fraxinus quadrangulata	blue ash
Nyssa sylvatica	black tupelo
Pinus echinata	short-leaf pine
Quercus coccinea	scarlet oak
Quercus falcata	southern red oak
Quercus imbricaria	shingle oak
Quercus marilandica	blackjack oak
Quercus muhlenbergii	chinkapin oak
Quercus shumardii	shumard's oak
Quercus stellata	post oak
Ulmus rubra	slippery elm

Woody Understory

Amelanchier arborea	downy service-berry
Ceanothus americanus	New Jersey-tea
Cercis canadensis	redbud
Cornus drummondi	rough-leaf dogwood
Cornus florida	flowering dogwood
Cornus racemosa	gray dogwood
Parthenocissus quinquefolia	Virginia-creeper
Rhus aromatica	fragnant sumac
Symphoricarpos orbiculatus	coral-berry
Ulmus alata	winged elm
Vaccinium arboreum	tree sparkle-berry
Vaccinium pallidum	early lowbush blueberry
Vaccinium stamineum	deerberry
Vitis aestivalis	summer grape

Herbaceous Understory

Antennaria plantaginifolia	woman's-tobacco
Asplenium platyneuron	ebony spleenwort
Aster patens	late purple aster
Carex pensylvanica	Pennsylvania sedge
Clitoria mariana	Atlantic pigeonwings
Cunila marina	common dittany
Danthonia spicata	poverty white oat grass
Desmodium nudiflorum	naked-flower tick-trefoil
Galium concinnum	shining bedstraw
Galium pilosum	hairy bedstraw
Helianthus divaricatus	woodland sunflower
Hieracium gronovii	queendevil
Podophyllum peltatum	may-apple

Polystichum acrostichoides	Christmas fern
Prenanthes alba	white rattlesnake-root
Prenanthes altissima	tall rattlesnake-root
Ranunculus hispidus	bristly buttercup
Silene caroliniana	sticky catchfly
Solidago hispida	hairy goldenrod
Tradescantia virginiana	Virgina spiderwort

Oak–Pine Forest

In this region Oak–Pine Forest occurs primarily in the Ozark Highlands or Ozark Plateaus. It occupies dry to xeric sites such as south and west facing slopes and ridgetops. In some ways it is similar to the Oak–Hickory forest type and shares many of the same species. However, pine is a dominant and conspicuous part of the overstory, sometimes occurring in pure stands, especially on acid soils. This community corresponds to Küchler #111.

Canopy
Characteristic Species
Carya texana	black hickory
Pinus echinata	short-leaf pine
Quercus alba	northern white oak
Quercus marilandica	blackjack oak
Quercus stellata	post oak
Quercus velutina	black oak

Associates
Carya ovalis	red hickory
Diospyros virginiana	common persimmon
Quercus coccinea	scarlet oak
Quercus falcata	southern red oak
Sassafras albidum	sassafras
Ulmus alata	winged elm

Woody Understory
Amelanchier arborea	downy service-berry
Ceanothus americanus	New Jersey-tea
Cornus florida	flowering dogwood
Frangula caroliniana	Carolina buckthorn
Hypericum hypericoides	St. Andrew's-cross
Ostrya virginiana	eastern hop-hornbeam
Rhus aromatica	fragrant sumac
Rhus copallinum	winged sumac
Rosa carolina	Carolina rose
Vaccinum arboreum	tree sparkle-berry
Vaccinum staminum	early lowbush blueberry

Herbaceous Understory
Antennaria plantaginifolia	woman's tobacco
Aster anomalus	many-ray aster
Aster linariifolius	flax-leaf white-top aster
Aster patens	late purple aster

Carex flaccosperma	thin-fruit sedge
Cunila marina	common dittany
Danthonia spicata	poverty wild oat grass
Dichanthelium dichotomum	cypress rosette grass
Helianthus divaricatus	woodland sunflower
Lespedeza procumbens	trailing bush-clover
Lespedeza repens	creeping bush-clover
Potentilla simplex	oldfield cinquefoil
Pteridium aquilinum	northern bracken fern
Ranunculus hispida	bristly buttercup
Silene virginica	fire-pink
Solidago buckleyi	Buckley's goldenrod
Solidago hispida	hairy goldenrod
Stylosanthes biflora	side-beak pencil-flower
Tradescantia virginiana	Virginia spiderwort
Viola pedata	bird-foot violet

Western Mesophytic Forest

Western Mesophytic Forest occurs throughout the region on rich, moist sites such as protected lower north slopes, deep ravines, and other areas of deep, rich, well drained soils. It has the highest species diversity of the forested communities in this region. This community corresponds, in part, to Küchler type #100.

Canopy
Characteristic Species

Acer saccharum	sugar maple
Carya cordiformis	bitter-nut hickory
Carya ovata	shag-bark hickory
Fagus grandifolia	American beech
Liriodendron tulipifera	tuliptree
Quercus alba	northern white oak
Quercus rubra	northern red oak
Tilia americana	American basswood

Associates

Aesculus glabra	Ohio buckeye
Celtis occidentalis	common hackberry
Fraxinus americana	white ash
Gymnocladus dioicus	Kentucky coffeetree
Juglans nigra	black walnut
Liquidambar styraciflua	sweet-gum
Magnolia acuminata	cucumber magnolia
Nyssa sylvatica	black tupelo
Platanus occidentalis	American sycamore
Prunus serotina	black cherry
Quercus shumardii	Shumard's oak
Ulmus rubra	slippery elm

Woody Understory

Asimina triloba	common pawpaw
Carpinus caroliniana	American hornbeam

Cercis canadensis	redbud
Cornus alternifolia	alternate-leaf dogwood
Cornus florida	flowering dogwood
Dirca palustris	eastern leatherwood
Hamamelis virginiana	American witch-hazel
Hydrangea arborescens	wild hydrangea
Lindera benzoin	northern spicebush
Ostrya virginiana	eastern hop-hornbeam
Sassafras albidium	sassafras
Staphylea trifolia	American bladdernut

Herbaceous Understory

Actaea pachypoda	white baneberry
Adiantum pedatum	northern maidenhair
Amphicarpaea bracteata	American hog-peanut
Amsonia tabernaemontana	eastern bluestar
Aquilegia canadensis	red columbine
Aralia racemosa	American spikenard
Arisaema triphyllum	jack-in-the-pulpit
Aruncus dioicus	bride's-feathers
Asarum canadense	Canadian wild ginger
Asplenium platyneuron	ebony spleenwort
Athyrium filix-femina	subarctic lady fern
Cardamine concatenata	cut-leaf toothwort
Chasmanthium latifolium	Indian wood-oats
Cimicifuga racemosa	black bugbane
Claytonia virginica	Virginia springbeauty
Cypripedium pubescens	greater yellow lady's-slipper
Diarrhena americana	American beakgrain
Dicentra canadensis	squirrel-corn
Dicentra cucullaria	Dutchman's-breeches
Dodecatheon meadia	eastern shootingstar
Dryopteris intermedia	evergreen wood fern
Dryopteris marginalis	marginal wood fern
Enemion biternatum	eastern false rue-anemone
Erythronium albidum	small white fawn-lily
Erythronium americanum	American trout-lily
Galearis spectabilis	showy orchid
Geranium maculatum	spotted crane's-bill
Hepatica nobilis	liverwort
Hydrophyllum appendiculatum	great waterleaf
Hydrophyllum canadense	blunt-leaf waterleaf
Hydrophyllum virginianum	Shawnee-salad
Jeffersonia diphylla	twinleaf
Maianthemum racemosum	feathery false Solomon's-seal
Mitella diphylla	two-leaf bishop's-cap
Onoclea sensibilis	sensitive fern
Osmunda cinnamomea	cinnamon fern
Panax quinquefolius	American ginseng

Phacelia bipinnatifida	fern-leaf scorpion-weed
Phlox divaricata	wild blue phlox
Polystichum acrostichoides	Christmas fern
Sanguinaria canadensis	bloodroot
Saxifraga virginiensis	early saxifrage
Silene virginica	fire-pink
Solidago caesia	wreath goldenrod
Solidago flexicaulis	zigzag goldenrod
Stylophorum diphyllum	celandine-poppy
Thalictrum thalictroides	rue-anemone
Tiarella cordifolia	heart-leaf foamflower
Trillium erectum	stinking-Benjamin
Trillium flexipes	nodding wakerobin
Trillium grandiflorum	large-flower wakerobin
Trillium recurvatum	bloody-butcher
Trillium sessile	toadshade
Viola canadensis	Canadian white violet
Viola pubescens	downy yellow violet
Viola sororia	hooded blue violet

Oak Barrens

Oak barrens, a savanna-like community of scattered, open grown oaks with a variably open understory composed of prairie and woodland species originally occurred over a broad area. Except for scattered remnants, this community type is all but gone from the landscape. This community corresponds to Küchler #82.

Canopy
Characteristic Species
Quercus alba	northern white oak
Quercus macrocarpa	burr oak
Quercus marilandica	blackjack oak
Quercus stellata	post oak

Associates
Carya texana	black hickory
Juniperus virginiana	eastern red cedar
Pinus echinata	short-leaf pine
Quercus imbricaria	shingle oak
Quercus velutina	black oak

Woody Understory
Cratagus spp.	hawthorn
Forestiera ligustrina	upland swamp-privet
Rhus aromatica	fragrant sumac

Herbaceous Understory
Andropogon gerardii	big bluestem
Baptisia bracteata	long-bract wild indigo
Blephilia ciliata	downy pagoda-plant
Bouteloua curtipendula	side-oats grama

Echinacea purpurea	eastern purple-coneflower
Gentiana puberulenta	downy gentian
Houstonia canadensis	Canadian summer bluet
Pedicularis canadensis	Canadian lousewort
Schizachyrium scoparium	little false bluestem
Silene regia	royal catchfly
Sorghastrum nutans	yellow Indian grass
Tephrosia virginiana	goat's-rue
Viola pedata	bird-foot violet

Bluestem Prairie

Bluestem Prairie once occupied millions of acres in this region. It occurred primarily as disjunct, variable sized prairie openings in an otherwise forested area. The grass dominated prairies were maintained by fire and grazing. The prairies ranged from wet to dry depending upon soil depth, moisture availability, aspect and other factors. The prairies were primarily grass dominated with forbs scattered throughout. Trees and shrubs occurred only as isolated individuals or in groves. This community corresponds to Küchler #74 and #82.

Characteristic Species

Andropogon gerardii	big bluestem
Aster novi-angliae	New England aster
Aster oolentangiensis	sky-blue aster
Aster pilosus	white oldfield aster
Baptisia alba	white wild indigo
Bouteloua curtipendula	side-oats grama
Chamaecrista fasciculata	sleepingplant
Chrysopsis mariana	Maryland golden-aster
Coreopsis lanceolata	lance-leaf tickseed
Dalea candida	white prairie-clover
Dalea purpurea	violet prairie-clover
Echinacea pallida	pale purple-coneflower
Eryngium yuccifolium	button eryngo
Euphorbia corollata	flowering spurge
Helianthus mollis	neglected sunflower
Heliopsis helianthoides	smooth oxeye
Lespedeza capitata	round-head bush-clover
Liatris aspera	tall gayfeather
Liatris pychnostachya	cat-tail gayfeather
Liatris spicata	dense gayfeather
Manfreda virginica	false aloe
Monarda fistulosa	Oswego-tea
Panicum virgatum	wand panic grass
Penstemon digitalis	foxglove beardtongue
Phlox pilosa	downy phlox
Physostegia virginiana	obedient-plant
Pycnanthemum tenuifolium	narrow-leaf mountain-mint
Ratibida pinnata	gray-head Mexican-hat
Rudbeckia hirta	black-eyed-Susan
Salvia azurea	azure-blue sage

Schizachyrium scoparium	little false bluestem
Silene regia	royal catchfly
Silphium compositum	kidney-leaf rosinweed
Silphium laciniatum	compassplant
Silphium terebinthinaceum	prairie rosinweed
Solidago nemoralis	gray goldenrod
Solidago rigida	hard-leaf goldenrod
Sorghastum nutans	yellow Indian grass
Spartina pectinata	freshwater cord grass
Sporobolus heterolepis	prairie dropseed
Vernonia gigantea	giant ironweed
Veronicastrum virginicum	culver's-root

Glade

Glade is a naturally open, grass and/or forb dominated area where bedrock is at or near the surface of the ground. Glade communities may occur on slopes of hills or in topographically flat areas. They are usually dry and droughty during the growing season but may be locally saturated in the spring. Glades are usually small but can be locally dominant in the central basin of Tennessee and in parts of Arkansas and Missouri in the Ozarks. Glade communities are often distinguished by bedrock type (i.e. sandstone, limestone, dolomite, etc.). Glades are floristically diverse and often harbor many unusual and rare species. They share many species of the prairie and often grade into dry prairies where soil deepens. This community corresponds to Küchler #83.

Characteristic Species

Aristida longespica	red three-awn
Aster sericeus	western silver aster
Bouteloua curtipendula	side-oats grama
Castilleja coccinea	scarlet Indian-paintbrush
Cheilanthes lanosa	hairy lip fern
Crotonopsis elliptica	egg-leaf rushfoil
Dalea candida	white prairie-clover
Dalea purpurea	violet prairie-clover
Danthonia spicata	poverty wild oat grass
Diodia teres	poorjoe
Echinacea pallida	pale purple-coneflower
Eragrostis spectabilis	petticoat climber
Glandularia canadensis	rose mock vervain
Heliotropium tenellum	pasture heliotrope
Hypericum gentianoides	orange-grass
Lechea mucronata	hairy pinweed
Lechea tenuifolia	narrow-leaf pinweed
Liatris aspera	tall gayfeather
Liatris cylindracea	Ontario gayfeather
Minuartia patula	Pitcher's stitchwort
Ophioglossum engelmannii	limestone adder's-tongue
Opuntia humifusa	eastern prickly-pear
Phlox pilosa	downy phlox
Sabatia angularis	rose-pink
Schizachyrum scoparium	little false bluestem

Sedum pulchellum	widow's cross
Senecio anonymus	Small's ragwort
Sorghastrum nutans	yellow Indian grass
Sporobolus asper	tall dropseed
Sporobolus heterolepis	prairie dropseed
Sporobolus vaginiflorus	poverty dropseed
Stylosanthes biflora	side-beak pencil-flower
Talinum parviflorum	sunbright
Tephrosia virginiana	goat's-rue

WETLAND SYSTEMS

Floodplain Forest

Floodplain Forest occurs throughout the region along large streams and rivers where floodplains have developed. The canopy composition is a variety of large deciduous trees; and, the understory and herbaceous layers range from well developed to poorly developed, depending on the duration of annual flooding. This community corresponds to Küchler #113.

Canopy
Characteristic species

Acer saccharinum	silver maple
Betula nigra	river birch
Carya laciniosa	shell-bark hickory
Celtis occidentalis	common hackberry
Liquidambar styraciflua	sweet-gum
Populus deltoides	eastern cottonwood
Quercus bicolor	swamp white oak
Quercus lyrata	overcup oak
Quercus macrocarpa	burr oak
Quercus pagoda	cherry-bark oak
Quercus palustris	pin oak
Ulmus americana	American elm

Associates

Acer negundo	ash-leaf maple
Acer rubrum	red maple
Carya cordiformis	bitter-nut hickory
Fraxinus pennsylvanica	green ash
Gleditsia triacanthos	honey-locust
Juglans nigra	black walnut
Nyssa sylvatica	black tupelo
Platanus occidentalis	American sycamore
Quercus michauxii	swamp chestnut oak
Salix nigra	black willow
Ulmus rubra	slippery elm

Woody Understory

Asimina triloba	common pawpaw
Bignonia capreolata	crossvine
Campsis radicans	trumpet-creeper
Carpinus caroliniana	American hornbeam
Cornus foemina	stiff dogwood
Ilex decidua	deciduous holly
Lindera benzoin	northern spicebush
Toxicodendron radicans	eastern poison-ivy
Vitis spp.	grape

Herbaceous Understory

Arundinaria gigantea	giant cane
Boehmeria cylindrica	small-spike false nettle
Carex grayi	Gray's sedge
Carex tribuloides	blunt broom sedge
Chelone glabra	white turtlehead
Cinna arundinacea	sweet wood-reed
Elymus virginicus	Virginia wild rye
Hymenocallis caroliniana	Carolina spider-lily
Impatiens capensis	spotted touch-me-not
Laportea canadensis	Canadian wood-nettle
Lobelia cardinalis	cardinal-flower
Lobelia siphilitica	great blue lobelia
Mertensia virginica	Virginia bluebells
Mimulus ringens	Allegheny monkey-flower
Monarda didyma	scarlet beebalm
Onoclea sensibilis	sensitive fern
Phacelia purshii	Miami-mist
Sanicula canadensis	Canadian black-snakeroot
Viola cucullata	marsh blue violet

Swamp Forest

Swamp Forest is uncommon and scattered throughout this region, usually associated with large floodplains of major rivers. Less common are upland swamps, usually associated with poorly drained depressions or sinkholes. Most swamps in this region are hardwood dominated although some can be dominated by southern bald-cypress.

Canopy
Characteristic species

Betula nigra	river birch
Nyssa aquatica	water tupelo
Populus heterophylla	swamp cottonwood
Quercus lyrata	overcup oak
Quercus palustris	pin oak
Salix nigra	black willow
Taxodium distichum	southern bald-cypress

Woody Understory

Cephalanthus occidentalis	common buttonbush
Decodon verticillatus	swamp-loosestrife
Ilex decidua	deciduous holly
Itea virginica	Virginia sweetspire
Rosa palustris	swamp rose

Herbaceous Understory

Ceratophyllum demursum	coontail
Iris virginica	Virginia blueflag
Lemna spp.	duckweed
Sagittaria latifolia	duck-potato
Saururus cernuus	lizard's-tail

Marsh

Marsh is primarily associated with floodplains of larger streams and rivers although it also occurs in upland depressions. These communities are shallowly flooded for much of the year. They are associated with Wet Prairie communities in dryer areas and Swamp Forest in deeper water areas.

Characteristic Species

Alisma subcordatum	Amercian water-plantain
Boltonia asteroides	white doll's-daisy
Carex frankii	Frank's sedge
Carex lupulina	hop sedge
Carex tribuloides	blunt broom sedge
Carex vulpinoidea	common fox sedge
Eleocharis acicularis	needle spike-rush
Eleocharis obtusa	blunt spike-rush
Hibiscus laevis	halherb-leaf rose-mallow
Hibiscus moscheutos	crimson-eyed rose-mallow
Iris brevicaulis	zigzag iris
Iris virginica	Virginia blueflag
Juncus effusus	lamp rush
Leersia virginica	white grass
Nelumbo lutea	Amercian lotus
Nuphar lutea	yellow pond-lily
Polygonum amphibium	water smartweed
Polygonum hydropiperoides	swamp smartwced
Polygonum pensylvanicum	pinkweed
Rumex verticillatus	swamp dock
Sagittaria latifolia	duck-potato
Scirpus americanus	chairmaker's bulrush
Scirpus atrovirens	dark-green bulrush
Scirpus tabernaemontani	soft-stem bulrush
Sparganium eurycarpum	broad-fruit burr-reed
Typha latifolia	broad-leaf cat-tail

Wet Prairie

Wet Prairie is often associated with marsh communities in floodplains of larger streams and in poorly drained depressions in the uplands. These grass dominated wetlands are essentially eradicated now with most areas converted to cropland.

Characteristic Species

Agalinis tenuifolia	slender-leaf false foxglove
Asclepias incarnata	swamp milkweed
Bidens aristosa	bearded beggarticks
Bidens cernua	nodding burr-marigold
Carex arkansana	Arkansas sedge
Carex vulpinoidea	common fox sedge
Cephalanthus occidentalis	common buttonbush
Cicuta maculata	spotted water-hemlock
Eupatorium coelestinum	blue mistflower
Eupatorium maculatum	spotted joe-pye-weed
Eupatorium perfoliatum	common boneset
Helenium autumnale	fall sneezeweed
Helianthus angustifolius	swamp sunflower
Panicum virgatum	wand panic grass
Rudbeckia laciniata	green-head coneflower
Sium suave	hemlock water-parsnip
Solidago rugosa	wrinkle-leaf goldenrod
Spartina pectinata	freshwater cord grass
Spiraea alba	white meadowsweet
Tripsacum dactyloides	eastern mock grama
Verbena hastata	simpler's-joy

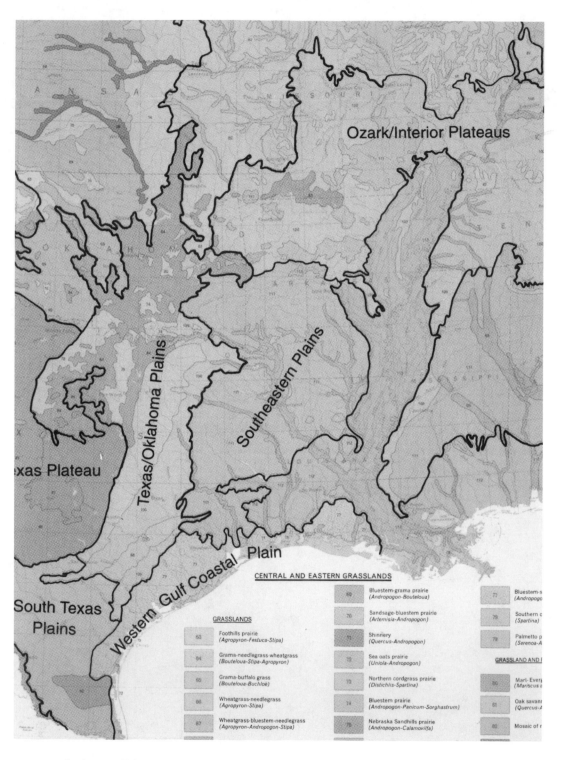

Southeastern Plains

Southeastern Plains

Introduction

The Southeastern Plains region extends from the Pine Barrens in New Jersey, south and east through the Coastal Plain and Piedmont physiographic regions of Virginia, and North and South Carolina, and into the northern half of Georgia, Alabama, Mississippi and Louisiana. The western boundary includes southern Arkansas and east Texas. Excluded from the region are the coastal zones of Georgia, Alabama, and Mississippi which are part of the Southern Coastal Plains region. The majority of the region is the relatively flat coastal plain, and the remaining encompasses the Piedmont, an area of gently rolling hills bordering the Appalachian highlands.

Vegetation is very diverse, ranging from closed canopy forest to shrublands, savannas, grasslands, and many freshwater wetlands. The impact of human activity has caused dramatic changes to the natural communities. The suppression of natural fires has led to changes in the vegetation. The forests throughout the region are presently dominated by shortleaf or longleaf pine. The region was originally dominated by a mixture of oak and hickory, as well as pine. Forested lands converted to agriculture and then abandoned have been reseeded, either intentionally or naturally, with the now dominant pine species. Much of the forest land is intensively managed by wood products industries which make large investments in the establishment and growth of pine timber.

Other natural communities, especially wetlands, have been dramatically changed or reduced in number by drainage and development. Marshes, lakes, and swamps are often associated with the streams that wind gently through the sloping topography of the region. Wetland communities not associated with rivers, or non-alluvial wetlands are Pocosin and Atlantic White-cedar Swamp. Wetlands associated with coastal conditions include Salt Shrub Thicket and Salt Marsh.

The primary sources used to develop descriptions and species lists are: Barbour and Billings 1988; Forman 1979; Martin et al. In press; Nelson 1986; Schafale and Weakley 1990; U.S. Fish and Wildlife Service 1984; Wharton 1989.

Dominant Ecological Communities

Upland Systems
Oak–Hickory–Pine Forest
Southern Mixed Hardwoods Forest
Mesic Pine Forest
Xeric Pine Forest
Pine Barrens
Live Oak Woodland
Blackbelt Prairie

Wetland Systems
Southern Floodplain Forest
Cypress–Tupelo Swamp Forest
Atlantic White-cedar Swamp
Pocosin
Freshwater Marsh

Estuarine Systems
Salt Shrub Thicket
Salt Marsh

UPLAND SYSTEMS

Oak–Hickory–Pine Forest

Oak–Hickory–Pine Forest was originally the most extensive forest type in this region. This forest type occurs throughout the Piedmont and the Southeastern Coastal Plain on slopes, ridges, upland flats, and other dry to dry-mesic sites. The dominant trees are hickories, short-leaf pine, loblolly pine, northern white oak, and post oak. Examples of original oak-hickory-pine are rare because most of the area is now used for agriculture, urban development, or is occupied by pine stands after past agriculture. Examples of the original forest, however, may be found in fragmented areas along rivers or creeks. This community corresponds to Küchler #111.

Canopy

Characteristic Species

Carya alba	mockernut hickory
Carya carolinae-septentrionalis	southern shag-bark hickory
Carya glabra	pignut hickory
Pinus echinata	short-leaf pine
Pinus taeda	loblolly pine
Quercus alba	northern white oak
Quercus coccinea	scarlet oak
Quercus marilandica	blackjack oak
Quercus rubra	northern red oak
Quercus stellata	post oak
Quercus velutina	black oak

Associates

Acer rubrum	red maple
Carya cordiformis	bitter-nut hickory
Carya ovalis	red hickory
Carya ovata	shag-bark hickory
Carya pallida	sand hickory
Diospyros virginiana	common persimmon
Fraxinus americana	white ash
Juglans nigra	black walnut
Liquidambar styraciflua	sweet-gum
Liriodendron tulipifera	tuliptree
Nyssa sylvatica	black tupelo
Persea borbonia	red bay
Pinus strobus	eastern white pine
Pinus virginiana	Virginia pine
Prunus serotina	black cherry
Quercus falcata	southern red oak
Quercus muhlenbergii	chinkapin oak
Quercus shumardii	Shumard's oak

Woody Understory

Acer leucoderme	chalk maple
Aesculus sylvatica	painted buckeye
Amelanchier spp.	service-berry
Asimina parviflora	small-flower pawpaw

Calycanthus floridus	eastern sweetshrub
Carpinus caroliniana	American hornbeam
Cercis canadensis	redbud
Chionanthus virginicus	white fringetree
Cornus florida	flowering dogwood
Evonymus americanus	American strawberry-bush
Hypericum hypericoides	St. Andrew's-cross
Ilex decidua	deciduous holly
Ostrya virginiana	eastern hop-hornbeam
Oxydendron arboreum	sourwood
Rhododendron canescens	mountain azalea
Rhododendron periclymenoides	early azalea
Rhus aromatica	fragrant sumac
Symphoricarpos orbiculatus	coral-berry
Symplocos tinctoria	horsesugar
Toxicodendron pubescens	Atlantic poison-oak
Vaccinium arboreum	tree sparkle-berry
Viburnum acerifolium	maple-leaf arrow-wood
Viburnum prunifolium	smooth blackhaw
Viburnum rafinesquianum	downy arrow-wood
Viburnum rufidulum	rusty blackhaw

Herbaceous Understory

Agrimonia gryposepala	tall hairy grooveburr
Amianthium muscaetoxicum	flypoison
Andropogon virginicus	broom-sedge
Aristolochia serpentaria	Virginia-snakeroot
Aster dumosus	rice button aster
Aster paternus	toothed white-top aster
Aster solidagineus	narrow-leaf white-top aster
Aureolaria flava	smooth yellow false-foxglove
Carex albicans	white-tinge sedge
Carex nigromarginata	black-edge sedge
Chimaphila maculata	striped prince's-pine
Chrysopsis mariana	Maryland golden-aster
Coreopsis major	greater tickseed
Cunila marima	common dittany
Cypripedium acaule	pink lady's-slipper
Desmodium laevigatum	smooth tick-trefoil
Desmodium nudiflorum	naked-flower tick-trefoil
Desmodium obtusum	stiff tick-trefoil
Desmodium perplexum	perplexed tick-trefoil
Desmodium rotundifolium	prostrate tick-trefoil
Dichanthelium sphaerocarpon	round-seed rosette grass
Elephantopus spp.	elephant's foot
Euphorbia corollata	flowering spurge
Galium circaezans	licorice bedstraw
Galium pilosum	hairy bedstraw
Goodyera pubescens	downy rattlesnake-plantain

Hexastylis arifolia	little-brown-jug
Hexastylis virginica	Virginia heartleaf
Hieracium gronovii	queendevil
Hieracium venosum	rattlesnake-weed
Lespedeza repens	creeping bush-clover
Panicum spp.	panic grass
Phryma leptostachya	American lopseed
Piptochaetium avenaceum	black-seed spear grass
Polygonatum biflorum	King Solomon's-seal
Pycnanthemum flexuosum	Appalachian mountain-mint
Rhynchosia tomentosa	twining snout-bean
Scleria oligantha	little-head nut-rush
Solidago nemoralis	gray goldenrod
Strophostyles umbellata	pink fuzzy-bean
Stylosanthes bilflora	side-beak pencil-flower
Tephrosia virginiana	goat's-rue
Tipularia discolor	crippled-cranefly
Trillium catsbaei	bashful wakerobin
Uvularia perifoliata	perfoliate bellwort
Uvularia sessilifolia	sessile-leaf bellwort

Southern Mixed Hardwoods Forest

Southern Mixed Hardwoods Forest is restricted to coves and gorges in this region. American beech, northern white oak, red maple, and sweet-gum are the dominant species. Southern Mixed Hardwoods Forest is more mesic than Oak–Hickory–Pine Forest, yet it is distinct from forests along river bottomlands. Small remnant old-growth stands can be found on slopes, islands in swamps, and on a few upland flats. This community corresponds to Küchler #112.

Canopy
Characteristic Species

Acer rubrum	red maple
Acer saccharum	sugar maple
Carya cordiformis	bitter-nut hickory
Carya pallida	sand hickory
Fagus grandifolia	American beech
Juglans nigra	black walnut
Liquidambar styraciflua	sweet-gum
Liriodendron tulipifera	tuliptree
Quercus alba	northern white oak
Quercus pagoda	cherry-bark oak
Quercus michauxii	swamp chestnut oak
Quercus rubra	northern red oak
Quercus shumardii	Shumard's oak
Ulmus americana	American elm
Ulmus rubra	slippery elm

Associates

Acer barbatum	Florida maple
Carya alba	mockernut hickory
Carya glabra	pignut hickory

Celtis laevigata	sugar-berry
Juglans nigra	black walnut
Liquidambar styraciflua	sweet-gum
Magnolia grandiflora	southern magnolia
Magnolia tripetala	umbrella magnolia
Persea borbonia	red bay
Pinus echinata	short-leaf pine
Pinus elliottii	slash pine
Pinus palustris	long-leaf pine
Pinus taeda	loblolly pine
Populus heterophylla	swamp cottonwood
Quercus falcata	southern red oak
Quercus incana	bluejack oak
Quercus laevis	turkey oak
Quercus laurifolia	laurel oak
Quercus marilandica	blackjack oak
Quercus stellata	post oak
Quercus virginiana	live oak
Tilia americana	American basswood

Woody Understory

Acer negundo	ash-leaf maple
Aesculus pavia	red buckeye
Aesculus sylvatica	painted buckeye
Asimina parviflora	small-flower pawpaw
Asimina triloba	common pawpaw
Calycanthus floridus	eastern sweetshrub
Carpinus caroliniana	American hornbeam
Cercis canadensis	redbud
Cornus florida	flowering dogwood
Evonymus americanus	American strawberry-bush
Evonymus atropurpurea	eastern wahoo
Hamamelis virginiana	Amercian witch-hazel
Hydrangea arborescens	wild hydrangea
Ilex glabra	inkberry
Ilex opaca	American holly
Lindera benzoin	northern spicebush
Menispermum canadense	Canadian moonseed
Myrica cerifera	southern bayberry
Ostrya virginiana	eastern hop-hornbeam
Philadelphus inodorus	scentless mock orange
Sabal palmetto	cabbage palmetto
Staphylea trifolia	American bladdernut
Stewartia malacodendron	silky-camellia
Styrax grandifolia	big-leaf snowbell
Symplocos tinctoria	horsesugar
Viburnum rufidulum	rusty blackhaw

Herbaceous Understory

Actaea pachypoda	white baneberry
Adiantum pedatum	northern maidenhair
Anemone virginiana	tall thimbleweed
Asarum canadense	Canadian wild ginger
Aureolaria flava	smooth yellow false-foxglove
Campanulastrum americana	American-bellflower
Cimicifuga racemosa	black bugbane
Corydalis flavula	yellow fumewort
Cypripedium pubescens	greater yellow lady's-slipper
Delphinium tricorne	dwarf larkspur
Dicentra cucullaria	Dutchman's-breeches
Enemion biternatum	eastern false rue-anemone
Epifagus virginiana	beechdrops
Hepatica nobilis	liverwort
Heuchera americana	American alumroot
Hybanthus concolor	eastern green-violet
Lathyrus venosus	veiny vetchling
Mitchella repens	partridge-berry
Panax quinquefolius	American ginseng
Podophyllum peltatum	may-apple
Polystichum acrostichoides	Christmas fern
Sanguinaria canadensis	bloodroot
Scutellaria ovata	heart-leaf skullcap
Silene stellata	widow's frill
Thaspium trifoliatum	purple meadow-parsnip
Tiarella cordifolia	heart-leaf foamflower
Tipularia discolor	crippled-cranefly
Trillium cuneatum	little-sweet-Betsy
Trillium erectum	stinking-Benjamin

Mesic Pine Forest

In the coastal plain, Mesic Pine Forest may occur on flat or rolling land. These forests are often referred to as "Flatwoods." In recent years the suppression of fire has led to changes in community structure as hardwood species invade and share dominance. The pine forests of the region are divided into mesic and xeric categories. These two types share many of the same species. The Mesic Pine Forest has a denser and more diverse herbaceous layer than the Xeric Pine Forest.

Canopy

Characteristic Species

Pinus echinata	short-leaf pine
Pinus palustris	long-leaf pine
Pinus taeda	loblolly pine

Associates

Carya alba	mockernut hickory
Carya pallida	sand hickory
Gordonia lasianthus	loblolly-bay

Liquidambar styraciflua	sweet-gum
Magnolia virginiana	sweet-bay
Quercus falcata	southern red oak
Quercus incana	bluejack oak
Quercus laurifolia	laurel oak
Quercus marilandica	blackjack oak
Quercus nigra	water oak
Quercus stellata	post oak

Woody Understory

Cyrilla racemiflora	swamp titi
Ilex coriacea	large gallberry
Ilex glabra	inkberry
Kalmia hirsuta	hairy-laurel
Myrica cerifera	southern wax-myrtle
Myrica inodora	odorless wax-myrtle
Vaccinium tenellum	small black blueberry
Viburnum nudum	possumhaw

Herbaceous Understory

Andropogon gerardii	big bluestem
Anthaenantia villosa	green silkyscale
Aristida stricta	pineland three-awn
Aster paludosus	southen swamp aster
Aster tortifolius	dixie white-top aster
Aster walteri	Walter's aster
Chaptalia tomentosa	woolly sunbonnets
Dalea pinnata	summer-farewell
Elephantopus carolinianus	Carolina elephant's-foot
Gymnopogon brevifolium	short-leaf skeleton grass
Helianthus angustifolius	swamp sunflower
Helianthus radula	rayless sunflower
Lespedeza capitata	round-head bush-clover
Panicum virgatum	wand panic grass
Paspalum bifidum	pitchfork crown grass
Pteridium aquilinum	northern bracken fern
Pterocaulon virgatum	wand blackroot
Schizachyrium scoparium	little false bluestem
Solidago odora	anise-scented goldenrod
Sorghastrum nutans	yellow Indian grass
Tephrosia spicata	spiked hoary-pea
Tephrosia virginica	goat's-rue

Xeric Pine Forest

Xeric Pine Forest is the driest community in the Southeastern Plains region. This community is often dominated by longleaf pine, turkey oak, and pineland three-awn (wiregrass). These xeric areas have been classified as "Sandhill Pine Forest," "Sandhill Pine Scrub," and "Xeric Sandhill Scrub." Xeric Pine Forests naturally experience frequent fires.

Canopy
Characteristic Species
    Pinus palustris   long-leaf pine
    Quercus laevis   turkey oak
Associate Species
    Diospyros virginiana   common persimmon
    Liquidamber styraciflua   sweet-gum
    Nyssa sylvatica   black tupelo
    Pinus echinata   short-leaf pine
    Pinus taeda   loblolly pine
    Quercus incana   bluejack oak
    Quercus marilandica   blackjack oak

Woody Understory
    Ceratiola ericoides   sand-heath
    Cornus florida   flowering dogwood
    Gaylussacia dumosa   dwarf huckleberry
    Gaylussacia frondosa   blue huckleberry
    Ilex vomitoria   yaupon
    Licania michauxii   gopher-apple
    Lyonia mariana   Piedmont staggerbush
    Opuntia humifusa   eastern prickly-pear
    Quercus margarettiae   sand post oak
    Quercus pumila   runner oak
    Sassafras albidum   sassafras
    Toxicodendron pubescens   Atlantic poison-oak

Herbaceous Understory
    Aristida stricta   pineland three-awn
    Baptisia lanceolata   gopherweed
    Chrysopsis gossypina   cottony golden-aster
    Cnidoscolus stimulosus   ginger-rot
    Dicranum condensatum   sandhill broom-moss
    Dicranum spurium   broom moss
    Eupatorium rotundifolium   round-leaf thoroughwort
    Euphorbia ipecacuanhae   American-ipecac
    Minuartia caroliniana   pine-barren stitchwort
    Pluchea rosea   rosy camphorweed
    Polygonella polygama   October-flower
    Rudebeckia hirta   black-eyed-Susan
    Schizachyrium scoparium   little false bluestem
    Selaginella arenicola   sand spike-moss
    Stillingia sylvatica   queen's-delight
    Stipulicida setacea   pineland scaly-pink
    Stylosanthes biflora   side-beak pencil-flower
    Tephrosia virginiana   goat's rue

Pine Barrens

Pine Barrens is a dwarf forest dominated by pitch pine (*Pinus rigida*). This forest type occurs north of the Delaware Bay 100-200 feet above sea level in gently rolling terrain. The largest and most uniform pine barrens community occurs in New Jersey and covers nearly one and a half million acres. Fires are an important factor in maintaining the structure and composition of Pine Barrens. Toward the south Pine Barrens is replaced by Live Oak Woodland. This community corresponds to Küchler #110.

Canopy
Characteristic Species
Pinus rigida	pitch pine

Associates
Pinus echinata	short-leaf pine
Quercus coccinea	scarlet oak
Quercus marilandica	blackjack oak
Quercus prinus	chestnut oak
Quercus stellata	post oak
Quercus velutina	black oak

Woody Understory
Arctostaphylos uva-ursi	red bearberry
Clethra alnifolia	coastal sweet-pepperbush
Comptonia peregrina	sweet-fern
Corema conradii	broom-crowberry
Epigaea repens	trailing-arbutus
Gaultheria procumbens	eastern teaberry
Gaylussacia baccata	black huckleberry
Gaylussacia dumosa	dwarf huckleberry
Gaylussacia frondosa	blue huckleberry
Ilex glabra	inkberry
Kalmia angustifolia	sheep-laurel
Kalmia latifolia	mountain-laurel
Leiophyllum buxifolium	sand-myrtle
Quercus ilicifolia	bear oak

Herbaceous Understory
Andropogon virginicus	broom-sedge
Cladonia atlantica	lichen
Cladonia caroliniana	lichen
Cladonia cristatella	lichen
Cladonia squamosa	lichen
Aureolaria pedicularia	fern-leaf yellow false-foxglove
Scleria triglomerata	whip nut-rush

Live Oak Woodland

Live Oak Woodland is associated with maritime conditions and is often referred to as "maritime forests." Live oak communities occur on the Barrier Islands and along the coast. Frequently live oaks grow on old stabilized dunes and flats, protected from salt water and flooding and the most extreme salt spray. The trees are characterized by their asymmetric growth resulting from a combination of wind and salt spray. Sea-oats are important in the Live Oak Woodland due to their role in stabilizing the dunes. This community corresponds to Küchler #90.

Canopy
Characteristic Species
Pinus elliottii	slash pine
Quercus virginiana	live oak
Sabal palmetto	cabbage palmetto

Associates
Carya glabra	pignut hickory
Pinus palustris	long-leaf pine
Pinus taeda	loblolly pine
Quercus falcata	southern red oak
Quercus hemisphaerica	Darlington's oak
Quercus laevis	turkey oak
Quercus laurifolia	laurel oak
Quercus nigra	water oak

Woody Understory
Ampelopsis arborea	peppervine
Baccharis halimifolia	groundseltree
Berchemia scandens	Alabama supplejack
Bignonia capreolata	crossvine
Callicarpa americana	American beauty-bush
Campsis radicans	trumpet-creeper
Carpinus caroliniana	Amerian hornbeam
Cornus florida	flowering dogwood
Gelsemium sempervirens	evening trumpet-flower
Hamamelis virginiana	American witch-hazel
Ilex opaca	American holly
Ilex vomitoria	yaupon
Iva frutescens	jesuit's-bark
Iva imbricata	seacoast marsh-elder
Juniperus virginiana	eastern red-cedar
Lyonia ferruginea	rusty staggerbush
Magnolia virginiana	sweet-bay
Myrica cerifera	southern wax-myrtle
Myrica pensylvanica	northern bayberry
Opuntia humifusa	eastern prickly-pear
Osmanthus americana	devilwood
Parthenocissus quinquefolia	Virginia-creeper
Persea borbonia	red bay
Prunus caroliniana	Carolina laurel cherry
Rhus copallinum	winged sumac

Sabal minor	dwarf palmetto
Sassafras albidum	sassafras
Serenoa repens	saw-palmetto
Smilax bona-nox	fringed greenbrier
Toxicodendron radicans	eastern poison-ivy
Vitis rotundifolia	muscadine
Yucca aloifolia	aloe yucca
Yucca filamentosa	Adam's-needle
Zanthoxylum clava-herculis	Hercules'-club

Herbaceous Understory

Ammophila breviligulata	American beach grass
Andropogon virginicus	broom-sedge
Asplenium platyneuron	ebony spleenwort
Cakile edentula	American searocket
Cenchrus tribuloides	sand-dune sandburr
Chamaesyce bombensis	dixie sandmat
Chamaesyce polygonifolia	seaside spurge
Chasmanthium laxum	slender wood-oats
Cnidoscolus stimulosus	finger-rot
Conyza canadensis	Canadian horseweed
Croton punctatus	gulf croton
Dichanthelium commutatum	variable rosette grass
Diodia teres	poor-joe
Elephantopus nudatus	smooth elephant's-foot
Eustrachys petraea	pinewoods finger grass
Galium pilosum	hairy bedstraw
Houstonia procumbens	round-leaf bluet
Hydrocotyle bonariensis	coastal marsh-pennywort
Juncus roemerianus	Roemer's rush
Kostleltskya virginica	Virginia fen-rose
Mitchella repens	partridge-berry
Oenothera humifusa	seaside evening-primrose
Panicum amarum	bitter panic grass
Passiflora incarnata	purple passion-flower
Passiflora lutea	yellow passion-flower
Physalis walteri	Walter's ground-cherry
Piptochaetium avenaceum	black-seed spear grass
Schizachyrium scoparium	little false bluestem
Scleria triglomerata	whip nut-rush
Spartina alternifolia	salt water cord grass
Spartina patens	salt-meadow cord grass
Stenotaphrum secundatum	St. Augustine grass
Strophostyles helvula	trailing fuzzy-bean
Triplasis purpurea	purple sand grass
Uniola paniculata	sea-oats

Blackbelt Prairie

The Blackbelt region of Alabama and Mississippi has been converted to agriculture. The natural vegetation was probably a prairie and oak savanna mosaic. Küchler (#89) calls the Blackbelt a *Liquidamber-Quercus-Juniperus* community. It is likely that the control of fire and eradication of grazing animals resulted in succession of the prairie to forest vegetation.

Characteristic Species

Andropogon gerardii	big bluestem
Andropogon virginicus	broom-sedge
Aristida purpurescens	arrow-feather three-awn
Aster dumosus	rice button aster
Aster patens	late purple aster
Aster pilosus	white oldfield aster
Chamaecrista fasciculata	sleepingplant
Dalea purpurea	violet prairie-clover
Echinacea purpurea	eastern purple-coneflower
Eupatorium altissimum	tall thoroughwort
Galactia volubilis	downy milk-pea
Gymnopogon brevifolius	short-leaf skeleton grass
Monarda fistulosa	Oswego-tea
Panicum anceps	beaked panic grass
Ratibita pinnata	gray-head Mexican-hat
Rudbeckia fulgida	orange coneflower
Sabatia angularis	rose-pink
Salvia lyrata	lyre-leaf sage
Schizachyrium scopraium	little false bluestem
Silphium asteriscus	starry rosinweed
Silphium laciniatum	compassplant
Sporobolus asper	tall dropseed
Sporobolus vaginiflorus	poverty dropseed
Tragia urticifolia	nettle-leaf noseburn
Tridens flavus	tall redtop

Associates

Asclepias verticillata	whorled milkweed
Aster undulatus	waxy-leaf aster
Bouteloua curtipendula	side-oats grama
Desmodium ciliare	hairy small-leaf tick-trefoil
Erigeron strigosus	prairie fleabane
Euphorbia corollata	flowering spurge
Gaillardia aestivalis	lance-leaf blanket-flower
Lobelia spicata	pale-spike lobelia
Panicum virgatum	wand panic grass
Pycnanthemum tenuifolium	narrow-leaf mountain-mint

WETLAND SYSTEMS
Southern Floodplain Forest

Southern Floodplain Forest occurs throughout the Coastal Plain along large and medium size rivers. There are many "zones" associated with floodplains based on the length of time the soils are saturated. The dominants and associates in floodplain areas are determined in large part by the degree of moisture. The zone that encompasses the greatest area is saturated during the winter and spring which accounts for 20 to 30 percent of the year. In these areas laurel oak is the dominant tree species. Willow oak, sweet-gum, green ash, and tuliptree may accompany laurel oak as a characteristic species. In higher areas swamp chestnut oak and cherry-bark oak will be dominant and in lower areas southern bald-cypress, water tupelo, and swamp tupelo are characteristic. This community corresponds to Küchler #113.

Canopy
Characteristic Species

Carya aquatica	water hickory
Carya cordiformis	bitter-nut hickory
Carya ovata	shag-bark hickory
Fraxinus pennsylvanica	green ash
Juglans nigra	black walnut
Liquidambar styraciflua	sweet-gum
Liriodendron tulipifera	tuliptree
Pinus taeda	loblolly pine
Quercus laurifolia	laurel oak
Quercus lyrata	overcup oak
Quercus michauxii	swamp chestnut oak
Quercus phellos	willow oak

Associates

Acer rubrum	red maple
Betula nigra	river birch
Celtis laevigata	sugar-berry
Chamaecyparis thyoides	Atlantic white-cedar
Fraxinus americana	white ash
Fraxinus caroliniana	Carolina ash
Fraxinus profunda	pumpkin ash
Gleditsia aquatica	water-locust
Nyssa aquatica	water tupelo
Nyssa biflora	swamp tupelo
Nyssa sylvatica	black tupelo
Plantanus occidentalis	American sycamore
Populus deltoides	eastern cottonwood
Populus heterophylla	swamp cottonwood
Quercus falcata	southern red oak
Quercus nigra	water oak
Quercus pagoda	cherry-bark oak
Quercus shumardii	Shumard's oak
Taxodium distichum	southern bald-cypress
Ulmus alata	winged elm
Ulmus americana	American elm

Woody Understory

Acer negundo	ash-leaf maple
Alnus serrulata	brookside alder
Ampelopsis arborea	peppervine
Arundinaria gigantea	giant cane
Asimina triloba	common pawpaw
Berchemia scandens	Alabama supplejack
Bignonia capreolata	crossvine
Campsis radicans	trumpet-creeper
Carpinus carolinianus	American hornbeam
Cephalanthus occidentalis	common buttonbush
Clematis virginiana	devil's-darning-needles
Clethra alnifolia	coastal sweet-pepperbush
Cornus foemina	stiff dogwood
Cyrilla racemiflora	swamp titi
Evonymous americanus	American strawberry-bush
Ilex decidua	deciduos holly
Ilex opaca	American holly
Itea virginica	Virginia sweetspire
Lindera benzoin	northern spicebush
Lyonia ligustrinia	maleberry
Magnolia virginiana	sweet-bay
Parthenocissus quinquefolia	Virginia-creeper
Persea borbonia	red bay
Persea palustis	swamp bay
Planera aquatica	planertree
Salix nigra	black willow
Smilax rotundifolia	horsebrier
Staphylea trifolia	American bladdernut
Toxicodendron pubescens	Atlantic poison-oak
Toxicodendron radicans	eastern poison-ivy
Vaccinium elliottii	Elliott's blueberry
Vaccinium stamineum	deerberry
Viburnum acerifolium	maple-leaf arrow-wood
Viburnum dentatum	southern arrow-wood
Viburnum prunifolium	smooth blackhaw
Vitis aestivalis	summer grape
Vitis rotundifolia	muscadine

Herbaceous Understory

Arisaema draconteum	greendragon
Asclepias perennis	Aquatic milkweed
Asplenium platyneuron	ebony spleenwort
Aster lateriflorus	farewell-summer
Boehmeria cylindrica	small-spike false nettle
Cayaponia quinqueloba	five-lobe-cucumber
Chasmanthium latifolium	Indian wood-oats
Chasmanthium laxum	slender wood-oats
Commelina virginica	Virginia dayflower

Dioscorea villosa	wild yam
Galium aparine	sticky-willy
Hymenocallis caroliniana	Carolina spider-lily
Leersia lenticularis	catchfly grass
Lysimachia quadrifolia	whorled yellow-loosestrife
Matelea gonocarpos	angular-fruit milkvine
Onoclea sensibilis	sensitive fern
Osmunda cinnamomea	cinnamon fern
Osmunda regalis	royal fern
Oxalis violacea	violet wood-sorrel
Pilea pumila	Canadian clearweed
Polygonum virginianum	jumpseed
Senecio glabellus	cress-leaf ragwort
Spiranthes cernua	white nodding ladies'-tresses
Thelypteris palustris	eastern marsh fern
Tradescantia virginiana	Virginia spiderwort
Viola affinis	sand violet
Viola lanceolata	bog white violet
Woodwardia areolata	netted chain fern
Woodwardia virginica	Virginia chain fern
Zepharanthes atamasco	atamasco-lily

Cypress–Tupelo Swamp Forest

Cypress–Tupelo Swamp Forest occurs in the lowest and wettest parts of floodplains. Southern bald-cypress is the most typical tree species of this habitat. A unique feature of the bald-cypress and tupelo are their buttressed bases and "cypress knees". Water tupelo is most common where water is relatively deep and inundation periods are long. In shallower, less frequently inundated areas swamp tupelo is abundant. This community corresponds, in part, to Küchler #113.

Canopy
Characteristic Species

Nyssa aquatica	water tupelo
Nyssa biflora	swamp tupelo
Taxodium ascendens	pond-cypress
Taxodium distichum	southern bald-cypress

Associates

Acer rubrum	red maple
Chamaecyparis thyoides	Atlantic white-cedar
Carya aquatica	water hickory
Fraxinus carolinana	Carolina ash
Fraxinus profunda	pumpkin ash
Pinus serotina	pond pine
Pinus taeda	loblolly pine
Populus heterophylla	swamp cottonwood
Quercus nigra	water oak
Salix nigra	black willow

Woody Understory

Berchemia scandens	Alabama supplejack
Brunnichia ovata	American buckwheatvine
Campsis radicans	trumpet-creeper
Cephalanthus occidentalis	common buttonbush
Clethra alnifolia	coastal sweet-pepperbush
Crataegus marshallii	parsley hawthorn
Cyrilla racemiflora	swamp titi
Forestiera acuminata	eastern swamp-privit
Gaylussacia frondosa	blue huckleberry
Gordonia lasianthus	loblolly-bay
Ilex coriacea	large gallberry
Ilex decidua	deciduos holly
Ilex glabra	inkberry
Lyonia ligustrina	maleberry
Lyonia lucida	shinyleaf
Magnolia virginiana	sweet-bay
Myrica cerifera	southern wax-myrtle
Myrica heterophylla	evergreen bayberry
Persea borbonia	red bay
Persea palustris	swamp bay
Planera aquatica	planertree

Herbaceous Understory

Azolla caroliniana	Carolina mosquito fern
Boehmeria cylindrica	small-spike false nettle
Carex gigantea	giant sedge
Centella asiatica	spadeleaf
Drosera capillaris	pink sundew
Dulichium arundinaceum	three-way sedge
Hydrocotyle verticillata	whorled marsh-pennywort
Lemna minor	common duckweed
Mayaca fluviatilis	stream bog-moss
Mikania scandens	climbing hempvine
Mitchella repens	partridge-berry
Peltandra virginica	green arrow-arum
Polygonum punctatum	dotted smartweed
Sarracenia flava	yellow pitcherplant
Sarracenia rubra	sweet pitcherplant
Saururus cernuus	lizard's-tail
Sphagnum spp.	moss
Utricularia subulata	zigzag bladderwort
Woodwardia areolata	netted chain fern

Atlantic White-cedar Swamp

White-cedar dominated swamp forests occur on deep peats often over sandy substrates. This community type ranges from New England to northern Florida. Atlantic White-cedar Swamp usually occurs in large, even stands due to uniform regeneration following a fire. Extensive stands are found in the New Jersey Pine Barrens and the lower terraces of the North Carolina and Virginia coastal plains.

Canopy
Characteristic Species

Chamaecyparis thyoides	Atlantic white-cedar

Associates

Acer rubrum	red maple
Nyssa biflora	swamp tupelo
Pinus serotina	pond pine
Pinus taeda	loblolly pine
Taxodium ascendens	pond-cypress

Woody Understory

Cyrilla racemiflora	swamp titi
Gaylussacia frondosa	blue huckleberry
Gordonia lasianthus	loblolly-bay
Ilex coriacea	large gallberry
Ilex glabra	inkberry
Lyonia ligustrina	maleberry
Lyonia lucida	shinyleaf
Magnolia virginiana	sweet-bay
Myrica cerifera	southern wax-myrtle
Myrica heterophylla	evergreen bayberry
Persea borbonia	red bay
Persea palustris	swamp bay

Herbaceous Understory

Drosera capillaris	pink sundew
Mayaca fluviatilis	stream bog-moss
Mitchella repens	partridge-berry
Peltandra virginica	green arrow-arum
Sarracenia flava	yellow pitcherplant
Sarracenia rubra	sweet pitcherplant
Sphagnum spp.	moss
Woodwardia areolata	netted chain fern

Pocosin

Shrub dominated wetlands or pocosins are common features of the Coastal Plain. These peatlands are dominated by a dense, nearly impenetrable cover of evergreen and deciduous shrubs usually between three and nine feet tall. Scattered emergent trees, especially loblolly-bay, sweet-bay and red bay may invade a pocosin and become a "Bay forest". Pocosins are often divided into three types: low, medium, and high pocosins depending on the percentage of shrub and tree cover. Pocosins are seasonally flooded or saturated, and extremely nutrient poor with nutrient input only from rainfall. Severe fires may occur periodically in pocosins. This community corresponds to Küchler #114.

Characteristic Woody Species

Aronia arbutifolia	red chokeberry
Chamaedaphne calyculata	leatherleaf
Clethra alnifolium	summer sweet clethra
Cyrilla racemiflora	swamp titi

Ilex coriacea	large gallberry
Ilex glabra	inkberry
Leucothoe racemosa	swamp doghobble
Lyonia lucida	shinyleaf
Myrica cerifera	southern wax-myrtle
Persea borbonia	red bay
Pinus serotina	pond pine
Rhododendron viscosum	clammy azalea
Smilax laurifolia	laurel-leaf greenbrier
Vaccinium corymbosum	highbush blueberry
Vaccinium fuscatum	black blueberry
Zenobia pulverulenta	honeycup

Associates

Acer rubrum	red maple
Gordonia lasianthus	loblolly-bay
Liquidambar styraciflua	sweet-gum
Magnolia virginiana	sweet-bay
Persea palustris	swamp bay
Pinus palustris	long-leaf pine
Vaccinium macrocarpon	large cranberry

Herbaceous Understory

Andropogon glomeratus	bushy bluestem
Carex stricta	uptight sedge
Sarracenia flava	yellow pitcherplant
Sphagnum spp.	moss
Woodwardia virginica	Virginian chain fern

Freshwater Marsh

Freshwater Marsh is located upstream from Salt Marsh and downstream from nontidal freshwater wetlands. It is characterized by near freshwater conditions, with the average salinity of 0.5 parts per trillion or below except during periods of drought. Chesapeake Bay and the South Carolina coast have many freshwater marshes. Off the coast of North Carolina swamps are more common than freshwater marshes. The characteristic vegetation of freshwater marshes consists of rushes, sedges, grasses, and cattails. Many of the marshes and associated swamps were diked, impounded, and converted to rice fields during the 18th and 19th centuries. Many of these impoundments remain intact and provide habitat for waterfowl.

Characteristic Species

Carex stricta	uptight sedge
Centella asiatica	spadeleaf
Cladium mariscus	swamp saw-grass
Eleocharis fallax	creeping spike-rush
Eleocharis rosetellata	beaked spike-rush
Fuirena squarrosa	hairy umbrella sedge
Impatiens capensis	spotted touch-me-not
Iris virginica	Virginia blueflag
Kosteletzkya virginica	Virginia fen-rose
Lachnanthes carolina	Carolina redroot

Lemna perpusilla	minute duckweed
Limnobium spongia	American spongeplant
Ludwigia palustris	marsh primrose-willow
Lythrum alatum	wing-angle loosestrife
Myriophyllum aquaticum	parrot's feather
Myriophyllum heterophyllum	two-leaf water-milfoil
Nuphar lutea	yellow pond-lily
Nymphoides cordata	little floatingheart
Orontium aquaticum	goldenclub
Osmunda regalis	royal fern
Panicum hemitomon	maiden-cane
Peltandra virginica	green arrow-arum
Phragmites australis	common reed
Pontederia cordata	pickerelweed
Sagittaria graminea	grass-leaf arrowhead
Sagittaria latifolia	duck-potato
Saururus cernuus	lizard's-tail
Scirpus americanus	chairmaker's bulrush
Scirpus cyperinus	cottongrass bulrush
Scirpus robustus	seaside bulrush
Sium suave	hemlock water-parsnip
Sparganium americanum	American burr-reed
Spartina cynosuroides	big cord grass
Typha angustifolia	narrow-leaf cat-tail
Typha domingensis	southern cat-tail
Typha latifolia	broad-leaf cat-tail
Zizania aquatica	Indian wild rice
Zizaniopsis miliacea	marsh-millet

Associates

Asclepias incarnata	swamp milkweed
Boltonia asteroides	white doll's-daisy
Carex alata	broad-wing sedge
Cicuta maculata	spotted water-hemlock
Echinochloa crus-galli	large barnyard grass
Echinochloa walteri	long-awn cock's-spur grass
Eleocharis albida	white spike-rush
Eleocharis flavescens	yellow spike-rush
Hibiscus moscheutos	crimson-eyed rose-mallow
Hydrocotyle umbellata	many-flower marsh-pennywort
Lythrum lineare	saltmarsh loosestrife
Myrica cerifera	southern bayberry
Phragmites australis	common reed
Physostegia virginiana	obedient-plant
Pluchea foetida	stinking camphorweed
Rhynchospora corniculata	short-bristle horned beak rush
Saccharum giganteum	giant plume grass
Scirpus tabernaemontani	soft-stem bulrush
Setaria magna	giant bristle grass
Taxodium distichum	southern bald-cypress
Thelypteris palustris	eastern marsh fern

ESTUARINE SYSTEMS

Salt Shrub Thicket

Salt Shrub Thicket occurs in the high areas of salt marshes. These communities are especially common on the barrier islands. Nutrients in these communities are primarily provided by salt or brackish water as well as salt spray. Periodic salt water flooding prevents invasion by trees and other shrubs. Fire, overwash, and sand deposition may play a role in community composition.

Characteristic Species
Baccharis angustifolia	saltwater false willow
Baccharis glomeruliflora	silverling
Baccharis halimifoila	groundseltree
Borrichia frutescens	bushy seaside-tansy
Myrica cerifera	southern wax-myrtle

Associates
Cynanchum angustifolium	Gulf coast swallow-wort
Iva frutescens	jesuit's-bark
Juncus roemerianus	Roemer's rush
Juniperus virginiana	eastern red cedar
Solidago sempervirens	seaside goldenrod
Spartina patens	salt-meadow cord grass

Salt Marsh

Salt Marsh occurs along the margins of sounds and estuaries, along the backs of barrier islands, and near closed inlets with regular salt water tides. These areas are regularly flooded and dominated by salt-tolerant grasses. Saltwater cord grass (smooth cord grass) is the most common characteristic species. Marshes dominated by cord grass are perhaps the most widely known estuarine community. This community corresponds to Küchler #73.

Characteristic Species
Distichlis spicata	coastal salt grass
Juncus roemerianus	Roemer's rush
Spartina alterniflora	saltwater cord grass
Spartina patens	salt-meadow cord grass

Associates
Agalinis maritima	gerardia
Borrichia frutescens	bushy seaside-tansy
Juncus gerardii	saltmarsh rush
Limonium carolinianum	Carolina sea-lavender
Plantago decipiens	seaside plantain
Salicornia virginica	woody saltwort
Triglochin maritimum	seaside arrow-grass

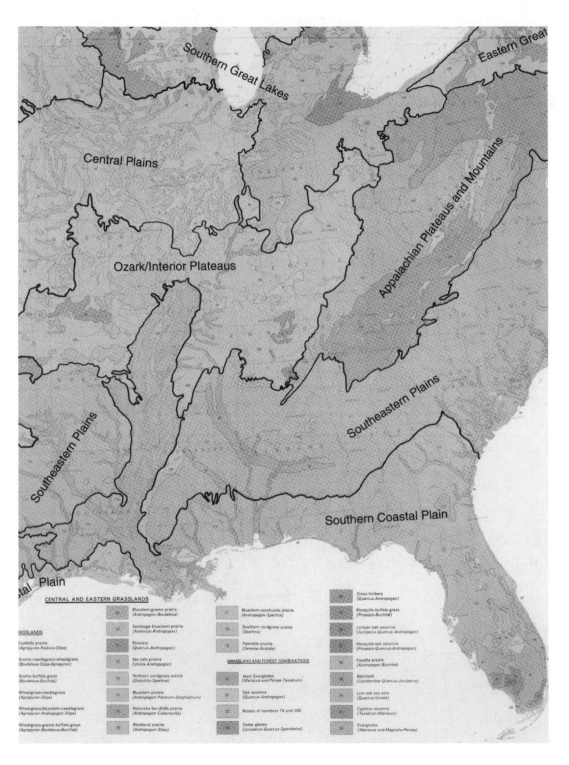

Southern Coastal Plain

Southern Coastal Plain

Introduction

This region occupies Florida, the southern portions of Georgia, Alabama, and Mississippi, and includes the Mississippi River Alluvial Plain from Lousiana north to extreme southern Illinois. It is underlain by limestone or alluvium, has sandy soils, and a low elevation. Fire and water have played a major role in plant community development in this region. Soils range from those with extensive organic development to soils with no organic content. The water regimes and natural flows, especially in Florida, have been highly altered by development. Extensive wetland areas have been drained and developed for agriculture and other purposes.

The vegetation ranges from dry pine dominated communities to swamp forests and wet prairies. This range of community types can sometimes occur over a small area. There are also extensive areas of certain communities, such as the Sawgrass Marsh of the Everglades. The vegetation of south Florida has a strong tropical influence. Several communities are only found south of Lake Okeechobee. In some cases community types occur throughout the region, but have some distinctive plant species in the southern tip of Florida and the Keys.

The primary sources used to develop descriptions and species lists are: Barbour and Billings 1988; Florida Natural Areas Inventory and Department of Natural Resources (no date); Martin et al. In press; Myers and Ewel 1990; Deborah White (pers. com.).

Dominant Ecological Communities

Upland Systems
Southern Mixed Hardwoods Forest
Rockland Hammock
Maritime Hammock
Sandhill
Pine Flatwoods
Pine Rockland
Scrub
Dry Prairie
Beach Dune

Wetland Systems
Southern Swamp Forest
Baygall Forest
Dome Swamp Forest
Floodplain Marsh
Coastal Grassland
Sawgrass Marsh
Marl Prairie
Wet Prairie
Upland Marsh (Basin/Depression Marshes)

Estuarine Systems
Mangrove
Salt Marsh

UPLAND SYSTEMS
Southern Mixed Hardwoods Forest

These forests are sometimes called hammocks. They are closed canopy forests in ravines, on slopes and upland rolling hills. A wide variety of species occur in these mesic forests with topography, moisture, and other abiotic factors determining species composition on a particular site. Species with northern affinities drop out on a southern gradient and are generally absent in peninsular Florida. This community corresponds to Küchler #111 and #112.

Canopy
Characteristic Species
Carya glabra	pignut hickory
Fagus grandifolia	American beech
Liquidambar styraciflua	sweet-gum
Magnolia grandiflora	southern magnolia
Morus rubra	red mulberry
Oxydendrum arboreum	sourwood
Persea borbonia	red bay
Pinus glabra	spruce pine
Pinus taeda	loblolly pine
Prunus caroliniana	Carolina laurel cherry
Quercus hemisphaerica	Darlington's oak
Quercus michauxii	swamp chestnut oak
Quercus nigra	water oak
Quercus virginiana	live oak

Associates
Carya pallida	sand hickory
Celtis laevigata	sugar-berry
Diospyros virginiana	common persimmon
Fraxinus americana	white ash
Liriodendron tulipifera	tuliptree
Magnolia pyramidata	pyramid magnolia
Quercus alba	northern white oak
Quercus austrina	bluff oak
Tilia americana	American basswood
Ulmus alata	winged elm
Ulmus americana	American elm

Woody Understory
Acer barbatum	Florida maple
Aralia spinosa	devil's-walkingstick
Callicarpa americana	American beauty-berry
Calycanthus floridus	eastern sweetshrub
Carpinus caroliniana	American hornbeam
Cercis canadensis	redbud
Chionanthus virginicus	white fringetree
Cornus florida	flowering dogwood
Dirca palustris	eastern leatherwood

Evonymus americana	American strawberry-bush
Hamamelis virginiana	American witch-hazel
Ilex ambigua	Carolina holly
Ilex opaca	American holly
Juniperus virginiana	eastern red cedar
Magnolia ashei	Ashe's magnolia
Osmanthus americanus	devilwood
Ostrya virginiana	eastern hop-hornbeam
Sabal palmetto	cabbage palmetto
Sebastiania fruticosa	Gulf sebastain-bush
Smilax bona-nox	fringed greenbrier
Smilax pumila	sarsaparilla-vine
Stewartia malacodendron	silky-camellia
Styrax grandifolius	big-leaf snowbell
Symplocos tinctoria	horsesugar
Vaccinium arboreum	tree sparkle-berry
Zanthoxylum clava-herculis	Hercules'-club

Herbaceous Understory

Actaea pachypoda	white baneberry
Adiantum pedatum	northern maidenhair
Campanula spp.	bellflower
Goodyera pubescens	downy rattlesnake-plantain
Hepatica nobilis	liverwort
Hexastylis arifolia	little-brown-jug
Mitchella repens	partridge-berry
Passiflora lutea	yellow passion-flower
Polygonatum biflorum	King Solomon's-seal
Polystichum acrostichoides	Christmas fern
Sanicula spp.	black-snakeroot
Trillium spp.	wakerobin
Uvularia spp.	bellwort

Rockland Hammock

Rockland Hammock is found in extreme southern Florida. This closed canopy forest of broad-leaved tropical and semi-tropical trees occurs on limestone that is exposed or near the surface. These species-rich areas do not normally flood or burn.

Canopy
Characteristic Species

Coccothrinax argentata	Florida silver palm
Eugenia foetida	box-leaf stopper
Eugenia rhombea	red stopper
Guapira discolor	beeftree
Myrcianthes fragrans	twinberry

Associates

Acer rubrum	red maple
Bursera simaruba	gumbo-limbo
Capparis cynophallophora	Jamaican caper

Capparis flexuosa	falseteeth
Celtis laevigata	sugar-berry
Chrysophyllum oliviforme	satinleaf
Coccoloba diversifolia	tietongue
Conocarpus erectus	button mangrove
Exostema caribaeum	Carribbean princewood
Exothea paniculata	butterbough
Ficus aurea	Florida strangler fig
Gouania lupuloides	whiteroot
Guajacum sanctum	holywood lignumvitae
Krugiodendron ferreum	leadwood
Lysiloma latisiliquum	false tamarind
Metopium toxiferum	Florida poisontree
Morus rubra	red mulberry
Persea borbonia	red bay
Piscidia piscipula	Florida fishpoison-tree
Quercus laurifolia	laurel oak
Quercus pumila	running oak
Quercus virginiana	live oak
Roystonea elata	Florida royal palm
Sabal palmetto	cabbage palmetto

Woody Understory

Acacia pinetorum	pineland acacia
Alvaradoa amorphoides	Mexican alvaradoa
Ampelopsis arborea	peppervine
Amyris elemifera	sea torchwood
Annona glabra	pond-apple
Ardisia escallonoides	island marl-berry
Baccharis angustifolia	softwater false willow
Baccharis glomeruliflora	silverling
Baccharis halimifolia	groundseltree
Berchemia scandens	Alabama supplejack
Bourreria ovata	Bahama strongbark
Bourreria succulenta	bodywood
Byrsonima lucida	long key locust-berry
Caesalpinia bonduc	yellow nicker
Caesalpinia crista	gray nicker
Callicarpa americana	American beauty-berry
Calyptranthes pallens	pale lidflower
Calyptranthes zuzygium	myrtle-of-the-river
Canella winteriana	pepper-cinnamon
Catesbaea parviflora	small-flower lilythorn
Cephalanthus occidentalis	common buttonbush
Chiococca alba	West Indian milkberry
Chrysobalanus icaco	icaco coco-plum
Cissus verticillata	seasonvine
Citharexylum fruticosum	Florida fiddlewood

Coccoloba uvifera	seaside-grape
Colubrina arborescens	greenheart
Colubrina cubensis	Cuban nakedwood
Colubrina elliptica	soldierwood
Cordia globosa	curaciao-bush
Cordia sebestena	large-leaf geigertree
Cornus foemina	stiff dogwood
Crossopetalum rhacoma	maiden-berry
Cupania glabra	Florida toadwood
Dalbergia brownii	Brown's Indian-rosewood
Dalbergia ecastaphyllum	coinvine
Dodonaea viscosa	Florida hopbush
Drypetes diversifolia	milkbark
Drypetes lateriflora	Guianna-plum
Erithalis fruticosa	blacktorch
Erythrina herbacea	red-cardinal
Eugenia axillaris	white stopper
Eugenia confusa	red-berry stopper
Ficus citrifolia	wild banyantree
Forestiera segregata	Florida swamp-privet
Guettarda eliptica	hammock velvetseed
Gyminda latifolia	West Indian false box
Gymnanthes lucida	oysterwood
Hamelia patens	scarletbush
Hippocratea volubilis	medicine-vine
Hippomane mancinella	manchineel
Hypelate trifoliata	inkwood
Ilex cassine	dahoon
Ilex krugiana	tawny-berry holly
Jacquinia keyensis	joewood
Lantana involucrata	button-sage
Magnolia virginiana	sweet-bay
Manilkara jaimiqui	wild dilly
Maytenus phyllanthoides	Florida mayten
Myrica cerifera	southern wax-myrtle
Myrsine floridana	guianese colicwood
Parthenocissus quinquefolia	Virginia-creeper
Pisonia aculeata	devil's-claw pisonia
Pisonia rotundata	smooth devil's-claws
Pithecellobium unguis-cati	cat's-claw blackbead
Prunus myrtifolia	West Indian cherry
Pseudophoenix sargentii	Florida cherry palm
Psidium longipes	mangroveberry
Psychotria ligustrifolia	Bahama wild coffee
Psychotria nervosa	Seminole balsamo
Randia aculeata	white indigo-berry
Reynosia septentrionalis	darling-plum
Rhus copallinum	winged sumac

Salix caroliniana	coastal-plain willow
Sapindus saponaria	wing-leaf soapberry
Savia bahamensis	Bahama-maidenbush
Schaefferia frutescens	Florida boxwood
Schoepfia chrysophylloides	island beefwood
Serenoa repens	saw-palmetto
Sideroxylon celastrinum	saffron-plum
Sideroxylon foetidissimum	false mastic
Sideroxylon reclinatum	Florida bully
Sideroxylon salicifolium	white bully
Simarouba glauca	paradise-tree
Smilax spp.	greenbrier
Solanum donianum	mullein nightshade
Solanum erianthum	potato-tree
Swietenia mahagoni	West Indian mahogany
Tetrazygia bicolor	Florida clover-ash
Thrinax morrisii	Key thatch palm
Thrinax radiata	Florida thatch palm
Tournefortia hirsutissima	chiggery-grapes
Tournefortia volubilis	twining soilderbush
Trema lamarckianum	pain-in-back
Trema micranthum	Jamaican nettletree
Vallesia glabra	pearlberry
Viburnum obovatum	small-leaf arrow-wood
Vitis labrusca	fox grape
Vitis rotundifolia	muscadine
Ximenia americana	tallow-wood
Zamia pumila	coontie
Zanthoxylum clava-herculis	Hercules'-club
Zanthoxylum fagara	lime prickly-ash

Herbaceous Understory

Eupatorium villosum	Florida Keys thoroughwort
Solanum bahamense	Bahama nightshade

Maritime Hammock

Maritime Hammock is a low salt-pruned forest that occurs interior to the dune system. This is the stable dune community of the coast. The trees form a dense canopy which allows for humus buildup and moisture retention. This community grades into coastal scrub toward the ocean. Soils are sandy and well drained. This community corresponds to Küchler #90.

Canopy
Characteristic Species

Ilex vomitoria	yaupon
Magnolia grandiflora	southern magnolia
Persea borbonia	red bay
Quercus virginiana	live oak

Sabal palmetto	cabbage palmetto
Associates	
Bursera simaruba	gumbo-limbo
Capparis spp.	caper tree
Celtis laevigata	sugar-berry
Ficus aurea	Florida strangler fig
Ilex opaca	American holly
Juniperus virginiana	eastern red cedar
Metopium toxiferum	Florida poisonwood
Myrsine floridana	guianese colicwood
Prunus serotina	black cherry
Quercus hemisphaerica	Darlington's oak
Simarouba glauca	paradise-tree

Woody Understory

Ardisia escallonioides	island marl-berry
Callicarpa americana	American beauty-berry
Coccoloba uvifera	seaside-grape
Erythrina herbacea	red-cardinal
Lyonia ferruginea	rusty staggerbush
Myrica cerifera	southern wax-myrtle
Osmanthus americana	devilwood
Psychotria nervosa	Seminole balsamo
Rivina humilis	rougeplant
Serenoa repens	saw-palmetto
Sideroxylon tenax	tough bully
Sideroxylon foetidissimum	false mastic
Smilax auriculata	ear-leaf greenbrier
Symphoricarpos albus	common snowberry
Vaccinium darrowi	Darrow's blueberry
Vitis munsoniana	little muscadine
Zamia pumila	coontie
Zanthoxylum clava-herculis	Hercule's-club

Herbaceous Understory

Salvia lyrata	lyre-leaf sage
Verbesina virginica	white crownbeard

Sandhill

Sandhill, also called high pine, is a vegetation type that occurs on rolling hills of sand throughout Florida north of Lake Okeechobee and into southern Georgia. It is generally an open, longleaf pine forest with a grass and oak shrub understory. Pineland three-awn (wiregrass), *Aristida stricta*, is the characteristic ground cover species and is important in facilitating low intensity ground fires. This vegetation type is highly tolerant of and requires fire on a regular basis. Slash pine has been brought in to replace longleaf pine on many sites. This community corresponds, in part, to Küchler #115.

Canopy
Characteristic Species
Pinus echinata	short-leaf pine
Pinus palustris	long-leaf pine
Quercus laevis	turkey oak

Associates
Carya alba	mockernut hickory
Diospyros virginiana	common persimmon
Quercus falcata	southern red oak
Quercus incana	bluejack oak
Quercus margarettiae	sand post oak
Quercus marilandica	blackjack oak
Quercus stellata	post oak
Sassafras albidum	sassafras
Vaccinium arboreum	tree sparkle-berry

Woody Understory
Asimina incana	woolly pawpaw
Gaylussacia dumosa	dwarf huckleberry
Gaylussacia frondosa	blue huckleberry
Gelsemium spp.	trumpet-flower
Ilex glabra	inkberry
Licania michauxii	gopher-apple
Opuntia spp.	prickly-pear
Quercus minima	dwarf live oak
Quercus pumila	runner oak
Rhus copallinum	winged sumac
Rubus cuneifolius	sand blackberry
Smilax laurifolia	laurel-leaf greenbrier
Vitis labrusca	fox grape

Herbaceous Understory
Andropogon gerardii	big bluestem
Andropogon ternarius	split-beard bluestem
Andropogon virginicus	broom-sedge
Aristida stricta	pineland three-awn
Aster spp.	aster
Aureolaria flava	smooth yellow false-foxglove
Balduina angustifolia	coastal-plain honeycomb-head
Berlandiera subacaulis	Florida greeneyes
Chamaecrista fasciculata	sleepingplant
Croton argyranthemus	healing croton
Dalea pinnata	summer farewell
Dyschoriste oblongifolia	oblong-leaf snakeherb
Eriogonum tomentosum	dog-tongue wild buckwheat
Galactia volubilis	milk peas
Indigofera spp.	indigo
Lechea spp.	pinweed

Liatris pauciflora	few-flower gayfeather
Liatris tenuifolia	short-leaf gayfeather
Muhlenbergia capillaris	hair-awn muhly
Pityopsis graminifolia	narrow-leaf silk-grass
Polanisia tenuifolia	slender-leaf clammeyweed
Pteridium aquilinum	northern bracken fern
Rhynchosia spp.	snout-bean
Sanicula spp.	black snakeroot
Solidago spp.	goldenrod
Sorghastrum nutans	yellow Indian grass
Sporobolus junceus	wire grass
Stillingia sylvatica	queen's-delight
Stylosanthes biflora	side-beak pencil-flower
Tephrosia virginiana	goat's-rue

Pine Flatwoods

Flatwoods range from open forests of scattered pines with little understory to dense pine stands with a rather dense undergrowth of grasses (particularly *Aristida*), saw palmettos, and other low shrubs. Flatwoods occur on level topography with poorly drained acidic sands. The dominant canopy species is usually *Pinus elliottii*, but can be other pine species depending upon latitude, soils, hydroperiod, and fire frequency.

Canopy
Characteristic Species

Pinus elliottii	slash pine

Associates

Coccothrinax argentata	Florida silver palm
Pinus palustris	long-leaf pine
Quercus chapmanii	Chapman's oak
Quercus geminata	sand live oak
Quercus inopina	sandhill oak
Quercus myrtifolia	myrtle oak
Quercus virginiana	live oak

Woody Understory

Befaria racemosa	tarflower
Garberia heterophylla	garberia
Gaylussacia dumosa	dwarf huckleberry
Hypericum spp.	St. John's-wort
Ilex glabra	inkberry
Kalmia hirsuta	hairy-laurel
Licania michauxii	gopher-apple
Lyonia ferruginea	rusty staggerbush
Lyonia fruticosa	coastal-plain staggerbush
Lyonia lucida	shinyleaf
Myrica cerifera	southern wax-myrtle
Persea humilis	silk bay
Quercus pumila	runner oak
Sabal etonia	scrub palmetto
Serenoa repens	saw-palmetto

Vaccinium arboreum	tree sparkle-berry
Vaccinium elliottii	Elliott's blueberry
Zamia pumila	coontie

Herbaceous Understory

Agalinis spp.	false foxglove
Aristida spp.	three-awn
Aster paternus	toothed white-topped aster
Chrysopsis spp.	golden aster
Cladonia spp.	lichen
Lachnocaulon spp.	bogbutton
Lechea spp.	pinweed
Panicum abscissum	cut-throat grass
Pterocaulon virgatum	wand blackroot
Solidago spp.	goldenrod
Verbesina virginica	white crownbeard
Xyris spp.	yellow-eyed-grass

Pine Rockland

This is an open canopy forest of slash pine with a shrub, palm, and grass understory. It occurs on limestone outcrops and is maintained by fire. This community corresponds to Küchler #116.

Canopy
Characteristic Species

Alvaradoa amorphoides	Mexican alvaradoa
Annona glabra	pond-apple
Bursera simaruba	gumbo-limbo
Chrysophyllum oliviforme	satinleaf
Citharexylum fruticosum	Florida fiddlewood
Conocarpus erectus	button mangrove
Diospyros virginiana	common persimmon
Erithalis fruticosa	blacktorch
Exothea paniculata	butterbough
Ficus aurea	Florida strangler fig
Guapira discolor	beeftree
Hypelate trifoliata	ironwood
Lysiloma latisiliquum	false tamarind
Metopium toxiferum	Florida poisonwood
Persea borbonia	red bay
Pinus elliottii	slash pine
Piscidia piscipula	Florida fishpoison-tree
Psidium longipes	mangroveberry
Quercus geminata	sand live oak
Quercus virginiana	live oak
Sabal palmetto	cabbage palmetto
Sideroxylon foetidissimum	false mastic
Sideroxylon salicifolium	white bully
Thrinax morrisii	Key thatch palm
Thrinax radiata	Florida thatch palm

Woody Understory

Acacia farnesiana	sweet acacia
Acacia pinetorum	pineland acacia
Amorpha herbacea	cluster-spike indigo-bush
Ardisia escallonoides	island marl-berry
Asimina reticulata	netted pawpaw
Baccharis angustifolia	saltwater false willow
Baccharis glomeruliflora	silverling
Baccharis halimifolia	groundseltree
Befaria racemosa	tarflower
Bourreria cassinifolia	smooth strongbark
Byrsonima lucida	long key locust-berry
Caesalpinia pauciflora	few-flower holdback
Callicarpa americana	American beauty-berry
Catesbaea parviflora	small-flower lilythorn
Cephalanthus occidentalis	common buttonbush
Chamaecrista fasciculata	sleepingplant
Chrysobalanus icaco	icaco coco-plum
Coccoloba diversifolia	tietongue
Coccoloba uvifera	seaside-grape
Coccothrinax argentata	Florida silver palm
Colubrina arborescens	greenheart
Colubrina cubensis	Cuban nakedwood
Crossopetalum rhacome	maiden-berry
Crotalaria spp.	rattlebox
Croton linearis	grannybush
Dodonaea viscosa	Florida hopbush
Drypetes diversifolia	milkbark
Echites umbellata	devil's-potato
Eugenia axillaris	white stopper
Eugenia foetida	box-leaf stopper
Ficus citrifolia	wild banyantree
Forestiera segregata	Florida swamp-privet
Guettarda elliptica	hammock velvetseed
Guettarda scabra	wild guave
Gymnanthes lucida	oysterwood
Hippomane mancinella	manchineel
Ilex cassine	dahoon
Ilex glabra	inkberry
Ilex krugiana	tawny-berry holly
Jacquinia keyensis	joewood
Lantana involucrata	button sage
Lyonia fruticosa	coastal-plain staggerbush
Magnolia virginiana	sweet-bay
Manilkara jaimiqui	wild dilly
Myrica cerifera	southern wax-myrtle
Myrcianthes fragrans	twinberry
Myrsine floridana	guianese colicwood

Pisonia rotundata	smooth devil's-claws
Pithecellobium keyense	Florida Keys blackbead
Psychotria nervosa	Seminole balsamo
Quercus minima	dwarf live oak
Quercus pumila	running oak
Randia aculeata	white indigo-berry
Reynosia septentrionalis	darling-plum
Rhus copallinum	winged sumac
Salix caroliniana	coastal-plain willow
Sambucus canadensis	American elder
Serenoa repens	saw-palmetto
Sideroxylon celastrinum	saffron-plum
Sideroxylon salicifolium	white bully
Sideroxylon reclinatum	Florida bully
Smilax spp.	greenbrier
Solanum donianum	mullein nightshade
Solanum erianthum	potato-tree
Symphoricarpos albus	common snowberry
Tetrazygia bicolor	Florida clover-ash
Trema lamarckianum	pain-in-back
Trema micranthum	Jamaican nettletree
Toxicodendron radicans	eastern poison-ivy
Vaccinium myrsinites	shiny blueberry
Ximenia americana	tallow-wood
Zamia pumila	coontie

Herbaceous Understory

Andropogon virginicus	broom-sedge
Anemia adiantifolia	pineland fern
Aristida spp.	three-awn
Eupatorium villosum	Florida Keys thoroughwort
Muhlenbergia spp.	muhly

Scrub

This is generally a shrub community dominated by a variety of evergreen oak species. It occurs on well-drained, sandy soils throughout Florida and into southern Georgia. Scrub may or may not have a pine overstory. Although the herbaceous layer is usually very sparse, the mid-story can form a dense thicket. Natural fire cycles are longer than in other pine-dominated communities in this region and fire events are intense. This community corresponds to Küchler #115.

Canopy
Characteristic Species

Carya floridana	scrub hickory
Ceratiola ericoides	sand-heath
Pinus clausa	sand pine
Quercus chapmanii	Chapman's oak
Quercus geminata	sand live oak
Quercus inopina	sandhill oak

Quercus myrtifolia	myrtle oak

Associates

Juniperus virginiana	eastern red-cedar
Magnolia grandiflora	southern magnolia
Persea borbonia	red bay
Pinus elliottii	slash pine
Piscidia piscipula	Florida fishpoison-tree
Quercus virginiana	live oak
Sabal palmetto	cabbage palm

Woody Understory

Ampelopsis arborea	peppervine
Baccharis halimifolia	groundseltree
Caesalpinia bonduc	yellow nicker
Chrysoma pauciflosculosa	woody goldenrod
Dalbergia ecastaphyllum	coinvine
Echites umbellata	devil's-potato
Erythrina herbacea	red-cardinal
Forestiera segregata	Florida swamp-privet
Garberia heterophylla	garberia
Ilex opaca	scrub holly
Ilex vomitoria	yaupon
Lantana involucrata	button-sage
Limonium spp.	sea-lavender
Lyonia ferruginea	rusty staggerbush
Lyonia fruticosa	coastal-plain staggerbush
Myrcianthes fragrans	twinberry
Myrica cerifera	southern wax-myrtle
Myrsine floridana	guianese colicwood
Opuntia stricta	erect prickly-pear
Osmanthus americanus	devilwood
Persea humilis	silk bay
Pithecellobium keyense	Florida Keys blackbead
Pithecellobium unguis-cati	cat-claw blackbeard
Randia aculeata	white indigo-berry
Sabal etonia	scrub palmetto
Serenoa repens	saw-palmetto
Sideroxylon celastrinum	saffron-plum
Sideroxylon tenax	tough bully
Smilax auriculata	ear-leaf greenbrier
Sophora tomentosa	yellow necklacepod
Toxicodendron radicans	eastern poison-ivy
Vaccinium arboreum	tree sparkle-berry
Vitis munsoniana	little muscadine
Ximenia americana	tallow-wood
Yucca aloifolia	aloe yucca
Zanthoxylum clava-herculis	Hercules'-club

Herbaceous Understory

Alternanthera flavescens	yellow joyweed
Ambrosia hispida	coastal ragweed
Andropogon floridanus	Florida bluestem
Andropogon glomeratus	bushy bluestem
Asclepias curtissii	Curtis's milkweed
Cladonia evansii	lichen
Cladonia leporina	lichen
Cladonia prostrata	lichen
Cladonia subtenuis	lichen
Croton glandulosus	vente-conmigo
Dichanthelium sabulorum	hemlock rosette grass
Euphorbia cyathophora	fire-on-the-mountain
Eustachys petraea	pinewoods finger grass
Flaveria floridana	Florida yellowtops
Galactia spp.	milk-pea
Heterotheca subaxillaris	camphorweed
Hydrocotyle bonariensis	coastal marsh-pennywort
Ipomoea pes-caprae	bay-hops
Lechea cernua	nodding pinweed
Oenothera humifusa	seaside evening-primrose
Palafoxia feayi	Feay's palafoxia
Physalis angustifolia	coastal ground-cherry
Rhynchospora megalocarpa	sandy-field beak sedge
Schizachyrium sanguineum	crimson false bluestem
Trichostema dichotomum	forked bluecurls

Dry Prairie

This is a treeless grass, saw palmetto, and low shrub vegetation type. It occurs on moderately to poorly drained soils. A fire frequency of one to four years appears necessary to maintain this vegetation type. This community corresponds to Küchler #79.

Characteristic Herbaceous Species

Andropogon virginicus	broom-sedge
Aristida purpurascens	arrow-feather three-awn
Aristida spiciformis	bottlebrush three-awn
Axonopus spp.	carpet grass
Eragrostis spp.	love grass
Hyptis alata	clustered bush-mint
Liatris spp.	gayfeather
Lilium catesbaei	southern red lily
Panicum virgatum	wand panic grass
Polygala spp.	milkwort
Pterocaulon virgatum	wand blackroot
Sabatia spp.	rose-gentian
Schizachyrium scoparium	little false bluestem
Solidago spp.	goldenrod
Sorghastrum nutans	yellow Indian grass

Characteristic Woody Species

Asimina spp.	pawpaw
Ilex glabra	inkberry
Lyonia ferruginea	rusty staggerbush
Lyonia lucida	shinyleaf
Myrica cerifera	southern wax-myrtle
Quercus pumila	runner oak
Serenoa repens	saw-palmetto
Vaccinium myrsinites	shiny blueberry

Beach Dune

This community is the foredune or upper beach zone along the coast. It is a dynamic community due to the wind and wave action that continually moves the coastal sands. Dunes are sandy, xeric soils. The vegetation must tolerate exposure to salt spray, blowing sand, and direct sunlight. The shrubs are scattered and do not become dominant in the community.

Characteristic Herbaceous Species

Alternanthera flavescens	yellow joyweed
Atriplex pentandra	crested saltbush
Cakile edentula	American searocket
Canavalia rosea	bay-bean
Cenchrus spp.	sandburr
Chamaesyce bombensis	dixie sandmat
Cnidoscolus stimulosus	finger-rot
Commelina erecta	white-mouth dayflower
Croton punctatus	gulf croton
Distichlis spicata	coastal salt grass
Eustachys petraea	pinewoods finger grass
Helianthus debilis	cucumber-leaf sunflower
Hydrocotyle bonariensis	coastal marsh-pennywort
Ipomoea imperati	beach morning-glory
Ipomoea pes-caprae	bay-hops
Oenothera humifusa	seaside evening-primrose
Okenia hypogaea	burrowing-four-o'clock
Panicum amarum	bitter panic grass
Paspalum distichum	jointed crown grass
Physalis walteri	Walter's ground-cherry
Sesuvium portulacastrum	shoreline sea-purslane
Spartina patens	salt-meadow cord grass
Sporobolus virginicus	seashore dropseed
Uniola paniculata	sea-oats

Characteristic Woody Species

Argusia gnaphalodes	sea-rosemary
Dalbergia ecastophyllum	coinvine
Iva imbricata	seacoast marsh-elder
Scaevola plumieri	gullfeed
Sophora tomentosa	yellow necklacepod
Suriana maritima	bay-cedar

WETLAND SYSTEMS

Southern Swamp Forest

For the purposes of this book the Southern Swamp Forest includes many types of forested wetlands including bottomland hardwood, cypress-tupelo, sloughs, and other forests of the floodplain. These forests are closed-canopy and have a variety of understories that range from dense shrub to a mix of herbs and grasses and on some sites very little cover. This community corresponds to Küchler #113.

Canopy
Characteristic Species

Acer negundo	ash-leaf maple
Acer rubrum	red maple
Acer saccharinum	silver maple
Annona glabra	pond-apple
Betula nigra	river birch
Carya aquatica	water hickory
Carya glabra	pignut hickory
Catalpa bignonioides	southern catalpa
Catalpa speciosa	northern catalpa
Celtis laevigata	sugar-berry
Chamaecyparis thyoides	Atlantic white-cedar
Chrysobalanus icaco	icaco coco-plum
Fagus grandifolia	American beech
Ficus aurea	Florida strangler fig
Fraxinus caroliniana	Carolina ash
Fraxinus pennsylvanica	green ash
Fraxinus profunda	pumpkin ash
Gleditsia aquatica	water-locust
Gordonia lasianthus	loblolly-bay
Halesia spp.	silverbell
Juniperus virginiana	eastern red cedar
Liquidambar styraciflua	sweet-gum
Magnolia grandiflora	southern magnolia
Nyssa aquatica	water tupelo
Nyssa ogeche	Ogeechee tupelo
Nyssa sylvatica	black tupelo
Persea borbonia	red bay
Pinus elliotti	slash pine
Pinus glabra	spruce pine
Pinus palustris	long-leaf pine
Pinus serotina	pond pine
Pinus taeda	loblolly pine
Platanus occidentalis	American sycamore
Populus deltoides	eastern cottonwood
Populus heterophylla	swamp cottonwood
Quercus laurifolia	laurel oak
Quercus lyrata	overcup oak
Quercus michauxii	swamp chestnut oak

Quercus nigra	water oak
Quercus phellos	willow oak
Quercus virginiana	live oak
Roystonea elata	Floridian royal palm
Sabal palmetto	cabbage palmetto
Taxodium distichum	southern bald-cypress
Ulmus americana	American elm

Woody Understory

Alnus serrulata	brookside alder
Ampelopsis arborea	peppervine
Aronia arbutifolia	red chokeberry
Aster carolinianus	climbing aster
Berchemia scandens	Alabama supplejack
Bignonia capreolata	crossvine
Carpinus caroliniana	American hornbeam
Cephyalanthus occidentalis	common buttonbush
Clethra alnifolia	coastal sweet-pepperbush
Cliftonia monophylla	buchwheat-tree
Cornus foemina	stiff dogwood
Crataegus marshallii	parsley hawthorn
Cyrilla racemiflora	swamp titi
Diospyros virginiana	common persimmon
Ficus citrifolia	wild banyantree
Forestiera acuminata	eastern swamp-privet
Gelsemium sempervirens	evening trumpet-flower
Ilex cassine	dahoon
Ilex coriacea	large gallberry
Ilex decidua	deciduous holly
Ilex glabra	inkberry
Ilex myrtifolia	myrtle dahoon
Ilex vomitoria	yaupon
Itea virginica	Virginia sweetspire
Leucothoe axillaris	coastal doghobble
Leucothoe racemosa	swamp doghobble
Lyonia ferruginea	rusty staggerbush
Lyonia lucida	shinyleaf
Magnolia virginiana	sweet-bay
Myrica cerifera	southern wax-myrtle
Myrica heterophylla	evergreen bayberry
Myrsine floridana	guianese colicwood
Persea palustris	swamp bay
Planera aquatica	planertree
Rhapidophyllum hystrix	needle palm
Rhododendron vaseyi	pink shell azalea
Rhododendron viscosum	clammy azalea
Rubus argutus	saw-tooth blackberry
Sabal minor	dwarf palmetto
Salix caroliniana	coastal-plain willow

Salix nigra	black willow
Sambucus canadensis	American elder
Smilax bona-nox	fringed greenbrier
Smilax glauca	sawbrier
Smilax laurifolia	laurel leaf greenbrier
Smilax walteri	coral greenbrier
Toxicodendron radicans	eastern poison-ivy
Vaccinium arboreum	tree sparkle-berry
Vaccinium corymbosum	highbush blueberry
Viburnum nudum	possumhaw
Viburnum obovatum	small-leaf arrow-wood
Vitis aestivalis	summer grape
Vitis rotundifolia	muscadine
Vitis shuttleworthii	calloose grape
Wisteria frutescens	American wisteria

Herbaceous Understory

Acrostichum danaeifolium	leather fern
Bacopa spp.	water hyssop
Canna flaccida	bandanna-of-the-everglades
Carex spp.	sedge
Cladium mariscus	swamp sawgrass
Crinum americanum	seven-sisters
Juncus effusus	lamp rush
Leersia virginica	white grass
Lemna spp.	duckweed
Limnobium spongia	American spongeplant
Ludwigia palustris	marsh primrose-willow
Nymphoides aquatica	big floatingheart
Oplismenus setarius	short-leaf basket grass
Osmunda regalis	royal fern
Panicum rigidulum	red-top panic grass
Peltandra spp.	arrow-arum
Pistia stratiotes	water-lettuce
Polygonum punctatum	dotted smartweed
Pontederia cordata	pickerelweed
Sagittaria spp.	arrowhead
Saururus cernuus	lizard's-tail
Thalia geniculata	bent alligator-flag
Thelypteris palustris	eastern marsh fern
Zizaniopsis miliacea	marsh-millet

Baygall Forest

This is a closed canopy evergreen forest found in poorly drained, peat-filled, shallow depressions. This community type typically forms at the base of a slope where soils are acidic (pH 3.5-4.5).

Canopy
Characteristic Species

Chamaecyparis thyoides	Atlantic white-cedar

Gordonia lasianthus	loblolly-bay
Ilex decidua	deciduos holly
Ilex myrtifolia	myrtle dahoon
Liquidambar styraciflua	sweet-gum
Persea palustris	swamp bay
Taxodium spp.	cypress

Woody Understory

Aronia arbutifolia	red chokeberry
Clethra spp.	sweet-pepperbush
Ilex cassine	dahoon
Ilex coriacea	large gallberry
Itea virginica	Virginia sweetspire
Leucothoe axillaris	coastal doghobble
Leucothoe racemosa	swamp doghobble
Lyonia ligustrina	maleberry
Lyonia lucida	shinyleaf
Magnolia virginiana	sweet-bay
Myrica cerifera	southern wax-myrtle
Myrica inodora	odorless wax-myrtle
Rhapidophyllum hystrix	needle palm
Smilax laurifolia	laurel leaf greenbrier
Toxicodendron radicans	eastern poison-ivy
Vitis spp.	grape

Herbaceous Understory

Osmunda cinnamomea	cinnamon fern
Woodwardia areolata	netted chain fern
Woodwardia virginica	chain fern

Dome Swamp Forest

Dome Swamp Forest (cypress dome or cypress hammock) is a forested wetland type that occurs in depressions. Tree height increases toward the center where the water is deeper. This gives these areas a dome appearance. These communities typically form in sandy flatwoods and sinkholes where sand has partially filled them.

Canopy
Characteristic Species

Acer barbatum	Florida maple
Annona glabra	pond-apple
Gordonia lasianthus	loblolly-bay
Persea palustris	swamp bay
Taxodium ascendens	pond-cypress

Associates

Acer rubrum	red maple
Nyssa biflora	swamp tupelo

Woody Understory

Cephalantus occidentalis	common buttonbush
Clethra alnifolia	coastal sweet-pepperbush
Cyrilla racemiflora	swamp titi
Decodon verticillatus	swamp-loosestrife
Hypericum spp.	St. John's-wort
Ilex cassine	dahoon
Ilex coriacea	large gallberry
Ilex glabra	inkberry
Itea virginica	Virginia sweetspire
Leucothoe racemosa	swamp doghobble
Magnolia virginiana	sweet-bay
Lyonia lucida	shinyleaf
Myrica cerifera	southern wax-myrtle
Salix caroliniana	coastal-plain willow
Smilax laurifolia	laurel-leaf greenbrier
Smilax walteri	coral greenbrier
Toxicodendron radicans	eastern poison-ivy
Vaccinium spp.	blueberry

Herbaceous Understory

Bacopa spp.	water hyssop
Cladium mariscus	swamp sawgrass
Lachnanthes caroliniana	Carolina redroot
Ludwigia palustris	marsh primrose-willow
Nymphoides aquatica	big floatingheart
Osmunda cinnamomea	cinnamon fern
Panicum hemitomon	maiden-cane
Peltandra spp.	arrow-arum
Saururus cernuus	lizard's-tail
Sphagnum spp.	sphagnum moss
Thalia geniculata	bent alligator-flag
Woodwardia areolata	netted chain fern
Woodwardia virginica	chain fern

Floodplain Marsh

Floodplain Marsh occurs in river floodplains and is dominated by shrubs and herbaceous plants.

Characteristic Herbaceous Species

Amaranthus australis	southern amaranth
Amphicarpum muhlenbergianum	perennial goober grass
Cabomba caroliniana	Carolina fanwort
Cladium mariscus	swamp sawgrass
Coreopsis spp.	tickseed
Crinum americanum	seven-sisters
Eleocharis equisetoides	horsetail-spike-rush
Eleocharis vivipara	viviparous spike-rush

Juncus acuminatus	knotty-leaf rush
Juncus effusus	lamp rush
Lachnanthes caroliniana	Carolina redroot
Leersia hexandra	southern cut grass
Ludwigia repens	creeping primrose-willow
Luziola fluitans	southern water grass
Nymphaea mexicana	banana water-lily
Nymphaea odorata	American white water-lily
Orontium aquaticum	goldenclub
Panicum hemitomon	maiden-cane
Panicum repens	torpedo grass
Peltandra virginica	green arrow-arum
Polygonum punctatum	dotted smartweed
Pontederia cordata	pickerelweed
Reimarochloa oligostachya	Florida reimar grass
Rhynchospora inundata	narrow-fruit horned beak sedge
Rhynchospora tracyi	Tracy's beak sedge
Sacciolepis striata	American glenwood grass
Sagittaria latifolia	duck-potato
Salicornia spp.	saltwort
Scirpus spp.	bulrush
Sesuvium spp.	sea-purslane
Spartina bakeri	bunch cord grass
Sporobolus virginicus	seashore dropseed
Thalia geniculata	bent alligator-flag
Typha spp.	cat-tail
Utricularia foliosa	leafy bladderwort

Characteristic Woody Species

Cephalanthus occidentalis	common buttonbush
Glottidium vesicarium	bagpod
Hibiscus grandiflorus	swamp rose-mallow

Coastal Grassland

Coastal Grassland occurs in low flat areas behind the foredunes. It is often covered by salt water during storms.

Characteristic Herbaceous Species

Andropogon glomeratus	bushy bluestem
Andropogon spp.	bluestem
Cenchrus spp.	sandburr
Cirsium horridulum	yellow thistle
Croton glandulosus	vente-conmigo
Cyperus spp.	sedge
Eragrostis spp.	love grass
Eustachys petraea	pinewood finger grass
Hydrocotyle spp.	pennywort
Ipomoea imperati	beach morning-glory

Ipomoea pes-caprae	bay-hops
Muhlenbergia spp.	muhly
Oenothera spp.	evening primrose
Panicum amarum	bitter panic grass
Pentalinon luteum	hammock vipertail
Physalis spp.	ground-cherry
Salicornia spp.	saltwort
Schizachyrium sanguineum	crimson false bluestem
Sesuvium spp.	sea-purslane
Spartina patens	saltmeadow cord grass
Sporobolus spp.	dropseed
Uniola paniculata	sea-oats
Chamaesyce garberi	Garber's sandmat

Characteristic Woody Species

Waltheria indica	basera-prieta
Opuntia stricta	erect prickly-pear
Borrichia frutescens	bushy seaside-tansy
Baccharis halimifolia	groundseltree
Iva imbricata	seacoast marsh-elder
Myrica cerifera	southern wax-myrtle

Sawgrass Marsh

Sawgrass Marsh is a predominant community type in the Florida Everglades. Sawgrass forms a nearly impenetrable mat on sites with deep organic soils. This community corresponds to Küchler #92.

Characteristic Herbaceous Species

Bacopa spp.	water hyssop
Cladium mariscus	swamp sawgrass
Crinum americanum	seven-sisters
Eleocharis elongata	slim spike-rush
Muhlenbergia spp.	muhly
Nymphaea odorata	American shite water-lily
Pontederia cordata	pickerelweed
Sagittaria spp.	arrowhead
Utricularia spp.	bladderwort
Ludwigia repens	creeping primrose-willow

Characteristic Woody Species

Cephalanthus occidentalis	common buttonbush
Salix caroliniana	coastal-plain willow

Marl Prairie

Marl Prairie occurs on seasonally flooded sites on alkaline soils with limestone or marl near the surface. The vegetation is sparse with widely scattered dwarf cypress. This community corresponds to Küchler #80 and #91.

Characteristic Herbaceous Species

Aletris spp.	colicroot
Aristida purpurascens	arrow-feather three-awn
Aster spp.	aster
Cladium mariscus	swamp sawgrass
Crinum americanum	seven-sisters
Cyrtopodium punctatum	cowhorn orchid
Eleocharis spp.	spike-rush
Eragrostis spp.	love grass
Eupatorium capillifolium	dogfennel
Hyptis alata	clustered bush-mint
Leersia spp.	cutgrass
Muhlenbergia capillaris	hair-awn muhly
Nymphaea odorata	American white water-lily
Polygala spp.	milkwort
Pontederia cordata	pickerelweed
Rhynchospora colorata	narrow-leaf white-top
Rhynchospora microcarpa	southern beak sedge
Schizachyrium rhizomatum	Florida false bluestem
Schoenus nigricans	black bog-rush
Spartina bakeri	bunch cord grass
Thalia geniculata	bent alligator-flag

Characteristic Woody Species

Taxodium ascendens	pond-cypress

Wet Prairie

This is a flat, poorly drained treeless community on soils saturated or underwater 50 to 150 days each year. The species in this community type vary with soils, fire, and hydroperiod. Species have a tolerance for both flooding and dry periods.

Characteristic Herbaceous Species

Aletris spp.	colicroot
Aristida spp.	three-awn
Cladium mariscus	swamp sawgrass
Coreopsis spp.	tickseed
Ctenium aromaticum	toothache grass
Drosera spp.	sundew
Eleocharis spp.	spike-rush
Eragrostis spp.	love grass
Eriocaulon spp.	pipewort
Helenium spp.	sneezeweed
Helianthus spp.	sunflower
Muhlenbergia capillaris	hair-awn muhly
Panicum hemitomon	maiden-cane
Panicum spp.	panic grass
Rhexia spp.	meadow beauty
Rhynchospora colorata	narrow-leaf white-top
Rhynchospora tracyi	Tracy's beak sedge

Rudbeckia hirta	black-eyed-Susan
Sabatia spp.	rose-gentian
Saccharum giganteum	giant plume grass
Sarracenia spp.	pitcherplant
Setaria corrugata	coastal bristle grass
Spartina bakeri	bunch cord grass
Verbesina chapmanii	Chapman's crownbeard
Xyris spp.	yellow-eyed-grass

Characteristic Woody Species

Hypericum fasciculatum	peel-bark St. John's-wort
Myrica cerifera	southern wax-myrtle

Upland Marsh

Upland Marsh occurs in basins or depressions located outside the floodplain, such as old lake beds, ponds, and sinkholes. The frequency of fire determines the degree of shrub invasion. Hydroperiod can vary from 50 days to all year.

Characteristic Herbaceous Species

Bidens bipinnata	Spanish-needles
Eleocharis spp.	spike-rush
Eupatorium capillifolium	dogfennel
Hydrocotyle spp.	marsh-pennywort
Juncus effusus	lamp rush
Lachnanthes caroliniana	Carolina redroot
Leersia spp.	cutgrass
Ludwigia palustris	marsh primrose-willow
Ludwigia repens	creeping primrose-willow
Luziola fluitans	southern water grass
Nelumbo lutea	American lotus
Panicum hemitomon	maiden-cane
Panicum spp.	panic grass
Phragmites australis	common reed
Pontederia cordata	pickerelweed
Sagittaria spp.	arrowhead
Thalia geniculata	bent alligator-flag
Utricularia spp.	bladderwort
Woodwardia spp.	chain fern
Xyris spp.	yellow-eyed-grass

Characteristic Woody Species

Baccharis spp.	false willow
Cephalanthus occidentalis	common buttonbush
Hypericum spp.	St. John's-wort
Myrica cerifera	southern wax-myrtle
Salix caroliniana	coastal-plain willow
Salix spp.	willow
Sambucus canadensis	American elder

ESTUARINE SYSTEMS

Mangrove

Mangrove is a shrub community composed of any of the following species: white mangrove, black mangrove, red mangrove, and buttonwood. Mangrove occurs in marine and estuarine tidal areas along the southern peninsula in a variety of soils that are saturated with brackish water and under water during high tide. This community corresponds to Küchler #105.

Canopy
Characteristic Species

Avicennia germinans	black mangrove
Borrichia frutescens	bushy seaside-tansy
Conocarpus erectus	button mangrove
Laguncularia racemosa	white mangrove
Rhizophora mangle	red mangrove

Herbaceous Understory

Batis maritima	turtleweed
Distichlis spicata	coastal salt grass
Eleocharis spp.	spike-rush
Juncus roemerianus	Roemer's rush
Salicornia spp.	saltwort
Sesuvium spp.	sea-purslane
Spartina spartinae	gulf cord grass

Salt Marsh

Salt Marsh is an intertidal coastal community type consisting of salt-tolerant grasses, rushes, sedges, and other halophytic herbs. This community corresponds to Küchler #78.

Characteristic Herbaceous Species

Acrostichum aureum	golden leather fern
Aster tenuifolius	perennial saltmarsh aster
Batis maritima	turtleweed
Boltonia diffusa	small-head doll's-daisy
Cladium mariscus	swamp sawgrass
Distichlis spicata	coastal salt grass
Heliotropium curassavicum	seaside heliotrope
Juncus effusus	lamp rush
Juncus roemerianus	Roemer's rush
Limonium carolinianum	Carolina sea-lavender
Monanthochloe littoralis	shore grass
Paspalum distichum	jointed crown grass
Paspalum vaginatum	talquezal
Pluchea spp.	camphorweed
Salicornia bigelovii	dwarf saltwort
Salicornia virginica	woody saltwort
Scripus spp.	bulrush
Sesuvium portulacastrum	sea-purslane

Solidago sempervirens	seaside goldenrod
Spartina alterniflora	smooth cord grass
Spartina bakeri	bunch cord grass
Spartina cynosuroides	big cord grass
Spartina patens	salt-meadow cord grass
Spartina spartinae	gulf cord grass
Sporobolus virginicus	seashore dropseed
Suaeda linearis	annual seepweed
Suaeda maritima	herbaceous seepweed
Typha spp.	cat-tail

Characteristic Woody Species

Avicennia germinans	black mangrove
Baccharis halimifolia	groundseltree
Borrichia arborescens	tree seaside-tansy
Borrichia frutescens	bushy seaside-tansy
Conocarpus erectus	button mangrove
Iva frutescens	jesuit's-bark
Laguncularia racemosa	white mangrove
Lycium carolinianum	Carolina desert-thorn

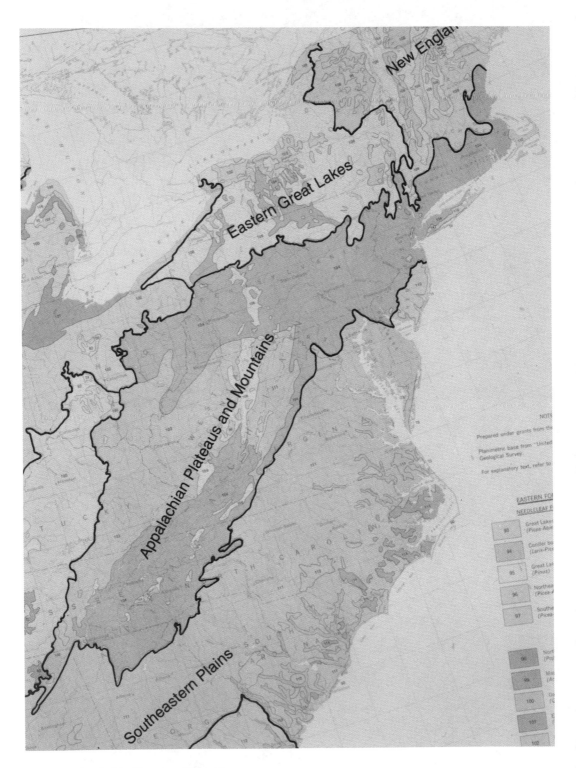

Appalachian Plateaus and Mountains

Appalachian Plateaus and Mountains

Introduction

This region occupies a long and relatively narrow area encompassing the central and southern Appalachian Mountains and the Cumberland and Appalachian plateaus. For the most part this region is rugged and mountainous. Elevations range from about 1300-1500 feet and go up to 6711 feet at the summit of Mt. Mitchell. Oak-chestnut once covered much of the region and is being replaced by predominantly oak forests with the loss of the American chestnut to the blight. The diverse topography has givern rise to many kinds of ecological communities in this region.

The primary sources used to develop descriptions and species lists are: Barbour and Billings 1988; Braun 1950.

Dominant Ecological Communities

Upland Systems
Northern Conifer Forest
Northern Hardwoods Forest
Appalachian Oak Forest
Mesophytic Forest
Pine-Oak Forest
Wetland Systems
Floodplain Forest

UPLAND SYSTEMS

Northern Conifer Forest

In this region Northern Conifer Forest is restricted to the highest elevations and is more widespread in the northern part of the region. In the Southern Appalachians Fraser's fir is endemic and restricted to the highest mountain slopes and peaks where it replaces balsam fir, which is characteristic of more northern mountain peaks. This community corresponds to Küchler #96 and #97.

Canopy
Characteristic Species
Abies balsamea	balsam fir
Abies fraseri	fraser's fir
Betula alleghaniensis	yellow birch
Picea rubens	red spruce
Pinus strobus	eastern white pine

Associates
Acer spicatum	mountain maple
Betula papyrifera	paper birch
Prunus pensylvanica	fire cherry
Sorbus americanus	American mountain-ash
Tsuga canadensis	eastern hemlock

Woody Understory

Ilex montana	mountain holly
Menziesia pilosa	minniebush
Rhododendron catawbiense	catawba rosebay
Rubus alleghaniensis	allegheny blackberry
Rubus canadensis	smooth blackberry
Rubus idaeus	common red raspberry
Vaccinium corymbosum	highbush blueberry
Vaccinium erythrocarpum	southern mountain-cranberrry
Viburnum lantanoides	hobblebush

Herbaceous Understory

Ageratima altissima	white snakeroot
Aster acuminatus	whorled wood aster
Aster divaricatus	white wood aster
Athyrium filix-femina	subarctic lady fern
Carex pensylvanica	Pennsylvania sedge
Chelone lyonii	pink turtlehead
Circaea alpina	small enchanter's-nightshade
Clintonia borealis	yellow bluebead-lily
Dryopteris camplyoptera	mountain wood fern
Huperzia lucidula	shining club-moss
Maianthemum canadense	false lily-of-the-valley
Oxalis montana	sleeping-beauty
Solidago glomerata	clustered goldenrod
Streptopus roseus	rosy twistedstalk
Viola macloskeyi	smooth white violet

Northern Hardwoods Forest

Northern Hardwoods Forest occurs throughout this region at higher elevations but usually below Northern Conifer Forest. It is generally found on mesic sites with high rainfall, abundant fog, and low temperatures. This community corresponds to Küchler #106.

Canopy

Characteristic Species

Acer saccharum	sugar maple
Aesculus flava	yellow buckeye
Betula alleghaniensis	yellow birch
Fagus grandifolia	American beech

Associates

Acer rubrum	red maple
Fraxinus americana	white ash
Magnolia acuminata	cucumber magnolia
Prunus serotina	black cherry
Tilia americana	American basswood

Woody Understory

Acer pensylvanicum	striped maple
Acer spicatum	mountain maple

Amelanchier laevis	allegheny service-berry
Cornus alternifolia	alternate-leaf dogwood
Hydrangea arborescens	wild hydrangea
Ostrya virginiana	eastern hop-hornbeam
Rhododendron catawbiense	catawba rosebay
Sorbus americana	American mountain-ash
Viburnum lantanoides	hobblebush

Herbaceous Understory

Actaea pachypoda	white baneberry
Ageratina altissima	white snakeroot
Anemone quinquefolia	nightcaps
Arisaema triphyllum	jack-in-the-pulpit
Arnoglossum muehlenbergii	great Indian-plantain
Aster cordifolius	common blue wood aster
Aster divaricatus	white wood aster
Athyrium filix-femina	subarctic lady fern
Cardamine concatenata	cut-leaf toothwort
Carex debilis	white-edge sedge
Carex pensylvanica	Pennsylvania sedge
Caulophyllum thalictroides	blue cohosh
Cimicifuga americana	mountain bugbane
Claytonia caroliniana	Carolina springbeauty
Collinsonia canadensis	richweed
Dryopteris goldiana	Goldie's wood fern
Dryopteris intermedia	evergreen wood fern
Dryopteris marginalis	marginal wood fern
Erythronium umbilicatum	dimpled trout-lily
Hydrophyllum canadense	blunt-leaf waterleaf
Hydrophyllum virginianum	Shawnee-salad
Impatiens pallida	pale touch-me-not
Laportea canadensis	Canadian wood-nettle
Lilium superbum	Turk's-cap lily
Maianthemum racemosum	feathery false Solomon's-seal
Monarda didyma	scarlet beebalm
Osmorhiza claytonii	hairy sweet-cicely
Phacelia bipinnatifida	fern-leaf scorpion-weed
Prenanthes altissima	tall rattlesnake-root
Rudbeckia laciniata	green-head coneflower
Stellaria pubera	great chickweed
Streptopus roseus	rosy twistedstalk
Trillium erectum	stinking-Benjamin
Trillium grandiflorum	large-flower wakerobin
Trillium luteum	yellow wakerobin
Viola blanda	sweet white violet
Viola canadensis	Canadian white violet
Viola hastata	halberd-leaf yellow violet
Viola rostrata	long-spur violet

Appalachian Oak Forest

Appalachian Oak Forest is widespread throughout this region and has many variants. It occupies lower elevation slopes and ridges that are well drained and range from dry to dry-mesic. Before chestnut blight eliminated the American chestnut, it was one of the most important canopy trees in this community and the region. This community corresponds to Küchler #104.

Canopy

Characteristic Species

Castanea dentata	American chestnut
Quercus alba	northern white oak
Quercus coccinea	scarlet oak
Quercus prinus	chestnut oak
Quercus velutina	black oak

Associates

Acer rubrum	red maple
Carya glabra	pignut hickory
Carya alba	mockernut hickory
Liriodendron tulipifera	tuliptree
Nyssa sylvatica	black tupelo
Pinus echinata	short-leaf pine
Pinus rigida	pitch pine
Quercus rubra	northern red oak
Quercus stellata	post oak

Woody Understory

Amelanchier arborea	downy service-berry
Clethra acuminata	mountain sweet-pepperbush
Cornus florida	flowering dogwood
Corylus cornuta	beaked hazalnut
Epigaea repens	trailing-arbutus
Gaultheria procumbens	eastern teaberry
Gaylussacia baccata	black huckleberry
Hamamelis virginiana	American witch-hazel
Kalmia latifolia	mountain-laurel
Oxydendrum arboreum	sourwood
Prunus pensylvanica	fire cherry
Pyrularia pubera	buffalo-nut
Quercus ilicifolia	bear oak
Rhododendrum calendulaceum	flame azalea
Rhododendrum maximum	great-laurel
Sassafras albidum	sassafras
Vaccinium corymbosum	highbush blueberry
Vaccinium stamineum	deerberry
Viburnum acerifolium	maple-leaf arrow-wood

Herbaceous Understory

Aureolaria laevigata	entire-leaf yellow false-foxglove
Chimaphila maculata	striped prince's-pine
Coreopsis major	greater tickseed

Galax urceolata	beetleweed
Goodyeara pubescens	downy rattlesnake-plantain
Heuchera longifolia	long-flower alumroot
Hieracium venosum	rattlesnake-weed
Lysimachia quadrifolia	whorled yellow-loosestrife
Maianthemum racemosum	feathery false Solomon's-seal
Medeola virginiana	Indian cucumber-root
Melanthium parviflorum	Appalachian bunchflower
Pedicularis canadensis	Canadian lousewort
Polygonatum biflorum	King Solomon's-seal
Prenanthes trifoliolata	gall-of-the-earth

Mesophytic Forest

In this region Mesophytic Forest is well developed. It is the richest and most diverse forest type occurring in the southern Appalachians and Cumberland Mountains. Dominance in these forests is often shared by many species, and numerous variants occur. This community corresponds to Küchler #103.

Canopy
Characteristic Species

Acer saccharum	sugar maple
Aesculus flava	yellow buckeye
Betula lenta	sweet birch
Fagus grandifolia	American beech
Fraxinus americana	white ash
Liriodendron tulipifera	tuliptree
Magnolia acuminata	cucumber magnolia
Quercus alba	northern white oak
Tilia americana	American basswood
Tsuga canadensis	eastern hemlock

Associates

Acer rubrum	red maple
Betula alleghaniensis	yellow birch
Carya cordiformis	bitter-nut hickory
Carya ovata	shag-bark hickory
Halesia carolina	Carolina silverbell
Juglans cinerea	white walnut
Juglans nigra	black walnut
Prunus serotina	black cherry
Quercus rubra	northern red oak
Tilia americana	American basswood
Ulmus rubra	slippery elm

Woody Understory

Acer pensylvanicum	striped maple
Acer spicatum	mountain maple
Asimina triloba	common pawpaw
Carpinus caroliniana	American hornbeam
Cornus florida	flowering dogwood

Hydrangea arborescens	wild hydrangea
Leucothe axillaris	coastal doghobble
Magnolia fraseri	Fraser's magnolia
Magnolia tripetala	umbrella magnolia
Ostrya virginiana	eastern hop-hornbeam
Rhododendrum maximum	great laurel

Herbaceous Understory

Actaea pachypoda	white baneberry
Adiantum pedatum	northern maidenhair
Ageratina altissima	white snakeroot
Arisaema triphyllum	jack-in-the-pulpit
Asarum canadense	Canadian wild ginger
Aster cordifolius	common blue wood aster
Cardamine concatenata	cut-leaf toothwort
Caulophyllum thalictroides	blue cohosh
Cimicifuga racemosa	black bugbane
Clintonia umbellata	white bluebead-lily
Dicentra canadensis	squirrel-corn
Dicentra cucullaria	Dutchman's-breeches
Dryopteris intermedia	evergreen wood fern
Galium triflorum	fragrant bedstraw
Hepatica nobilis	liverwort
Hydrophyllum canadense	blunt-leaf waterleaf
Hydrophyllum virginianum	Shawnee-salad
Impatiens capensis	spotted touch-me-not
Impatiens pallida	pale touch-me-not
Laportea canadensis	Canadian wood-nettle
Meehania cordata	Meehan's-mint
Mitchella repens	partridge-berry
Mitella diphylla	two-leaf bishop's-cap
Osmorhiza claytonii	hairy sweet-cicely
Panax quinquefolius	American ginseng
Podophyllum peltatum	may-apple
Polystichum acrostichoides	Christmas fern
Sedum ternatum	woodland stonecrop
Stellaria pubera	great chickweed
Thalictrum clavatum	mountain meadow-rue
Thelypteris noveboracensis	New York fern
Tiarella cordifolia	heart-leaf foamflower
Trillium erectum	stinking-Benjamin
Trillium grandiflorum	large-flower wakerobin
Viola canadensis	Canadian white violet
Viola rostrata	long-spur violet
Viola rotundifolia	round-leaf yellow violet

Pine–Oak Forest

Pine and oak dominated forests occur throughout this region on infertile and excessively well drained, sandy or gravelly sites on upper slopes and other exposed or south-facing ridges. Some sites can be dominated exclusively by pine. This community corresponds in part to Küchler #110.

Canopy
Characteristic Species
Pinus echinata	short-leaf pine
Pinus pungens	table mountain pine
Pinus rigida	pitch pine
Pinus virginiana	Virginia pine
Quercus coccinea	scarlet oak
Quercus prinus	chestnut oak

Associates
Acer rubrum	red maple
Castanea dentata	American chestnut
Nyssa sylvatica	black tupelo
Oxydendrum arboreum	sourwood
Robinia hispida	bristly locust
Robinia pseudo-acacia	black locust
Sassafras albidum	sassafras
Tsuga caroliniana	Carolina hemlock

Woody Understory
Castanea pumila	allegheny-chinkapin
Comptonia peregrina	sweet-fern
Epigea repens	trailing-arbutus
Gaultheria procumbens	eastern teaberry
Gaylussacia baccata	black huckleberry
Gaylussacia ursina	bear huckleberry
Kalmia latifolia	mountain-laurel
Leucothoe recurva	red-twig doghobble
Quercus ilicifolia	bear oak
Rhododendron catawbiense	catawba rosebay
Rhododendron maximum	great-laurel
Smilax glauca	sawbrier
Symplocos tinctoria	horsesugar
Vaccinium pallidum	early lowbush blueberry
Vaccinium stamineum	deerberry

Herbaceous Understory
Chimaphila maculata	striped prince's-pine
Coreopsis major	greater tickseed
Cypripedium acaule	pink lady's-slipper
Galax urceolata	beetleweed
Melampyrum lineare	American cow-wheat
Pteridium aquilinum	northern bracken fern
Schizachyrium scoparium	little false bluestem
Tephrosia virginiana	goat's-rue
Uvularia puberula	mountain bellwort
Xerophyllum asphodeloides	eastern turkeybeard

WETLAND SYSTEMS

Floodplain Forest

Floodplain Forest occurs primarily along the larger streams and rivers where a relatively large valley bottom has developed. Floodplain forests can vary considerably in composition depending upon substrate, drainage, and duration of flooding.

Canopy
Characteristic Species

Acer saccharinum	silver maple
Betula nigra	river birch
Celtis laevigata	sugar-berry
Fraxinus americana	white ash
Fraxinus pennsylvanica	green ash
Liquidambar styraciflua	sweet-gum
Platanus occidentalis	American sycamore
Ulmus americana	American elm

Associates

Acer rubrum	red maple
Carya cordiformis	bitter-nut hickory
Carya ovata	shag-bark hickory
Juglans nigra	black walnut
Liriodendron tulipifera	tuliptree
Quercus bicolor	swamp white oak
Quercus michauxii	swamp chestnut oak
Quercus pagoda	cherry-bark oak

Woody Understory

Acer negundo	ash-leaf maple
Alnus serrulata	brookside alder
Arundinaria gigantea	giant cane
Asimina triloba	common pawpaw
Bignonia capreolata	crossvine
Campsis radicans	trumpet-creeper
Carpinus caroliniana	American hornbeam
Cornus amomum	silky dogwood
Cornus florida	flowering dogwood
Evonymous americanus	American strawberry-bush
Ilex opaca	American holly
Leucothoe recurva	red-twig doghobble
Lindera benzoin	northern spicebush
Menispermun canadense	Canadian moonseed
Parthenocissus quinquefolia	Virginia creeper
Physocarpus opulifolius	Atlantic ninbark
Rhododendron maximum	great-laurel
Toxicodendron radicans	eastern poison-ivy
Xanthorhiza simplicissima	shrub yellowroot

Herbaceous Understory

Arisaema triphyllum	jack-in-the-pulpit
Aster divaricatus	white wood aster
Boehmeria cylindrica	small-spike false nettle
Carex laxiflora	broad loose-flower sedge
Chasmanthium latifolium	Indian wood-oats
Corydalis flavula	yellow fumewort
Cryptotaenia canadensis	Canadian honewort
Dichanthelium dichotomum	cypress rosette grass
Elymus hystrix	eastern bottle-brush grass
Elymus virginicus	Virginia wild rye
Impatiens pallida	pale touch-me-not
Laportea canadensis	Canadian wood-nettle
Lobelia cardinalis	cardinal-flower
Mertensia virginica	Virginia bluebells
Osmunda cinnamomea	cinnamon fern
Polemonium reptans	greek-valerian
Polygonum virginianum	jumpseed
Rudbeckia laciniata	green-head coneflower
Senecio aureus	golden ragwort
Solidago caesia	wreath goldenrod
Stellaria pubera	great chickweed
Verbesina alternifolia	wingstem

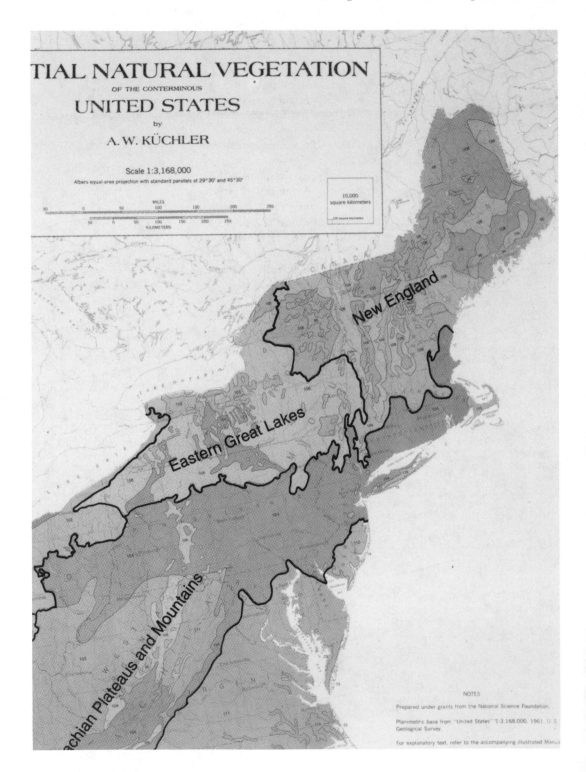

New England

New England

Introduction

The New England region encompasses Maine, New Hampshire, Vermont, Massachusetts, and eastern New York. This region is primarily vegetated with closed canopy forest. The most common upland community type is the Northern Hardwoods–Conifer Forest. On higher elevations, exposed sites, and cool flats, spruce-fir forests occur, often mixed with yellow and white birch. Oak, oak–hickory, and oak–pine forests are not extensive but do occur on dry slopes, especially in the southern part of the region. Pine and spruce forests and woodlands occupy narrow zones along the coast.

The dominant wetland community in New England is Floodplain Forest which is dominated by combinations of red and silver maple with ash, cottonwood, sycamore, and other flood tolerant species. Swamps dominated by red maple or conifers such as spruce, fir, or white-cedar also occur. Other wetland types which occur but are generally localized or small in extent include shrub swamps, marshes, bogs, fens, and estuarine salt and tidal marshes.

Specialized or localized communities, usually very limited in extent, include alpine ridges and krummholz at the highest elevations; heath, deciduous, and coniferous barrens or woodlands; pine forests of red and/or white pine; coastal dune/shoreline communities; and many others.

The primary sources used to develop descriptions and species lists are: Barbour and Billings 1988; Maine Natural Heritage Program 1991; Reschke 1990.

Dominant Ecological Communities

Upland Systems
Northeastern Spruce–Fir Forest
Northern Hardwoods–Conifer Forest
Oak-Pine-Hickory Forest
Beech–Maple Forest
Coniferous Woodland
Deciduous Woodland

Wetland Systems
Floodplain Forest
Deciduous Swamp Forest
Coniferous Swamp Forest
Forested Bog
Shrub Bog/Fen
Shrub Swamp
Herbaceous Bog/Fen
Mineral Soil Marsh

Estuarine Systems
Brackish Tidal Marsh
Freshwater Tidal Marsh

UPLAND SYSTEMS
Northeastern Spruce–Fir Forest

Northeastern Spruce–Fir Forest occurs on high-elevation slopes in mountainous areas such as the Adirondack high peaks and northern Appalachians (the Green and White Mountains). It also occurs along the coast of Maine where white and black spruce are common, and on moist, poorly drained to well drained soils on low flats. This is a broadly defined forest type with many variants and segregates dependant on elevation, exposure, and drainage. Spruce–fir forests include spruce flats, balsam flats, maritime spruce-fir, spruce slopes, and mountain-fir forests. This community corresponds to Küchler #96.

Canopy
Characteristic Species
Abies balsamea	balsam fir
Picea glauca	white spruce
Picea mariana	black spruce
Picea rubens	red spruce

Associates
Acer rubrum	red maple
Betula alleghaniensis	yellow birch
Betula papyrifera	paper birch
Pinus strobus	eastern white pine
Prunus serotina	black cherry
Sorbus americana	American mountain-ash
Tsuga canadensis	eastern hemlock

Woody Understory
Acer pensylvanicum	striped maple
Acer spicatum	mountain maple
Alnus viridis	sitka alder
Gaultheria hispidula	creeping-snowberry
Kalmia angustifolia	sheep-laurel
Ledum groenlandicum	rusty Laborador-tea
Lonicera canadensis	American fly-honeysuckle
Nemopanthus mucronatus	catberry
Prunus pensylvanica	fire cherry
Ribes glandulosum	skunk currant
Rubus idaeus	common red raspberry
Rubus pubescens	dwarf red raspberry
Sorbus americana	American mountain-ash
Vaccinium angustifolium	late lowbush blueberry
Vaccinium myrtilloides	shiny blueberry
Viburnum lantanoides	hobblebush
Viburnum nudum	possumhaw

Herbaceous Understory
Aralia nudicaulis	wild sarsaparilla
Aster acuminatus	whorled wood aster
Athyrium filix-femina	subarctic lady fern

Clintonia borealis	yellow bluebead-lily
Coptis trifolia	three-leaf goldthread
Cornus canadensis	Canadian bunchberry
Dalibarda repens	robin-run-away
Dryopteris campyloptera	mountain wood fern
Dryopteris carthusiana	spinulose wood fern
Huperzia lucidula	shining club moss
Maianthemum canadense	false lily-of-the-valley
Oxalis montana	sleeping-beauty
Solidago macrophylla	large-leaf goldenrod
Streptopus amplexifolius	clasping twistedstalk

Northern Hardwoods–Conifer Forest

Northern Hardwoods–Conifer Forest is the most common forest community in the New England region. It occupies lower and mid elevation slopes and well drained upland and lowland flats. This broadly defined community has many regional and edaphic variants and plant associations within it. The dominant species include hardwoods (sugar maple, beech, and yellow birch), and conifers (hemlock, spruce, and white pine). The characteristic species composition varies according to available moisture, elevation, and soil conditions. This community corresponds to Küchler #108.

Canopy
Characteristic Species

Acer rubrum	red maple
Acer saccharum	sugar maple
Betula alleghaniensis	yellow birch
Fagus grandifolia	American beech
Picea rubens	red spruce
Pinus resinosa	red pine
Pinus strobus	eastern white pine
Tsuga canadensis	eastern hemlock

Associates

Abies balsamea	balsam fir
Betula lenta	sweet birch
Betula papyrifera	paper birch
Fraxinus americana	white ash
Picea glauca	white spruce
Populus tremuloides	quaking aspen
Prunus serotina	black cherry
Quercus rubra	northern red oak
Tilia americana	American basswood
Ulmus americana	American elm

Woody Understory

Acer pensylvanicum	striped maple
Acer spicatum	mountain maple
Amelanchier canadensis	Canadian service-berry
Carpinus caroliniana	American hornbeam
Cornus alternifolia	alternate-leaf dogwood
Corylus cornuta	beaked hazelnut

Epigaea repens	trailing-arbutus
Gaultheria procumbens	eastern teaberry
Hamamelis virginiana	American witch-hazel
Kalmia angustifolia	sheep-laurel
Kalmia latifolia	mountain-laurel
Lonicera canadensis	American fly-honeysuckle
Ostrya virginiana	eastern hop-hornbeam
Taxus canadensis	American yew
Vaccinium angustifolium	late lowbush blueberry
Vaccinium myrtilloides	velvet-leaf blueberry
Viburnum acerifolium	maple-leaf arrow-wood
Viburnum dentatum	southern arrow-wood
Viburnum lantanoides	hobblebush
Viburnum nudum	possumhaw

Herbaceous Understory

Aralia nudicaulis	wild sarsaparilla
Aster macrophyllus	large-leaf aster
Carex pensylvanica	Pennsylvania sedge
Clintonia borealis	yellow bluebead-lily
Cornus canadensis	Canadian bunchberry
Coptis trifolia	three-leaf goldthread
Cypripedium acaule	pink lady's-slipper
Deparia acrostichoides	silver false spleenwort
Dryopteris campyloptera	mountain wood fern
Dryopteris goldiana	Goldie's wood fern
Dryopteris intermedia	evergreen wood fern
Huperzia lucidula	shining club-moss
Lycopodium obscurum	princess-pine
Maianthemum canadense	false lily-of-the-valley
Medeola virginiana	Indian cucumber-root
Melampyrum lineare	American cow-wheat
Mitchella repens	partridge-berry
Oryzopsis asperifolia	white-grain mountain-rice grass
Oxalis montana	sleeping-beauty
Polystichum acrostichoides	Christmas fern
Pteridium aquilinum	northern bracken fern
Streptopus roseus	rosy twistedstalk
Tiarella cordifolia	heart-leaf foamflower
Trientalis borealis	American starflower
Trillium erectum	stinking-Benjamin
Trillium undulatum	painted wakerobin
Uvularia sessilifolia	sessile-leaf bellwort
Viola rotundifolia	round-leaf yellow violet

Oak–Pine–Hickory Forest

Oak–Pine–Hickory Forest occurs on south- and west-facing slopes and ridgetops where the soil is sandy or rocky. Limited moisture and poor soil formation are important factors in maintaining the characteristic mix of oak, pine, and hickory in the canopy.

Canopy
Characteristic Species

Carya glabra	pignut hickory
Carya ovalis	red hickory
Carya ovata	shag-bark hickory
Pinus rigida	pitch pine
Pinus strobus	eastern white pine
Quercus alba	northern white oak
Quercus coccinea	scarlet oak
Quercus prinus	chestnut oak
Quercus rubra	northern red oak
Quercus velutina	black oak

Associates

Acer rubrum	red maple
Betula lenta	sweet birch
Fagus grandifolia	American beech
Fraxinus americana	white ash
Prunus serotina	black cherry
Tilia americana	American basswood
Tsuga canadensis	eastern hemlock

Woody Understory

Amelanchier arborea	downy service-berry
Cornus florida	flowering dogwood
Cornus foemina	stiff dogwood
Corylus cornuta	beaked hazelnut
Gaultheria procumbens	eastern teaberry
Gaylussacia baccata	black huckleberry
Hamamelis virginiana	American witch-hazel
Kalmia latifolia	mountian-laurel
Ostrya virginiana	eastern hop-hornbeam
Prunus virginiana	choke cherry
Quercus ilicifolia	bear oak
Rubus idaeus	common red raspberry
Vaccinium angustifolium	late lowbush blueberry
Vaccinium pallidum	early lowbush blueberry
Viburnum acerifolium	maple-leaf arrow-wood

Herbaceous Understory

Aralia nudicaulis	wild sarsaparilla
Carex pensylvanica	Pennsylvania sedge
Chimaphila maculata	striped prince's-pine
Cimicifuga racemosa	black bugbane
Desmodium glutinosum	pointed-leaf tick-trefoil

Desmodium paniculatum	panicled-leaf tick-trefoil
Hepatica nobilis	liverwort
Maianthemum racemosum	feathery false Solomon's-seal
Prenanthes alba	white rattlesnake-root
Pteridium aquilinum	northern bracken fern
Smilax rotundifolia	horsebrier
Solidago bicolor	white goldenrod

Beech–Maple Forest

Beech–Maple Forest occurs on sheltered, low to mid elevation sites and on east or north exposures. The soil is generally loamy, high in fertility, moist, and well drained. The most characteristic species include sugar maple, beech, and basswood. This community corresponds to Küchler #102.

Canopy
Characteristic Species

Acer saccharum	sugar maple
Fagus grandifolia	American beech
Tilia americana	American basswood

Associates

Acer rubrum	red maple
Betula alleghaniensis	yellow birch
Fraxinus americana	white ash
Quercus rubra	northern red oak
Ulmus americana	American elm

Woody Understory

Acer pensylvanicum	striped maple
Carpinus caroliniana	American hornbeam
Cornus alternifolia	alternate-leaf dogwood
Hamamelis virginiana	American witch-hazel
Ostrya virginiana	eastern hop-hornbeam
Viburnum lantanoides	hobblebush

Herbaceous Understory

Actaea pachypoda	white baneberry
Allium tricoccum	ramp
Arisaema triphyllum	jack-in-the-pulpit
Asarum canadense	Canadian wild ginger
Carex plantaginea	broad scale sedge
Carex platyphylla	plantain-leaf sedge
Caulophyllum thalictroides	blue cohosh
Dicentra cucullaria	Dutchman's-breeches
Dryopteris goldiana	Goldie's wood fern
Impatiens pallida	pale touch-me-not
Maianthemum racemosum	feathery false Solomon's-seal
Panax quinquefolius	American ginseng
Polystichum acrostichoides	Christmas fern
Sanguinaria canadensis	bloodroot

Coniferous Woodland

Coniferous Woodland occurs on gravelly slopes, sandy and rocky soils, dunes, and rocky areas. These sites generally have nutrient-poor soils and are excessively well drained. In the coastal areas and along lake shores, pitch pine or jack pine is usually the dominant species. Fire may have played a role in maintaining the coniferous woodland communities. Woodlands and barrens will be less distinct as the forest canopy closes in areas where fire is suppressed.

Canopy
Characteristic Species
Picea mariana	black spruce
Picea rubens	red spruce
Pinus banksiana	jack pine
Pinus resinosa	red pine
Pinus rigida	pitch pine
Pinus strobus	eastern white pine

Associates
Abies balsamea	balsam fir
Acer rubrum	red maple
Betula papyrifera	paper birch
Betula populifolia	gray birch
Corema conradii	broom-crowberry
Picea glauca	white spruce
Populus grandidentata	big-tooth aspen
Populus tremuloides	quaking aspen
Quercus coccinea	scarlet oak
Quercus rubra	northern red oak
Thuja occidentalis	eastern arborvitae

Woody Understory
Aronia melanocarpa	black chokeberry
Chamaedaphne calyculata	leatherleaf
Comptonia peregrina	sweet-fern
Corema conradii	broom-crowberry
Cornus foemina	stiff dogwood
Gaultheria procumbens	eastern teaberry
Gaylussacia baccata	black huckleberry
Kalmia angustifolia	sheep-laurel
Lonicera dioica	limber honeysuckle
Quercus ilicifolia	bear oak
Rhamnus alnifolia	alder-leaf buckthorn
Ribes cynosbati	eastern prickly gooseberry
Rubus idaeus	common red raspberry
Rubus occidentalis	black raspberry
Staphylea trifolia	American bladdernut
Toxicodendron radicans	eastern poison-ivy
Vaccinium angustifolium	late lowbush blueberry
Vaccinium myrtilloides	shiny blueberry
Vaccinium pallidum	early lowbush blueberry

Herbaceous Understory

Aralia nudicaulis	wild sarsaparilla
Asplenium trichomanes	maidenhair spleenwort
Aster macrophyllus	large-leaf aster
Botrychium virginianum	rattlesnake fern
Carex eburnea	bristle-leaf sedge
Carex pensylvanica	Pennsylvania sedge
Carex platyphylla	plantain-leaf sedge
Cypripedium acaule	pink lady's-slipper
Danthonia spicata	poverty wild oat grass
Deschampsia flexuosa	wavy hair grass
Dryopteris marginalis	marginal wood fern
Fragaria virginiana	Virginia strawberry
Geranium robertianum	herbrobert
Hudsonia tomentosa	sand golden-heather
Maianthemum canadense	false lily-of-the-valley
Maianthemum racemosum	feathery false Solomon's-seal
Melampyrum lineare	American cow-wheat
Polypodium virginanum	rock polypody
Pteridium aquilinum	northern bracken fern
Sanicula marilandica	Maryland black-snakeroot
Solidago caesia	wreath goldenrod
Thalictrum dioicum	early meadow-rue
Trillium grandiflorum	large-flower wakerobin
Waldsteinia fragarioides	Appalachian barren-strawberry

Deciduous Woodland

Deciduous Woodland occurs on shallow soils over bedrock, usually with numerous outcrops. Trees occur scattered or in groves but never with a closed canopy. The characteristic species vary according to soil type and moisture availability. Deciduous woodlands may need fire in certain areas to maintain the distinct woodland composition.

Canopy

Characteristic Species

Carya glabra	pignut hickory
Fraxinus americana	white ash
Juniperus virginiana	eastern red cedar
Ostrya virginiana	eastern hop-hornbeam
Pinus strobus	eastern white pine
Quercus alba	northern white oak
Quercus prinus	chestnut oak
Quercus rubra	northern red oak

Associates

Acer saccharum	sugar maple
Carya ovata	shag-bark hickory
Quercus macrocarpa	burr oak
Thuja occidentalis	eastern arborvitae
Tilia americana	American basswood

Woody Understory

Acer pensylvanicum	striped maple
Acer spicatum	mountain maple
Cornus foemina	stiff dogwood
Cornus rugosa	round-leaf dogwood
Gaultheria procumbens	eastern teaberry
Gaylussacia baccata	black huckleberry
Juniperus communis	common juniper
Kalmia angustifolia	sheep-laurel
Lonicera dioica	limber honeysuckle
Quercus ilicifolia	bear oak
Quercus priniodes	dwarf chinkapin oak
Rhamnus alnifolia	alder-leaf buckthorn
Rhus glabra	smooth sumac
Ribes cynosbati	eastern prickly gooseberry
Rubus idaeus	common red raspberry
Rubus occidentalis	black raspberry
Staphylea trifolia	American bladdernut
Toxicodendron radicans	eastern poison-ivy
Vaccinium angustifolium	late lowbush blueberry
Viburnum rafinesquianum	downy arrow-wood
Zanthoxylum americanum	toothachetree

Herbaceous Understory

Actaea pachypoda	white baneberry
Adiantum pedatum	northern maidenhair
Antennaria plantaginifolia	woman's-tobacco
Asarum canadense	Canadian wild ginger
Asplenium rhizophyllum	walking fern
Asplenium trichomanes	maidenhair spleenwort
Aster divaricatus	white wood aster
Aster macrophyllus	large-leaf aster
Athyrium filix-femina	subarctic lady fern
Botrychium virginianum	rattlesnake fern
Carex eburnea	bristle-leaf sedge
Carex pensylvanica	Pennsylvania sedge
Carex platyphylla	plantain-leaf sedge
Caulophyllum thalictroides	blue cohosh
Cystopteris bulbifera	bulblet bladder fern
Cystopteris fragilis	brittle bladder fern
Deparia acrostichoides	silver false spleenwort
Deschampsia flexuosa	wavy hair grass
Dryopteris marginalis	marginal wood fern
Elymus hystrix	eastern bottle-brush grass
Fragaria virginiana	Virginia strawberry
Geranium robertianum	herbrobert
Hieracium venosum	rattlesnake-weed
Lycopodium sabinifolium	savin-leaf ground-pine
Maianthemum canadense	false lily-of-the-valley

Maianthemum racemosum	feathery false Solomon's-seal
Oryzopsis racemosa	black-seed mountain-rice grass
Panax quinquefolius	American ginseng
Penstemon hirsutus	hairy beardtongue
Polygonatum pubescens	hairy Solomon's-seal
Polystichum acrostichoides	Christmas fern
Pteridium aquilinum	northern bracken fern
Sanguinaria canadensis	bloodroot
Sanicula marilandica	Maryland black-snakeroot
Schizachyrium scoparium	little false bluestem
Sibbaldiopsis tridentata	shrubby-fivefingers
Solidago caesia	wreath goldenrod
Solidago flexicaulis	zigzag goldenrod
Thalictrum dioicum	early meadow-rue
Trillium grandiflorum	large-flower wakerobin
Waldsteinia fragarioides	Appalachian barren-strawberry

WETLAND SYSTEMS

Floodplain Forest

Floodplain Forest occurs on low terraces of river floodplains and river deltas throughout the region. These areas are seasonally flooded, usually in the spring. The soils are generally mineral soils. The composition of Floodplain Forest changes in relation to flood frequency and elevation of floodplain terraces along large rivers. The characteristic species are dominant throughout the region but some of the associate species become characteristic in specific areas. Cottonwood, for example, occurs in the floodplain forest in northern New York as a characteristic species but not in Maine.

Canopy
Characteristic Species
Acer rubrum	red maple
Acer saccharinum	silver maple
Fraxinus nigra	black ash
Juglans cinerea	white walnut
Salix nigra	black willow

Associates
Carya cordiformis	bitter-nut hickory
Fraxinus americana	white ash
Fraxinus pennsylvanica	green ash
Nyssa sylvatica	black tupelo
Platanus occidentalis	American sycamore
Populus deltoides	eastern cottonwood
Quercus bicolor	swamp white oak
Quercus macrocarpa	burr oak
Tilia americana	American basswood
Ulmus americana	American elm

Woody Understory

Clematis virginiana	devil's-darning-needles
Lindera benzoin	northern spicebush
Parthenocissus quinquefolia	Virginia-creeper
Toxicodendron radicans	eastern poison-ivy

Herbaceous Understory

Ageratina altissima	white snakeroot
Allium tricoccum	ramp
Anemone quinquefolia	nightcaps
Caulophyllum thalictroides	blue cohosh
Erythronium americanum	American trout-lily
Impatiens capensis	spotted touch-me-not
Matteuccia struthiopteris	ostrich fern
Onoclea sensibilis	sensitive fern
Polygonum virginianum	jumpseed
Sanguinaria canadensis	bloodroot
Solidago canadensis	Canadian goldenrod

Deciduous Swamp Forest

Deciduous Swamp Forest occurs in poorly drained basins and along lake shores, streams, and rivers throughout the region. The characteristic species include red maple, black and green ash, swamp white oak, and American elm. Species composition varies according to moisture and soil conditions. Soils are hydric, usually saturated, and inorganic.

Canopy

Characteristic Species

Acer rubrum	red maple
Fraxinus nigra	black ash
Fraxinus pennsylvanica	green ash
Quercus bicolor	swamp white oak
Ulmus americana	American elm

Associates

Acer saccharinum	silver maple
Betula alleghaniensis	yellow birch
Carya cordiformis	bitternut hickory
Fraxinus americana	white ash
Juglans cinerea	white walnut
Pinus rigida	pitch pine
Pinus strobus	eastern white pine
Quercus alba	northern white oak
Quercus coccinea	scarlet oak
Salix nigra	black willow
Tsuga canadensis	eastern hemlock

Woody Understory

Aronia melanocarpa	black chokeberry
Cornus sericea	redosier
Gaylussacia baccata	black huckleberry

Ilex verticillata	common winterberry
Lindera benzoin	northern spicebush
Nemopanthus mucronatus	catberry
Parthenocissus quinquefolia	Virginia-creeper
Rhododendron periclymenoides	pink azalea
Toxicodendron radicans	eastern poison-ivy
Vaccinium angustifolium	late lowbush blueberry
Vaccinium corymbosum	highbush blueberry
Viburnum dentatum	southern arrow-wood
Viburnum nudum	possumhaw

Herbaceous Understory

Carex intumescens	great bladder sedge
Carex lacustris	lakebank sedge
Dryopteris carthusiana	spinulose wood fern
Dryopteris cristata	crested wood fern
Glyceria striata	fowl manna grass
Impatiens capensis	spotted touch-me-not
Laportea canadensis	Canadian wood-nettle
Onoclea sensibilis	sensitive fern
Osmunda cinnamomea	cinnamon fern
Osmunda claytoniana	interrupted fern
Osmunda regalis	royal fern
Scirpus cyperinus	cottongrass bulrush
Scutellaria galericulata	hooded skullcap
Symplocarpus foetidus	skunk-cabbage
Thalictrum pubescens	king-of-the-meadow
Thelypteris palustris	eastern marsh fern

Coniferous Swamp Forest

Coniferous Swamp Forest occurs in stagnant basins or bordering small streams. Coniferous swamps are distinguished from upland coniferous forests by their hydric soils, lower elevation, and greater importance of sphagnum in the ground layer. Coniferous swamps include both basin swamps, with somewhat stagnant water, and seepage swamps on gentle slopes, where soils remain saturated through groundwater seepage. In the Adirondacks these swamps are often found in drainage basins occasionally flooded by beavers. Coniferous swamps are supplied with water containing a high concentration of minerals from the substrate. The high mineral content sets them apart from Forested Bog which occurs in peat soils and which is fed with relatively mineral poor water.

Canopy
Characteristic Species

Abies balsamea	balsam fir
Picea glauca	white spruce
Picea mariana	black spruce
Picea rubens	red spruce
Thuja occidentalis	eastern arborvitae

Associates
Acer rubrum	red maple
Larix laricina	American larch

Woody Understory
Alnus viridis	sitka alder
Clethra alnifolium	summer sweet clethra
Gaultheria hispidula	creeping-snowberry
Ilex laevigata	smooth winterberry
Ilex verticillata	common winterberry
Sorbus americana	American mountain-ash
Vaccinium corymbosum	highbush blueberry
Viburnum nudum	possumhaw

Herbaceous Understory
Coptis trifoila	three-leaf goldthread
Dalibarda repens	robin-run-away
Dryopteris campyloptera	mountain wood fern
Osmunda cinnamomea	cinnamon fern
Oxalis montana	sleeping-beauty
Sphagnum spp.	moss

Forested Bog

Forested Bog develops mainly on accumulated peat, fine grained marl, and organic muck. American larch (tamarack) and black spruce are very common characteristic species. Bogs get most of their moisture through rainfall rather than more nutrient-rich streams or rivers. The lack of nutrients in the peat contributes to the slow growth of trees in bogs.

Canopy
Characteristic Species
Larix laricina	American larch
Picea mariana	black spruce
Pinus strobus	eastern white pine
Thuja occidentalis	eastern arborvitae

Associates
Abies balsamea	balsam fir
Acer rubrum	red maple
Betula alleghaniensis	yellow birch
Chamaecyparis thyoides	Atlantic white-cedar
Fraxinus nigra	black ash
Pinus banksiana	jack pine
Pinus rigida	pitch pine

Woody Understory
Alnus incana	speckled alder
Alnus serrulata	brookside alder
Aronia melanocarpa	black chokeberry
Betula pumila	bog birch

Chamaedaphne calyculata	leatherleaf
Cornus sericea	redosier
Gaultheria procumbens	eastern teaberry
Ilex verticillata	common winterberry
Kalmia polifolia	bog-laurel
Ledum groenlandicum	Laborador tea
Lonicera oblongifolia	swamp fly-honeysuckle
Nemopanthus mucronatus	catberry
Pentaphylloides floribunda	golden-hardhack
Rhamnus alnifolia	alder-leaf buckthorn
Rubus pubescens	dwarf red raspberry
Spiraea alba	white meadowsweet
Toxicodendron vernix	poison-sumac
Vaccinium corymbosum	highbush blueberry
Vaccinium oxycoccus	small cranberry

Herbaceous Understory

Caltha palustris	yellow marsh-marigold
Carex lacustris	lakebank sedge
Carex leptalea	bristly-stalk sedge
Carex stricta	uptight sedge
Carex trisperma	three-seed sedge
Coptis trifolia	three-leaf goldthread
Dryopteris cristata	crested wood fern
Osmunda regalis	royal fern
Sarracenia purpurea	purple pitcherplant
Solidago patula	round-leaf goldenrod
Thelypteris palustris	eastern marsh fern

Shrub Bog/Fen

The Shrub Bog/Fen community type occurs on peat substrate. These areas are generally fed by fog, precipitation, and water drainage but may also be fed by springs. There are many characteristic shrubs which depend on specific conditions. Bog-rosemary, leatherleaf, bog-laurel, and highbush blueberry are among the most common characteristic species occurring in both nutrient poor and nutrient rich areas. Shrub bogs and fens often occupy a band that is a transition or succession between forested and open bogs.

Characteristic Woody Species

Acer rubrum	red maple
Alnus incana	speckled alder
Andromeda polifolia	bog-rosemary
Chamaedaphne calyculata	leatherleaf
Gaylussacia baccata	black huckleberry
Kalmia angustifolia	sheep-laurel
Kalmia polifolia	bog-laurel
Ledum groenlandicum	rusty Laborador-tea
Salix candida	sage willow
Vaccinium corymbosom	highbush blueberry
Vaccinium oxycoccos	small cranberry

Associates

Aronia melanocarpa	black chokeberry
Betula pumila	bog birch
Clethra alnifolia	coastal sweet-pepperbush
Cornus sericea	redosier
Decodon verticillatus	swamp-loosestrife
Ilex laevigata	smooth winterberry
Ilex verticillata	common winterberry
Larix laricina	American larch
Lonicera oblongifolia	swamp fly-honeysuckle
Myrica gale	sweet gale
Nemopanthus mucronatus	catberry
Pentaphylloides floribunda	golden hardhack
Picea mariana	black spruce
Pinus rigida	pitch pine
Pinus strobus	eastern white pine
Rhamnus alnifolia	alder-leaf buckthorn
Rubus chamaemorus	cloudberry
Toxicodendron vernix	poison-sumac
Vaccinium angustifolium	late lowbush blueberry
Vaccinium macrocarpon	large cranberry

Herbaceous Understory

Calla palustris	water-dragon
Carex aquatilis	leafy tussock sedge
Carex canescens	hoary sedge
Carex exilis	coastal sedge
Carex lacustris	lakebank sedge
Carex oligosperma	few-seed sedge
Carex trisperma	three-seed sedge
Drosera intermedia	spoon-leaf sundew
Drosera rotundifolia	round-leaf sundew
Eriophorum vaginatum	tussock cotton-grass
Eriophorum virginicum	tawny cotton-grass
Geocaulon lividum	false toadflax
Iris versicolor	harlequin blueflag
Maianthemum trifolium	three-leaf false Solomon's-seal
Menyanthes trifoliata	buck-bean
Osmunda cinnamomea	cinnamon fern
Osmunda regalis	royal fern
Peltandra virginica	green arrow-arum
Rhynchospora alba	white beak sedge
Sarracenia purpurea	purple pitcherplant
Scheuchzeria palustris	rannoch-rush
Scirpus acutus	hard-stem bulrush
Scirpus cespitosus	tufted bulrush
Sphagnum angustifolim	moss
Sphagnum centrale	moss
Sphagnum cuspidatum	moss

Sphagnum fallax	moss
Sphagnum fimbriatum	moss
Sphagnum magellanicum	moss
Sphagnum majus	moss
Sphagnum nemoreum	moss
Sphagnum papillosum	moss
Sphagnum rubellum	moss
Thelypteris palustris	eastern marsh fern
Triadenum virginicum	Virginia marsh-St. John's-wort
Woodwardia virginica	Virginia chain fern

Shrub Swamp

Shrub Swamp occurs on mineral soils in areas that are flooded too long and too deeply for trees to tolerate or as successional transition zones between forested and open wetlands. Often shrub swamps occur around the margins of ponds and bogs where the water may reach a depth of six inches or more.

Characteristic Woody Species

Alnus incana	speckled alder
Cornus amomum	silky dogwood
Cornus sericea	redosier
Myrica gale	sweet gale

Associates

Alnus serrulata	brookside alder
Cephalanthus occidentalis	common buttonbush
Cornus racemosa	gray dogwood
Decodon verticillatus	swamp loosestrife
Lindera benzoin	northern spicebush
Lyonia ligustrina	maleberry
Rhododendron viscosum	clammy azalea
Salix bebbiana	long-beak willow
Salix discolor	tall pussy willow
Salix lucida	shining willow
Salix petiolaris	meadow willow
Spiraea alba	white meadowsweet
Spiraea tomentosa	steeplebush
Vaccinium corymbosum	highbush blueberry
Viburnum dentatum	southern arrow-wood
Viburnum nudum	possumhaw

Herbaceous Understory

Saxifraga pensylvanica	eastern swamp saxifrage

Herbaceous Bog/Fen

The Herbaceous Bog/Fen community type is an open wetland on organic soils of peat or muck. The dominant species include many sedges, grasses, and rushes. Shrubs and trees may also occur but woody species cover is less than 50 percent of the area.

Characteristic Species

Acorus americanus	sweetflag
Angelica atropurpurea	purple-stem angelica
Aster umbellatus	parasol flat-top white aster
Aulacomnium palustre	moss
Calamagrostis canadensis	bluejoint
Carex aquatilis	leafy tussock sedge
Carex diandra	lesser tussock sedge
Carex flava	yellow-green sedge
Carex hystericina	porcupine sedge
Carex livida	livid sedge
Carex magellanica	boreal-bog sedge
Carex oligosperma	few-seed sedge
Carex prairea	prairie sedge
Carex stricta	uptight sedge
Cladium mariscoides	swamp saw-grass
Drosera rotundifolia	round-leaf sundew
Dulichium arundinaceum	three-way sedge
Eleocharis rosetellata	beaked spike-rush
Equisetum arvense	field horsetail
Eupatorium maculatum	spotted joe-pye-weed
Iris versicolor	harlequin blueflag
Juncus stygius	moor rush
Menyanthes trifoliata	buck-bean
Muhlenbergia glomerata	spiked muhly
Osmunda regalis	royal fern
Parnassia glauca	fen grass-of-Parnassus
Pogonia ophioglossoides	snake-mouth orchid
Rhynchospora alba	white beak rush
Sarracenia purpurea	purple pitcher-plant
Scheuchzeria palustris	rannoch-rush
Scirpus atrovirens	dark-green bulrush
Spiraea alba	white meadowsweet
Thalictrum pubescens	king-of-the-meadow
Thelypteris palustris	eastern marsh fern
Tomenthypnum nitens	moss
Typha angustifolia	narrow-leaf cat-tail
Typha latifolia	broad-leaf cat-tail
Utricularia minor	lesser bladderwort

Associates

Andromeda polifolia	bog rosemary
Cornus racemosa	gray dogwood
Cornus sericea	redosier
Machaerium revolvens	moss
Myrica pensylvanica	northern bayberry
Pentaphylloides floribunda	golden hardhack
Rhamnus alnifolia	alder-leaf buckthorn
Salix candida	sage willow
Scorpidium scorpioides	moss

Sphagnum contortum	moss
Sphagnum subsecundum	moss
Vaccinium macrocarpon	large cranberry

Mineral Soil Marsh

Mineral Soil Marsh occurs in areas periodically inundated with standing or slow moving water on mineral soils with little or no peat accumulation. Species composition varies according to available moisture. Some emergent marshes are permanently saturated while others are seasonally flooded. Emergent marshes may have water up to six feet deep and support species such as yellow pond-lily and American white water-lily. Other marsh communities may occur along the shores of lakes and ponds, and along river or stream channels where disturbance prevents peat accumulation.

Characteristic Species

Acorus americanus	sweetflag
Alisma plantago-aquatica	water plantain
Armoracia lacustris	lakecress
Calamagrostis canadensis	bluejoint
Caltha palustris	yellow marsh-marigold
Campanula aparinoides	marsh bellflower
Carex lacustris	lakebank sedge
Carex stricta	uptight sedge
Cyperus squarrosus	awned flat sedge
Dulichium arundinaceum	three-way sedge
Eleocharis acicularis	needle spike-rush
Eleocharis obtusa	blunt spike-rush
Eleocharis palustris	pale spike-rush
Fimbristylis autumnalis	slender fimbry
Glyceria canadensis	rattlesnake manna grass
Gratiola neglecta	clammy hedge-hyssop
Heteranthera dubia	grass-leaf mud-plantain
Iris versicolor	harlequin blueflag
Juncus canadensis	Canadian rush
Leersia oryzoides	rice cut grass
Lobelia dortmanna	water lobelia
Ludwigia palustris	marsh primrose-willow
Lythrum thrysiflora	thyme-leaf loosestrife
Nuphar lutea	yellow pond-lily
Nymphaea odorata	American white water-lily
Peltandra virginica	green arrow-arum
Polygonum amphibium	water smartweed
Polygonum pensylvanicum	pinkweed
Ranunculus longirostris	long-beak water-crowfoot
Ranunculus reptans	lesser creeping spearwort
Scripus acutus	hard-stem bulrush
Scripus atrovirens	dark-green bulrush
Scripus cyperinus	cottongrass bulrush
Scripus microcarpus	red-tinge bulrush
Scripus tabernaemontanii	soft-stem bulrush
Sparganium eurycarpum	broad-fruit burr-reed

Typha angustifolia	narrow-leaf cat-tail
Typha latifolia	broad-leaf cat-tail
Veratrum viride	American false hellebore
Zizania aquatica	Indian wild rice

ESTUARINE SYSTEMS

Brackish Tidal Marsh

Brackish Tidal Marsh occurs in coastal tidal areas where the salinity ranges from 0.5 to 18 parts per trillion and where water is less that six feet deep at high tide. Within this broadly defined marsh community there may be up to three distinct zones: broad mudflats, marshes dominated by tall graminoids, and muddy, gravel, or rock shores. Each of these zones supports a different type of herbaceous vegetation.

Characteristic Species

Cardamine longii	Long's bittercress
Lilaeopsis chinensis	eastern grasswort
Limosella australis	Welsh mudwort
Sagittaria calycina	hooded arrowhead
Sagittaria latifolia	duck-potato
Samolus valerandi	seaside brookweed
Sium suave	hemlock water-parsnip
Spartina alterniflora	saltwater cord grass
Zizania aquatica	Indian wild rice

Freshwater Tidal Marsh

Freshwater Tidal Marsh occurs in shallow bays, shoals, and the mouths of tributaries of large tidal river systems where the water is usually fresh. Salinity in these marshes is less than 0.5 parts per trillion. Freshwater Tidal Marsh has up to three distinctive zones: mudflats, marshes, and muddy or rocky shores, each with a characteristic species composition.

Characteristic Species

Crassula aquatica	water pygmyweed
Eriocaulon parkeri	estuary pipewort
Limosella australis	Welsh mudwort
Lobelia cardinalis	cardinal-flower
Samolus valerandi	seaside brookweed
Scirpus pungens	three-square
Typha angustifolia	narrow-leaf cat-tail
Zizania aquatica	Indian wild rice

APPENDIX B

Woody and Herbaceous Plant Matrices

This appendix contains woody and herbaceous plant matrices that provide seven categories of information for each plant species in Appendix A. The matrices were compiled using state and regional floras, references on gardening and landscaping, and ecological studies of individual species as well as the authors' own observations. This information is intended to assist the restorationist and landscape designer in selecting appropriate species for a given planning unit or site. The Wildflower Research Center in Austin, Texas provides lists of native plants recommended for landscaping for each state.

The seven categories of information are plant type, environmental tolerance, aesthetic value, wildlife value, flower color, bloom period, and suggested landscape uses. Letter codes are used in each category, alone or in combination, to characterize each species.

The user will find that some of the categories are very closely related. For example, short perennials (plant type) often make excellent groundcovers (landscape use); annuals (plant type) that tolerate shade and flooding (environmental tolerances) may be suitable to rapidly stabilize wooded streambanks (landscape use).

Each category and the letter codes used in the matrices are described below. A " –" denotes we could find no documented, significant, or otherwise known value. An "X" indicates the category is not applicable to that species.

PLANT TYPE

Plant type refers to the life cycle (e. g., annual, biennial, perennial) as well as plant height and other physical attributes that help characterize plant species. Height codes for both woody and herbaceous plants refer to the maximum height achieved in favorable habitat. Woody plants are perennial species that generally increase annually in size up to their maximum height. Those which achieve the greatest height comprise the canopy or overstory in a forest community. Understory trees reach a maximum height at maturity that is beneath that of canopy species but taller than shrub species. Shrubs comprise the lower layer in a forest community, or may be the sole woody component in a shrub or scrub community. For herbaceous plants, the 'small' code includes species with trailing, reclining, or procumbent habits. It should be noted that species will sometimes exceed the maximum height when used in a managed landscape where competition is reduced and other favorable factors exist.

Since woody plants are perennial, the life cycle code applies only to herbaceous plants. Herbaceous plants may complete all stages of their life cycle in a single season or live for many years. The life cycle code refers to the normal growth pattern exhibited within a species' natural range. The life cycle outside a species' natural range may change in response to climate. For example, a perennial species such as California poppy will often act as an annual when used in colder climates outside its native range.

The letter code 'G' is used to distinguish grasses from forbs because many landscape situations call for the use of grasses or forbs, or a balanced combination of both. Included in this delineation are sedges, rushes, and other grass-like plants.

Additional letter codes are used for miscellaneous codes that help to further characterize each species.

Woody Plants—Height Codes

LC   large canopy tree (over 75 feet)
SC   small canopy tree (50 to 75 feet)
LU   large understory tree (35 to 50 feet)
SU   small understory tree (20 to 35 feet)
LS   large shrub (12 to 20 feet)
MS   medium shrub (6 to 12 feet)
SS   small shrub (less than 6 feet)
WV   woody vine (height variable)
S   shrub (maximum height unknown)

Herbaceous Plants—Height Codes

L   large (over 4 feet)
M   medium (2 to 4 feet)
S   small (less than 2 feet)
HV   herbaceous vine (height variable)

Herbaceous Plants—Life Cycle Codes

A   annual—plants that live one season only, producing flowers and seeds the first season.
B   biennial—plants that live two seasons, producing flowers and seeds in both the first and second seasons or only the second season.
P   perennial—plants that live more than two seasons and generally produce flowers and seeds beginning the second season.

Miscellaneous Codes

AQ   aquatic—includes emergent plants with floating leaves and free-floating plants
C   cactus
c   coniferous (evergreen)
e   evergreen (not coniferous)
G   grass or grass-like plant (grasses, sedges, and rushes)
m   moss

ENVIRONMENTAL TOLERANCE

The tolerance of a plant species to specific environmental conditions can greatly influence its use in a managed landscape. For example, species which tolerate drought, "D," are often suitable for use in xeriscaping. Those which tolerate flooding, "F," may be suitable for streambank restoration, and those which tolerate wet soil, "W," may be suitable for wetland restoration or water gardening. Those which tolerate shade, "s," can be grown beneath mature trees, while species which tolerate both shade and sun, "Ss," are often best suited for use in woodland and savannah restoration or in gardens that receive shade part of the day. Plants tolerant of salt, "Na," may be used in coastal, brackish, or saline conditions.

D	drought	Na	salt	s	shade
F	flood	S	sun	W	wet soil

AESTHETIC VALUE

This category refers to the notable ornamental value of a species. While this category tends to be subjective, it is based on generally recognized aesthetic attributes. As botanists, we can find almost any physical characteristic to be of aesthetic interest or value. As landscapers, we look for characteristics which distinguish a plant and make it outstanding in a setting, such as a showy flower or striking autumn coloration. Many wildflowers that produce stunning displays when grown in drifts or masses are identified with the "F" code. This category is intended as a guide only. Since one person's weed is another's rose, we encourage all users of this manual to become familiar with the species native to their region and to draw their own conclusions in this regard.

A	autumn coloration	F	flowers
B	bark, twigs, or stems	f	fruit
D	dried specimens	L	foliage

WILDLIFE VALUE

It is important to recognize that nearly all plants, native or not, provide cover for wildlife species, from minute insects to large mammals. This category is intended to identify specific groups of animals that use native plants for food. Many butterflies and moths, "B," are nectar feeders while their caterpillars can be very host-specific and feed more extensively on sap or other plant parts. Hummingbirds are also nectar feeders, while ground birds and songbirds rely more extensively on seeds. Mammals use many plant parts for food, with browsing mammals relying most heavily on stems and leaves. Browsing mammals include rabbits and deer; large mammals include muskrat, raccoon, and beaver; small mammals include squirrels, mice, and moles; ground birds include grouse and quail; songbirds include finches and orioles; waterfowl and shorebirds include herons, ducks, and geese. Providing habitat for these groups will also attract larger predatory wildlife such as hawks, owls, and foxes.

The benefits of native plants to wildlife have long been recognized by biologists, but such information remains largely undocumented for many species. Most information on plant use by wildlife is derived from food habit studies of particular wildlife species. In the past, such studies focused primarily on game mammals while other species received little attention. With the increasing popularity of gardening to attract butterflies, hummingbirds, songbirds, and other desirable wildlife, more information on uses of specific plants is becoming available. Where information was available for a genus or a particular species, we often inferred wildlife value for other closely related species having similar attributes.

B	butterflies and moths	h	honeybees	S	songbirds
C	caterpillars	L	large mammals	W	waterfowl, shorebirds
G	upland ground birds	M	browsing mammals	U	unknown
H	hummingbirds	m	small mammals		

FLOWER COLOR

Often, a species will exhibit a range of flower color, or the color may grade from one shade to another. Many species will therefore have more than one color code.

B	blue	P	pink
Br	brown	Pu	purple
Bu	burgundy	R	red
G	green	W	white
Gr	gray	Y	yellow
L	lavender	yg	yellow-green
O	orange		

BLOOM PERIOD

The period of time during which a species produces flowers may encompass one season or a range of seasons. The bloom period may also vary from one region to another in response to climatic and other factors. For most species, a range of bloom periods is provided.

Sp	spring	F	fall
Su	summer	W	winter

LANDSCAPE USE

Landscape use is closely related to the other categories and refers to the various ways a plant can be successfully used in a designed landscape. There is little information identifying specific landscape uses for most native species; therefore, this information was derived from analyzing the information in the other categories. The use of letter codes was somewhat arbitrary and we hope it will not be confusing to the user. Some of the codes are so closely related that with perfect hindsight, we might have combined them; for example, quick cover, "C," and erosion control, "E." The accent specimen, "A," code is reserved for plants which, because of their showy flowers or other outstanding ornamental appeal, can be used alone as a focal point in a landscape design.

A   accent specimen (outstanding aesthetic quality)
B   wooded buffer, border, woodland, or savannah, western riparian and other partially open sites
b   bird and butterfly garden
C   quick cover
E   erosion control
F   foundation planting (suitable for use around building foundations)
G   groundcover (low cover)
g   garden bed or border
H   hedge
I   interior forest (moderate to deep shade)
M   meadow, includes deserts, glades, prairies, and other dry to mesic, open sites such as along roadsides
N   nut or fruit crop (for human consumption)
P   physical barrier (dense, thorny, stinging)
R   rocks (able to grow on rocks in dry or wet sites)
S   streambank, shoreline including sandy beaches, dunes subject to flood
s   screening (dense growth habit or evergreen)
T   shade tree
W   areas of wet soil including wet meadow, swamp, bog, marshy pond, or lake margins
wg   water garden

Woody Plant Matrix

PLANT LIST	Plant Type	Env. Tol.	Aesthetic Value	Wildlife Value	Flower Color	Bloom Period	Landscape Uses
Abies amabilis Pacific silver fir	cLC	Ss	L	GLMmS	Pu	Sp	ABIs
Abies balsamea balsam fir	cSC	FSs	L	GLMmS	PuRY	Sp	ABIsW
Abies concolor white fir	cLC	DSs	BL	GLMmS	R	SpSu	ABITs
Abies fraseri Fraser's fir	cSC	DS	L	GLMmS	—	SpSu	ABIs
Abies grandis grand fir	cLC	FS	L	GLMmS	Y	Sp	ABIs
Abies lasiocarpa subalpine fir	cLC	Ss	L	MmS	BPu	Su	ABIs
Abies magnifica California red fir	cLC	Ss	BfL	GLMmS	Pu	Sp	ABIs
Abies procera noble fir	cLC	S	L	GLMmS	PPu	—	As
Acacia angustissima prairie wattle	SS	Ss	FL	GMm	WY	SpSu	BM
Acacia berlandieri guajillo	eLS	DS	F	HhM	W	WSp	ABHMs
Acacia constricta mescat wattle	MS	DS	FB	GhMm	Y	Su	ABM
Acacia farnesiana mealy wattle	LS	DFS	F	GhMm	OY	Su	ABM
Acacia greggii long-flower catclaw	LS	DS	F	GhMm	WY	SpSu	ABMP
Acacia minuta coastal-scrub wattle	LS	DS	F	GhMm	Y	SpSu	ABM
Acacia neovernicosa trans-pecos wattle	MS	DS	F	GhMm	Y	Su	ABM
Acacia pinetorum pineland wattle	SS	DS	F	GhMm	Y	Sp	BI
Acacia rigidula chaparro-prieto	LS	DS	F	GhMm	WY	Sp	ABEP
Acacia schaffneri Schaffner's wattle	SU	DS	B	GhMm	OY	Sp	AB
Acacia tortuosa poponax	MS	DS	BF	GhMm	OY	Sp	AB
Acamptopappus shockleyi Shockley's goldenhead	SS	DS	F	M	Y	SpF	BM
Acer barbatum Florida maple	SU	FS	ABf	GHmS	yg	Sp	ST
Acer circinatum vine maple	SU	FSs	A	LM	PuR	Sp	A
Acer glabrum Rocky Mountain maple	SU	S	AL	M	yg	SpSu	AE
Acer grandidentatum canyon maple	SC	S	A	M	Y	Sp	BIT

PLANT LIST	Plant Type	Env. Tol.	Aesthetic Value	Wildlife Value	Flower Color	Bloom Period	Landscape Uses
Acer leucoderme chalk maple	SU	DS	AL	GHmS	yg	Sp	HMS
Acer macrophyllum big-leaf maple	SC	FSs	ABFL	GhLMmS	Y	Sp	ABST
Acer negundo ash-leaf maple	LU	DFS	AL	CGMmSW	yg	Sp	SWT
Acer nigrum black maple	LC	s	AL	GLmS	yg	Sp	IST
Acer pensylvanicum striped maple	LU	s	AB	GMmS	Y	Sp	AI
Acer rubrum red maple	LC	FS	AL	HmSW	R	Sp	AIWT
Acer saccharinum silver maple	LC	FS	B	HmSW	RY	Sp	CISWT
Acer saccharum sugar maple	LC	Ss	ABf	GHmS	yg	Sp	AST
Acer spicatum mountain maple	SU	Ss	A	GMmS	yg	Sp	AI
Adenostoma fasciculatum common chamise	eMS	S	BF	MmS	W	SpSu	BMs
Adenostoma sparsifolium redshank	eLS	S	B	MmS	W	Su	BMs
Aesculus californica California buckeye	LS	DS	BFfL	m	W	Su	AB
Aesculus flava yellow buckeye	LC	FSs	ABFL	m	Y	Sp	AIT
Aesculus glabra Ohio buckeye	LU	DFSs	AFfL	hm	Y	Sp	AbIT
Aesculus pavia red buckeye	LS	Ss	FL	m	R	Sp	ABS
Aesculus sylvatica painted buckeye	LS	s	F	m	PRyg	Sp	AI
Agave lechuguilla lechuguilla	eLS	DS	FfL	G	Ryg	Su	AMP
Agave neomexicana New Mexico century-plant	eLS	DS	FfL	G	yg	Su	AMP
Agave palmeri Palmer's century-plant	eLS	DS	FfL	G	GPu	Su	AMP
Agave parryi Parry's century-plant	eLS	DS	FfL	G	Ryg	Su	AMP
Agave parviflora small-flower century-plant	eLS	DS	FfL	G	PW	Su	AMP
Agave scabra rough century-plant	eLS	DS	FfL	G	Y	Su	AMP
Agave schottii Schott's century-plant	eMS	DS	FfL	G	Y	Su	AMP
Agave utahensis Utah century-plant	eLP	DS	FfL	G	Y	SpSu	AMP
Ageratina wrightii Wright's snakeroot	SS	DS	—	BS	W	F	bM

PLANT LIST	Plant Type	Env. Tol.	Aesthetic Value	Wildlife Value	Flower Color	Bloom Period	Landscape Uses
Allenrolfea occidentalis iodinebush	MS	FNaS	—	U	G	Su	W
Alnus arrulata smooth alder	LU	FS	B	GLMmS W	PuR	Sp	W
Alnus incana speckled alder	LS	FS	BL	GLMmS W	Pu	Sp	SW
Alnus oblongifolia Arizona alder	LU	Fs	AL	GLMS	RY	Sp	ES
Alnus rhombifolia white alder	SC	FSs	ABL	GLMS	G	FW	S
Alnus rubra red alder	SC	S	ABL	GLMS	R	Sp	IS
Alnus serrulata brookside alder	LS	FSW	AL	GMmS W	Y	Sp	SW
Alnus viridis sitka alder	MS	FSsW	BFL	GLMS	G	Sp	SW
Aloysia gratissima whitebrush	MS	DSs	FL	h	W	SpSuF	ABFHMR
Aloysia ligustrina beebrush	MS	DSs	FL	h	PuW	SpSuF	ABFHMR
Aloysia wrightii Wright's beebrush	MS	DS	FL	hM	W	Sp	ABFHMR
Alvaradoa amorphoides Mexican alvaradoa	eSC	Ss	—	U	GY	WF	AI
Ambrosia deltoidea triangle burr-ragweed	SS	DS	—	GMmS W	G	Sp	BM
Ambrosia dumosa white burrobush	SS	D3		GMmS W	W	SpSu	BM
Amelanchier alnifolia Saskatoon service-berry	SS	DS	FfL	GLMmS	W	Sp	BIN
Amelanchier arborea downy service-berry	SU	DS	ABF	GLMmS	W	Sp	ABINS
Amelanchier canadensis Canadian service-berry	LU	Ss	AFL	GLMmS	W	Sp	ABINS
Amelanchier laevis Allegheny service-berry	SU	Ss	AFL	GLMmS	W	Sp	BINS
Amelanchier pallida pale service-berry	SS	DS	AFL	GLMmS	W	Sp	BINS
Amelanchier stolonifera running service-berry	SS	S	Ff	GLMmS	W	Sp	B
Amelanchier utahensis Utah service-berry	SU	DS	Ff	LMmS	PW	SpSu	Ab
Amorpha canescens leadplant	SS	DSs	F	B	BPu	SpSu	bEgM
Amorpha fruticosa false indigo-bush	LS	S	F	GS	BPu	Su	AES
Amorpha herbacea cluster-spike indigo-blue	eSS	D	—	GS	Pu	—	E
Ampelopsis arborea peppervine	WV	DFSs	AfL	GLmS	G	Su	IW

PLANT LIST	Plant Type	Env. Tol.	Aesthetic Value	Wildlife Value	Flower Color	Bloom Period	Landscape Uses
Ampelopsis cordata heart-leaf peppervine	WV	Fs	AfL	GLmS	G	Sp	IS
Amyris elemifera sea torchwood	eSU	Ss	F	U	W	WSpSu F	AI
Andromeda polifolia bog-rosemary	eSS	FSs	FL	m	PW	Sp	BCW
Anisacanthus thurberi Thurber's desert-honeysuckle	SS	DS	B	M	BOR	Sp	M
Annona glabra pond-apple	eSC	FSW	F	mS	W	Sp	NW
Aplopappus laricifolius turpentine bush	SS	NaS	F	U	Y	F	BM
Aralia spinosa devil's-walkingstick	SU	Ss	FfL	GMS	W	Su	ABI
Arbutus arizonica Arizona madrone	eLU	S	B	GMmS	WP	Sp	A
Arbutus menziesii Pacific madrone	eLC	S	ABFL	GMmS	W	Sp	AB
Arctostaphylos canescens hoary manzanita	eMS	DS	B	GLMmS	WP	WSp	BM
Arctostaphylos glandulosa Eastwood's manzanita	eMS	DS	BF	GLMmS	WP	WSp	ABM
Arctostaphylos glauca big-berry manzanita	eLS	DS	BF	GLMmS	W	WSp	ABEM
Arctostaphylos manzanita big manzanita	eSU	DS	BF	GLMmS	PW	WSp	ABEM
Arctostaphylos myrtifolia ione manzanita	eSS	DS	BF	GLMmS	PW	WSP	BM
Arctostaphylos nevadensis pinemat manzanita	eSS	S	BfL	GLMmS	PW	Sp	BCGI
Arctostaphylos nummularia Fort Bragg manzanita	eSS	S	BL	GLMms	W	WSp	BM
Arctostaphylos parryana pineland manzanita	eMS	DS	BL	GLMmS	PW	Sp	B
Arctostaphylos patula green-leaf manzanita	eMS	Ss	BL	GLMmS	P	Sp	B
Arctostaphylos pringlei pink-bract manzanita	eSU	DS	BF	GLMmS	W	W	E
Arctostaphylos pungens Mexican manzanita	eMS	DS	BL	GLMm	PW	WSp	BEMN
Arctostaphylos stanfordiana Stanford's manzanita	eMS	S	BL	GLMmS	PPu	WSp	BM
Arctostaphylos tomentosa hairy manzanita	eSS	S	BL	GLMmS	PW	WSp	BM
Arctostaphylos uva-ursi red bearberry	eSS	DS	BFfL	hLMm	PW	Sp	bGM
Arctostaphylos viscida white-leaf manzanita	eMS	DS	BFL	GLMmS	P	WSp	AB
Ardisia escallonoides island marl-berry	eSU	DSs	BFf	S	W	SpF	BAI

PLANT LIST	Plant Type	Env. Tol.	Aesthetic Value	Wildlife Value	Flower Color	Bloom Period	Landscape Uses
Argusia gnaphalodes sea-rosemary	eMS	DS	F	U	W	WSpSuF	EgS
Aronia arbutifolia red chokeberry	MS	DFSs	AFfL	GLMmS	W	Sp	AgNW
Aronia melanocarpa black chokeberry	MS	FSs	AFfL	GLMmS	W	SpSu	AgNW
Artemisia arbuscula dwarf sagebrush	eSS	DSs	L	GMm	Br	Su	BM
Artemisia bigelovii flat sagebrush	eSS	DS	BL	GMm	Y	SuF	BgM
Artemisia californica coastal sagebrush	eSS	DS	L	GLMm	PuY	SuF	M
Artemisia cana hoary sagebrush	eSS	DS	BL	M	WY	Su	ABgM
Artemisia filifolia silver sagebrush	SS	DS	L	GLMm	WY	SpF	ABEgM
Artemisia frigida prairie sagebrush	SS	DS	L	GM	Y	SuF	BM
Artemisia nova black sagebrush	SS	DNaS	L	GLMm	BrG	SuF	M
Artemisia pedatifida big-foot sagebrush	SS	DS	L	GLMm	BrG	SpSu	M
Artemisia rothrockii timberline sagebrush	eSS	S	BL	GLMm	PuY	SuF	BM
Artemisia spinescens bud sagebrush	eSS	DNaS	BL	GLMm	PY	SpSu	GgM
Artemisia tridentata big sagebrush	eMS	DNaS	BL	GLMm	BrY	SuF	BM
Artemisia tripartita three-tip sagebrush	SS	DS	L	GLMm	Br	Su	M
Arundinaria gigantea giant cane	eLPG	DFSs	BL	MS	G	SpSu	BEIMPSsW
Asimina incana woolly pawpaw	MS	Ss	F	Lm	W	Sp	IN
Asimina parviflora small-flower pawpaw	MS	Ss	F	Lm	Pu	Sp	IN
Asimina reticulata netted pawpaw	SS	S	F	Lm	W	Sp	I
Asimina triloba common pawpaw	SU	Ss	FfL	Lm	R	Sp	BINS
Aster carolinianus climbing aster	WV	FW	F	GMmS	PPu	WSpSuF	W
Atriplex canescens four-wing saltbush	eSS	DNaS	f	GMm	—	SuF	EM
Atriplex confertifolia shadscale	SS	DNaS	f	GLMmSW	—	SpSu	M
Atriplex gardneri Gardner's saltbush	MS	DNaS	f	GLMmSW	Br	SuF	BMW
Atriplex hymenelytra desert-holly	SS	DS	fL	GMsSW	—	SuF	M

PLANT LIST	Plant Type	Env. Tol.	Aesthetic Value	Wildlife Value	Flower Color	Bloom Period	Landscape Uses
Atriplex lentiformis quailbush	MS	DNaS	f	GLMmS W	—	SuF	M
Atriplex nuttallii Nuttall's saltbush	SS	DNaS	f	GLMmS W	—	Su	M
Atriplex polycarpa cattle-spinach	SS	DFNaS	f	GLMmS W	—	SuF	M
Atriplex spinifera spinescale	SS	DNaS	—	GLMmS W	—	SuF	M
Avicennia germinans black mangrove	LS	NaSW	f	h	WY	Su	W
Baccharis angustifolia saltwater false willow	MS	FNaSW	F	M	WY	WSpSuF	W
Baccharis glomeruliflora silverling	LS	FNaSW	F	M	WY	WSpSuF	W
Baccharis halimifolia groundseltree	MS	DFNaS	AFfL	SW	GW	F	ESW
Baccharis neglecta Roosevelt-weed	MS	—	—	M	Br	—	—
Baccharis pilularis coyotebrush	SS	DS	F	M	WY	SuF	BE
Baccharis sarothroides rosinbush	SS	DNaS	BFf	M	WY	SuF	AEM
Baccharis sergiloides squaw's false willow	SS	DS	F	M	WY	SPSUF	BM
Befaria racemosa tarflower	eMS	DSS	F	U	PW	WSp	ABgI
Berchemia scandens Alabama supplejack	WV	DFS	AfL	GMmS	W	Sp	BW
Betula alleghaniensis yellow birch	LC	Ss	AB	CGLMmS	yg	Sp	ABI
Betula glandulosa scrub birch	SS	FSW	L	CGLMmS	G	Sp	BW
Betula lenta sweet birch	SC	DSs	A	CGLMmS	yg	Sp	AIT
Betula nigra river birch	SC	DFS	ABL	C	Br	Sp	ABSsT
Betula occidentalis water birch	SU	FSW	ABL	M	G	Sp	ABSW
Betula papyrifera paper birch	SC	DS	ABL	CGMmS	yg	Sp	ABI
Betula populifolia gray birch	LU	FS	ABL	CMmSW	yg	SpF	BCEW
Betula pumila bog birch	LS	FSW	A	CGmSW	yg	Sp	W
Bignonia capreolata crossvine	eWV	S	F	H	OR	Su	BI
Borrichia arborescens tree seaside-tansy	SS	FNaSW	F	U	Y	WSpSuF	SW
Borrichia frutescens bushy seaside-tansy	SS	FNaSW	F	U	Y	SpF	SMW

PLANT LIST	Plant Type	Env. Tol.	Aesthetic Value	Wildlife Value	Flower Color	Bloom Period	Landscape Uses
Bourreria cassinifolia smooth strongbark	eSU	DSs	F	U	W	WSpSu F	ABI
Bourreria ovata Bahama strongbark	eSU	Ss	F	U	W	WSpSu F	ABI
Bourreria succulenta bodywood	eSU	DSs	F	U	W	WSpSu F	ABI
Brickellia californica California brickellbush	SS	FDS	F	G	GY	Su	BRS
Brickellia laciniata split-leaf brickellbush	SS	D	—	G	GWY	—	—
Brunnichia ovata American buckwheatvine	WV	F	—	GMmS	G	Su	B
Buddleja racemosa wand butterfly-bush	SS	DS	F	M	Y	Sp	—
Buddleja scordioides escobilla butterfly-bush	SS	DS	F	M	GW	SpSuF	bRM
Bursera microphylla elephant tree	LS	DS	B	U	W	Su	ABM
Bursera simaruba gumbo-limbo	SC	DS	B	U	G	SpSu	ABI
Byrsonima lucida long key locust-berry	eLU	DFS	Ff	U	PPuW	WSpSu F	AIB
Caesalpinia bonduc yellow nicker	WV	DFNaS	F	U	Y	WSpSu F	B
Caesalpinia crista gray nicker	SS	DNaS	F	U	Y	SpSu	BSM
Caesalpinia pauciflora few-flower nicker	SS	DSs	F	U	Y	Su	BFI
Calliandra eriophylla fairy-duster	SS	DS	F	GLM	PuW	Sp	AM
Callicarpa americana American beauty-berry	MS	DS	FfL	GLMmS	PPu	SpSu	ABFgHM
Calocedrus decurrens incense-cedar	cLC	DSs	FfL	M	—	—	ABIST
Calycanthus floridus eastern sweetshrub	MS	FNaSs	F	U	BrR	SpSu	ABfg
Calyptranthes pallens pale lidflower	eSU	s	B	U	Br	SpSu	BFI
Calyptranthes zuzygium myrtle-of-the-river	eSU	s	BL	U	W	Su	BI
Campsis radicans trumpet-creeper	WV	DFS	FL	HT	OR	SuF	BbSs
Canella winteriana pepper-cinnamon	eSC	Ss	BFf	U	PuR	SuF	AI
Canotia holacantha crucifixion-thorn	LS	DS	B	U	W	Su	BM
Capparis cynophallophora Jamaican caper	SC	Ss	L	GMmS	W	SpSu	AI
Capparis flexuosa falseteeth	SC	Ss	L	GMmS	PW	SpSu	AI

PLANT LIST	Plant Type	Env. Tol.	Aesthetic Value	Wildlife Value	Flower Color	Bloom Period	Landscape Uses
Carnegia gigantea saguaro	C	DS	B	GMmS	W	Sp	AM
Carpinus caroliniana American hornbeam	LU	FS	AB	SW	R	Sp	ABISW
Carya alba mockernut hickory	LC	DS	B	GLMmS W	yg	Sp	AINT
Carya aquatica water hickory	LC	FSW	B	GLMmS W	BY	Sp	ITW
Carya carolinae-septentrionalis southern shag-bark hickory	LC	DFS	ABL	GLMmS W	yg	Sp	INT
Carya cordiformis bitter-nut hickory	LC	FSs	AL	GLMmS W	yg	Sp	IT
Carya floridana scrub hickory	SC	DS	AL	GLMmS W	yg	Sp	BI
Carya glabra pignut hickory	LC	DS	AL	GLMmS W	yg	Sp	IT
Carya illinoinensis pecan	LC	FS	AL	GLMmS	yg	Sp	INST
Carya laciniosa shell-bark hickory	LC	S	AL	GLMmS	yg	Sp	INT
Carya ovalis red hickory	LC	DFS	AL	GLMmS W	yg	Sp	IT
Carya ovata shag-bark hickory	LC	DFS	ABL	GLMmS W	yg	Sp	INT
Carya pallida sand hickory	LC	S	AB	GLMmS W	B	Sp	IT
Carya texana black hickory	SC	DFS W	AL	GLMmS W	—	Sp	ITW
Casasia ligustrina seven-year-apple	eSU	D	—	U	W	WSpSu F	BS
Castanea dentata American chestnut	LC	Ss	Ff	GMmS	Y	Su	AINT
Castanea pumila Allegheny-chinkpin	SU	DS	Ff	GMmS	Y	Su	BIN
Castanopsis chrysophylla golden chinkapin	eLC	DS	BF	GMS	W	Su	BNS
Castanopsis sempervirens Sierran chinkapin	eMS	DS	F	GMS	W	Su	Bs
Castela emoryi thorn-of-Christ	MS	DS	Ff	U	PuR	Sp	gM
Castela erecta goatbush	SS	DS	Ff	U	OR	Sp	BM
Catalpa bignonioides southern catalpa	LU	FS	Ff	C	W	Su	ABT
Catalpa speciosa nothern catalpa	LC	FSW	Ff	C	W	Sp	ASTW
Catesbaea parviflora small-flower lilythorn	MS	DSs	f	U	W	SpSuF	BPS
Ceanothus americanus New Jersey-tea	SS	DSs	FL	GhMmS	W	SpSu	BFgM

PLANT LIST	Plant Type	Env. Tol.	Aesthetic Value	Wildlife Value	Flower Color	Bloom Period	Landscape Uses
Ceanothus cordulatus mountain whitethorn	SS	DS	BF	GhLMm	W	SpSu	BgP
Ceanothus crassifolius snowball	MS	DS	F	GhLMm	W	SpSu	Bg
Ceanothus cuneatus sedge-leaf buckbrush	MS	DS	F	GhLMm	W	SpSu	BMP
Ceanothus dentatus sandscrub	eSS	S	F	GhLMm	B	SpSu	BgM
Ceanothus diversifolius pinemat	eSS	Ss	FL	GhLMm	B	SpSu	BgI
Ceanothus fendleri Fendler's buckbrush	SS	Ss	F	GhLMm	W	SpSu	BFgR
Ceanothus fresnensis fresnomat	SS	S	F	GhLMm	B	—	BM
Ceanothus greggii Mojave buckbrush	SS	DS	F	GhLMm	W	SpSu	BHMR
Ceanothus herbaceous prairie redroot	SS	FSs	FfL	GHhMmS	W	Su	BbgM
Ceanothus impressus Santa Barbara buckbrush	eSS	Ss	F	GhLMm	B	—	BgM
Ceanothus integerrimus deerbrush	MS	Ss	BF	GhLMm	BW	SuF	ABg
Ceanothus jepsonii muskbush	SS	S	F	GhLMm	BW		B
Ceanothus leucodermis jackbrush	S	S	—	GMm	BW	SuF	—
Ceanothus oliganthus explorer's-bush	MS	DS	F	GhLMm	BPuW	—	Bg
Ceanothus palmeri cuyamaca-bush	MS	DS	BF	GhLMm	BW	Sp	Bg
Ceanothus parryi ladybloom	eMS	Ss	F	GhLMm	B	—	Bgs
Ceanothus parvifolius cattlebush	SS	Ss	F	GhLMm	B	—	Bg
Ceanothus pinetorum Kern River buckbrush	SS	Ss	F	GhLMm	BW	—	BI
Ceanothus prostratus squawcarpet	SS	Ss	BFL	GhLMm	B	SpSu	BGI
Ceanothus sanguineus Oregon teatree	LS	Ss	BF	GhLMm	W	SpSu	ABg
Ceanothus spinosus redheart	eSU	DS	BF	GhLMm	BW	Sp	Bgs
Ceanothus thyrsiflorus bluebrush	eSU	Ss	F	GhLMm	BW	Sp	BgIS
Ceanothus tomentosus ionebush	MS	DS	BFL	GhLMm	B	—	Bg
Ceanothus velutinus tobacco-brush	eSS	Ss	FL	GhLMm	W	Su	BgI
Ceanothus verrucosus barranca-bush	SS	DS	F	GhLMm	W	Su	BgM

PLANT LIST	Plant Type	Env. Tol.	Aesthetic Value	Wildlife Value	Flower Color	Bloom Period	Landscape Uses
Celastrus scandens American bittersweet	WV	DFSs	AfL	GmS	G	Sp	BI
Celtis laevigata sugar-berry	SC	FSs	AB	S	G	Sp	ABISTW
Celtis occidentalis common hackberry	LC	DFSs	B	BmS	yg	Sp	AbNST
Celtis pallida shiny hackberry	eLS	DS	B	BGhLMS	W	—	BMs
Cephalanthus occidentali common buttonbush	MS	FSW	FL	BFhMmSW	W	Su	SWwg
Ceratiola ericoides sand-heath	eMS	DS	FL	U	RY	SpSuF	BFHM
Cercis canadensis redbud	SU	DFSs	ABFL	Hh	P	Sp	ABbgI
Cercocarpus intricatus little-leaf mountain-mahogany	S	DS	—	GM	—	—	B
Cercocarpus ledifolius curl-leaf mountain-mahogany	eSU	DS	L	GM	—	Su	BS
Cercocarpus montanus alder-leaf mountain-mahogany	MS	DS	fL	GM	G	Sp	B
Chamaebatia foliolosa Sierran mountain-misery	eSS	s	L	U	W	—	GI
Chamaebatiaria millifolium fernbush	SS	DS	FL	U	W	Su	FgMR
Chamaecyparis lawsoniana Port Orford-cedar	cLC	Ss	L	LMS	R	Sp	ABFH
Chamaecyparis nootkatensis Alaska-cedar	cLC	S	L	LMS	BY	Sp	A
Chamaecyparis thyoides Atlantic white-cedar	cLU	FS	L	LMS	Ryg	Sp	wg
Chamaedaphne calyculata leatherleaf	eSS	FSW	L	GMS	W	SpSu	W
Chilopsis linearis desert-willow	SU	DS	F	hS	PPu	Su	A
Chiococca alba West Indian milkberry	eSS	Ss	L	U	WY	WSpSuF	ABI
Chionanthus virginicus white fringetree	SU	Ss	AFL	S	W	Sp	ABFg
Chrysobalanus icaco icaco coco-plum	eSU	Na	—	U	G	Sp	Is
Chrysoma pauciflosculosa woody goldenrod	SS	DS	—	U	Y	SpSu	BG
Chrysophyllum oliviforme satinleaf	eSC	DSs	L	U	G	WF	As
Chrysothamnus depressus long-flower rabbitbrush	SS	DS	F	MmS	Y	Su	M
Chrysothamnus nauseosus rubber rabbitbrush	MS	DFNaS	FL	hLMmS	WY	SuF	Eg
Chrysothamnus paniculatus dotted rabbitbrush	SS	DS	F	MmS	Y	Su	BM

PLANT LIST	Plant Type	Env. Tol.	Aesthetic Value	Wildlife Value	Flower Color	Bloom Period	Landscape Uses
Chrysothamnus parryi Parry's rabbitbrush	SS	DS	F	MmS	Y	Su	BM
Chrysothamnus pumilis rabbitbrush	SS	DS	BF	MmS	Y	Su	BM
Chrysothamnus teretifolius needle-leaf rabbitbrush	SS	DS	F	LMmS	Y	Su	BM
Chrysothamnus vaseyi Vasey's rabbitbrush	SS	DS	F	MmS	Y	Su	BM
Chrysothamnus viscidiflorus green rabbitbrush	MS	DS	BF	MmS	Y	Su	M
Cissus verticillata seasonvine	WV	—	—	U	GW	SpSu	—
Citharexylum fruticosum Florida fiddlewood	eSU	Ss	F	U	W	WSpSuF	BIS
Clematis columbiana Columbian virgin's-bower	WV	S	F	U	BPu	Su	B
Clematis ligusticifolia deciduous traveler's-joy	WV	DS	F	M	W	SpSuF	Bg
Clematis virginiana devil's-darning-needles	WV	DFSs	FL	S	W	SuF	BW
Cleome isomeris bladder-pod spider-flower	S	—	—	U	Y	WSpSuF	—
Clethra acuminata mountain sweet-pepperbush	MS	s	AFL	C	W	Su	BFI
Clethra alnifolia coastal sweet-pepperbush	MS	FSsW	AFL	BGmSW	PW	SuF	bIWwg
Cliftonia monophylla buckwheat-tree	eSU		Ff	hM	R	WSp	AWs
Coccoloba diversifolia tietongue	eSC	FS	fL	U	W	Su	BEs
Coccoloba uvifera seaside-grape	eLS	S	L	U	W	Su	ABFSs
Coccothrinax argentata Florida silver palm	eSU	DS	L	S	W	Su	ABs
Coleogyne ramosissima blackbrush	SS	DS	F	M	WY	Sp	E
Colubrina arborescens greenheart	eSU	DS	—	L	G	SuF	Is
Colubrina cubensis Cuban nakedwood	eSU	Ss	—	L	G	Su	Is
Colubrina elliptica soldierwood	eSU	Ss	B	L	yg	SpF	AIs
Colubrina texensis hog-plum	MS	DS	—	L	yg	Sp	H
Comptonia peregrina sweet-fern	SS	DS	L	GMm	Br	Sp	EI
Condalia ericoides javelin-bush	SS	DS	—	U	—	—	M
Condalia hookeri Brazilian bluewood	eSU	Ss	FL	S	G	Sp	Hs

PLANT LIST	Plant Type	Env. Tol.	Aesthetic Value	Wildlife Value	Flower Color	Bloom Period	Landscape Uses
Condalia spathulata squawbush	eMS	DS	—	GM	G	—	Ms
Conocarpus erectus button mangrove	eSU	FNaSW	L	U	G	WSpSuF	Ws
Cordia globosa curaciao-bush	eSS	Ss	F	U	W	WSpSuF	Bl
Cordia sebestena large-leaf geigertree	eSU	NaS	F	U	R	WSpSuF	ABFs
Corema conradii broom-crowberry	eSS	Ss	FL	U	BrPu	Sp	BEs
Cornus alternifolia alternate-leaf dogwood	SU	FSs	AFf	BGMmSW	W	Sp	ABFIS
Cornus amomum silky dogwood	MS	FS	ABFL	BMmSW	W	Su	BEgISW
Cornus drummondii rough-leaf dogwood	MS	Ss	L	GLMmS	W	Sp	B
Cornus florida flowering dogwood	LU	DSs	AFf	BGLMmS	WY	Sp	ABI
Cornus foemina stiff dogwood	LS	FS	ABF	BGLMmS	W	Sp	BW
Cornus glabrata smooth-leaf dogwood	SU	FSs	A	GLMmS	W	Sp	BS
Cornus nuttalli Pacific flowering dogwood	SU	s	FfL	GLMmSW	W	Sp	BI
Cornus racemosa gray dogwood	LS	DFSs	ABF	BGMmSW	W	Sp	BbFg
Cornus rugosa round-leaf dogwood	MS	Ss	AfL	BGLMmS	W	Su	Bl
Cornus sericea redosier	MS	FSs	ABL	BLMmSW	W	SpSu	BSW
Cornus stolonifera redosier dogwood	SS	FsW	AB	GLMmS	W	Su	SW
Corylus americana American hazelnut	MS	DSs	Ff	GLMmS	BrR	Sp	ABIN
Corylus cornuta beaked hazelnut	SS	DSs	AL	GLMmS	BrR	Sp	BHNs
Coryphantha cornifera rhinoceros cactus	C	DS	BF	U	Y	SpSu	gM
Coryphantha macromeris nipple beehive cactus	C	DS	BF	U	PuR	SpSu	gM
Coryphantha ramillosa whiskerbush	C	DS	BF	U	PPu	SpSu	gM
Coryphantha recurvata Santa Cruz beehive cactus	C	DS	BF	U	RY	SpSu	gM
Coryphantha scheeri long-tubercle beehive cactus	C	DS	BF	U	RY	SpSu	gM
Coryphantha sulcata pineapple cactus	C	DS	BF	U	RY	SpSu	gM
Coursetia glandulosa rosary baby-bonnets	Ss	DSs	BF	U	PW	SpSuF	gM

PLANT LIST	Plant Type	Env. Tol.	Aesthetic Value	Wildlife Value	Flower Color	Bloom Period	Landscape Uses
Crataegus douglasii black hawthorn	LS	DFS	BFfL	GhLMm SW	W	Sp	BbFS
Crataegus marshallii parsley hawthorn	LS	FS	BFfL	GhLMm SW	W	Sp	b
Crataegus spathulata little-hip hawthorn	LS	Ss	L	GhLMm SW	W	Sp	Bb
Crossopetalum rhacoma maiden-berry	SU	s	—	U	GR	SpSu	I
Crossosoma bigelovii ragged rockflower	SS	DS	—	U	PuW	Sp	—
Croton linearis grannybush	SS	DSs	—	GmS	—	WSpSuF	BMS
Cupania glabra Florida toadwood	eSU	Ss	—	U	—	F	s
Cupressus arizonica Arizona cypress	cSC	DS	BfL	Mm	Y	Sp	AEs
Cupressus bakeri Modoc cypress	cSC	DS	L	Mm	—	—	AHs
Cupressus forbesii Tecate cypress	c	DS	BL	Mm	—	—	AHs
Cupressus glabra Arizona smooth cypress	cSC	DNaS	BL	Mm	—	—	AHs
Cupressus goveniana Gowen cypress	cSC	S	BL	Mm	—	—	AHs
Cupressus macnabiana MacNab's cypress	cLU	DS	BL	Mm	yg	Sp	AHs
Cupressus macrocarpa Monterey cypress	cSC	NaS	BL	Mm	—	—	AHs
Cupressus nevadensis Paiute cypress	cLU	S	L	Mm	Y	WSp	AHs
Cupressus pygmaea Mendocino cypress	cSC	DS	L	Mm	—	—	AHs
Cupressus sargentii Sargent's cypress	cMS	DS	L	Mm	—	—	AHs
Cupressus stephensonii Cuyamaca cypress		S	L	Mm	—	—	AHs
Cyrilla racemiflora swamp titi	eSU	DFS	AFL	hMSW	W	Su	bgW
Dalbergia brownii Brown's Indian-rosewood	SS	DSs	F	U	PW	—	BgP
Dalbergia ecastaphyllum coinvine	MS	DSW	Ff	U	PW	Sp	BSW
Dalea formosa featherplume	SS	DS	F	m	Pu	SpSuF	AM
Dasylirion leiophyllum green sotol	SS	DS	L	GM	WY	Su	AM
Dasylirion wheeleri common sotol	SS	DS	L	GM	WY	Su	AM
Decodon verticillatus swamp-loosetrife	LS	FSW	F	m	P	Su	Wwg

PLANT LIST	Plant Type	Env. Tol.	Aesthetic Value	Wildlife Value	Flower Color	Bloom Period	Landscape Uses
Diervilla lonicera northern bush-honeysuckle	SS	DSs	AFL	BHS	R	Su	bI
Diospyros texana Texas persimmon	eLU	DS	BL	BGLMmS	GW	Sp	ABNs
Diospyros virginiana common persimmon	SC	DFS	BLf	BGLMmS	Y	Su	BNT
Diplacus longiflorus southern bush-monkey-flower	eSS	S	—	U	PY	SpSu	—
Dirca palustris eastern leatherwood	SS	Ss	AL	GMS	Y	Sp	IS
Dodonaea viscosa Florida hopbush	eSU	FS	—	U	yg	WF	AWs
Drypetes diversifolia milkbark	eSU	S	—	U	yg	Su	Is
Drypetes lateriflora Guiana-plum	eSU	Ss	—	U	yg	WSp	Is
Echinocactus horizonthalonius devil's-head	C	DS	BF	mS	PY	Sp	AgM
Echinocactus polycephalus cotton-top cactus	C	DS	BF	mS	Y	Sp	AgM
Echinocactus texensis horse-crippler	C	DS	BF	mS	PuR	Sp	AgM
Echinocereus chloranthus brown-spine hedgehog cactus	C	DS	BF	mS	BrGR	Sp	AgM
Echinocereus coccineus scarlet hedgehog cactus	C	DS	BF	mS	R	Sp	AgM
Echinocereus engelmannii saints cactus	C	DS	BF	mS	PPu	Sp	AgMR
Echinocereus enneacanthus pitaya	C	DS	BF	mS	Pu	Sp	AgMR
Echinocereus fendleri pink-flower hedgehog cactus	C	DS	BF	mS	PuR	Sp	AgMR
Echinocereus pectinatus Texas rainbow cactus	C	DS	BF	mS	LPuY	Sp	Agm
Echinocereus reichenbachii lace hedgehog cactus	C	DS	BF	mS	PPu	SpSu	AgM
Echinocereus rigidissimus rainbow hedgehog cactus	C	DS	BF	mS	—	Sp	AgM
Echinocereus stramineus strawberry hedgehog cactus	C	DS	BF	mS	—	Sp	AgM
Echinocereus triglochidiatus king-cup cactus	C	DS	BF	mS	R	Sp	AgM
Echites umbellata devil's-potato	Wv	Ss	F	U	W	WSpSuF	B
Ehretia anacua knockaway	eSC	Ss	AB	GhLMS	W	Sp	ABITs
Elaeagnus commutata American silver-berry	MS	DNaS	BF	GMS	Y	Sp	AMW
Encelia californica California brittlebush	SS	DS	F	U	PuY	Sp	gM

PLANT LIST	Plant Type	Env. Tol.	Aesthetic Value	Wildlife Value	Flower Color	Bloom Period	Landscape Uses
Encelia farinosa goldenhills	SS	DS	FL	U	Y	Sp	gM
Encelia virginensis virgin river brittlebush	SS	DSs	L	U	Y	Sp	M
Ephedra antisyphilitica clapweed	eSS	DS	B	GLM	Y	Sp	BgM
Ephedra californica California joint-fir	SS	DS	B	GLMm	—	Sp	gM
Ephedra nevadensis Nevada joint-fir	SS	DS	B	GLM	—	Sp	gM
Ephedra torreyana Torrey's joint-fir	SS	DS	B	GLM	Y	Sp	gM
Ephedra trifurca long-leaf joint-fir	MS	DS	B	GLM	Y	Sp	gM
Ephedra viridis Mormon-tea	SS	DS	B	GLM	BG	SpSu	gM
Epigaea repens trailing-arbutus	eSS	DSs	FL	GMm	PW	Sp	BGgI
Epithelantha micromeris ping-pong-ball cactus	C	DS	B	S	P	—	gM
Ericameria cooperi Cooper's heath-goldenrod	SS	DS	F	M	Y	—	M
Ericameria cuneata cliff heath-goldenrod	eSS	DS	F	M	Y	—	MR
Ericameria gilmanii white-flower heath-goldenrod	S	DS	F	M	WY	SuF	M
Ericameria laricifolia turpentine-bush	eSS	DS	F	M	Y	F	BGM
Ericameria linearifolius narrow-leaf heath-goldenrod	S	DS	F	M	Y	Sp	M
Eriodictyon angustifolium narrow-leaf yerba-santa	eMS	DS	F	M	W	Sp	BgMs
Eriodictyon californicum California yerba-santa	eMS	DS	F	M	BW	Sp	gMs
Eriodictyon trichocalyx hairy yerba-santa	MS	DS	F	M	BW	Sp	gMs
Eriogonum elongatum long-stem wild buckwheat	SS	DS	—	GLMmS	W	Su	BM
Eriogonum fasciculatum eastern Mojave wild buckwheat	SS	DS	—	GhLMmS	W	SuF	BgM
Eriogonum heermannii Heermann's wild buckwheat	SS	DS	—	GLMmS	Y	Su	BM
Eriogonum heracleoides Parsnip-flower wild buckwheat	SS	DS	—	GLMmS	W	Su	BM
Eriogonum microthecum slender wild buckwheat	SS	DS	—	GLMmS	PWY	Su	BM
Eriogonum niveum snow wild buckwheat	SS	L	—	GLMmS	W	Su	BgM
Eriogonum ovalifolium cushion wild buckwheat	SS	S	BL	GLMmS	RW	Su	gMR

PLANT LIST	Plant Type	Env. Tol.	Aesthetic Value	Wildlife Value	Flower Color	Bloom Period	Landscape Uses
Eriogonum umbellatum sulphur-flower wild buckwheat	SS	DS	FL	GLMmS	Y	Su	CgMR
Eriogonum wrightii hastard-sage	SS	DS	F	GLMmS	PW	Su	BFGR
Erithalis fruticosa blacktorch	SC	Ss	—	U	W	WSpSu F	BIS
Erythrina flabelliformis coral-bean	SU	DS	F	U	R	Sp	ABH
Erythrina herbacea red-cardinal	LS	S	F	U	R	SpSuF	ABHT
Escobaria orcuttii Orcutt's fox-tail cactus	C	DS	B	mS	—	—	gM
Escobaria tuberculosa white-column fox-tail cactus	C	DS	B	mS	—	—	gM
Escobaria vivipara spinystar	C	DS	B	Ms	P	—	gM
Eugenia axillaris white stopper	eSU	Ss	Ff	U	W	SuF	ABIs
Eugenia confusa red-berry stopper	eSU	Ss	Ff	U	W	Su	ABIs
Eugenia foetida box-leaf stopper	eSU	Ss	Ff	U	W	SuF	ABIs
Eugenia rhombea red stopper	eSU	Ss	Ff	U	W	SuF	ABFIs
Eupatorium azureum blue boneset	MS	Ss	F	BGS	B	WSpSu	Bb
Evonymus americanus American strawberry-bush	MS	Ss	f	GmS	Pu	Su	I
Evonymus atropurpureus eastern wahoo	SU	FSs	AfL	GS	R	Su	BSs
Exostema caribaeum Caribbean princewood	eSC	Ss	—	U	W	Su	BFIs
Exothea paniculata butterbough	eSC	Ss	F	U	W	SpSu	ABFIs
Eysenhardtia orthocarpa Tahitian kidneywood	SU	DS	—	U	W	Sp	—
Eysenhardtia texana Texas kidneywood	LS	DS	—	h	W	SpSu	Ab
Fagus grandifolia American beech	LC	Ss	AB	GLMmS	yg	Sp	AIT
Fallugia paradoxa Apache-plume	MS	DS	Ff	M	W	Su	E
Fendlerella utahensis Utah-fendlerbush	SS	DS	B	M	W	Su	BM
Ferocactus cylindraceus California barrel cactus	C	DS	BF	mS	Y	SpSu	AgRM
Ferocactus hamatacanthus turk's head	C	DS	BF	mS	Y	SpSu	AgM
Ferocactus wislizeni candy barrel cactus	C	DS	BF	mS	OY	SpSu	AgM

PLANT LIST	Plant Type	Env. Tol.	Aesthetic Value	Wildlife Value	Flower Color	Bloom Period	Landscape Uses
Ficus aurea Florida strangler fig	eSC	DSs	BL	mS	—	SpSuFW	ABIs
Ficus citrifolia wild banyantree	eSU	FS	B	mS	R	WSpSuF	ABs
Flourensia cernua American tarwort	SS	DS	—	U	Y	WF	M
Forestiera acuminata eastern swamp-privit	LS	FSsW	L	GMSW	G	Sp	SW
Forestiera angustifolia Texas swamp-privet	eSU	NaS	—	GMS	G	Sp	BMs
Forestiera ligustrina upland swamp-privet	MS	DSs	L	GMSW	G	Su	BgS
Forestiera pubescens stretchberry	MS	FSs	—	GMmS	G	Sp	BES
Forestiera segregata Florida swamp-privet	eSU	FS	L	GMSW	Y	Sp	BIs
Fouquieria splendens ocotillo	LS	DS	BF	S	OR	WSpSuF	AH
Frangula alnus alder-buckthorn	MS	S	L	h	G	Sp	H
Frangula betulifolia birch-leaf buckthorn	MS	—	L	GLMmS	—	—	—
Frangula californica California coffee berry	eSS	DS	L	GLMmS	G	Su	B
Frangula caroliniana Carolina buckthorn	LS	FSsW	FL	GLMmS	W	SpSu	ABS
Frangula purshiana cascara sagrada	LS	S	—	GLMmS	G	—	—
Frankenia salina alkali sea-heath	SS	S	L	U	P	—	—
Fraxinus americana white ash	LC	DFS	A	GLMmSW	Pu	Sp	IT
Fraxinus anomala single-leaf ash	SC	DS	L	GMmNS	G	Sp	A
Fraxinus berlandieriana Mexican ash	SC	F	L	GLMmS	G	Sp	AT
Fraxinus caroliniana Carolina ash	LU	FS	L	GLMmSW	yg	Sp	W
Fraxinus dipetala two-petal ash	MS	DS	F	GLMmSW	W	Sp	B
Fraxinus latifolia Oregon ash	SC	S	L	GLMmSW	—	Sp	T
Fraxinus nigra black ash	SC	FS	AL	GLMmSW	Pu	Sp	bSW
Fraxinus pennsylvanica green ash	LC	DFS	A	GLMmSW	Pu	Sp	IT
Fraxinus profunda pumpkin ash	LC	FSW	L	GLMmSW	—	—	W
Fraxinus quadrangulata blue ash	SC	DSs	AL	GLMmSW	Pu	Sp	BIST

PLANT LIST	Plant Type	Env. Tol.	Aesthetic Value	Wildlife Value	Flower Color	Bloom Period	Landscape Uses
Fraxinus texensis Texas ash	LU	DS	AL	GLMmS	Y	Sp	AT
Fraxinus velutina velvet ash	SC	S	L	GLMmS	yg	Sp	T
Fremontodendron californicum California flannelbush	eSU	S	—	U	Y	Sp	—
Garberia heterophylla garberia	eMS	DS	F	U	P	Su	BIs
Garrya buxifolia dwarf silktassel	eSS	DS	L	GM	—	—	—
Garrya elliptica wavy-leaf silktassel	eMS	S	FL	GM	—	W	s
Garrya flavescens ashy silktassel	eMS	DS	L	GM	—	W	s
Garrya fremontii bearbush	eMS	DS	L	GM	—	—	s
Garrya ovata lindheimer silktassel	eLS	DSs	L	GM	—	Sp	BR
Garrya veatchii canyon silktassel	SS	DS	L	GM	—	W	—
Garrya wrightii Wright's silktassel	eMS	DSs	L	GM	—	SpSu	BRs
Gaultheria hispidula creeping-snowberry	eSS	s	FfL	GLMmS	W	Sp	FGIW
Gaultheria procumbens eastern teaberry	eSS	DFSs	L	GLMm	W	SpSu	BGIW
Gaultheria shallon salal	eSS	—	L	GLMmS	W	—	BG
Gaylussacia baccata black huckleberry	SS	DSs	L	GLMmS	W	Sp	GN
Gaylussacia dumosa dwarf huckleberry	SS	FS	L	GLMmS	PW	Su	N
Gaylussacia frondosa blue huckleberry	SS	DSs	L	GLMmS	PuW	SpSu	N
Gaylussacia ursina bear huckleberry	SS	Ss	fL	GLMmS	GPW	Sp	BFIN
Gelsemium sempervirens evening trumpet-flower	eWV	Ss	FL	GM	Y	Sp	Gs
Gleditsia aquatica water-locust	LU	FSW	—	GhLM	—	Su	AW
Gleditsia triacanthos honey-locust	SC	FDS	AL	GhLM	yg	Su	AT
Glossopetalon spinescens spiny greasebush	SS	DS	—	U	W	—	R
Glottidium vesicarium bagpod	MS	FS	—	U	Y	SpSuF	—
Gordonia lasianthus loblolly-bay	eLU	FSW	FL	U	W	SpF	As
Gouania lupuloides whiteroot	WV	Fs	—	U	YG	SpSu	BI

PLANT LIST	Plant Type	Env. Tol.	Aesthetic Value	Wildlife Value	Flower Color	Bloom Period	Landscape Uses
Grayia spinosa spiny hop-sage	SS	DNaS	L	U	—	—	M
Guajacum angustifolium Texas lignumvitae	eMS	S	FL	U	PuW	SpSuF	As
Guajacum sanctum holywood lignumvitae	SU	DSs	BFL	U	BPu	SpSu	AI
Guapira discolor beeftree	SU	DSs	—	U	yg	Su	AI
Guettarda elliptica hammock velvetseed	SC	S	F	U	W	Su	BI
Guettarda scabra wild guave	SU	DSs	—	U	W	Su	BI
Gutierrezia microcephala small-head snakeweed	SS	DS	—	GLMm	Y	SuF	—
Gutierrezia sarothrae kindlingweed	SS	DS	F	GLMm	Y	SuF	—
Gyminda latifolia West Indian false box	eSU	Ss	—	U	W	Su	BIs
Gymnanthes lucida oysterwood	eSU	S	—	U	yg	SpF	ABFIs
Gymnocladus dioicus Kentucky coffeetree	LC	FS	AL	mS	GW	Su	AST
Hulesia carolina Carolina silverbell	LU	Ss	AF	U	W	Sp	ABIg
Hamamelis virginiana American witch-hazel	SU	Ss	ABF	MmS	Y	F	ABbISW
Hamelia patens scarletbush	eSS	DS	F	U	R	SpSuF W	BF
Haploesthes greggii false broomweed	SS	DNaS	—	U	GY	—	B
Havardia pallens haujillo	MS	DSs	F	U	WY	Su	B
Hazardia squarrosa saw-tooth bristleweed	SS	DS	—	GLMmS	Y	F	g
Hechtia texensis Texas false agave	MS	DS	—	U	—	—	—
Heteromeles arbutifolia California-Christmas-berry	eMS	DS	FfL	GmS	W	Su	A
Hibiscus denudatus paleface	SS	DS	FfL	U	LW	Sp	A
Hibiscus grandiflorus swamp rose-mallow	LS	FSW	F	U	P	SpSu	—
Hippocratea volubilis medicine-vine	WV	—	—	U	—	SpSu	—
Hippomane mancinella manchineel	SU	FSs	—	U	W	Sp	BI
Holodiscus boursieri Boursier's oceanspray	MS	DSs	BL	U	—	SuF	B
Holodiscus discolor hillside oceanspray	SS	DS	F	U	W	Su	A

PLANT LIST	Plant Type	Env. Tol.	Aesthetic Value	Wildlife Value	Flower Color	Bloom Period	Landscape Uses
Holodiscus dumosus glandular oceanspray	SS	DS	F	U	PW	—	AH
Hydrangea arborescens wild hydrangea	SS	s	FL	GMS	W	Su	BgI
Hymenoclea monogyra single-whorl cheesebush	SS	FS	—	U	—	—	E
Hymenoclea salsola white cheesebush	SS	FDS	—	U	—	Sp	—
Hypelate trifoliata inkwood	SC	Ss	—	U	G	SpSu	BI
Hypericum fasciculatum peel-bark St. John's-wort	eLS	FW	F	U	Y	SpSu	AW
Hypericum hypericoides St. Andrew's-cross	SS	FS	FL	U	Y	SpF	SW
Ilex ambigua Carolina holly	LS	s	fL	GLMmS	W	Sp	BIS
Ilex cassine dahoon	eSU	sW	fL	GLMmS W	W	Su	ABISsW
Ilex coriacea large gallberry	eMS	FSsW	fL	GLMmS W	W	Sp	ABISsW
Ilex decidua deciduos holly	SU	DFSs	BfL	GLMmS W	GW	Sp	BISW
Ilex glabra inkberry	eMS	FSs	fL	GLmSW	W	Sp	FHWs
Ilex krugiana tawny-berry holly	eSU	FSs	fL	GLMS	W	SpSu	AIs
Ilex laevigata smooth winterberry	MS	FSs	AfL	GLMmS W	W	Sp	SW
Ilex montana mountain holly	LS	s	A	GLMmS	W	Sp	ABI
Ilex myrtifolia myrtle dahoon	eSU	SsW	fL	GLMmS	W	Sp	ABSsW
Ilex opaca American holly	eLU	SsW	fL	GLMmS W	W	Sp	AIsW
Ilex verticillata common winterberry	MS	FSs	fL	GLMmS W	W	Su	BSW
Ilex vomitoria yaupon	eLS	DFSs	BfL	GLMmS W	W	Sp	AFHPsW
Isocoma acradenia alkali jimmyweed	SS	DNaS	F	U	Y	SuF	gM
Isocoma menziesii jimmyweed	SS	—	F	U	Y	—	—
Isocoma pluriflora southern jimmyweed	SS	DS	F	U	Y	Su	gM
Isocoma tenuisecta shrine jimmyweed	SS	DS	F	U	Y	SuF	M
Itea virginica Virginia sweetspire	MS	DFSs W	AFL	GmSW	W	Su	gSW
Iva frutescens jesuit's-bark	MS	FS	—	U	W	SuF	W

PLANT LIST	Plant Type	Env. Tol.	Aesthetic Value	Wildlife Value	Flower Color	Bloom Period	Landscape Uses
Iva imbricata seacoast marsh-elder	SS	NaS	—	U	W	SuF	W
Jacquinia keyensis joewood	eLS	FNaS	FL	U	WY	SuF	AEIs
Jamesia americana five-petal cliffbush	MS	DS	A	U	W	Su	ABH
Jatropha cardiophylla sangre-de-cristo	SS	DS	—	U	—	Su	BM
Jatropha dioica leatherstem	SS	DS	—	U	PW	Su	BM
Juglans californica Southern California walnut	SU	FSs	L	LS	Y	Sp	BS
Juglans cinerea white walnut	LC	FS	AL	mS	yg	Sp	IN
Juglans major Arizona walnut	LU	FS	f	m	yg	Sp	BNT
Juglans microcarpa little walnut	SU	FS	L	m	G	Sp	SBN
Juglans nigra black walnut	LC	DFS	AL	m	yg	Sp	ANPT
Juniperus ashei Ashe's juniper	cSU	DS	tL	GLMmS	—	—	ABRM
Juniperus californica California juniper	cLS	DS	L	GLMmS	—		BEMP
Juniperus communis common juniper	cSU	DS	L	GLmS	Y	Sp	CEGg
Juniperus deppeana alligator juniper	cSC	DS	B	GLMmS	—	WSp	BM
Juniperus erythrocarpa red-berry juniper	cLS	DS	L	GLMmS	—	—	DM
Juniperus flaccida drooping juniper	cSU	DSs	BL	GLMmS	—	—	ABMR
Juniperus monosperma one-seed juniper	cSC	DS	BL	GLMmS	Y	Sp	ABM
Juniperus occidentalis western juniper	cLU	DS	BL	GLMmS	—	—	BMPR
Juniperus osteosperma Utah juniper	cLS	DS	L	GLMmS	—	—	BP
Juniperus pinchotii Pinchot's juniper	cSU	DS	L	GLMmS	—	—	B
Juniperus scopulorum Rocky Mountain juniper	cSU	DS	L	GLMmS	Y	Sp	ABM
Juniperus virginiana eastern red-cedar	cSC	DSs	fL	GLMmS	PuY	Sp	ABCEFHIPs
Kalmia angustifolia sheep-laurel	eSS	FSs	FL	Gm	PR	Su	BW
Kalmia hirsuta hairy-laurel	SS	FS	—	Gm	—	—	W
Kalmia latifolia mountian-laurel	eLS	DFSs	LF	GLMm	PW	Sp	BgW

PLANT LIST	Plant Type	Env. Tol.	Aesthetic Value	Wildlife Value	Flower Color	Bloom Period	Landscape Uses
Kalmia polifolia bog-laurel	eSS	FSsW	LF	Gm	P	Su	W
Karwinskia humboldtiana coyotillo	eSU	DS	L	U	—	—	A
Koeberlinia spinosa crown-of-thorns	SU	DS	—	GM	GW	Sp	EHP
Krameria grayi white ratany	SS	DS	FL	GM	Pu	SpSuF	EM
Krascheninnikovia lantata winterfat	SS	DFNaS	f	Mm	G	SpSuF	ES
Krugiodendron ferreum leadwood	eSC	Ss	L	U	G	Su	BFI
Laguncularia racemosa white mangrove	SC	FNaSsW	BL	U	W	WSpSuF	W
Lantana involucrata button-sage	eMS	DS	F	U	L	WSpSuF	BEFs
Larix laricina American larch	cSC	FS	L	GMmS	RY	Sp	BSW
Larix lyallii subalpine larch	cSC	S	L	GMmS	—	Sp	—
Larix occidentalis western larch	cLC	S	BL	GMmS	—	Sp	—
Larrea tridentata creosote-bush	eSS	DS	L	m	Y	SpSu	A
Ledum glandulosum glandular Labrador tea	eSS	—	—	U	W	Sp	—
Ledum groenlandicum rusty Labrador-tea	eSS	FS	FL	BGS	W	Sp	W
Leiophyllum buxifolium sand-myrtle	eSS	DFSs	FL	GmS	W	Sp	CGg
Lepidospartum latisquamum scalebroom	MS	DS	—	U	—	—	—
Leptodactylon pungens granite prickly-phlox	SS	DS	F	U	PW	SpSu	GgR
Leucaena pulverulenta great leadtree	SC	F	L	U	W	Sp	AST
Leucophyllum frutescens Texas barometer-bush	MS	S	FL	U	PPuW	Su	AH
Leucophyllum minus Big Bend barometer-bush	MS	—	FL	U	PPu		AH
Leucothoe axillaris coastal doghobble	eMS	SW	AFL	U	W	WSp	AsW
Leucothoe racemosa swamp doghobble	eSS	SsW	AFL	M	W	Sp	AFHW
Leucothoe recurva red-twig doghobble	eLS	Fs	ABFL	U	W	Sp	ASs
Licania michauxii gopher-apple	eSS	DS	L	RS	W	Sp	B
Lindera benzoin northern spicebush	MS	DS	AFf	CGMS	Y	Sp	BIN

PLANT LIST	Plant Type	Env. Tol.	Aesthetic Value	Wildlife Value	Flower Color	Bloom Period	Landscape Uses
Linnaea borealis American twinflower	eSS	Ss	F	M	PuW	SpSu	C
Liquidambar styraciflua sweet-gum	LC	FS	AL	GLmSW	yg	Sp	AISTW
Liriodendron tulipifera tuliptree	LC	Ss	AFL	HhLmS	yg	Su	AIT
Lithocarpus densiflorus tan-oak	eLC	Ss	BL	—	W	—	BIs
Lonicera albiflora white honeysuckle	WV	DS	F	GS	W	—	—
Lonicera canadensis American fly-honeysuckle	SS	DSs	Ff	BGHmS	O	Sp	bNW
Lonicera conjugialis purple-flower honeysuckle	SS	s	Ff	Hh	Pu	Su	I
Lonicera dioica limber honeysuckle	SS	DFSs	Ff	BGHmS	Y	Sp	bgM
Lonicera hirsuta hairy honeysuckle	WV	S	Ff	BH	Y	Su	I
Lonicera hispidula pink honeysuckle	eMS	—	F	GS	RY	Su	As
Lonicera interrupta chaparral honeysuckle	SS	DS	Ff	—	Y	—	Bg
Lonicera involucrata four-line honeysuckle	MS	s	F	GS	GPuR	Su	II
Lonicera oblongifolia swamp fly-honeysuckle	SS	FS	Ff	BH	W	Sp	W
Lonicera sempervirens trumpet honeysuckle	WV	—	—	—	ROY	Sp	I
Lonicera subspicata Santa Barbara honeysuckle	SS	DS	Ff	—	Y	—	Bg
Lycium andersonii red-berry desert-thorn	MS	DNaS	F	GHM	PuW	WSpSu	BbM
Lycium berlandieri silver desert-thorn	MS	DNaS	BF	GHM	BPu	SpSuF	BMR
Lycium carolinianum Carolina desert-thorn	SS	NaSW	F	MW	BPu	SpSu	BgSW
Lycium cooperi peachthorn	MS	DS	B	GMmW	W	SpSuF	BMP
Lycium fremontii Fremont's desert-thorn	MS	DS	Ff	GHM	PuW	WSp	BgMN
Lycium pallidum pale desert-thorn	SS	DS	BLf	M	W	WSP	MPR
Lycium richii Santa Catalina desert-thorn	MS	DS	Ff	GMmW	Pu	WSp	BMP
Lyonia ferruginea rusty staggerbush	SU	DFS	—	mS	W	—	SW
Lyonia fruticosa coastal-plain staggerbush	MS	DFS	—	mS	W	Sp	SW
Lyonia ligustrina maleberry	LS	DFSW	AL	mS	W	SpSu	SW

PLANT LIST	Plant Type	Env. Tol.	Aesthetic Value	Wildlife Value	Flower Color	Bloom Period	Landscape Uses
Lyonia lucida shinyleaf	eSS	FSsW	FL	mS	W	Sp	IW
Lyonia mariana Piedmont staggerbush	SS	SsW	F	U	PW	SpSu	BM
Lysiloma latisiliquum false tamarind	eSC	S	L	U	W	SpSu	ABFIs
Lysiloma watsonii little-leaf false tamarind	LS	—	—	U	W	—	—
Maclura pomifera osage-orange	LC	DFS	f	GLMm	G	Su	H
Magnolia acuminanta cucumber magnolia	LC	Ss	FfL	MmS	yg	Sp	ABIT
Magnolia ashei Ashe's magnolia	SU	Ss	FfL	MmS	W	Sp	A
Magnolia fraseri Fraser's magnolia	SU	s	FL	MmS	YW	Sp	ABI
Magnolia grandiflora southern magnolia	eSC	Ss	FfL	MmS	W	SpSu	AHsT
Magnolia pyramidata pyramid magnolia	SU	Fs	FL	MmS	W	Sp	ABT
Magnolia tripetala umbrella magnolia	SU	Fs	FfL	MmS	W	Sp	ABI
Magnolia virginiana sweet-bay	eLS	FSs	FL	MmS	W	SpSu	ASsW
Mahonia fremontii desert Oregon-grape	eMS	DS	L	LM	Y	Su	As
Mahonia haematocarpa red Oregon-grape	eMS	DS	L	GS	Y	Su	As
Mahonia nervosa Cascade Oregon-grape	eSS	s	L	GS	Y	Sp	G
Mahonia repens creeping Oregon-grape	eSS	s	FL	GMS	Y	Sp	EG
Mahonia trifoliata Laredo Oregon-grape	eMS	DS	L	GhS	GY	Sp	Hs
Malosma laurina laurel-sumac	MS	S	FL	GhLMmS	—	—	Bg
Malpighia glabra wild crape-myrtle	SS	Ss	Ff	U	PPu	SpSuF	Bg
Malus ioensis prairie crabapple	LU	S	FL	GLMmS	PW	Sp	B
Malvaviscus drummondii Texas wax-mallow	MS	Ss	F	U	R	WSpSuF	BFg
Mammillaria grahamii Graham's nipple cactus	C	DS	BFf	U	PPuW	—	GgMR
Mammillaria heyderi little nipple cactus	C	DS	BF	U	PPu	—	M
Mammillaria mainiae counter-clockwise nipple cactus	C	DS	BFf	U	RW	—	GgMR
Mammillaria pottsii rat-tail nipple cactus	C	DS	BFf	U	PuR	—	M

PLANT LIST	Plant Type	Env. Tol.	Aesthetic Value	Wildlife Value	Flower Color	Bloom Period	Landscape Uses
Mammillaria tetrancistra corkseed cactus	C	DS	BF	U	PPu	—	M
Mammillaria viridiflora green-flower nipple cactus	C	DS	BF	U	PPu	—	M
Mammillaria wrightii Wright's nipple cactus	C	DS	BF	U	P	—	M
Manilkara jaimiqui wild dilly	SU	DS	—	h	Y	SpF	BF
Maytenus phyllanthoides Florida mayten	eSU	DS	f	U	GW	WSp	BFs
Menispermum canadense Canadian moonseed	WV	FSs	AL	GLmS	Wyg	Su	s
Menodora scabra rough menodora	SS	DS	FL	M	Y	SpSuF	B
Menodora spinescens spiny menodora	SS	DS	—	U	W	Su	ABP
Menziesia ferruginea fool's-huckleberry	LS	FSs	FL	U	GPu	Su	BS
Menziesia pilosa minniebush	SS	DFSs	L	U	PW	SpSu	W
Metopium toxiferum Florida poisontree	SC	Ss	—	U	W	SpSu	B
Mimosa biuncifera cat-claw mimosa	MS	DS	F	GLMm	PW	Su	EH
Mimosa borealis fragrant mimosa	SS	S	F	GLMm	P	Sp	A
Mimosa dysocarpa velvet-pod mimosa	SS	DS	F	GLMm	P	Su	A
Mimosa pigra black mimosa	SS	F	F	GLMm	P	—	A
Mortonia sempervirens Rio Grande saddlebush	SS	DS	—	U	W	SpSuF	E
Morus microphylla Texas mulberry	SU	DS	f	GLMS	G	Sp	N
Morus rubra red mulberry	LU	DFSs	AfL	GLmS	yg	Sp	INS
Myrcianthes fragrans twinberry	eSU	DNaSs	FL	U	W	—	ABs
Myrica californica Pacific bayberry	eSU	FSs	BL	U	—	Sp	AsW
Myrica cerifera southern bayberry	eSU	FSsW	BL	GLMSW	yg	Sp	AFsW
Myrica gale sweetgale	eSS	FSW	L	GLMSW	—	—	AsW
Myrica heterophylla evergreen bayberry	eLS	FSsW	L	GLMSW	—	WSp	AsW
Myrica inodora odorless bayberry	eSU	DF	L	GLMSW	G	Sp	As
Myrica pensylvanica northern bayberry	MS	DFS	fL	GLMSW	yg	Sp	BEFNSW

PLANT LIST	Plant Type	Env. Tol.	Aesthetic Value	Wildlife Value	Flower Color	Bloom Period	Landscape Uses
Myrsine floridana guianese colicwood	eSU	DSs	L	U	RW	WSp	BFIs
Nemopanthus mucronatus catberry	MS	WFSs	f	U	Y	Sp	BIW
Nolina erumpens foothill bear-grass	eSS	DS	FL	U	PW	SpSu	AM
Nolina microcarpa sacahuista bear-grass	eSS	DS	L	U	PuW	SpSu	AM
Nolina texana Texas bear-grass	eSS	DS	L	U	W	SpSu	AM
Nyssa aquatica water tupelo	LC	FSW	L	GhMS	G	Sp	Wwg
Nyssa biflora swamp tupelo	LC	FSW	L	GhLMm SW	—	Sp	Wwg
Nyssa ogeche Ogeechee tupelo	MC	FSsW	f	GhLMm SW	—	Sp	SW
Nyssa sylvatica black tupelo	LC	DFS W	AL	GhLMm SW	W	Sp	ABISTW
Oemleria cerasiformis oso-berry	LS	—	—	S	G	Sp	—
Olneya tesota desert-ironwood	eLU	S	FL	HhMS	BPu	Su	AMs
Oplopanax horridus devil's-club	MS	Fs	—	U	—	Su	BPS
Opuntia acanthocarpa buck-horn cholla	C	DS	BF	GMmS	R	SpSu	AMP
Opuntia basilaris beaver-tail cactus	C	DS	BF	GLMmS	PR	Sp	gMR
Opuntia bigelovii teddy-bear cholla	C	DS	BF	GMmS	yg	SpSu	AMP
Opuntia chlorotica clock-face prickly-pear	C	DS	B	GMmS	Y	SpSu	M
Opuntia echinocarpa golden cholla	C	DS	BF	GMmS	Y	SpSu	AMP
Opuntia engelmannii cactus-apple	C	DS	B	GMmS	Y	Sp	AM
Opuntia erinacea oldman cactus	C	DS	BF	GMmS	RY	SpSu	AMP
Opuntia fragilis pygmy prickly-pear	C	DS	B	S	yg	SpSu	MR
Opuntia fulgida jumping cholla	C	DS	BFf	GMmS	PPuRW	Su	AM
Opuntia gosseliniana violet prickly-pear	C	DS	B	GLMmS	—	SpSu	M
Opuntia humifusa eastern prickly-pear	C	DS	BF	GLMmS	Y	SpSu	BgPRS
Opuntia imbricata tree cholla	C	DS	B	GLMmS	Pu	SpSu	M
Opuntia kleiniae candle cholla	C	DS	BF	GLMmS	Pu	SpSu	AM

PLANT LIST	Plant Type	Env. Tol.	Aesthetic Value	Wildlife Value	Flower Color	Bloom Period	Landscape Uses
Opuntia kunzei devil's cholla	C	DS	B	GLMmS	—	SpSu	M
Opuntia leptocaulis Christmas cholla	C	DS	BF	GLMmS	yg	Su	M
Opuntia littoralis coastal prickly-pear	C	DS	B	GLMmS	—	SpSu	M
Opuntia macrocentra purple prickly-pear	C	DS	B	GLMmS	Y	SpSu	AM
Opuntia macrorhiza twist-spine prickly-pear	C	DS	B	GLMmS	—	SpSu	M
Opuntia parishii matted cholla	C	DS	B	GLMmS	RY	SpSu	M
Opuntia phaeacantha tulip prickly-pear	C	DS	B	GLMmS	—	SpSu	M
Opuntia polyacantha hair-spine prickly-pear	C	DS	B	GLMmS	—	SpSu	M
Opuntia ramosissima darning-needle cholla	C	DS	BF	GLMmS	Pu	SpSu	AP
Opuntia santa-rita Santa Rita prickly-pear	C	DS	B	GLMmS	—	SpSu	M
Opuntia schottii dog cholla	C	DS	B	GLMmS	—	SpSu	M
Opuntia spinosior walkingstick cactus	C	DS	B	GLMmS	PPuW Y	Sp	M
Opuntia tetracantha Tucson prickly-pear	C	DS	B	GLMmS	—	SpSu	M
Opuntia tunicata thistle cholla	C	DS	BF	GLMmS	yg	SpSu	AM
Opuntia versicolor stag-horn cholla	C	DS	B	GLMmS	RY	SpSu	M
Opuntia whipplei rat-tail cholla	C	DS	B	GLMmS	—	SpSu	M
Osmanthus americanus devilwood	eSU	F	FfL	U	W	Sp	SWs
Ostrya virginiana eastern hop-hornbeam	LU	DSs	AL	GmS	R	Sp	AFI
Oxalis frutescens shrubby wood-sorrel	S	—	—	U	Y	SpSuF	—
Oxydendron arboreum sourwood	LU	Ss	AFL	GmS	W	Su	A
Pachycereus schottii senita	C	DS	B	U	—	—	M
Pachystima myrsinites myrtle boxleaf	eSS	S	F	Gm	G	SpSu	BG
Parkinsonia aculeata Jerusalem-thorn	SU	NaS	BL	hMm	Y	SpSuF	AH
Parkinsonia florida blue palo-verde	SU	DS	B	hMm	Y	SpSu	A
Parkinsonia microphylla yellow palo-verde	MS	DS	BF	hMm	Y	Sp	A

PLANT LIST	Plant Type	Env. Tol.	Aesthetic Value	Wildlife Value	Flower Color	Bloom Period	Landscape Uses
Parkinsonia texana Texas palo-verde	SU	DS	B	hMm	Y	SpSu	A
Parthenium argentatum guayule	SS	DS	—	U	W	—	M
Parthenium incanum mariola	SS	DS	—	U	W	—	M
Parthenocissus quinquefolia Virginia-creeper	WV	DFSs	ALF	GLmS	W	Su	BIW
Parthenocissus vitacea thicket-creeper	WV	DSs	AL	GLS	G	Su	R
Peniocereus greggii night-blooming-cereus	C	DS	B	GS	W	Su	A
Pentaphylloides floribunda golden-hardhack	SS	DFS	FL	GLMmS	Y	Su	BFgHW
Persea borbonia red bay	eLU	FS	L	S	Y	Sp	sW
Persea humilis silk bay	eSU	DS	L	S	Y	Sp	Is
Persea palustris swamp bay	eSU	FSW	L	S	—	Sp	sWwg
Petradoria pumila grassy rock-goldenrod	P	DS	F	U	Y	Su	M
Petrophyton caespitosum rockmat	SS	DS	—	U	W	Sp	gMR
Peucephyllum schottii Schott's pygmy-cedar	MS	DS	—	U	Y	—	M
Phaulothamnus spinescens devilqueen	MS	—	—	U	—	F	—
Philadelphus inodorus scentless mock orange	SS	Ss	F	m	W	Sp	BS
Philadelphus lewisii Lewis' mock orange	MS	Ss	F	m	W	Su	AB
Philadelphus microphyllus little-leaf mock orange	SS	DS	FL	m	W	Su	AM
Phyllodoce breweri red mountain-heath	SS	Ss	FL	u	P	Su	BGI
Phyllodoce empetriformis pink mountain-heath	eSS	SW	FL	u	R	—	GgsW
Physocarpus malvaceus mallow-leaf ninebark	MS	DSs	L	M	W	Su	Bm
Physocarpus monogynus mountain ninebark	SS	DS	FL	Gm	PW	Su	BMs
Physocarpus opulifolius Atlantic ninebark	MS	DFS	Bf	GmW	W	SpSu	BMSs
Picea engelmannii Engelmann's spruce	cLC	Ss	L	MmS	PuR	Su	A
Picea glauca white spruce	cSC	FSs	L	GLMmS	Pu	Sp	AHPSs
Picea mariana black spruce	cSC	FSs	L	GLMmS	R	Su	SsW

PLANT LIST	Plant Type	Env. Tol.	Aesthetic Value	Wildlife Value	Flower Color	Bloom Period	Landscape Uses
Picea pungens blue spruce	cLC	FS	L	GLMmS	yg	Sp	AHPs
Picea rubens red spruce	cSC	S	L	GLMmS	R	—	AMs
Picea sitchensis sitka spruce	cLC	FSs	L	GLMmS	R	—	As
Pickeringia montana stingaree-bush	eMS	DS	F	U	Pu	SpSu	Ps
Pinus albicaulis white-bark pine	cSC	—	L	GMmS	X	X	s
Pinus aristata bristle-cone pine	cLU	DS	BL	GMmS	X	X	AFs
Pinus attenuata knob-cone pine	cSU	DS	FL	GLMmS	X	X	Is
Pinus banksiana jack pine	cSC	DS	L	GMmS	X	X	Ps
Pinus cembroides Mexican pinyon	cLU	S	LN	GLMmS	X	X	As
Pinus clausa sand pine	cMC	DS	L	GMmS	X	X	s
Pinus contorta lodgepole pine	cSC	DNaS	B	GLMmS	X	X	Es
Pinus coulteri Coulter's pine	cLC	DSs	BL	GLMmS	X	X	ABIsT
Pinus echinata short-leaf pine	cLC	DS	BL	GLMmS	X	X	gTsW
Pinus edulis two-needle pinyon	cLS	DS	BLN	GLMmS	X	X	AENs
Pinus elliottii slash pine	cSU	DSW	L	GLMmS	X	X	AsWwg
Pinus engelmannii Apache pine	cSC	S	L	GMmS	X	X	s
Pinus flexilis limber pine	cLS	DS	BL	GLMmS	X	X	Fs
Pinus glabra spruce pine	cLC	FS	L	GMmS	X	X	BsT
Pinus jeffreyi Jeffrey pine	cLC	DSs	L	GLMmS	X	X	AIsT
Pinus lambertiana sugar pine	cLC	DS	BL	GLMmS	X	X	AIsT
Pinus leiophylla Chihuahuan pine	cSC	DS	—	GMmS	X	X	s
Pinus longaeva Intermountain bristle-cone pine	cSC	DS	BL	GMmS	X	X	ABs
Pinus monophylla single-leaf pinyon	cLS	DS	L	GLMmS	X	X	BNs
Pinus monticola western white pine	cLC	DSs	BL	GLMmS	X	X	BIsT
Pinus muricata Bishop pine	cLU	Na	L	GLMmS	X	X	Bs

PLANT LIST	Plant Type	Env. Tol.	Aesthetic Value	Wildlife Value	Flower Color	Bloom Period	Landscape Uses
Pinus palustris long-leaf pine	cLC	FS	L	GLMmS	X	X	BsT
Pinus ponderosa ponderosa pine	cLC	DSs	BL.	GLMmS	X	X	BIsT
Pinus pungens Table Mountain pine	cSC	DS	L	GMmS	X	X	ABs
Pinus quadrifolia four-leaf pinyon	cSU	DS	L	GLMmS	X	X	BNs
Pinus radiata Monterey pine	cSC	D	L	GMmS	X	X	ABbsT
Pinus remota paper-shell pinyon	cLC	S	BfL	GLMmS	X	X	ABNsT
Pinus resinosa red pine	cLC	DSs	BL	GLMmS	X	X	BPsT
Pinus rigida pitch pine	cSC	DS	L	GLMmS	X	X	BEIs
Pinus sabiniana digger pine	cSC	DS	f	GLMmS	X	X	BNs
Pinus serotina pond pine	cLU	F	L	GLMmS	X	X	BsW
Pinus strobiformis southwestern white pine	cLC	DS	L	GMmS	X	X	BsT
Pinus strobus eastern white pine	cLC	Ss	BLf	GLMmS	X	X	ABCIsT
Pinus taeda loblolly pine	cLC	S	L	GLMmS	X	X	BCSsT
Pinus torreyana Torrey pine	cSU	DS	BfL	GMmS	X	X	ABs
Pinus virginiana Virginia pine	cSU	DS	L	GLMmS	X	X	BCs
Piscidia piscipula Florida fishpoison-tree	SC	S	—	U	PW	Su	ABs
Pisonia aculeata devil's-claw pisonia	SS	S	—	U	PuY	SpSu	B
Pisonia rotundata smooth devil's-claws	LS	DS	—	U	G	SpSu	I
Pithecellobium ebano ebony blackbead	eSU	DS	L	h	W	SpSuF	BHSs
Pithecellobium keyense Florida Keys blackbead	eSU	DS	F	U	PW	WSuSp F	Bs
Pithecellobium unguis-cati cat-claw blackbead	SU	FSs	F	U	P	SpF	BP
Planera aquatica planertree	SU	FSW	B	MW	GY	Sp	SWwg
Platanus occidentalis American sycamore	LC	DFS	BLf	LMS	yg	Sp	ABIST
Platanus racemosa California sycamore	LC	FS	BFL	LS	BrY	Sp	AST
Platanus wrightii Arizona sycamore	SC	FS	BFL	LS	R	Sp	AT

PLANT LIST	Plant Type	Env. Tol.	Aesthetic Value	Wildlife Value	Flower Color	Bloom Period	Landscape Uses
Pluchea sericea arrow-weed	SS	FNaS	BF	hM	PuW	SpSu	gS
Poliomintha incana hoary rosemary-mint	SS	DNaS	L	U	PuW	SpSuF	AB
Populus angustifolia narrow-leaf cottonwood	LU	FS	L	LM	Br	Sp	AT
Populus balsamifera balsam poplar	LC	FSW	L	CGLMmS	G	Sp	SW
Populus deltoides eastern cottonwood	LC	DFS	ABL	CGLMmSW	R	Sp	ABCESTW
Populus fremontii Fremont's cottonwood	LC	FS	BL	GLMmS	G	Sp	AST
Populus grandidentata big-tooth aspen	SC	S	AL	CGLMmS	G	Sp	AB
Populus heterophylla swamp cottonwood	LC	FSW	AL	CGLMmS	G	Sp	ASWwg
Populus tremuloides quaking aspen	LU	S	AL	CGLMmS	G	Sp	ABS
Prosopis glandulosa honey mesquite	SU	S	L	GLMmS	yg	SuF	ABT
Prosopis pubescens American screw-bean	LU	SF	FL	GLMmS	W	Su	ABT
Prosopis velutina velvet mesquite	SU	S	L	GLMmS	yg	SuF	AB
Prunus americana American plum	SU	S	AFf	GLMmS	W	Sp	A
Prunus angustifolia chickasaw plum	LS	S	Ff	GLMmS	W	Sp	B
Prunus caroliniana Carolina laurel cherry	eLU	S	ABFfL	GLMmS	W	Sp	DFIs
Prunus emarginata bitter cherry	LS	FS	F	GLMmS	OW	Sp	BS
Prunus fasciculata desert almond	SS	DS	F	GLMmS	W	Sp	BM
Prunus ilicifolia holly-leaf cherry	eSU	DS	fL	GLMmS	W	Sp	ABgPs
Prunus mexicana bigtree plum	LU	FS	FL	GLMmS	W	Sp	AB
Prunus myrtifolia West Indian cherry	eSU	Ss	F	GLMmS	W	WSp	ABFIs
Prunus pensylvanica fire cherry	SU	DS	ABFfL	BGLMmS	W	Sp	BN
Prunus pumila Great Lakes sand cherry	SS	FW	AfL	BGLMmS	W	Sp	ENS
Prunus serotina black cherry	SC	DFS	ABFfL	BGLMmS	W	Sp	BNIW
Prunus texana peachbush	SS	—	FL	GLMmS	W	Sp	AB
Prunus virginiana choke cherry	LU	DSs	ABFfL	BGLMmS	W	Sp	BN

PLANT LIST	Plant Type	Env. Tol.	Aesthetic Value	Wildlife Value	Flower Color	Bloom Period	Landscape Uses
Pseudophoenix sargentii Florida cherry palm	SU	S	FL	mS	Y	WSpSuF	ABFI
Pseudotsuga macrocarpa big-cone douglas fir	cLC	s	L	GLMmS	yg	—	ABsT
Pseudotsuga menziesii Douglas-fir	cLC	S	L	GLMmS	OR	SpSu	ABIsT
Psidium longipes mangroveberry	eLS	DSs	F	U	W	SuF	Is
Psorothamnus arborescens Mojave smokebush	MS	DSs	F	m	B	—	BMP
Psorothamnus emoryi Emory's smokebush	SS	DS	F	m	Pu	Sp	BP
Psorothamnus fremontii Fremont's smokebush	SS	DS	F	m	Pu	SpSu	BP
Psorothamnus schottii indigo bush	S	FSs	FL	m	B	Sp	BPS
Psorothamnus spinosus smokethorn	SU	FS	BF	m	BPu	Su	BPS
Psychotria ligustrifolia Bahama wild coffee	SU	s	f	U	W	SpSu	I
Psychotria nervosa Seminole balsamo	SS	s	L	U	W	WSpSuF	BFgI
Ptelea trifoliata common hoptree	SU	Ss	L	U	W	SpSu	AB
Purshia glandulosa antelope-brush	SS	DS	B	Mm	W	Su	AB
Purshia mexicana Mexican cliff-rose	eSS	DS	Ff	Mm	Y	Su	ABFR
Purshia tridentata bitterbrush	SS	DS	F	LMm	Y	Su	B
Pyrularia pubera buffalo-nut	MS	s	—	U	BrG	Sp	gI
Quercus agrifolia coastal live oak	eSC	DS	BL	GLMmSW	—	—	AFTs
Quercus alba northern white oak	LC	DSs	ABL	CGMmS	yg	Sp	AINT
Quercus arizonica Arizona white oak	SC	S	L	CGMmS	Y	—	AT
Quercus austrina bluff oak	LC	S	L	CGMmSW	Y	Sp	ABIT
Quercus bicolor swamp white oak	LC	DFSsW	AL	CGMmSW	yg	Sp	INSWwg
Quercus buckleyi Buckley's oak	SU	—	—	CGMmS	Y	Sp	—
Quercus chapmanii Chapman's oak	SC	DSs	BL	CGMmSW	yg	Sp	BIT
Quercus chrysolepis canyon live oak	eLC	DSs	BL	GLMmSW	RY	Su	ABIT
Quercus coccinea scarlet oak	SC	DS	AL	CGMmS	yg	Sp	ABIT

PLANT LIST	Plant Type	Env. Tol.	Aesthetic Value	Wildlife Value	Flower Color	Bloom Period	Landscape Uses
Quercus douglasii blue oak	SC	DS	BL	GLMmS W	yg	Sp	ABT
Quercus dumosa California scrub oak	eSS	DS	L	GLMmS W	yg	Sp	BM
Quercus durata leather oak	SS	S	L	GLMmS W	yg	Sp	B
Quercus ellipsoidalis northern pin oak	SC	DS	AL	CGMmS	yg	Sp	BT
Quercus emoryi Emory's oak	eSC	DS	BL	CGMmS	Y	Sp	ABNT
Quercus engelmannii Engelmann's oak	eLU	DS	L	GLMmS W	yg	Sp	ABET
Quercus falcata southern red oak	SC	DS	BL	CGMmS	R	Sp	ABT
Quercus fusiformis plateau oak	eLU	DS	L	GMmS	yg	Sp	AB
Quercus gambelii Gambel's oak	SU	DS	A	CGMmS W	Br	Sp	AB
Quercus garryana Oregon white oak	LC	FS	BL	CGMmS W	yg	Sp	BIST
Quercus geminata sand live oak	SC	DS	—	CGMmS W	Br	Sp	BI
Quercus gravesii Graves' oak	LU	S	AL	GMmS	Br	Sp	AT
Quercus grisea gray oak	SC	DS	L	CGMmS	yg	Sp	B
Quercus havardii Havard's oak	SS	DS	DS	GLS	yg	Sp	BM
Quercus hemisphaerica Darlington's oak	eSC	FS	L	CGMmS W	yg	Sp	ABSsTW
Quercus hypoleucoides silver-leaf oak	eSU	S	BL	GLS	RG	Sp	ABs
Quercus ilicifolia bear oak	LS	DS	AL	CGLmS W	yg	Sp	BEN
Quercus imbricaria shingle oak	LU	DFSs	AL	CGMmS W	yg	Sp	ABIT
Quercus incana bluejack oak	LU	DS	L	CGMmS W	RY	Sp	BT
Quercus inopina sandhill oak	LS	DS	L	CGMmS W	Br	Sp	BI
Quercus kelloggii California black oak	SC	DS	AL	GLMmS W	yg	Sp	ABT
Quercus laceyi Lacey's oak	LU	DS	AL	GLMmS	yg	Sp	ABT
Quercus laevis turkey oak	SC	DS	L	CGMmS W	R	Sp	BT
Quercus laurifolia laurel oak	SC	FSW	L	CMmSW	R	Sp	ASTW
Quercus lobata valley oak	LC	S	BL	GLMmS W	Y	Sp	ABT

PLANT LIST	Plant Type	Env. Tol.	Aesthetic Value	Wildlife Value	Flower Color	Bloom Period	Landscape Uses
Quercus lyrata overcup oak	SC	FSW	L	CMmSW	Y	Sp	SW
Quercus macrocarpa burr oak	LC	DFS	BL	CGmSW	yg	Sp	ABIT
Quercus margarettiae sand post oak	MS	DFS	BL	CGMmS W	yg	Sp	AI
Quercus marilandica blackjack oak	LU	DFS	L	CGMmS W	yg	Sp	AB
Quercus michauxii swamp chestnut oak	LC	S	L	CGMmS W	yg	Sp	AIT
Quercus minima dwarf live oak	MS	DS	L	CGMmS W	yg	Sp	ABIS
Quercus mohriana Mohr's oak	LS	DS	BL	CGMmS	yg	Sp	AB
Quercus muehlenbergii chinkapin oak	LC	DS	L	CGMmS W	yg	Sp	ABT
Quercus myrtifolia myrtle oak	eSU	DS	L	CGMmS W	R	Sp	BIs
Quercus nigra water oak	SC	FSW	L	CGMmS W	Br	Sp	AST
Quercus oblongifolia Mexican blue oak	eSC	DS	B	CGMmS	yg	Sp	ABTs
Quercus pagoda cherry-bark oak	LC	FSs	BL	CGMmS W	yg	Sp	AIW
Quercus palustris pin oak	LC	FSW	AL	CGMmS W	yg	Sp	AITW
Quercus phellos willow oak	SC	DFS W	AL	CGMmS W	yg	Sp	AIT
Quercus prinoides dwarf chinkapin oak	LS	DS	AL	CGLmS W	yg	Sp	B
Quercus prinus chestnut oak	SC	DSs	AL	CGLMm SW	yg	Sp	ABIT
Quercus pumila running oak	SS	DS	—	CGLMm SW	Y	Sp	BI
Quercus pungens sandpaper oak	eSU	DS	L	CGLMm S	yg	Sp	AT
Quercus rubra northern red oak	LC	Ss	ABL	CGMmS W	yg	Sp	ABIT
Quercus rugosa net-leaf oak	eSU	S	L	CGLMm S	yg	Sp	AB
Quercus sadleriana deer oak	eMS	Ss	L	CGLMm S	yg	Sp	AB
Quercus shumardii Shumard's oak	SC	DS	AL	CGmSW	yg	Sp	STW
Quercus sinuata bastard oak	MC	Fs	L	CGMm W	yg	Sp	S
Quercus stellata post oak	LU	DS	L	CGMmS W	yg	Sp	AB
Quercus texana Texas red oak	SU	DS	AL	CGLMm S	R	Sp	ABT

PLANT LIST	Plant Type	Env. Tol.	Aesthetic Value	Wildlife Value	Flower Color	Bloom Period	Landscape Uses
Quercus toumeyi Toumey's oak	eSU	DS	L	CGLMmS	yg	Sp	B
Quercus turbinella shrub live oak	eLS	DS	L	GLMmSW	Y	Sp	AB
Quercus vacciniifolia huckleberry oak	eSS	S	L	GLMmSW	yg	Sp	BM
Quercus velutina black oak	LC	DSs	AL	CGMmSW	yg	Sp	BT
Quercus virginiana live oak	eSC	DFS	BL	CGMmSW	Y	Sp	AITs
Quercus wislizenii interior live oak	eSC	S	BL	GLMmSW	yg	—	ABTs
Randia aculeata white indigo-berry	eSC	DFSs	f	U	W	Su	ABFIs
Reynosia septentrionalis darling-plum	eSU	DS	—	U	yg	SpSu	BFIs
Rhamnus alnifolia alder-leaf buckthorn	SS	FS	L	hS	GW	—	W
Rhamnus crocea holly-leaf buckthorn	eLS	DS	fL	GLMmS	GY	Sp	Bs
Rhapidophyllum hystrix needle palm	eMS	Fs	L	U	W	Sp	Ws
Rhizophora mangle red mangrove	eSC	SsW	L	W	Y	WSpSuF	SsW
Rhododendron albiflorum Cascade azalea	SS	Fs	FL	GLMm	W	—	ABIS
Rhododendron calendulaceum flame azalea	MS	Ss	AFL	BHGLMmS	O	SpSu	ABI
Rhododendron canescens mountain azalea	LS	Ss	FL	bGHMmS	PW	Sp	BIS
Rhododendron catawbiense catawba rosebay	eLS	DS	FL	GMmS	PPu	SpSu	ABs
Rhododendron macrophyllum California rhododendron	eSU	Ss	FI	GMmS	PPu	Sp	ABs
Rhododendron maximum great-laurel	eSU	FSs	FL	BHmS	P	Su	BIW
Rhododendron periclymenoides pink azalea	MS	DFSs	FL	BGHmS	PuW	Sp	BISW
Rhododendron vaseyi pink-shell azalea	LS	FSs	AFL	BGHLMmS	P	Sp	ABIS
Rhododendron viscosum clammy azalea	MS	FSs	FL	BGHLMmW	W	Su	ABW
Rhus aromatica fragrant sumac	MS	DS	AfL	GLMmS	Y	Sp	ABGN
Rhus copallinum winged sumac	SU	DS	AfL	GLmS	yg	Su	ABg
Rhus glabra smooth sumac	MS	S	AfL	GLMmS	G	Su	ABCEP
Rhus integrifolia lemonade sumac	eMS	NaS	AFL	GLMmS	W	Sp	B

PLANT LIST	Plant Type	Env. Tol.	Aesthetic Value	Wildlife Value	Flower Color	Bloom Period	Landscape Uses
Rhus microphylla little-leaf sumac	MS	DS	A	Mm	GW	Sp	AB
Rhus ovata sugar sumac	eMS	DS	L	GLMmS	—	Sp	E
Rhus trilobata ill-scented sumac	MS	S	AfL	mS	G	Sp	AH
Rhus virens evergreen sumac	eMS	S	FfL	GMmS	W	Su	bH
Ribes amarum bitter gooseberry	MS	DS	L	GLMmS W	Pu	Su	BNP
Ribes americanum wild black currant	SS	FSs	AL	GLMmS W	W	Sp	ABNW
Ribes aureum golden currant	MS	Fs	FfL	GLMmS	Y	Su	EISN
Ribes californicum California gooseberry	SS	DS	L	GLMmS W	W	Su	ABPN
Ribes cereum white squaw currant	SS	S	F	GLMmS W	PW	Su	ABN
Ribes cynosbati eastern prickly gooseberry	SS	DFSs	AL	GLMmS W	GW	Sp	ABHIPNW
Ribes glandulosum skunk currant	SS	FS	L	GLMmS W	—	Sp	AINW
Ribes hirtellum hairy-stem gooseberry	SS	FS	L	GLMmS W	—	Sp	IN
Ribes indecorum white-flower currant	S	—	—	GLMmS W	W	WSpF	—
Ribes lacustre bristly black gooseberry	SS	FS	L	GLMmS W	G	Sp	ANPW
Ribes malvaceum chaparral currant	SS	Ss	L	GLMmS W	P	WSp	ABINP
Ribes missouriense Missouri gooseberry	SS	Ss	f	GLMS	GW	Sp	AINP
Ribes montigenum western prickly gooseberry	SS	DS	f	GLMmS W	R	Su	ANP
Ribes pinetorum orange gooseberry	MS	s	f	GLMmS W	OR	Su	AFNP
Ribes roezlii Sierran gooseberry	SS	S	Ff	GLMmS W	R	Su	NP
Ribes velutinum desert gooseberry	SS	Ss	BfL	GLMmS	Y	Sp	ABIP
Ribes viburnifolium Santa Catalina currant	eSS	DS	L	GLMmS W	P	Su	N
Ribes viscosissimum sticky currant	SS	s	B	GLMmS W	W	Su	BN
Ribes wolfii winaha currant	MS	s	L	GLMmS	PW	Su	IN
Rivina humilis rougeplant	SS	s	L	M	PW	—	BI
Robinia hispida bristly locust	SS	DS	F	mS	Pu	Sp	ABE

PLANT LIST	Plant Type	Env. Tol.	Aesthetic Value	Wildlife Value	Flower Color	Bloom Period	Landscape Uses
Robinia neomexicana New Mexico locust	SU	S	F	GMm	PW	Su	AE
Robinia pseudo-acacia black locust	LC	S	L	mS	W	Su	E
Rosa arkansana prairie rose	SS	DS	F	BGLMmS	P	SpSu	bHM
Rosa blanda smooth rose	SS	S	Ff	BGLMmS	P	Sp	bHM
Rosa carolina Carolina rose	SS	DS	Ff	BGLMmS	PW	Su	BbEFhG
Rosa gymnocarpa wood rose	SS	s	F	GLMmS	P	SpSu	HIS
Rosa nutkana Nootka rose	MS	S	FL	BGLMmS	P	Sp	Bbg
Rosa palustris swamp rose	SS	FSW	F	BGLMmS	P	Su	SWwg
Rosa woodsii Woods' rose	SS	DS	F	BGLMmS	P	Su	AbHM
Roystonea elata Florida royal palm	eSC	S	L	mS	W	—	A
Rubus allegheniensis allegheny blackberry	MS	Ds	FfL	GLMmS	W	SpSu	NP
Rubus argutus saw-tooth blackberry	SS	D	FfL	GLMmS	W	Sp	NP
Rubus canadensis smooth blackberry	SS	S	FfL	GLMmS	W	Su	NP
Rubus chamaemorus cloudberry	SS	FS	FfL	BGLMmSW	W	SpSu	GNSW
Rubus cuneifolius sand blackberry	SS	F	FfL	BGLMmS	W	SpSu	NP
Rubus flagellaris whiplash dewberry	SS	D	FfL	BGLMmS	W	Su	NP
Rubus idaeus common red raspberry	MS	DFSs	AFfL	BCGLMmSW	W	SpSu	BgINW
Rubus lasiococcus hairy-fruit smooth dewberry	SS	DS	FfL	GLMmS	W	SpSu	BGIN
Rubus leucodermis white-stem raspberry	SS	Ss	FfL	GLMmS	W	Sp	BN
Rubus occidentalis black raspberry	SS	DFSs	FfL	BGLMmS	W	Sp	BIN
Rubus parviflorus western thimble-berry	SS	DSs	FfL	BGLMmS	W	SpSu	BN
Rubus pedatus strawberry-leaf raspberry	SS	Ss	FfL	BGLMmS	W	SpSu	GN
Rubus pubescens dwarf red raspberry	eSS	FS	FfL	BGLMmSW	W	SpSu	INW
Rubus spectabilis salmon raspberry	SS	FsW	BFfL	S	PR	Sp	BNSW
Rubus trivialis southern dewberry	MS	Ss	FfL	GLMmS	W	Sp	N

PLANT LIST	Plant Type	Env. Tol.	Aesthetic Value	Wildlife Value	Flower Color	Bloom Period	Landscape Uses
Rubus ursinis California Dewberry	SS	Ss	FfL	GLMmS	W	SpSu	MNP
Rubus vitifolius Pacific dewberry	eSS	FS	FfL	GLMmS	W	Sp	NS
Sabal etonia scrub palmetto	eMS	DS	L	mS	W	SpSu	AB
Sabal mexicana Rio Grande palmetto	eLU	S	L	mS	W	Su	AB
Sabal minor dwarf palmetto	LU	FSW	BL	LMS	W	Su	ABIW
Sabal palmetto cabbage palmetto	LC	DFSW	BL	LMS	W	SpSu	ABT
Sageretia wrightii Wright's mock buckthorn	MS	DS	—	U	W	SpSuF	B
Salazaria mexicana Mexican bladder-sage	SS	DFS	Ff	M	BPu	Sp	BgP
Salix amygdaloides peach-leaf willow	LU	FS	L	GLMmSW	yg	Sp	SW
Salix arctica stout arctic willow	SS	S	L	U	G	Sp	B
Salix bebbiana long-beak willow	SU	DFS	F	GLMmSW	yg	Sp	SW
Salix bonplandiana Bonpland's willow	eLS	FS	L	GMmS	GrY	—	S
Salix candida sage willow	MS	FSsW	BL	BGhLMmS	GW	SpSu	BSW
Salix caroliniana coastal-plain willow	SU	FSW	L	GLMmS	Y	Su	SW
Salix discolor tall pussy willow	SU	DFS	LF	BGhLMmSW	Gr	Sp	gSW
Salix drummondiana Drummond's willow	MS	FSW	L	GLMmS	yg	Sp	SW
Salix eriocephala Missouri willow	LS	FS	—	GLMmS	yg	Sp	SW
Salix exigua sandbar willow	SU	FNaS	L	GLMmS	Y	Sp	SW
Salix geyeriana Geyer's willow	LS	FSW	L	GLMmS	Y	Sp	SW
Salix gooddingii Goodding's willow	LU	FS	—	GLMmS	Y	Sp	ST
Salix hindsiana sandbar willow	LS	FS	—	GLMmS	yg	Sp	ES
Salix hookeriana coastal willow	LS	FNa	FL	GLMmS	Y	Sp	SW
Salix humilis small pussy willow	MS	DFS	L	CGhLMmSW	yg	Sp	gMW
Salix interior sandbar willow	LS	FSW	L	GLMmSW	Y	Sp	CESW
Salix lasiolepis arroyo willow	LS	FS	BL	GLMmS	—	WSp	S

PLANT LIST	Plant Type	Env. Tol.	Aesthetic Value	Wildlife Value	Flower Color	Bloom Period	Landscape Uses
Salix lucida shining willow	LS	DFS	L	GLMmS W	Gr	Sp	BSW
Salix lutea yellow willow	MS	DFS	—	GLMmS	—	Sp	S
Salix melanopsis dusky willow	LS	FS	—	GLMmS	—	Sp	S
Salix monticola mountain willow	LU	FW	L	GLMmS	Y	Sp	W
Salix nigra black willow	LU	DFS W	L	BCGhL MmSW	yg	Sp	ABCESW
Salix petiolaris meadow willow	LS	FS	L	GLMmS	—	Sp	SW
Salix scouleriana Scouler's willow	LU	s	L	GLMmS	—	Sp	I
Salix sericea silky willow	LS	FS	L	GLMmS	—	Sp	ABS
Salix sessilifolia sessile-leaf willow	SU	FS	L	GLMmS	Y	Sp	S
Salix sitchensis sitka willow	SU	FS	L	GLMmS	yg	SP	ST
Salvia apiana California white sage	MS	DS	FL	GS	W	—	BgM
Salvia dorrii gray ball sage	SS	DSs	FL	GS	BPu	SpSuF	BgM
Salvia funerea Death Valley sage	SS	DS	F	GHS	Pu	Sp	gM
Salvia leucophylla San Luis purple sage	SS	DS	F	GS	Pu	Sp	BgM
Salvia mellifera California black sage	SS	DS	F	GhS	W	Sp	BgM
Salvia mohavensis Mojave sage	SS	DS	F	GHS	B	SpSu	gM
Salvia pachyphylla rose sage	SS	DS	F	GHS	—	Su	E
Salvia vaseyi bristle sage	SS	DS	F	GHS	W	Sp	gM
Sambucus canadensis American elder	MS	DFSs	FL	GLMmS W	W	SuF	BNW
Sambucus cerulea blue elder	SU	FS	FL	GLMmS	W	SpSuF	A
Sapindus saponaria wing-leaf soapberry	SC	FS	AF	S	W	SpSu	AST
Sapium biloculare Mexican jumping-bean	SU	DFS	F	U	G	SpSuF	MS
Sarcobatus vermiculatus greasewood	MS	NaS	B	LMm	G	SuF	EM
Sassafras albidum sassafras	LU	D	AL	GLMS	Y	Sp	AB
Savia bahamensis Bahama-maidenbush	SU	Ss	—	U	—	SpF	I

PLANT LIST	Plant Type	Env. Tol.	Aesthetic Value	Wildlife Value	Flower Color	Bloom Period	Landscape Uses
Scaevola plumieri gullfeed	eLS	S	F	U	W	WSpSu F	E
Schaefferia cuneifolia desert-yaupon	eSS	S	f	U	GY	Su	AH
Schaefferia frutescens Florida boxwood	SU	—	—	U	—	SpSu	I
Schoepfia chrysophylloides island beefwood	SU	Ss	—	U	GR	FW	I
Sclerocactus erectocentrus red-spine fish-hook cactus	C	DS	BF	mS	PPuW Y	—	gM
Sclerocactus intertextus white fish-hook cactus	C	DS	BF	mS	PPuW Y	—	gM
Sclerocactus scheeri Scheer's fish-hook cactus	C	DS	BF	mS	PPuW Y	—	gM
Sclerocactus uncinatus Chihuahuan fish-hook cactus	C	DS	BF	mS	PPuW Y	—	gM
Sebastiania fruticosa Gulf sebastian-bush	SS	F	A	U	yg	SpSuF	AS
Senna armata desert wild sensitive plant	SS	FS	F	U	PY	Su	MS
Sequoia sempervirens redwood	cLC	F	B	mS	X	X	BITs
Serenoa repens saw-palmetto	SS	DFNaS	—	hmS	W	SpSu	W
Serjania brachycarpa little-fruit slipplejack	WV	Ss	—	U	GWY	WSp	B
Shepherdia canadensis russet buffalo-berry	MS	DS	f	GLmS	Y	Sp	E
Sideroxylon celastrinum saffron-plum	SU	FS	—	U	yg	WF	W
Sideroxylon foetidissimum false mastic	eSC	DSs	B	U	Y	WSpSuF	ABIs
Sideroxylon lanuginosum gum bully	SU	DSs	—	U	Y	Su	ABI
Sideroxylon reclinatum Florida bully	LS	FS	—	U	—	SpSu	B
Sideroxylon salicifolium white bully	SC	DS	—	U	Y	WSp	B
Sideroxylon tenax tough bully	SU	DS	—	U	W	Sp	ABI
Simarouba glauca paradise-tree	SC	DSs	F	U	yg	Sp	ABI
Simmondsia chinensis jojoba	MS	DS	—	G	—	WSp	BM
Smilax auriculata ear-leaf greenbrier	WV	DS	—	GLMmS	yg	Su	I
Smilax bona-nox fringed greenbrier	WV	DFSW	—	GLMmS W	G	SpSu	BIW
Smilax glauca sawbrier	WV	Ss	—	GLMS	G	Su	BI

PLANT LIST	Plant Type	Env. Tol.	Aesthetic Value	Wildlife Value	Flower Color	Bloom Period	Landscape Uses
Smilax laurifolia laurel-leaf greenbrier	eWV	FSW	L	GLMmSW	GW	Su	BW
Smilax pumila sarsparilla-vine	WV	DS	—	GLMmSW	G	Su	BIM
Smilax rotundifolia horsebrier	WV	DFSs	fL	GLMmSW	Ryg	SpSu	BIPW
Smilax tamnoides chinaroot	WV	Ss	L	GLMmSW	G	Sp	BI
Smilax walteri coral greenbrier	WV	F	L	MmS	G	SpSu	BI
Solanum donianum mullien nightshade	SU	—	—	U	B	WSpSuF	—
Solanum dulcamara climbing nightshade	MS	S	F	GLmSW	G	SpSu	B
Solanum erianthum potato-tree	MS	Ss	FL	GLmS	W	SpSuF	B
Sophora affinis Eve's mecklacepod	LS	Ss	—	U	PW	—	—
Sophora secundiflora mescal-bean	eLS	Ss	FL	U	BPu	—	—
Sophora tomentosa yellow necklacepod	eMS	DFS	F	U	Y	WSpSuF	gMs
Sorbus americana American mountain-ash	SU	FS	FfL	GLMmS	W	Sp	W
Sorbus decora northern mountain-ash	SU	FS	ABfL	GLMmSW	W	Sp	BW
Sorbus scopulina Cascade Mountain-ash	SS	DS	fL	GLMmS	W	Su	B
Sphaeralcea ambigua apricot globe-mallow	SS	DS	F	Mm	OR	SpSuF	BgM
Sphaeralcea rosea desert mallow	SS	DS	F	Mm	P	SpSu	BgM
Sphaeromeria cana wire-lettuce	SS	DS	FL	Mm	OR	SuF	BgM
Spiraea alba white meadowsweet	SS	SW	BF	BGM	W	SU	ABWwg
Spiraea douglasii Douglas' meadowsweet	MS	FS	B	GM	P	Su	A
Spiraea tomentosa steeplebush	SS	FSW	Ff	BGMmSW	PPu	Su	BWwg
Staphylea trifolia American bladdernut	MS	FSs	ABL	U	W	Sp	BISW
Stenocereus thurberi organ-pipe cactus	C	DS	BF	mS	PuR	Sp	AMPs
Stenotus acaulis stemless mock goldenweed	eSS	DS	FL	U	Y	SpSu	GgMR
Stewartia malacodendron silky-camellia	SU	s	BF	U	W	SpSu	ABI
Styrax grandifolius big-leaf snowbell	LS	FSs	F	W	W	Sp	AgIS

PLANT LIST	Plant Type	Env. Tol.	Aesthetic Value	Wildlife Value	Flower Color	Bloom Period	Landscape Uses
Suaeda californica broom seepweed	SS	FNaS	B	W	—	F	ESW
Suaeda moquinii shrubby seepweed	SS	DNaS	—	W	—	—	M
Suriana maritima bay-cedar	MS	DNaS	F	U	Y	Sp	ES
Swietenia mahogani West Indian mahogany	SC	—	Ff	U	yg	SpSu	AI
Symphoricarpos albus common snowberry	MS	DSs	f	GLMmS	P	SpSu	BEI
Symphoricarpos longiflorus desert snowberry	SS	DFS	f	GLMmS	P	Su	ES
Symphoricarpos mollis creeping snowberry	SS	Ss	f	GLMmS	RW	Sp	Bg
Symphoricarpos occidentalis western snowberry	SS	DS	FL	GhLMmS	P	Su	AB
Symphoricarpos orbiculatus coral-berry	SS	DSs	f	GLMmS	G	Su	BE
Symphoricarpos oreophilus mountain snowberry	SS	S	Ff	GLMmS	W	Sp	B
Symphoricarpos rotundifolius round-leaf snowberry	SS	S	Ff	GLMmS	P	Sp	AB
Symplocos tinctoria horsesugar	LS	FS	L	MS	Y	Sp	IW
Taxodium ascendens pond-cypress	LC	FS	L	W	—	Sp	ATW
Taxodium distichum southern bald-cypress	cLC	FSW	ABL	W	Pu	Sp	ATW
Taxus brevifolia Pacific yew	cSU	Ss	BfL	LS	Y	—	AI
Taxus canadensis American yew	cSS	s	L	GS	yg	Sp	EFGI
Tetradymia axillaris cottonthorn	SS	NaSs	F	U	Y	SuF	BM
Tetradymia canescens spineless horsebrush	SS	DS	F	U	Y	SuF	MR
Tetradymia glabrata little-leaf horsebrush	SS	DSs	F	U	Y	Su	BM
Tetradymia spinosa short-spine horsebrush	SS	DSs	F	U	Y	Su	BM
Tetrazygia bicolor Florida clover-ash	LS	DS	F	U	Y	SpSu	BFI
Thamnosma montana turpentine-broom	SS	DS	—	U	Pu	—	M
Thelocactus bicolor glory-of-Texas	C	DS	F	U	R	—	R
Thelocactus setispinus miniature-barrel cactus	C	DS	—	U	—	—	R
Thrinax morrisii Key thatch palm	SC	S	L	mS	Y	WSpSuF	ABI

PLANT LIST	Plant Type	Env. Tol.	Aesthetic Value	Wildlife Value	Flower Color	Bloom Period	Landscape Uses
Thrinax radiata Florida thatch palm	SC	S	L	mS	—	—	ABI
Thuja occidentalis eastern arborvitae	cSC	DFSs	L	MmS	X	X	AFHPSs
Thuja plicata western arborvitae	cLC	FSs	L	MmS	X	X	sT
Tilia americana American basswood	LC	Ss	AL	GhLMm	Y	Su	ABIT
Tiquilia canescens woody crinklemat	SS	Ss	FL	U	PR	—	BGgM
Tiquilia greggii plumed crinklemat	SS	DS	FL	U	PW	—	GgM
Torreya californica California-nutmeg	cLU	Fs	L	U	—	—	ABISs
Tournefortia hirsutissima chiggery-grapes	WV	Ss	F	U	W	WSpSuF	BI
Tournefortia volubilis twining soilderbush	WV	Ss	—	U	Wyg	WSpSu	BI
Toxicodendron diversilobum Pacific poison-oak	SS	Ss	AfL	GLMmS	G	—	BI
Toxicodendron pubescens Atlantic poison-oak	MS	FSs	L	GLMmS	Gr	—	BI
Toxicodendron radicans eastern poison-ivy	WV	DFSs	AL	GLMmS	GW	Sp	DI
Toxicodendron vernix poison-sumac	MS	FSs	AL	GLMmS	GW	—	W
Trema lamarckianum pain-in-back	cSU	DSs	B	S	PW	WSpSuF	BIS
Trema micranthum Jamaican nettletree	cSU	DSs	B	S	PW	—	BIS
Tsuga canadensis eastern hemlock	cLC	Ss	BL	MmS	X	X	ABFHIs
Tsuga caroliniana Carolina hemlock	cLC	Ss	BL	GMmS	X	X	ABHITS
Tsuga heterophylla western hemlock	cLC	Ss	BL	GMmS	X	X	ABIT
Tsuga mertensiana mountain hemlock	cLC	Ss	BL	GLMmS	X	X	ABIT
Ulmus alata winged elm	LU	Ss	L	GLMSW	GR	W	ABT
Ulmus americana American elm	LC	DFSs	AL	GLMmSW	BrG	Sp	ABITW
Ulmus crassifolia cedar elm	LC	DFS	L	GMmS	GR	Su	AT
Ulmus rubra slippery elm	LC	S	AL	GLMSW	yg	WSp	BIW
Ulmus thomasii rock elm	LC	Fs	L	GLMSW	BrR	Sp	BI
Umbellularia californica California-laurel	eSU	DFSs	L	mS	Y	WSp	BgRsT

PLANT LIST	Plant Type	Env. Tol.	Aesthetic Value	Wildlife Value	Flower Color	Bloom Period	Landscape Uses
Ungnadia speciosa Mexican-buckeye	LU	DFS	F	h	P	Sp	ABS
Vaccinium angustifolium late lowbush blueberry	SS	DFSs	AL	CGLmSW	W	Sp	N
Vaccinium arboreum tree sparkle-berry	eLS	DSs	BL	GLMmSW	W	Sp	BIg
Vaccinium cespitosum dwarf blueberry	SS	Ss	Lf	GLMmS	PW	SpSu	BMN
Vaccinium corymbosum highbush blueberry	MS	DFSsW	AL	CGLMmSW	W	Sp	BMN
Vaccinium crassifolium creeping blueberry	eSS	FSs	fL	GLMmSW	P	Sp	BGgsW
Vaccinium darrowii Darrow's blueberry	eSS	DS	L	LMmR	RW	Sp	BgIs
Vaccinium deliciosum rainier blueberry	SS	DSs	Lf	GLMmS	PW	Sp	BgI
Vaccinium elliottii Elliott's blueberry	SS	DFSs	L	GLMmSW	PW	Su	BISW
Vaccinium erythrocarpum southern mountain-cranberry	SS	Ss	Ff	GLMmS	PW	SpSu	BINR
Vaccinium fuscatum black blueberry	MS	FS	L	GLMmSW	W	Su	W
Vaccinium macrocarpon large cranberry	eSS	FSsW	AFL	CGLMmSW	WP	Su	MNsW
Vaccinium membranaceum square-twig blueberry	SS	Ss	L	GLMmS	GW	Sp	BIN
Vaccinium myrsinites shiny blueberry	eSS	DSs	FL	GLMmS	PW	Sp	BgM
Vaccinium myrtilloides velvet-leaf blueberry	SS	FSsW	F	GLMmSW	PW	Su	BW
Vaccinium myrtillus whortle-berry	SS	DSs	f	GLMS	P	Sp	BG
Vaccinium ovalifolium oval-leaf blueberry	MS	Ss	—	GLMmS	PW	Sp	BI
Vaccinium ovatum evergreen blueberry	eMS	Ss	Lf	GLMmS	PW	Sp	BgIN
Vaccinium oxycoccos small cranberry	eSS	FSsW	L	GLMMSW	PW	Su	W
Vaccinium pallidum early lowbush blueberry	SS	DSs	—	GLMmSW	PW	Sp	BI
Vaccinium parvifolium red blueberry	LS	Ss	f	GLMmS	G	Sp	BIN
Vaccinium scoparium grouseberry	SS	Ss	—	GLMmSW	W	Su	BI
Vaccinium stamineum deerberry	MS	DSs	Ff	GLMmSW	W	Sp	B
Vaccinium tenellum small black blueberry	SS	S	F	GLMmSW	PR	Sp	B
Vaccinium vitis-idaea northern mountain-cranberry	eSS	DFSW	L	GLMmSW	W	Sp	BINRW

PLANT LIST	Plant Type	Env. Tol.	Aesthetic Value	Wildlife Value	Flower Color	Bloom Period	Landscape Uses
Vallesia glabra pearlberry	MS	Ss	—	U	W	SpSuF	BI
Vauquelinia californica Arizona-rosewood	eSU	DS	FL	U	W	Su	Bgs
Viburnum acerifolium maple-leaf arrow-wood	SS	Ds	AFfL	BGLMmS	W	Sp	AbIN
Viburnum dentatum southern arrow-wood	MS	FfsW	AFfL	BGmS	W	Sp	AbgHIsW
Viburnum edule squashberry	SS	Ss	Ff	GLMmS	W	SpSu	Ig
Viburnum lantanoides hobblebush	MS	s	AL	BGLMmS	W	Sp	bGHIs
Viburnum lentago nanny-berry	LS	FSs	FfL	BS	W	Sp	ABbs
Viburnum nudum possumhaw	LS	FDSsW	AFfL	BGLmSW	W	SpSu	ABbgINW
Viburnum obovatum small-leaf arrow-wood	SU	s	Ff	BGLmSW	W	Sp	I
Viburnum prunifolium smooth blackhaw	SU	DS	AfL	BGMmS	W	Sp	ABbg
Viburnum rafinesquianum downy arrow-wood	SS	DSs	AFL	BGLMmS	W	Sp	ABbgl
Viburnum rufidulum rusty blackhaw	SU	DSs	AFfL	BGLSs	W	Sp	ABbg
Viguiera deltoidea triangle goldeneye	SS	DS	F	U	Y	SpSu	M
Viguiera stenoloba resinbush	SS	DS	F	BS	Y	Su	M
Vitis aestivalis summer grape	WV	DSs	fL	GLmSW	W	SpSu	BINP
Vitis arizonica canyon grape	WV	DSs	fL	GLMS	W	SpSu	BEN
Vitis californica California grape	WV	FS	FfL	GLMSW	W	Sp	BS
Vitis labrusca fox grape	WV	FSs	fL	GLMSW	GW	Su	BN
Vitis monticola sweet mountain grape	WV	S	fL	GLMmS	—	—	BN
Vitis munsoniana little muscadine	WV	DSs	f	GLMmS	G	SpSuF	BIN
Vitis mustangensis mustang grape	WV	DFS	L	GLMmS	R	Sp	BN
Vitis riparia river-bank grape	WV	DFSs	AL	GLmSW	yg	Sp	INS
Vitis rotundifolia muscadine	WV	FSs	L	MS	G	Su	BINS
Vitis shuttleworthii calloose grape	WV	Ss	f	GLMmS	G	—	BI
Vitis vulpina frost grape	WV	FSs	L	GLMmS	—	Su	N

PLANT LIST	Plant Type	Env. Tol.	Aesthetic Value	Wildlife Value	Flower Color	Bloom Period	Landscape Uses
Waltheria indica basora-prieta	SS	DS	F	Mm	Y	WSp	ABM
Washingtonia filifera California fan palm	eSU	FS	L	mS	W	Su	ABM
Wisteria frutescens American wisteria	WV	Ss	F	U	Pu	Su	AB
Xanthorhiza simplicissima shrub yellowroot	SS	FSs	L	U	BPu	Sp	GIS
Ximenia americana tallow-wood	SU	DSs	F	U	Y	SpF	BI
Yucca aloifolia aloe yucca	eMS	DS	—	mS	W	—	—
Yucca arkansana Arkansas yucca	eMS	DS	FL	HmS	W	—	AM
Yucca baccata banana yucca	eSS	DS	F	hm	W	Sp	AMP
Yucca brevifolia Joshua-tree	eSU	DS	BFL	mRT	yg	Sp	AM
Yucca campestris Plains yucca	eSS	DS	FL	HmS	PGW	Sp	AM
Yucca constricta Buckley's yucca	SS	DS	FL	HmS	GW	Sp	AM
Yucca elata soaptree yucca	eSU	DS	FL	HMmS	W	Su	AM
Yucca faxoniana Eve's-needle	eLS	S	FL	HmS	W	SpSu	AM
Yucca filamentosa Adam's-needle	eSS	DS	FL	HmS	W	Su	AbgM
Yucca glauca soapweed yucca	eMS	DS	FL	HmS	W	Su	AgM
Yucca schidigera Mojave yucca	eLS	DS	L	HmS	W	Sp	AM
Yucca schottii hoary yucca	eSU	DS	FL	HmS	W	SuF	AM
Yucca thompsoniana Thompson's yucca	eSU	DS	FL	HmS	W	Su	AM
Yucca torreyi Torrey's yucca	eSU	DS	FL	HmS	W	Sp	ABM
Yucca treculeana Don Quixote's-lace	eSU	DS	FL	HmS	W	WSp	ABM
Yucca whipplei Our-Lord's-candle	eMS	DS	FL	HmS	W	Sp	AM
Zamia pumila coontie	eSS	DS	LF	U	R	Su	BFg
Zanthoxylum americanum toothachetree	SU	DFS	AL	GmS	yg	Sp	BP
Zanthoxylum clava-herculis Hercules'-club	SU	Ss	—	GS	GW	Sp	I
Zanthoxylum fagara lime prickly-ash	eSU	Ss	—	GS	yg	WSpSu	BI

PLANT LIST	Plant Type	Env. Tol.	Aesthetic Value	Wildlife Value	Flower Color	Bloom Period	Landscape Uses
Zanthoxylum hirsutum Texas hercules'-club	LS	S	S	GS	yg	—	B
Zenobia pulverulenta honeycup	SS	FSs	AL	GmS	W	Su	BIW
Ziziphus obtusifolia lotebush	SS	DS	—	GmS	—	Su	BM

Herbaceous Plant Matrix

PLANT LIST	Plant Type	Env. Tol.	Aesthetic Value	Wildlife Value	Flower Color	Bloom Period	Landscape Uses
Acalypha gracilens slender three-seed-mercury	SA	DS	—	GS	G	SuF	M
Achlys triphylla sweet-after-death	SP	Ss	DF	U	PuR	Su	BIS
Acleisanthes anisophylla oblique-leaf trumpets	SP	S	—	U	W	SpSuF	M
Acleisanthes longiflora angel's trumpets	SP	DS	F	B	PuW	SpSuF	bEM
Aconitum columbianum Columbian monkshood	MP	SF	FL	U	BW	SW	gSW
Acorus americanus sweetflag	MP	FSW	L	Lm	Y	Su	Wwg
Acourtia runcinata feather-leaf desert-peony	SP	Ss	F	U	PPu	SpSuF	BE
Acrostichum aureum golden leather fern	MP	FS	L	U	X	X	W
Acrostichum danaeifolium inland leather fern	MP	FS	L	U	X	X	W
Actaea pachypoda white baneberry	MP	s	FfL	Gm	W	Su	BgI
Actaea rubra red baneberry	SP	Ss	FfL	GM	W	SpSu	BgI
Adenocaulon bicolor American trailplant	MP	s	L	U	W	Su	I
Adiantum pedatum northern maidenhair	SP	s	L	M	X	X	BgI
Agalinis maritima salt marsh false foxglove	SA	FNaSW	FL	B	P	SpSu	bCSWwg
Agalinis tenuifolia slender-leaf false foxglove	SP	FSs	F	U	P	SuF	WMBg
Agastache urticifolia nettle-leaf giant-hyssop	LP	Ds	F	U	LPu	Su	BgI
Ageratina altissima white snakeroot	MP	DSs	F	BGS	W	SuF	BIW
Agoseris glauca pale goat-chicory	SP	S	F	U	Y	SpSu	gM
Agrimonia gryposepala tall hairy grooveburr	LP	Ss	F	U	Y	Su	B
Agrostis diegoensis leafy bent	SPG	Ss	—	U	Gr	—	BM
Agrostis elliottiana Elliot's bent	SAG	S	—	M	G	Sp	M
Agrostis gigantea black bent	MPG	Fs	—	U	Gr	—	BIS

PLANT LIST	Plant Type	Env. Tol.	Aesthetic Value	Wildlife Value	Flower Color	Bloom Period	Landscape Uses
Agrostis hallii Hall's bent	MPG	s	—	U	Gr	—	BI
Agrostis hyemalis winter bent	MPG	DSs	—	U	Gr	—	M
Agrostis idahoensis Idaho bent	SPG	S	—	U	Gr	—	M
Agrostis scabra rough bent	MPG	DSs	—	U	Gr	—	M
Alisma plantago-aquatica water plantain	MP	FSW	FL	Lm	W	Su	Wwg
Alisma subcordatum American water-plantain	MP	FSW	FL	LM	W	Su	Wwg
Allionia incarnata trailing windmills	MP	DS	—	U	PPuW	SpSu	M
Allium acuminatum taper-tip onion	SP	DS	F	B	P	—	Bb
Allium canadense meadow garlic	SP	FSs	—	GHhS	PW	SpSu	BM
Allium cernuum nodding onion	MP	DS	F	B	P	Su	bM
Allium textile white wild onion	SP	DS	F	B	PW	SpSu	bM
Allium tricoccum ramp	MP	s	FL	B	G	Su	BgI
Alopecurus aequalis short-awn meadow-foxtail	MPG	FSW	F	GS	Gr	—	Wwg
Alopecurus borealis meadow-foxtail	PG	—	—	U	yg	SpSu	—
Alopecurus saccatus Pacific meadow-foxtail	SG	FSW	F	GS	X	X	MW
Alophia drummondii propeller-flower	SP	S	F	U	LPu	Sp	gM
Alternanthera flavescens yellow joyweed	P	—	—	U	YW	WSpSuF	—
Alyssum desertorum desert madwort	P	—	—	U	Y	Su	—
Amaranthus australis southern amaranth	LP	FNaS	—	GLMmSW	—	—	—
Amaranthus palmeri Palmer's amaranth	MA	DS	—	GLMmSW	—	—	—
Amblyolepis setigera huisache-daisy	SA	S	F	BC	Y	Sp	bCGgM
Amblyopappus pusillus dwarf coastweed	SA	FNaS	F	U	Y	Su	CSW
Ambrosia acanthicarpa flat-spine burr-ragweed	SA	S	—	GS	G	SuF	C
Ambrosia artemisiifolia annual ragweed	LA	DS	—	GS	G	SuF	CS

PLANT LIST	Plant Type	Env. Tol.	Aesthetic Value	Wildlife Value	Flower Color	Bloom Period	Landscape Uses
Ambrosia confertiflora weak-leaf burr-ragweed	LP	S	—	GMmS	G	SuF	EM
Ambrosia hispida coastal ragweed	MA	FS	—	GS	G	SuF	CS
Ambrosia psilostachya western ragweed	SAP	DS	—	GS	G	SuF	C
Amianthium muscitoxicum flypoison	MP	FS	F	U	W	Su	BWwg
Ammophila breviligulata American beach grass	MG	S	—	GS	Br	SuF	CES
Amphicarpaea bracteata American hog-peanut	HV	Ss	L	LS	Pu	SuF	CGI
Amphicarpum muhlenbergianum perennial goober grass	MPG	FS	—	U	Gr	SuF	W
Amsonia illustris Ozark bluestar	MP	FS	F	U	B	Sp	W
Amsonia tabernaemontana eastern bluestar	MP	Ss	F	U	B	SpSu	Bg
Andropogon floridanus Florida bluestem	MPG	DS	AL	GL	W	F	M
Andropogon gerardii big bluestem	LPG	DS	ABL	GL	GPu	SuF	EgM
Andropogon glomeratus bushy bluestem	LPG	FNaS	AFL	GL	GW	SuF	SW
Andropogon hallii sand bluestem	MPG	SD	AL	GL	GW	SuF	—
Andropogon ternarius split-beard bluestem	MPG	SF	AFL	GL	W	F	BM
Andropogon virginicus broom-sedge	MPG	S	ABFL	GL	W	SuF	EM
Androsace occidentalis western rock-jasmine	SA	DS	F	U	PW	Sp	Cg
Anemia adiantifolia pineland fern	SP	DS	F	U	—	SpSu	Bg
Anemone berlandieri ten-petal thimbleweed	P	—	—	U	PuW	Sp	—
Anemone canadensis round-leaf thimbleweed	SP	S	F	h	BW	Sp	BgM
Anemone caroliniana Carolina thimbleweed	SP	S	F	h	BW	Sp	BgM
Anemone cylindrica long-head thimbleweed	MP	DSs	FL	h	W	Sp	BgM
Anemone edwardsiana plateau thimbleweed	SP	Ss	FL	h	W	Sp	R
Anemone lyallii little mountain thimbleweed	P	—	—	U	BPW	Sp	—
Anemone piperi Piper's windflower	P	—	—	U	BPW	Sp	—

PLANT LIST	Plant Type	Env. Tol.	Aesthetic Value	Wildlife Value	Flower Color	Bloom Period	Landscape Uses
Anemone quinquefolia nightcaps	SP	S	FL	h	W	Sp	BgM
Anemone virginiana tall thimbleweed	MP	S	F	h	W	Su	BgM
Anemopsis californica yerba-mansa	SP	FNaS	FL	U	W	SpSu	gSW
Angelica atropurpurea purple-stem angelica	LP	FSW	FL	B	W	Su	gSW
Angelica pinnata small-leaf angelica	P	FW	—	U	PW	Su	W
Anisocoma acaulis scalebud	SA	DS	F	U	W	Sp	Cg
Antennaria dimorpha cushion pussytoes	SP	Ss	L	GLMm	—	SpSu	BG
Antennaria neglecta field pussytoes	SP	DS	L	GLMm	W	Sp	BGM
Antennaria parlinii Parlin's pussytoes	SP	DSs	FL	GMm	W	SpSu	BGgMR
Antennaria plantaginifolia woman's-tobacco	SP	Ds	AL	GLMm	W	Sp	BGR
Antennaria rosea rosy pussytoes	SP	S	F	GLMm	P	Su	G
Anthaenantia villosa green silkyscale	MPG	DSs	F	U	G	SuF	B
Aphanostephus ramosissimus plains dozedaisy	SA	S	F	B	LPPu	SpSu	CM
Aphanostephus skirrhobasis Arkansas dozedaisy	SA	DS	F	U	LW	SpSu	gM
Apios americana groundnut	HV	FSs	F	m	Br	SuF	GgI
Apocynum androsaemifolium spreading dogbane	MP	S	F	BC	P	Su	B
Aquilegia canadensis red columbine	SP	S	FL	Hh	RY	SpSu	Bbl
Aquilegia chrysantha golden columbine	MP	S	FL	h	Y	Su	BgR
Aquilegia coerulea Colorado blue columbine	MP	S	FL	h	B	Su	BbM
Aquilegia formosa crimson columbine	MP	S	FL	Hh	R	Su	BbM
Arabis breweri Brewer's rockcress	SP	S	—	CS	PuW	—	R
Arabis drummondii Canadian rockcress	MP	DSs	—	U	W	SpSu	B
Arabis holboellii Holboell's rockcress	SP	DS	—	CS	PW	Su	b
Arabis lignifera Owens Valley rockcress	P	—	—	U	PPu	Sp	—

PLANT LIST	Plant Type	Env. Tol.	Aesthetic Value	Wildlife Value	Flower Color	Bloom Period	Landscape Uses
Arabis lyrata lyre-leaf rockcress	SP	S	F	C	W	Sp	B
Arabis platysperma pioneer rockcress	SP	S	—	CS	PW	Su	B
Arabis repanda Yosemite rockcress	SB	S	—	CS	W	Su	B
Arabis sparsiflora elegant rockcress	BP	—	—	U	Pu	SpSu	—
Aralia californica California spikenard	LP	s	FfL	GMS	R	Sn	gIS
Aralia nudicaulis wild sarsaparilla	SP	S	L	U	GW	Su	BI
Aralia racemosa American spikenard	LP	Ss	fL	U	W	Su	BgI
Arenaria hookeri Hooker's sandwort	P	—	—	U	W	Su	—
Arenaria kingii King's sandwort	P	—	—	U	WP	Su	—
Argentina anserina common silverweed	SP	FS	FL	U	Y	Su	GSW
Argentina egedii Pacific silverweed	P	—	—	U	Y	SpSu	—
Arisaema dracontium greendragon	MP	FS	LF	GS	yg	Sp	BI
Arisaema triphyllum jack-in-the-pulpit	SP	s	FfL	GS	GPu	Sp	BgI
Aristida californica California three-awn	SPG	DS	F	LMmS	Br	Su	M
Aristida divaricata poverty three-awn	SPG	DS	F	LMmS	Br	Su	M
Aristida longespica red three-awn	MAG	DS	F	LMmS	Pu	SuF	M
Aristida oligantha prairie three-awn	SAG	DS	F	LMmS	GPu	SuF	M
Aristida orcuttiana single-awn three-awn	PG	—	—	U	yg	SuF	M
Aristida purpurascens arrow-feather three-awn	MPG	DS	F	LMmS	Br	SuF	BM
Aristida purpurea purple three-awn	MPG	DS	F	LMmS	Br	SuF	BM
Aristida spiciformis bottlebrush three-awn	MPG	DS	F	LMmS	Br	F	B
Aristida stricta pineland three-awn	SPG	DS	F	LMmS	Br	SuF	BM
Aristida ternipes spider grass	SPG	DS	F	LMmS	Br	SuF	M
Aristolochia serpentaria Virginia-snakeroot	HV	Ss	F	U	PuR	SpSu	BI

PLANT LIST	Plant Type	Env. Tol.	Aesthetic Value	Wildlife Value	Flower Color	Bloom Period	Landscape Uses
Armeria maritima sea thrift	eSP	—	—	U	P	SuSp	—
Armoracia lacustris lakecress	AP	W	—	U	W	SpSu	wg
Arnica chamissonis leafy leopard-bane	P	FW	F	U	Y	Su	W
Arnica cordifolia heart-leaf leopard-bane	SP	Ds	F	U	Y	Su	B
Arnica latifolia daffodil leopard-bane	SP	Ss	F	U	Y	Su	B
Arnoglossum muehlenbergii great Indian-plantain	LP	S	—	U	W	Su	BI
Artemisia campestris Pacific wormwood	SBP	DS	—	U	WY	SuF	—
Artemisia dracunculus dragon wormwood	LP	—	L	GMm	WY	F	—
Artemisia ludoviciana white sagebrush	MP	SD	L	GMm	yg	SuF	M
Artemisia michauxiana Michaux's wormwood	P	—	—	GMm	Y	SpSu	—
Artemisia parryi Parry's wormwood	P	—	—	GMm	Y	Su	—
Artemisia tripartita three-tip sagebrush	eP	—	—	GMm	BrW	Su	—
Arthrocnemum subterminale Parish's glasswort	SP	NaS	—	W	—	—	S
Aruncus dioicus bride's-feathers	MP	Ss	FL	U	W	Su	BgI
Asarum canadense Canadian wild ginger	SP	s	L	U	Bu	Sp	BGgI
Asarum caudatum long-tail wild ginger	SP	s	L	U	Pu	Sp	BGgI
Asarum hartwegii Hartweg's wild ginger	SP	s	FL	U	Br	SpSu	GI
Asclepias arenaria sand milkweed	SP	S	F	B	GW	Su	bM
Asclepias asperula spider antelope-horns	SP	DSs	F	BC	Puyg	SpSu	BbgM
Asclepias curtissii Curtis' milkweed	MP	DS	F	B	W	SpSuF	b
Asclepias eriocarpa Indian milkweed	MP	DS	Ff	BM	WP	Su	bM
Asclepias incarnata swamp milkweed	MP	FS	Ff	BCh	P	Su	bWwg
Asclepias lanuginosa side-cluster milkweed	MP	S	Ff	BC	P	SpSu	M
Asclepias latifolia broad-leaf milkweed	MP	DS	Ff	BC	G	Su	M

PLANT LIST	Plant Type	Env. Tol.	Aesthetic Value	Wildlife Value	Flower Color	Bloom Period	Landscape Uses
Asclepias ovalifolia oval-leaf milkweed	SP	S	Ff	BCh	GW	Su	b
Asclepias perennis aquatic milkweed	MP	FSW	Ff	BCh	W	SpSu	blW
Asclepias speciosa showy milkweed	MP	S	Ff	BCh	P	SpSu	BbS
Asclepias stenophylla slim-leaf milkweed	MP	DS	Ff	BC	GW	SU	bMR
Asclepias subulata rush milkweed	LP	DFS	F	BM	WY	SpSu	bMW
Asclepias syriaca common milkweed	LP	DS	Ff	BCh	Pu	Su	bM
Asclepias tuberosa butterfly milkweed	MP	DS	Ff	BCh	O	SuF	bM
Asclepias verticillata whorled milkweed	MP	DS	F	BC	W	Su	bgM
Asclepias viridiflora green comet milkweed	MP	DS	F	BC	G	SU	bM
Asplenium platyneuron ebony spleenwort	eSP	s	L	U	X	X	Bbl
Asplenium rhizophyllum walking fern	SP	s	L	U	X	X	BlR
Asplenium trichomanes maidenhair spleenwort	SP	s	L	U	X	X	Bgl
Aster acuminatus whorled wood aster	MP	S	F	BCGhL MmS	W	SuF	Bb
Aster alpigenus tundra aster	P	FW	F	GLMmS	BPu	SuF	bW
Aster anomalus many-ray aster	MP	Ds	F	BCGhL MmS	BP	F	BbEg
Aster breweri Brewer's aster	P	—	F	GLMmS ch	B	SuF	b
Aster ciliolatus Lindley's aster	MP	Ss	F	DCGhL MmS	B	SuF	b
Aster conspicuus eastern showy aster	P	—	F	U	Pu	Su	b
Aster cordifolius common blue wood aster	MP	S	F	CBh	Pu	F	Bb
Aster divaricatus white wood aster	MP	s	F	BGLMm CSh	W	SuF	BblW
Aster drummondii Drummond's aster	MP	DSs	F	BCGMm S	BP	SuF	BbgM
Aster dumosus rice button aster	MP	FSs	F	BCGhL MmS	BPuW	SuF	b
Aster ericoides white heath aster	MP	DS	F	BCGhL MmS	W	SuF	bM
Aster laevis smooth blue aster	MP	S	F	BCL	B	SuF	bM

PLANT LIST	Plant Type	Env. Tol.	Aesthetic Value	Wildlife Value	Flower Color	Bloom Period	Landscape Uses
Aster lanceolatus white panicle aster	MP	FS	Ch	BC	W	SuF	bW
Aster lateriflorus farewell-summer	LP	S	F	BCh	PuW	SuF	b
Aster linariifolius flax-leaf white-top aster	SP	S	F	BCh	B	SuF	bM
Aster macrophyllus large-leaf aster	LP	S	F	BCGLM mSh	Pu	SuF	b
Aster novi-angliae New England aster	LP	S	F	BS	Pu	F	bM
Aster occidentalis western mountain aster	P	FW	—	U	LPu	SuF	W
Aster oolentangiensis sky blue aster	MP	S	F	BCGhL MmS	B	SuF	bM
Aster paludosus southern swamp aster	SP	S	F	BCh	Pu	SuF	BbM
Aster patens late purple aster	MP	DSs	F	BCGhL MmS	BPu	F	BbEgM
Aster paternus toothed white-top aster	SP	S	F	BCGhL MmS	W	Su	BI
Aster pilosus white oldfield aster	MP	DS	F	BS	W	F	bM
Aster puniceus purple-stem aster	LP	FSW	F	BCh	Pu	SuF	bW
Aster sericeus western silver aster	MP	DS	F	BS	Pu	F	bW
Aster solidagineus narrow-leaf white-top aster	MP	S	F	BCGHh LMmS	W	SuF	b
Aster tenuifolius perennial saltmarsh aster	SP	FSW	F	BGMmS	BNP	F	bW
Aster tortifolius dixie white-top aster	MP	DS	F	BCh	W	SuF	BbM
Aster undulatus waxy-leaf aster	MP	DSs	F	BCGhM mS	B	SuF	BbgM
Aster umbellatus parasol flat-top white aster	LP	FS	FL	BCGhL MmS	W	SuF	bW
Aster walteri Walter's aster	SP	DS	F	BCh	Pu	F	BbM
Astragalus adsurgens standing milk-vetch	SP	DS	F	GLMm	Pu	Su	BEM
Astragalus amphioxys Aladdin's-slippers	SAP	—	—	GLMm	PPu	SpSu	E
Astragalus arrectus palouse milk-vetch	P	—	—	GLMm	WY	SpSu	EM
Astragalus castaneiformis chestnut milk-vetch	P	—	—	GLMm	W	SpSu	E
Astragalus crassicarpus ground-plum	P	DS	F	GLMm	Pu	Sp	EM

PLANT LIST	Plant Type	Env. Tol.	Aesthetic Value	Wildlife Value	Flower Color	Bloom Period	Landscape Uses
Astragalus kentrophyta spiny milk-vetch	P	—	—	GLMm	PPuW	SuF	—
Astragalus miser timber milk-vetch	P	—	—	GLMm	Y	Sp	—
Astragalus missouriensis Missouri milk-vetch	SP	DS	F	U	PPu	Sp	GM
Astragalus mollissimus woolly milk-vetch	SP	DS	—	GLMm	Pu	SpSu	—
Astragalus nuttallianus turkey-pea	SA	DS	DF	GMm	PPu	Sp	GgM
Astragalus pectinatus narrow-leaf milk-vetch	P	—	—	GLMm	YW	SpSu	—
Astragalus platytropis broad-keel milk-vetch	SP	S	F	GLMm	PuY	Su	Fg
Astragalus purshii Pursh's milk-vetch	SP	DS	FL	GLMm	WPu	SpSu	EM
Astragalus spaldingii Spalding's milk-vetch	MP	—	L	GLMm	—	—	EM
Astragalus spatulatus tufted milk-vetch	P	—	—	GLMm	PPu	SpSu	—
Astragalus tener alkali milk-vetch	SP	DNaS	F	GLMm	Pu	Sp	EM
Astragalus tephrodes ashen milk-vetch	P	—	—	GLMm	PPu	SpSu	—
Astragalus troglodytus creeping milk-vetch	P	—	—	GLMm	PuR	SpSu	—
Astragalus wootonii Wooton's milk-vetch	SAB	DS	F	GMm	PRW	Sp	GgM
Athyrium filix-femina subarctic lady fern	MP	s	L	U	X	X	DgI
Atrichoseris platyphylla parachute-plant	A	—	—	U	PW	Sp	—
Atriplex argentea silverscale	SA	DS	—	GLMmS	G	SuF	C
Atriplex fruticulosa ball saltbush	SP	DNaS	—	GLMmS W	G	SuF	—
Atriplex patula halberd-leaf orache	SA	FNaS	L	GLMmS W	G	SuF	CSW
Atriplex pentandra crested saltbush	SAP	FNaS	—	GLMmS W	G	SuF	C
Atriplex phyllostegia arrow saltbush	SP	DS	—	GLMmS W	G	SuF	—
Atriplex powellii Powell's orache	SP	DNaS	L	GLMmS W	G	SuF	M
Atriplex tularensis Bakersfield saltbush	SP	DNaS	f	GLMmS W	—	SuF	M
Atriplex watsonii Watson's saltbush	SP	FSW	—	GLMmS W	G	Su	W

PLANT LIST	Plant Type	Env. Tol.	Aesthetic Value	Wildlife Value	Flower Color	Bloom Period	Landscape Uses
Aulacomnium palustre moss	m	FSs	—	U	X	X	IW
Aureolaria flava smooth yellow false-foxglove	LP	s	F	U	Y	Su	Bgl
Aureolaria laevigata entire-leaf yellow false-foxglove	MP	s	F	U	Y	Su	BI
Aureolaria pedicularia fern-leaf yellow false-foxglove	MA	DSs	F	U	Y	F	CBI
Aureolaria virginica downy yellow false-foxglove	MP	Ss	F	U	Y	SpSu	Bl
Azolla caroliniana Carolina mosquito fern	AQP	SW	LA	W	X	X	Wwg
Baileya multiradiata showy desert-marigold	SAP	DS	F	U	Y	Su	CgM
Balduina angustifolia coastal-plain honeycomb-head	MP	DS	—	U	Y	SuF	—
Balsamorhiza incana hoary balsamroot	SP	DS	F	U	Y	SpSu	BgM
Balsamorhiza sagittata arrow-leaf balsamroot	MP	DS	FL	U	Y	SpSu	BM
Baptisia alba white wild indigo	LP	DS	FL	B	W	SpSu	ABgM
Baptisia bracteata long-bract wild indigo	MP	DS	FL	B	WY	SpSu	ABgM
Baptisia lanceolata gopherweed	MP	S	FL	B	Y	Sp	ABgM
Barbarea orthoceras American yellow-rocket	S	FWs	F	GS	Y	Su	BSW
Batis maritima turtleweed	MP	NaS	—	U	W	Su	ES
Berlandiera subacaulis Florida greeneyes	SP	DS	F	BS	Y	SpSu	bM
Berlandiera texana Texas greeneyes	MP	FSs	F	U	OY	SpSu	BS
Berula erecta cat-leaf water-parsnip	MP	FSW	DL	U	W	SuF	SWwg
Besseya wyomingensis Wyoming coraldrops	P	—	—	U	Pu	Sp	—
Bidens aristosa bearded beggarticks	MP	DFS	FL	BGmSW	Y	SuF	BbCgMW
Bidens bipinnata Spanish-needles	MA	FSs	FL	BGmSW	Y	SuF	C
Bidens cernua nodding burr-marigold	MP	DFS	F	BS	Y	SuF	BbgMW
Bidens frondosa devil's-pitchfork	MP	FS	—	GmSW	yg	SuF	MW
Bifora americana prairie bishop	MA	S	—	U	W	SpSu	M

PLANT LIST	Plant Type	Env. Tol.	Aesthetic Value	Wildlife Value	Flower Color	Bloom Period	Landscape Uses
Blechnum spicant deerfern	eP	FW	—	U	X	X	W
Blennosperma nanum common stickyseed	AP	FW	—	U	YPuW	Sp	W
Blepharoneuron tricholepis pine-dropseed	PG	—	—	U	G	Su	—
Blephilia ciliata downy pagode-plant	SP	DS	FL	B	LPu	SpSu	BbgM
Boehmeria cylindrica small-spike false nettle	MP	FSs	—	U	G	SuF	IW
Boisduvalia glabella smooth spike-primrose	SA	S	FL	U	PuW	Sp	M
Boltonia asteroides white doll's-daisy	LP	FNaSW	F	B	PuW	SuF	bMW
Boltonia diffusa small-head doll's-daisy	MP	FSs	F	B	PuW	F	BM
Bothriochloa barbinodis cane beard grass	MPG	DS	F	GL	W	Su	AM
Bothriochloa saccharoides plumed beard grass	MPG	DS	F	GL	W	Su	AM
Botrychium virginianum rattlesnake fern	eSP	s	L	GLM	X	X	Bgl
Bouteloua breviseta gypsum grama	SPG	DS	F	GLMmS	G	Su	M
Bouteloua chondrosioides spruce-top grama	SPG	DS	F	GLMmS	G	Su	M
Bouteloua curtipendula side oats grama	MG	DS	F	GLMmS	GPu	SuF	M
Bouteloua eriopoda black grama	SPG	DS	F	GLMmS	G	Su	M
Bouteloua gracilis blue grama	SPG	DS	F	GLMmS	Br	Su	M
Bouteloua hirsuta hairy grama	SPG	DS	F	GLMmS	Br	Su	M
Bouteloua pectinata tall grama	MPG	S	—	m	G	SpSuF	M
Bouteloua ramosa chino grama	MPG	DS	F	GLMmS	G	Si	MR
Bouteloua repens slender grama	SPG	DS	F	GLMmS	G	Su	MR
Bouteloua rigidiseta Texas grama	SPG	DS	F	GLMmS	G	Su	MR
Bouteloua trifida red grama	SPG	DS	F	GLMmS	G	Su	MR
Brachiaria ciliatissima fringed signal grass	LPG	S	F	U	G	SpSuF	EM
Brachyelytrum erectum bearded shorthusk	MPG	Ss	—	U	G	Su	BI

PLANT LIST	Plant Type	Env. Tol.	Aesthetic Value	Wildlife Value	Flower Color	Bloom Period	Landscape Uses
Brickellia cylindraceae gravel-bar brickellbush	MP	Ss	—	G	GW	SuF	M
Brickellia eupatarioides false boneset	LP	S	f	U	WY	SuF	gM
Brickellia oblongifolia narrow-leaf brickelbush	SP	DS	—	U	GPuW	SuF	M
Bromus anomalus nodding brome	SPG	DS	—	GLMmS	G	Su	EM
Bromus ciliatus fringed brome	MPG	Ss	—	GLMmS	G	Su	BES
Bromus diandrus ripgut brome	PG	—	—	GLMmS	yg	SpSu	—
Bromus laevipes woodland brome	PG	—	—	GLMmS	yg	SpSu	—
Bromus marginatus large mountain brome	MPG	DS	—	GLMmS	G	Su	BEM
Bromus orcuttianus Chinook brome	MPG	DSs	—	GLMmS	G	Su	BEI
Bromus pubescens hairy woodland brome	MPG	DSs	—	GLMmS	G	Su	BEI
Bromus vulgaris Columbian brome	MPG	Ss	—	GLMmS	G	Su	BE
Buchloë dactyloides buffalo grass	SPG	DS	F	LSW	G	Su	EM
Buchnera americana American bluehearts	MP	DFSs W	F	U	Pu	WSuF	BMWwg
Cabomba caroliniana Carolina fanwort	AQP	SsW	L	U	W	SpSu	Wwg
Cacalia atriplicifolia pale Indian-plantain	LP	Ss	L	U	W	Su	BgM
Cakile edentula American searocket	SA	FNaS	L	U	Y	SpF	CEW
Calamagrostis breweri short-hair reed grass	SPG	S	L	LM	Pu	Su	M
Calamagrostis canadensis bluejoint	LPG	FSW	L	LM	Pu	Su	W
Calamagrostis nutkaensis nootka reed grass	LPG	Fs	L	LM	Pu	Su	W
Calamagrostis rubescens pinegrass	MPG	DS	L	LM	Pu	Su	BM
Calamagrostis stricta slim-stem reedgrass	MPG	FSW	L	LM	Pu	Su	W
Calamovilfa gigantea giant sand-reed	LPG	DS	—	LM	G	SuF	S
Calamovilfa longifolia prairie sand-reed	LPG	DS	—	LM	G	SuF	M
Calla palustris water-dragon	SP	SW	FfL	U	WY	SpSu	Wwg

PLANT LIST	Plant Type	Env. Tol.	Aesthetic Value	Wildlife Value	Flower Color	Bloom Period	Landscape Uses
Callirhoe involucrata purple poppy-mallow	SP	Ss	F	B	PuR	Sp	BgM
Calochortus ambiguus doubting mariposa-lily	P	—	—	U	GrP	SpSu	—
Calochortus invenustus plain mariposa-lily	SP	S	FL	U	Pu	Sp	gM
Calochortus luteus yellow mariposa-lily	SP	DS	F	U	OY	SpSu	gM
Calochortus nuttallii sego-lily	SP	DS	F	U	PuW	SpSu	gM
Calopogon tuberosus tubercus grass-pink	SP	FS	FL	U	P	Su	gW
Caltha leptosepala white marsh-marigold	SP	FS	F	hL	W	SpSu	SWwg
Caltha palustris yellow marsh-marigold	SP	FSsW	FL	hL	Y	Su	Wwg
Calycoseris parryi yellow tackstem	SA	DS	F	U	Y	Sp	C
Calylophus berlandieri Berlandier's sundrops	SAP	DS	F	U	Y	SpSu	gM
Calylophus hartwegii Hartweg's sundrops	SP	DS	F	U	Y	SpSu	gMR
Calylophus serrulatus yellow sundrops	MP	DS	—	U	Y	Su	M
Calystegia occidentalis chaparral false bindweed	PHV	—	—	U	P	SpSu	—
Calystegia sepium hedge false bindweed	HV	FS	FL	GLm	P	SpF	BS
Camassia quamash small camas	SP	FS	F	U	BW	Sp	MW
Camassia scilloides Atlantic camas	MP	s	F	U	B	Sp	BgI
Camissonia boothii shredding suncup	A			U	PW	Su	—
Camissonia brevipes golden suncup	A	—	—	U	Y	Sp	—
Camissonia chamaenerioides long-capsule suncup	SA	DS	—	U	W	Sp	—
Camissonia claviformis browneyes	A	—	—	U	RW	Sp	—
Camissonia scapoidea Paiute suncup	A	S	—	U	Y	Sp	—
Campanula aparinoides marsh bellflower	SP	FS	F	hS	BW	Su	gW
Campanula rotundifolia bluebell-of-Scotland	SP	S	F	hS	B	SuF	gM
Campanulastrum americanum American-bellflower	LA	s	F	U	B	Su	gI

PLANT LIST	Plant Type	Env. Tol.	Aesthetic Value	Wildlife Value	Flower Color	Bloom Period	Landscape Uses
Canavalia rosea bay-bean	MP	NaS	F	U	P	SpSuF	S
Canna flaccida bandanna-of-the-Everglades	MP	FSW	F	U	Y	SpSu	Wwg
Cardamine breweri Sierran bittercress	SP	S	F	U	W	Sp	M
Cardamine concatenata cut-leaf toothwort	SP	Fs	F	U	W	Sp	IS
Cardamine cordifolia large mountain bittercress	S	Fs	F	U	W	Sp	E
Cardamine diphylla crinkleroot	SP	Ss	L	U	W	Sp	SG
Cardamine longii Long's bittercress	SP	FNa SW	F	U	W	SuF	SW
Cardaria draba heart-pod hoarycress	SP	—	—	U	W	SP	—
Cardiospermum corindum faux-persil	HV	Ss	—	U	WY	SuF	BGM
Carex alata broad-wing sedge	MPG	SW	L	CGLMm SW	G	Su	W
Carex albicans white-tinge sedge	MPG	DsS	L	CGLMm S	G	SpSu	BI
Carex albursina white bear sedge	MPG	s	L	CGLMm S	G	Sp	I
Carex amphibola eastern narrow-leaf sedge	MPG	FSs	—	GLMmS	G	SpSu	BIMW
Carex aquatilis leafy tussock sedge	MPG	FSW	L	CGLMm SW	G	Su	Wwg
Carex arctata drooping woodland sedge	MPG	Ss	L	CGLMm S	G	Su	BI
Carex arkansana Arkansas sedge	MPG	S	L	CGLMm SW	BG	Su	MW
Carex atlantica prickly bog sedge	MPG	FSsW	L	GLMmS W	G	SpSu	BIW
Carex aurea golden-fruit sedge	SPG	FS	L	CGLMm S	G	Su	MS
Carex bebbii Bebb's sedge	MPG	S	L	CGLMm S	G	Su	M
Carex bicknellii Bicknell's sedge	SPG	DS	L	CGLMm SW	BG	SW	MW
Carex bolanderi Bolander's sedge	MPG	DS	L	CGLMm S	Br	Su	M
Carex brittoniana Britton's sedge	MPG	S	—	U	G	SpSu	EM
Carex bromoides brome-like sedge	MPG	FSs	L	CGLMm SW	G	SpSu	IMW
Carex canescens hoary sedge	MPG	FSW	L	CGLMm S	G	SpSu	Wwg

PLANT LIST	Plant Type	Env. Tol.	Aesthetic Value	Wildlife Value	Flower Color	Bloom Period	Landscape Uses
Carex cephalophora oval-leaf sedge	SPG	FSs	—	GLMmS	G	Sp	SW
Carex cherokeensis Cherokee sedge	MPG	Ss	—	U	G	Sp	BE
Carex comosa bearded sedge	MPG	WS	L	CGLMm SW	G	Su	W
Carex concinna low northern sedge	MPG	s	L	CGLMm S	G	Su	I
Carex concinnoides northwestern sedge	SPG	D	L	CGLMm SW	G	Su	M
Carex crinita fringed sedge	MPG	SW	FfL	CGLMm SW	G	Su	W
Carex debilis white-edge sedge	MPG	s	L	GLMmS	G	Su	BI
Carex diandra lesser tussock sedge	MPG	SW	L	CGLMm SW	G	SpSu	W
Carex disperma soft-leaf sedge	SPG	Ss	L	CGLMm S	G	SpSu	BI
Carex duriuscula spike-rush sedge	P	—	L	CGLMm S	G	Su	—
Carex eburnea bristle-leaf sedge	SPG	S	L	CGLMm S	G	SpSu	M
Carex emoryi Emory's sedge	MPG	FSs	—	GLMmS	G	Sp	SW
Carex exilis coastal sedge	MPG	FSW	L	CGLMm SW	G	SpSu	W
Carex exserta short-hair sedge	SPG	DS	L	CGLMm S	Br	Su	M
Carex festucacea fescue sedge	MPG	FSs	L	CGLMm S	G	SpSu	MW
Carex filifolia thread-leaf sedge	SPG	DS	L	CGLMm S	G	Su	M
Carex flaccosperma thin-fruit sedge	SPG	sW	—	GLMmS W	G	Sp	BIW
Carex flava yellow-green sedge	MPG	FS	L	CGLMm S	yg	Su	MS
Carex foenea dry-spike sedge	P	—	L	CGLMm S	G	Su	—
Carex folliculata northern long sedge	MPG	FSsW	L	CGLMm SW	G	Su	BIW
Carex frankii Frank's sedge	MPG	Ss	L	CGLMm S	G	Su	BIM
Carex geophila white mountain sedge	P	—	L	CGLMm S	G	Su	—
Carex geyeri Geyer's sedge	SPG	Ss	L	CGLMm S	G	Sp	BI
Carex gigantea giant sedge	MPG	FSW	L	CGLMm SW	G	SpF	W

PLANT LIST	Plant Type	Env. Tol.	Aesthetic Value	Wildlife Value	Flower Color	Bloom Period	Landscape Uses
Carex granularis limestone-meadow sedge	MPG	Ss	L	GLMmS	G	Su	BIM
Carex gravida heavy sedge	MPG	S	L	GLMmS	BrG	SpSu	M
Carex grayi Gray's sedge	MPG	Ss	L	GLMmS	G	SuF	BIM
Carex hassei Hasse's sedge	MPG	FS	L	GLMmS W	BrPu	Su	SW
Carex haydenii cloud sedge	MPG	SW	L	GLMmS W	G	SpSu	BIW
Carex heteroneura different-nerve sedge	MPG	S	L	GLMmS	G	Su	M
Carex hyalinolepis shoreline sedge	SPG	FSW	L	CGLMm SW	BrG	Su	MW
Carex hystericina porcupine sedge	MPG	FSW	L	GLMmS W	G	SuF	SW
Carex inops long-stolon sedge	SPG	D	L	GLMmS	G	Su	B
Carex interior inland sedge	SPG	FS	L	GLMmS W	G	SpSu	W
Carex intumescens great bladder sedge	MPG	Ss	L	GLMmS	G	SpF	BIM
Carex jonesii Jones' sedge	SPG	S	L	GLMmS	G	SpSu	M
Carex lacustris lakebank sedge	MPG	SW	L	GLMmS W	G	Su	W
Carex lanuginosa woolly sedge	MPG	FSW	L	GLMmS W	Br	SpSu	MWS
Carex laxiflora broad loose-flower sedge	MPG	s	L	GLMmS	G	SpSu	BI
Carex leptalea bristly-stalk sedge	SPG	FSs	L	GLMmS	G	Su	BIM
Carex livida livid sedge	SPG	FSW	L	GLMmS W	G	SpSu	MW
Carex lupulina hop sedge	MPG	SW	L	GLMmS W	G	Su	W
Carex lurida shallow sedge	MPG	SW	L	GLMmS W	G	Su	W
Carex lyngbyei Lyngbye's sedge	MPG	DS	L	GLMmS	G	SpSu	M
Carex macloviana Falkland Island sedge	SPG	S	L	GLMmS	Br	Su	M
Carex magellanica boreal-bog sedge	MPG	SsW	L	GLMmS	G	Su	BW
Carex meadii Mead's sedge	MPG	DS	L	GLMmS	G	Su	M
Carex microdonta little-tooth sedge	SPG	DS	—	GLMmS	G	Su	M

PLANT LIST	Plant Type	Env. Tol.	Aesthetic Value	Wildlife Value	Flower Color	Bloom Period	Landscape Uses
Carex microptera small-wing sedge	P	FW	L	GLM mSW	G	Su	W
Carex muhlenbergii Muhlenberg's sedge	SPG	s	—	GLMms	G	Sp	EI
Carex multicaulis many-stem sedge	SPG	DFS	L	GLMmS W	G	Su	MS
Carex nebrascensis Nebraska sedge	MPG	FSW	L	GLMmS W	G	Su	MW
Carex nigromarginata black-edge sedge	SPG	Ss	L	GLMmS	PuG	Sp	BIM
Carex obnupta slough sedge	MPG	S	L	GLMmS W	Bl	Su	M
Carex obtusata blunt sedge	SPG	DS	L	GLMmS	G	Su	M
Carex occidentalis western sedge	P	—	L	GLMmS	G	Su	—
Carex oligosperma few-seed sedge	MPG	FSW	L	GLMmS W	G	Su	W
Carex pedunculata long-stalk sedge	SPG	s	L	GLMmS	G	Sp	I
Carex pensylvanica Pennsylvania sedge	SPG	S	L	GLMmS	G	Sp	B
Carex planostachys cedar sedge	SPG	DSs	—	GLMmS	G	Sp	B
Carex plantaginea broad scale sedge	SPG	s	L	GLMmS	G	Sp	I
Carex platyphylla plantain-leaf sedge	SPG	s	L	GLMmS	G	Sp	I
Carex prairea prairie sedge	MPG	FSW	L	GLMmS W	G	SpSu	SW
Carex rosea rosy sedge	MPG	Ss	L	GLMmS	G	SpSu	BI
Carex rossii Ross' sedge	SPG	DS	L	GLMmS	G	SpSu	BM
Carex rostrata swollen beaked sedge	MPG	SW	L	GLMmS W	G	Su	W
Carex scabrata eastern rough sedge	MPG	FSs	L	GLMmS W	G	Su	BIMS
Carex schottii Schott's sedge	MPG	S	L	GLMmS	B	Su	M
Carex schweinitzii Schweinitz's sedge	MPG	FSsW	L	GLMmS W	G	SpSu	BIMW
Carex scoparia pointed broom sedge	MPG	NaSW	L	GLMmS W	G	Su	SW
Carex scopulorum Holm's Rocky Mountain sedge	SPG	S	L	GLMmS	G	Su	M
Carex senta western rough sedge	MPG	DS	L	GLMmS	G	Su	M

PLANT LIST	Plant Type	Env. Tol.	Aesthetic Value	Wildlife Value	Flower Color	Bloom Period	Landscape Uses
Carex sprengelii long-beak sedge	P	FW	L	GLMmSW	G	Su	W
Carex squarrosa squarrose sedge	MPG	FSs	L	GLMmSW	G	SuF	BIMW
Carex sterilis dioecious sedge	SPG	FS	L	GLMmSW	G	SpSu	MW
Carex stricta uptight sedge	MPG	SW	L	GLMmSW	G	Su	W
Carex teneriformis Sierran slender sedge	SPG	DS	L	GLMmS	Br	Su	M
Carex tetanica rigid sedge	MPG	FSsW	L	GLMmSW	PuBr	SpSu	BIMW
Carex tribuloides blunt broom sedge	MPG	FSs	L	GLMmSW	G	SuF	BIMSW
Carex trichocarpa hairy-fruit sedge	MPG	FS	L	GLMmSW	Pu	Su	SW
Carex trisperma three-seed sedge	MPG	FSsW	L	GLMmSW	G	Su	BIW
Carex tumulicola foothill sedge	MPG	DSs	L	GLMmSW	Br	Su	BW
Carex typhina cat-tail sedge	MPG	FSsW	L	GLMmSW	G	SuF	IMW
Carex vesicaria lesser bladder sedge	MPG	SW	—	GLMmSW	GBr	Su	W
Carex viridula little green sedge	SPG	FS	L	GLMmSW	G	SuF	MW
Carex vulpinoidea common fox sedge	MPG	SsW	L	GLMmSW	G	Su	IW
Carpobrotus aequilateralus baby sun-rose	P	S	FL	U	Pu	SpF	EGg
Castilleja angustifolia northwestern Indian-paintbrush	MP	DS	F	U	R	Su	—
Castilleja applegatei wavy-leaf Indian-paintbrush	SP	DS	F	U	R	SpSu	MR
Castilleja coccinea scarlet Indian-paintbrush	SAB	SW	F	H	RY	SpSu	MW
Castilleja exilis small-flower annual Indian-paintbrush	MA	SW	F	U	R	SpSu	MW
Castilleja flava lemon-yellow Indian-paintbrush	SP	S	F	U	Y	SpSu	M
Castilleja indivisa entire-leaf Indian-paintbrush	SA	SW	F	BH	R	SpSu	bWwg
Castilleja integra squawfeather	SP	s	F	U	R	SpSu	I
Castilleja linariifolia Wyoming Indian-paintbrush	SP	Ss	F	HM	R	Su	BbM

PLANT LIST	Plant Type	Env. Tol.	Aesthetic Value	Wildlife Value	Flower Color	Bloom Period	Landscape Uses
Castilleja lutescens stiff yellow Indian-paintbrush	SP	—	F	HM	Y	Su	—
Castilleja martinii Martin's Indian-paintbrush	SP	DS	F	HM	—	—	—
Castilleja miniata great red Indian-paintbrush	MP	S	F	HM	R	SpF	BbM
Castilleja minor alkali Indian-paintbrush	SP	SW	F	HM	OPR	SpSu	MW
Castilleja rhexiifolia rosy Indian-paintbrush	P	FW	F	U	PR	Su	W
Castilleja sulphurea sulphur Indian-paintbrush	SP	S	P	HM	Y	SpSu	bM
Catabrosa aquatica water whorl grass	AQ SPG	SW	—	U	BrY	Su	W
Caulanthus amplexicaulis clasping-leaf wild cabbage	MP	S	—	U	Pu	SpSu	—
Caulophyllum thalictroides blue cohosh	MP	s	L	U	G	Su	Bl
Cayaponia quinqueloba five-lobe-cucumber	HV	FS	—	U	GW	Su	B
Cenchrus carolinianus coastal sand burr	MPG	FSs	—	MS	G	SuF	EMS
Cenchrus tribuloides sand-dune sandburr	SA	S	—	SM	Br	SuF	BEM
Centaurea americana American star-thistle	LA	S	F	BGhS	PW	SpSu	bCgM
Centaurium exaltatum desert centaury	SA	S	F	U	P	Su	M
Centella asiatica spadeleaf	SP	FS	L	W	W	SpF	W
Centrosema virginianum spurred butterfly-pea	PHV	DSs	F	U	LPu	SpSuF	BgM
Cerastium arvense field mouse-ear chickweed	SP	S	—	U	W	SpSu	M
Cerastium beeringianum Bering Sea mouse-ear chickweed	SP	S	—	U	W	Su	M
Ceratophyllum demersum coontail	AQP	W	L	W	G	Su	wg
Chaenactis carphoclinia pebble pincushion	SA	DS	F	U	WY	Sp	M
Chaenactis fremontii morningbride	SA	DS	F	U	WY	Sp	M
Chaenactis santolinoides Santolina pincushion	SP	DSs	F	U	WY	Su	BM
Chaerophyllum procumbens spreading chevril	SA	s	—	U	W	Sp	I
Chaetopappa asteroides Arkansas leastdaisy	SA	DS	F	B	BP	SpSu	bCGM

PLANT LIST	Plant Type	Env. Tol.	Aesthetic Value	Wildlife Value	Flower Color	Bloom Period	Landscape Uses
Chaetopappa bellidifolia white-ray leastdaisy	SA	S	F	B	LVY	Sp	bGgM
Chaetopappa effusa spreading leastdaisy	MP	S	F	S	WY	SuF	M
Chamaecrista fasciculata sleepingplant	MP	DS	F	U	Y	SpSu	BM
Chamaesaracha sordida hairy five-eyes	P	—	—	U	W	SpSuF	—
Chamaesyce angusta blackfoot sandmat	SP	S	—	GMmS	W	SpSuF	BM
Chamaesyce bombensis dixie sandmat	SA	S	L	GMmS	G	SpF	CGM
Chamaesyce cordifolia heart-leaf sandmat	SA	DS	—	GMmS	W	SuF	CGM
Chamaesyce fendleri Fendler's sandmat	SP	DS	—	GMmS	W	SpSuF	M
Chamaesyce garberi Garber's sandmat	A	—	—	GMmS	W	WSpSuF	—
Chamaesyce geyeri Geyer's sandmat	SP	DS	—	GMmS	W	SuF	EM
Chamaesyce missurica prairie sandmat	SA	DS	—	GMmS	W	Su	CEG
Chamaesyce polygonifolia seaside spurge	SA	S	L	GMmS	G	SpF	CS
Chamaesyce serpens matted sandmat	SA	S	—	GMmS	W	SpSuF	CM
Chamaesyce serpyllifolia thyme-leaf sandmat	SA	DS	—	GMmS	W	SuF	CGM
Chaptalia tomentosa woolly sunbonnets	SP	FS	—	U	W	Sp	W
Chasmanthium latifolium Indian wood-oats	MPG	FSs	DF	U	BrG	SuF	BElgs
Chasmanthium laxum slender wood-oats	MPG	FS	DF	U	BrG	SuF	SW
Cheilanthes lanosa hairy lip fern	SP	DS	L	M	X	X	R
Chelone glabra white turtlehead	MP	FSs	F	Bh	W	SuF	BbIW
Chelone lyonii pink turtlehead	MP	FSs	F	Bh	Pu	SuF	BbIW
Chenopodium atrovirens pinyon goosefoot	SA	—	—	GMmS	W	Su	C
Chenopodium desiccatum arid-land goosefoot	SA	DS	—	GMmS	W	SuF	CM
Chenopodium leptophyllum narrow-leaf goosefoot	MA	DS	—	GMmS	G	Su	CM
Chimaphila maculata striped prince's-pine	eSP	s	FL	U	W	Su	GI

PLANT LIST	Plant Type	Env. Tol.	Aesthetic Value	Wildlife Value	Flower Color	Bloom Period	Landscape Uses
Chimaphila menziesii little prince's-pine	eSP	s	FL	U	W	Su	GI
Chimaphila umbellata pipsissewa	eSP	s	L	U	P	Su	GI
Chloracantha spinosa Mexican devilweed	P	—	—	U	W	SuF	—
Chloris ciliata fringed windmill grass	MPG	S	DF	U	G	SpSuF	M
Chloris cucullata hooded windmill grass	MPG	DS	—	U	G	SpSuF	EM
Chloris pluriflora multi-flower windmill grass	MPG	DSs	DF	M	GW	SuF	ABgM
Chloris verticillata tumble windmill grass	SPG	DS	F	U	G	SuF	EMR
Chorizanthe brevicornu brittle spineflower	SA	DS	F	U	W	—	CM
Chorizanthe rigida devil's spineflower	SA	DS	F	U	Y	Sp	CR
Chrysopsis gossypina cottony golden-aster	MP	S	F	BS	Y	F	BEM
Chrysopsis mariana Maryland golden-aster	SP	Ss	F	BS	Y	SuF	BhgM
Cicuta bulbifera bulblet-bearing water-hemlock	MP	FSW	FL	U	W	SuF	Wwg
Cicuta maculata spotted water-hemlock	LP	FSW	FL	U	W	SuF	W
Cimicifuga americana mountain bugbane	MP	s	FL	U	W	SuF	BgI
Cimicifuga racemosa black bugbane	LP	s	FL	U	W	Su	BgI
Cinna arundinacea sweet wood-reed	LPG	s	FL	U	G	SuF	BI
Circaea alpina small enchanter's-nightshade	SP	s	—	U	W	SpSu	I
Circaea lutetiana broad-leaf enchanter's-nightshade	MP	s	—	U	W	Su	I
Cirsium canescens prairie thistle	SBP	SW	F	BHS	PuR	SuF	MW
Cirsium discolor field thistle	LB	S	F	BS	P	SuF	BM
Cirsium flodmanii Flodman's thistle	MB	S	F	BS	Pu	SuF	M
Cirsium horridulum yellow thistle	MP	FS	F	L	LY	SpSu	MW
Cirsium muticum swamp thistle	LP	FSW	F	BSW	P	SuF	W
Cistanthe umbellata Mt. Hood pussypaws	SP	DFSs	LF	U	PW	Su	IMR

PLANT LIST	Plant Type	Env. Tol.	Aesthetic Value	Wildlife Value	Flower Color	Bloom Period	Landscape Uses
Cladium mariscoides smooth saw-grass	MPG	FNaS W	—	U	Br	SuF	SWwg
Cladium mariscus swamp saw-grass	MPG	FNaS W	—	U	Br	SuF	W
Cladonia evansii lichen	m	DS	—	Mm	X	X	IR
Cladonia leporina lichen	m	DS	—	Mm	X	X	IR
Cladonia prostrata lichen	m	DS	—	Mm	X	X	IR
Cladonia subtenuis lichen	m	DS	—	Mm	X	X	IR
Clarkia rhomboidea diamond fairyfan	MA	DS	F	U	PPu	SpSu	CEM
Claytonia caroliniana Carolina springbeauty	SP	s	F	U	PW	Sp	BgI
Claytonia lanceolata lance-leaf springbeauty	SP	Ss	F	U	PWY	SpSu	BgIM
Claytonia perfoliata miner's-lettuce	SA	Ss	F	U	PW	SpSu	BgIM
Claytonia sibirica Siberian springbeauty	SA	Ss	F	U	PW	Sp	BgIM
Claytonia virginica Virginia springbeauty	SP	s	F	U	PW	Sp	BgI
Clematis drummondii Texas virgin's-bower	PHV	DSs	DF	U	W	SpSuF	Bs
Clematis fremontii Fremont's leather-flower	SP	DS	F	B	BPuY	Sp	hM
Clematis pitcheri bluebill	PHV	Ss	F	U	BPu	Su	B
Clintonia borealis yellow bluebead-lily	SP	Fs	Ff	U	yg	Sp	IW
Clintonia umbellulata white bluebead-lily	SP	s	FL	U	W	Sp	I
Clintonia uniflora bride's bonnet	SP	s	F	U	W	SpSu	gI
Clitoria mariana Atlantic pigeonwings	HV	DSs	F	U	B	Su	BGg
Cnidoscolus stimulosus finger-rot	MP	DSs	F	U	W	SpF	BM
Cnidoscolus texanus Texas bull-nettle	MP	DS	F	U	W	SpSuF	gM
Cocculus diverisifolius snailseed	LP	Ss	Ff	U	WY	Su	BM
Coelorachis cylindrica Carolina joint-tail grass	MPG	Ss	—	U	G	—	BM
Collinsia childii child's blue-eyed Mary	SA	S	F	G	BPu	SuSp	CM

PLANT LIST	Plant Type	Env. Tol.	Aesthetic Value	Wildlife Value	Flower Color	Bloom Period	Landscape Uses
Collinsia parviflora small-flower blue-eyed Mary	SA	S	L	G	BW	Sp	gR
Collinsia torreyi Torrey's blue-eyed Mary	SA	S	F	G	BY	SpSu	CM
Collinsonia canadensis richweed	MP	s	—	G	Y	SuF	CgI
Collomia grandiflora large-flower mountain-trumpet	MA	S	F	U	P	Su	CB
Collomia heterophylla variable-leaf mountain-trumpet	SA	s	F	U	PuR	Sp	CI
Collomia linearis narrow-leaf mountain-trumpet	SAB	DS	F	U	BP	SpSu	CMS
Comandra umbellata bastard-toadflax	SP	FSs	FL	U	W	SpSu	BIM
Comarum palustre purple marshlocks	SP	FSW	F	GLMmS	R	Su	Wwg
Commelina erecta white-mouth dayflower	SP	DS	F	U	BW	Su	BM
Commelina virginica Virginia dayflower	MP	FS	F	GMS	B	Su	BS
Conopholis americana American squawroot	SP	s	B	M	yg	Sp	I
Conyza canadensis Canadian horseweed	MP	S	—	U	WY	SuF	E
Coptis aspleniifolia fern-leaf goldthread	SP	s	fL	U	W	SpSu	GgI
Coptis laciniata Oregon goldthread	SP	s	fL	U	W	SpSu	GgI
Coptis occidentalis Idaho goldthread	SP	s	fL	U	W	SpSu	GgI
Coptis trifolia three-leaf goldthread	eSP	FSs	L	U	W	SpSu	GgIW
Corallorrhiza maculata summer coralroot	MP	s	F	U	BrRY	SpF	I
Cordia podocephala Texas manjack	SP	DSs	F	U	W	SpSuF	BM
Cordylanthus maritimus saltmarsh bird's-beak	SA	NaSW	—	U	W	Su	MSW
Cordylanthus nevinii Nevin's bird's-beak	SA	S	—	U	PuY	SuF	M
Cordylanthus ramosus bushy bird's-beak	SA	—	—	U	Y	Su	—
Cordylanthus rigidus stiff-branch bird's beak	MA	DS	—	U	PuWY	Su	—
Coreopsis basalis golden-mane tickseed	SA	S	F	BS	Y	Sp	bCM
Coreopsis lanceolata lance-leaf tickseed	MP	DS	F	BS	Y	SpSu	bgM

PLANT LIST	Plant Type	Env. Tol.	Aesthetic Value	Wildlife Value	Flower Color	Bloom Period	Landscape Uses
Coreopsis major greater tickseed	MP	S	F	h	Y	Su	Bg
Coreopsis palmata stiff tickseed	MP	DS	F	h	Y	Su	gM
Coreopsis tripteris tall tickseed	LP	SD	F	BGmS	Y	Su	BbgM
Cornus canadensis Canadian bunchberry	SP	FSs	AFfL	BGS	WY	SpSu	BGl
Corydalis flavula yellow fumewort	SP	s	F	U	Y	Sp	BgI
Corydalis micrantha small-flower fumewort	SA	FSs	FL	U	Y	Sp	BC
Cotula coronopifolia common brassbuttons	SP	FNaSW	F	U	Y	WSp	Wwg
Crassula aquatica water pygmyweed	SA	FNaSW	—	U	GW	SuF	Wwg
Crepis acuminata long-leaf hawk's-beard	SP	DSs	FL	U	Y	SuSp	B
Crepis modocensis siskiyou hawk's-beard	P	—	—	U	Y	Su	—
Crepis occidentalis large-flower hawk's-beard	AP	—	—	U	Y	Su	—
Crepis runcinata fiddle-leaf hawk's-beard	SP	NaS	FL	U	W	Su	M
Cressa truxillensis spreading alkali-weed	SP	FS	—	U	W	SpSu	—
Crinum americanum seven-sisters	MP	FSsW	—	U	W	SuF	—
Croton argyranthemus healing croton	SP	S	—	GMmS	G	SuF	M
Croton capitatus hogwort	LA	DS	—	GMmS	W	SuF	CM
Croton dioicus grassland croton	SP	S	—	GMmS	W	SuF	M
Croton glandulosus vente-conmigo	SA	Ss	F	GMmS	G	SuF	BC
Croton punctatus Gulf croton	MP	S	L	GMmS	G	SpW	E
Crotonopsis elliptica egg-leaf rushfoil	SA	DFS	—	U	W	Su	CB
Cryptantha affinis quill cat's-eye	SA	S	—	U	W	Su	CBM
Cryptantha ambigua basin cat's-eye	SA	S	—	U	W	Su	CBM
Cryptantha circumscissa cushion cat's-eye	SA	—	—	U	W	SpSu	—
Cryptantha hoffmannii Hoffmann's cat's-eye	BP	—	—	S	W	Su	—

PLANT LIST	Plant Type	Env. Tol.	Aesthetic Value	Wildlife Value	Flower Color	Bloom Period	Landscape Uses
Cryptantha maritima Guadalupe cat's-eye	A	—	—	U	W	Sp	—
Cryptantha roosiorum bristle-cone cat's-eye	P	—	—	S	W	Su	—
Cryptantha watsonii Watson's cat's-eye	A	—	—	U	W	SpSu	—
Cryptogramma acrostichoides American rockbrake	SP	S	L	GLM	X	X	R
Cryptotaenia canadensis Canadian honewort	MP	s	L	U	W	SuF	BI
Ctenium aromaticum toothache grass	MPG	FSs	F	U	G	SuF	BW
Cunila marina common dittany	SP	DSs	FL	U	BPu	SuF	BI
Cymopterus bulbosus bulbous spring-parsley	SP	DS	—	U	PPu	Sp	M
Cymopterus cinerarius gray spring-parsley	SP	Ss	—	U	Pu	Sp	B
Cymopterus longipes long-stalk spring-parsley	P	S	—	U	YW	Sp	M
Cymopterus montanus mountain spring-parsley	SP	S	—	U	PuW	Sp	MW
Cynanchum angustifolium Gulf coast swallow-wort	HV	FNaSW	F	U	GW	SpSu	Wwg
Cyperus bipartitus shining flat sedge	SPG	FS	L	GSW	G	SuF	SWwg
Cyperus eragrostis tall flat sedge	MPG	S	L	GLmSW	G	Su	W
Cyperus esculentus chufa	SPG	S	L	GLmSW	G	Su	Wwg
Cyperus fendlerianus Fendler's flat sedge	MPG	S	L	GLmSW	Br	Su	M
Cyperus filiformis wiry flat sedge	P	S	L	GSW	G	Su	M
Cyperus schweinitzii sand flat sedge	SPG	DS	L	GLmS	G	Su	M
Cyperus squarrosus awned flat sedge	SAG	FS	L	GSW	G	Su	Wwg
Cypripedium acaule pink lady's-slipper	SP	s	FL	U	P	Su	gI
Cypripedium arietinum ram-head lady's-slipper	SP	FsW	FL	U	R	Sp	IW
Cypripedium calceolus showy lady's slipper	MP	FSs	FL	U	Y	SpSu	gIW
Cypripedium parviflorum lesser yellow lady's-slipper	MP	FSs	FL	U	Y	Sp	BgIW
Cypripedium pubescens greater yellow lady's-slipper	MP	s	F	U	Y	Sp	gI

PLANT LIST	Plant Type	Env. Tol.	Aesthetic Value	Wildlife Value	Flower Color	Bloom Period	Landscape Uses
Cyrtopodium punctatum cowhorn orchid	SP	FsW	F	U	W	SpSu	I
Cystopteris bulbifera bulblet bladder fern	SP	s	L	M	X	X	I
Cystopteris fragilis brittle bladder fern	SP	FSs	L	GLM	X	X	BIS
Dalea albiflora white-flower prairie-clover	P	DS	F	BGLM	W	Su	bM
Dalea aurea golden prairie-clover	SP	DS	F	B	Y	Su	gM
Dalea candida white prairie-clover	SP	DS	F	BGLM	W	Su	bM
Dalea compacta compact prairie-clover	MP	S	F	Bm	Y	Su	M
Dalea enneandra nine-anther prairie-clover	MP	DS	F	B	W	Su	Bg
Dalea multiflora round-head prairie-clover	SP	S	F	Bm	W	Su	M
Dalea pinnata summer-farewell	MP	DS	F	m	W	F	BgM
Dalea purpurea violet prairie-clover	MP	DS	F	BGLM	Pu	SuF	bM
Dalea versicolor oakwoods prairie-clover	P	—	F	BG	YW	SpSuF	M
Dalea villosa silky prairie-clover	MP	DS	F	BL	P	Su	bM
Dalibarda repens robin-run-away	SP	FSW	F	U	W	Su	gIW
Danthonia californica California wild oat grass	SPG	DSs	FL	M	G	Su	BM
Danthonia compressa flattened wild oat grass	MPG	S	FL	M	G	Su	BM
Danthonia intermedia timber wild oat grass	SPG	SW	FL	M	G	Su	MW
Danthonia spicata poverty wild oat grass	SPG	S	FL	M	G	Su	BM
Danthonia unispicata few-flower wild oat grass	SPG	DSs	—	U	—	Su	BgR
Delphinium andersonii desert larkspur	SP	DSs	F	U	B	—	BgI
Delphinium barbeyi subalpine larkspur	P	Ss	F	U	—	—	BgI
Delphinium bicolor flat-head larkspur	SP	Ss	F	U	BPu	SpSu	BgI
Delphinium carolinianum Carolina larkspur	MP	S	F	U	W	SpSu	BgM
Delphinium geyeri Geyer's larkspur	P	Ss	F	U	W	Su	BgI

PLANT LIST	Plant Type	Env. Tol.	Aesthetic Value	Wildlife Value	Flower Color	Bloom Period	Landscape Uses
Delphinium nuttallianum two-lobe larkspur	SP	DS	F	U	W	Su	M
Delphinium occidentale dunce-cap larkspur	LP	s	F	U	B	Su	gI
Delphinium tricorne dwarf larkspur	SP	Ss	F	U	B	Sp	BgI
Deparia acrostichoides silver false spleenwort	LP	s	L	M	X	X	I
Deschampsia cespitosa tufted hair grass	MPG	FSW	L	M	G	Su	MW
Deschampsia danthonioides annual hair grass	MAG	S	L	M	G	Su	M
Deschampsia flexuosa wavy hair grass	MPG	DSs	L	M	G	Su	BIM
Descurainia incana mountain tansy mustard	AB	—	—	U	Y	SpSu	—
Descurainia pinnata western tansy mustard	MA	DS	—	U	W	SpSu	CM
Desmanthus illinoensis prairie bundle-flower	MP	DFS	FfL	Gm	W	Su	CEgM
Desmodium canadense showy tick-trefoil	LP	S	F	GMm	P	Su	B
Desmodium ciliare hairy small-leaf tick-trefoil	SP	DSs	GMmS	GS	PuV	Su	BM
Desmodium glabellum Dillenius' tick-trefoil	LP	Ss	F	GMm	Pu	Su	BI
Desmodium glutinosum pointed-leaf tick-trefoil	MP	s	FL	GMmS	W	Su	I
Desmodium illinoense Illinois tick-trefoil	LP	DS	F	GMm	PuW	Su	M
Desmodium laevigatum smooth tick-trefoil	MP	DSs	F	GMm	Pu	Su	BIM
Desmodium nudiflorum naked-flower tick-trefoil	MP	s	F	GMm	PuW	Su	I
Desmodium obtusum stiff tick-trefoil	MP	DS	F	GMm	Pu	Su	—
Desmodium paniculatum panicled-leaf tick-trefoil	MP	DS	F	GMmS	Pu	Su	M
Desmodium perplexum perplexed tick-trefoil	MP	S	F	GMm	PPu	SuF	B
Desmodium psilophyllum simple-leaf tick-trefoil	MP	Ss	—	GMm	P	SpF	BM
Desmodium rotundifolium prostrate tick-trefoil	SP	Ds	F	GMm	PuW	SuF	I
Desmodium sessilifolium sessil-leaf tick-trefoil	MP	DS	F	GMmS	LP	SpSu	BM
Diarrhena americana American beakgrain	MG	s	BL	M	G	SuF	IS

PLANT LIST	Plant Type	Env. Tol.	Aesthetic Value	Wildlife Value	Flower Color	Bloom Period	Landscape Uses
Dicentra canadensis squirrel-corn	SP	Ss	FL	m	PW	Sp	BgI
Dicentra cucullaria Dutchman's breeches	SP	Ss	FL	hm	W	Sp	Bgl
Dichanthelium acuminatum tapered rosette grass	SPG	Ss	—	GMS	G	Su	BM
Dichanthelium commutatum variable rosette grass	MPG	s	L	GLMS	G	Su	BI
Dichanthelium dichotomum cypress rosette grass	MPG	Ds	FL	GLMS	G	Su	BI
Dichanthelium laxiflorum open-flower rosette grass	MPG	s	—	GW	G	Su	EIS
Dichanthelium leibergii Leiberg's rosette grass	MPG	DS	L	GLMS	G	Su	M
Dichanthelium linearifolium slim-leaf rosette grass	SPG	Ds	—	GMS	G	Su	BI
Dichanthelium oligosanthes Heller's rosette grass	SPG	s	L	GLMS	G	Su	BI
Dichanthelium pedicellatum cedar rosette grass	SPG	DS	—	GLMS	G	SpF	EM
Dichanthelium ravenelii Ravenel's rosette grass	MPG	DSs	—	G	G	Su	BEM
Dichanthelium sabulorum hemlock rosette grass	SPG	Ds	L	GLMSW	G	Su	BI
Dichanthelium sphaerocarpon round-seed rosette grass	MPG	FSsW	L	GLMSW	G	SuF	BIW
Dichelostemma pulchellum bluedicks	P	—	—	U	PuW	Sp	—
Dicliptera brachiata branched foldwing	MP	Fs	F	U	PuW	SuF	ISW
Dicranum polysetum moss	m	s	—	U	X	X	l
Dicranum undulatum feather moss	m	FsW	—	U	X	X	W
Digitaria californica California crab grass	MG	DS	—	U	G	Su	M
Digitaria texana Texas crab grass	MPG	S	—	GMS	G	WSpF	EM
Diodia teres poorjoe	SA	DS	F	GM	W	SuF	B
Dioscorea villosa wild yam	SP	FS	L	M	Y	Su	B
Disporum hookeri drops-of-gold	SP	Fs	FL	U	GW	SpSu	gIS
Disporum lanuginosum yellow fairybells	SP	s	Ff	U	Y	Sp	gI
Disporum smithii large-flower fairybells	P	—	F	U	W	Sp	—

PLANT LIST	Plant Type	Env. Tol.	Aesthetic Value	Wildlife Value	Flower Color	Bloom Period	Landscape Uses
Distichlis spicata coastal salt grass	MPG	DFNa SW	FL	MmW	G	SuF	SWwg
Dodecatheon jeffreyi tall mountain shootingstar	SP	FS	F	U	PR	Su	MS
Dodecatheon meadia eastern shootingstar	SP	DSs	FL	U	PW	Sp	gIM
Dodecatheon pulchellum dark-throated shootingstar	SP	Fs	F	U	P	Sp	M
Dodecatheon redolens scented shootingstar	SP	FS	FL	U	Pu	Sp	gM
Downingia bella Hoover's calico-flower	A	FW	—	U	B	SpSu	W
Draba albertina slender whitlow-grass	SBPG	FS	—	M	W	SpSu	MW
Draba cinera gray-leaf whitlow-grass	P	—	—	U	W	SpSu	—
Draba corrugata southern California whitlow-grass	SPG	Ss	FL	M	Y	SpSu	BIM
Draba verna spring whitlow-grass	SPG	DS	—	M	W	Sp	M
Dracocephalum parviflorum American dragonhead	MABP	DS	F	U	BL	SpSu	M
Drepanocladus revolvens moss	m	FSW	L	M	X	X	W
Drosera capillaris pink sundew	SP	FS	F	U	—	SpSu	W
Drosera intermedia spoon-leaf sundew	SP	FS	F	U	W	SpSu	W
Drosera rotundifolia round-leaf sundew	SP	FSW	F	U	W	Su	W
Dryopteris campyloptera mountain wood fern	MP	s	L	U	X	X	BgI
Dryopteris carthusiana spinulose wood fern	MP	FsW	L	U	X	X	BIW
Dryopteris cristata crested wood fern	eMP	FSs	L	U	X	X	BIW
Dryopteris goldiana Goldie's wood fern	MP	s	L	U	X	X	BgI
Dryopteris intermedia evergreen wood fern	MP	s	L	U	X	X	BgI
Dryopteris marginalis marginal wood fern	MP	s	L	U	X	X	BgI
Dudleya farinosa powdery live-forever	SP	DS	FL	U	W	SuF	gRM
Dugaldia hoopesii owl's-claws	LP	D	F	U	OY	Su	M

PLANT LIST	Plant Type	Env. Tol.	Aesthetic Value	Wildlife Value	Flower Color	Bloom Period	Landscape Uses
Dulichium arundinaceum three-way sedge	MPG	FS	L	U	G	Su	Wwg
Dyschoriste linearis polkadots	SP	DS	F	U	Pu	SpSu	GM
Dyschoriste oblongifolia oblong-leaf snakeherb	SP	DS	F	U	Pu	Su	—
Echinacea angustifolia blacksamson	MP	DS	F	BS	Pu	SpF	bM
Echinacea pallida pale purple-coneflower	MP	DS	F	BS	P	Su	bM
Echinacea purpurea eastern purple-coneflower	MP	DSs	F	BS	PPu	SuF	BbgM
Echinochloa crus-galli large barnyard grass	MAG	FSW	L	GLSW	G	SuF	Wwg
Echinochloa walteri long-awn cock's-spur grass	MAG	FSW	L	GLSW	G	SuF	Wwg
Echinocystis lobata wild cucumber	HV	FSs	FL	M	GW	SuF	S
Eleocharis acicularis neddle spike-rush	SPG	FS	L	LW	G	SuF	W
Eleocharis albida white spike-rush	MPG	FNaSW	L	LW	G	SuF	W
Eleocharis bella delicate spike-rush	MPG	SW	L	LW	G	SuF	MW
Eleocharis compressa flat-stem spike-rush	MPG	FS	L	LW	BrPu	SuF	Wwg
Eleocharis elliptica elliptic spike-rush	MPG	FS	L	LW	G	SpF	EW
Eleocharis elongata slim spike-rush	MPG	SW	L	LW	G	SuF	MW
Eleocharis equisetoides horsetail-spike-rush	SPG	FWS	L	LW	G	SuF	Wwg
Eleocharis erythropoda bald spike-rush	MPG	FS	L	LW	G	SuF	Wwg
Eleocharis fallax creeping spike-rush	MPG	FNaS	L	LW	G	Su	SW
Eleocharis flavescens yellow spike-rush	SPG	FS	L	LW	G	SuF	Wwg
Eleocharis intermedia matted spike-rush	SAG	FS	L	LW	G	SuF	CMSW
Eleocharis obtusa blunt spike-rush	MPG	FNaS	L	LW	G	Su	W
Eleocharis palustris pale spike-rush	MPG	FNaSW	L	LW	G	Su	Wwg
Eleocharis parvula little-head spike-rush	SAG	FSW	L	LW	G	SpSuF	CSW
Eleocharis quinqueflora few-flower spike-rush	MPG	SW	L	LW	G	Su	Wwg

PLANT LIST	Plant Type	Env. Tol.	Aesthetic Value	Wildlife Value	Flower Color	Bloom Period	Landscape Uses
Eleocharis rostellata beaked spike-rush	MPG	FNaS	L	LW	G	SuF	W
Eleocharis smallii Small's spike-rush	MPG	FNaS	L	LW	G	SuF	W
Eleocharis vivipara viviparous spike-rush	SPG	F	L	LW	G	SuF	Wwg
Elephantopus carolinianus Carolina elephant's-foot	SP	s	FL	B	PPu	SuF	I
Elephantopus nudatus smooth elephant's-foot	SP	FSs	FL	B	PPu	SuF	IW
Elymus canadensis nodding wild rye	LPG	DSs	FfL	LMS	G	Su	EMS
Elymus elymoides western bottle-brush grass	MPG	DS	L	LMS	G	Su	EM
Elymus glaucus blue wild rye	MPG	DFS	DFL	LMS	G	Su	BMS
Elymus hystrix eastern bottle-brush grass	LPG	DSs	DFL	LMS	G	Su	BIM
Elymus lanceolatus streamside wild rye	MPG	FS	L	LMS	G	Su	MS
Elymus trachycaulus slender wild rye	SPG	DS	L	LMS	G	Su	M
Elymus virginicus Virginia wild rye	MPG	FSs	DFL	LMS	G	SuF	BIMS
Elyonurus barbiculmis wool-spike grass	MPG	DS	FL	LMS	G	SuF	M
Elyonurus tripsacoides pan-American balsamscale	MPG	FS	FL	LMS	G	SuF	MS
Emmenanthe penduliflora yellow whispering-bells	SA	DS	FL	U	Y	Su	BgM
Encelia farinosa goldenhills	LP	DS	F	U	Y	Sp	M
Enemion biternatum eastern false rue-anemone	SP	s	FL	U	W	Sp	gI
Engelmannia pinnatifida Englemann's daisy	SB	S	F	U	Y	WSpSu	M
Epifagus virginiana beechdrops	SP	s	B	Mm	Br	SuF	I
Epilobium angustifolium fireweed	LP	S	FL	Mm	P	SuF	g
Epilobium brachycarpum tall annual willowherb	SA	DS	F	Mm	PW	SuF	gM
Epilobium ciliatum fringed willowherb	SA	Fs	F	Mm	PuW	SuF	IW
Epilobium glaberrimum glaucous willowherb	MA	FS	F	Mm	PuW	SuF	BW
Epilobium palustre marsh willowherb	SP	DS	F	Mm	PW	Su	W

PLANT LIST	Plant Type	Env. Tol.	Aesthetic Value	Wildlife Value	Flower Color	Bloom Period	Landscape Uses
Epilobium strictum downy willowherb	SP	FSW	F	Mm	PR	SuF	W
Equisetum arvense field horsetail	MP	FS	L	LMW	X	X	SWwg
Equisetum fluviatile water horsetail	MP	FSW	L	LMW	X	X	SWwg
Equisetum hyemale tall scouring-rush	MP	SF	L	LMW	X	X	SWwg
Equisetum sylvaticum woodland horsetail	SP	Ss	L	LM	X	X	BI
Equisetum variegatum varigated scouring-rush	SP	FSW	L	LMW	X	X	SWwg
Eragrostis intermedia plains love grass	MPG	S	FL	MS	GPu	SuF	EM
Eragrostis secundiflora red love grass	MPG	DS	DF	U	G	Su	EM
Eragrostis spectabilis petticoat-climber	SPG	DS	FL	MS	GPu	SuF	EIM
Eragrostis trichodes sand love grass	MPG	DS	FL	MS	GPu	SuF	EM
Eriastrum densifolium giant woolstar	P	—	—	U	BYW	Su	—
Erigeron arizonicus Arizona fleabane	P	—	—	U	PW	Su	—
Erigeron bellidiastrum western daisy fleabane	MA	DS	F	B	PW	SpSu	BbM
Erigeron breweri Brewer's fleabane	SP	DS	F	B	Pu	Su	bGM
Erigeron caespitosus tufted fleabane	SP	SD	F	B	PW	SpSu	BbM
Erigeron compositus dwarf mountain fleabane	SP	DS	F	B	BPW	Su	bGgM
Erigeron concinnus Navajo fleabane	SP	DS	F	B	BW	Su	bEGM
Erigeron divergens spreading fleabane	SAP	DS	F	B	—	Su	bEM
Erigeron engelmannii Engelmann's fleabane	SP	DS	F	B	W	SpSu	BbM
Erigeron eximius spruce-fir fleabane	P	S	F	B	BP	Su	gM
Erigeron flagellaris trailing fleabane	SP	DS	F	B	W	Sp	bEGM
Erigeron formosissimus beautiful fleabane	SP	S	F	B	BPW	Su	M
Erigeron glaucus seaside fleabane	SP	DFS	F	B	LPu	Su	bGMS
Erigeron lemmonii Lemmon's fleabane	P	—	—	B	PW	SpSuF	—

PLANT LIST	Plant Type	Env. Tol.	Aesthetic Value	Wildlife Value	Flower Color	Bloom Period	Landscape Uses
Erigeron linearis desert yellow fleabane	SP	DS	F	B	Y	Su	bGM
Erigeron nematophyllus needle-leaf fleabane	SP	DS	F	B	W	Sp	BbM
Erigeron neomexicanus New Mexico fleabane	P	—	—	B	PW	SuF	—
Erigeron oreophilus chaparral fleabane	P	—	—	B	PW	SuF	—
Erigeron parishii Parish's fleabane	SP	DS	FL	U	PuV	Sp	gM
Erigeron platyphyllus broad-leaf fleabane	P	—	—	B	P	SuF	—
Erigeron poliospermus purple cushion fleabane	SP	DS	F	B	PuW	Su	bGM
Erigeron pumilus shaggy fleabane	SP	DS	F	B	PW	Sp	BbM
Erigeron strigosus prairie fleabane	MP	DS	F	B	W	SuSp	BbM
Erigeron ursinus Bear River fleabane	SP	Ss	F	B	PuW	Su	BbGM
Eriocaulon parkeri estuary pipewort	SP	FSW	B	U	W	SuF	Wwg
Eriogonum abertianum Abert's wild buckwheat	MA	DS	—	GMmS	WY	SpSuF	M
Eriogonum alatum winged wild buckwheat	SP	DS	—	U	Y	SuF	M
Eriogonum annuum annual wild buckwheat	SAB	DS	F	GLMmS	PW	SpSuF	GgMR
Eriogonum baileyi Bailey's wild buckwheat	SP	DS	F	GLMmS	WY	Su	GgMR
Eriogonum caespitosum matted wild buckwheat	SP	DS	—	U	Y	Su	—
Eriogonum cernuum nodding wild buckwheat	SA	DS	F	G	W	SpSu	—
Eriogonum compositum arrow-leaf wild buckwheat	SP	DS	F	GLMmS	WY	Su	GgMR
Eriogonum flavum alpine golden wild buckwheat	SP	DS	F	GLMmS	Y	Su	GgMR
Eriogonum heracleoides parsnip-flower wild buckwheat	SP	DS	F	GLMmS	RWY	Su	GgMR
Eriogonum incanum frosted wild buckwheat	SP	DS	F	GLMmS	RY	Su	GgMR
Eriogonum inflatum Indian-pipeweed	MAP	DNaS	—	GMmS	RY	SpSuF	M
Eriogonum kennedyi Kennedy's wild buckwheat	SP	DS	F	GLMmS	PW	Su	GgMR
Eriogonum nudum naked wild buckwheat	MP	DS	F	GLMmS	W	SuF	gMR

PLANT LIST	Plant Type	Env. Tol.	Aesthetic Value	Wildlife Value	Flower Color	Bloom Period	Landscape Uses
Eriogonum ovalifolium cushion wild buckwheat	SP	DS	F	GLMmS	Y	Su	GgMR
Eriogonum parishii mountainmist	SP	DS	F	GLMmS	P	Su	GgMR
Eriogonum rotundifolium round-leaf wild buckwheat	SA	DS	—	GMmS	W	SpSuF	M
Eriogonum saxatile hoary wild buckwheat	SP	S	F	GLMmS	WY	Su	GgM
Eriogonum tenellum tall wild buckwheat	SP	DS	—	GMmS	PW	SuF	MR
Eriogonum tomentosum dog-tongue wild buckwheat	MP	DS	F	GLMmS	W	SuF	GgM
Eriogonum trichopes little desert trumpet	SA	DS	F	U	Y	SpSu	—
Erioneuron pilosum hairy woolly grass	SGP	DS	—	U	GPu	Su	GgM
Erioneuron pulchellum low woolly grass	SGP	DS	—	U	GPu	SpSu	GgM
Eriophorum cringerum fringed cotton-grass	P	—	—	U	G	Su	—
Eriophorum gracile slender cotton-grass	MPG	SW	F	U	W	SpSu	SWwg
Eriophorum vaginatum tussock cotton-grass	MPG	FSW	F	U	W	SpSu	Wwg
Eriophorum virginicum tawny cotton-grass	MPG	FSW	F	U	OY	SuF	Wwg
Eriophorum viridicarinatum tassel cotton-grass	SPG	FSW	F	U	W	SpSu	GWwg
Eriophyllum confertiflorum yellow-yarrow	SP	DS	F	U	Y	Su	GgM
Eriophyllum lanatum common wooly-sunflower	SP	DS	F	U	Y	SpSu	GgM
Eriophyllum stoechadifolium seaside woolly-sunflower	MP	DS	F	U	Y	Su	gM
Eryngium leavenworthii Leavenworth's eryngo	MP	DS	L	h	W	SuF	M
Eryngium yuccifolium button eryngo	LP	S	DL	h	GW	Su	gM
Erysimum asperum plains wallflower	MP	DS	F	U	ORY	SpSu	gM
Erythronium albidum small white fawn-lily	SP	s	F	U	W	Sp	I
Erythronium americanum American trout-lily	SP	s	FL	U	Y	Sp	gl
Erythronium grandiflorum yellow avalanche-lily	SP	S	FL	U	Y	SpSu	BM
Erythronium montanum white avalanche-lily	P	—	F	U	W	Su	—

PLANT LIST	Plant Type	Env. Tol.	Aesthetic Value	Wildlife Value	Flower Color	Bloom Period	Landscape Uses
Erythronium umbilicatum dimpled trout-lily	SP	s	FL	U	Y	Sp	EGgI
Eschscholzia californica California-poppy	SP	DS	F	GmS	O	WSu	gM
Eupatorium betonicifolium betony-leaf thoroughwort	MP	SsW	F	B	B	SuF	Wwg
Eupatorium capillifolium dogfennel	MP	DSs	—	U	GPW	SuF	BM
Eupatorium coelestinum blue mistflower	MP	FS	F	B	B	SuF	BbMW
Eupatorium maculatum spotted joe-pye-weed	LP	FS	F	BS	P	Su	BbW
Eupatorium perfoliatum common boneset	MP	FS	F	BhS	W	SuF	bW
Eupatorium rotundifolium round-leaf thoroughwort	MP	FSs	—	S	W	SuF	BM
Eupatorium serotinum late-flowering thoroughwort	MP	Ss	F	Bh	W	SuF	BgIM
Eupatorium villosum Florida Keys thoroughwort	P	—	—	U	PW	WSpSuF	—
Euphorbia corollata flowering spurge	MP	S	F	GMmS	W	SuF	M
Euphorbia cyathophora fire-on-the-mountain	MA	s	L	GMmS	W	Su	I
Euphorbia dentata toothed spurge	SA	DS	L	U	G	SpSuF	CM
Euphorbia hexagona six-angle spurge	SA	DS	—	U	W	SuF	MSW
Euphorbia ipecacuanhae American ipecac	SP	DSs	—	GMmS	G	SpSu	BM
Euphorbia roemeriana Roemer's spurge	SA	Ss	—	GMmS	W	Sp	BCM
Euphorbia tetrapora weak spurge	SA	DS	—	U	X	Sp	CM
Eustachys petraea pinewoods finger grass	MPG	Ds	F	U	Br	SuF	SW
Euthamia graminifolia flat-top goldentop	MP	S	F	BGLMmS	Y	SuF	bg
Evax caulescens involucrate pygmy-cudweed	SA	DFS	F	U	G	Su	CMS
Festuca arizonica Arizona fescue	SPG	Ss	—	GLMmS	G	Su	B
Festuca brachyphylla short-leaf fescue	SGP	S	—	GLMmS	G	Su	EGM
Festuca californica California fescue	LPG	DSs	—	GLMmS	G	Su	BM
Festuca campestris prairie fescue	MPG	S	—	GLMmS	G	Su	EM

PLANT LIST	Plant Type	Env. Tol.	Aesthetic Value	Wildlife Value	Flower Color	Bloom Period	Landscape Uses
Festuca idahoensis bluebunch fescue	MPG	Ss	—	GLMmS	G	Su	BM
Festuca kingii King's fescue	LPG	DS	—	GLMmS	G	Su	EM
Festuca occidentalis western fescue	MPG	DSs	—	GLMmS	G	Su	BI
Festuca rubra red fescue	MPG	FSW	—	GLMmS	Gr	Su	MW
Fimbristylis autumnalis slender fimbry	SAG	SW	—	U	G	SuF	CEGSW
Fimbristylis caroliniana Carolina fimbry	LPG	FNaS	F	U	G	SuF	BEgS
Fimbristylis castanea marsh fimbry	LPG	FSW	—	U	G	SpSuF	ESW
Fimbristylis puberula hairy fimbry	MG	DS	—	U	G	Su	M
Flaveria floridana Florida yellowtops	MP	DS	—	U	Y	F	M
Florestina tripteris sticky florestina	SA	Ss	—	U	PuW	SuF	BC
Fragaria chiloensis beach strawberry	SP	FS	F	B	W	SpSu	EGS
Fragaria vesca woodland strawberry	SP	Ss	Ff	GLMmS	W	SpSu	BM
Fragaria virginiana Virginia strawberry	SP	DSs	FN	BGLMmS	W	SpSu	bEG
Frasera albicaulis white-stem elkweed	SP	DS	F	U	W	—	gM
Frasera albomarginata desert elkweed	SP	DS	F	U	G	—	gM
Frasera caroliniensis American-columbo	MP	s	F	U	GY	Su	gIM
Frasera speciosa monument plant	LP	DS	F	M	GW	SuF	gM
Fremontodendron californicum California flannelbush	eLS	DSs	F	U	Y	—	ABF
Fritillaria pinetorum pinewoods missionbells	SP	s	F	U	Pu	Su	BI
Froelichia floridana plains snake-cotton	LA	DS	F	U	W	SuF	CM
Froelichia gracilis slender snake-cotton	SA	DS	—	U	W	SpSuF	M
Fuirena squarrosa hairy umbrella sedge	MPG	FSW	L	U	G	SuF	SW
Gaillardia aestivalis lance-leaf blanket-flower	MP	DSs	F	Bh	RY	SpSu	BbM
Gaillardia pulchella firewheel	SA	DS	F	B	PuRY	SpSu	bCgM

PLANT LIST	Plant Type	Env. Tol.	Aesthetic Value	Wildlife Value	Flower Color	Bloom Period	Landscape Uses
Gaillardia suavis perfumeballs	MP	S	F	Bh	RY	SpSu	bM
Galactia canescens hoary milk-pea	PHV	DS	F	U	P	SpSu	M
Galactia volubilis downy milk-pea	SP	DS	—	S	PPu	Su	B
Galax urceolata beetleweed	SP	s	L	M	W	SpSu	BIE
Galearis spectabilis showy orchid	SP	s	F	U	PW	Su	I
Galium aparine sticky-willy	MP	S	—	mW	W	SpSu	B
Galium asprellum rough bedstraw	MP	sW	—	M	W	Su	IW
Galium bifolium twin-leaf bedstraw	SA	S	—	m	W	Su	—
Galium boreale northern bedstraw	MP	FS	—	m	W	Su	S
Galium californicum California bedstraw	P	—	—	m	Y	SpSu	—
Galium circaezans bedstraw licorice	SP	s	L	m	W	Su	I
Galium concinnum shining bedstraw	SP	s	—	m	W	Su	I
Galium hypotrichium alpine bedstraw	P	—	—	m	yg	Su	—
Galium johnstonii Johnston's bedstraw	P	—		m	GW	Su	—
Galium obtusum blunt-leaf bedstraw	SP	FSsW	—	m	W	SpSu	W
Galium parishii Parish's bedstraw	SP	—	—	m	W	—	—
Galium pilosum hairy bedstraw	MP	s	—	m	W	Su	I
Galium sparsiflorum Sequoia bedstraw	SP	S	—	m	W	Su	M
Galium texense Texas bedstraw	SA	Ss	—	U	W	Sp	B
Galium tinctorium stiff marsh bedstraw	SP	FSW	—	m	W	SuF	W
Galium trifidum three-petal bedstraw	MP	s	—	m	W	Su	I
Galium triflorum fragrant bedstraw	SP	s	—	m	W	Su	I
Gaura coccinea scarlet beeblossom	SP	DS	F	B	R	SpSu	bM
Gaura parviflora velvetweed	MP	DS	F	B	W	Su	bM

PLANT LIST	Plant Type	Env. Tol.	Aesthetic Value	Wildlife Value	Flower Color	Bloom Period	Landscape Uses
Gaura villosa woolly beeblossom	P	—	—	B	W	SpSu	—
Gayophytum diffusum spreading groundsmoke	SA	DS	F	U	PW	Su	gM
Gayophytum heterozygum zigzag groundsmoke	SA	—	—	U	PW	Su	—
Gayophytum humile dwarf groundsmoke	SA	Ds	—	U	PW	Su	I
Gayophytum ramosissimum pinyon groundsmoke	A	DSs	—	U	PW	SpSu	B
Gentiana andrewsii closed bottle gentian	MP	FWSs	F	H	BW	SuF	BWwg
Gentiana newberryi alpine gentian	SP	S	F	H	B	Su	M
Gentiana puberulenta downy gentian	SP	DS	F	H	B	SuF	M
Gentiana saponaria harvestbells	MP	FSs	F	H	B	F	MW
Geocaulon lividum false toadflax	SP	Fs	—	U	Pu	SpSu	IW
Geranium caespitosum purple cluster crane's-bill	MP	Ss	F	U	PPuW	SpSu	BgI
Geranium maculatum spotted crane's-bill	MP	Ss	FL	GMmS	PPu	SpSu	BgI
Geranium richardsonii white crane's-bill	SP	Ss	F	GMmS	WL	SpSu	Bg
Geranium robertianum herbrobert	SP	S	FL	GMmS	P	SpF	BgI
Geranium viscosissimum sticky purple crane's-bill	MP	S	FL	GMmS	Pu	SpSu	B
Geum canadense white avens	SP	S	F	Gm	W	Su	B
Geum rivale purple avens	SP	FS	F	Gm	PuY	SpSu	W
Geum triflorum old-man's-whiskers	SP	DS	F	Gm	Pu	Sp	gM
Gilia clivorum purple-spot gily-flower	A	—	—	GMm	Y	Sp	—
Gilia interior inland gily-flower	SA	DS	—	GMm	B	SpSu	M
Gilia minor little gily-flower	SA	DS	—	GMm	B	SpSu	M
Gilia scopulorum rock gily-flower	SP	DS	—	GMm	LPY	SpSu	MR
Gilia splendens splendid gily-flower	A	—	—	HGMm	PR	SpSu	g
Gilia tricolor bird's-eyes	SA	S	F	GMm	BY	SpSu	gM

PLANT LIST	Plant Type	Env. Tol.	Aesthetic Value	Wildlife Value	Flower Color	Bloom Period	Landscape Uses
Glandularia bipinnatifida Dakota mock vervain	MP	—	F	U	PPu	WSp	gM
Glandularia canadensis rose mock vervain	MP	DS	F	U	PuW	WSpSu F	M
Glandularia wrightii Davis Mountain mock vervain	SP	DS	F	U	PPu	SpSuF	M
Glaux maritima sea-milkwort	SP	FNaSW	—	U	PW	Su	SW
Glyceria canadensis rattlesnake manna grass	MG	FS	L	W	—	Su	W
Glyceria elata tall manna grass	MG	FSs	L	W	—	Su	MIW
Glyceria grandis American manna grass	MG	FS	L	W	—	Su	SW
Glyceria melicaria melic manna grass	MG	FSs	L	W	—	Su	IW
Glyceria striata fowl manna grass	MG	SF	FL	W	—	Su	W
Glycyrrhiza lepidota American licorice	MP	S	—	U	W	SpSu	M
Goodyera oblongifolia green-leaf rattlesnake-plantain	SP	s	F	U	W	Su	I
Goodyera pubescens downy rattlesnake-plantain	SP	s	L	U	W	SpF	I
Gratiola ebracteata bractless hedge-hyssop	SA	FS	—	U	WY	Su	MW
Gratiola neglecta clammy hedge-hyssop	SP	FS	—	U	WY	SpF	W
Grayia spinosa spiny hop-sage	SS	DS	—	U	W	Sp	M
Grindelia camporum great valley gumweed	MP	DS	F	M	Y	SuF	M
Grindelia hirsutula hairy gumweed	P	—	F	M	Y	SpSu	—
Grindelia integrifolia Pudget Sound gumweed	MP	DS	F	U	Y	SuF	gMS
Grindelia paludosa Suisun Marsh gumweed	P	W	F	U	Y	SuSp	M
Grindelia squarrosa curly-cup gumweed	MBP	DS	F	U	Y	SuF	gMS
Gymnocarpium dryopteris western oak fern	SP	Fs	L	U	X	X	GIS
Gymnopogon brevifolius short-leaf skeleton grass	SPG	S	L	m	Gr	SuF	M
Hackelia patens spotted stickseed	MP	DS	—	U	W	Su	M
Hackelia virginiana beggar's-lice	MP	s	—	U	BW	SuF	I

PLANT LIST	Plant Type	Env. Tol.	Aesthetic Value	Wildlife Value	Flower Color	Bloom Period	Landscape Uses
Hainardia cylindrica barb grass	AG	—	—	U	G	Su	—
Halodule beaudettei shoalweed	P	Na	—	U	BrG	Su	—
Harbouria trachypleura whiskybroom-parsley	SP	—	—	U	Y	—	—
Hedeoma acinoides slender false pennyroyal	SA	S	—	U	BPuW	Sp	GM
Hedeoma costatum ribbed false pennyroyal	SP	DS	—	U	—	SpSu	R
Hedeoma dentatum Arizona false pennyroyal	SAP	DS	—	U	P	Sp	M
Hedeoma drummondii Drummond's false pennyroyal	SAP	DS	—	U	B	SpSuF	R
Hedeoma hispidum rough false pennyroyal	SA	DS	—	U	B	SpSu	M
Hedeoma hyssopifolium aromatic false pennyroyal	P	—	—	U	P	F	—
Hedeoma oblongifolium oblong-leaf false pennyroyal	P	—	—	U	PPu	F	—
Hedyotis nigricans diamond-flowers	SP	DS	L	B	PPu	SuF	bM
Helenium amarum yellowdicks	SA	S	F	B	Y	SpSu	bgM
Helenium autumnale fall sneezeweed	MP	DFS	F	B	Y	Su	bMW
Helenium bigelovii Bigelow's sneezeweed	MP	FS	F	B	Y	SuF	BMW
Helianthella uniflora Rocky Mountain dwarf-sunflower	MP	DS	F	B	Y	Su	BbgM
Helianthemum canadense long-branch frostweed	SP	DS	F	B	Y	SpSu	BbM
Helianthemum georgianum Georgia frostweed	SP	DSs	F	U	Y	SpSu	BgM
Helianthus angustifolius swamp sunflower	LP	FS	F	BGLMmS	Y	SuF	BbgW
Helianthus annuus common sunflower	LA	DS	F	BGLmS	Y	SuF	M
Helianthus anomalus western sunflower	MA	DS	F	BGLMmS	Y	Su	BbgM
Helianthus argophyllus silver-leaf sunflower	LA	S	F	BmS	Pu	SuF	CM
Helianthus ciliaris Texas-blueweed	MP	FS	F	BGLmS	Y	SuF	bMS
Helianthus debilis cucumber-leaf sunflower	MP	DS	F	BGLMmS	Y	Su	BbgM
Helianthus divaricatus woodland sunflower	LP	DSs	F	BGLMms	Y	SuF	Bg

PLANT LIST	Plant Type	Env. Tol.	Aesthetic Value	Wildlife Value	Flower Color	Bloom Period	Landscape Uses
Helianthus grosseserratus saw-tooth sunflower	LP	DS	F	BGLMmS	Y	SuF	BbgM
Helianthus maximiliani Michaelmas-daisy	LP	DS	F	BGLMmS	Y	SuF	BbgM
Helianthus mollis neglected sunflower	LP	DS	F	BGLMmS	Y	SuF	BbGM
Helianthus occidentalis few-leaf sunflower	LP	DS	F	BGLMmS	Y	SuF	BbgM
Helianthus pauciflorus stiff sunflower	LP	DS	F	BGLMmS	Y	SuF	BbM
Helianthus petiolaris prairie sunflower	MA	DS	F	BGLMm	Y	Su	BbM
Helianthus radula rayless sunflower	LP	FS	F	BGLMmS	Y	SuF	Bb
Helianthus strumosus pale-leaf woodland sunflower	LP	DS	F	BGLMmS	Y	SuF	Bb
Helianthus tuberosus Jerusalem-artichoke	LP	FSs	F	BGLMmS	Y	SuF	BEMSW
Heliomeris multiflora Nevada showy false goldeneye	MPA	NaS	F	BGS	Y	Su	BbMS
Heliopsis helianthoides smooth oxeye	LP	DS	F	BS	Y	SpSu	BbCEgM
Heliotropium convolvulaceum wide-flower heliotrope	SA	DS	—	G	W	SuF	M
Heliotropium curassavicum seaside heliotrope	SAP	DNaS	F	G	PuW	SpF	M
Heliotropium tenellum pasture heliotrope	SA	DS	—	U	W	Su	M
Hepatica nobilis liverwort	SP	s	F	U	WP	Sp	gI
Heracleum maximum cow-parsnip	LP	FSs	F	M	W	WSuF	BIMW
Heracleum sphondylium eltrot	LP	FS	FL	U	W	Su	M
Heteranthera dubia grass-leaf mud-plantain	SP	FSW	F	W	Y	SuF	Wwg
Heteromeles arbutifolia California-Christmas-berry	eLS	Ss	FfL	GmS	W	Su	AB
Heteropogon contortus twisted tanglehead	PG	—	—	U	G	Su	—
Heterotheca bolanderi Bolander's false golden-aster	P	—	—	U	Y	SuF	—
Heterotheca subaxillaris camphorweed	MAB	DS	F	B	Y	SuF	CbgM
Heterotheca villosa hairy false golden-aster	MP	DS	F	B	Y	SpSuF	BgM
Heuchera abramsii San Gabriel alumroot	P	—	—	U	PPu	Sp	—

PLANT LIST	Plant Type	Env. Tol.	Aesthetic Value	Wildlife Value	Flower Color	Bloom Period	Landscape Uses
Heuchera americana American alumroot	MP	s	FL	U	yg	Sp	GI
Heuchera longiflora long-flower alumroot	SP	s	L	H	PPuW	SpSu	GI
Heuchera parviflora little-flower alumroot	SP	s	L	U	PW	SuF	GI
Heuchera richardsonii Richardson's alumroot	SP	DS	L	U	GW	Sp	GM
Heuchera rubescens pink alumroot	SP	DS	L	H	PuR	SpF	GR
Hexastylis arifolia little-brown-jug	eSP	s	L	U	Br	Sp	GI
Hexastylis virginica Virginia heartleaf	SP	s	L	U	Br	Sp	GI
Hibiscus laevis halberd-leaf rose-mallow	LP	FSW	F	H	PW	Su	SWwg
Hibiscus moscheutos crimson-eyed rose-mallow	LP	FSW	F	Hh	PW	Su	bWwg
Hieracium albiflorum white-flower hawkweed	MP	DS	F	GLM	W	Su	B
Hieracium cynoglossoides hound-tongue hawkweed	SP	DS	F	GLM	Y	Su	gM
Hieracium gronovii queendevil	LP	DSs	F	GLMm	Y	SuF	BIM
Hieracium venosum rattlesnake-weed	MP	SD	F	GLM	Y	SpSu	gM
Hilaria belangeri curly-mesquite	SPG	DS	—	M	G	SuF	EM
Hilaria jamesii James' galleta	SPG	DS	F	M	G	SuF	EM
Hilaria mutica tobosa grass	SPG	DS	—	M	G	SuF	EM
Hilaria rigida big galleta	MPG	DS	F	Mm	G	SuF	EM
Hoita orbicularis round-leaf leather-root	P	—	—	U	Y	SuF	—
Hordeum brachyantherum meadow barley	MPG	FS	F	GLMmS	BrPu	Su	MW
Hordeum jubatum fox-tail barley	MPG	FS	f	GMSW	GPu	Su	MW
Hordeum pusillum little barley	SAG	DS	F	GLMmS	—	Su	M
Horkelia cuneata wedge-leaf honeydew	SP	S	—	U	W	—	M
Houstonia canadensis Canadian summer bluet	SP	DSs	F	U	BW	SpSuF	BgM
Houstonia longifolia long-leaf summer bluet	SP	S	F	S	PuW	Su	BgG

PLANT LIST	Plant Type	Env. Tol.	Aesthetic Value	Wildlife Value	Flower Color	Bloom Period	Landscape Uses
Houstonia procumbens round-leaf bluet	SP	DS	F	B	W	SpSu	BbEGg
Houstonia pusilla tiny bluet	SA	DS	F	U	BV	Sp	CgM
Hudsonia tomentosa sand golden-heather	SP	DS	F	U	Y	SpSu	E
Huperzia lucidula shining club-moss	eSP	s	L	U	X	X	GI
Hutchinsia procumbens ovalpurse	SA	W	—	U	W	SpSuF	W
Hybanthus concolor eastern green-violet	MP	FSs	—	U	G	Sp	I
Hydrocotyle bonariensis coastal marsh-pennywort	SP	FSW	L	U	GW	SpF	W
Hydrocotyle umbellata many-flower marsh-pennywort	SP	FSW	L	U	yg	SpF	W
Hydrocotyle verticillata whorled marsh-pennywort	SP	DFSW	L	U	yg	SpF	W
Hydrophyllum appendiculatum great waterleaf	SP	s	FL	U	P	SpSu	gI
Hydrophyllum canadense blunt-leaf waterleaf	SP	s	F	U	PW	SpSu	gI
Hydrophyllum capitatum cat's-breeches	SP	Ss	—	U	BW	SpSu	M
Hydrophyllum virginianum Shawnee-salad	SB	s	FL	U	B	SpSu	BIg
Hylocomium splendens feathermoss	ııı	Fs	L	U	—	—	GIW
Hymenocallis caroliniana Carolina spider-lily	SP	FSs	FL	U	W	Sp	gI
Hymenopappus artemisiifolius old-plains-man	MB	S	F	U	R	Sp	M
Hymenopappus filifolius fine-leaf woollywhite	MP	DS	—	U	WY	SpSuF	M
Hymenopappus scabiosaeus Carolina woollywhite	MB	S	F	B	W	SpSu	bM
Hymenoxys bigelovii Bigelow's rubberweed	MBP	DS	—	U	Y	Su	M
Hymenoxys cooperi Cooper's rubberweed	MBP	DS	—	U	Y	SuF	M
Hymenoxys quinquesquamata Ricon rubberweed	P	—	—	U	Y	SuF	—
Hymenoxys richardsonii Colorado rubberweed	MP	DS	—	U	Y	Su	M
Hypericum anagalloides tinker's penny	SP	FS	F	U	Y	Su	W
Hypericum drummondii nits-and-lice	SA	DS	—	U	OY	SuF	MR

PLANT LIST	Plant Type	Env. Tol.	Aesthetic Value	Wildlife Value	Flower Color	Bloom Period	Landscape Uses
Hypericum gentianoides orange-grass	SP	DS	F	U	Y	SuF	BgM
Hypericum majus greater Canadian St. John's-wort	SP	FS	F	U	Y	Su	SW
Hypnum circinale moss	m	—	—	U	X	X	GI
Hypoxis hirsuta eastern yellow star-grass	SP	DS	F	U	Y	SpSu	gM
Hyptis alata clustered bush-mint	LP	SsW	—	U	PuW	SpSu	gM
Impatiens capensis spotted touch-me-not	MP	FSsW	FL	BGHhLmS	O	SuF	bISWwg
Impatiens pallida pale touch-me-not	MP	FSsW	FL	BGHhLmS	Y	SuF	IbWwg
Ipomoea imperati beach morning-glory	HV	W	—	U	W	SpSuF	W
Ipomoea pes-caprae bay-hops	PV	DNaS	—	U	Pu	SuF	E
Ipomopsis aggregata scarlet skyrocket	MB	DS	F	U	BPRW	SuF	AgMR
Ipomopsis longiflora white-flower skyrocket	MP	DS	F	U	B	SpF	gM
Ipomopsis pumila low skyrocket	SA	DS	—	U	LW	Sp	R
Ipomopsis rubra standing-cypress	LB	DSs	F	BH	R	SuF	BbM
Ipomopsis spicata spiked skyrocket	SP	DS	F	U	WY	—	gM
Iris brevicaulis zigzag iris	SP	FSW	FL	GHLW	BPu	SpSu	AbWwg
Iris douglasiana mountain iris	P	—	FL	BHL	PuRW	Sp	—
Iris hartwegii rainbow iris	SP	S	FL	BHL	PuY	—	Bbg
Iris lacustris dwarf lake iris	SP	FS	FL	BHLW	B	Sp	AWwg
Iris missouriensis Rocky Mountain iris	SP	FS	FL	BHLW	BPu	SpSu	AbMSWwg
Iris tenax tough-leaf iris	MP	S	FL	BHL	LPu	Su	ABbM
Iris versicolor harlequin blueflag	MP	FSW	FL	BHLW	B	Su	AbWwg
Iris virginica Virginia blueflag	SP	FSW	FL	BHLW	B	Su	AbWwg
Isocoma drummondii Drummond's jimmyweed	MP	Ss	F	U	Y	SpSuF	BM
Isocoma pluriflora southern jimmyweed	MP	NaS	F	B	Y	SuF	gM

PLANT LIST	Plant Type	Env. Tol.	Aesthetic Value	Wildlife Value	Flower Color	Bloom Period	Landscape Uses
Isoetes howellii Howell's quillwort	MP	FS	—	U	X	X	SW
Iva axillaris deer-root	SP	DNaS	—	U	GW	SuF	MW
Iva imbricata seacoast marsh-elder	MP	DNaS	—	U	Y	SuF	E
Iva nevadensis Nevada marsh-elder	A	—	—	U	W	SuF	—
Ivesia purpurascens summit mousetail	P	—	FL	U	PuW	Su	R
Ivesia santolinoides Sierran mousetail	P	—	—	U	W	Su	—
Jaumea carnosa marsh jaumea	SP	FNaSW	F	U	Y	SuF	SW
Jeffersonia diphylla twinleaf	SP	s	FL	U	W	Sp	I
Juncus acuminatus knotty-leaf rush	MPG	FS	FL	L	Br	SpSu	W
Juncus acutus spiny rush	MPG	DS	—	L	Br	Su	M
Juncus alpinoarticulatus northern green rush	SAG	FSW	—	L	Br	Su	W
Juncus balticus Baltic rush	MPG	DFSW	—	L	BrG	SpF	Wwg
Juncus bufonius toad rush	SAG	FSW	—	GLm	G	SpF	W
Juncus canadensis Canadian rush	MPG	FSW	—	L	Br	Su	SW
Juncus cooperi Cooper's rush	MPG	NaSW	—	L	G	Su	W
Juncus covillei Coville's rush	MPG	—	—	L	Br	Su	—
Juncus dudleyi Dudley's rush	MPG	FS	—	L	Br	SuF	W
Juncus effusus lamp rush	MPG	FSW	FL	L	Br	SuF	Wwg
Juncus gerardii saltmarsh rush	MPG	FNaSW	—	L	Br	SuF	SW
Juncus interior inland rush	SPG	DS	D	L	BG	Su	W
Juncus lesueurii salt rush	PG	Na	—	L	BrG	SpSu	W
Juncus longistylis long-style rush	MPG	FSW	—	L	Br	Su	W
Juncus marginatus grass-leaf rush	MPG	FSW	—	L	Br	Su	W
Juncus mexicanus Mexican rush	MG	DS	—	L	Br	Su	M

PLANT LIST	Plant Type	Env. Tol.	Aesthetic Value	Wildlife Value	Flower Color	Bloom Period	Landscape Uses
Juncus nevadensis Sierran rush	SG	FS	—	L	Br	Su	MW
Juncus nodosus knotted rush	SPG	FSW	—	L	Br	Su	W
Juncus orthophyllus straight-leaf rush	PG	W	—	L	BrG	Su	W
Juncus pelocarpus brown-fruit rush	SPG	FSW	—	L	G	SuF	W
Juncus roemerianus Roemer's rush	MPG	FNaSW	—	L	Br	SpF	W
Juncus stygius moor rush	SG	SW	—	L	W	Su	W
Juncus tenuis poverty rush	SPG	FSsW	—	LM	Br	SuF	BEGW
Juncus torreyi Torrey's rush	MG	S	—	L	Br	SuF	M
Keckiella antirrhinoides chaparral bush-beardtongue	P	—	—	U	Y	Sp	—
Kochia americana greenmolly	SP	DNaS	L	H	W	SuF	M
Kochia californica California summer-cypress	SP	Ss	BL	U	R	—	BM
Koeleria macrantha prairie Koeler's grass	SG	DS	fL	M	G	SpSu	AEM
Kosteletzkya virginica Virginia fen-rose	LP	DFNaSW	F	U	P	SuF	BgWwg
Krigia biflora two-flowered dwarf-dandelion	SP	S	F	B	Y	SpSu	Bg
Lachnanthes caroliniana Carolina redroot	MP	FS	F	W	Y	Su	gW
Lactuca canadensis Florida blue lettuce	LP	S	F	GMmS	Y	SuF	B
Laennecia schiedeana pineland marshtail	A	—	—	U	W	F	—
Langloisia setosissma bristly-calico	SA	S	—	U	LPu	SpSu	BM
Laportea canadensis Canadian wood-nettle	MP	Fs	F	U	G	Su	IS
Lappula occidentalis flat-spine sheepburr	SA	DSs	—	U	B	Su	CBM
Lasthenia californica California goldfields	SA	S	F	U	Y	Sp	CgM
Lasthenia glabrata yellow-ray goldfields	SA	FNaS	F	U	Y	Sp	CW
Lasthenia minor coastal goldfields	A	—	—	U	Y	Sp	—
Lathyrus graminifolius grass-leaf vetchling	SP	Ss	F	h	BPW	Sp	B

PLANT LIST	Plant Type	Env. Tol.	Aesthetic Value	Wildlife Value	Flower Color	Bloom Period	Landscape Uses
Lathyrus lanszwertii Nevada vetchling	HVP	—	—	U	BPu	SpSu	—
Lathyrus ochroleucus cream vetchling	MP	Ds	F	h	W	SpSu	Bl
Lathyrus palustris marsh vetchling	MP	FSW	F	h	Pu	Su	W
Lathyrus polyphyllus leafy vetchling	MP	—	F	h	Pu	Su	—
Lathyrus venosus veiny vetchling	MP	FsW	F	h	Pu	SpSu	gISW
Layia chrysanthemoides smooth tidytips	SA	S	F	U	Y	SpSu	CgM
Layia glandulosa white tidytips	SA	DS	F	U	W	SpSu	CgM
Lechea cernua nodding pinweed	SP	DS	—	S	R	Su	M
Lechea mucronata hairy pinweed	MP	DSs	—	S	R	Su	BM
Lechea san-sabeana San Saba pinwheel	SP	Ss	—	U	R	Sp	BM
Lechea tenuifolia narrow-leaf pinweed	SP	DSs	—	S	R	Su	BM
Leersia hexandra southern cut grass	MPG	SW	—	LSW	G	Su	ESW
Leersia lenticularis catchfly grass	LPG	FSW	F	LSW	G	F	EW
Leersia oryzoides rice cut grass	MPG	FSW	—	LSW	G	Su	EPSW
Leersia virginica white grass	MPG	FSs	F	LSW	G	SuF	IW
Lemna aequinoctialis lesser duckweed	AQ	FSW	—	W	X	X	Wwg
Lemna minor common duckweed	AQP	SW	L	W	G	Su	Wwg
Lemna perpusilla minute duckweed	AQP	SW	L	W	G	Su	Wwg
Lepidium densiflorum miner's pepperwort	SAB	DS	—	MmSW	GW	Su	M
Lepidium fremontii bush pepperwort	MP	DS	—	MmS	W	Su	M
Lepidium lasiocarpum hairy-pod pepperwort	SAB	DNaS	—	MmS	W	Sp	BM
Lepidium latipes San Diego pepperwort	SA	FNaS	—	MmSW	G	Sp	M
Leptochloa dubia green sprangletop	MPG	DS	—	U	G	SpF	MR
Leptodactylon pungens granite prickly-phlox	SP	DS	FL	B	P	Sp	BbGgMR

PLANT LIST	Plant Type	Env. Tol.	Aesthetic Value	Wildlife Value	Flower Color	Bloom Period	Landscape Uses
Lespedeza capitata round-head bush-clover	LP	DS	L	GhMS	W	Su	CEM
Lespedeza hirta hairy bush-clover	LP	S	L	GMS	YW	Su	CEM
Lespedeza procumbens trailing bush-clover	SP	DS	F	GMS	P	SuF	EB
Lespedeza repens creeping bush-clover	SP	DS	F	GMS	PPu	SpF	EB
Lespedeza stuevei tall bush-clover	MP	DS	F	GMS	Pu	SuF	EM
Lespedeza texana Texas bush-clover	SA	Fs	F	GhMS	BPu	SuF	CIS
Lespedeza violacea violet bush-clover	SP	DSs	F	GMS	V	Su	BgM
Lesquerella gordonii Gordon's bladderpod	SA	DS	—	U	Y	Sp	M
Lesquerella ludoviciana Louisiana bladderpod	SP	DSs	F	U	Y	Sp	BI
Leucobryum glaucum white moss	em	s	L	U	X	X	GI
Leucocrinum montanum star-lily	MP	Ds	F	U	W	SpSu	BI
Lewisia nevadensis Nevada bitter-root	SP	S	F	S	PW	Su	BIM
Leymus cinereus Great Basin lyme grass	MPG	DSsW	DF	GS	G	SpSu	BEIMSW
Leymus condensatus giant lyme grass	MPG	DFS	—	GS	G	Su	EMSW
Leymus salinus salinas lyme grass	LPG	DSs	DF	GS	G	Su	BEIM
Leymus triticoides beardless lyme grass	MPG	FNaS	DF	GS	G	Su	ESW
Liatris aspera tall gayfeather	LP	DS	F	BHS	PPu	SuF	bgM
Liatris cylindracea Ontario gayfeather	SP	DS	DF	BHS	PPu	SuF	bgM
Liatris elegans pink-scale gayfeather	MP	S	DF	BS	PuW	SuF	bM
Liatris mucronata cusp gayfeather	MP	DS	F	BHS	Pu	SuF	bM
Liatris pauciflora few-flower gayfeather	MP	DS	F	BHS	Pu	SuF	bgM
Liatris punctata dotted gayfeather	MP	DS	F	BHS	PR	SuF	bgM
Liatris pycnostachya cat-tail gayfeather	MP	DS	F	BHS	Pu	SuF	M
Liatris scariosa devil's-bite	LP	S	F	BHS	P	SuF	bgM

PLANT LIST	Plant Type	Env. Tol.	Aesthetic Value	Wildlife Value	Flower Color	Bloom Period	Landscape Uses
Liatris spicata dense gayfeather	LP	FS	F	BHS	P	SuF	bgM
Liatris squarrosa scaly gayfeather	MP	DS	F	BHS	PPu	Su	bgM
Liatris tenuifolia short-leaf gayfeather	MP	DS	DF	BHS	Pu	SuF	bgM
Ligusticum filicinum fern-leaf wild lovage	MP	DSs	L	U	W	Su	BM
Ligusticum porteri Porter's wild lovage	MP	Ss	L	U	W	Su	BM
Lilaea scilloides flowering-quillwort	A	SW	L	U	G	SpSu	Wwg
Lilaeopsis chinensis eastern grasswort	SP	FS	L	U	W	SpF	W
Lilium catesbaei southern red lily	SP	FS	F	BHS	O	Su	bW
Lilium parryi lemon lily	MP	FS	FL	BS	Y	Su	bM
Lilium philadelphicum wood lily	MP	S	F	BHS	OR	Su	Bbgl
Lilium superbum Turk's-cap lily	LP	FS	F	BHS	OR	Su	BW
Limnanthes douglasii Douglas' meadowfoam	SP	FS	FL	U	WY	Sp	BgMW
Limnobium spongia American spongeplant	AQP	SW	L	U	G	SuF	Wwg
Limnodea arkansana Ozark grass	SAG	DS		U	G	Sp	M
Limonium californicum marsh-rosemary	SP	FNaS	F	U	Pu	SuW	SW
Limonium carolinianum Carolina sea-lavender	SP	NaSW	DF	B	Pu	SuF	SWwg
Limosella aquatica awl-leaf mudwort	SP	FS	—	U	PuW	Su	W
Limosella australis Welsh mudwort	SP	FNaS W	—	U	W	SuF	W
Linanthis nuttallii Nuttall's desert-trumpets	SP	Ss	F	U	PW	—	Bg
Linanthus ciliatus whiskerbrush	SA	S	F	U	PuR	—	Bg
Linum hudsonioides Texas flax	SA	DS	F	U	Y	SpSuF	gM
Linum lewisii prairie flay	SP	DS	F	B	B	SpSuF	bMR
Linum rigidum large-flower yellow flax	SA	DNaS	F	B	Y	Su	BbM
Liparis loeselii yellow wide-lip orchid	SP	FSs	FL	m	GY	SpSu	IW

PLANT LIST	Plant Type	Env. Tol.	Aesthetic Value	Wildlife Value	Flower Color	Bloom Period	Landscape Uses
Listera caurina northwestern twayblade	SP	Ss	F	U	GPu	SpSu	IM
Listera convallarioides broad-tip twayblade	SP	Fs	F	U	yg	SpSu	gI
Lithophragma glabrum bulbous woodlandstar	SP	Ss	F	U	P	Sp	BI
Lithophragma parviflorum prairie woodlandstar	SP	Ss	F	U	P	Sp	MR
Lithophragma tenellum slender woodlandstar	SP	Ss	F	U	P	Sp	MR
Lithospermum canescens hoary puccoon	SP	DS	F	U	OY	Sp	gM
Lithospermum caroliniense hairy puccoon	SP	Ss	F	U	OY	SpSu	BM
Lithospermum incisum fringed gromwell	SP	DS	F	U	OY	Sp	M
Lithospermum ruderale Columbian puccoon	SP	Ss	F	U	Y	Sp	BM
Lobelia cardinalis cardinal-flower	MP	FSs	F	Hh	R	SuF	ABbgIWS
Lobelia dortmanna water lobelia	SP	SW	F	B	Pu	SuF	bWwg
Lobelia kalmii brook lobelia	SP	FS	F	B	B	SuF	bWwy
Lobelia siphilitica great blue lobelia	MP	FSs	F	Bh	B	SuF	BbMSW
Lobelia spicata pale-spike lobelia	MP	DS	F	Bh	BW	SuF	BbM
Lomatium foeniculaceum carrot-leaf desert-parsley	SP	DS	—	U	Y	Su	BM
Lomatium triternatum nine-leaf desert-parsley	SP	S	—	U	Y	Su	M
Lotus nevadensis Nevada bird's-foot-trefoil	SP	S	F	GLMm	Y	SpSu	M
Lotus oblongifolius streambank bird's-foot-trefoil	SP	FS	F	GLMm	Y	SpF	S
Lotus plebus long-bract bird's-foot-trefoil	SP	FSs	F	GLMm	Y	Sp	B
Lotus rigidus broom bird's-foot-trefoil	SP	DS	F	GLMm	WY	Sp	M
Lotus salsuginosus coastal bird's-foot-trefoil	SP	DS	F	GLMm	Y	SpSu	M
Lotus wrightii scrub bird's-foot-trefoil	SP	DS	F	GLMm	Y	Sp	M
Ludwigia palustris marsh primrose-willow	MP	FSW	F	W	Y	Su	W
Ludwigia repens creeping primrose-willow	SP	FSsW	F	W	Y	Su	SW

PLANT LIST	Plant Type	Env. Tol.	Aesthetic Value	Wildlife Value	Flower Color	Bloom Period	Landscape Uses
Lupinus argenteus silver-stem lupine	MP	DSs	FL	GLMmS	B	Su	BgM
Lupinus arizonicus Arizona lupine	SA	S	FL	GLMmS	PuR	Sp	gM
Lupinus bicolor miniature annual lupine	SA	S	FL	GLMmS	BW	Sp	CgM
Lupinus brevicaulis short-stem lupine	SA	DNaSs	FL	GLMmS	B	SpSu	CBgM
Lupinus breweri matted lupine	SP	DS	FL	BCGMmS	B	Su	bM
Lupinus caudatus Kellogg's spurred lupine	SP	Ss	FL	GLMmS	B	Sp	BgM
Lupinus elatus tall silky lupine	SP	Ss	FL	GLMmS	PuW	SpSu	Bg
Lupinus excubitus interior bush lupine	MP	DFS	FL	GLMmS	B	SpSu	gM
Lupinus formosus summer lupine	MP	Ss	FL	GLMmS	BPuW	Su	BgM
Lupinus huachucanus Huachuca Mountain lupine	SP	Ss	F	GLMmS	BPu	Sp	BgM
Lupinus latifolius broad-leaf lupine	MP	S	F	CGHLMmS	Pu	SpSu	gM
Lupinus luteolus butter lupine	MA	DS	F	CGHLMmS	Y	SpSu	BgM
Lupinus neomexicanus New Mexico lupine	SP	S	F	CGHLMmS	L	SpSuF	gM
Lupinus palmeri Palmer's lupine	MP	S	F	CGHLMmS	Pu	SpSuF	gM
Lupinus peirsonii long lupine	P	—	F	BCH	Y	Sp	bg
Lupinus perennis sundial lupine	SP	DS	FL	BCGHLMmS	B	SpSu	bgM
Lupinus polyphyllus blue-pod lupine	MP	FS	F	CGLMmSH	BRY	SpSu	gMW
Lupinus sericeus Pursh's silky lupine	SP	S	FL	CGHLMmS	B	SpSu	gM
Lupinus subcarnosus Texas bluebonnet	SA	S	FL	GMmS	B	Sp	CbM
Lupinus texensis Texas lupine	SA	DS	F	BC	B	Sp	gM
Lupinus versicolor Lindley's varied lupine	SP	S	F	BCGH	BPPuY	SpSu	bM
Luziola fluitans southern water grass	G	W	—	U	—	—	wg
Luzula congesta heath wood-rush	SG	S	—	U	Br	—	M
Lycopodium clavatum running ground-pine	eSP	Ss	L	M	X	X	BGI

PLANT LIST	Plant Type	Env. Tol.	Aesthetic Value	Wildlife Value	Flower Color	Bloom Period	Landscape Uses
Lycopodium obscurum princess-pine	eSP	Ss	L	M	X	X	BGI
Lycopodium sabinifolium savin-leaf ground pine	eSP	Ss	L	M	X	X	BGI
Lycopus americanus cut-leaf water-horehound	MP	FSW	—	U	W	SuF	W
Lycopus asper rough water-horehound	SP	FSW	—	U	W	SuF	W
Lycopus uniflorus northern water-horehound	SP	FS	—	U	W	SuF	W
Lycopus virginicus Virginia water-horehound	SP	FSW	—	U	W	SuF	W
Lycurus phleoides common wolf's-tail	SPG	DS	F	U	G	Su	MR
Lygodesmia juncea rush skeleton-plant	MP	DS	F	U	BPPu	Su	M
Lysichiton americanus yellow skunk-cabbage	MP	SW	FL	GW	Y	Su	Wwg
Lysimachia ciliata fringed yellow-loosestrife	MP	FSs	F	mW	Y	Su	BgSW
Lysimachia quadrifolia whorled yellow-loosestrife	MP	S	F	m	Y	Su	gM
Lysimachia thyrsiflora tufted yellow-loosestrife	MP	FW	F	U	Y	Su	Wwg
Lythrum alatum wing-angle loosestrife	MP	FSW	F	U	P	SuF	Wwg
Lythrum lineare saltmarsh loosestrife	MP	FNaSW	F	U	P	SuF	Wwg
Machaeranthera canescens hoary tansy-aster	MBP	DNaSs	F	B	PPuW	SuF	BbM
Machaeranthera phyllocephala camphor-daisy	A	FS	F	B	Y	—	bMS
Machaeranthera pinnatifida lacy tansy-aster	SP	DS	F	B	Y	SpSuF	bM
Machaeranthera tanacetifolia takhoka-daisy	SA	DS	F	B	BPPu	SpSu	CbM
Machaerocarpus californicus fringed-water-plantain	SP	FSW	F	U	PW	SpSu	Wwg
Madia exigua little tarplant	SA	S	F	GLmS	Y	Sp	CBM
Madia gracilis grassy tarplant	MA	S	F	GLmS	Y	Sp	CBM
Maianthemum canadense false lily-of-the-valley	SP	Ss	FL	GLm	W	Sp	BEGgI
Maianthemum dilatatum two-leaf false Solomon's-seal	SP	SW	Ff	G	W	Sp	IWwg
Maianthemum racemosum feathery false Solomon's-seal	MP	s	F	GmS	WG	Sp	BI

PLANT LIST	Plant Type	Env. Tol.	Aesthetic Value	Wildlife Value	Flower Color	Bloom Period	Landscape Uses
Maianthemum stellatum starry false Solomon's-seal	SP	DS	Ff	GLM	W	SpSu	B
Maianthemum trifolium three-leaf false Solomon's-seal	SP	sW	Ff	GLM	W	SpSu	IWwg
Malacothrix glabrata smooth desert-dandelion	SA	DS	F	U	Y	Sp	gM
Manfreda virginica false aloe	LP	DS	L	U	yg	Su	gM
Marshallia caespitosa puffballs	SP	DS	F	U	LWY	Sp	M
Marsilea vestita hairy water-clover	AQP	FSW	L	W	X	X	Wwg
Matelea edwardsensis plateau milkvine	PHV	DSs	—	U	G	Sp	BI
Matelea gonocarpa angular-fruit milkvine	HVP	s	F	BC	BrPu	Su	bI
Matelea reticulata netted milkvine	PHV	DSs	—	U	G	SpSuF	B
Matteuccia struthiopteris ostrich fern	LP	FSW	L	U	X	X	BSW
Mayaca fluviatilis stream bog-moss	AQ	SW	L	U	PW	SpSu	W
Medeola virginiana Indian cucumber-root	SP	s	FfL	S	yg	Sp	gI
Meehania cordata Meehan's-mint	SP	s	L	U	BL	SuF	I
Melampodium leucanthum plains blackfoot	SP	Ss	F	U	W	SpSuF	BM
Melampyrum lineare American cow-wheat	SP	DFS	F	U	W	Su	W
Melanthium parviflorum Appalachian bunchflower	LP	s	—	U	yg	SuF	I
Melica bulbosa onion grass	SPG	s	—	MS	G	Su	I
Melica californica California melic grass	MPG	Ss	—	MS	G	Su	BM
Melica harfordii Harford's melic grass	SPG	Ss	—	MS	G	Su	B
Melica imperfecta coast range melic grass	MPG	DSs	—	MS	G	Su	B
Melica stricta rock melic grass	SG	S	—	MS	G	Su	MS
Melothria pendula Guadeloupe-cucumber	HPV	FSs	—	U	yg	SpF	B
Mentha arvensis American wild mint	SP	FS	F	U	BW	SuF	W
Mentzelia albicaulis white-stem blazingstar	SA	DS	BF	G	Y	Sp	CgMR

PLANT LIST	Plant Type	Env. Tol.	Aesthetic Value	Wildlife Value	Flower Color	Bloom Period	Landscape Uses
Mentzelia involucrata white-bract blazingstar	SAB	DFS	BF	U	RWY	Sp	gMR
Mentzelia multiflora Adonia blazingstar	SAB	DS	BF	U	Y	Sp	gM
Mentzelia pumila golden blazingstar	SAB	DS	BF	U	Y	SpSuF	gM
Menyanthes trifoliata buck-bean	SP	FSW	F	U	W	Su	SW
Mertensia arizonica aspen bluebells	SP	Ss	F	Hh	B	SpSu	Bbg
Mertensia ciliata tall fringe bluebells	MP	Ss	F	Hh	B	SpSu	Bbg
Mertensia lanceolata prairie bluebells	SP	Ss	F	Hh	B	SpSu	Bbg
Mertensia oblongifolia languid-lady	SP	Ss	F	Hh	B	SpSu	Bbg
Mertensia virginica Virginia bluebells	SP	Fs	F	Hh	B	Sp	bgIW
Mesembryanthemum nodiflorum slender-leaf iceplant	SA	S	F	U	W	SpSu	gM
Mikania scandens climbing hempvine	HV	FSsW	F	U	LPu	SuF	BSW
Mimulus bigelovii yellow-throat monkey-flower	SA	Ss	F	U	BPu	—	B
Mimulus guttatus seep monkey-flower	MP	F	F	U	Y	Su	W
Mimulus moschatus muskflower	SP	FS	F	U	Y	—	SW
Mimulus primuloides yellow creeping monkey-flower	SP	S	FL	U	Y	Su	gM
Mimulus ringens Allegheny monkey-flower	SP	Fs	F	U	BW	SuF	BgI
Mimulus suksdorfii miniature monkey-flower	SP	SW	F	U	Y	SpSu	gMWwg
Mimulus tricolor tricolor monkey-flower	SP	FS	F	U	Pu	Sp	W
Minuartia californica California stitchwort	SA	DS	—	U	W	Sp	GR
Minuartia caroliniana pine-barren stitchwort	SP	Ss	L	U	Pw	SpSu	BMG
Minuartia nuttallii brittle stitchwort	SA	Ss	—	U	W	SpSu	BGE
Minuartia patula Pitcher's stitchwort	SA	DS	—	U	W	SpSu	GM
Mirabilis albida white four-o'clock	MP	DS	F	BHs	PW	SpSuF	bM
Mirabilis alipes winged four-o'clock	SP	NaSs	F	BHS	Ppu	SuF	BbM

PLANT LIST	Plant Type	Env. Tol.	Aesthetic Value	Wildlife Value	Flower Color	Bloom Period	Landscape Uses
Mirabilis bigelovii desert wishbonebush	SP	Ss	F	BHS	Ppu	SuF	Bb
Mirabilis hirsuta hairy four-o'clock	MP	DS	F	S	PPu	SuF	BgR
Mirabilis linearis narrow-leaf four-o'clock	LP	DS	F	S	PPu	SuF	BgR
Mitchella repens partridge-berry	SP	s	FL	GL	W	Sp	BGgI
Mitella diphylla two-leaf bishop's-cap	SP	s	FL	G	W	Sp	BGgI
Mitella nuda bare-stem bishop's-cap	SP	s	FL	U	BrG	SpSu	BGgI
Mitella stauropetala side-flower bishop's-cap	SP	S	L	U	W	SpSu	GgI
Moehringia macrophylla big-leaf grove-sandwort	SP	SsW	—	U	W	SpSu	BW
Monanthochloe littoralis shore grass	SPG	FNaS	—	U	G	Sp	EW
Monarda citriodora lemon beebalm	MP	Ss	F	Bh	PW	SpSuF	BbM
Monarda clinopodioides basil beebalm	SA	S	F	Bh	PW	SpSu	BCM
Monarda didyma scarlet beebalm	MP	FSs	F	H	PuR	SuF	BbSW
Monarda fistulosa Oswego-tea	MP	DSs	DF	BHL	L	Su	BbM
Monarda punctata spotted beebalm	MP	DS	DF	Bh	LPu	SuF	bM
Monardella cinerea gray mountainbalm	SP	S	F	U	PuW	Su	M
Monardella linoides flax-leaf mountainbalm	SP	S	F	U	PuW	Su	gM
Monardella odoratissima alpine mountainbalm	SP	DS	F	U	PuW	SuF	M
Monolepis nuttalliana Nuttall's poverty-weed	SA	DS	—	U	GR	W	M
Monotropa hypopithys many-flower Indian-pipe	SP	s	F	U	P	SpSu	I
Monotropa uniflora one-flower Indian-pipe	SP	s	F	U	W	SpSu	I
Monroa squarrosa false buffalo grass	G	—	—	U	G	Su	—
Montia linearis linear-leaf candy-flower	SA	FS	L	mGS	W	SuF	Swg
Muhlenbergia capillaris hair-awn muhly	MPG	Ds	—	GLM	G	SuF	BI
Muhlenbergia cuspidata stony-hills muhly	MPG	DS	—	GLM	G	SuF	M

PLANT LIST	Plant Type	Env. Tol.	Aesthetic Value	Wildlife Value	Flower Color	Bloom Period	Landscape Uses
Muhlenbergia emersleyi bull grass	SPG	S	—	GLM	G	SuF	R
Muhlenbergia filiculmis slim-stem muhly	PG	—	—	GLM	G	Su	—
Muhlenbergia filiformis pullup muhly	SPG	S	—	GM	G	SuF	BM
Muhlenbergia frondosa wire-stem muhly	MPG	DS	—	GLM	G	SuF	M
Muhlenbergia glomerata spiked muhly	MPG	FSW	—	GLM	G	SuF	W
Muhlenbergia lindheimeri Lindheimer's muhly	LPG	FSs	—	GM	G	F	BES
Muhlenbergia minutissima least muhly	SAG	DS	—	GLM	G	SuF	R
Muhlenbergia montana mountain muhly	SPG	DSs	—	GLM	G	F	BR
Muhlenbergia porteri bush muhly	SPG	DSs	—	GLM	G	SuF	BM
Muhlenbergia pungens sandhill muhly	SPG	DSs	—	GLM	G	Su	BM
Muhlenbergia racemosa green muhly	MPG	DFSs	—	GLM	G	SuF	BEMSW
Muhlenbergia reverchonii seep muhly	SPG	DS	—	GLM	G	SuF	M
Muhlenbergia richardsonis matted muhly	SG	DSNa	—	GLM	G	SuF	EM
Muhlenbergia schreberi nimblewill	SPG	sW	—	GM	G	F	BEI
Muhlenbergia torreyi ringed muhly	MPG	DSs	—	GLM	G	SuF	BM
Muhlenbergia utilis aparejo grass	SPG	FSs	—	GM	G	F	SW
Muhlenbergia virescens screw leaf muhly	SPG	DSs	—	GLM	G	SuF	BM
Muhlenbergia wrightii Wright's muhly	SPG	S	—	GLM	G	SuF	M
Musineon divaricatum leafy wild parsley	SP	DNaS	—	C	Y	—	M
Myosotis verna spring forget-me-not	SA	FSs	—	U	W	Sp	BCMS
Myosurus minimus tiny mousetail	SA	FS	—	U	WY	SpSu	CM
Myriophyllum aquaticum parrot's feather	AQP	FSW	L	W	W	Su	Wwg
Myriophyllum heterophyllum two-leaf water-milfoil	AQP	FSW	L	W	W	Su	Wwg
Najas marina holly-leaf waternymph	AQP	W	L	W	Br	—	wg

PLANT LIST	Plant Type	Env. Tol.	Aesthetic Value	Wildlife Value	Flower Color	Bloom Period	Landscape Uses
Nassella cernua tussock grass	MPG	S	L	LMmS	—	—	M
Nassella lepida tussock grass	MPG	S	L	LMmS	—	—	M
Nassella leucotricha Texas wintergrass	MPG	DS	L	LMmS	Br	—	M
Nassella pulchra tussock grass	MPG	DS	L	LMmS	Pu	—	M
Nassella viridula green tussock grass	MPG	DS	L	LMmS	BrG	—	M
Navarretia intertexta needle-leaf pincushion-plant	SA	S	F	U	PuW	Sp	M
Navarretia leucocephala white-flower pincushion-plant	SA	FS	F	U	W	Su	CGgMW
Nelumbo lutea American lotus	AQP	SW	FL	LMW	Y	Su	wg
Nemastylis geminiflora prairie pleatleaf	SP	S	F	U	B	Sp	gM
Nemophila breviflora Great Basin baby-blue-eyes	SA	Ss	F	U	W	SpSu	BCGI
Nemophila phacelioides large-flower baby-blue-eyes	A	Ss	F	U	BPu	Sp	Bg
Neostapfia colusana colusa grass	SAG	DFs	—	U	G	Su	MS
Neptunia lutea yellow puff	SP	DS	F	U	Y	SpSuF	gM
Nitrophila occidentalis boraxweed	SP	DNaS	—	U	PW	Su	EM
Nolina bigelovii bigelow's bear-grass	LP	DS	—	U	—	Sp	M
Nothoscordum bivalve cowpoison	SP	DS	F	U	W	SpSuF	BgMR
Nuphar lutea yellow pond-lily	AQP	SW	FL	LW	Y	Su	Wwg
Nuttalanthus texanus Texas-toadflax	AB	—	—	U	BL	SpSu	—
Nyctaginia capitata devil's-bouquet	SP	S	F	H	PR	SpSuF	bGM
Nymphaea mexicana banana water-lily	AQP	SW	FL	LW	Y	Su	Wwg
Nymphaea odorata American white water-lily	AQP	SW	FL	LMW	W	Su	Wwg
Nymphoides aquatica big floatingheart	AQP	SW	FL	LMW	W	Su	Wwg
Nymphoides cordata little floatingheart	AQP	SW	FL	LMW	W	Su	Wwg
Oenanthe sarmentosa Pacific water-dropwort	AQP	W	—	U	W	SuF	W

PLANT LIST	Plant Type	Env. Tol.	Aesthetic Value	Wildlife Value	Flower Color	Bloom Period	Landscape Uses
Oenothera albicaulis white-stem evening-primrose	MA	Ss	F	HMS	PW	SpSu	Bb
Oenothera biennis king's-cureall	LP	DS	F	MS	Y	SuF	bM
Oenothera cespitosa tufted evening-primrose	SP	DS	F	HMS	PW	Su	bEMR
Oenothera deltoides devil's lantern	SA	Ss	F	HMS	PW	SpSu	Bb
Oenothera drummondii beach evening-primrose	MP	S	F	B	Y	WSpSu	bMS
Oenothera elata Hooker's evening-primrose	SB	FSs	F	HMS	Y	SpSu	BbI
Oenothera humifusa seaside evening-primrose	SP	DNaS	FL	MS	Y	SpF	bE
Oenothera pallida white-pole evening-primrose	SPA	Ss	F	MS	LPW	SpSuF	BI
Oenothera rhombipetala greater four-point evening-primrose	MA	S	F	MS	Y	Su	M
Oenothera speciosa pinkladies	SP	DS	F	B	P	SpSu	bgM
Okenia hypogaea burrowing-four-o'clock	MP	DS	—	U	—	SuF	E
Onoclea sensibilis sensitive fern	MP	SsW	fL	U	X	X	BCWI
Ophioglossum engelmannii limestone adder's tongue	SP	FSs	L	U	X	X	BMR
Oplismenus setarius short-leaf basket grass	SPG	Fs	—	U	G	SuF	IS
Oreonana vestita woolly mountain-parsley	SP	S	—	U	W	SpSuF	M
Orobanche fasciculata clustered broom-rape	SP	SsF	F	U	Y	Sp	IM
Orobanche ludoviciana Louisiana broom-rape	SP	FS	F	U	Pu	SuF	S
Orontium aquaticum goldenclub	AQP	SW	FL	U	Y	Sp	Wwg
Orthilia secunda sidebells	eSP	s	LF	G	W	Su	GI
Orthocarpus attenuatus valley-tassels	SAP	DS	F	U	WY	Sp	gM
Orthocarpus campestris field owl-clover	SA	DS	F	U	W	Sp	gM
Orthocarpus erianthus Johnnytuck	SA	DS	F	U	Y	Sp	gM
Orthocarpus linearilobus pale owl-clover	SA	DS	F	U	W	Sp	gM

PLANT LIST	Plant Type	Env. Tol.	Aesthetic Value	Wildlife Value	Flower Color	Bloom Period	Landscape Uses
Orthocarpus luteus golden-tongue osa-clover	SA	DS	F	U	Y	SuF	gM
Orthocarpus purpurascens red owl-clover	SP	S	F	U	PY	Sp	BM
Orthocarpus tolmiei Tolmie's owl-clover	A	—	—	U	G	Su	—
Oryzopsis asperifolia white-grain mountain-rice grass	MPG	Ds	—	GMmS	G	Su	BIE
Oryzopsis hymenoides Indian mountain-rice grass	MG	DS	—	GMmS	G	SpSu	EM
Oryzopsis pungens short-awn mountain-rice grass	SPG	DS	—	GMmS	G	Su	EM
Oryzopsis racemosa black-seed mountain-rice grass	MPG	s	—	GMmS	G	Su	EI
Osmorhiza chilensis mountain sweet-cicely	MP	Ss	FL	U	W	Su	BgIS
Osmorhiza claytonii hairy sweet-cicely	MP	s	FL	U	W	Su	BgI
Osmorhiza depauperata blunt-fruit sweet-cicely	MP	FSs	FL	U	W	Su	BgIS
Osmorhiza occidentalis Sierran sweet-cicely	MP	FSs	F	U	GW	Su	BIS
Osmunda cinnamomea cinnamon fern	LP	FSsW	fL	m	X	X	ABgIWwg
Osmunda claytoniana interrupted fern	MP	s	L	m	X	X	BgI
Osmunda regalis royal fern	MP	FsW	fL	m	X	X	ABgISWwg
Oxalis dichondraefolia peony-leaf wood-sorrel	SP	Ss	FL	CGMS	Y	WSpSuF	G
Oxalis montana sleeping-beauty	SP	Ss	FL	GLMS	W	SpSu	BgI
Oxalis oregana redwood-sorrel	P	—	—	GLMS	PuW	WSpSu	—
Oxalis violacea violet wood-sorrel	SP	Ss	FL	GLMS	Pu	Sp	gM
Oxytropis lagopus hare-foot locoweed	P	—	—	U	PPu	Su	—
Oxytropis lamberti stemless locoweed	SP	DSs	F	U	PPuW	SpSu	BM
Oxytropis parryi Parry's locoweed	SP	S	F	U	PPu	SpSu	M
Palafoxia feayi Feay's palafox	MP	DS	F	U	P	F	BI
Palafoxia rosea rosy palafox	SA	S	—	U	P	SuF	M
Palafoxia texana Texas palafox	SA	S	F	U	P	SpSuF	CGM

PLANT LIST	Plant Type	Env. Tol.	Aesthetic Value	Wildlife Value	Flower Color	Bloom Period	Landscape Uses
Panax quinquefolius American ginseng	SP	s	FfL	U	W	Su	BgI
Panax trifolius dwarf ginseng	SP	FSs	FL	U	W	SpSu	BgI
Panicum abscissum cut-throat grass	MPG	FS	—	GLMS	G	SuSpF	W
Panicum amarum bitter panic grass	MPG	DNaS	—	GLMS	G	SuF	ES
Panicum anceps beaked panic grass	MPG	DSs	—	GMS	G	SuF	BM
Panicum bulbosum bulb panic grass	SPG	Ss	—	GLMS	G	SuF	BM
Panicum flexile wiry panic grass	SPG	S	—	GLMS	G	SuF	BM
Panicum hallii Hall's panic grass	SPG	DFSs	—	GLMmS W	G	—	BEM
Panicum hemitomon maiden-cane	MPG	FSW	—	GLMSW	G	SuF	Wwg
Panicum obtusum blunt panic grass	SPG	FS	—	GLMSW	G	SuF	EMS
Panicum philadelphicum Philadelphia panic grass	SPG	DS	—	GLMS	G	SuF	M
Panicum repens torpedo grass	MPG	FSW	—	GLMS	G	SpSuF	S
Panicum rigidulum red-top panic grass	MPG	FS	—	GLMS	G	WSpSu F	W
Panicum virgatum wand panic grass	LPG	DFNa SsW	A	GLMSW	G	SuF	EMW
Pappophorum bicolor pink pappus grass	MPG	S	—	U	GP	SpSu	M
Pappophorum vaginatum whiplash pappus grass	G	—	—	U	G	Su	—
Parietaria pensylvanica Pennsylvania pellitory	SA	s	—	U	G	Sp	IRS
Parnassia glauca fen grass-of-Parnassus	SP	FS	FL	U	W	SuF	MgSW
Paronychia drummondii Drummond's nailwort	SAB	Ds	—	U	W	SpSuF	CBI
Paronychia jamesii James' nailwort	SP	DFS	—	U	—	SpSuF	EMRS
Paronychia sessiliflora low nailwort	S	DSs	—	U	—	SpSu	GMR
Parthenium hysterophorus Santa Maria feverfew	MA	S	F	U	W	SuF	M
Parthenium integrifolium wild quinine	MP	DS	FD	U	W	Su	BgM
Pascopyrum smithii western-wheat grass	MG	DS	—	U	G	Su	M

PLANT LIST	Plant Type	Env. Tol.	Aesthetic Value	Wildlife Value	Flower Color	Bloom Period	Landscape Uses
Paspalum bifidum pitchfork crown grass	MPG	Ss	—	GLMSW	G	F	BI
Paspalum dilatatum golden crown grass	LPG	SW	—	MS	G	Su	BMW
Paspalum distichum jointed crown grass	MPG	FS	—	GLMSW	G	SpSuF	s
Paspalum floridanum Florida crown grass	LPG	S	—	GLMSW	G	SpSuF	s
Paspalum monostachyum Gulf dune crown grass	LPG	FS	—	GLMSW	G	SuF	BIs
Paspalum plicatulum brown-seed crown grass	MPG	DS	—	GLMSW	G	SpSuF	M
Paspalum pubiflorum hairy-seed crown grass	MPG	SsW	—	MS	G	SpSu	BEMW
Paspalum setaceum slender crown grass	MPG	FS	—	GLMSW	G	WSpSu F	sW
Paspalum vaginatum talquezal	SPG	FNaS W	—	GLMSW	G	WSuF	W
Passiflora affinis bracted passion-flower	PHV	Ss	F	U	yg	Su	Bg
Passiflora foetida scalet-fruit passion-flower	PHV	NaSs	F	C	PuW	SpSuF	BbM
Passiflora incarnata purple passion-flower	HV	Ss	FL	H	L	Su	bB
Passiflora lutea yellow passion-flower	HV	Ss	FL	H	Y	Su	bBI
Passiflora tenuiloba bird-wing passion-flower	PHV	Ss	F	U	G	SpF	Bg
Pedicularis canadensis Canadian lousewort	SP	Ss	F	U	RY	Sp	DI
Pedicularis groenlandica bull elephant's-head	MP	SsW	F	U	BPu	Sp	BgMI
Pedicularis procera giant lousewort	MP	Ss	F	U	Y	Sp	BgM
Pedicularis racemosa parrot's-beak	SP	Ss	F	U	PuWY	Sp	BgI
Pedicularis semibarbata pinewoods lousewort	SP	Ds	L	H	Y	SpSu	bGI
Pediocactus simpsonii snowball cactus	C	DS	B	U	Pu	Sp	gM
Pediomelum argophyllum silver-leaf Indian-breadroot	SP	S	FL	U	B	Su	M
Pediomelum cuspidatum large-bract Indian-breadroot	SP	DS	FL	U	B	Su	M
Pediomelum esculentum large-Indian-breadroot	SP	DS	L	B	B	SpSu	b
Pellaea breweri Brewer's cliffbrake	eSP	s	L	U	X	X	gIR

PLANT LIST	Plant Type	Env. Tol.	Aesthetic Value	Wildlife Value	Flower Color	Bloom Period	Landscape Uses
Pellaea mucronata bird-foot cliffbrake	eSP	DS	L	U	X	X	gIR
Peltandra virginica green arrow arum	SP	FSW	L	W	G	SpSu	Wwg
Penstemon albidus red-line beardtongue	MP	DS	F	Hh	W	SpSu	bgM
Penstemon angustifolius broad-beard beardtongue	SP	S	F	Hh	BWY	SpSu	bgM
Penstemon arenicola red desert beardtongue	SP	DS	F	Hh	BPu	Su	bgM
Penstemon australis Eustis Lake beardtongue	MP	DSs	F	MmS	PuRY	SpSu	Bg
Penstemon barbatus beard-lip beardtongue	MP	DS	F	HMmS	R	SuF	bgM
Penstemon caesius San Bernardino beardtongue	SP	S	F	HMmS	B	Su	bgM
Penstemon cobaea cobaea beardtongue	MP	S	F	MmS	Pu	SpSu	BgM
Penstemon davidsonii timberline beardtongue	SP	S	FL	HMmS	B	Su	bGgR
Penstemon digitalis foxglove beardtongue	LP	DS	F	HhS	W	Su	bM
Penstemon eatonii Eaton's beardtongue	SP	DS	F	HhMmS	R	Su	bgM
Penstemon fremontii Fremont's beardtongue	SP	DSs	F	HMmS	BW	Su	BbgM
Penstemon gracilis lilac beardtongue	SP	S	F	HMmS	BPu	Su	bgM
Penstemon grinnellii Grinnell's beardtongue	P	—	F	HMmS	BPuW	SpSu	bg
Penstemon hirsutus hairy beardtongue	MP	DSs	F	BHMmS	BW	SpSu	BbgR
Penstemon humilis low beardtongue	SP	Ss	F	BMmS	B	Su	bBg
Penstemon labrosus San Gabriel beardtongue	MP	DSs	F	HMmS	R	Su	BbgI
Penstemon linarioides toadflax beardtongue	SP	S	F	HhMmS	Pu	Su	bgM
Penstemon palmeri scented beardtongue	MP	DSs	F	HhMmS	WY	Su	BbgM
Penstemon rostriflorus beaked beardtongue	MP	Ss	F	HMmS	ORY	Su	BbgM
Penstemon rydbergii meadow beardtongue	SP	Ss	F	HhMmS	Pu	Su	BbgM
Penstemon speciosus royal beardtongue	SP	S	F	HhMmS	BPu	SpSu	bgM
Penstemon subglaber Utah smooth beardtongue	SP	Ss	F	HhMmS	PW	Su	BbgM

PLANT LIST	Plant Type	Env. Tol.	Aesthetic Value	Wildlife Value	Flower Color	Bloom Period	Landscape Uses
Penstemon tubiflorus white wand beardtongue	LP	S	F	MmS	W	SpSu	gM
Penstemon virgatus upright blue beardtongue	SP	Ss	F	HhMmS	BLPu	Su	BbgM
Penstemon watsonii Watson's beardtongue	SP	DS	F	HhMmS	BPu	Su	bgM
Penstemon whippleanus dark beardtongue	MP	Ss	F	HhMmS	BPuW	Su	Bbgm
Pentalinon luteum hammock vipertail	HVP	—	—	U	Y	WSpSuF	—
Perideridia parishii Parish's yampah	P	—	—	U	PW	SuF	—
Perityle emoryi Emory's rockdaisy	SAB	DSs	F	B	WY	SpSu	bCgMR
Phacelia austromontana southern sierran scorpion-weed	SA	Ss	F	Mm	BL	SpSu	CGgI
Phacelia bipinnatifida fern-leaf scorpion-weed	SB	Ss	FL	Bm	BL	Sp	BbCGgI
Phacelia crenulata notch-leaf scorpion-weed	SA	S	F	m	Pu	WSp	CR
Phacelia distans distant scorpion-weed	SP	Ss	F	m	BPuW	SpSu	Bg
Phacelia imbricata imbricate scorpion-weed	P	—	—	m	W	SpSu	—
Phacelia patuliflora sand scorpion-weed	SA	Ss	F	U	LV	Sp	BGg
Phacelia purshii Miami-mist	SA	Fs	F	m	B	SpSu	BCgS
Phacelia sericea purplefringe	SP	Ss	F	m	BPu	Su	BgI
Phegopteris connectilis narrow beech fern	SP	s	L	m	X	X	I
Phleum alpinum mountain timothy	SPG	FSW	—	MS	G	SuF	W
Phlox caespitosa clustered phlox	SP	S	F	HMS	PuW	Sp	bgM
Phlox covillei Coville's phlox	P	—	—	HMS	PW	SuF	—
Phlox divaricata wild blue phlox	SP	s	FL	BHMS	B	Sp	BbGI
Phlox drummondii annual phlox	MA	DS	F	BHS	R	Su	CbgM
Phlox gracilis slender phlox	SP	s	F	HMS	PuW	Sp	bGgI
Phlox hoodii carpet phlox	SP	DSs	F	BHMS	LW	SpSu	BbGgM
Phlox longifolia long-leaf phlox	SP	DS	F	HMS	PPuW	SpSu	bGgM

PLANT LIST	Plant Type	Env. Tol.	Aesthetic Value	Wildlife Value	Flower Color	Bloom Period	Landscape Uses
Phlox multiflora Rocky Mountain phlox	SP	DSs	F	BHMS	PW	SpSu	BbGIM
Phlox pilosa downy phlox	SP	DS	F	BhMS	BP	Su	bGgM
Phragmites australis common reed	LPG	FSW	FL	U	GrR	SuF	W
Phryma leptostachya American lopseed	MP	S	F	U	PuW	SuF	BI
Phyllanthus abnormis Drummond's leaf-flower	SA	DS	—	U	W	SpSuF	M
Phyllanthus polygonoides smartweed leaf-flower	SP	DS	—	U	G	SpSuF	M
Physalis angustifolia coastal ground-cherry	SP	DS	—	GLm	W	WSpSuF	M
Physalis virginiana Virginia ground-cherry	SP	Ss	f	GLm	Y	Su	BI
Physalis walteri Walter's ground-cherry	SP	DNaS	—	GLm	W	SpSu	—
Physostegia intermedia slender false dragonhead	LP	FSW	F	h	L	SpSu	Wwg
Physostegia virginiana obedient-plant	MP	FS	FL	hS	P	SuF	bgMW
Pilea pumila Canadian clearweed	SP	Fs	L	U	W	SuF	IS
Pilularia americana American pillwort	SP	FSW	—	U	X	X	RWwg
Pinaropappus roseus white rock-lettuce	SP	DS	—	U	LRW	Sp	MR
Piptochaetium avenaceum black-seed spear grass	MPG	s	F	MmS	Br	Sp	BI
Piptochaetium fimbriatum pinyon spear grass	MPG	S	F	MmS	G	SuF	MR
Piptochaetium pringlei pringle's spear grass	MPG	s	F	MmS	Br	Sp	BI
Pistia stratiotes water-lettuce	AQP	SW	L	U	Y	WSpSuF	wg
Pityopsis graminifolia golden-aster	MP	DS	—	U	Y	SpSu	M
Plagiobothrys acanthocarpus adobe popcorn-flower	SA	—	—	U	W	—	C
Plagiobothrys distantiflorus California popcorn-flower	A	—	—	U	YW	SpSu	—
Plagiobothrys humistratus dwarf popcorn-flower	SA	—	—	U	W	—	—
Plagiobothrys hystriculus bearded popcorn-flower	A	—	—	U	YW	Sp	—
Plagiobothrys jonesii Mojave popcorn-flower	SA	DS	—	U	—	—	CM

PLANT LIST	Plant Type	Env. Tol.	Aesthetic Value	Wildlife Value	Flower Color	Bloom Period	Landscape Uses
Plagiobothrys kingii Great Basin popcorn-flower	SA	DS	—	U	W	Sp	CM
Plagiobothrys leptocladus alkali popcorn-flower	SA	SW	—	U	W	—	CW
Plagiobothrys nothofulvus rusty popcorn-flower	SP	S	—	U	W	Sp	M
Plagiobothrys stipitatus stalked popcorn-flower	SA	S	—	U	W	Sp	M
Plantago decipiens seaside plantain	SP	FNaS W	—	GLMmS	W	SuF	W
Plantago eriopoda red-woolly plantain	SP	FNaS	—	GLMmS	W	SuF	W
Plantago maritima goosetongue	SP	FS	—	GLMmS	W	SuF	W
Plantago ovata blond plantain	A	—	—	GLMmS	G	Sp	—
Plantago patagonica woolly plantain	SA	DS	—	GLMmS	PuW	SuF	M
Platanthera blephariglottis white fringed orchid	SP	FSW	F	M	W	SuF	Wwg
Platanthera dilatata scentbottle	MP	FS	F	M	W	SpF	W
Platanthera grandiflora greater purple fringed orchid	MP	FS	F	M	Pu	Su	W
Platanthera leucophaea prairie white fringed orchid	MP	FS	F	M	W	Su	W
Platanthera leucostachys sierra rein orchid	MP	FS	F	M	W	Su	BMW
Platanthera sparsiflora canyon bog orchid	SP	FS	F	M	G	Su	W
Pleurozium schreberi feather moss	m	FSsW	—	U	X	X	BGIW
Pluchea camphorata plowman's wort	LP	FS	F	U	P	SuF	W
Pluchea foetida stinking camphorweed	MP	FSW	F	U	W	SuF	Wwg
Pluchea rosea rosy camphorweed	MP	FSW	F	m	P	SuF	Wwg
Poa alpina alpine blue grass	SPG	FS	—	GLMmS	G	Sp	EM
Poa arachnifera Texas blue grass	MPG	S	—	U	G	F	M
Poa bolanderi Bolander's blue grass	SG	Ss	—	GLMmS	G	Sp	BEM
Poa fendleriana mutton grass	SPG	DSs	—	GLMmS	G	Sp	BEM
Poa glauca white blue grass	SG	S	—	GLMmS	G	SuF	EMR

PLANT LIST	Plant Type	Env. Tol.	Aesthetic Value	Wildlife Value	Flower Color	Bloom Period	Landscape Uses
Poa nervosa Hooker's blue grass	SPG	Ss	—	GLMmS	G	SpSu	BE
Poa palustris fowl blue grass	MG	S	—	GLMmS	G	SpSu	EM
Poa reflexa nodding blue grass	SPG	S	—	GLMmS	G	SpSu	EM
Poa secunda curly blue grass	MPG	DSs	—	GLMmS	G	SpSu	EBM
Podophyllum peltatum may-apple	SP	Ss	FfL	U	W	Sp	I
Pogogyne ziziphoroides Sacramento mesa-mint	SA	FS	—	U	Pu	Sp	M
Pogonia ophioglossoides snake-mouth orchid	SP	FSW	FL	U	P	SpSu	W
Polanisia tenuifolia slender-leaf clammeyweed	MP	DS	—	U	W	Su	B
Polemonium foliosissimum towering Jacob's-ladder	MP	Ss	FL	U	BPuW	Sp	Bg
Polemonium pulcherrimum beautiful Jacob's-ladder	SP	Ss	FL	U	BPuW	Sp	BgM
Polemonium reptans Greek-valerian	SP	Ss	F	U	L	Sp	BgIM
Polygala alba white milkwort	SA	DS	F	U	W	SpSu	gM
Polygala lindheimeri shrubby milkwort	SP	DSs	—	U	P	SpF	BM
Polygala nuttallii Nuttall's milkwort	SP	DS	F	U	Pu	SuF	gM
Polygala ovatifolia egg-leaf milkwort	SP	DSs	F	U	PW	SpSu	BM
Polygala paucifolia gaywings	SP	s	FL	U	P	Sp	BgI
Polygala verticillata whorled milkwort	SA	DS	F	U	P	Su	GM
Polygonatum biflorum King Solomon's-seal	LP	FSs	FL	G	W	Sp	BgIS
Polygonatum pubescens hairy Solomon's-seal	MP	s	F	G	GW	Sp	gI
Polygonella articulata coastal jointweed	SA	DS	F	U	PW	SuF	gM
Polygonella polygama October-flower	SP	DSs	—	U	PY	F	BM
Polygonum amphibium water smartweed	MP	FSW	BF	GLmSW	PR	SuF	Wwg
Polygonum bistortoides American bistort	MP	Ss	F	GmS	PW	Su	BM
Polygonum douglasii Douglas' knotweed	SA	Ss	—	GLmS	GPW	Su	B

PLANT LIST	Plant Type	Env. Tol.	Aesthetic Value	Wildlife Value	Flower Color	Bloom Period	Landscape Uses
Polygonum hydropiperoides swamp smartweed	SP	SW	—	GMmSW	PW	Su	Wwg
Polygonum pensylvanicum pinkweed	MP	FSW	F	GLmSW	P	SpF	Wwg
Polygonum punctatum dotted smartweed	MP	FSW	F	GLmSW	W	SuF	Wwg
Polygonum saggittatum arrow-leaf tearthumb	SP	FNaSW	FL	GLmSW	W	SuF	Wwg
Polygonum virginianum jumpseed	MP	s	—	GLmS	P	Su	I
Polypodium hesperium western polypody	eSP	s	L	GLM	X	X	gIR
Polypodium virginianum rock polypody	SP	Ds	L	GLM	X	X	gIR
Polypremum procumbens juniper-leaf	SAP	DS	—	U	W	SpSuF	BM
Polystichum acrostichoides Christmas fern	eSP	s	L	GLM	X	X	BgI
Polystichum munitum pineland sword fern	eMP	s	L	GLM	X	X	BgI
Polytaenia texana Texas false-parsley	MP	S	DF	U	Y	SpSu	M
Polytrichum strictum feather moss	m	FSW	—	U	X	X	W
Pontederia cordata pickerelweed	MP	FSW	FL	LW	B	SuF	Wwg
Potentilla arguta tall cinquefoil	MP	DS	F	GLMmS	WY	Su	gM
Potentilla breweri Sierran cinquefoil	SP	S	F	GLMmS	Y	Su	gM
Potentilla crinita bearded cinquefoil	SP	Ss	F	BGLMmS	Y	Su	BbgM
Potentilla glandulosa sticky cinquefoil	SP	DS	F	BGLMmS	Y	SpSu	bgM
Potentilla gracilis graceful cinquefoil	SP	DS	F	BGLMmS	WY	Su	bgM
Potentilla hippiana woolly cinquefoil	SP	DS	F	BGLMmS	Y	Su	bgM
Potentilla paradoxa bushy cinquefoil	SAP	FSW	FL	BGLMmS	Y	SuF	bgMW
Potentilla simplex oldfield cinquefoil	SP	S	F	BGmLMS	Y	Sp	BbgM
Potentilla thurberi scarlet cinquefoil	P	W	F	BGLMmS	R	SuF	W
Prenanthella exigua brightwhite	SA	S	F	U	PW	SpSu	BM
Prenanthes alba white rattlesnake-root	LP	Ss	F	U	W	Su	BI

PLANT LIST	Plant Type	Env. Tol.	Aesthetic Value	Wildlife Value	Flower Color	Bloom Period	Landscape Uses
Prenanthes altissima tall rattlesnake-root	LP	s	—	U	W	SuF	BI
Prenanthes racemosa purple rattlesnake-root	LP	FSW	F	U	P	SuF	MWS
Prenanthes trifoliolata gall-of-the-earth	LP	DSs	F	U	W	F	B
Primula parryi brook primrose	SP	Ss	F	U	PuR	—	gM
Proboscidea louisianica ram's-horn	MA	S	f	U	WY	Su	BgM
Pseudocymopterus montanus alpine false mountain-parsley	SP	DS	—	U	Y	Su	BM
Pseudoroegneria spicata bluebunch-wheat grass	MPG	DS	—	U	Gr	Su	M
Pseudostellaria jamesiana sticky-starwort	P	—	—	U	W	SpSu	—
Psoralidium tenuiflorum slender-flower lemonweed	MP	DS	—	U	Pu	Su	BM
Psorothamnus fremontii Fremont's smokebush	MS	DS	FL	U	B	Su	BgM
Pteridium aquilinum northern bracken fern	MP	DSs	L	GLM	X	X	BgI
Pterocaulon virgatum wand blackroot	SP	S	L	U	yg	Sp	M
Pterospora andromedea pine drops	MA	s	F	U	W	SuF	gI
Ptilagrostis kingii Sierran false needle grass	PG	—	—	U	G	Su	—
Ptilium crista-castrensis feathermoss	m	s	L	U	X	X	GI
Puccinellia kurilensis dwarf alkali grass	PG	—	—	U	G	Su	—
Puccinellia nuttalliana Nuttall's alkali grass	SPG	S	—	U	G	—	EM
Pulsatilla patens American pasqueflower	SP	DS	F	h	BPuW	Sp	bgM
Pycnanthemum californicum California mountain-mint	MP	DS	FL	B	W	Su	bgM
Pycnanthemum flexuosum Appalachian mountain-mint	MP	DFS	FL	B	W	SuF	BbgSW
Pycnanthemum tenuifolium narrow-leaf mountain-mint	SP	DSs	DF	B	W	Su	BbgM
Pycnanthemum virginianum Virginia mountain-mint	MP	Ss	F	Bh	PuW	Su	Bbg
Pyrola asarifolia pink wintergreen	eSP	sW	FL	G	PPu	Su	GgIWwg
Pyrola chlorantha green-flower wintergreen	eSP	sW	FL	G	PW	Su	GgIWwg

PLANT LIST	Plant Type	Env. Tol.	Aesthetic Value	Wildlife Value	Flower Color	Bloom Period	Landscape Uses
Pyrola elliptica shinleaf	eSP	s	FL	G	GW	Su	GgI
Pyrola picta white vein wintergreen	eSP	s	FL	G	GWY	Su	GgI
Pyrrocoma recemosa clustered goldenweed	SP	NaS	F	u	Y	Su	gM
Rafinesquia neomexicana New Mexico plumseed	SA	DSs	F	U	PPuW	Sp	BCG
Ranunculus abortivus kidney-leaf buttercup	SP	S	—	GLMmS	Y	SpSu	M
Ranunculus californicus California buttercup	SP	S	F	GLMmS	Y	SpSu	gM
Ranunculus cymbalaria alkali buttercup	SP	NaS	FL	GLMmS	Y	SpF	gMS
Ranunculus fascicularis early buttercup	SP	Ss	F	GLmS	Y	Sp	BgIM
Ranunculus glaberrimus sagebrush buttercup	SP	S	FL	GLMmS	Y	Sp	BgM
Ranunculus hispidus bristly buttercut	SP	Ss	F	U	Y	Sp	BgI
Ranunculus longirostris long-beak water-crowfoot	P	SsW	F	GLMmS W	W	SpSu	Wwg
Ranunculus macranthus large buttercup	MP	FSsW	F	GMmW	Y	Sp	IW
Ranunculus recurvatus blisterwort	SP	s	F	GLMmS	Y	Sp	gI
Ranunculus reptans lesser creeping spearwort	SP	FS	F	GLMmS W	Y	Su	gMS
Rununculus sceleratus cursed buttercup	MAP	SW	F	GLMmS W	Y	SpSu	Wwg
Ratibida columnifera red-spike Mexican-hat	LP	DS	F	BS	Y	SuF	bgM
Ratibida pinnata gray-head Mexican-hat	LP	DS	F	BS	Y	Su	bgM
Redfieldia flexuosa blowout grass	PG	—	—	U	G	Su	—
Reimarochloa oligostachya Florida reimar grass	MPG	DS	—	U	Gr	SpSu	W
Rhexia mariana Maryland meadow-beauty	SP	FSW	F	U	PuR	Su	MW
Rhynchosia americana American snout-bean	PHV	Ss	F	U	Y	SpSuF	B
Rhynchosia tomentosa twining snout-bean	MP	DSs	—	U	O	SpSu	BM
Rhynchospora alba white beak sedge	LPG	Ss	—	GLMSW	W	Su	W
Rhynchospora capillacea needle beak sedge	SPG	FSW	—	GLMSW	G	SuF	W

PLANT LIST	Plant Type	Env. Tol.	Aesthetic Value	Wildlife Value	Flower Color	Bloom Period	Landscape Uses
Rhynchospora colorata narrow-leaf whitetop	SPG	FS	—	GLMSW	G	Su	W
Rhynchospora corniculata short-bristle horned beak sedge	MPG	FNaS W	—	GLMSW	G	SuF	W
Rhynchospora harveyi Harvey's beak sedge	MPG	FSs	—	GMmS W	G	SpSu	BEMW
Rhynchospora inundata narrow-fruit horned beak sedge	SAPG	FS	—	GLMSW	G	Su	W
Rhynchospora megalocarpa sandy-field beak sedge	MPG	DS	—	GLMS	G	Su	M
Rhynchospora microcarpa southern beak sedge	MPG	FSsW	—	GLMSW	G	Su	W
Rhynchospora tracyi Tracy's beak sedge	MPG	FSW	—	GLMSW	G	SuF	W
Rivina humilis rougeplant	LP	FSs	Ff	U	PW	SpF	B
Rorippa teres southern marsh yellowcress	SA	SsW	—	U	Y	WSp	W
Rudbeckia fulgida orange coneflower	MP	Ss	F	BGS	OY	Su	BgM
Rudbeckia hirta black-eyed-Susan	MBP	DS	F	BCS	Y	SuF	BbgM
Rudbeckia laciniata green-head coneflower	LP	FS	F	BS	Y	SuF	bMW
Rudbeckia occidentalis western coneflower	LP	Fs	F	BS	Y	Su	BbIS
Ruellia caroliniensis Carolina wild petunia	MP	Ss	F	GS	B	SpSuF	BbgM
Ruellia drummondiana Drummond's wild petunia	MP	Ss	F	U	L	SuF	BRS
Ruellia humilis fringe-leaf wild petunia	MP	Ss	F	GS	BL	Su	BgM
Ruellia nudiflora violet wild petunia	MP	Ss	F	GS	BPu	SpSuF	BbgM
Rumex maritimus golden dock	SA	FNaS	—	CGLMm SW	G	Su	C
Rumex orbiculatus greater water dock	LP	SW	L	CGLMm SW	G	SuF	BWwg
Rumex verticillatus swamp dock	LP	FSW	—	CGMmS W	BrG	Su	W
Ruppia maritima beaked ditch-grass	AQPG	NaW	—	U	—	WSpSu F	Wwg
Sabatia angularis rose-pink	MBP	DS	F	U	P	SuF	BgM
Sabatia arenicola sand rose-gentian	SA	Ss	F	B	P	SpSu	BbGM
Sabatia campestris Texas-star	SP	S	F	U	Y	SuF	M

PLANT LIST	Plant Type	Env. Tol.	Aesthetic Value	Wildlife Value	Flower Color	Bloom Period	Landscape Uses
Saccharum giganteum giant plume grass	PG	W	—	U	G	Su	W
Sacciolepis striata American glenwood grass	LPG	FSsW	—	U	G	SuF	ESW
Sagittaria calycina hooded arrowhead	P	SsW	FL	LW	W	Su	Wwg
Sagittaria graminea grass-leaf arrowhead	SP	SW	FL	LW	W	SuF	Wwg
Sagittaria lancifolia bull-tongue arrowhead	P	FW	FL	MW	W	SpSuF	Wwg
Sagittaria latifolia duck-potato	P	Ss	FL	LW	W	Su	Wwg
Sagittaria papillosa nipple-bract arrowhead	P	FNaW	FL	MW	W	SpSuF	Wwg
Salicornia bigelovii dwarf saltwort	SA	DNaS	—	W	W	SuF	W
Salicornia maritima sea saltwort	A	NaSW	—	W	G	SuF	W
Salicornia rubra red saltwort	SA	DNaS W	—	W	G	SuF	W
Salicornia virginica woody saltwort	SP	FNaS W	—	W	G	SuF	W
Salvia azurea azure-blue sage	LP	DS	F	BH	B	SuF	bgM
Salvia coccinea blood sage	MAP	Ss	F	BHhS	R	SpSuF	BbgM
Salvia columbariae California sage	SA	S	F	U	BPu	Sp	M
Salvia lyrata lyre-leaf sage	SP	DS	F	U	BPu	SpSu	BgM
Salvia roemeriana cedar sedge	MP	Ss	F	HhS	R	SpSu	Bb
Salvia spathacea hummingbird sage	MA	S	F	GHS	R	Sp	bg
Samolus ebracteatus limewater brookweed	SP	FNaS W	F	U	PW	SpSuF	MW
Samolus valerandi seaside brookweed	SP	SF	—	U	W	SpSu	W
Sanguinaria canadensis bloodroot	SP	s	FL	ANTS	W	Sp	gI
Sanicula arctopoides footsteps-of-spring	SP	S	—	U	Y	Su	GM
Sanicula bipinnatifida purple black-snakeroot	SP	S	L	U	Y	Su	M
Sanicula canadensis Canadian black-snakeroot	MBP	DSs	L	U	W	SpSu	BI
Sanicula marilandica Maryland black-snakeroot	MP	s	L	U	GW	Su	BI

PLANT LIST	Plant Type	Env. Tol.	Aesthetic Value	Wildlife Value	Flower Color	Bloom Period	Landscape Uses
Sanicula odorata clustered black-snakeroot	P	W	—	U	W	SpSu	W
Sarcocornia pacifica Pacific swampfire	SP	NaSW	—	U	—	—	EW
Sarcodes sanguinea snowplant	SP	s	FL	U	R	SpSu	I
Sarracenia flava yellow pitcherplant	MP	SW	FL	U	Y	Sp	Wwg
Sarracenia purpurea purple pitcherplant	SP	SW	FL	U	R	SpSu	W
Sarracenia rubra sweet pitcherplant	SP	FS	FL	U	R	Sp	W
Satureja douglasii Oregon-tea	P	—	—	U	PuW	SpSuF	—
Saururus cernuus lizard's-tail	LP	FSW	FL	U	W	SuF	SWwg
Saxifraga odontoloma streambank saxifrage	MP	FSW	FL	U	Pu	SpSu	SWwg
Saxifraga pensylvanica eastern swamp saxifrage	MP	FSW	F	m	yg	Sp	Wwg
Saxifraga virginiensis early saxifrage	SP	s	FL	U	W	Sp	BgIR
Scheuchzeria palustris rannoch-rush	SPG	Fs	—	U	W	Sp	EW
Schizachne purpurascens false melic grass	MPG	DSs	F	U	—	Su	BgRI
Schizachyrium cirratum Texas false bluestem	MPG	S	B	GMmS	W	SuF	EM
Schizachyrium rhizomatum Florida false bluestem	MPG	S	FL	GMmS	G	Su	M
Schizachyrium sanguineum crimson false bluestem	MPG	DS	FL	GMmS	W	SuF	EM
Schizachyrium scoparium little false bluestem	MPG	DS	AFL	GMmS	W	SuF	BEgM
Schizachyrium tenerum slender false bluestem	MPG	s	FL	U	W	SuF	EI
Schoenocrambe linifolia Salmon River plains-mustard	P	—	—	U	Y	SpSu	—
Schoenus nigricans black bog-rush	SPG	DFS	—	U	Br	SpSu	SW
Schrankia microphylla little-leaf sensitive-briar	SP	DS	FL	U	P	SpF	BM
Scirpus acutus hard-stem bulrush	LPG	FNaSW	L	GLmSW	G	SuF	Wwg
Scirpus americanus chairmaker's bulrush	LPG	FNaSW	L	GLmSW	BrG	SuF	Wwg
Scirpus atrovirens dark-green bulrush	LPG	FSW	DL	GLmSW	G	Su	MW

PLANT LIST	Plant Type	Env. Tol.	Aesthetic Value	Wildlife Value	Flower Color	Bloom Period	Landscape Uses
Scirpus californicus California bulrush	LPG	FNaSW	L	GLmSW	Br	Su	Wwg
Scirpus cespitosus tufted bulrush	MPG	FSW	L	GLmSW	G	Su	Wwg
Scirpus congdonii Congdon's bulrush	MG	FSW	L	GLMsW	G	Su	SW
Scirpus cyperinus cottongrass bulrush	LPG	FSW	DL	GLmSW	G	SuF	SWwg
Scirpus fluviatilis river bulrush	LPG	FSW	L	GLmSW	G	SuF	Wwg
Scirpus heterochaetus pale great bulrush	LPG	FSW	L	GLmSW	G	SuF	Wwg
Scirpus lineatus drooping bulrush	MPG	FS	L	GLmSW	G	Su	MW
Scirpus maritimus saltmarsh bulrush	LPG	FS	L	GLmSW	G	SuF	W
Scirpus microcarpus red-tinge bulrush	MPG	FSW	L	GLmSW	G	Su	MsW
Scirpus pallidus pale bulrush	MPG	SW	L	GLmSW	G	Su	W
Scirpus pungens three-square	MPG	FNaSW	L	GLmSW	Br	SuF	Wwg
Scirpus robustus seaside bulrush	LPG	FNaSW	L	GLmSW	Br	SuF	Wwg
Scirpus tabernaemontani soft-stem bulrush	LPG	FNaSW	DL	GLmSW	BrG	SuF	SWwg
Scleria oligantha little-head nut-rush	MPG	FSs	—	GSW	Br	SpSu	BIM
Scleria triglomerata whip nut-rush	MPG	Ss	—	GSW	Br	SpF	BI
Scleria verticillata low nut-rush	SPG	FSW	—	GSW	Br	SuF	W
Scleropogon brevifolius burro grass	SPG	Ss	FL	M	G	—	BEM
Scorpidium scorpioides moss	m	SW	L	U	X	X	Wwg
Scrophularia lanceolata lance-leaf figwort	LP	Ss	—	U	yg	Su	B
Scrophularia parviflora pineland figwort	P	—	—	U	RG	SuF	—
Scutellaria drummondii Drummond's skullcap	SA	DSs	F	H	BPu	SpSu	BMR
Scutellaria galericulata hooded skullcap	MP	FS	F	U	B	Su	BW
Scutellaria lateriflora mad dog skullcap	MP	FS	F	U	BW	SuF	W
Scutellaria ovata heart-leaf skullcap	MP	s	F	U	B	Su	I

PLANT LIST	Plant Type	Env. Tol.	Aesthetic Value	Wildlife Value	Flower Color	Bloom Period	Landscape Uses
Scutellaria resinosa resin-dot skullcap	SP	DS	F	U	BPu	SpSuF	MR
Sedum niveum Davidson's stonecrop	P	—	—	U	W	Su	—
Sedum nuttallianum yellow stonecrop	SA	DS	FL	BC	Y	SpSu	GgMR
Sedum pulchellum widow's cross	SABP	DSs	FL	U	PW	SpSu	GgR
Sedum rhodanthum queen's-crown	SP	Ss	FL	U	PW	SpSu	GgM
Sedum stenopetalum worm-leaf stonecrop	SP	Ss	F	U	Y	—	Gg
Sedum ternatum woodland stonecrop	SP	DSs	FL	U	W	Sp	EGgIR
Selaginella arenicola sand spike moss	SPm	DS	L	U	X	X	Gg
Senecio ampullaceus Texas ragwort	MA	DS	F	B	Y	Sp	M
Senecio anonymus Small's ragwort	MP	S	FL	B	Y	SpSu	bM
Senecio aureus golden ragwort	SP	FSW	FL	B	Y	SpSu	bW
Senecio canus silver-woolly ragwort	SP	DSs	FL	B	Y	SpSu	BbM
Senecio cynthioides white mountain ragwort	P	—	FL	B	Y	Su	b
Senecio eremophilus desert ragwort	MP	Ss	FL	B	Y	SpSu	BbEm
Senecio flaccidus thread-leaf ragwort	P	—	FL	B	Y	SpSu	b
Senecio glabellus cress-leaf ragwort	MP	FS	F	B	Y	Sp	bSW
Senecio multilobatus lobe-leaf ragwort	SBP	Ss	FL	B	Y	SpSu	Bb
Senecio parryi mountain ragwort	SA	—	—	B	Y	F	—
Senecio pauperculus balsam ragwort	MP	DS	F	B	Y	Su	BbW
Senecio plattensis prairie ragwort	MP	DSs	F	B	Y	SpSu	bMR
Senecio riddellii Riddell's ragwort	MP	S	F	B	Y	SuF	bM
Senecio scorzonella Sierran ragwort	SP	S	FL	BM	Y	—	bM
Senecio spartioides broom-like ragwort	MP	FNaS	FL	B	Y	SuF	BbS
Senecio triangularis arrow-leaf ragwort	LP	FS	FL	B	Y	SuF	bSW

PLANT LIST	Plant Type	Env. Tol.	Aesthetic Value	Wildlife Value	Flower Color	Bloom Period	Landscape Uses
Senna bauhinioides shrubby wild sensitive-plant	SP	S	F	GMm	Y	Sp	M
Senna hirsuta woolly wild sensitive-plant	P	—	—	U	Y	Su	—
Senna roemeriana two-leaved wild sensitive-plant	SP	Ss	L	GmS	Y	Su	BgM
Sesuvium portulacastrum shoreline sea-purslane	SP	DNaS	F	U	PPu	WSpSuF	GgM
Setaria corrugata coastal bristle grass	MAG	FSs	—	GLmS	G	Su	CS
Setaria leucopila strembed bristle grass	MPG	DFS	—	U	G	SuF	MS
Setaria macrostachya plains bristle grass	MPG	S	—	GLmS	G	SuF	EM
Setaria magna giant bristle grass	LAG	FNaSW	—	GLmSW	G	SuF	EW
Setaria ramiseta Rio Grande bristle grass	SPG	DS	—	GLmS	G	SpSuF	EM
Setaria scheelei southwestern bristle grass	MPG	s	DF	U	G	SpSuF	IS
Sibbaldia procumbens creeping-glow-wort	SP	Ss	—	U	Y	Su	BGM
Sibbaldiopsis tridentata shrubby-fivefingers	MP	FSs	—	mS	W	Su	gR
Sicyos angulatus one-seed burr-cucumber	HV	FS	L	U	W	SuF	B
Silene caroliniana sticky catchfly	SP	s	F	HmS	PW	Sp	BGgI
Silene douglasii seabluff catchfly	SP	Ss	F	U	GPW	SpSu	BM
Silene lemmonii Lemmon's catchfly	SP	S	F	mS	W	—	BGgM
Silene parishii Parish's catchfly	SP	Ss	F	mS	WY	—	BGgI
Silene regia royal catchfly	MP	DSs	F	HS	R	Su	BbgM
Silene stellata widow's-frill	MP	SD	FL	BmS	W	SuF	BbM
Silene verecunda San Francisco catchfly	P	S	G	mS	P	—	gM
Silene virginica fire-pink	SP	s	F	H	R	SpSu	BgI
Silphium asteriscus starry rosinweed	LP	DSs	F	BGS	Y	Su	Bbg
Silphium compositum kidney-leaf rosinweed	LP	DS	F	BS	Y	SuF	bM
Silphium integrifolium entire-leaf rosinweed	LP	DS	F	BS	Y	Su	bM

PLANT LIST	Plant Type	Env. Tol.	Aesthetic Value	Wildlife Value	Flower Color	Bloom Period	Landscape Uses
Silphium laciniatum compassplant	LP	DS	FL	BS	Y	Su	bM
Silphium radula rough stem rosinweed	P	DS	F	BS	Y	Su	—
Silphium terebinthinaceum prairie rosinweed	LP	DS	FL	BS	Y	Su	bM
Simsia calva awnless bush-sunflower	SP	S	F	U	Y	SpSuF	BM
Siphonoglossa pilosella hairy tubetongue	SP	DFSs	F	U	BPuW	SpSuF	BMS
Sisyrinchium albidum white blue-eyed-grass	SP	DS	F	U	VW	Sp	BgM
Sisyrinchium angustifolium narrow-leaf blue-eyed-grass	SP	Ss	FL	U	B	Sp	gM
Sisyrinchium bellum California blue-eyed-grass	SP	S	FL	U	B	Sp	gM
Sisyrinchium douglasii grasswindows	SP	DS	F	U	PuW	Sp	BM
Sium suave hemlock water-parsnip	LP	FSW	F	U	W	Su	W
Smilax ecirrata upright carrion-flower	HPV	s	—	MS	G	Sp	I
Smilax herbacea smooth carrion-flower	HPV	s	—	MS	G	Sp	I
Solanum bahamense Bahama nightshade	P	—	—	U	BW	WSpSuF	—
Solanum elaeagnifolium silver-leaf nightshade	MP	DSs	—	GS	BPuW	SpSuF	BM
Solanum xantii chaparral nightshade	SP	DS	F	GLmSW	B	—	GgM
Solidago bicolor white goldenrod	MP	DS	F	BGLMmS	W	F	BgIR
Solidago buckleyi Buckley's goldenrod	MP	Ss	F	BCS	Y	F	BbI
Solidago caesia wreath goldenrod	MP	s	F	BGLMmS	Y	F	BbI
Solidago californica northern California goldenrod	MP	DS	F	GLMmS	Y	F	M
Solidago canadensis Canadian goldenrod	LP	FS	F	BGLMmS	Y	SuF	bMW
Solidago flexicaulis zigzag goldenrod	MP	s	F	BGLMmS	Y	SuF	bI
Solidago gigantea late goldenrod	LP	S	F	BGLMmS	Y	SuF	Bb
Solidago glomerata clustered goldenrod	MP	FS	F	GLMmS	Y	F	W
Solidago hispida hairy goldenrod	MP	S	F	BGLMmS	Y	SuF	bM

PLANT LIST	Plant Type	Env. Tol.	Aesthetic Value	Wildlife Value	Flower Color	Bloom Period	Landscape Uses
Solidago juncea early goldenrod	MP	DSs	F	BGLMmS	Y	SuF	BbM
Solidago macrophylla large-leaf goldenrod	MP	s	F	BGLMmS	Y	SuF	Bb
Solidago missouriensis Missouri goldenrod	MP	S	F	BGLMmS	Y	SpF	BbM
Solidago mollis velvet goldenrod	SP	DS	F	BGLMmS	Y	SuF	bM
Solidago multiradiata Rocky Mountain goldenrod	MP	S	F	BGLMmS	Y	SuF	bM
Solidago nemoralis gray goldenrod	SP	S	F	BGLMmS	Y	SuF	bM
Solidago odora anise-scented goldenrod	MP	S	F	BGLMmS	Y	SuF	bM
Solidago ohioensis Ohio goldenrod	MP	FS	F	BGLMmS	Y	SuF	bMW
Solidago patula round-leaf goldenrod	MP	FS	F	BGLMmS	Y	F	bMW
Solidago ptarmicoides prairie goldenrod	MP	DS	F	BGLMmS	Y	F	bM
Solidago rigida hard-leaf goldenrod	LP	DS	F	BGLMmS	Y	SuF	bM
Solidago rugosa wrinkle-leaf goldenrod	MP	FSW	F	BGMmS	Y	F	bMW
Solidago sempervirens seaside goldenrod	LP	FNaS	F	BGLMmS	Y	SuF	bW
Solidago spathulata coastal-dune goldenrod	SP	Ss	F	BGLMmS	Y	F	BbG
Solidago speciosa showy goldenrod	LP	DS	F	BGLMmS	Y	SuF	BbM
Solidago uliginosa bog goldenrod	LP	FS	F	BGLMmS	Y	SuF	bMW
Solidago velutina three-nerve goldenrod	P	—	F	BGLMmS	Y	SuF	—
Solidago wrightii Wright's goldenrod	MP	DSs	F	BGLMmS	Y	SuF	BbM
Sorghastrum nutans yellow Indian grass	LPG	DFS	L	L	Y	SuF	M
Sparganium americanum American burr-reed	MPG	SW	L	LmSW	G	SpSu	Wwg
Sparganium eurycarpum broad-fruit burr-reed	LP	FSs	DL	LW	G	Su	SWwg
Spartina alterniflora saltwater cord grass	LPG	FNaSW	L	LMSW	G	SuF	W
Spartina bakeri bunch cord grass	LPG	FS	L	LMSW	G	WSpF	W
Spartina cynosuroides big cord grass	LG	FNaSW	L	LMSW	G	SuF	Wwg

PLANT LIST	Plant Type	Env. Tol.	Aesthetic Value	Wildlife Value	Flower Color	Bloom Period	Landscape Uses
Spartina foliosa California cord grass	MPG	FNaSW	L	MmSW	G	SuF	Wwg
Spartina gracilis alkali cord grass	MG	FS	FL	LMSW	G	SuF	Wwg
Spartina patens salt-meadow cord grass	MG	FNaSW	L	LMSW	G	SuF	Wwg
Spartina pectinata freshwater cord grass	LG	FNaSW	L	LMSW	G	SuF	W
Spartina spartinae gulf cord grass	LG	FNaSW	L	LMSW	G	SuF	W
Spergularia salina sandspurrey	SA	DFNaSW	—	U	PuW	SpSu	CW
Sphaeralcea angustifolia copper globe-mallow	SP	DS	DF	U	LPuR	WSpSuF	GgRM
Sphaeralcea coccinea scarlet globe-mallow	SP	DS	DF	U	LR	SpSu	GgM
Sphaeralcea emoryi Emory's globe-mallow	P	—	DF	U	O	SpSuF	—
Sphaeralcea fendleri thicket globe-mallow	SP	DS	DF	U	LPuR	SpSuF	GgMR
Sphaeralcea grossulariifolia currant-leaf globe-mallow	MP	Ss	FL	U	OP	—	BgM
Sphaeralcea incana soft globe-mallow	LP	DS	F	U	P	SuF	gMR
Sphaeralcea leptophylla scaly globe-mallow	SP	Ss	DF	U	R	SpSu	BGgM
Sphagnum angustifolim moss	m	SsW	L	mR	X	X	W
Sphagnum capillifolium moss	m	FSs	L	mR	X	X	SW
Sphagnum centrale moss	m	FSs	L	GW	X	X	IW
Sphagnum contortum moss	m	FSsW	L	mR	X	X	WM
Sphagnum cuspidatum moss	m	FSW	L	mR	X	X	Wwg
Sphagnum fallax moss	m	FSW	L	mR	X	X	W
Sphagnum fimbriatum moss	m	FSsW	L	mR	X	X	W
Sphagnum fuscum moss	m	FSsW	L	mR	X	X	W
Sphagnum magellanicum moss	m	FSsW	L	mR	X	X	W
Sphagnum majus moss	m	FSsW	L	mR	X	X	Wwg
Sphagnum nemoreum moss	m	FSsW	L	mR	X	X	W

PLANT LIST	Plant Type	Env. Tol.	Aesthetic Value	Wildlife Value	Flower Color	Bloom Period	Landscape Uses
Sphagnum papillosum moss	m	FSsW	L	mR	X	X	W
Sphagnum recurvum moss	m	FSsW	L	mR	X	X	BW
Sphagnum rubellum moss	m	FSsW	L	mR	X	X	W
Sphagnum russowii moss	m	FSsW	L	mR	X	X	BW
Sphagnum subsecundum moss	m	FSsW	L	mR	X	X	MWwg
Sphagnum teres moss	m	FSsW	L	mR	X	X	Wwg
Sphagnum warnstorfii moss	m	FSsW	L	mR	X	X	BW
Sphenosciadium capitellatum swamp whiteheads	LP	FSW	F	U	W	Su	MW
Spiranthes cernua white nodding ladies'-tresses	SP	FS	F	M	W	SuF	gMW
Spiranthes lucida shining ladies'-tresses	SP	S	F	M	Y	Su	BgM
Spiranthes romanzoffiana hooded ladies'-tresses	SP	FSsW	F	M	W	SuF	gMW
Sporobolus airoides alkali-sacaton	MPG	FNaS	FL	GMmS	G	SuF	EM
Sporobolus asper tall dropseed	MPG	S	L	GMmS	G	SuF	EM
Sporobolus contractus narrow-spike dropseed	MPG	DFNaSs	L	GMmS	G	SuF	BM
Sporobolus cryptandrus sand dropseed	MPG	DS	L	GMmS	G	SuF	M
Sporobolus flexuosus mesa dropseed	MPG	S	L	GMmS	G	SuF	M
Sporobolus giganteus giant dropseed	LPG	DSs	L	GMmS	G	Su	BEM
Sporobolus heterolepis prairie dropseed	MPG	DS	L	GMmS	G	SuF	EM
Sporobolus indicus smut grass	MPG	DS	L	GMmS	G	Su	EM
Sporobolus junceus wire grass	MPG	DSs	L	GMmS	G	SuF	BEM
Sporobolus pyramidatus whorled dropseed	MPG	NaS	—	GMmS	G	SuF	EM
Sporobolus silveanus Silvens' dropseed	MPG	Ss	L	GMmS	G	SuF	BE
Sporobolus vaginiflorus poverty dropseed	SAG	DS	L	GMmS	G	SuF	EM
Sporobolus virginicus seashore dropseed	SPG	FNaS	L	GMmS	G	SuF	ESW

PLANT LIST	Plant Type	Env. Tol.	Aesthetic Value	Wildlife Value	Flower Color	Bloom Period	Landscape Uses
Sporobolus wrightii Wright's dropseed	MPG	DNaSs	FL	GMmS	G	SuF	BEM
Stachys drummondii Drummond's hedge nettle	MAB	Ss	F	U	LP	WSpSu	B
Stachys mexicana Mexican hedge-nettle	P	W	—	U	Pu	Su	W
Stachys palustris woundwort	SP	S	F	U	Pu	Su	M
Stachys tenuifolia smooth hedge-nettle	LP	FS	F	U	P	SuF	W
Stellaria nitens shiny starwort	SA	FSs	—	m	W	Su	BM
Stellaria prostrata prostrate starwort	SA	Fs	—	U	W	SpSuF	GIS
Stellaria pubera great chickweed	SP	s	—	GMmS	W	Sp	BI
Stenosiphon linifolius false gaura	LP	DS	—	U	W	SuF	R
Stenotaphrum secundatum St. Augustine grass	SPG	FS	—	U	R	SuF	MS
Stenotus acaulis stemless mock goldenweed	P	—	—	U	Y	SpSu	—
Stephanomeria pauciflora brown-plume wire-lettuce	SP	DNaSs	—	U	PW	SuF	BEM
Stillingia sylvatica queen's-delight	MP	S	L	G	Y	SpSu	B
Stillingia texana Texas toothleaf	SP	S	—	G	G	Sp	BM
Stipa comata needle-and-thread	SPG	DS	F	MmS	G	Sp	GM
Stipa coronata giant needle grass	LPG	DS	F	MmS	Pu	SpSu	M
Stipa lettermanii Letterman's needle grass	SPG	DS	—	LMmS	G	Su	GM
Stipa nelsonii Nelson's needle grass	P	—	—	MmS	G	Su	—
Stipa neomexicana New Mexico needle grass	MPG	DSs	—	MmS	G	SuF	BM
Stipa occidentalis western needle grass	SPG	DS	F	MmS	G	Su	BEM
Stipa pinetorum pine-forest needle grass	SPG	Ss	—	MmS	G	Su	BE
Stipa spartea porcupine grass	MPG	DS	F	LMmS	G	Sp	EM
Stipa speciosa desert needle grass	SPG	DS	F	MmS	G	Sp	EGM
Stipa thurberiana Thurber's needle grass	SPG	DS	F	MmS	G	Su	EM

PLANT LIST	Plant Type	Env. Tol.	Aesthetic Value	Wildlife Value	Flower Color	Bloom Period	Landscape Uses
Stipulicida setacea pineland scaly-pink	SP	Ss	F	U	—	SpSuF	BgM
Streptanthus bernardinus Laguna Mountain jewelflower	MP	Ss	F	U	PuW	—	Bg
Streptopus amplexifolius clasping twistedstalk	MP	s	FL	U	GW	SpSu	gI
Streptopus roseus rosy twistedstalk	MP	s	FL	U	P	SpSu	gI
Strophostyles helvula trailing fuzzy-bean	HVA	FS	F	G	PPu	SuF	BEGS
Strophostyles leiosperma slick-seed fuzzy-bean	HVA	DS	F	G	PPu	SuF	BEG
Strophostyles umbellata pink fuzzy-bean	HVP	S	F	G	P	SuF	BG
Stylisma pickeringii Pickering's dawnflower	PHV	S	F	U	W	SuF	gM
Stylocline micropoides woolly-head neststraw	SA	DS	B	U	U	Sp	—
Stylophorum diphyllum celandine-poppy	SP	s	FL	U	Y	Sp	BgI
Stylosanthes biflora side-beak pencil-flower	SP	DS	F	U	Y	SpF	gRM
Suaeda californica broom seepweed	MP	FNaSW	F	U		F	W
Suaeda linearis annual seepweed	MA	FNaSW	F	U	—	SuF	SW
Suaeda maritima herbaceous seepweed	SA	FNaS	F	U	W	SuF	—
Symplocarpus foetidus skunk-cabbage	SP	SW	FL	GW	GPu	WSp	W
Synthyris reniformis snowqueen	P	—	—	U	BPu	Sp	—
Talinum parviflorum sunbright	SP	DS	FL	U	PW	Su	gR
Talinum teretifolium quill fameflower	SP	DS	FL	U	PPu	Su	gR
Tellima grandiflora fragrant fringecup	MP	s	FL	U	RW	SP	EgI
Tephrosia lindheimeri Lindheimer's hoary-pea	MP	S	FL	BG	Pu	SpSuF	EGM
Tephrosia spicata spiked hoary-pea	SP	S	FL	BG	WP	SpSu	EBG
Tephrosia virginiana goat's-rue	SP	S	FL	BG	PY	SpSu	EBG
Tetragonotheca ludoviciana Louisiana neveray	LP	S	F	U	Y	SuF	gI
Tetraneuris acaulis stemless four-nerve-daisy	SP	DS	F	B	Y	SpSu	MR

PLANT LIST	Plant Type	Env. Tol.	Aesthetic Value	Wildlife Value	Flower Color	Bloom Period	Landscape Uses
Teucrium canadense American germander	MP	FSs	F	U	P	SuF	BS
Thalia geniculata bent alligator-flag	AQP	FSW	L	U	W	SuF	Wwg
Thalictrum clavatum mountain meadow-rue	MP	FSs	L	B	W	SpSu	BlS
Thalictrum dasycarpum purple meadow-rue	LP	FS	FL	B	Wyg	Su	BgS
Thalictrum dioicum early meadow-rue	LP	Ss	FL	B	W	Sp	Bb
Thalictrum fendleri Fendler's meadow-rue	MP	Ss	FL	B	W	SpSu	Bb
Thalictrum occidentale western meadow-rue	MP	s	FL	B	W	Su	BbI
Thalictrum pubescens king-of-the-meadow	LP	Fs	FL	B	W	Su	BbIW
Thalictrum thalictroides rue-anemone	SP	s	FL	B	PW	Sp	BbI
Thamnosma texanum rue-of-the-mountains	MP	S	FL	U	PuY	SpF	gM
Thaspium trifoliatum purple meadow-parsnip	MP	FSs	F	B	Y	SpSu	BbMW
Thelesperma megapotamicum Hopi-tea	MP	S	F	U	Y	SpSu	M
Thelesperma nuecense Rio Grand greenthread	MA	S	F	B	Y	SpSuF	C
Thelesperma simplicifolium slender greenthread	MP	DS	F	U	Y	Su	EgM
Thelespermia filifolium stiff greenthread	MA	S	F	U	Y	SpSu	CgM
Thelypodiopsis elegans westwater tumble-mustard	MAB	Ss	F	U	LPW	—	BC
Thelypodium sagittatum arrowhead thelypody	SB	NaS	L	U	PuW	—	GM
Thelypteris noveboracensis New York fern	MP	Fs	L	M	X	X	BgIS
Thelypteris palustris eastern marsh fern	MP	FSsW	L	M	X	X	BgW
Thermopsis rhombifolia prairie golden-banner	SP	Ss	F	U	Y	—	BEGg
Thymophylla acerosa American pricklyleaf	SP	Ss	F	U	Y	—	BGg
Thymophylla pentachaeta five-needle pricklyleaf	SP	Ss	F	U	Y	—	BGg
Tiarella cordifolia heart-leaf foamflower	SP	s	FL	G	W	SpSu	GgI
Tiarella trifoliata three-leaf foamflower	SP	s	FL	G	W	SpSu	GgI

PLANT LIST	Plant Type	Env. Tol.	Aesthetic Value	Wildlife Value	Flower Color	Bloom Period	Landscape Uses
Tinantia anomala widow's-tears	MA	Ss	F	U	BL	SpSu	BCR
Tipularia discolor crippled-cranefly	SP	s	FL	U	G	Su	GgI
Tiquilia canescens woody crinklemat	SP	S	F	U	P	SpSu	M
Tolmiea menziesii piggyback-plant	MP	Ss	L	U	BrGPu	—	BgIS
Tomenthypnum nitens moss	m	FSW	—	GMmW	X	X	W
Tortula brevipes moss	m	—	—	GMmW	X	X	—
Tortula princeps moss	m	—	—	GMmW	X	X	—
Tortula ruralis moss	m	DS	L	GMmW	X	X	ERS
Trachypogon secundus one-sided crinkle-awn grass	MPG	Ss	—	U	G	SuF	BEM
Tradescantia edwardsiana plateau spiderwort	MP	s	F	B	PW	Sp	gI
Tradescantia gigantea giant spiderwort	MP	S	F	U	BP	Sp	gM
Tradescantia occidentalis prairie spiderwort	SP	DS	F	U	BP	SpSu	gM
Tradescantia ohiensis bluejacket	SP	S	LF	U	BP	Su	gM
Tradescantia virginiana Virginia spiderwort	SP	Ss	FL	U	B	SpSu	BgI
Tragia ramosa branched noseburn	SP	Ss	—	U	G	SpSuF	BP
Tragia urticifolia nettle-leaf noseburn	MP	DS	—	U	—	Su	BM
Triadenum virginicum Virginia marsh-St. John's-wort	MP	3W	L	W	P	Su	W
Trichocolea tomentella leafy liverwort	m	—	—	U	X	X	—
Trichoneura elegans Silveus' grass	MAG	DS	—	U	G	SpF	EM
Trichoptilium incisum yellowdome	SA	DS	L	U	W	Su	M
Trichostema dichotomum forked bluecurls	SA	DS	F	G	BP	SuF	CgM
Tridens eragrostoides love fluff grass	MPG	Ss	—	U	G	SpSuF	E
Tridens flavus tall redtop	LPG	DSs	DF	U	GPu	SuF	BEM
Tridens muticus awnless fluff grass	SPG	DS	—	U	GPu	SuF	M

PLANT LIST	Plant Type	Env. Tol.	Aesthetic Value	Wildlife Value	Flower Color	Bloom Period	Landscape Uses
Tridens strictus long-spike fluff grass	MG	Ss	—	U	Pu	Su	BIW
Trientalis borealis American starflower	SP	sW	F	U	W	Sp	gI
Trifolium albopurpureum rancheria clover	SP	DS	F	GLMmS W	Pu	Sp	GM
Trifolium barbigerum bearded clover	SP	S	FL	GLMmS W	P	Sp	GM
Trifolium cyathiferum bowl clover	SP	DS	FL	GLMmS W	PW	SpSu	GM
Trifolium depauperatum balloon sack clover	MP	S	FL	GLMmS W	WPY	Sp	M
Trifolium fucatum sour clover	MP	FNaS	F	GLMmS W	PW	Sp	MS
Trifolium gracilentum pin-point clover	SP	S	FL	GLMmS W	P	Sp	GM
Trifolium gymnocarpon holly-leaf clover	SP	Ss	F	GLMmS W	LPPu	Su	BGM
Trifolium microdon valparaiso clover	SP	S	L	GLMmS W	PW	Sp	GM
Trifolium monanthum mountain carpet clover	SP	FS	FL	GLMmS W	PW	Sp	GMS
Trifolium olivaceum olive clover	SP	S	FL	GLMmS W	PuW	Sp	GM
Trifolium variegatum white-tip clover	SP	FSs	FL	GLMmS W	Pu	Su	MS
Triglochin concinnum slender arrow-grass	SPG	NaSW	—	W	G	SpSu	W
Triglochin maritimum seaside arrow-grass	SPG	FNaS W	—	W	G	SpSu	W
Triglochin palustre marsh arrow-grass	SPG	FNaS W	—	W	G	SpSu	SW
Trillium catesbaei bashful wakerobin	SP	s	FL	U	P	Sp	gI
Trillium cernuum whip-poor-will-flower	SP	Fs	F	U	W	SpSu	gIW
Trillium cuneatum little-sweet-Betsy	SP	s	F	U	R	Sp	gI
Trillium erectum stinking-Benjamin	SP	s	F	U	R	Sp	gI
Trillium flexipes nodding wakerobin	SP	s	F	U	W	SpSu	gI
Trillium grandiflorum large-flower wakerobin	SP	s	F	U	W	Sp	gI
Trillium luteum yellow wakerobin	SP	s	FL	U	Y	Sp	gI
Trillium nivale dwarf white wakerobin	SP	s	F	U	W	Sp	gI

PLANT LIST	Plant Type	Env. Tol.	Aesthetic Value	Wildlife Value	Flower Color	Bloom Period	Landscape Uses
Trillium ovatum western wakerobin	SP	s	F	U	RW	Sp	gI
Trillium recurvatum bloody-butcher	SP	s	F	U	R	Sp	gI
Trillium sessile toadshade	SP	s	FL	U	Br	SpSu	gI
Trillium undulatum painted wakerobin	SP	s	F	U	W	Sp	gI
Triplasis purpurea purple sand grass	MPG	DS	B	S	G	SuF	BEM
Tripsacum dactyloides eastern mock grama	LPG	FS	—	U	G	SpF	SW
Trisetum spicatum narrow false oat	SPG	S	F	U	Pu	Su	M
Triteleia grandiflora large-flower triplet-lily	MP	Ss	F	U	B	SpSu	B
Trollius laxus American globeflower	SP	FS	F	U	Y	SpSu	gW
Typha angustifolia narrow-leaf cat-tail	LPG	FSW	FfL	LW	Br	Su	Wwg
Typha domingensis southern cat-tail	LPG	SF	FfL	LW	Br	SpSu	Wwg
Typha latifolia broad-leaf cat-tail	LPG	FSW	FfL	LW	Br	Su	Wwg
Uniola paniculata sea-oats	LG	S	DFfL	U	G	Su	ECS
Urtica chamaedryoides heart-leaf nettle	MA	s	—	U	G	SpSu	CI
Urtica dioica stinging nettle	MP	DS	—	U	G	SuF	MP
Utricularia cornuta horned bladderwort	AQ	W	—	U	Y	Su	Wwg
Utricularia foliosa leafy bladderwort	AQP	SW		U	Y	WSpSuF	Wwg
Utricularia minor lesser bladderwort	AQP	Ss	FL	U	Y	Su	Wwg
Utricularia subulata zigzag bladderwort	AQP	SW	F	U	Y	SpF	Wwg
Uvularia grandiflora large-flower bellwort	SP	Ss	FL	U	Y	Sp	gI
Uvularia perfoliata perfoliate bellwort	SP	s	FL	U	Y	Sp	gI
Uvularia puberula mountain bellwort	SP	s	FL	U	Y	Sp	BgI
Uvularia sessilifolia sessile-leaf bellwort	MP	s	FL	U	Y	Sp	BgI
Valeriana arizonica Arizona valerian	SP	Ss	FL	U	PW	Su	BgM

PLANT LIST	Plant Type	Env. Tol.	Aesthetic Value	Wildlife Value	Flower Color	Bloom Period	Landscape Uses
Valeriana occidentalis small-flower valerian	MP	Ss	—	U	W	SpSu	BM
Valeriana sitchensis Sitka valerian	MP	S	F	U	W	Su	gM
Valerianella stenocarpa narrow-cell cornsalad	SA	S	—	U	W	Sp	MRS
Valerianella texana Edwards plateau cornsalad	SA	FSs	—	U	W	Sp	BS
Vancouveria hexandra white inside-out-flower	SP	Ss	FL	U	W	SpSu	BGI
Vaseychloa multinervosa Texas grass	MPG	s	—	U	G	SpSuF	EI
Veratrum californicum California false hellebore	LP	FSsW	FL	U	GW	Su	Wwg
Veratrum fimbriatum fringed false hellebore	LP	S	F	U	GW	Su	BgM
Veratrum viride American false hellebore	LP	SsW	F	U	W	Su	Wwg
Verbena bonariensis purple-top vervain	LP	DS	F	LS	Pu	Su	gM
Verbena halei Texas vervain	LP	Ss	F	MS	BPu	SpSuF	gM
Verbena hastata simpler's-joy	LP	FS	F	LSW	B	SuF	gMW
Verbena stricta hoary vervain	MP	S	F	mS	BPu	Su	BgM
Verbesina alternifolia wingstem	LP	Fs	F	B	Y	SuF	MS
Verbesina chapmanii Chapman's crownbeard	MP	FS	F	B	Y	Su	bMW
Verbesina encelioides shrubby seepweed	SA	DS	F	GMS	Y	SpSuF	gMS
Verbesina microptera Texas crownbeard	LP	S	F	BGmS	WY	SuF	bM
Verbesina virginica white crownbeard	LP	FSs	F	B	W	SuF	BMS
Vernonia baldwinii western ironweed	LP	DS	F	B	PuW	SuF	M
Vernonia fasciculata prairie ironweed	LP	DS	F	B	Pu	SuF	M
Vernonia gigantea grant ironweed	LP	DS	F	B	Pu	Su	M
Vernonia texana Texas ironweed	MP	S	F	B	Pu	Su	bM
Veronica americana American-brooklime	SP	FsW	F	h	B	SpSu	W
Veronica peregrina neckweed	SP	FS	F	h	W	SpSu	MW

PLANT LIST	Plant Type	Env. Tol.	Aesthetic Value	Wildlife Value	Flower Color	Bloom Period	Landscape Uses
Veronicastrum virginicum culver's-root	MP	DS	F	H	PW	Su	bM
Vicia americana American purple vetch	MP	FS	F	BCGSm	Pu	SpSu	bMS
Vigna luteola piedmont cow-pea	SP	SW	F	U	Y	SpSuF	W
Viola adunca hook-spur violet	SP	Ss	FL	CGLmS	Pu	SpSu	BGgI
Viola affinis sand violet	SP	FSs	FL	CGLmS	W	Sp	BGgIMS
Viola beckwithii western pansy	SP	Ss	FL	CGLmS	RPu	SpSu	BGgM
Viola blanda sweet white violet	SP	s	FL	CGLmS	W	Sp	bGgI
Viola canadensis Canadian white violet	SP	s	FL	CGLmS	W	Sp	BGgI
Viola conspersa American dog violet	SP	Ss	F	CGLmS	Pu	SpSu	BGgI
Viola cucullata marsh blue violet	SP	FS	FL	CGLmS	B	Sp	Wwg
Viola glabella pioneer violet	SP	Fs	FL	CGLmS	Y	SpSu	GgIS
Viola hastata halberd-leaf yellow violet	SP	s	F	GmS	Y	Sp	gI
Viola lanceolata bog white violet	SP	FS	FL	CGLmS	W	Sp	GgSWwg
Viola lobata moose-horn violet	SP	S	FL	GLmS	Y	SpSu	BGg
Viola macloskeyi smooth white violet	SP	FsW	FL	GmMS	W	SpSu	GgW
Viola missouriensis Missouri violet	SP	Fs	L	GCmS	B	Sp	EgIS
Viola nephrophylla northern bog violet	SP	FW	FL	GMmS	B	SpSu	GWwg
Viola palmata early blue violet	SP	s	FL	CGLmS	Pu	Sp	BGgI
Viola pedata bird-foot violet	SP	SD	FL	BCGhLmS	B	Sp	GgbR
Viola pedatifida crow-foot violet	SP	S	FL	CGLmS	Pu	Sp	GgM
Viola pubescens downy yellow violet	SP	s	FL	CGLmS	Y	Sp	GgI
Viola purpurea goose-foot yellow violet	SP	Ss	FL	GLmS	Y	SpSu	BGgM
Viola rostrata long-spur violet	SP	s	FL	GmMS	L	Sp	BGgI
Viola rotundifolia round-leaf yellow violet	SP	s	FL	CGLmS	Y	Sp	BGgI

PLANT LIST	Plant Type	Env. Tol.	Aesthetic Value	Wildlife Value	Flower Color	Bloom Period	Landscape Uses
Viola sempervirens redwood violet	SP	s	FL	CGLmS	Y	Sp	GgI
Viola sororia hooded blue violet	SP	s	FL	CGLmS	Pu	SpSu	GgI
Viola umbraticola ponderosa violet	SP	—	FL	CGLmS	—	—	GgI
Vulpia microstachys small six-weeks grass	SAG	S	—	GLMmS	G	Su	EM
Vulpia myuros rat-tail six-weeks grass	SPG	S	—	MS	G	SuF	M
Vulpia octoflora eight-flower six-weeks grass	SAG	S	FL	GLMmS	G	Sp	EM
Waldsteinia fragarioides Appalachian barren-strawberry	SP	s	F	GLMmS	Y	Sp	BG
Wedelia hispida hairy creeping-oxeye	P	—	—	U	Y	SuF	—
Whipplea modesta modesty	SP	Ss	—	U	W	SpSu	B
Woodsia oregana Oregon cliff fern	SP	s	L	GLM	X	X	GI
Woodsia scopulina Rocky Mountain cliff fern	SP	s	L	GLM	X	X	GI
Woodwardia areolata netted chain fern	MP	SsW	L	GLM	X	X	gIW
Woodwardia virginica Virginian chain fern	MP	SsW	L	GLM	X	X	gIW
Wyethia amplexicaulis northern mule's-ears	SP	S	FL	Gm	Y	SpSu	GM
Wyethia mollis wooly mule's-ears	MP	DS	FL	Gm	Y	Su	BM
Xanthisma texanum Texas sleepy-daisy	MA	DS	F	—	Y	SpSuF	gM
Xerophyllum asphodeloides eastern turkeybeard	MP	Ss	F	U	W	Su	BI
Xerophyllum tenax western turkeybeard	MP	DS	—	U	W	Su	BM
Xylorhiza glabriuscula smooth woody-aster	SP	NaS	F	U	PW	Su	gM
Xyris montana northern yellow-eye-grass	SP	FSW	L	U	Y	SuF	W
Zephyranthes atamasca atamasco-lily	SP	Ss	F	U	W	Sp	BgI
Zigadenus elegans mountain deathcamas	MP	S	F	U	GWY	Su	gM
Zigadenus paniculatus sand-corn	MP	Ss	F	U	WY	Su	B
Zigadenus venenosus meadow deathcamas	MP	FSs	F	U	WY	Su	BgMS

PLANT LIST	Plant Type	Env. Tol.	Aesthetic Value	Wildlife Value	Flower Color	Bloom Period	Landscape Uses
Zinnia acerosa white zinnia	SP	DS	F	BS	W	SuF	bgM
Zinnia grandiflora little golden zinnia	SP	DS	F	BS	GRY	SuSpF	bgM
Zizania aquatica Indian wild rice	MA	SW	L	SW	G	Su	W
Zizaniopsis miliacea marsh-millet	MG	FS	L	W	—	Su	SW
Zizia aptera heart-leaf alexanders	SP	DSs	F	U	Y	SpSu	BgI

APPENDIX C

Nursery Sources for Native Plants and Seeds

Introduction

The nurseries in this appendix responded to a survey that was sent to over 500 nurseries throughout the United States. The addresses were gathered from a number of published sources that gave the address of nurseries interested in native plants and seeds or listed a nursery as a general reference for information. We received over 220 responses. The survey asked what percent of the species offered are native and to which region are they native. This information can be found listed under each nursery in this appendix. We believe that the percent of native stock offered will grow as the demand grows. An attempt was made to include only sources that sell nursery–propagated material.

Each source is listed by state in alphabetical order. All listings include an address and telephone number. The italicized type corresponds to a question on the survey followed by the nursery's respective answer. If there was no response to a question on the survey, the code N/A indicates this or, in some cases, a nursery catalog was sent without the survey. Every effort was made to provide accurate and complete information.

This list is not inclusive of all native plant nurseries or of all nurseries offering native species. The intention is to help you get in touch with sources offering native plant material or information. Use Appendix A to identify species native to your region. Appendix B, the plant matrices, will give you an idea of native species that will best suit your landscaping needs. Many of the nurseries listed in Appendix C offer consultation services. Use this list to get started on naturalizing your area, whether through restoration or natural landscaping. Additional sources of information can be found in the National Wildflower Research Center's *Widlflower Handbook*.

Alabama

Byers Nursery Co., Inc.
6001 Moores Mill Road
Huntsville, AL 35811 (205) 859-0690
Sales type: wholesale
Type of stock: trees, shrubs, seeds
Native stock: 50% +
Regional focus: southeastern U.S.
Services: N/A
Comments: We offer excellent landscape trees and shrubs.

Arkansas

Holland Wildflower Farm
290 O'Neal Lane
Elkins, AR 72727 (501) 643-2622
Sales type: mail-order, retail
Type of stock: trees, shrubs, herbaceous plants, seeds,
seed mixes
Native stock: 80%
Regional focus: southeastern U.S.
Services: landscaping and custom design of flower beds.
Comments: We are beginning to use native trees and
shrubs.

Pittman Wholesale Nursery
P.O. Box 606
Magnolia, AR 71753 1-800-553-6661
Sales type: wholesale
Type of stock: trees, shrubs, herbaceous plants
Native stock: 25%
Regional focus: N/A
Services: N/A
Comments: We offer a large selection of perennials.

Arizona

Desert Enterprises
P.O. Box 23
Morristown, AZ 85342 (602) 388-2448
Sales type: retail, wholesale
Type of stock: trees, shrubs, herbaceous plants, seeds,
seed mixes
Native stock: 100%
Regional focus: Southwest
Services: habitat restoration, reclamation, and
revegetation
Comments: We provide seeds only of plants (cacti, trees,
wildflowers) native to southwestern U.S. and Sonora,
Mexico.

Desert Tree Farm
2744 E. Utopia
Phoenix, AZ 85024 (602) 992-0400
Sales type: wholesale
Type of stock: trees, shrubs, herbaceous plants
Native stock: 50%
Regional focus: Arizona, New Mexico, Texas, deserts of
the southwest
Services: N/A
Comments: We offer containerized desert trees, shrubs,
and groundcovers.

Hildegard Nase
2540 E. Ross Place
Tucson, AZ 85716 (602) 326-1651
Sales type: wholesale
Type of stock: seeds
Native stock: 80%
Regional focus: North and South America, Africa
Services: N/A
Comments: We specialize in cacti and succulent seeds
and other drought resisting plants.

Silver Bell Nursery
2730 N. Silverbell Road
Tucson, AZ 85745 (602) 622-3894
Sales type: retail, wholesale
Type of stock: trees, shrubs, herbaceous plants, seeds,
seed mixes
Native stock: 50% +
Regional focus: southwest U.S. and Sonoran desert
Services: landscaping and make artificial rocks
Comments: We propagate a large variety of native and
non-native groundcovers, shrubs, and trees.

Southwestern Native Seeds
P.O. Box 50503
Tucson, AZ 85703
Sales type: mail-order (catalog is $1.00)
Type of stock: seeds, seed mixes
Native stock: N/A
Regional focus: Arizona, New Mexico, southwest U.S.
Services: N/A
Comments: We do not sell seeds of endangered species,
and are careful not to have any effect on plant commu-
nities as a result of our collecting.

Wild Seed
2073 East ASU Circle
Tempe, AZ 85284 (602) 345-0669
Sales type: mail-order, retail, wholesale
Type of stock: seeds
Native stock: N/A
Regional focus: southwest U.S.
Services: habitat restoration
Comments: We have the largest available selection of
native western wildflower, grass, tree, and shrub seed.

California

Albright Seed Co.
487 Dawson Drive
Camarillo, CA 93012   (805) 484-0551
Sales type: wholesale
Type of stock: seeds, seed mixes, custom collection of seed
Native stock: 75%
Regional focus: southwest U.S., Pacific Coast
Services: habitat and wetland restoration
Comments: We've been selling and collecting native seed for 25 years with an emphasis on erosion control.

All Season's Wholesale Nursery and Seed Co.
10656 Sheldon Woods Way
Elk Grove, CA 95624   (916) 682-8154
Sales type: wholesale
Type of stock: trees and shrubs, seeds
Native stock: 85%
Regional focus: west, midwest, east, southwest, south
Services: habitat and wetland restoration
Comments: We offer 35 species of oaks, sapling-sized seedlings, and containerized oaks.

Anderson Valley Nursery
18151 Mountain View Road, Box 504
Boonville, CA 95415   (707) 895-3853
Sales type: retail, wholesale
Type of stock: trees, shrubs, herbaceous plants
Native stock: N/A
Regional focus: northern and central California
Services: consultation
Comments: We specialize in water-conserving plants, using mostly woody species native to California.

Appleton Forestry Native Plant Nursery
1369 Tilton Road
Sebastopol, CA 95472   (707) 823-3776
Sales type: retail, wholesale
Type of stock: trees, shrubs
Native stock: 100%
Regional focus: northwest California
Services: habitat and wetland restoration
Comments: We specialize in revegetation species and contract growing of site-specific species.

Blue Oak Nursery
2731 Mountain Oak Lane
Rescue, CA 95672   (916) 677-2111
Sales type: mail-order, retail, wholesale
Type of stock: trees, shrubs
Native stock: 75%
Regional focus: western states
Services: contract grower
Comments: We offer a large variety of native plants found in the western U.S.

C. H. Baccus
900 Boynton Avenue
San Jose, CA 95117   (408) 244-2923
Sales type: mail-order, retail
Type of stock: herbaceous plants and bulbs
Native stock: 100%
Regional focus: western U.S.
Services: contract growing
Comments: We are a small mail-order grower selling 100% seed grown stock.

California Flora Nursery
P.O. Box 3
Fulton, CA 95439   (707) 528-8813
Sales type: retail, wholesale
Type of stock: trees, shrubs, perennials, and grasses
Native stock: 33%
Regional focus: Mediterranean climates, including California
Services: delivery available in the Bay Area
Comments: We specialize in California native plants.

Christensen Nursery Co.
16000 Sanborn Road
Saratoga, CA 95070-9707   (408) 867-4181
Sales type: wholesale
Type of stock: trees, shrubs, herbaceous plants, seeds, seed mixes
Native stock: N/A
Regional focus: N/A
Services: N/A
Comments: N/A

Circuit Rider Productions
9619 Old Redwood Hwy.
Windsor, CA 95492   (707) 838-6641
Sales type: wholesale
Type of stock: trees, shrubs
Native stock: 100%
Regional focus: northern California
Services: wetland and habitat restoration
Comments: We specialize in northern California woody plants for restoration and revegetation work.

Clotilde Merlo Forest Tree Nursery
1508 Crannell Road
Trinidad, CA 95570   (707) 677-0911
Sales type: mail-order, retail, wholesale
Type of stock: reforestation size tree seedlings and liners
Native stock: N/A
Regional focus: western U.S.
Services: reforestation following logging
Comments: We deal with reforestation conifer species native to CA., the Northern Sierra and Pacific NW.

Clyde Robin Seed Co., Inc.
3670 Enterprise Ave.
Hayward, CA 94545   (510) 785-0425
Sales type: mail-order, retail, wholesale
Type of stock: native wildflower seeds, seed mixes
Native stock: N/A
Regional focus: west, mid-west, southeast U.S.
Services: habitat restoration and consultation
Comments: Established in 1934, we offer species native
   to most of the U.S.

Conservaseed
P.O. Box 455
Rio Vista, CA 94571   (916) 775-1646
Sales type: retail, wholesale
Type of stock: trees, shrubs, herbaceous plants, seeds,
   seed mixes
Native stock: 90%
Regional focus: CA, AZ, OR, WA
Services: habitat and wetland restoration, erosion
   control, construction
Comments: We are moving towards California native
   bunch grasses that are area specific.

Cornflower Farms
P.O. Box 896
Elkgrove, CA 95759   (916) 689-1015
Sales type: wholesale
Type of stock: trees, shrubs, herbaceous plants
Native stock: 80%
Regional focus: California
Services: habitat and wetland restoration
Comments: We propagate native ornamentals and reveg-
   etation natives for California landscapes.

Endangered Species
P.O. Box 1830
Tustin, CA 92680   (714) 544-9505
Sales type: mail-order, retail, wholesale
Type of stock: trees, shrubs, palms, bamboo, cycads,
   grasses
Native stock: 30%
Regional focus: FL, LA, TX, CA
Services: habitat and wetland restoration, landscaping
Comments: We have a huge selection of hardy, tropical
   bamboo, native palms, and rare ornamentals.

Environmental Seed Producers
P.O. Box 2709, 1851 W. Olive Ave.
Lompoc, CA 93438-2709   (805) 735-8888
Sales type: wholesale
Type of stock: seeds and custom wildflower seed mixes
Native stock: 50%
Regional focus: species from all over the U.S.
Services: custom wildflower seed mixes
Comments: We offer over 130 species of wildflowers,
   native and ornamental grasses to choose from.

Forest Seeds of California
1100 Indian Hill Road
Placerville, CA 95667   (916) 621-1551
Sales type: mail-order, wholesale
Type of stock: seeds
Native stock: 95%
Regional focus: west coast
Services: habitat restoration, weed control, forestry
   services
Comments: We offer tree and shrub seed collection and
   processing and are a licensed pest control operator.

Freshwater Farms
5851 Myrtle Avenue
Freshwater, CA 95501   (707) 444-8261
Sales type: mail-order, retail, wholesale
Type of stock: trees and shrubs, herbaceous plants, and
   wetland plants
Native stock: 90%
Regional focus: Pacific coast
Services: habitat and wetland restoration, irrigation, land-
   scaping
Comments: We specialize in wetland plants used in bio-
   filtration systems.

Habitat Restoration
3234 "H" Ashford St.
San Diego, CA 92111   (619) 279-8769
Sales type: wholesale
Type of stock: herbaceous plants, seeds, seed mixes
Native stock: 98%
Regional focus: southwest
Services: habitat and wetland restoration, mitigation land-
   scaping
Comments: Habitat restoration specializing in the endan-
   gered habitats of coastal San Diego County.

Hardscrabble Seed Co.
Route 2, Box 255
Springville, CA 93265   (209) 539-2635
Sales type: mail-order, wholesale
Type of stock: seeds
Native stock: 100%
Regional focus: the west
Comments: We deal only in Sequoiadendron, separated
   by grove.

J. L. Hudson, Seedsman
P.O. Box 1058
Redwood City, CA 94064
Sales type: mail-order (catalog is $1.00)
Type of stock: seeds
Native stock: 100%
Regional focus: all regions, all continents except Antarc-
   tica. One World!
Services: consulting
Comments: I offer a large selection of seeds—worldwide
   collection and distribution to all regions.

KSA Jojoba
19025 – EF Parthenia
Northridge, CA 91324 (818) 701-1534
Sales type: mail-order, wholesale
Type of stock: Jojoba seeds
Native stock: 100%
Regional focus: Sonoran Desert area of California, Arizona, Mexico
Services: N/A
Comments: We provide a free catalog for sending a self-addressed stamped (2 stamps) envelope.

Larner Seeds
P.O. Box 407
Bolinas, CA 94924 (415) 868-9407
Sales type: mail-order, retail, wholesale
Type of stock: trees, shrubs, herbaceous plants, seeds, seed mixes
Native stock: 100%
Regional focus: California
Services: habitat restoration and landscaping
Comments: We concentrate on coastal areas in habitat restoration and landscaping. Consultation is available.

Las Pilitas Nursery
Las Pilitas Road
Santa Margarita, CA 93453 (805) 438-5992
Sales type: mail-order, retail, wholesale (catalog—$4.00, price list free)
Type of stock: trees, shrubs, herbaceous plants, seeds, seed mixes
Native stock: 100%
Regional focus: California
Services: habitat and wetland restoration, landscaping
Comments: We offer site specific consultation, habitat restoration, and landscaping services.

Mockingbird Nurseries, Inc.
1670 Jackson Street
Riverside, CA 92504 (714) 780-3571
Sales type: retail, wholesale
Type of stock: trees, shrubs, herbaceous plants, seeds, seed mixes
Native stock: 95%
Regional focus: southwest, California
Services: grow species for habitat and wetland restoration
Comments: We specialize in sustainable landscape plants and habitat and wetland restoration plants.

Mostly Natives Nursery
27215 Highway 1, P.O. Box 258
Tomales, CA 94971 (707) 878-2009
Sales type: mail-order, retail, wholesale
Type of stock: trees, shrubs, herbaceous plants
Native stock: 50%
Regional focus: west coast
Comments: We specialize in coastal native plants.

Native Sons Nursery
379 West El Campo Road
Arroyo Grande, CA 93420 (805) 481-5996
Sales type: wholesale
Type of stock: trees, shrubs, herbaceous plants
Native stock: 50%
Regional focus: all regions
Comments: We offer a large selection of California natives and Mediterranean perennials.

Olle Olsson Nurseries, Inc.
2154 Peck Road
Monrovia, CA 91016 1-800-752-6873
Sales type: wholesale
Type of stock: trees and shrubs
Native stock: N/A
Regional focus: N/A
Comments: N/A

Pacific Open Space, Inc./ Northcoast Native Nursery
P.O. Box 744
Petaluma, CA 94953 (707) 769-1213
Sales type: wholesale
Type of stock: trees, shrubs, herbaceous plants, native grass seeds, seed mixes
Native stock: 100%
Regional focus: California, Pacific northcoast
Services: habitat and wetland restoration, landscaping
Comments: Northcoast Native Nursery, a division of Pacific Open Space, offers ecological and environmental consultation, including propagation of native plants and seed and offer land management planning.

Pacific Coast Seed, Inc.
7074 D Commerce Circle
Pleasanton, CA 94588 (510) 463-1188
Sales type: wholesale
Type of stock: seeds, custom seed mixes
Native stock: 60%
Regional focus: northern California, western Nevada
Services: habitat and wetland restoration, landscaping
Comments: We specialize in California native grasses, native shrubs, trees, and wildflowers.

Pacific Southwest Nursery
P.O. Box 985
National City, CA 91951-0985 (619) 477-5333
Sales type: mail-order, retail, wholesale
Type of stock: trees, shrubs, herbaceous plants
Native stock: 70%
Regional focus: coastal southern California
Services: habitat and wetland restoration
Comments: We focus on native habitat restoration plants as well as drought tolerant native and exotic plants.

Pecoff Bros. Nursery & Seed, Inc.
20220 Elfin Forest Road
Escondido, CA 92029   (619) 744-3120
Sales type: wholesale
Type of stock: trees, shrubs, herbaceous plants, seeds,
    seed mixes
Native stock: 30%
Regional focus: southwestern U. S., Australia
Services: habitat and wetland restoration, landscaping
Comments: We offer Washington robust palm trees.

Redwood City Seed Co.
P.O. Box 361
Redwood City, CA 94064   (415) 325-7333
Sales type: mail-order, retail, wholesale
Type of stock: grass plugs of California native perennial
    bunchgrass
Native stock: 100%
Regional focus: California
Services: habitat restoration, landscaping, bunchgrasses
    for lawns
Comments: We use 100% native grass plugs in habitat
    restoration and landscaping.

S & S Seeds
P.O. Box 1275
Carpinteria, CA 93013   (805) 684-0436
Sales type: wholesale
Type of stock: seeds
Native stock: 75%
Regional focus: California, Arizona
Services: site specific seed collection
Comments: We offer all types of seeds used in erosion
    control, revegetation, and landscaping.

San Simeon Nursery
HCR 33 Villa Creek Road
Cayucos, CA 93430   (805) 995-2466
Sales type: wholesale
Type of stock: trees, shrubs, herbaceous plants, cacti, and
    succulents
Native stock: 60%
Regional focus: California, southwest
Services: habitat restoration, landscaping
Comments: We offer drought adaptive species from tem-
    perate and semi-arid regions.

Santa Barbara Botanic Garden
1212 Mission Canyon Road
Santa Barbara, CA 93105   (805) 682-4726
Sales type: retail
Type of stock: trees, shrubs, herbaceous plants
Native stock: 60%
Regional focus: California
Comments: We have a large selection of drought-tolerant
    plants from mediterranean climates.

Sunset Coast Nursery
P.O. Box 221/ 2745 Tierra Way
Watsonville, CA 95076   (408) 726-1672
Sales type: retail, wholesale
Type of stock: trees, shrubs, herbaceous plants, bare root,
    grasses
Native stock: 100%
Regional focus: California, southwest
Services: habitat and wetland restoration, site specific
    services
Comments: We specialize in coastal plants native to the
    Monterey Bay area.

Taylor's Herb Garden
1535 Lone Oak Road
Vista, CA 92084   (619) 727-3485
Sales type: mail-order, retail, wholesale
Type of stock: herbaceous plants, seeds, wreaths
Native stock: 50%
Regional focus: southwest
Services: offer to ship live plants in U.S.
Comments: We specialize in growing many varieties of
    herbs for gardeners around the world.

The Living Desert
47900 Portola Ave.
Palm Desert, CA 92260   (619) 346-5694
Sales type: retail, wholesale
Type of stock: trees, shrubs, herbaceous plants
Native stock: 90%
Regional focus: southwest U.S.
Comments: We have a zoological garden with a small
    retail nursery.

Theodore Payne Foundation
10459 Tuxford Street
Sun Valley, CA 91352   (818) 768-1802
Sales type: mail-order, retail (offer discount to landscap-
    ers)
Type of stock: trees, shrubs, herbaceous plants, seeds,
    seed mixes, books
Native stock: 100%
Regional focus: California and southwest
Services: provide referrals on habitat and wetland resto-
    ration, landscaping
Comments: We are a non-profit, membership organiza-
    tion. We emphasize rare and endangered species.

Village Nurseries
P.O. Box 25509
Anaheim, CA 92825-5509   (714) 282-5880
Sales type: wholesale
Type of stock: trees, shrubs, herbaceous plants
Native stock: 10%
Regional focus: California
Services: habitat and wetland restoration
Comments: Our 300 acre nursery offers native and drought
    tolerant plants in sizes from liners to 48" boxes.

Wapumne Native Plant Nursery Co.
8305 Cedar Crest Way
Sacramento, CA 95826 (916) 645-9737
Sales type: retail, wholesale
Type of stock: trees, shrubs, herbaceous plants, seeds,
    grasses
Native stock: 100%
Regional focus: northern California
Services: consultation
Comments: We are a small but experienced (18 yrs.)
    nursery; knowledgeable of natural environments.

Colorado

Applewood Seed Co.
5380 Vivian Street
Arvada, CO 80002 (303) 431-6283
Sales type: wholesale
Type of stock: seeds, seed mixes
Native stock: 80%
Regional focus: offer different regional mixes
Services: horticultural consultation
Comments: Applewood specializes in wildflower seeds,
    wildflower mixtures, and herb seeds.

Arkansas Valley Seed Co.
4625 Colorado Blvd.
Denver, CO 80216 (303) 320-7500
Sales type: wholesale
Type of stock: seeds
Native stock: 20%
Regional focus: intermountain, semi-arid regions
Comments: We are a wholesale supplier of rangeland
    grasses, turfgrass, and pasture grass seed.

Edge of the Rockies
133 Hunna Road
Bayfield, CO 81122-9758 (303) 884-9003
Sales type: mail-order, wholesale
Type of stock: trees and shrubs, herbaceous plants, seeds,
    seed mixes
Native stock: 100%
Regional focus: Four Corners region (NM, CO, UT, AZ)
Services: habitat restoration, landscaping, consulting
Comments: We offer a wide variety of seeds from alpine
    to high desert plateaus of the region.

Rocky Mountain Rare Plants
P.O. Box 20483
Denver, CO 80220-0483 (303) 322-1410
Sales type: mail-order
Type of stock: seeds
Native stock: 75%
Regional focus: Colorado, Wyoming, Idaho, Utah
Comments: We offer primarily perennials under 12" tall,
    which are natives to steppe and alpine habitats.

Wild Things
218 Quincy
Pueblo, CO 81004 (719) 543-2722
Sales type: wholesale
Type of stock: shrubs, herbaceous plants
Native stock: 100%
Regional focus: mostly southwest
Services: N/A
Comments: I mostly grow drought tolerant flowers and
    prairie species that are hardy to Colorado.

Connecticut

Broken Arrow Nursery
13 Broken Arrow Road
Hamden, CT 06518 (203) 288-1026
Sales type: mail-order, retail, wholesale
Type of stock: trees, shrubs
Native stock: 10%
Regional focus: eastern U.S.
Comments: We specialize in varieties of mountain laurel
    and have a large selection of natives and exotics.

Kathleen Nelson Perennials
55 Mud Pond Road
Gaylordsville, CT 06755 (203) 355-1547
Sales type: retail
Type of stock: herbaceous plants
Native stock: 30–40%
Regional focus: northeastern U.S.
Services: small scale landscaping and wetland restoration
Comments: We have a good selection of native grasses
    and herbaceous perennials native to NE wetlands.

Oliver Nurseries
1159 Bronson Road
Fairfield, CT 06430
Sales type: retail
Type of stock: trees, shrubs, herbaceous plants
Native stock: 40%
Regional focus: northeastern U.S.
Services: landscaping
Comments: We specialize in dwarf conifers, alpines, and
    unusual cultivars.

Select Seeds
Hill Road
180 Stickney
Union, CT 06076 (203) 684-5655
Sales type: mail-order, retail, wholesale
Type of stock: seeds
Native stock: 10%
Regional focus: N. America
Comments: We specialize in seeds for garden flowers,
    including native species.

The Gilded Lily
495 Westover Road
Stamford, CT 06902   (203) 348-8886
Sales type: mail-order, retail, wholesale
Type of stock: only daylilies
Native stock: unknown
Regional focus: all regions of U.S.
Services: landscaping
Comments: We specialize in naturalizing daylilies. They are perfect on water tees and near rocky entrances.

Florida

Birdsong Nursery
511 Royal Oak Road
Webster, FL 33597-9725
Sales type: mail-order, retail
Type of stock: trees and shrubs
Native stock: 60%
Regional focus: southeastern U.S.
Services: habitat and wetland restoration, landscaping
Comments: We offer large sizes of both trees and shrubs.

Blake's Nursery
Route 2, Box 971
Madison, FL 32340   (904) 971-5003
Sales type: mail-order, retail
Type of stock: trees, shrubs
Native stock: 90-95%
Regional focus: Florida, Georgia, Alabama
Services: Xeriscape design
Comments: We specialize in area-endemic species, all seed grown in our nursery.

Bullbay Creek Farm
1033 Old Bumpy Road
Tallahassee, FL 32311
Sales type: wholesale
Type of stock: trees, shrubs, herbaceous plants
Native stock: 95%
Regional focus: southeastern U.S.
Services: grower only
Comments: We are strictly growers, specializing in wildflowers and ferns.

Central Florida Native Flora, Inc.
P.O. Box 1045
San Antonio, FL 33576   (904) 588-3687
Sales type: wholesale
Type of stock: trees, shrubs, herbaceous plants, wildflowers
Native stock: 100%
Regional focus: southeastern U.S., specifically Florida
Services: restoration, landscaping, consulting
Comments: We offer upland, wetland, and transitional species in containers in sizes from 1-65 gallons.

Daylily Discounters
Route 2, Box 24
Alachua, FL 32615   (904) 462-1539
Sales type: mail-order, retail, wholesale
Type of stock: herbaceous plants
Native stock: 33%
Regional focus: southeastern U.S.
Comments: Apart from daylilies (non-native plant that has been naturalized widely in the U.S.), we carry Louisiana iris, excellent for boggy areas.

Farnsworth Farms Nursery
7080 Hypoluxo Farms Road
Lake Worth, FL 33463   (407) 965-2657
Sales type: retail, wholesale
Type of stock: trees, shrubs
Native stock: 85%
Regional focus: tropical and subtropical regions of Florida
Comments: We specialize in tropical hammock species and have a large variety of native plants.

Gann's Tropical Greenery & Natives
22140 SW 152nd Avenue
Goulds, FL 33170   (305) 248-5529
Sales type: mail-order, retail, wholesale
Type of stock: trees, shrubs, groundcovers, wildflowers
Native stock: 99%
Regional focus: Florida
Services: habitat and wetland restoration, landscaping
Comments: We are a pioneer South Florida native nursery. We sell pineland, hammock, salt, and freshwater species.

Gone Native Nursery
P.O. Box 1122
Jensen Beach, FL 34958-1122   (407) 283-8420
Sales type: mail-order, wholesale
Type of stock: trees, shrubs, herbaceous plants
Native stock: 100%
Regional focus: southeast
Services: habitat and wetland restoration
Comments: Our emphasis is on wetlands, littoral zones, mangrove/cypress swamps, space, and SE hydric hammocks.

Horticultural Systems, Inc.
Golf Course Road, P.O. Box 70
Parrish, FL 34219   (813) 776-1760/1-800-771-4114
Sales type: mail-order, retail, wholesale
Type of stock: trees, shrubs, herbaceous plants, seeds, seed mixes
Native stock: 95%
Regional focus: N. and S. East, S. Gulf of Mexico
Services: habitat and wetland restoration, landscaping
Comments: We work with beach, freshwater aquatics and saline esturine and upland habitats.

The Liner Farm
P.O. Box 701369
St. Cloud, FL 34770-1369   1-800-330-1484
Sales type: wholesale
Type of stock: trees, shrubs, herbaceous plants, aquatic,
   and wetland plants
Native stock: 20%
Regional focus: Florida, southeastern U.S.
Services: custom propagation
Comments: We offer a free catalog of over 600 types of
   potted seedlings and starter plants.

Mandarin Native Plants
13500 Mandarin Road
Jacksonville, FL 32223   (904) 268-2904
Sales type: retail, wholesale
Type of stock: trees, shrubs, herbaceous plants
Native stock: 70%
Regional focus: southeastern U.S.
Services: N/A
Comments: We sell native plants which are typical Florida
   natives.

Native Green Cay
Route 1, Box 331 B
Boynton Beach, FL 33437   (407) 496-1415
Sales type: wholesale
Type of stock: trees, shrubs
Native stock: 100%
Regional focus: southern Florida
Services: grow only S. Florida native trees and shrubs
Comments: We sell upland and wetland field grown
   material and some container shrubs and trees.

Native Tree Nursery, Inc.
17250 SW 232nd Street
Goulds, FL 33030   (305) 247-4499
Sales type: wholesale
Type of stock: trees, shrubs
Native stock: 80%
Regional focus: N/A
Services: N/A
Comments: Our experience over the last 10 years enables
   us to consistently produce top quality stock.

Plants for Tomorrow, Inc.
16361 Norris Road
Loxahatchee, FL 33470 (407)790-1422/1-800-448-2525
Sales type: wholesale
Type of stock: trees, shrubs, groundcover, vines, aquatic
   plants, native grasses
Native stock: 80%
Regional focus: Florida
Services: habitat and wetland restoration, landscaping,
   erosion control
Comments: We are one of America's premiere wetlands
   restoration specialist.

Slocum Water Gardens
1101 Cypress Gardens Blvd.
Winter Haven, FL 33884   (813) 293-7151
Sales type: mail-order, retail, wholesale
Type of stock: aquatic plants
Native stock: 20%
Regional focus: southeast
Services: sales, consulting
Comments: We are a full-service mail-order aquatic plant
   nursery. A sixty page colored catalog available.

Superior Trees, Inc.
P.O. Box 9325
Lee, FL 32059   (904) 971-5159
Sales type: wholesale
Type of stock: trees, shrubs
Native stock: 99%
Regional focus: southeast
Services: N/A
Comments: We sell native trees and shrubs, bareroot
   seedlings and 1-3 gallon containers.

The Natives
2929 J.B. Carter Road
Davenport, FL 33837   (813) 422-6664
Sales type: retail, wholesale
Type of stock: trees, shrubs, herbaceous plants
Native stock: 100%
Regional focus: Florida
Services: habitat and wetland restoration, landscaping
Comments: We offer sand scrub, sandhill and many
   wildflowers

The Wetlands Company, Inc.
7650 South Tamiami Trail #10
Sarasota, FL 34231   (813) 921-6609
Sales type: retail, wholesale
Type of stock: trees, shrubs, herbaceous plants
Native stock: 100%
Regional focus: southeast, Gulf Coast, east coast, Cali-
   fornia
Services: habitat and wetland restoration
Comments: We have over 200 acres of aquatic plant
   ponds with over 40 varieties of wetland species.

Georgia

Cedar Lane Farms
3790 Sandy Creek Road
Madison, GA 30650   (404) 342-2626
Sales type: wholesale
Type of stock: trees, shrubs, herbaceous plants
Native stock: 50%
Regional focus: southeast
Services: wholesaler
Comments: We want you to know that all our plants are
   nursery propagated.

Transplant Nursery
Rt. 2 Parkertown Road
Lavonia, GA 30553   (404) 356-8947
Sales type: mail-order, retail, wholesale
Type of stock: eastern native azaleas
Native stock: 15%
Regional focus: eastern seaboard
Services: landscaping
Comments: We offer native deciduous azaleas, evergreen
    azaleas, rhododendrons, and companion plants.

Twisted Oaks Nursery
Box 10
Waynesboro, GA 30830 (404) 554-3040/1-800-868-1015
Sales type: wholesale
Type of stock: trees, shrubs
Native stock: 20%
Regional focus: southeast
Services: landscaping, wetland restoration
Comments: We develop new cultivars of native plant
    material, like Myrica pumila *Fairfax*.

Iowa

Cascade Forestry Nursery
Rt. 2
Cascade, IA 52033   (319) 852-3042
Sales type: mail-order, retail, wholesale
Type of stock: trees, shrubs, seeds
Native stock: 95%
Regional focus: northern midwest
Services: habitat and wetland restoration, consultation
Comments: Our staff includes professional foresters who
    have experience in native habitat establishment.

Ion Exchange
RR. #1, Box 48C
Harpers Ferry, IA 52146   (319) 535-7231
Sales type: mail-order, retail, wholesale
Type of stock: herbaceous plants, seeds, seed mixes
Native stock: 99%
Regional focus: midwest
Services: prairie and wetland restoration, landscaping,
    consulting
Comments: We offer a large selection of prairie and
    savannah species, wet and dry.

Iowa Prairie Seed Co.
RR 1, Box 259
Cresco, IA 52136   (319) 547-3824
Sales type: mail-order, retail, wholesale
Type of stock: herbaceous plants, seeds, seed mixes
Native stock: 90%
Regional focus: midwest
Services: habitat restoration, landscaping
Comments: We deal almost exclusively in prairie species.

Smith Nursery Co.
P.O. Box 515
Charles City, IA 50616   (515) 228-3239
Sales type: retail, wholesale
Type of stock: trees, shrubs, seeds
Native stock: 40%
Regional focus: midwest, east, northwest
Services: habitat and wetland restoration, landscaping
Comments: We offer a large selection of seedlings, most
    are native to the U.S.

Wildflowers From Nature's Way
RR1, Box 62
Woodburn, IA 50275   (515) 342-6246
Sales type: mail-order, retail
Type of stock: herbaceous plants, seeds, seed mixes
Native stock: 99%
Regional focus: exclusively Iowa
Services: landscaping, consulting
Comments: We naturalize yards in urban areas and en-
    courage the use of wildflower in flower beds and
    butterfly gardens.

Idaho

Fantasy Farms Nursery
Box 157
Peck, ID 83545   (208) 486-6841 OR 486-7751
Sales type: mail-order, wholesale
Type of stock: trees, shrubs
Native stock: 30%
Regional focus: northwest and southwest
Services: N/A
Comments: We have mostly tree species for landscaping
    and Christmas trees, also windbreak species.

High Altitude Gardens
P.O. Box 4619
Ketchum, ID 83340   1-800-874-7333
Sales type: mail-order
Type of stock: seeds and seed mixes for wildflowers and
    vegetables
Native stock: 30%
Regional focus: regions at high elevations
Services: N/A
Comments: We offer species native to higher elevations.

Northplan Seed Producers
P.O. Box 9107
Moscow, ID 83843 (208) 882-8040
Sales type: mail-order
Type of stock: seeds, seed mixes
Native stock: 95%
Regional focus: northwest, prairie
Services: N/A
Comments: We supply seeds for habitat and wetland restoration, xeriscaping, and erosion control.

Reggear Tree Farm
1495 Dent Bridge Rd.
Orofino, ID 83544 (208) 476-7364
Sales type: wholesale
Type of stock: trees, shrubs, herbaceous plants
Native stock: 85%
Regional focus: northwest, mountains, prairie
Services: habitat, wetland restoration, landscaping, tree moving
Comments: Our climate can be harsh; making for a late spring flush and hardy material.

Winterfield Ranch Seed
P.O. Box 97
Swan Valley, ID 83449 (208) 483-3683
Sales type: wholesale
Type of stock: seeds
Native stock: 50%
Regional focus: northern Rockies, Pacific Northwest
Services: consulting
Comments: Winterfield Ranch is a small private farm operation and have some hand collected native species.

Illinois

Bluestem Prairie Nursery
Route 2, Box 92
Hillsboro, IL 62049 (217) 532-6344
Sales type: mail-order
Type of stock: herbaceous plants, seeds, seed mixes
Native stock: 100%
Regional focus: Illinois, midwest
Services: prairie/savanna, habitat and wetland restoration, landscaping
Comments: We stress diversity. Plants are shipped in the Spring bare root.

Country Road Greenhouses, Inc.
RR 1, Box 62
Malta, IL 60150 (815) 825-2305
Sales type: wholesale
Type of stock: herbaceous plants
Native stock: 100%
Regional focus: midwest
Services: contract growing, consultation
Comments: We grow large quantities of savanna, prairie, and wetland species.

Genesis Nursery
RR 1, Box 32
Walnut, IL 61376 (815) 379-9060
Sales type: mail-order, retail, wholesale
Type of stock: herbaceous plants, seeds, seed mixes
Native stock: 100%
Regional focus: midwest
Services: habitat and wetland restoration, landscaping, consulting, monitoring
Comments: We offer a large variety of savanna, wetland, and prairie species.

LaFayette Home Nursery, Inc.
Rt 1, Box 1A
LaFayette, IL 61449 (309) 995-3311
Sales type: landscape retail sales
Type of stock: trees, shrubs, herbaceous plants, seeds, seed mixes
Native stock: 100% seeds, 33% other
Regional focus: midwest
Services: habitat and wetland restoration, landscaping, consulting, design
Comments: Family business since 1887, offering native grasses, wildflowers, wetland plants, and nursery stock.

Purple Prairie Farm
RR #2, Box 176
Wyoming, IL 61491 (309) 286-7356
Sales type: wholesale
Type of stock: seeds
Native stock: 100%
Regional focus: Illinois Grand Prairie
Services: N/A
Comments: We have a moderate selection of wetland and prairie species.

The Natural Garden
38 W. 443 Hwy 64
St. Charles, IL 60174 (708) 584-0150
Sales type: mail-order, retail, wholesale
Type of stock: trees, shrubs, herbaceous plants, seeds, seed mixes
Native stock: 20%
Regional focus: northern Illinois
Services: habitat and wetland restoration, landscaping
Comments: We offer over 150 species of native plants to northern Illinois.

Kansas

Glen Snell/Quivira Management
300 N. Adams
Medicine Lodge, KS 67104   (316) 886-5075/1-800-821-2365
Sales type: mail-order, retail, wholesale
Type of stock: seeds, seed mixes
Native stock: 100%
Regional focus: Kansas
Services: prairie wildflower planting
Comments: We offer about 40 native wildflower species.

Kentucky

Akinback Farm
2501 Hwy 53 South
LaGrange, KY 40031   (502) 222-5791
Sales type: retail
Type of stock: herbaceous perennials
Native stock: 40%
Regional focus: midwest, southeast
Services: display gardens available for viewing
Comments: We carry over 1000 perennials, 350 varieties of native and ornamental herbs.

Dabney Herbs
P.O. Box 22061
Louisville, KY 40252   (502) 893-5198
Sales type: mail-order, wholesale
Type of stock: trees, shrubs, herbaceous plants, seeds
Native stock: 45%
Regional focus: midwest, Appalachia
Services: habitat restoration, landscaping information
Comments: We offer nursery propagated plants, medicinal herbs, and shade plants.

Jane's Native Seeds
1860 Kays Branch Road
Owenton, KY 40359 (502) 484-2044
Sales type: retail only
Type of stock: seeds of wetlands, some upland species
Native stock: 100%
Regional focus: N/A
Services: N/A
Comments: N/A

Nolin River Nut Tree Nursery
797 Port Wooden Road
Upton, KY 42784   (502) 369-8551
Sales type: mail-order
Type of stock: trees, shrubs
Native stock: 85%
Regional focus: eastern U.S.
Services: custom grafting of nut trees, retail (1993)
Comments: N/A

Nurtured Gardens Nursery
8150 Lower Licking Road
Morehead, KY 40351   (606) 784-4769
Sales type: wholesale, contract grower
Type of stock: trees, shrubs (native, woody ornamentals)
Native stock: 80%
Regional focus: Appalachian, southeast
Services: habitat and wetland restoration, landscape, design
Comments: We are dedicated to the preservation of Kentucky wildlife. We offer 37 native, woody species.

Shooting Star Nursery
444 Bates Road
Frankfort, KY 40601   (502) 223-1679
Sales type: mail-order, retail, wholesale
Type of stock: trees, shrubs, herbaceous plants, seeds, seed mixes
Native stock: 99%
Regional focus: midwest, eastern U.S.
Services: habitat restoration, landscaping, contract growing
Comments: We have over 200 species of nursery propagated woodland, prairie, and wetland species.

Stinson Rhododendron Nursery
10400 Florian Rd.
Louisville, KY 40223   (502) 244-9459
Sales type: wholesale
Type of stock: trees, shrubs
Native stock: 75%
Regional focus: Appalachian Mountain Range
Services: N/A
Comments: We offer flowering shrubs.

Louisiana

Louisiana Nature and Science Center
P.O. Box 870610
New Orleans, LA 70187-0610
Sales type: mail-order, retail, wholesale
Type of stock: trees, shrubs, herbaceous plants, seeds, seed mixes
Native stock: N/A
Regional focus: N/A
Services: N/A
Comments: N/A

Louisiana Nursery
Rt. 7, Box 43
Opelousas, LA 70570 (318) 948-3696
Sales type: mail-order, retail
Type of stock: trees, shrubs, herbaceous plants, vines, magnolias
Native stock: 10%
Regional focus: most regions of U.S.
Services: books, information
Comments: We have hundreds of Louisiana iris and other native Iris bog plants, perennials, trees and shrubs.

Natives Nurseries
23322 North Gretchen
Covington, LA 70433 (504) 892-5424
Sales type: retail, wholesale
Type of stock: trees, shrubs, herbaceous plants
Native stock: 85%
Regional focus: southeastern U.S.
Services: habitat and wetland restoration, landscaping
Comments: We work to educate the public on native plants and habitats.

Prairie Basse Native Plants
Rt. 2, Box 491 F
Carencro, LA 70520 (318) 896-9187
Sales type: mail-order, retail
Type of stock: trees, shrubs, herbaceous plants
Native stock: 95%
Regional focus: Gulf Coastal Plain
Services: habitat and wetland restoration, landscaping
Comments: We specialize in habitat enrichment/restoration and do ecological consultation.

Sherwood Akin's Greenhouses
P.O. Box 6
Sibley, LA 71073 (318) 377-3653
Sales type: mail-order, retail
Type of stock: trees, shrubs, herbaceous plants
Native stock: N/A
Regional focus: N/A
Services: grow superior fruited mayhaws
Comments: We are a small nursery specializing in unusual, edible landscaping plants.

Massachusetts

Botanicals, Inc.
219 Concord Road
Wayland, MA 01778 (508) 358-4846
Sales type: mail-order, retail, wholesale
Type of stock: trees, shrubs, herbaceous plants
Native stock: N/A
Regional focus: north and southeast, southern prairie
Services: N/A
Comments: We emphasize adaptive plants which are useful in a variety of open or woodland situations.

Briarwood Gardens
14 Gully Lane, RFD #3
East Sandwich, MA 02537 (508) 888-2146
Sales type: mail-order, retail, wholesale
Type of stock: trees, shrubs, rhododendrons
Native stock: .5 %
Regional focus: east coast
Services: expert advice, landscape design
Comments: Experienced wholesaler and dealer in landscaping plants with a large selection of rhododendrons.

Donaroma's Nursery & Landscape Services
Box 2189, Upper Main St.
Edgartown, MA 02539 (508) 627-3036
Sales type: mail-order, retail, wholesale
Type of stock: herbaceous plants
Native stock: 50%
Regional focus: New England
Services: landscaping, wetland restoration
Comments: We offer mainly wildflowers and perennials.

F. W. Schumacher Co., Inc.
36 Spring Hill Road
Sandwich, MA 02563-1023 (508) 888-0659
Sales type: mail-order, retail, wholesale
Type of stock: seeds
Native stock: 70%
Regional focus: all regions
Services: habitat and wetland restoration, landscaping
Comments: We offer ornamental landscaping and sell seeds of trees and shrubs.

New England Wildflower Society
Garden in the Woods
Hemenway Road
Framingham, MA 01701   (508) 877-7630
Sales type: retail
Type of stock: trees, shrubs, herbaceous plants, seeds,
    seed mixes
Native stock: 99%
Regional focus: eastern U.S.
Services: N/A
Comments: We are non-profit and offer field trips and
    botany and horticulture courses.

Rock Spray Nursery, Inc.
P.O. Box 693
Truro, MA 02666-0693   (508) 349-6769
Sales type: mail-order, retail, wholesale (send $1.00 for
    catalog)
Type of stock: heath, heather
Native stock: 100%
Regional focus: U.S., Canada
Services: growers of heather
Comments: We grow over 120 varieties of heath and
    heather, hardy to zone 4.

Weston Nurseries, Inc.
East Main St., P.O. Box 186
Hopkinton, MA 01748   (508) 435-3414
Sales type: retail, wholesale
Type of stock: trees, shrubs, herbaceous plants
Native stock: 10 -20 %
Regional focus: N/A
Services: landscaping
Comments: New England's largest selection of land-
    scape-size plants, trees, and shrubs.

Maryland

Environmental Concern, Inc.
210 West Chew Avenue, P.O. Box P
St. Michaels, MD 21663   (410) 745-9620
Sales type: wholesale
Type of stock: trees, shrubs, herbaceous plants, seeds
Native stock: 100% (herbaceous), 30% (woody)
Regional focus: NE, coastal Maryland, Delaware,
    Virginia
Services: habitat, wetland restoration, landscaping
Comments: The nursery specializes in herbaceous and
    woody wetland species. Consulting specializes in
    wetland, stream, and upland forest restoration.

Maryland Aquatic Nurseries
3427 N. Furnace Road
Jarrettsville, MD 21084   (410) 557-7615
Sales type: mail-order, wholesale
Type of stock: aquatic plants, moisture-loving perennials
    and grasses
Native stock: 25%
Regional focus: eastern seaboard
Services: landscaping, specializing in pond design
Comments: We offer a broad selection of aquatic plants
    as well as exclusive M.A.N.-made products.

Native Seeds, Inc.
14590 Triadelphia Mill Road
Dayton, MD 21036   (301) 596-9818
Sales type: mail-order, retail, wholesale
Type of stock: seeds, wildflower seed mixes
Native stock: 70%
Regional focus: N/A
Services: landscaping
Comments: Both bulk and seed packet quantities of
    wildflower seeds are offered.

Sylva Native Nursery & Seed Co.
1927 York Road
Timonium, MD 21093   (301) 560-2504
Sales type: wholesale
Type of stock: trees, shrubs, herbaceous plants, seeds,
    seed mixes
Native stock: 100%
Regional focus: mid-Atlantic, northeast
Services: landscaping, habitat, wetland, and stream resto-
    ration
Comments: We have developed seed mixes especially for
    wet areas and for shoreline and beaches.

Wildflower
6 Oaklyn Court
Potomac, MD 20854   (301) 983-2607
Sales type: retail, wholesale
Type of stock: shrubs, herbaceous plants
Native stock: 90%
Regional focus: north and southeast, midwest
Services: N/A
Comments: We propagate both sun and shade loving
    perennials which thrive in the mid-Atlantic region.

Maine

Fieldstone Gardens
620 Quaker Lane
Vassalboro, ME 04989-9713 (207) 923-3836
Sales type: mail-order, retail
Type of stock: herbaceous plants
Native stock: 10 - 15%
Regional focus: cold climate states
Services: N/A
Comments: We offer over 600 varieties of rock garden, border, shade, and full sun plants.

Michigan

BioEnt Enterprises
14174 Hoffman Rd.
Three Rivers, MI 49093 (616) 278-3075
Sales type: retail, wholesale
Type of stock: trees, shrubs, herbaceous plants, seeds, seed mixes
Native stock: 80%
Regional focus: Great Lakes region
Services: habitat and wetland restoration, landscaping
Comments: We offer both wetland and dryland native species.

Far North Gardens
16785 Harrison
Livonia, MI 48154
Sales type: mail-order
Type of stock: seeds, seed mixes
Native stock: N/A
Regional focus: north and southeast
Services: N/A
Comments: We offer thousands of rare flower species of seed and many native species.

Grootendorst Nurseries, Inc./Southmeadow Fruit Gardens
15310 Red Arrow Hwy.
Lakeside, MI 49116 (616) 469-2865
Sales type: mail-order, wholesale
Type of stock: trees, shrubs
Native stock: N/A
Regional focus: N/A
Services: N/A
Comments: We offer choice and unusual fruit varieties for the connoisseur and home gardener.

The Michigan Wildflower Farm
11770 Cutler Road
Portland, MI 48875-9452 (517) 647-6010
Sales type: mail-order, retail, wholesale
Type of stock: herbaceous plants, seeds, seed mixes
Native stock: 100%
Regional focus: Michigan
Services: habitat restoration, landscaping, consultation
Comments: We offer native Michigan species, especially dryland and woodland edge seeds.

The Wildside
4815 Valley Avenue
Hudsonville, MI 49426 (616) 669-3256
Sales type: mail-order, retail, wholesale
Type of stock: trees, shrubs, herbaceous plants, seeds
Native stock: 98%
Regional focus: Great Lakes, midwest
Services: consultation, installation
Comments: We have a growing variety of woodland, prairie, and wetland species.

Vans Pines, Inc.
7550 144th Avenue
West Olive, MI 49460 (616) 399-1620
Sales type: mail order, wholesale
Type of stock: trees, shrubs, tree seeds
Native stock: 80%
Regional focus: midwest
Services: native dune grass installation
Comments: Growers of 120 species of native and non-native forest tree seedlings and transplants.

Wavecrest Nursery
2509 Lakeshore Drive
Fennville, MI 49408 (616) 543-4175
Sales type: mail-order, retail, wholesale
Type of stock: trees, shrubs, herbaceous plants
Native stock: 10%
Regional focus: midwest
Services: habitat and wetland restoration, landscaping
Comments: We offer a large selection of shade loving woodland plants and many prairie grasses.

Minnesota

Landscape Alternatives, Inc.
1465 Pascal St.
St. Paul, MN 55108 (612) 488-3142
Sales type: mail-order, retail, wholesale
Type of stock: herbaceous plants, seeds
Native stock: 95%
Regional focus: upper midwest, Minnesota
Services: habitat restoration, landscape, design
Comments: We offer over 100 species of prairie wild-
flowers and grasses as well as many woodland spe-
cies.

Orchid Gardens
2232 139th Ave. NW
Andover, MN 55304 (612) 755-0205, no collect calls
Sales type: mail-order
Type of stock: trees, shrubs, herbaceous plants
Native stock: N/A
Regional focus: Midwest
Services: habitat restoration, landscaping
Comments: We deal exclusively with plants native to
Minnesota, mostly wildflowers.

Prairie Hill Wildflowers
Rt. 1, Box 191-A
Ellendale, MN 56026 (507) 451-7791
Sales type: retail, wholesale
Type of stock: herbaceous plants, seeds, custom seed
mixes
Native stock: 100%
Regional focus: upper midwest
Services: habitat, wetland, prairie restoration
Comments: We offer a good selection of prairie and
wetland species.

Prairie Moon Nursery
Route 3, Box 163
Winona, MN 55987 (507) 452-1362
Sales type: mail-order, retail, wholesale (catalog price is
$2.00)
Type of stock: herbaceous plants, seeds, seed mixes, grasses
and sedges
Native stock: 100%
Regional focus: upper midwest
Services: consultation
Comments: We offer 100% indigenous native prairie,
wetland, and woodland species.

Prairie Restoration, Inc.
P.O. Box 327
Princeton, MN 55371 (612) 389-4342
Sales type: mail-order, retail, wholesale
Type of stock: trees, shrubs, herbaceous plants, seeds,
seed mixes
Native stock: 100%
Regional focus: midwest
Services: habitat and wetland restoration
Comments: We are ecologists dedicated to native plant
community restoration.

The Environmental Collaborative
P.O. Box 539
Osseo, MN 55369
Sales type: mail-order
Type of stock: trees, shrubs
Native stock: 95%
Regional focus: northeast, midwest, north central
Services: N/A
Comments: We offer over 50 species of hardwoods,
conifers, and shrubs.

Wildlife Habitat
Route 3, Box 178
Owatonna, MN 55060 (507) 451-6771
Sales type: mail-order, retail, wholesale
Type of stock: seeds, seed mixes, ground prairie grass
mulch
Native stock: 100%
Regional focus: Minnesota, Iowa, Wisconsin, South and
North Dakota
Services: N/A
Comments: We grow and condition six species of warm
season native prairie grasses.

Missouri

Elixer Farm Botanicals
General Delivery
Brixey, MO 65618 (417) 261-2393
Sales type: mail-order
Type of stock: herbaceous plants (bare root only), seeds,
seed mixes
Native stock: 75%
Regional focus: Ozarks Bioregion
Services: grow medicinal plants
Comments: We specialize in Chinese and indigenous
medicinal plant seed.

Forrest Keeling Nursery
Hwy 79 S., P.O. Box 135
Elsberry, MO 63343 (314) 898-5571
Sales type: wholesale
Type of stock: trees, shrubs, herbaceous plants, groundcovers and vines
Native stock: 20%
Regional focus: Midwest, north central
Services: landscaping, special packaging, promotional services
Comments: We offer a large selection of native trees and shrubs, especially oaks, dogwoods, and maples.

Hamilton Seeds and Wildflowers
HCR 9, Box 138
Elk Creek, MO 65464 (417) 967-2190
Sales type: mail-order, retail, wholesale
Type of stock: herbaceous plants (bare root, potted plants), seeds, seed mixes
Native stock: 95%
Regional focus: Midwest
Services: custom mixing
Comments: We offer predominately prairie species with some woodland species.

Missouri Wildflowers Nursery
9814 Pleasant Hill Road
Jefferson City, MO 65109
Sales type: mail order, retail
Type of stock: shrubs, herbaceous plants, seeds, seed mixes, glade perennials
Native stock: 100%
Regional focus: Missouri and surrounding states
Services: landscaping
Comments: We have the showiest glade and prairie species Missouri has to offer.

Sharp Bros. Seed Co.
Rt. 4, P.O. Box 237A
Clinton, MO 64735 (816) 885-6845
Sales type: mail-order, retail, wholesale
Type of stock: seeds, seed mixes
Native stock: 90%
Regional focus: central, Great Plains
Services: N/A
Comments: We have specialized in native grasses and wildflowers for over 30 years.

Montana

Bitterroot Native Growers, Inc.
445 Quast Lane
Corvallis, MT 59828 (406) 961-4991
Sales type: mail-order, wholesale
Type of stock: trees, shrubs, herbaceous plants, wetland species
Native stock: 100%
Regional focus: west of Miss. River
Services: habitat and wetland restoration, landscaping, custom growing
Comments: BNG offers a wide variety of plants and services including site planning and installation.

Four Winds Nursery
5853 East Shore Rt.
Polson, MT 59860 (406) 887-2215
Sales type: mail-order, retail
Type of stock: trees, shrubs, herbaceous plants, seeds, seed mixes
Native stock: 20%
Regional focus: N. Rocky Mtns., Northern Plains
Services: landscaping of alpine, rock, bog gardens
Comments: We are a small mom and pop business and carry a large variety of hardy, regional plants.

Valley Nursery
P.O. Box 4845
Helena, MT 59604 (406) 442-8460
Sales type: mail-order, retail, wholesale
Type of stock: trees, shrubs, herbaceous plants, seeds
Native stock: 10% +
Regional focus: Northern Plains
Services: habitat restoration
Comments: We offer plants for cold climates.

Wild Flower Seeds
16100 Highway 10 A, West
Anaconda, MT 59711 (406) 563-8048
Sales type: mail-order, retail, wholesale
Type of stock: seeds
Native stock: 100%
Regional focus: N. Rocky Mtns., high elevations
Services: home landscaping
Comments: This is a small home landscaping business offering a variety of wildflower seeds.

North Carolina

Appalachian Trees
P.O. Box 92
Glendale Springs, NC 28629   (919)982-2377
Sales type: wholesale
Type of stock: trees, shrubs
Native stock: 50%
Regional focus: southeast, eastern U.S.
Services: N/A
Comments: We are a liner producer of mostly deciduous trees and shrub material from seeds and cuttings.

Argura Nurseries, Inc.
7000 Canada Road
Tuckasegee, NC 28783 (704) 293-5550
Sales type: mail-order, wholesale
Type of stock: trees, shrubs, groundcovers
Native stock: 90%
Regional focus: eastern U.S.
Services: habitat and wetland restoration
Comments: We offer conifer seedlings, transplants, field trees, and deciduous liners.

Gardens of the Blue Ridge
P.O. Box 10
Pineola, NC 28662 (704) 733-2417
Sales type: mail-order, retail, wholesale
Type of stock: trees, shrubs, herbaceous plants, seeds, seed mixes, native wildflowers
Native stock: 100%
Regional focus: eastern U.S.
Services: N/A
Comments: We specialize in native wildflowers, trees, and shrubs.

Griffey's Nursery
1670 Hwy 25/70
Marshall, NC 28753 (704) 656-2334
Sales type: mail-order, wholesale
Type of stock: trees, shrubs, herbaceous plants, vines
Native stock: N/A
Regional focus: N/A
Services: N/A
Comments: We offer rhododendrons, azaleas, evergreens and more.

Lamtree Farm
Rte. 1, Box 162
Warrensville, NC 28693 (919) 385-6144
Sales type: mail-order, wholesale
Type of stock: trees, shrubs
Native stock: 90%
Regional focus: Mtns. of North Carolina, SE and NE U.S
Services: landscaping, contract growing
Comments: We offer native rhododendrons, azaleas, kalmia, stewartias, styrax and much more.

Niche Gardens
1111 Dawson Road
Chapel Hill, NC 27516   (919) 967-0078
Sales type: mail-order, retail, wholesale
Type of stock: trees, shrubs, herbaceous plants, seeds, seed mixes
Native stock: 80%
Regional focus: N. and S. East
Services: habitat restoration, landscaping
Comments: We specialize in nursery propagated N. American native plants with a special emphasis on southeastern natives. We also offer custom growing services.

Nebraska

P. E. Allen Farm Supply
Rt. 2, Box 8
Bristow, NE 68719-9407   (402) 583-9924
Sales type: mail-order, retail, wholesale
Type of stock: seeds
Native stock: 100%
Regional focus: Central U.S.
Services: N/A
Comments: All seed is collected in the wild with an emphasis on Amorpha canescens.

Stock Seed Farms, Inc.
28008 Mill Road
Murdock, NE 68407-2350 (402) 867-3771
Sales type: mail-order, retail, wholesale
Type of stock: seeds, seed mixes
Native stock: 90%
Regional focus: Great Plains through the northeast
Services: N/A
Comments: We have 35 years of working with native prairie grasses and wildflowers.

New Jersey

Hess' Nurseries, Inc.
P.O. Box 326, Rt. 553
Cedarville, NJ 08311   (609) 447-4213
Sales type: wholesale
Type of stock: trees, shrubs, seeds
Native stock: 90%
Regional focus: northeast
Services: wetland restoration
Comments: N/A

Princeton Nurseries
P.O. Box 191
Princeton, NJ 08542 (609) 924-1776
Sales type: wholesale
Type of stock: trees, shrubs
Native stock: 25%
Regional focus: northeast
Services: N/A
Comments: We offer native woody plants bare root, in containers or B&B.

Well-Sweep Herb Farm
317 Mt. Bethel Road
Port Murray, NJ 07865 (908) 852-5390
Sales type: mail-order, retail
Type of stock: herbaceous plants, seeds
Native stock: N/A
Regional focus: north coast
Services: lectures, classes
Comments: We offer a large selection of wild and native herb plants.

New Mexico

Curtis & Curtis, Inc.
Star Route, Box 8A
Clovis, NM 88101 1-800-933-2774
Sales type: retail, wholesale
Type of stock: seeds, seed mixes
Native stock: 80%
Regional focus: southwest
Services: N/A
Comments: We specialize in native plant seeds.

Desert Moon Nursery
P. O. Box 600
Veguita, NM 87062 (505) 864-0614
Sales type: mail-order, retail, wholesale
Type of stock: trees, shrubs, herbaceous plants, cacti, succulents
Native stock: 99%
Regional focus: southwestern U.S.
Services: landscaping, habitat restoration, consultation
Comments: We specialize in southwest plants and carry a large selection of hardy cacti, agaves, and yuccas.

Plants of the Southwest
Rt. 6, Box 11-A
Santa Fe, NM 87501 (505) 438-8888
Sales type: mail-order, retail, wholesale
Type of stock: trees, shrubs, herbaceous plants, seeds, seeds mixes
Native stock: 100%
Regional focus: southwestern
Services: landscaping, habitat and wetland restoration
Comments: We hope you enjoy our catalog which is photographically dedicated to shrubs.

New York

John H. Gordon Jr.
1385 Campbell Blvd.
Amherst, NY 14228-1404 (716) 691-9371
Sales type: mail-order, retail
Type of stock: trees, shrubs, seeds, nut trees, pawpaw, persimmon
Native stock: N/A
Regional focus: northeast, midwest
Services: habitat and wetland restoration
Comments: We specialize in nut trees, pawpaw, and persimmons.

Panfield Nurseries, Inc.
322 Southdown Road
Huntington, NY 11743 (516) 427-0112
Sales type: retail, wholesale
Type of stock: meadow wildflowers (100% propagated), woodland plants and ferns
Native stock: 20%
Regional focus: northeast
Services: habitat restoration, landscaping, consultation
Comments: Established in 1931, we have a large assortment of perennials, native and woodland plants.

S. Scherer & Sons
104 Waterside Road
Northport, NY 11768 (516) 261-7432
Sales type: mail-order, retail, wholesale
Type of stock: trees, shrubs, herbaceous plants, seeds, seed mixes
Native stock: N/A
Regional focus: N/A
Services: grower of aquatic plants
Comments: We offer aquatic plants and water garden accessories.

Wildginger Woodlands
P.O. Box 1091
Webster, NY 14580
Sales type: mail-order, please send $1.00 for descriptive catalog
Type of stock: herbaceous plants, seeds
Native stock: N/A
Regional focus: N/A
Services: N/A
Comments: We are a small and expanding nursery, catering to the home gardener. We offer a large variety.

Ohio

Bekatha's Garden
P.O. Box 615, 3354 Lebanon Road
Lebanon, OH 45036   (513) 932-1070
Sales type: mail-order, retail, wholesale
Type of stock: trees, shrubs, herbaceous plants, seeds,
    seed mixes
Native stock: N/A
Regional focus: N/A
Services: habitat and wetland restoration, landscaping
Comments: N/A

Oklahoma

Grasslander
Rt. 1, Box 56
Hennessey, OK 73742   (405) 853-2607
Sales type: N/A
Type of stock: grasses
Native stock: N/A
Regional focus: N/A
Services: propagate and harvest grasses
Comments: We make the best grass seeder on the market.

Oregon

Balance Restoration Nursery
27995 Chambers Mill Road
Lorane, OR 97451   (503) 942-5530
Sales type: mail-order, wholesale
Type of stock: trees, shrubs, herbaceous plants, emergants
Native stock: 94%
Regional focus: northwest
Services: consultation
Comments: We specialize in native wetland plants.

Forestfarm
990 Tetherow Road
Williams, OR 97544   (503) 864-6963
Sales type: mail-order
Type of stock: trees, shrubs, herbaceous plants
Native stock: N/A
Regional focus: all regions, especially the west
Services: N/A
Comments: We offer extensive selection of American
    native plants for sunny meadows, shady woodlands,
    and wet and dry conditions.

Greer Gardens
1280 Goodpasture Island Road
Eugene, OR 97401   (503) 686-8266
Sales type: mail-order, retail
Type of stock: trees, shrubs, herbaceous plants
Native stock: 5 - 10%
Regional focus: all over
Services: N/A
Comments: We offer rare and unusual plants

Nature's Garden
40611 Highway 226
Scio, OR 97374-9351   (503) 394-3217
Sales type: mail-order, retail, wholesale
Type of stock: trees, shrubs, herbaceous plants
Native stock: 10%
Regional focus: mid-Atlantic to New England
Services: commercial agriculture
Comments: We grow mostly iris, Campanulas and
    Sisyrinchium, but do have some woodland plants.

Sevenoaks Native Nursery
2320 N. W. Huntington Drive
Corvallis, OR 97330   (503) 745-5540
Sales type: wholesale
Type of stock: trees, shrubs (all propagated)
Native stock: 100%
Regional focus: north and southwest, Rocky Mtns. area
Services: habitat and wetland restoration, landscaping
Comments: Grower of Populas tremuloides and other
    high elevation, ornamental and wildlife plants.

Turf Seed, Inc.
P.O. Box 250
Hubbard, OR 97032   (503) 651-2130
Sales type: wholesale
Type of stock: seeds, seed mixes
Native stock: N/A
Regional focus: northern tier states
Services: seed production
Comments: We offer a large selection of turfgrass seed
    for golf course use, cool season species. Many of our
    varieties contain "endophyte" for natural insect resis-
    tance without herbicides.

Pennsylvania

Appalachian Wildflower Nursery
Rte.1, Box 275A
Reedsville, PA 17084 (717) 667-6998
Sales type: mail-order, retail
Type of stock: trees, shrubs, herbaceous plants, seeds, seed mixes
Native stock: 45%
Regional focus: Intermountain West, Rockies, Cascades, Arizona, midwest, northeast
Services: none
Comments: To receive a descriptive catalog, please send $2.00 which is deductible from order.

Carino Nurseries
P.O. Box 538
Indiana, PA 15701 (412) 463-3350
Sales type: mail-order, retail, wholesale (now shipping to customers in 46 states)
Type of stock: trees, shrubs
Native stock: N/A
Regional focus: most of the U.S.
Services: habitat and wetland restoration, landscaping, soil conservation
Comments: We offer an abundance of bareroot seedlings and transplants, conifers and deciduous.

Flickingers' Nursery
P.O. Box 245
Sagamore, PA 16250 (412)783-6528
Sales type: mail-order, wholesale
Type of stock: trees, shrubs, groundcover (Vinca Minor *Myrtle*)
Native stock: 90%
Regional focus: northeast, midwest
Services: habitat restoration
Comments: We offer a complete selection of bare root pines, spruce, fir and Canadian hemlock.

Johnston Nurseries
RD 1, Box 100
Creekside, PA 15732 (412) 463-8456
Sales type: mail-order
Type of stock: trees, shrubs, Christmas trees (all bare root nursery stock)
Native stock: 50%
Regional focus: northeast, southeast, midwest
Services: N/A
Comments: We specialize in reforestation and conservation planting.

Musser Forests, Inc.
Dept. EF, Box 340
Indiana, PA 15701-0340 (412) 465-5685
Sales type: mail-order, retail, wholesale
Type of stock: trees, shrubs, herbaceous plants
Native stock: 10%
Regional focus: northeast, midwest
Services: N/A
Comments: N/A

Primrose Path
R.D. 2, Box 110
Scottsdale, PA 15683 (412) 887-6756
Sales type: mail-order, retail
Type of stock: herbaceous plants (all plants are nursery propagated)
Native stock: 60%
Regional focus: northern two-thirds of the U.S.
Services: garden installation and design
Comments: We specialize in phlox, woodland plants, western plants amenable to the northeast.

The Rosemary House
120 S. Market St.
Mechanicsburg, PA 17055 (717) 697-5111
Sales type: mail-order, retail
Type of stock: herbaceous plants, herb seeds
Native stock: 10%
Regional focus: northern U.S.
Services: garden design
Comments: We specialize in herbs for all purposes.

Wildflower Patch
442 Brookside Drive
Walnutport, PA 18088 (215) 767-3195
Sales type: mail-order, retail
Type of stock: seeds, seed mixes
Native stock: 80%
Regional focus: most of the U.S.
Services: N/A
Comments: We mail-order single varieties and specialized mixes for geographic areas, specific applications, and customized uses.

South Carolina

Charlestown Aquatic Nurseries
4624 Hwy 162
Hollywood, SC 29449 (803) 766-1511
Sales type: mail-order, wholesale
Type of stock: aquatic plants, moisture-loving perennials
  and grasses
Native stock: 25%
Regional focus: eastern seaboard
Services: landscaping, specializing in pond design
Comments: We offer a broad selection of aquatic plants
  and specialize in golf course beautification.

Coastal Gardens & Nursery
4611 Socastee Boulevard
Myrtle Beach, SC 29575 (803) 293-2000
Sales type: mail-order, retail, wholesale
Type of stock: shrubs, herbaceous plants
Native stock: 10%
Regional focus: southeast, southern U.S.
Services: landscaping, wetland restoration
Comments: We offer shade and ornamental wetland
  plants.

Park Seed Co., Inc.
P.O. Box 31, Cokesburg Road
Greenwood, SC 29647-0001 (803) 223-8555, ext. 232
Sales type: mail-order
Type of stock: herbaceous plants, seeds
Native stock: 100%
Regional focus: N/A
Services: N/A
Comments: N/A

Wayside Gardens
1 Garden Lane
Hodges, SC 29695-0001 (803) 223-8555, ext. 232
Sales type: mail-order
Type of stock: trees, shrubs, herbaceous plants
Native stock: 100%
Regional focus: N/A
Services: N/A
Comments: N/A

Woodlanders, Inc.
1128 Colleton Avenue
Aiken, SC 29801 (803) 648-7522
Sales type: N/A
Type of stock: trees, shrubs, herbaceous plants
Native stock: 60%
Regional focus: southeastern and southwestern U.S.
Services: N/A
Comments: We offer over one thousand species of trees,
  shrubs, vines, perennials, mostly uncommon or rare.

Tennessee

Hidden Springs Nursery
Rt. 14, Box 159
Cookeville, TN 38501 (615) 268-9889
Sales type: mail-order, retail
Type of stock: trees, shrubs, herbaceous plants
Native stock: 50%
Regional focus: midwest, southwest, northeast
Services: N/A
Comments: We offer improved varieties of native and
  low-input fruits and nuts, and nitrogen fixing shrubs.

Fred's Plant Farm
P.O. Box 707
Dresden, TN 38225 (901) 364-3754/1-800-243-9377
Sales type: mail-order, wholesale
Type of stock: sweet potato seeds and plants
Native stock: 50%
Regional focus: All states except California and Arizona
Services: N/A
Comments: We grow sweet potato and ship the seed and
  plants from May to July.

Mountain Ornamental Nursery
P.O. Box 268
Altamont, TN 37301 (615) 692-3424
Sales type: wholesale
Type of stock: trees, shrubs, herbaceous plants, seeds
Native stock: 4%
Regional focus: northern states, some western
Services: N/A
Comments: We can supply large quantities of most items
  listed in catalog and a variety of tree/shrub seed.

Native Gardens
5737 Fisher Lane
Greenback, TN 37742 (615) 856-3350
Sales type: mail-order, retail, wholesale
Type of stock: trees, shrubs, herbaceous plants, seeds
Native stock: 99%
Regional focus: eastern woodland
Services: consultation/design, contract growing
Comments: We began propagating native plants in 1984
  and now offer over 150 species of plants.

Texas

Aldridge Nursery, Inc.
P.O. Box 1299
Von Ormy, TX 78073 (512) 622-3491
Sales type: wholesale
Type of stock: trees, shrubs
Native stock: 30%
Regional focus: south and central U.S.
Services: N/A
Comments: We specialize in shade and ornamental trees.

Dallas Nature Center
7171 Mountain Creek Parkway
Dallas, TX 75249 (214) 296-2476
Sales type: mail-order, retail, wholesale
Type of stock: trees, shrubs, herbaceous plants, seeds
Native stock: 100%
Regional focus: Dallas Co., Texas Blacklands
Services: habitat and prairie restoration, landscaping
Comments: We sell only what we grow ourselves.

Doremus Wholesale Nursery
Rt. 2, Box 750
Warren, TX 77664 (409) 547-3536
Sales type: wholesale
Type of stock: trees, shrubs, herbaceous plants
Native stock: 60%
Regional focus: south and southeastern Texas
Services: N/A
Comments: We offer a large selection of uncommon native trees.

Gardens
1818 West 35th Street
Austin, TX 78703 (512) 451-5490
Sales type: retail
Type of stock: trees, shrubs, herbaceous plants
Native stock: 60%
Regional focus: Texas
Services: landscaping, landscape design
Comments: N/A

Gunsight Mountain Ranch & Nursery
P.O. Box 86, Williams Creek Road
Tarpley, TX 78883 (512) 562-3225
Sales type: retail, wholesale
Type of stock: trees, shrubs, herbaceous plants
Native stock: 100%
Regional focus: Texas, except east Texas
Services: habitat restoration, landscaping
Comments: We specialize in seed grown or cuttings for arid Texas. Our own ranch provides much material. We specialize in Edwards Plateau plants.

Heep's Nursery
1705 Jason
Edinburg, TX 78539 (512) 381-8813
Sales type: retail, wholesale
Type of stock: trees, shrubs, herbaceous plants, grasses
Native stock: 100%
Regional focus: south Texas
Services: habitat restoration, landscaping
Comments: We offer over 100 species native to south Texas. All plants are propagated by seed or cuttings.

Island Botanics Environmental Consultants
3734 Flour Bluff Drive
Corpus Christi, TX 78418 (512) 937-4873
Sales type: contract grower only, consulting
Type of stock: grasses, dune species
Native stock: 100%
Regional focus: Texas Gulf Coast
Services: habitat and wetland restoration, consulting
Comments: N/A

J'Don Seeds International
P.O. Box 10998-533
Austin, TX 78766 1-800-848-1641
Sales type: mail-order, wholesale
Type of stock: seeds, seed mixes
Native stock: 40%
Regional focus: all regions
Services: N/A
Comments: We offer a large selection of native wildflower seed, regional mixes, and custom mixes.

Lone Star Growers
7960 Cagnon Road
San Antonio, TX 78252-2202 (512) 677-8020
Sales type: wholesale
Type of stock: trees, shrubs, herbaceous plants
Native stock: 10%
Regional focus: southwestern and southern U.S.
Services: N/A
Comments: We specialize in container grown southwestern and southern prairie natives.

Madrone Nursery
2318 Hilliard Road
San Marcos, TX 78666 (512) 353-3944
Sales type: wholesale
Type of stock: trees, shrubs, herbaceous plants, seeds
Native stock: 98%
Regional focus: Trans Pecos, Edwards Plateau, Cross Timbers, Blackland Prairie
Services: habitat restoration, landscaping
Comments: We propagate plants native to Texas and never wild collect.

Native American Seed
3400 Long Prairie
Flower Mound, TX 75028   (214) 539-0534
Sales type: mail-order, wholesale
Type of stock: seeds
Native stock: 100%
Regional focus: Texas
Services: habitat and wetland restoration
Comments: We offer prairie restoration using wildflow-
ers and native grasses.

Native Ornamentals
Box 997
Mertzon, TX 76941   (915) 835-2021
Sales type: retail
Type of stock: trees and shrubs, herbaceous plants, seeds,
wildflowers
Native stock: 100%
Regional focus: southwest and west Texas
Services: landscaping
Comments: We specialize in native, drought tolerant
plants to add beauty and conserve water.

Shades of Green
334 W. Sunset Road
San Antonio, TX 78209-1734   (512) 824-3772
Sales type: retail
Type of stock: trees and shrubs, herbaceous plants, seeds
Native stock: 25%
Regional focus: Texas/southwest
Services: N/A
Comments: We emphasize proper planting as well as
plant selection. 100% nursery grown and propagated.

W.H. Anton Seed Co., Inc.
P.O. Box 667
Lockhart, TX 78644   (512) 398-2433
Sales type: mail-order, retail, wholesale
Type of stock: seeds
Native stock: 1%
Regional focus: central and west Texas
Services: adapted seeds for central and west Texas
Comments: Our objective is to supply adapted grasses,
clovers, legumes, and buffalograss as a lawn estab-
lishment in areas where intensive care is not practical.

Wildseed Farms, Inc.
P.O. Box 308
Eagle Lake, TX 77434   1-800-848-0078
Sales type: mail-order, retail, wholesale
Type of stock: herbaceous plants, seeds, seed mixes
Native stock: 90%
Regional focus: all U.S.
Services: habitat restoration, landscaping, custom seed
mixes
Comments: We have a large inventory of wildflower
species. Our 48 page, color catalog is $2.00.

Utah

Granite Seed Co.
P.O. Box 177
Lehi, UT 84043   (801) 768-4422
Sales type: wholesale
Type of stock: seeds, seed mixes
Native stock: 85%
Regional focus: west of the Mississippi
Services: consultation, erosion control
Comments: We offer a diverse selection of native and
domesticated grasses, turfgrasses and wildflowers.

Intermountain Cactus
1478 No. 750 East
Kaysville, UT 84037   (801) 546-2006
Sales type: mail-order
Type of stock: herbaceous plants
Native stock: 100%
Regional focus: western U.S.
Services: N/A
Comments: We offer a large selection of winter hardy
cactus.

Maple Leaf Industries, Inc.
480 South 50 East
Ephraim, UT 84627   (801) 283-4701
Sales type: mail-order, retail, wholesale
Type of stock: seeds, seed mixes, some root stock
Native stock: 80%
Regional focus: Rocky Mtns. area
Services: habitat and wetland restoration, landscaping,
consulting
Comments: We have a large selection of native seeds,
grasses, shrubs, and flowers, most Rocky mtns. na-
tives.

Virginia

Andre Viette Farm and Nursery
Route 608
Fishersville, VA 22939   (703) 943-2315
Sales type: mail-order, retail, wholesale
Type of stock: herbaceous plants
Native stock: .5 %
Regional focus: southeast and northeast
Services: landscaping, consultation
Comments: We are collectors of rare and exotic plants.
We propagate 99% of our stock.

Edible Landscaping
P.O. Box 77
Afton, VA 22920
Sales type: mail-order, retail, wholesale
Type of stock: trees, shrubs, herbaceous plants
Native stock: 40%
Regional focus: north, south, eastern U.S.
Services: N/A
Comments: We offer less care edibles for beauty and bounty.

Holley's Hobbies
Rt. 4, Box 270A
Warrenton, VA 22186 (703) 347-7663
Sales type: retail, wholesale
Type of stock: herbaceous plants
Native stock: 50%
Regional focus: Virginia
Services: landscaping
Comments: We specialize in landscaping in the shade.

Ingleside Plantation Nurseries
P.O. Box 1038
Oak Grove, VA 22443 (804) 224-7111
Sales type: wholesale
Type of stock: trees, shrubs
Native stock: 60%
Regional focus: northeast, southeast
Services: N/A
Comments: We are the largest wholesale grower of woody ornamental nursery stock in Virginia.

Virginia Natives
Wildside, Box 18
Hume, VA 22639 (703) 364-1665 or 364-1001
Sales type: retail, wholesale (catalogues are available for $1.00)
Type of stock: herbaceous plants, seeds
Native stock: 95%
Regional focus: east and southeast
Services: habitat and wetland restoration, landscaping
Comments: We offer herbaceous perennial wildflowers, ferns, native and ornamental grasses.

Virginia Wilde Farms
Rt. 2, Box 1512
Hanover, VA 23069 (804) 643-0021
Sales type: mail-order, retail, wholesale
Type of stock: trees, shrubs, herbaceous plants, seeds, seed mixes
Native stock: 55%
Regional focus: southeast and Florida
Services: landscaping, garden design
Comments: The nursery is dedicated to expanding the use of "useful natives" which require limited care to survive in Virginia's challenging climate. Consulting services are available.

Vermont

Cady's Falls Nursery
R.D. 3, Box 2100
Morrisville, VT 05661 (802) 888-5559
Sales type: retail, wholesale (to landscapers only)
Type of stock: trees, shrubs, herbaceous plants
Native stock: N/A
Regional focus: mainly northeast
Services: N/A
Comments: We are mainly a perennial nursery but carry some native plants. None are wild collected.

Washington

Abundant Life Seed Foundation
P.O. Box 772
Port Townsend, WA 98368 (206) 385-5660
Sales type: mail-order, retail, wholesale
Type of stock: seeds, seed mixes
Native stock: 25%
Regional focus: Pacific Northwest
Services: N/A
Comments: We offer seeds of native and naturalized trees, shrubs, wildflowers and of herbs and flowers.

Aldrich Berry Farm and Nursery, Inc.
190 Aldrich Road
Mossyrock, WA 98564 (206) 983-3138
Sales type: wholesale
Type of stock: trees, shrubs
Native stock: 80%
Regional focus: Pacific Northwest
Services: contract growing
Comments: N/A

Bear Creek Nursery
P.O. Box 411, Bear Creek Road
Northport, WA 99157-0411
Sales type: mail-order
Type of stock: trees, shrubs
Native stock: 50%
Regional focus: northwest, west, Rocky Mtns.
Services: N/A
Comments: We have one of the largest apple collections in the world.

Davenport Seed Corp.
1404 4th St., P.O. Box 187
Davenport, WA 99122   1-800 828-8873
Sales type: wholesale
Type of stock: seeds, seed mixes
Native stock: N/A
Regional focus: NW, SW, NE, and Midwestern U.S.
Services: habitat restoration
Comments: We produce and clean reclamation and native
    grass species at Davenport Seed.

Foliage Gardens
2003 128th Avenue SE
Bellevue, WA 98005   (206) 747-2998
Sales type: mail-order, retail (color catalog, $2.00)
Type of stock: ferns
Native stock: 37%
Regional focus: all regions
Services: N/A
Comments: We offer a selection of native and exotic
    woodland ferns as well as rock garden species.

Frosty Hollow Nursery
Box 53
Langley, WA 98260   (206) 221-2332
Sales type: mail-order, retail, wholesale
Type of stock: seeds (for a seed list, send a self-addressed
    envelope)
Native stock: 100%
Regional focus: Pacific Northwest
Services: habitat and wetland restoration, consultation
Comments: Consultation services available to managers
    of golf courses wishing to increase diversity and
    improve wildlife habitat at existing courses.

Henry's Plant Farm
4522 132nd St. NE
Snohomish, WA 98290   (509) 466-0230
Sales type: mail-order, wholesale
Type of stock: seeds
Native stock: N/A
Regional focus: Pacific Northwest, N. Rockies, N. Cas-
    cades, Olympics
Services: N/A
Comments: N/A

J'Don Seeds International
2633 E. Beaver Lake Dr. SE
Issaquah, WA 98027   1-800-848-1641
Sales type: mail-order, wholesale
Type of stock: seeds, seed mixes
Native stock: 40%
Regional focus: all regions
Services: N/A
Comments: We offer a large selection of native wild-
    flower seed, regional mixes, and custom mixes.

McLaughlin's Seeds
Buttercup's Acre, P.O. Box 550
Mead, WA 99021-0550   (509) 466-0230
Sales type: mail-order, wholesale
Type of stock: seeds
Native stock: N/A
Regional focus: Pacific Northwest, N. Rockies, N. Cas-
    cades, Olympics
Comments: Established in 1929, we have been a pioneer
    in the production and marketing of authentic native
    wildflower, alpine and rock plant seeds in consign-
    ment packets and by mail order.

Plants of the Wild
P.O. Box 866
Tekoa, WA 99033   (509) 284-2848
Sales type: mail-order, retail, wholesale
Type of stock: trees, shrubs, herbaceous plants
Native stock: 90%
Regional focus: northwest
Comments: We offer over 100 species, from wildflowers
    to tall trees.

Wisconsin

Applied Ecological Service, Inc.
P.O. 256/ Rt. 3, Smith Road
Brodhead, WI 53520
Sales type: mail-order, retail, wholesale
Type of stock: seeds, seed mixes
Native stock: 100%
Regional focus: Wisconsin, Iowa, Illinois
Services: habitat, wetland restoration, land use planning,
    site selection
Comments: Our staff of botanists/ecologists offer con-
    sulting and contracting services on natural area resto-
    ration.

Country Wetlands Nursery & Consulting, Ltd.
S. 75- W. 20755 Field Dr.
Muskego, WI 53150   (414)679-1268
Sales type: mail-order, retail
Type of stock: shrubs, herbaceous plants, seeds, seed
    mixes
Native stock: 100%
Regional focus: east, west, midwest
Services: habitat, wetland restoration, landscaping, edu-
    cation
Comments: CWNC designs and executes natural land-
    scaping projects which include prairie and woodland
    systems.

Hauser's Superior View Farm
Rt. 1, Box 199
Bayfield, WI 54814 (715) 779-5404
Sales type: mail-order, retail, wholesale
Type of stock: herbaceous plants
Native stock: 80%
Regional focus: midwest, northeast
Services: The best plants at low prices
Comments: Established in 1908, Hauser's sells only one
　　to two year old, field grown plants.

J.W. Jung Seed Co.
335 S. High St.
Randolph, WI 53957 (414) 326-3121
Sales type: mail-order, retail
Type of stock: trees, shrubs, herbaceous plants, seeds,
　　seed mixes, bulbs
Native stock: 85%
Regional focus: midwest
Services: landscaping, home gardens
Comments: We offer well adapted species for the midwest.

Kettle Moraine Natural Landscaping
W996 Birchwood Dr.
Campbellsport, WI 53010 (414) 533-8939
Sales type: mail-order, retail (catalog is $1.50)
Type of stock: seeds, seed mixes
Native stock: 100%
Regional focus: southern Wisconsin
Services: habitat restoration, landscaping, consulting
Comments: We offer a large selection of prairie forb
　　seeds with complete planting instructions.

Little Valley Farm
Rt. 3, Box 544
Spring Green, WI 53588 (608) 935-3324
Sales type: mail-order, retail
Type of stock: shrubs, herbaceous plants, some seeds
Native stock: 100%
Regional focus: midwest
Services: landscaping
Comments: We offer landscaping with native shrubs, and
　　a select group of woodland and prairie species.

Milaeger's Gardens
4838 Douglass Ave.
Racine, WI 53402-2498 (414) 639-2371
Sales type: mail-order, retail
Type of stock: herbaceous plants
Native stock: 10%
Regional focus: prairie regions
Services: landscaping
Comments: We offer a large selection of native prairie
　　species as well as exotic perennials.

Prairie Future Seed Company
P.O. Box 644
Menomonee Falls, WI 53052-0644 (414) 491-0685
Sales type: mail-order, retail, wholesale
Type of stock: herbaceous plants, seeds, seed mixes
Native stock: 93%
Regional focus: midwest
Services: landscaping, consultation
Comments: We offer over 200 native prairie species to
　　select from in 1992.

Prairie Nursery
P.O. Box 306
Westfield, WI 53964 (608) 296-3679
Sales type: mail-order
Type of stock: herbaceous plants, seeds, seed mixes
Native stock: 100%
Regional focus: northeast, midwest, mid-Atlantic
Services: habitat, prairie restoration, landscaping, design
Comments: We are experts in prairie restoration and offer
　　numerous native prairie plants and seed.

Prairie Ridge Nursery
9738 Overland Road
Mt. Horeb, WI 53572 (608) 437-5245
Sales type: mail-order, retail, wholesale
Type of stock: herbaceous plants, seeds, seed mixes
Native stock: 100%
Regional focus: Midwest
Services: habitat, wetland and woodland restoration
Comments: We offer complete consulting, planting and
　　management services for prairie, wetland and wood-
　　land restorations and gardens. All plants are propa-
　　gated at our nursery.

Reeseville Ridge Nursery
P.O. Box 171, 309 S. Main St.
Reeseville, WI 53579 (414) 927-3291
Sales type: mail-order, wholesale
Type of stock: trees, shrubs, some herbaceous plants,
　　seeds
Native stock: 50%
Regional focus: states northeast of the Rockies and Ap-
　　palachian mtns.
Services: native plant community consultation
Comments: Nearly all plant material in lining out sizes,
　　no B&B stock available.

Wehr Nature Center
9701 W. College Avenue
Franklin, WI 53132 (414) 425-8500
Sales type: retail
Type of stock: seed mixes
Native stock: 100%
Regional focus: upper midwest, Wisconsin
Services: N/A
Comments: Our 1992 mix includes 38 native prairie forb
　　species harvested from prairies in SE Wisconsin.

No. 628

The

HARVARD
SONG BOOK

Compiled and Edited

by

ELLIOT FORBES

E. C. SCHIRMER MUSIC COMPANY

600 Washington Street   Boston, Mass.

Table of Contents

I

HARVARD SONGS

II

SONGS OF OTHER COLLEGES

v

III

Traditional Songs

IV

Traditional Songs of the Harvard Glee Club

V

Motets

Preface

It was 107 years ago that the first Harvard song book appeared with the title "College Song Book. A Collection of American College Songs", compiled and arranged by C. Wistar Stevens '60 and dedicated "To My Classmates, the Class of '60 at Harvard and to all music-loving students of American Colleges." Mr. Stevens' Preface makes such charming and nostalgic reading that the present editor feels obliged to share it with you:

> It is a source of pleasure to see the vigorous efforts put forth in Yale, Williams, and Dartmouth Colleges, to increase the number and quality of College songs. To collect the songs made hallowed by time, and to endeavor to raise the tone and merit of College poems generally, are worthy objects. And the Editor of the Collection hopes that he has accomplished something to further this project.

> This volume is intended as a companion to College Words and Customs. It has been the Editor's aim to select nearly all the melodies of all Colleges which cultivate music. In the choice of poems, he has been guided by their intrinsic worth, and especially by the light which they throw on permanent College customs. It is hoped that the new feature of piano-forte accompaniments will be acceptable to amateurs, both those within the College walls, by whom instrumental music is cultivated, and to all graduates, to the latter of whom the songs of *Alma Mater* must be dear. How cheering to forget now and then the cares and bustle of active life, and sing over the songs, which are associated with all the merry-makings and festivals of College life — which are whistled through the College year, and hummed while "digging" over Greek tragedies, sung in Glee Clubs and in the nightly serenade. The melodies and words bring back familiar faces and sports, and the wearied heart feels young again, and realizes the force of Horace's advice:

> Misce stultitiam consiliis brevem:
> Dulce est desipere in loco.

> Although this is the first published Collection of Harvard Songs, yet music is by no means neglected by the students here; on the contrary it is pursued with much enthusiasm. The concerts of the PIERIAN SODALITY, and HARVARD GLEE CLUB, the past winter, gave ample evidence how great success can be attained by systematic practice. The oldest graduates of the University inform the Editor that thirty years ago musical societies existed here, and the students sang with great gusto the popular airs of the day, as well as selections from the German masters. It has been found impossible to obtain many Harvard songs, because many have been forgotten, and many are confined to secret societies. The present Collection has been handed down orally, a fact that will account for whatever imperfections may be found in it.

> To the Editor's classmates, and particularly to Mr. S. W. Langmaid, of the Class of '59, and Mr. Levi P. Homer, the accomplished instructor in music, he would render hearty thanks for the ready assistance which they have uniformly given him.

> C. WISTAR STEVENS.

Harvard University, Oct. 5th, 1859

At this time the Harvard Glee Club was a year old, the Pierian Sodality had just celebrated its fiftieth birthday, and Mr. Homer, mentioned above, had already taught for four years in the Music Department. His place was taken by John Knowles Paine in 1862. Ten years later music as an academic subject had received official recognition by the college, but there were to be another forty years before there was any direct relation between Harvard singing and the Music Department.

During that time there appeared the following collections of Harvard song books:

1886 "Music — Sung by the Alumni at the Two Hundred and Fiftieth Anniversary of the Foundation of Harvard University, November 7 (1636–1886)."

1886 "Songs of Harvard", compiled by H. D. Sleeper, '89, with a foreword by Sleeper and H. E. Everett '89, and dedicated "to members of the Harvard Glee Club, past, present and future and to students and alumni of Harvard University."

1892 "The New Harvard Song Book", compiled by R. T. Whitehouse '91 and Frederick Bruegger '92 (revised by Whitehouse in 1896), and dedicated "To the Glee Club of Harvard University."

1902 "Harvard University Songs", compiled by E. F. DuBois '03, and dedicated to the Harvard Union.

1913 "Songs of Harvard", compiled by Lloyd Adams Noble '14 without dedication but including "A Word from Dean Briggs."

Just a year before this last edition Archibald T. Davison '06 had been asked by the members of the Harvard Glee Club to coach their singing. Then in 1919 came the big step, which was to confirm officially the new phase of singing at Harvard: "Doc" Davison was persuaded to conduct the Glee Club in the serious music that they performed in public, and at the same time the Glee Club disassociated itself with its long-time companion, the Mandolin Society.

Three years later the final Harvard Song Book, before this present edition, was published by the Glee Club and dedicated to its conductor, with a "word" from President Lowell. It was the work primarily of Abbot Low Moffat '23 and Henry Clough-Leighter, Editor-in-Chief of E. C. Schirmer Music Co.

The contents of the 1922 Song Book were similar to those of all preceding editions in that they were all college songs, social songs and popular songs. The modern Glee Club era then was only a few years old, too soon for the new tastes in Harvard singing to be represented. Doc's exciting years of pioneering were followed, starting in 1933, with the twenty-five years of dynamic growth under G. Wallace Woodworth which so many of us have experienced directly.

Inasmuch as there are now some fifty generations of Glee Club alumni who have experienced the kind of singing inaugurated by Doc, the present editor has felt that it is time for a Harvard Song Book that represents some of the music that has provided this experience along with the most durable of the college songs and popular songs of old. The joy that comes from singing music of substance and real beauty is an experience that has been shared by lovers of music across the land; and thanks to the great advance in the teaching of music in schools, the ability to read music has increased enormously. Thus, the purpose of this book is to supply a collection of worthwhile songs, which have become favorites at Harvard, for alumni and their friends as they gather around the piano for that especial delight of making music together. Certain of the traditional songs from the old song book are designated for mixed company. To sing these with men's voices let the second tenors and basses take the lower clef and the first tenors and basses the upper. For easy reference the music has been divided into the following categories: Harvard songs, songs of other colleges, traditional songs, Glee Club favorites, and motets.

After the happy collaboration with Henry Clough-Leighter of E. C. Schirmer Music Co. in the editing of the 1922 Song Book, it was logical to turn to this firm for the publication of the present book. The editor's task has been made easy by the spirit of cheerful cooperation from this company's President, Robert MacWilliams, to whom we wish to extend thanks for the large part that he has played in bringing this book to print. Our thanks go also to "Woody" for his advice in the selection of songs, and to Ruth Abbott, R. Bruce Archibald, Bernard E. Kreger, Allan D. Miller and William F. Russell for their permission to use their arrangements and harmonizations. We are grateful to Hans W. Heinsheimer of G. Schirmer, Inc. for permission to print a number of choruses from their catalogue.

ELLIOT FORBES

Cambridge, Massachusetts
July, 1966

In the last hundred years of Harvard history there have been published a number of collections of Harvard songs, but none more famous than *The Harvard Song Book* which originally appeared under Harvard Glee Club auspices in 1922. This volume quickly established itself as a standard and went through five editions. The volume was significant for the care with which it was assembled and for the emphasis placed on the musical worth of the selections.

American choral singing has come of age in the interval of forty odd years since *The Harvard Song Book* first appeared. Here in Cambridge our maturing taste has been influenced by three remarkable men — the pioneer, Archibald T. Davison, followed by "the Doc's" pupil, G. Wallace Woodworth, and now "Woody's" pupil, Elliot Forbes. Thanks to their labors and influence, there is a new appreciation here and elsewhere of what is excellent and enduring in choral music. Their teaching and their writing have played a part in an emerging awareness of music that is both good to know and good to sing.

It seems, therefore, most appropriate that there should be a fresh edition of *The Harvard Song Book* and inevitable changes in its contents. Students come to college today with far more educated tastes than did their fathers and grandfathers, and it is not strange that the lovely Liebeslieder Waltzes of Brahms should be represented, while songs like "Gin'ral Grant" and "Jingle Bells" have been dropped from the roster. The emphasis is on singing — not necessarily singing by trained voices but singing for the pleasure of it. We need more song in American life, and it will be satisfying if this new Song Book, containing as it does both the old, familiar Harvard songs as well as new selections popular in the present, can contribute to that end.

Nathan M. Pusey

Composers and Sources

Fair Harvard

Thomas Moore
Arranged

SOPRANO
ALTO

TENOR
BASS

1. Fair Harvard! thy sons to thy ju-bi-lee throng, And with bless-ings sur-rend-er thee o'er, By these fes-ti-val rites, from the age that is past, To the age that is wait-ing be-

2. To thy bow'rs we were led in the bloom of our youth, From the home of our in-fan-tile years, When our fa-thers had warn'd, and our moth-ers had pray'd, And our sis-ters had blest thro' their

3. When as pil-grims we come to re-vis-it thy halls, To what kind-lings the sea-son gives birth! Thy shades are more sooth-ing, thy sun-light more dear, Than de-scend on less priv-i-leged

4. Fare-well! be thy des-ti-nies on-ward and bright! To thy chil-dren the les-son still give, With free-dom to think, and with pa-tience to bear, And for right ev-er brave-ly to

2

fore._____ O rel - ic and type of our
tears._____ Thou then wert our pa - rent, the
earth._____ For the good and the great, in their
live._____ Let not moss - cov - er'd er - ror move

an - ces - tors' worth, That has long kept their mem - o - ry
nurse of our soul; We were mold - ed to man - hood by
beau - ti - ful prime, Thro' thy pre - cincts have mus - ing - ly
thee at its side, As the world on truth's cur - rent glides

warm,_____ First____ flow'r of their wil - der - ness!
thee,_____ Till____ freight - ed with treas - ure - thoughts,
trod,_____ As they gird - ed their spir - its or
by, _____ Be the her - ald of light, and the

poco rall.

star of their night! Calm__ ris - ing thro' change and thro' storm.__
friend-ships and hopes, Thou didst launch us on Des - ti - ny's sea.__
deep - en'd the streams That make glad the fair ci - ty of God.__
bear - er of love, Till the stock of the Pur - i - tans die.__

poco rall.

Harvard Hymn

James Bradstreet Greenough, '56　　　　　　　　　　John Knowles Paine, '69

1. De - us __ o - mni - um __ cre - a - tor,
2. Pa - tres __ no - stri huc __ per - la - ti,
3. Qua de __ spe fac te __ pre - ca - mur,
4. Sic dum ci - vi - tas __ man - e - bit,

Re - rum mun - di mo - de - ra - tor, Cres - cat cu - ius
Tu - o mo - ni - tu, per - gra - ti, De - di - ca - runt
In e - ven - tu ne fal - la - mur Sed ma - io - ra
Cla - rum lu - men hic lu - ce - bit, Lu - ce an - gu -

es fun - da - tor, No - stra U - ni - ver - si - tas,
ve - ri - ta - ti Par - vum tum col - le - gi - um,
dum co - na - mur Fa - ve - as la - bo - ri - bus,
los re - ple - bit, Fu - ge - rit ob - scu - ri - tas,

4

In - te - gri sint cu - ra - to - res, E - ru - di - ti
Id - que tu - o post fa - vo - re Au - ctum sem - per
Si - mul gra - ti - as ha - be - mus Quod tam di - u
Er - ror ter - ri - tus la - te - bit, Vir - tus vi - vi

pro - fes - so - res, Lar - gi - an - tur do - na - to - res
et a - mo - re Bo - nam spem o - sten - tat fo - re
iam flo - re - mus Nec au - di - re re - mit - te - mus
da va - le - bit, Et in - sig - ni - or flo - re - bit

Be - ne par - tas co - pi - as.
Tem - plum qua - si re - gi - um.
Ve - ri - ta - tis mo - ni - tus.
Nos - tra U - ni - ver - si - tas. A - men.

E.C.S. No 2018

Seventy-eighth Psalm

Give ear, ye children, to my law

St. Martin's C.M.
William Tansur
(1700-1783)

Nahum Tate (1652-1715)
Nicholas Brady (1659-1726)
Isaac Watts (1674-1748)
Jeremy Belknap (1744-1798)

1. Give ear, ye children, to my law De-vout at-ten-tion lend, Let the in-struc-tions of my mouth Deep in your hearts de-scend.
2. My tongue, by in-spi-ra-tion taught, Shall par-a-bles un-fold: Dark or-a-cles but un-der-stood And owned for truths of old,
3. Which we from sa-cred re-gis-ters Of an-cient times have known, And our fore-fa-thers' pi-ous care To us has hand-ed down.
4. Let chil-dren learn the migh-ty deeds Which God per-formed of old, Which, in our young-er years, we saw, And which our fa-thers told.
5. Our lips shall tell them to our sons, And they a-gain to theirs, That gen-e-ra-tions yet un-born May teach them to their heirs. A-men.

Domine salvum fac

Charles Gounod
(1818-1893)

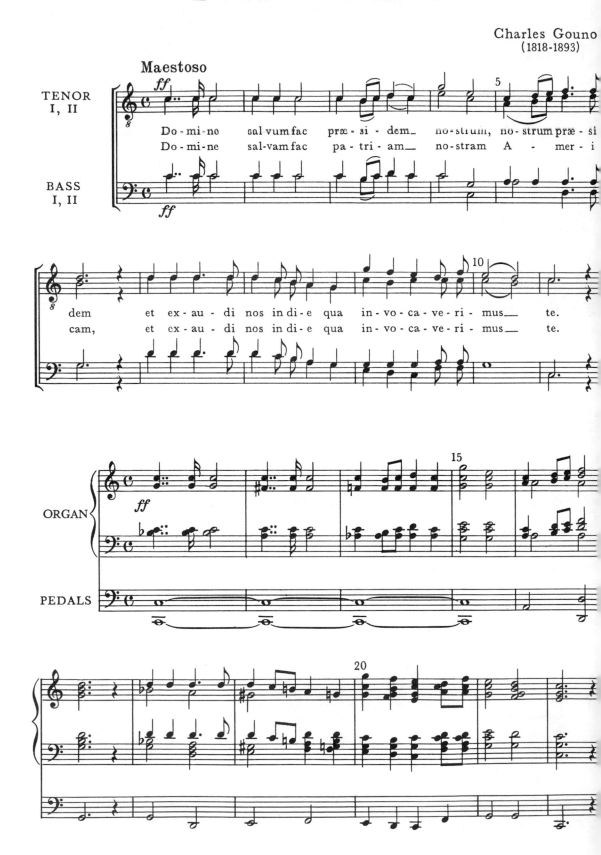

TENOR I, II — Do - mi - ne sal-vum fac præ - si - dem_ no - strum, no-strum præ - si -
Do - mi - ne sal-vam fac pa - tri - am_ no - stram A - mer - i

BASS I, II

ORGAN

PEDALS

dem   et ex - au - di nos in di - e qua in - vo - ca - ve - ri - mus_ te.
cam,   et ex - au - di nos in di - e qua in - vo - ca - ve - ri - mus_ te.

Harvardiana*

R.G. Williams, '11
Piano part arranged by R.S. Childe, '22, and
adjusted to fit vocal arrangement by Allan D. Miller, '54
Vocal arrangement by A.D.M.

*) "Harvardiana," "The Gridiron King," and "Soldiers Field" are so arranged that they may be played and sung as one pi

E - li's hopes we are dash - ing_____ In - to

E - li's hopes we are dash - ing_____ In - to

blue ob - scu - ri - ty._____ Re -

blue ob - scu - ri - ty, ob - scu - ri - ty. Our__

sist - less our team sweeps goal - ward_____ with the

team,_____ our team sweeps goal-ward with the

E - li's hopes we are dash - ing_____ In - to

E - li's hopes we are dash - ing_____ In - to

blue ob - scu - ri - ty_____ Re -

blue ob - scu - ri - ty_____ Re -

sist - less our team sweeps goal - ward_____ With the

sist - less our team sweeps goal - ward_____ With the

14

fu - ry of the blast_____ We'll
of the blast_____ We'll_____
fu - ry_____ of the blast_____ We'll

fight for the name of Har - vard_____ Till the
fight for the name of Har - vard_____ Till the

poco ritard.
last white line is passed._____
poco ritard.
last white line is passed._____
poco ritard.
(attacca)

The Gridiron King *

Richmond K. Fletcher '08
Voice parts arranged by Allan D. Miller, '54

Richmond K. Fletcher,'08

*) "Harvardiana," "The Gridiron King," and "Soldiers Field" are so arranged that they may be played and sung as one piece.
E.C.S. Nº 2018

16

show the sons_____ of E - li_____ that the

show the sons_____ of E - li_____

crim - son still holds sway._____

that the crim - son still holds sway._____

f Sweep down_____ the field a - gain,_____

f Sweep down_____ the field a - gain,_____

Victory or die! And we'll give the grand old cheer boys, When the Harvard team goes by.

poco ritard.

(attacca)

Soldiers Field*

W.W. Gallagher,'04
Henry Davenport,'04

Richmond K. Fletcher, '08
Piano part adjusted to fit
voice arrangement by Allan D. Miller, '54
Vocal arrangement by A.D.M.

See the crim - son tide is turn - ing

See the crim - son tide is turn - ing

Gain-ing more and more! Then fight, fight, fight! For we

Gain-ing more and more! Then fight, fight, fight! For we

win, to - night! Old Har-vard for ev - er - more!

win, to - night! Old Har-vard for ev - er - more!

Ten thousand men of Harvard

A. Putnam,'18

Murray Taylor, '18
Refrain
arranged by W. F. Russell

For years past the teams of Crim - son have won tri - umph af - ter tri - umph from her foe, Her glo - ry has ne'er di - min - ish'd; To de - feat the men of Crim - son can - not

go. _____ Then vic - t'ry _____ must now be

cer - tain, _____ For the loy - al sons of Har - vard know no

fear. _____ All rise _____ for Har - vard _____

— And we'll give her cheer on cheer! _____

22

TENORS I,II

BASS I, II

Ten thou - sand men of Har - vard_____ want

vic - t'ry_____ to - day,_____ For they

know that o'er old E - li_____ fair

Har - vard _____ holds sway; _____ So then we'll

con - quer _____ old E - li's men _____ And when the

game ends _____ we'll sing a - gain _____ Ten

thou - sand men of Har - vard _____ gain'd

24

E. C. S. Nº 2018

26

game ends _____ we'll sing _____ a - gain: Ten

game ends _____ we'll sing a - gain: _____ Ten

thou - sand men of Har - vard _____ gain'd

Har - vard _____

thou - sand men of Har - - vard gain'd

vic - t'ry _____ to - day. _____

vic - t'ry _____ to - day. _____

Our Director

F. E. Bigelow
Arranged by W. F. Russell
Piano part arranged by
Bernard E. Kreger,'59

luck _____ for poor old E - li!

luck _____ for poor old E - li!

Tough on the blue; _____

Tough on the blue; _____

Three cheers for Har - vard! and down with

Three cheers for Har - vard! and down with

Yale! Rah! Rah! Rah! down with Yale!___

Yale! Rah! Rah! Rah! down with Yale!___

(Shouted)

(Shouted)

Up the Street

W.L.W. Field, '98

R.G. Morse, '96
Arranged by R.S. Childe, '22
Voice parts arranged by A.D. Miller's

vic - to - ry   a - gain, March - ing with drum - beat and with   song;   Hear the re -

vic - to - ry   a - gain, March - ing with drum - beat and with   song;   Oh

frain,_____   as   it thun-ders a - long, as   it thun-ders a - long. Look where the

hear___ the re - frain,   a - long, as   it thun-ders a - long. Look where the

long. Be - hold,_____   they come   in   view,   who

long. Be - hold,_____   they come   in   view,   who

34

Veritas March

John H. Densmore, '04

John H. Densmore, '04
Arranged by W. F. Russell

bleach - ers blue turn pale with fright;_____ Send a

bleach - ers blue turn pale with fright;_____ Send a

cheer a cross to bleach 'em nice and white! Oh, look at the

cheer a cross to bleach 'em nice and white! Oh, look at the

way we smash and rib 'em through _____ While the

way we smash and rib 'em through _____ While the

blue bull - dog howls, "Boo - la, boo - la, Boo!" Let out your

blue bull - dog howls, "Boo - la, boo - la, Boo!" Let out your

voic - es now so loud and hale,_____ 'Tis a

voic - es now so loud and hale,_____ 'Tis a

fun' - ral ode we sing to E - li Yale. Oh, give us a

fun' - ral ode we sing to E - li Yale. Oh, give us a

yell, Hi! Hi! for Har - vard _____ For the

yell, Hi! Hi! for Har - vard _____ For the

martellato

martellato

Crim - son _____ to - day! _____ We

Crim - son _____ to - day! _____ We

44

Crim - - - son _____ to -

Crim - - - son _____ to -

day! _____

day! _____

Yo Ho, the good ship Harvard

Richmond K. Fletcher, '08

Richmond K. Fletcher, '08
Arranged by Allan D. Miller, '54
Revised by Elliot Forbes, '40
Piano part by Bernard E. Kreger, '59

Yo Ho, _____ the good ship

Yo Ho, _____ the good ship

Har - vard is goal - ward bound a - gain.

Har - vard is goal - ward bound a - gain. All the

All the crew at the hal - yards,

crew_____ are at the hal - yards, Here's a

hail for John Har-vard's men. Bright

hail for John-ny Har-vard's men. Bright

crim - son at the fore - - peak rides

crim - - son at the fore - peak rides

48

high a - bove the foam, _____ we sweep thru

high _____ a-bove the foam, While we sweep thru the

deep blue, Har - vard strikes home.

deep blue, Har-vard strikes home.

Yo

TENOR I,II

crim - son at the fore - peak rides high_____ a-bove the

BASS I,II

crim - son at the fore - peak rides high_____ a-bove the

foam, While we sweep thru the deep blue, Har-vard strikes home.

foam,__ While we sweep thru the deep blue, Har-vard strikes home.

Crimson Triumph

Paul Lord, '14

Ralph L. Blaikie, '14

1. We_____ are 'sons of dear old Har - vard, we're
2. When_____ the team is on the field, boys, we'll

here_____ to sing a song to thee._____
cheer_____ them each and ev - 'ry one._____

To her and to her teams
Watch_____ the backs go tear - ing through,

we'll show our loy - al - ty; So,
smash - ing the line of Blue, For

boys, _____ we'll drink a toast to Har - vard, her
they _____ are fight - ing for the Crim - son and

men, and mem - o - ries so sweet; _____ We'll
theirs the vic - to - ry to - day! _____ Watch,

sing a song to her when e'er
see them swell the score as Yale

54

Harvard, in deepest wine

E. L. Viets, '11

E. L. Viets, '11
Arranged by W. F. Russell

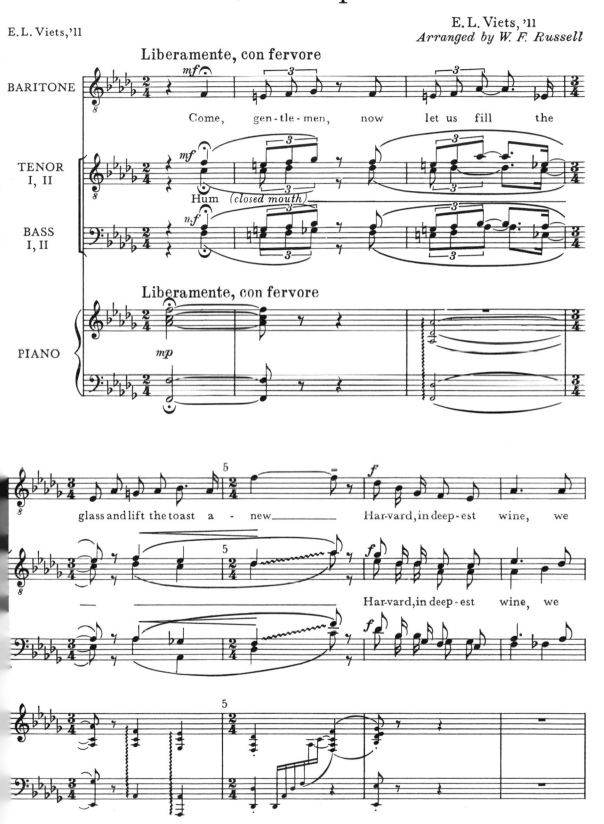

Johnny Harvard

E.C.S. No 2018

60

Jol - ly boys are we, ___ Free from care and de-spair, What care we 'Tis

wine di-vine, That brings us jol - li - ty. Oh, here's to John-ny Har - vard!

Tempo I

fill him up a full glass, Fill him up a glass to his

name and fame, And at the same time don't for-get his true love;

Fill her up a bum - per to the brim. Then

drink, drink, drink, drink, Pass the wine cup free; Drink, drink, drink, drink,

drink, drink,

Jol - ly boys are we, ___ Free from care and des-pair, What care we; Here's to

wine di - vine, That brings us jol - li - ty. Drink, drink, drink,

drink, drink, drink, drink, drink, drink, drink, drink, drink, drink, drink, drink, drink,

drink, drink, drink, drink, drink, Yes, drink.

drink, drink, drink, drink, drink,

Old Harvard

David T. W. Mc Cord, '21

F. Campenhout*
Arranged

1. Be-fore old E - li had come in - to the world,___ Or___ Prince - ton's found-a - tion was laid, Har - vard, with ban - ner fair un - furl'd___ The__ Pil - grim's wil - der-ness sur - vey'd. And her day shall nev - er, nev - er wane,___ Fore-most to-mor - row as of

2. And like a torch that has burn'd through-out the past,___ In__ thought and in wis - dom she shone; Loy - al her sons un - to the last,___ Each__ class and gen - er - a - tion on! So that light shall nev - er, nev - er wane,___:

* "The Brabançonne"

E.C.S. № 2018

Onward to the goal

Frank R. Hancock,'12

Frank R. Hancock, '12

Row, Yale, Row!

Stephen Foster

1. New Lon-don race-course four miles long, Sing a-
2. The Har-vard crew got stuck in the grass, Sing a-
3. But the Har-vard crew it shook it-self loose, Sing a-

doo - dah! Sing a - doo - dah! And the Har - vard crew is
doo - dah! Sing a - doo - dah! And the E - li crew went
doo - dah! Sing a - doo - dah! And the E - lis saw it

row - ing strong. Oh, Doo - dah day!
slow - ly past. Oh, Doo - dah day!
was - n't an - y use. Oh, Doo - dah day!

CHORUS

SOPRANO and ALTO

G'wine to row all night! G'wine to row all day! I'll__ bet my mon-ey on the Har-vard crew, Some-bo-dy bet on Yale. Where, oh, where is Yale? They're com-ing, They're com-ing, But they're com-ing ver-y slow; Oh, can't you hear those E-lis shout-ing "Row, Yale, row!"

TENOR and BASS

Score

J. S. Reed, '10

J. W. Adams, '10

70

wail!_____ It might be worse, boys,

call up a hearse for poor old

Yale. Yale._____

The sun of victory

Frank R. Hancock,'12

Frank R. Hancock, '12

Har - vard's hopes beat high;_____ Watch the

cresc.

spir - it of old Har - vard, Driv - ing ev - er t'ward the

goal,_____ Give them a yell, Hol_____ Down the field they

go - o, While the Crim - son thun - ders roll._____

As the backs go tearing by

(Dartmouth College)

John Thomas Keady

Carl W. Blaisdell
Vocal arrangement by Elliot Forbes

Con anima

TENOR I, II

As the backs go tear-ing by On the

BASS I, II

way to do or die. Ma-ny sighs and man-y tears, Min-gle

with the Har-vard cheers, As the backs go tear-ing by_____ mak-ing

Used with permission of Dartmouth College.

gain on stead-y gain, ech - o swells the sweet re -

frain,_____ Dart-mouth's going to win to - day, Dart-mouth

sure must win to - day, as the backs go tear-ing by.

Bright college years
(Yale University)

H.S. Durand

Carl Wilhelm
Edited by Marshall Bartholomew

Maestoso

TENOR I, II

BASS I, II

1. Bright col-lege years, with plea-sure rife, The short-est, glad-dest years of life; How
2. In af-ter years, should trou-bles rise, To cloud the blue of sun-ny skies, How

swift - ly are ye glid-ing by! Oh, why doth time so quick-ly fly? The
bright will seem, thro' mem-'ry's haze, The hap-py, gold-en, by-gone days! Oh,

poco a poco cresc.

sempre cresc.

sea-sons come, the sea-sons go, The earth is green or white with snow, But time and
let us strive that ev-er we May let these words our watch-cry be, Wher - e'er up-

poco allarg.

change shall naught a - vail, To break the friend - ships formed at Yale.
on life's sea we sail: For God, for Coun - try, and for Yale."

poco allarg.

E.C.S. Nº 2018

Bull-Dog
(Yale University)

Cole Porter

'Way down, 'way down in New Ha - ven town, Lives Mis - ter Yale, old E - li Yale, No one ev - er cares to come a - round, Just be - cause of his pet "bow - wow,"

Poor old Har-vard tries it once a year, Al-ways goes back,

tied up in black, For when Old Yale sicks that big bull - dog

on, He rais - es an aw - ful row.

CHORUS, unisoni

Bull-dog! Bull-dog! Bow, wow, wow, E - li Yale,

Bull-dog! Bull-dog! Bow, wow, wow, Our team can nev - er fail.___

___ When the sons of E - li break through the line, That is the sign we

hail,___ Bull-dog! Bull-dog! Bow, wow, wow,

E - li Yale!___ Yale!___

Far above Cayuga's waters

(Cornell University)

Archibald Croswell Weeks
and Wilmot Moses Smith

H. S. Thompson

1. Far a-bove Ca-yu-ga's wa-ters, With its waves of blue,
2. Far a-bove the bu-sy hum-ming Of the bust-ling town,

Stands our no - ble Al - ma Ma - ter, Glo - ri-ous to view.
Reared a-gainst the arch of heav-en, Looks she proud-ly down.

Refrain

Lift the cho - rus, speed it on - ward, Loud her prais - es tell;

Hail to thee, our Al - ma Ma - ter! Hail, all hail, Cor - nell!

Al - ma Ma - ter! Hail, all hail, Cor - nell!

Lord Jeffery Amherst
(Amherst College)

J. S. Hamilton

J. S. Hamilton

1. Oh,— Lord Jeff-er-y Am-herst was a sol-dier of the King, And he came from a-cross— the sea,— To— the French-men and the In-di-ans he did-n't do a thing, In the wilds of this

2. Oh,— Lord Jeff-er-y Am-herst was the man who gave his name To our col-lege up-on— the hill,— And the sto-ry of— his loy-al-ty and bra-ve-ry and fame A - bides here a-

E.C.S. Nº 2018   Used with permission of Amherst College

wild coun - try, _____ In the wilds of this wild coun - try. _____ And
mong us still, _____ A - bides here a - mong us still. _____ You may

for His Roy - al Ma - jes - ty he fought with all his might, For he was a sol - dier
talk a - bout your John - nies and your E - lis and the rest, For they are names that

loy - al and true, _____ And _ he con - quered all _ the en - e - mies that
time can nev - er dim, _____ But _ give us our on - ly Jeff - 'ry, he's the

came with - in his sight, And he looked a - round for more when he was through. _____
no - blest and the best, To the end we will stand fast by him. _____

CHORUS

Old Nassau

(Princeton University)

Karl Langlotz
Arranged by W. L. Nollner

H.P. Peck

1. Tune ev - 'ry heart and ev - 'ry voice, bid ev - 'ry care with-draw: Let
2. Till then with joy our songs we'll bring, and while a breath we draw: We'll

all with one ac - cord re-joice in praise of old Nas - sau.
all u - nite to shout and sing: long life to old Nas - sau.

Refrain
(Più mosso)

In praise of old Nas - sau, my boys, Hur - rah! Hur-rah! Hur rah!__ Her__
Long life to old Nas - sau, my boys, Hur - rah! Hur-rah! Hur rah!__ Her__

meno mosso

sons will give, while they shall live, three cheers for old Nas - sau.__
sons will give, while they shall live, long life to old Nas - sau.__

E.C.S. № 2018   Used with permission of G. Schirmer, Inc.

The Orange and the Black

(Princeton University)

Tune *"Sadie Ray"*
Arranged by J. Merrill Knapp

Clarence B. Mitchell

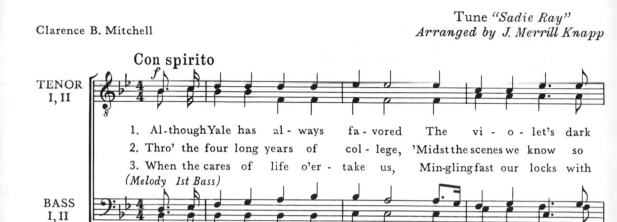

Con spirito

TENOR I, II

1. Al-though Yale has al - ways fa - vored The vi - o - let's dark
2. Thro' the four long years of col - lege, 'Midst the scenes we know so
3. When the cares of life o'er - take us, Min-gling fast our locks with

(Melody 1st Bass)

BASS I, II

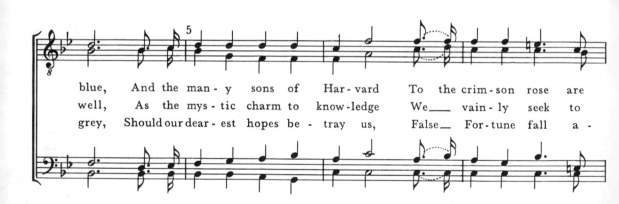

blue, And the man - y sons of Har - vard To the crim - son rose are
well, As the mys - tic charm to know - ledge We___ vain - ly seek to
grey, Should our dear - est hopes be - tray us, False___ For - tune fall a -

true, We will own the lil - ies slen - der, Nor hon - or shall they
spell; Or, we win ath - let - ic vic - t'ries On the foot - ball-field or
way, Still we'll ban - ish care and sad - ness As we turn our mem - 'ries

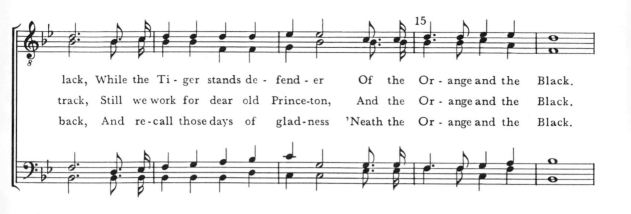

lack, While the Ti - ger stands de - fend - er   Of the Or - ange and the   Black.
track, Still we work for dear old Prince-ton,   And the Or - ange and the   Black.
back, And re - call those days of glad - ness 'Neath the Or - ange and the   Black.

We   will own the lil - ies slen - der,   Nor hon - or shall   they
Or,   we win ath - let - ic vic - t'ries   On the foot - ball - field   or
Still   we'll ban - ish care and sad - ness   As we turn our mem - 'ries

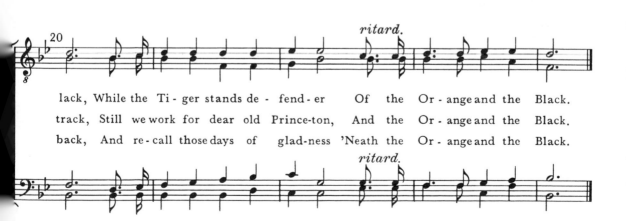

lack, While the Ti - ger stands de - fend - er   Of the Or - ange and the   Black.
track, Still we work for dear old Prince-ton,   And the Or - ange and the   Black.
back, And re - call those days of glad - ness 'Neath the Or - ange and the   Black.

Auld Lang Syne

Robert Burns

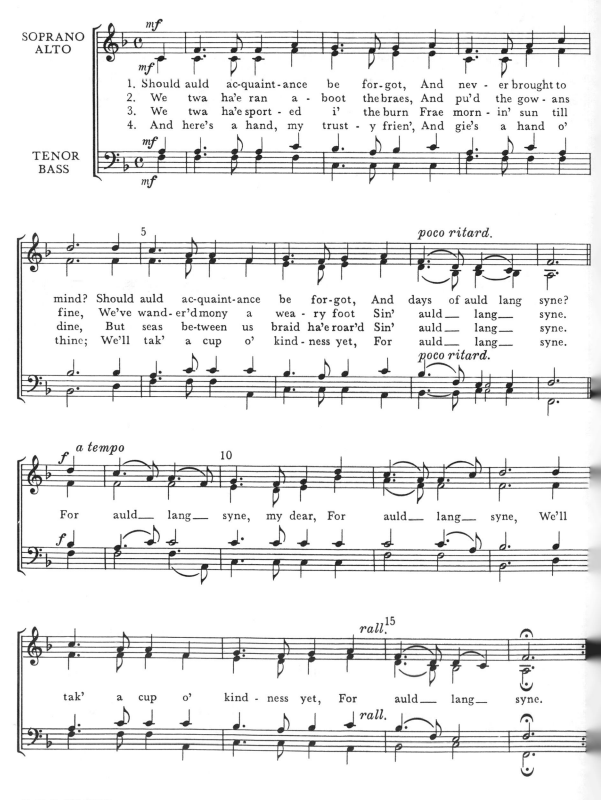

Gaudeamus igitur

Traditional

CHORUS

TENOR I, II

1. Gau - de - a - mus   i - gi - tur,   Ju - ve - nes dum   su - mus;
2. U - bi sunt, qui   an - te nos   In mun - do fu -   e - re?
3. Vi - ta nos - tra   bre - vis est,   Bre - vi fi - ni -   e - tur,
4. Vi - vat a - ca -   de - mi - a,   Vi - vant pro - fes -   so - res,
5. Vi - vant om - nes   vir - gi - nes   Fa - ci - les, for -   mo - sæ,
6. Vi - vat et re -   pu - bli - ca,   Et qui il - lam   re - git,
7. Pe - re - at tris -   ti - ti - a,   Pe - re - ant o -   so - res,
8. Quis con - flu - xus   ho - di - e   A - ca - de - mi -   co - rum?
9. Al - ma Ma - ter   flo - re - at   Quæ nos e - du -   ca - vit,

BASS I, II

QUARTET

Gau - de - a - mus   i - gi - tur,   Ju - ve - nes dum   su - mus;
U - bi sunt, qui   an - te nos   In mun - do fu -   e - re?
Vi - ta nos - tra   bre - vis est,   Bre - vi fi - ni -   e - tur,
Vi - vat a - ca -   de - mi - a,   Vi - vant pro - fes -   so - res,
Vi - vant om - nes   vir - gi - nes   Fa - ci - les, for -   mo - sæ,
Vi - vat et re -   pu - bli - ca,   Et qui il - lam   re - git,
Pe - re - at tris -   ti - ti - a,   Pe - re - ant o -   so - res,
Quis con - flu - xus   ho - di - e   A - ca - de - mi -   co - rum?
Al - ma Ma - ter   flo - re - at   Quæ nos e - du -   ca - vit,

CHORUS

Post ju - cun - dam   ju - ven - tu - tem,   Post mo - les - tam   se - nec - tu - tem,
Trans - e - as ad   su - pe - ros,   A - be - as ad   in - fe - ros,
Ve - nit mors ve -   lo - ci - ter,   Ra - pit nos a -   tro - ci - ter,
Vi - vat mem - brum quod li - bet,   Vi - vant mem - bra quæ - li - bet,
Vi - vant et mu -   li - e - res,   Te - ne - ræ a -   ma - bi - les,
Vi - vat nos - tra   ci - vi - tas,   Mæ - ce - na - tum   ca - ri - tas,
Pe - re - at di -   a - bo - lus,   Qui - vis an - ti -   bur - schi - us
E lon - gin - quo   con - ve - ne - runt   Pro - ti - nus - que   suc - ces - se - runt
Ca - ros et com -   mi - li - to - nes,   Dis - si - tas in   re - gi - o - nes

rall.

Nos ha - be - bit   hu -   mus,   Nos ha - be - bit   hu -   mus.
Quos si vis vi -   de -   re,   Quos si vis vi -   de -   re.
Ne - mi - ni par - ce -   tur,   Ne - mi - ni par - ce -   tur.
Sem - per sint in   flo -   re,   Sem - per sint in   flo -   re.
Bo - næ la - bo - ri - o -   sæ,   Bo - næ la - bo - ri - o -   sæ.
Quæ nos hic pro - te -   git,   Quæ nos hic pro - te -   git.
At - que ir - ri - so -   res,   At - que ir - ri - so -   res.
In com - mu - ne   fo -   rum,   In com - mu - ne   fo -   rum.
Spar - sos con - gre - ga -   vit,   Spar - sos con - gre - ga -   vit.

Integer vitæ

Horatii Flacci
Lib. I, Ode XXII

Friedrich F. Flemming, 1810

TENOR I, II

BASS I, II

1. In - te - ger vi - tæ sce - le - ris - que pu - rus,
2. Si - ve per Syr - tes i - ter æst - u - os - as,
3. Nam - que me sil - va lu - pus in Sa - bi - na,
4. Qua - le por - ten - tum ne - que mi - li - ta - ris
5. Po - ne me, pi - gris u - bi nul - la cam - pis
6. Po - ne sub cur - ru ni - mi - um pro - pin - qui

Non e - get Mau - ri ja - cu - lis, nec ar - cu, Nec ve - ne -
Si - ve fact - ur - us per in - hos - pi - ta - lem Cau - ca - sum,
Dum me - am can - to La - la - gen, et ul - tra, Ter - mi - num
Da - u - nias la - tis a - lit æ - scu - le - tis, Nec Ju - bæ
Ar - bor æ - sti - va re - cre - a - tur au - ra, Quod la - tus
So - lis, in ter - ra do - mi - bus ne - ga - ta; Dul - ce ri -

rall.

na - tis gra - vi - da sa - git - tis, Fus - ce, pha - re - tra.
vel quæ lo - ca fab - u - los - us, Lam - bit Hy - das - pes.
cu - ris va - gor ex - pe - di - tus, Fu - git i - ner - men.
tel - lus ge - ne - rat, le - o - num A - ri - da nu - trix.
mun - di ne - bu - læ ma - lu - sque Ju - pi - ter ur - get;
den - tem La - la - gen a - ma - bo Dul - ce lo - quen - tem.

rall.

Australia

Arranged by Frank R. Hancock, '12

Drink to me only with thine eyes

Ben Jonson

Old English Air
Arranged

SOPRANO
ALTO

TENOR
BASS

1. Drink to me on - ly with thine eyes, And I_ will pledge with mine,_
2. I sent thee late a ros - y wreath, Not so much hon'ring thee,_

Or leave a kiss with - in_ the cup, And I'll_ not ask for wine;_ The
As giv - ing it a hope that there It could not with - er'd be;_ But

thirst that from the soul doth rise Doth ask a drink di - vine;_
thou there - on did'st on - ly breathe And send'st it back to me;_

But might I of Jove's nec - tar sip_ I would not change for thine.__
Since when it grows and smells, I swear, Not of_ it - self but thee.__

Good-night, ladies

Juanita

October
(Harrow School Song)

Edward E. Bowen

John Farmer

1. The months are met, with their crown-lets on, As Ju-li-us Cæ-sar crown'd them; With slaves, the gen-tle-men
2. "I vote for March, may it please you," cries A stu-dent pale and mea-gre; "He gives us theme and
3. "For May! for May!" the girls all say, "How mild the air that blows is! How nice-ly sweet the
4. Oc-to-ber brings the cold-weath-er down, When the wind and the rain con-tin-ue, He nerves the limbs that are

CHORUS

Prayer of Thanksgiving

English version by
Dr. Theo. Baker

Netherlands Folk-song
Arranged

1. We gath-er to-geth-er to ask the Lord's bless-ing, He chas-tens and has-tens His will to make known; The wick-ed op-press-ing cease them from dis-tress-ing, Sing
2. Be-side us to guide us, our God with us join-ing, Or-dain-ing, main-tain-ing His King-dom di-vine, So from the be-gin-ning the fight we were win-ning; Thou,
3. We all do ex-tol Thee, Thou lead-er in bat-tle, And pray that Thou still our De-fen-der wilt be. Let Thy con-gre-ga-tion es-cape trib-u-la-tion: Thy

Schneider's Band

A. G. Mason, '86

102

CHORUS

E.C.S. № 2018

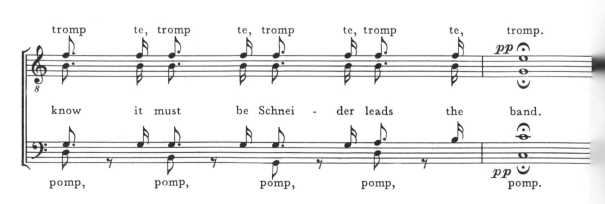

Vive l'amour

Glorious Apollo

Glee

Samuel Webbe
(1740-1816)
Arranged by Archibald T. Davison

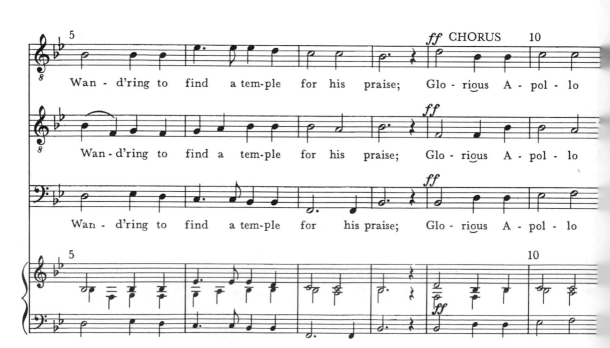

Published also for Women's Voices S.S.A. (E.C.S. No. 1970) and Mixed Voices S.A.B. (No. 2296). "Glorious Apollo" was written in 1784 for the original Glee Club and was sung ever afterward at the opening of its concerts.

E.C.S. No. 2018

A lieta vita

Giovanni Giacomo Gastoldi
(1556-1622)
Arranged by G. Wallace Woodworth

Of unknown authorship

Tutti venite armati
Villanella Napolitana

Of unknown authorship

Giovanni Giacomo Gastoldi
(1556-1622)
Arranged by G. Wallace Woodworth

From *Balletti a cinque voci*, 1591

E.C.S. Nº 2018

Marching to Pretoria

South African Veld Song

Josef Marais
Arranged by Ruth E. Abbott, 1949

As we march a - long._____ We are march-ing to Pre -

As we march a - long._____ We are march-ing to Pre -

to - ri - a,_____ Pre - to-ri - a,_____ Pre - to-ri - a;_____

to - ri - a,_____ Pre - to-ri - a,_____ Pre - to-ri - a;_____

So let us sing to-geth- er As we march a - long.

So let us sing to-geth- er As we march a - long.

124

E.C.S. N⁰ 2018

The silver moon is shining

Tu mi vuoi tanto bene

English version by
K.K. Davis

Italian Folk-song
Arranged by Archibald T. Davison

E.C.S. Nº 2018

lovely is the moonlight Between the shadows breaking! My
do - te ti prepara, La do - te ti pre-pa-ra, La

heart would ease its aching If thou wert near me.
do - te ti pre-pa-ra, Ed io ti spo-so.

Bacchanal

Gioacchino Cocchi
(ca. 1715-1804)

Bacchanale

Henri Meilhac and Ludovic Halévy
English version by G.W.W.

Jacques Offenbach
(1819-1880)
Edited by G. Wallace Woodworth

1. Hail our gi-gan-tic Bac-cha-na-le, Hail Ve-nus, Ve-nus As-tar-
C'est une im-men-se Bac-cha-na-le, Et Vé-nus, Vé-nus As-tar-

From *La belle Hélène*

E.C.S. Nº 2018

té! Strike up the dance from hell in - fer - nal, Sing to our
té A - ni - me la ronde in - fer - na - le, Tout est plai -

Bac - cha - na - lian Day! Our vir - tue, du - ty, laws, and
sir et vo - lup - té! Ver - tu, de - voir, hon - neur, mo -

hon - or, All for - got in the flood of joy!
ra - le, Par le flot tout est em - por - té!

p subito

dan - ces, Which we were taught so long a - go, Danc - es so
rhy - que, Qu'au - tre - fois on nous en - sei - gna, Dan - se____

no - ble, so clas - si - que, Look what a dance we dance to -
no - ble, dan - se clas - si - que, En tous lieux main - te - nant voi -

day. Ec - cen - tric, stiff, bi - zarre, fan - tas - tic, So bar -
là. Qu'on danse u - ne chose ex - cen - trique Et sans nom,

bar - ic, it goes like this...
qui____ res - semble à ça!

138

Come, sirrah Jack ho

Thomas Weelkes
(1575-1623)
Edited and adapted for male voices by
Edmund H. Fellowes

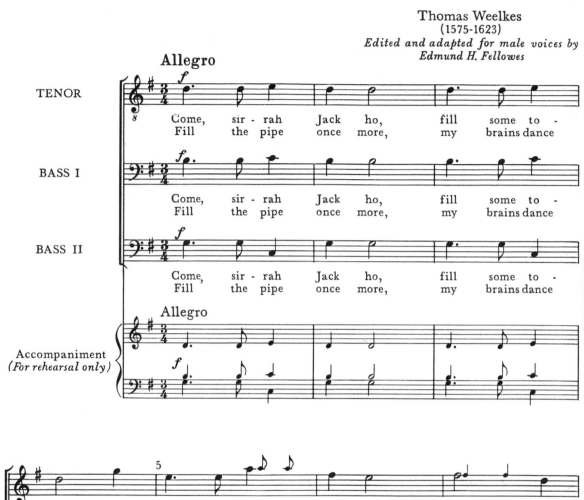

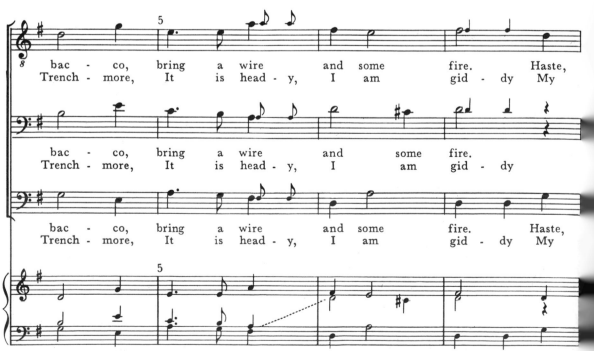

From *Airs to Three Voices*, 1608

NOTE.- This Air may be sung a semitone lower. The words of the second verse are not to be sung until both sections of the Air have been sung, with the repeats, to the words of the first verse. "Trenchmore" was a lively country-dance.

E.C.S.N. 2018 Used with permission of Galaxy Music Corp.

haste a-way, quick, I say, do not stay, shun de - lay,
head and brains, back and reins, joints and veins, from all pains,

Haste, haste a - way, quick, I say, do not stay, shun de -
My head and brains, back and reins, joints and veins, from all

haste a - way, quick, I say, do not stay, shun de - lay,
head and brains, back and reins, joints and veins, from all pains,

for I drank none good to - day. day. I
it doth well purge and make clean. clean. Then

lay, for I drank none good to - day. day. I
pains, it doth well purge and make clean. clean. Then

for I drank none good to - day. day. I
it doth well purge and make clean. clean. Then

142

swear that this to - bac - co it's per - fect Trin - i -
those that do con - demn it, or such as not com -

swear that this to - bac - co it's per - fect Trin i -
those that do con - demn it, or such as not com -

swear that this to - bac - co it's per - fect Trin - i -
those that do con - demn it, or such as not com -

da - do. By the ve - ry ve - ry Mass nev - er nev - er nev - er was bet - ter
mend it, nev - er were so wise to learn good to - bac - co to dis - cern, let them

da - do. By the ve - ry ve - ry Mass nev - er nev - er nev - er was bet - ter
mend it, nev - er were so wise to learn good to - bac - co to dis - cern, let them

da - do. By the ve - ry Mass nev - er was
mend it, nev - er were so wise let them go

E. C. S. Nº 2018

gear than is here; by the rood, for the blood it is
go pluck a crow, and not know as I do the_____

gear than is here; by the rood, for the blood it is
go pluck a crow, and not know as I do the_____

cresc.

bet - ter gear than is here
pluck a crow, and not know

cresc.

25

1.   2.

ve - ry, ve - ry good 'tis ve - ry good.   I   good.
sweet, the sweet, the sweet of Trin - i - da-do.   Then   da-do.

ve - ry, ve - ry good 'tis ve - ry good.   I   good.
sweet, the sweet, the sweet of Trin - i - da-do.   Then   da-do.

for the blood 'tis ve - ry good.   I   good.
the_____ sweet of Trin - i - da-do.   Then   da-do.

25

1.   2.

f

The Trysting Place
Der Gang zum Liebchen

English version by
W. G. Rothery

Johannes Brahms
(1833-1897)
Arranged by Archibald T. Davison

From *Drei Quartette*, Op. 31 (Nº 3)

Published also for *Mixed Voices* (*E.C.S. Choral Music*, Nº 391)

win - - dow, to - night shall we meet. ___
Le - - ben, im Le - ben wird seh'n. ___

win - dow, to - night ___ to - night shall we meet. ___
Le - ben wird seh'n, ___ im Le - ben wird seh'n.

win - dow, to - night to - night shall we meet.
Le - ben wird seh'n, im Le - ben wird seh'n.

win - dow, to - night ___ to - night shall we meet.
Le - ben wird seh'n, ___ im Le - ben wird seh'n.

(poco ritard.) *a tempo* ***pp*** *dolce e teneramente* 40

The stars are ap - pear - ing, Our
Es ging der Mond un - ter, ich

(poco ritard.) ***pp*** *dolce e teneramente*

The stars are ap - pear - ing, Our
Es ging der Mond un - ter, ich

(poco ritard.) ***pp*** *dolce e teneramente*

The stars are ap - pear - ing, Our
Es ging der Mond un - ter, ich

(poco ritard.) ***pp*** *dolce e teneramente*

The stars are ap - pear - ing, Our
Es ging der Mond un - ter, ich

poco ritard. *a tempo* 40

dim. ***pp*** *dolce*

150

The Hunters' Farewell

Der Jäger Abschied

Josef von Eichendorff (1788-1857)
English version anonymous
Edited by H. Clough-Leighter

Felix Mendelssohn-Bartholdy
(1809-1847)
Op. 50, Nº 2

Published, 1931, by E.C. Schirmer Music Co.

158

Done foun' my los' sheep

Negro Spiritual
Arranged by Elliot Forbes

In dat Res - sur - rec - tion Day   sin-ner can't fin'   no hid - in' place,

Go to de moun-tain, de moun-tain move;   Run to de hill,   de   hill run too.

TENOR I

Run to de hill,   de   hill run too.

TENOR II

Run to de hill,   de   hill run too.

BASS I

Run to de hill,   de   hill run too.

BASS II

Run to de hill,   de   hill run too.

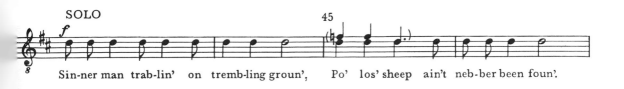

SOLO

Sin-ner man trab-lin' on tremb-ling groun',   Po' los' sheep ain't neb-ber been foun'.

Entrance and March of Peers

W. S. Gilbert

Arthur Seymour Sullivan
(1842-1900)
Piano Accompaniment
arranged by F. W. R. Jr.

From *Iolanthe*

Orchestra parts may be obtained from the Publisher. Published also for Mixed Voices (CHORAL SONGS, Nº 357)

Proud-ly bang the sound-ing brass-es,___ As up-on the

Proud-ly bang the sound-ing brass-es,___ Tzing boom! As up-on the

lord-ly__ way This u-nique pro - ces-sion pass-es. Tan-tan-ta-ra,

lord - ly way This u-nique pro - ces - sion pass-es. Tzing

ra! Tzing boom! Bow, bow, ye low-er mid-dle class-es!

ra! Tzing boom!

Bow, bow, ye trades-men, bow ye mass-es! Blow the__ trum-pets!

bang the brass-es, Tan - tan - ta-ra! Tzing boom!

Bow, bow, ye

low - er mid-dle class - es, Bow, bow, ye trades-men, bow, ye mass - es!

174

Blow, blow the trum-pets, bang the brass-es!

Blow, blow the trum-pets, bang the brass-es!

Blow, blow the trum-pets, Blow, blow the trum-pets!

Blow, blow the trum-pets, Blow, blow the trum-pets!

Tan - ta - ra ta ta ta ta ta ta ta!

Tzing boom, tzing boom!

Bow, ye low - er mid - dle class - es! Bow, ye trades-men, bow, ye

Bow, ye low - er mid - dle class - es! Bow, ye trades-men, bow, ye

mass - es! Bow, ye low - er mid - dle class - es! Bow, ye trades-men, bow, ye

mass - es! Bow, ye low - er mid - dle class - es! Bow, ye trades-men, bow, ye

mass - es! Tan - tan-ta - ra, Tan - tan-ta - ra, tan - tan-ta -

mass - es! Tan - tan-ta - ra, Tan - tan-ta - ra, tan - tan-ta -

ra, tan-ta-ra, tan-ta-ra, tan-ta-ra, tan-ta-ra, ra, ra, ra,

ra, tan-ta-ra, tan-ta-ra, tan-ta-ra, tan-ta-ra, ra, ra, ra,

ra!   Tan - ta - ra!

ra!   Tan - ta - ra!

Tan - ta - ra!

Tan - ta - ra!

The E-RI-E

American Great Lakes Folk Tune
Arranged by Elliot Forbes

Traditional

Con moto

BARITONE (Solo)

TENOR I

We were for-ty miles from Al- ba-ny, for-

TENOR II

BASS I

BASS II

PIANO

get it, I nev- er shall, What a ter-ri-ble storm we had one night on the

© 1959, by G. Schirmer, Inc.- Used with permission

BARITONE Solo

The cook she was a kind old soul, she had a rag-ged dress, We
heist-ed her up-on a pole as a sig-nal of dis-tress.

The winds be-gin to whis-tle, and the waves be-gin to roll, And we

had to reef our roy-als on the rag - ing ca - nawl.

75
git a drink till we get to Buf - fa - lo - o - o, till we get to Buf - fa -
git a drink till we get to Buf - fa - lo - o - o, till we get to Buf - fa -
git a drink till we get to Buf - fa - lo - o - o, till we get to Buf - fa -
git a drink till we get to Buf - fa - lo - o - o, till we get to Buf - fa -
75
8va
BARITONE Solo
p
80
Oh, when we got to Sy - ra - cuse, the
lo.
lo.
lo.
lo.
80
p

ris - in' and the gin was a-git-tin' low, And I

ris - in' and the gin was a-git-tin' low, And I

ris - in' and the gin was a-git-tin' low, And I

ris - in' and the gin was a-git-tin' low, And I

100

scarce-ly think we'll git a drink till we get to Buf - fa -

scarce-ly think we'll git a drink till we get to Buf - fa -

scarce-ly think we'll git a drink till we get to Buf - fa -

scarce-ly think we'll git a drink till we get to Buf - fa -

100

Fire, fire, my heart

Thomas Morley
(1557-1603)
Arranged by Archibald T. Davison

From *First Book of Ballets to Five Voices*, 1595

E.C.S. No 2018

Hark! all ye lovely saints above

Of unknown authorship

Thomas Weelkes
(1578?-1623)
Arranged by Archibald T. Davison

TENOR I

TENOR II

BASS I

BASS II

Accompaniment
(For rehearsal only)

1. Hark! all ye love-ly saints a-bove, Di-
2. See, see! your Mis-tress bids you cease, And

an - a hath a - greed with love, hath a - greed with love, ___ his
wel - come love with ___ love's in-crease, love with ___ love's in - crease, ___ Di -

From *Ballets and Madrigals to Five Voices*, 1598
Published *also for Mixed Voices* (E.C.S. No. 1787)

E.C.S. Nº 2018

216

The Hundred Pipers

Scottish Folk-song
Arranged by Arthur Whiting

Lady Nairne

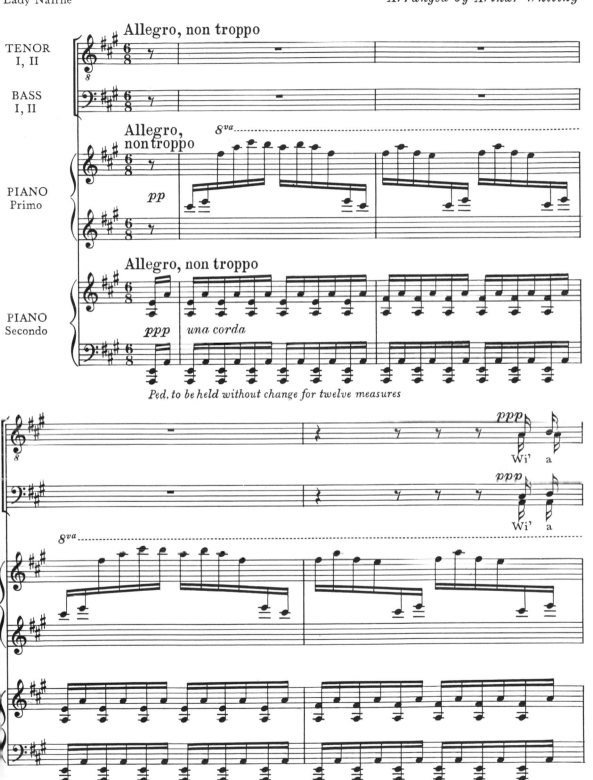

Ped. to be held without change for twelve measures

up an' gie them a blaw, a blaw, Wi' a

up an' gie them a blaw, a blaw, Wi' a

hun - dred pi - pers an' a', an' a', Oh! it's

hun - dred pi - pers an' a', an' a', Oh! it's

220

222

up an' gie them a blaw, a blaw, Wi' a hun - dred pi - pers an'

up an' gie them a blaw, a blaw, Wi' a hun - dred pi - pers an'

a', an' a'.

a', an' a'.

E. C. S. Nọ 2018

sight - ed San - dy looked fu' wae, And mith - ers grat when they

sight - ed San - dy looked fu' wae, __ And mith - ers grat when they

marched a - way. Wi' a hun - dred pi - pers an' a', an' a', Wi' a

marched a - way. Wi' a hun - dred pi - pers an' a', an' a', Wi' a

hun - dred pi - pers an' a', an' a', We'll_ up an' gie them a

hun - dred pi - pers an' a', an' a', We'll up an' gie them a

pp

pp

Ped. ✳ Ped. ✳ Ped. ✳ Ped. ✳ Ped. ✳

senza ritard.

ppp

blaw, a blaw, Wi' a hun - dred pi - pers an' a', an' a'.

senza ritard.

blaw, a blaw, Wi' a hun - dred pi - pers an' a', an' a'.

senza ritard.

ppp

senza ritard.

ppp

Ped. Ped. ✳ Ped. ✳

I gave her cakes

Catch

Henry Purcell
(1659-1695)

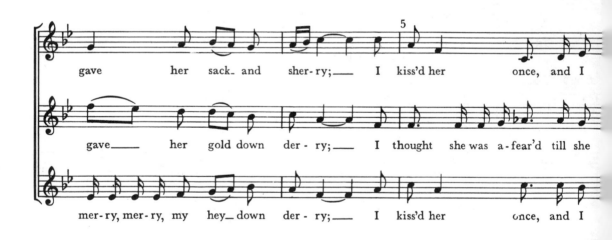

Once, twice, thrice, I Julia tried

Catch

Henry Purcell
(1659-1695)

J'ay le rebours

Chanson

Pierre Certon
(c. 1510-1572)
Edited by Elliot Forbes

Jesu, Joy of Man's Desiring

Wohl mir, dass ich Jesum habe

Johann Sebastian Bach
(1685-1750)
Arranged by Bruce Archibald

From Cantata № 147, *Herz und Mund und Tat und Leben*
* To be played as ♩♪, according to Baroque procedure.
E.C.S. № 2018

round_ Thy___ throne.
joys__ un - known.
Her - ze___ bricht.
und__ Ge - sicht.

Lasst uns mit geschlungnen Händen

Wolfgang Amadeus Mozart
(1756-1791)

Masonic Song to Close the Meeting of the Lodge (Vienna, 1785) as appended to Cantata *Laut verkünde unsre Freude* (K. 623

Es um-schlin-ge die-se_ Ket-te, so wie die - se
Seht, die Wei - he ist vol-len-det; wär' doch auch das
Dann strömt nicht al - lein in_ O - sten, dann strömt nicht al -

Es um-schlin-ge die-se_ Ket-te, so wie die - se
Seht, die Wei - he ist vol-len-det; wär' doch auch das
Dann strömt nicht al - lein in_ O - sten, dann strömt nicht al -

heil' - ge_ Stät - te, auch den gan - zen Er - den - ball.
Werk ge - en - det, wel - ches uns - re Her - zen weiht!
lein in_ We - sten, auch in Süd und Nor - den Licht.

heil' - ge_ Stät - te, auch den gan - zen Er - den - ball.
Werk ge - en - det, wel - ches uns - re Her - zen weiht!
lein in_ We - sten, auch in Süd und Nor - den Licht.

Coro dal segno

Let their celestial concerts all unite

Georg Friedrich Händel
(1685-1759)
Arranged by Archibald T. Davison

From *Samson*, 1743.
Orchestra parts obtainable from the publisher. Published also for Mixed Voices, E.C.S. Choral Music Nº 312

E.C.S. Nº 2018

244

248

E.C.S. No 2018

Dark-eye'd maiden

O die Frauen

from *Polydora* by Daumer
English version by
Natalia Macfarren

Johannes Brahms
(1833-1897)

TENOR

Dark - eye'd mai - den, dark - eye'd mai - den
O die Frau - en, o die Frau - en,

BASS

Dark - eye'd mai - den, dark - eye'd mai - den
O die Frau - en, o die Frau - en,

PIANO Primo

PIANO Secondo

with all fond de - lights o'er - la - den!
wie sie Won - ne, Won - ne tau - en!

with all fond de - lights o'er - la - den!
wie sie Won - ne, Won - ne tau - en!

From *Liebeslieder Walzer*, Opus 52 (Nº 3)
E.C.S. Nº 2018

20

not un - done_____ me, un - done_____ me!
nicht die Frau - en, die Frau - en!

not un - done_____ me, un - done_____ me!
nicht die Frau - en, die Frau - en!

20

25

Long the staff and cowl had won me
Wä - re lang ein Mönch ge - wor - den,

Long the staff and cowl had won me
Wä - re lang ein Mönch ge - wor - den,

25

25

25

had thy witch - ing not un - done me, hadst thou
wä - re lang ein Mönch ge - wor - den; wä - ren

had thy witch - ing not un - done me, hadst thou
wä - re lang ein Mönch ge - wor - den; wä - ren

not un - done me, un - done me!
nicht die Frau - en, die Frau - en!

not un - done me, un - done me!
nicht die Frau - en, die Frau - en!

Bright thy sheen, oh lucent wave

Sieh', wie ist die Welle klar

from *Polydora* by Daumer
English version by
Natalia Macfarren

Johannes Brahms
(1833-1897)

Thou, whose heart a- lone I crave,
Die du mei - ne Lie - be bist,

Thou, whose heart a- lone I crave,
Die du mei - ne Lie - be bist,

maid - en dear - est, love me!
lie - be du mich wie - - der!

maid - en dear - est, love me!
lie - be du mich wie - - der!

Nightingale, thy sweetest song

Nachtigall, sie singt so schön

from *Polydora* by Daumer
English version by
Natalia Macfarren

Johannes Brahms
(1833-1897)
Arranged by
Archibald T. Davison

From *Liebeslieder Walzer*, Opus 52 (No 15)

E.C.S. No. 2018

From yon hills the torrent speeds

Vom Gebirge Well' auf Well'

from *Polydora* by Daumer
English version by
Natalia Macfarren

Johannes Brahms
(1833-1897)
Arranged by
Archibald T. Davison

From *Liebeslieder Walzer* Opus 65 (No 7)

E.C.S. No 2018

tor - rent speeds, And the rain ne'er ceas - es Would that I might
Well' auf Well' kom - men Re - gen - güs - se Und ich gä - be

tor - rent speeds, And the rain ne'er ceas - es Would that I might
Well' auf Well' kom - men Re - gen - güs - se Und ich gä - be

cresc.

cresc.

give to thee Hun - dred thou - sand kiss - es.
dir so gern hun - dert - tau - send Küs - se.

give to thee Hun - dred thou - sand kiss - es.
dir so gern hun - dert - tau - send Küs - se.

The Maiden in the Wood

Mägdlein im Walde

Slovak Folk-song

Th. Cursch-Bühren
English version by
G. Wallace Woodworth

Antonin Dvořák
Op. 43, Nº 3

E.C.S. Nº 2018

heart, that her heart may yet find com - fort,
Herz den er - sehn - ten Frie-den fän - de,

heart, that her heart may yet find fort,
Herz den er-sehn-ten Frie den fän - de,

Ah, that her heart, that her heart may yet find
dass doch ihr Herz den er - sehn - ten Frie - den

Ah, that her heart, that her heart may yet find
dass doch ihr Herz den er - sehn - ten Frie - den

272

live my life a - lone; Still I sit by the
nun so ganz al - lein, still sitz' ich am—

live my life a - lone; Still I sit by the
nun so ganz al - lein, still sitz' ich am—

brook - let, Mourn - ing, ev - er—
Bäch - lein mit be - trüb - ten—

brook - let, Mourn - ing, ev - er
Bäch - lein mit be - trüb - ten

274

E.C.S. Nº 2018

Voice (8va):
grief of heart.
Her - zens - pein!

Voice (bass, 8va):
grief of heart.
Her - zens - pein!

Voice (8va):
Ah me, so bit - - ter, so
Ach, wie so bit - - ter, wie

Voice (bass, 8va):
Ah me, so bit - - ter, so
Ach, wie so bit - - ter, wie

deep is now my grief of heart."
weh ist___ doch Her - zens - pein!

deep is now my grief of heart."
weh ist___ doch Her - zens - pein!

(senza rall.)

colle voci

(senza rall.)

colle voci

dim.

Men of Harlech!

Welsh Folk-song
Arranged by Archibald T. Davison

William Duthie

E.C.S. Nº 2018

My Lord, what a morning!*

Negro Spiritual
Arranged by John W. Work

E.C.S. Nº 2018 Copyright, 1929 by Theodore Presser Co.- Used with permission

1. You'll hear the trum-pet sound, — To wake the na-tions un-der ground.
2. You'll hear the sin-ner cry, — To wake the na-tions un-der ground.
3. You'll hear the Christian shout, — To wake the na-tions un-der ground.

Look-ing to my God's right hand.
Look-ing to my God's right hand.
Look-ing to my God's right hand.

When the stars be-gin to fall.
When the stars be-gin to fall.
When the stars be-gin to fall.
When the stars be-gin to fall.

Now let every tongue adore Thee

Gloria sei dir gesungen

Philipp Nicolai
Translated by Paul English

Johann Sebastian Bach
(1685-1750)
Arranged by Archibald T. Davison

From Cantata Nº 140, *Wachet auf, ruft uns die Stimme*

Orchestra parts obtainable from the publishers.

Also published for Mixed Voices: Commonwealth Series, No. 354, and for Women's Voices, Concord Series No. 807. Also Women's Voices (G.& E.) E.C.S. Choral Music No. 1510

286

Let harps and cym - bals now u - nite.
mit Har - fen und mit Cym - beln schon.

Let harps and cym - bals now u - nite.
mit Har - fen und mit Cym - beln schon.

Let harps and cym - bals now u - nite.
mit Har - fen und mit Cym - beln schon.

Let harps and cym - bals now u - nite.
mit Har - fen und mit Cym - beln schon.

All Thy gates with pearl are glo - - rious,
Von zwölf Per - len sind die Pfor - - ten

All Thy gates with pearl are glo - - rious,
Von zwölf Per - len sind die Pfor - - ten

All Thy gates with pearl are glo - - rious,
Von zwölf Per - len sind die Pfor - - ten

All Thy gates with pearl are glo - - rious,
Von zwölf Per - len sind die Pfor - - ten

288

E.C.S. No 2018

O du eselhafter Martin

Canon

Wolfgang Amadeus Mozart
(1756-1791)
K. 560 b

Oh, why camest thou before me

Of unknown authorship

Welsh Folk-song
Arranged by Archibald T. Davison

.C.S. No 2018

Say, dear, will you not have me?

Thomas Morley
(1557-1602)
Edited by Elliot Forbes

rom Canzonets to Three Voices, 1593

E. C. S. № 2018

296

Sit down, servant

Negro Spiritual
Harmonized by John W. Work
Arranged for Men's Voices by
G. Wallace Woodworth

* The Refrain is to be sung before and after each verse.

E.C.S. No 2018

Studentenschmauss

Two Student Songs for the University of Leipzig (1626)

I

Johann Hermann Schein
(1516-1636)

Arranged by G. Wallace Woodworth

© Copyright, 1957, by G. Schirmer, Inc.-Used with permission

302

II

Allegro giocoso

TENOR I

1. Hol-la, gut G'sell, ich will dir san, Ein schwe-rer Ca-sus
2. Der Ca-sus ist mir e-ben schwer, Doch gib das Gläs-lein
3. Ich hab den Ca-sum de-ci-dirt, Le-gi-ti-me, wie

TENOR II

1. Hol-la, gut G'sell, ich will dir san, Ein schwe-rer Ca-sus
2. Der Ca-sus ist mir e-ben schwer, Doch gib das Gläs-lein
3. Ich hab den Ca-sum de-ci-dirt, Le-gi-ti-me, wie

BASS I

1. Hol-la, gut G'sell, ich will dir san, Ein schwe-rer Ca-sus
2. Der Ca-sus ist mir e-ben schwer, Doch gib das Gläs-lein
3. Ich hab den Ca-sum de-ci-dirt, Le-gi-ti-me, wie

BASS II

1. Hol-la, gut G'sell, ich will dir san, Ein schwe-rer Ca-sus
2. Der Ca-sus ist mir e-ben schwer, Doch gib das Gläs-lein
3. Ich hab den Ca-sum de-ci-dirt, Le-gi-ti-me, wie

Accompaniment
(For rehearsal only)

Allegro giocoso

hebt sich an, Run-da-di-nel-la, Run-da-di-nel -
im-mer her, Run-da-di-nel-la, Run-da-di-nel -
sich's ge-bührt,

hebt sich an, Run-da-di-nel-la, Run-da-di-nel -
im-mer her, Run-da-di-nel-la, Run-da-di-nel -
sich's ge-bührt,

hebt sich an, Run-da-di-nel-la, Run-da-di-nel -
im-mer her, Run-da-di-nel-la, Run-da-di-nel -
sich's ge-bührt,

hebt sich an, Run-da-di-nel-la, Run-da-di-nel -
im-mer her,
sich's ge-bührt,

Viva tutti

Canzonetta

Anonymous 18th Century

From *A Collection of Catches, Canons, Glees Duets, etc. Selected from the works of the most Eminent Composers Ancient and Modern, Vol. I, London, printed by Muzio Clementi and Co.*

E.C.S. Nº 2018

Choruses from "The Yeomen of the Guard"

W. S. Gilbert (1836-1911)

Arthur Seymour Sullivan
(1842-1900)
Arranged by Archibald T. Davison

Oh, Ser-geant Mer-yll, is it true— The wel-come news we read in

Oh, Ser-geant Mer-yll, is it true— The wel-come news we read in

Oh, Ser-geant Mer-yll, is it true— The wel-come news we read in

Oh, Ser-geant Mer-yll, is it true— The wel-come news we read in

we may fit - ly greet him, And wel - come his ar - ri - val here With

we may fit - ly greet him, And wel - come his ar - ri - val here With

we may fit - ly greet him, And wel - come his ar - ri - val here With

we may fit - ly greet him, And wel - come his ar - ri - val here With

shout on shout and cheer on cheer, Hur - rah! Hur - rah!

shout on shout and cheer on cheer, Hur - rah! Hur - rah!

shout on shout and cheer on cheer, Hur - rah! Hur - rah!

shout on shout and cheer on cheer, Hur - rah! Hur - rah!

To the Tow - er, wel - come thou!

To the Tow - er, wel - come thou!

To the Tow - er, wel - come thou!

To the Tow - er, wel - come thou!

Andante

As es-cort for the pris-on-er We

As es-cort for the pris-on-er We

Allegro brillante

With hap - pi - ness my soul is cloy'd_____

With hap - pi - ness my soul is cloy'd_____

songs maids sing, Who love with a love life - long, O! It's the

song of a mer - ry maid, nest - ling near Who lov'd her lord, but who

dropp'd a tear At the moan of a mer - ry - man, mop - ing mum, Whose

soul was sad and whose glance was glum, Who sipp'd no sup, and who

crav'd no crumb, As he sigh'd for the love of a la - dye!

Adoramus te, Christe

Antiphonal Motet

Felice Anerio
(c.1560-1614)
Arranged by
Archibald T. Davison

Copyright,1922, by E.C. Schirmer Music Co.
ⓒ Copyright renewed,1950, by E.C. Schirmer Music Co.

E.C.S. Nº 2018

CHORUS I

et be - ne - di - ci - mus ti - bi,

CHORUS II

et be - ne - di - ci - mus ti - bi.

CHORUS I *(or both* CHORUS I *and* II *to the end)*

Adoramus te, Christe

Motet

Jacques Clément (Clemens non Papa)
(c.1510-c.1556)
Arranged by Archibald T. Davison

E.C.S. Nº 2018

354

Adoramus te, Christe

Motet

Orlando di Lasso
(1532-1594)
Edited by Archibald T. Davison

* *A higher key should be used if possible. The indications* Tenors I, II, and III *do not refer to the range covered by any one part. The assignment of a few First Tenors to each of the three parts is advisable.*

E.C.S. No. 2018   Published, 1935, by E.C. Schirmer Music Co.

Cantate Domino

Motet

Psalm 149

Hans Leo Hassler
(1564-1612)
Arranged by Archibald T. Davison

Also published for Mixed Voices (A Cappella Nº 1131) and for Women's Voices (Concord Series Nº 821)
Also published for Mixed Voices with Latin and English texts (St. Dunstan Edition, Nº 1262)

E.C.S. Nº 2018

Diffusa est gratia

Christmas Motet

Giovanni Maria Nanino
(c.1545-1607)
Arranged by Archibald T. Davison

Psalm 45: verses 2 and 8

E.C.S. No 2018

Jesu dulcis memoria
Motet

Ludovico Tommaso da Vittoria
(1564-1645)
Arranged by Archibald T. Davison

Copyright, 1924, by E.C. Schirmer Music Co.
For all countries
© Copyright renewed, 1951, by E.C. Schirmer Music Co.

Lætentur cœli

Motet

Psalm 95: verses 11 to 13

Hans Leo Hassler
(1564-1612)
Edited by Elliot Forbes

372

E.C.S. No 2018

Miserere*
Motet

Psalm 51: verses 1, 2, 4 and 6

Gregorio Allegri
(1580-1652)
Arranged by Archibald T. Davison

* Four of the eleven verses of the "Miserere" are included in this arrangement.

E.C.S. Nº 2018

Non vos relinquam orphanos

Motet

John 14:18 and 28
Antiphon to the Magnificat
at 1st Vespers of Pentecost

William Byrd
Arranged by Archibald T. Davison

From *Gradualia, Liber Secundus*, London, 1610

E.C.S. No. 2018

Salvation belongeth to our God

Motet

Pavel Grigorevich Tchesnokov
(1877-1944)
Arranged by Archibald T. Davison

Published also for Women's Voices S.S.A.A. (*E.C.S. No.1925*)

E.C.S. N° 2018

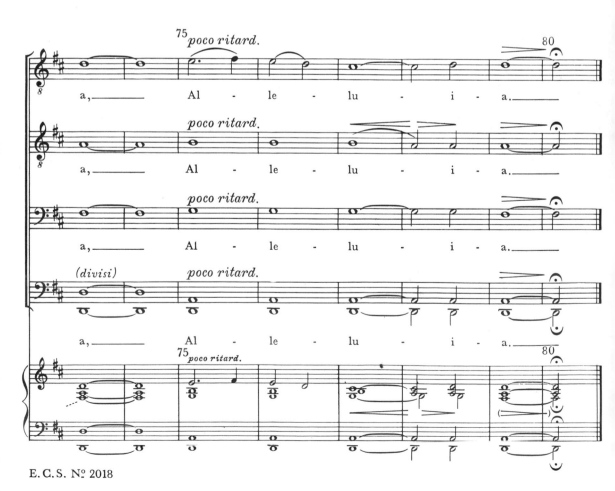

Alphabetical Index of Titles